Political Science Methods

G. David Garson
Tufts University

Political Science Methods

Holbrook Press, Inc.
Boston

Printed in the United States of America.

Library of Congress Cataloging in Publication Data

Garson, G   David.
    Political science methods.

    Includes index.
    1. Political science—Methodology.   I. Title
JA73.G37   320'.01'8   75-30507
ISBN 0-205-04867-6

to Cindy, with love

Contents

Choosing a Topic Forming an Outline Setting up the Hypothesis Gathering Evidence Presenting Evidence on the Hypothesis Using Control Variables Accepting or Rejecting Your Hypothesis Drawing Implications

Preface

An introductory text is a curious work, validly subject to the criticisms of tempting the student into pat formulas and instant analysis on one hand, and of numbing him or her to the enormity of the field on the other. This book *is* an introduction, and presumes further study. Not dependent on any particular text, it is designed for political and social science methods and statistics courses at beginning and intermediate levels. Various general topics, such as structural-functionalism, are presented for purposes of methodological instruction, for illustration, and for discussion. To treat each of these topics on its own terms, in its own complexity, is beyond the scope of this work.

There are as many political science methods as there are political scientists. A few methods are discussed here, and these only briefly. The annotated bibliography in each section is, therefore, an integral part of this volume, directing the student toward more profound treatment of each topic.

That political science methods are both qualitative and quantitative, both normative and empirical quickly becomes evident when reading the literature of political science. These methods often are presented as polarities, warring on some imaginary battlefield. A different perspective is taken in this book. Rather than confining methods to a set of statistical techniques, or, in contrast, limiting the text to the philosophy of social science, this book seeks to show the complementarity—indeed, interdependence—of normative and empirical theory.

If it is possible for a textbook of political science methods to have a thesis, the thesis of this book is that there is no substitute for pursuing multiple approaches to the same question. This seems a simple observation. Yet, the history of political science is a history of the search for the one, "right" framework for analysis—whether it be group theory, communications theory, systems theory, Marxism, or jurisprudence. The rapid succession of frameworks claiming the single, unifying theory is astounding.

Seeking to establish general, political categories into which all political data might fit, the search for the "right" framework misidentifies the nature of political theory. Diverse as they are in other respects, Marxism, phenomenology, and systems analysis set forth categories for interpreting our observations of politics. The more general the categories, the less the possibility that observations cannot be reconciled with the framework. Those frameworks having an extremely high level of generalization of categories are those that are most "right": observed data do not contradict the framework.

Though such theorizing might lead to useful, "right" categories, it is premised on a peculiar concept. *The purpose of theory is to simplify reality by sifting data, thereby enabling the human mind to cope with it.* Here, we must ask, "cope" for what reason? If the mind's purpose is cataloguing data, then the search for the one, right framework may have some validity. If, however, the purpose is prediction, then the theory must sacrifice typologically useful generality in favor of more limited political models that have the advantage of narrowing the predictors to a manageable number.

Thus, Marxism suffers as a theory because its level of generalization is relatively easily falsified by data. Similarly, its categories are too specific to reconcile all variants of phenomena that might be studied. For example, the Marxist categories of social class strain the reality of possible, social stratification types. Yet, the very simplicity of the model enhances its applicability as a predictive model. The simplifications from a general framework, such as systems theory, to an intermediate framework, such as Marxism, involve choices of emphasis that always carry normative implications. This is not to deny that all frameworks, even the most general, carry such implications, but normative aspects become more determined as the level of generalization decreases. Therefore, predictive empirical theory is always closely associated with normative theory, either implicitly or explicitly. By making the connection explicit, political scientists are placed in a position of either advocating a given normative theory, or advocating multiple approaches (each having its own normative implications) to the same political question.

Political theory is an essential aid in creatively forming hypotheses—the first step in any sound, political science research project. Though this would seem commonplace, it is a belief not commonly acted upon. This book is a modest attempt at remediation, re-emphasizing the rightful role of political theory as an integral part of political science methodology. The two have long been separate, but I believe that the thoughtful student will find this approach valuable.

Although part of the content of this book is not to be found elsewhere, in general, it seeks to explain and apply the work of others. The list of authors to whom I and all political scientists are indebted would fill a volume; many are cited in the reading suggestions following each chapter. Appreciation must also be expressed to the authors and publishers who kindly granted permission to use the tables contained in the appendix, including the Literary Executor of the late Sir Ronald A. Fisher, F.R.S.; Dr. Frank Yates, F.R.S.; and Oliver & Boyd Ltd., Edinburgh, for permission to reprint Tables 3, 4, 5, and 7 from *Statistical Tables for Biological, Agricultural and Medical Research.*

D.G.

Introduction

The study of politics is not a science, and there is no one "correct" political science methodology. In fact, political scientists are behind as often as they are ahead of informed journalists in their ability to anticipate important political changes. Yet the study of political science methods is rapidly becoming mandatory for graduate and undergraduate students in the field. Why is this so?

Some have attributed the changes in the field to a desire to construct a complicated intellectual framework as a form of protection from charges that political science deals merely with the obvious. No doubt there is some truth to the argument that frustration in our attempts to answer the classic political questions of democracy and welfare, for example, has led the field to retreat into narrow techniques in order to learn lesser things about our political system, if only because these things *can* be determined. Perhaps there is even a measure of status seeking involved in the spread of complicated political methodologies.

These, however, seem only subsidiary reasons for the change. The paramount reason for the emphasis on method is simply that as larger issues are dealt with more and more systematically, the ways of gathering information, processing it, and interpreting it have become increasingly complex. The fact that many have used old or new methods for trivial or even incorrect purposes should not obscure the greater purposes involved.

THE CHALLENGE TO POLITICAL SCIENCE

Strange as it may seem, there is a romantic dream at stake here. That dream envisions the use of information about the past and present to predict and shape the future. It conceives of the ability to specify the likely consequences of alternative policies, alternatives the consequences of which are now only dimly perceived. B. F. Skinner, a founder of behavioralism, emphasized that social planning requires a predictive social science. The meaning of democracy will always have a flawed aspect until the practical implications of existing and proposed political actions and policies can be stated with greater clarity and assurance.

As political scientists, we need not accept the full challenge of this dream, which equates science with the ability to employ predictive theories, but we must recognize that it is a challenge of substantial importance. Explanations of the past and present, and predictions of the future, will occur regardless because decision making requires it. A president claims his foreign policies will bring peace. Unions proclaim that current business practices will bring economic depression. A local editor asserts that the permissive policies of the national government are leading to urban rioting. How are we to respond to these assertions?

Fortunately, the challenge to social scientists is not to immediately construct a total explanatory system, but only to improve upon the results of current reasoning. As political scientists, we share a part of that task; many have already begun through methods described in this book.[1]

POLITICAL SCIENCE AND OTHER SOCIAL SCIENCES

The study of politics has no definite boundaries and is not clearly differentiated from other social sciences. Many of the methods used in political science are also used (and were originated) in history, economics, sociology, psychology, philosophy, mathematics, and engineering. Increasingly, the student needs a smattering of several of these fields. While recognizing the arbitrariness of any fine distinctions between fields, it may nonetheless be shown that political science is differentiated in two areas, although more in the first than the second.

Power

The primary domain of political science is the study of rule, authority, and power—terms that have been defined in many ways. The questions raised by these concepts permeate our political system: distribution of power, control over policies, effect on the "public interest," the competition and

[1] For further reading, see Thomas S. Kuhn, *The Structure of Scientific Revolutions* (Chicago: Univ. of Chicago Press, 1964).

cooperation of public and private powers, power used for narrow or long-term self-interest, power used directly or indirectly, formally or informally, with or without intended results. Questions are raised of how decisions are made and "who benefits? who decides? and what difference does it make?"[2]

Policy

The first domain easily merges with the second, that of policy. The study of decisions is not easily divorced from the study of decision outcomes. Just as the study of power is made complex by the fact that actors may participate in decisions individually or by way of groups or even social classes, so policy results may be either narrow and technical or highly diffuse. Political scientists have traditionally been more inclined to focus on areas where policy outputs are diffuse, such as foreign policy, rather than on areas like transportation policy, where technical factors become prominent. The student must decide for him- or herself to what extent he or she is competent to enter the many technical fields that impinge on political science.[3]

POLITICAL SCIENCE AND THE REAL WORLD

The basic method of political science and of all science is simplification. In essence, political reality is so complex that the human mind cannot perceive it directly, but can understand it only by means of simplifications. Whether a concept or hypothesis is a simplification or an oversimplification depends on its usefulness for the purposes at hand. The division of the American population into Democrats, Republicans, and Independents may well be a useful simplification for analyzing the civil rights movement. What is a simplification in one context is often an oversimplification in another.

Simplification begins with the naming of variables and the development of typologies. Just to talk about what interests us we must attach labels, and

[2] For further reading, see R. Bell, D. Edwards, and R.H. Wagner, eds., *Political Power: A Reader in Theory and Research* (New York: Free Press, 1969); R. Dahl, "The Concept of Power," *Behavioral Science* 2 (July 1957): 201—215; K. Dolbeare, ed., *Power and Change in the United States: Empirical Findings and Their Implications* (New York: John Wiley & Sons, 1969); K. Dolbeare and M. Edelman, *American Politics* (Lexington, Mass: D.C. Heath, 1971), ch. 16; A. Isaak, *Scope and Methods of Political Science* (Homewood, Ill.: Dorsey, 1969), ch. 16; M. Olsen, ed., *Power in Societies* (N.Y.: Macmillan, 1970).

[3] For further reading, see T. Dye, *Understanding Public Policy* (Englewood Cliffs, N.J.: Prentice-Hall, 1972); D. Gil, *Unravelling Social Policy* (Cambridge, Mass.: Schenkman, 1973); D. Lerner and H. Lasswell, eds., *The Policy Sciences* (Stanford: Stanford Univ. Press, 1965; orig. pub. 1951); A. Ranney, ed., *Political Science and Public Policy* (Chicago: Markham, 1968); I. Sharkansky, ed., *Policy Analysis in Political Science* (Chicago: Markham, 1970).

these place items or people into arbitrary categories. For example, the same citizenry may be divided into conservatives and liberals, moralists and amoralists, voters and nonvoters. These and any labels carry analytic implications that need to be made explicit.

The dividing of a citizenry into conservatives and liberals often implies that the researcher considers a partisan policy dimension most salient, while the moralist-amoralist distinction emphasizes cultural and psychological causes. What is labelled a drunken brawl from one perspective may be labelled class struggle from another. No label or typology is invalid in itself, but some are more helpful than others. Usefulness has to do with the extent of clear operational definitions, comprehensiveness of scope, ideological connotations, and many other factors discussed in the sections that follow.

Simplification continues with the development of hypotheses. We may assert that X causes Y, but we must then specify whether necessary or sufficient causation (or both) is involved, whether causation occurs only in a limited context, under what conditions exceptions occur, and many related issues. A hypothesis that is appropriate in one research situation may not be useful in another. In one time period, for example, it might be true that capitalism leads to imperialism, while the same relationship might not hold in another.

The fine line between necessary simplification and oversimplification is difficult to draw. The researcher must consider not only labels and typologies, and the causal nature of the hypothesis, but also the level of generalization on which he or she wishes to operate. He or she must seek to identify the dynamic element in his or her overall explanation: are political changes to be linked to changes in production, to demographic changes, to "great events" or "great men," or perhaps even to changes in human nature?[4]

NORMATIVE AND EMPIRICAL POLITICAL THEORY

Students in political science are exposed to a number of concepts that seem, somewhat mysteriously, to generate a great deal of heat within the discipline. Often these concepts are counterposed: normative versus empirical theory, traditionalism versus behaviorism, and so on. These distinctions have a long history, going under many labels, but all versions share a common focal point: the problem of objectivity in applying a criterion for simplification.

---

[4]For further reading, see J. McKinney, *Constructive Typology and Social Theory* (New York: Appleton-Century-Crofts, 1966); A. Stinchombe, *Constructing Social Theories* (New York: Harcourt, Brace & World: 1968), esp. chs. 3 and 4.

In nineteenth-century American political science, when jurisprudence was dominant, the enormous inflow of data was simplified by sifting it through a number of legal-normative categories: monarchy, constitutional monarchy, republic, democracy, etc. This mode of data selection was inherent in a legalistic theory concerned with gathering information pertinent to understanding the institutional framework of government. Around the turn of the century, however, many American political scientists came to feel that this procedure of political analysis was biased; it was felt to constrict attention to the formalities of government, blinding its followers to the sometimes unpleasant realities of courthouse politics, influence peddling, and other informal processes.

Under the rationale of a more balanced treatment of formal and informal political processes, early twentieth-century American political science encompassed many whose implicit criterion for selection of data was relevance of the information selected to reform. Before American entrance into World War One, for example, Jesse Macy, a president of the American Political Science Association, addressed the 1916 annual meeting of that body on the topic of "The Scientific Spirit in Politics," equating political science with placing the knowledge of our discipline at the service of government reform.

After the Great War, however, American political science shared in the general mood of disillusion with reform that characterized the 1920s. In this period, there was much emphasis on descriptive political science, emphasizing knowledge for its own sake rather than for the sake of reform. Associated with names such as Charles Merriam and Harold Lasswell, this tradition prefigured the development of behavioralism during and after World War Two. Later, during the 1960s, the discipline saw the emergence of a renewed emphasis on normative theory and an insistence, associated with such groups as the Caucus for a New Political Science, that research monies and journal articles apply the standard of relevance to political values or goals and not simply relevance to intellectual attempts to construct scientific theories of politics.

Throughout the history of American political science there has been a pendulum-like movement between concern for normative relevance on the one hand and descriptive accuracy and the uncovering of empirical relationships on the other. As students of political science, how are we to think about this issue? Is it really necessary to take sides?

How a new generation of political scientists answers these questions is of momentous importance to political science. At one extreme, one may imagine further polarization: normative concerns becoming the province of political theory courses, divorced from the study of American politics, comparative government, and international relations; those concerned with political relevance splitting from the American Political Science Association to form their own organization, with separate meetings and separate journals: narrow empiricism coming to dominate policy analysis and many other areas within political science. All these possible trends are observable today.

Alternatively, American political science may not polarize but may remain splintered. With the enormous information explosion of the last decade, it is not difficult to discern the possibility of a highly eclectic political science, neither specifically normative nor empirical but instead composed of an infinite variety of approaches, perspectives, substantive concerns, theories, and value premises. To those who strive for an integrating theory of politics, such diversity is already disconcerting; it reduces political science from a unified discipline to a mere umbrella label for a variety of diverse approaches. In such a future, American political science could eventually be whittled away as a discipline as each subgroup that *does* share a unifying set of theories separates off to form its own associations, journals, and academic departments and schools, which *do* cohere intellectually. This process too is already at work.

Finally, and this is the challenge which we share as new and as older political scientists, it may be possible that there is more common ground than has traditionally been thought. The scope of this question goes far beyond the scope of a single textbook, but it underlies all of this book.

WAYS OF THINKING ABOUT VALUES
IN POLITICAL ANALYSIS

In constructing theory, it is often helpful to identify strong propositions, even though the simplifications they involve are sufficiently extreme that most political scientists prefer to endorse a combination of these propositions. For purposes of clarification, however, one may identify a number of distinct perspectives on the use of values in political analysis:

1. Pure empiricism: the belief that it is possible to separate value statements from objectively observable or subjectively observable data and that political science should confine itself to the latter, leaving value statements to the field of philosophy.
2. Pure behaviorism: similar to pure empiricism, but more extreme in that attention is confined to objective data alone, ruling out subjective data (e.g., self-ratings in attitude questionnaires. Note that in political science, behaviorism is usually used in a much broader sense, often equated with empiricism).
3. Scientific value relativism: the belief that value statements are separable from factual data, but that political science must be concerned not only with the latter but also with examining the factual basis of propositions underpinning value statements and with spelling out the normative consequences of alternative political actions.
4. Pure normative theory: an orientation toward analysis in which a described system or process is evaluated in terms of an intellectual construct made explicit

by the analyst. (Note that in political science, normative theory is usually used in a much broader sense, including all modes of analysis involving evaluation by some standard.)

5. Data relativism: the belief that the categories through which data are measured inherently constitute a normative base for perception; hence also the belief that measurement and observation of data cannot be separated from value statements.

Of these perspectives, as Kalleberg has noted, pure behaviorism, as associated with the early work of Arthur Bentley or Charles Merriam, has largely disappeared from political science. The behaviorists have become behavioralists, or empiricists, deeply concerned with how objectively verifiable theory may be based on subjective meaning-structures. That is, through attitudinal research they have become more and more involved with measurement of subjective phenomena: attraction, identification, trust, efficacy, alienation, etc. As this trend has come to the fore, so have the problems associated with it, such as the arbitrary nature of measurement tools. By what categories can we measure a concept like "trust"? A focus on such basic problems of meaning has brought a rise in data relativism, with methodologies sometimes tied to symbolic interactionism or phenomenology.

At the same time, there has occurred what David Easton has called the post-behavioral revolution, whose adherents have disparaged pure behaviorism and empiricism, calling for an emphasis on substance rather than technique and emphasizing the social responsibility of the intellectual to become involved with essentially normative concerns. Ironically, the re-emergence of normative theory (in the sense of comparing described systems with intellectually constructed systems) recalls the origins of American political science, when, under jurispurdence, scholars were concerned with the application of legal models to American politics. Though the legalistic constraints have been thrown off, modern normative theory has more in common with American political science before WWI than it has with the period of greatest behavioral influence, after WWII.

Normative theory is not speculation in the sense of statements in the absence of evidence. Rather, it involves an ethical standard, and in the narrow sense of the term "normative theory," it involves a model by which observed data may be evaluated. It thereby provides a criterion for the selection of data. Data relativists will insist that analysis proceed through each of several normatively-premised frameworks, but in all versions of normative theory the process of theory construction—simplification of reality by selection and therefore loss of data—is made an object of purposive choice. As MacRae has noted with regard to the study of public policy, emphasis on the relation of observed data (e.g., public policies) to normative theories can provide the themes to unite an otherwise disparate field of political study. This sort of interdependence between empirical description and normative theory is emphasized in the following chapters.[5]

Part One of the book takes up a number of the most commonly used frameworks for analysis of politics. In general, a data relativist position is taken: the student is urged to analyze a question from the points of view of each of a series of alternative frameworks, each with its own normative implications. Part Two begins where Part One leaves off—with the problem of evaluating alternative answers to the same question. Basic techniques are introduced, with emphasis on the assumptions and problems commonly associated with each. Part Three deals with complex analysis, examining various intermediate techniques and eventually returning to the problem of causation and the nature of proof in social science.[6]

---

[5] For further reading, see K. Baker, S. Hajjar, and A. Schenker, "A Note on Behavioralists and Post-Behavioralists in Political Science," *PS* 5 no. 3 (Summer 1972): 271—273; Howard S. Becker and I.L. Horowitz, "Radical Politics and Sociological Research: Observations on Methodology and Ideology," *American Journal of Sociology* 78, no. 1 (July 1972): 48—66; A. Brecht, *Political Theory: The Foundations of Twentieth-Century Political Thought* (Princeton, N.J.: Princeton Univ. Press, 1959); R. Dahl, "The Behavioral Approach in Political Science: Epitaph for a Monument to a Successful Protest," *American Political Science Review* 55, no. 4 (December 1961): 763—772; K. Deutsch, "On Political Theory and Political Action," *American Political Science Review* 65, no. 1 (March 1971): 11—27; D. Easton, "The New Revolution in Political Science," *American Political Science Review* 63, no. 4 (December 1969): 1051—1061; J. Gunnell, "Deduction, Explanation, and Social Scientific Inquiry," *American political Science Review* 63, no. 4 (December 1969): 1233—1246; A. Kalleberg, "Concept Formation in Normative and Empirical Studies: Toward Reconciliation in Political Theory," *American Political Science Review* 63, no. 1 (March 1969): 26—39; A. Kaplan, *The Conduct of Inquiry* (San Francisco: Chandler, 1964); H. Kariel, "Creating Political Reality," *American Political Science Review* 64, no. 4 (December 1970): 1088—1098; E. Meehan, *The Theory and Method of Political Analysis* (Homewood, Ill.: Dorsey, 1965); S. Wolin, "Political Theory as a Vocation," *American Political Science Review* 63, no. 4 (December 1969): 1062—1082.

[6] For a survey of political science, see J. Charlesworth, ed., *Contemporary Political Analysis* (New York: Free Press, 1967); I. de Sola Pool, ed., *Contemporary Political Science: Toward Empirical Theory* (New York: McGraw-Hill, in cooperation with the American Political Science Association, 1967; R. Dahl, *Modern Political Analysis* (Englewood Cliffs, N.J.: Prentice-Hall, 1963); R. Golembiewski, W. Welsh, and W. Crotty, *Methodological Primer for Political Scientists* (Chicago: Rand McNally, 1969); O. Young, *Systems of Political Science* (Englewood Cliffs, N.J.: Prentice-Hall, 1968); M. Haas and H. Kariel, *Approaches to the Study of Political Science* (New York: Chandler, 1970).

See also M. Conway and F. Feigert, *Political Analysis: An Introduction* (Boston: Allyn & Bacon, 1972); D. Everson and J. Paine, *An Introduction to Systematic Political Science* (Homewood, Ill.: Dorsey, 1973); A. Isaak, *Scope and Methods of Political Science* (Homewood, Ill.: Dorsey, 1969).

For a more critical view, see R. Blackburn, *Ideology in Social Science* (New York: Vintage 1973); G. Graham and G. Carey, eds., *The Post-Behavioral Era: Perspectives on Political Science* (New York: McKay, 1972); P. Green and S. Levinson, *Power and Community: Dissenting Essays in Political Science* (New York: Vintage, 1969); R. Lyne, *Knowledge for What? The Place of Social Science in American Culture* (New York: Grove, 1964; orig. pub. 1939); C. McCoy and J. Playford, eds., *Apolitical Politics: A Critique of Behavioralism* (New York: Crowell, 1967); C.W. Mills, *The Sociological Imagination* (New York: Grove, 1959); B. Moore, *Political Power and Social Theory* (Cambridge, Mass.: Harvard Univ. Press, 1958).

For an instructive case, see G.W. Domhoff and H.B. Ballard, eds., *C. Wright Mills and "The Power Elite"* (Boston: Beacon, 1969). This volume usefully presents classic essays on both sides of the important elitism-pluralism debate in American political and social science.

one

Perspectives

1 | Marxism as Methodology

In American political science, important social theories, such as Marxism, have become isolated in courses on "political theory," appearing only briefly in standard courses on such topics as the legislative process, parties, or public administration. This tendency has perpetuated the practice of contrasting "political philosophy" with "empirical social science" rather than seeking to understand the interdependence of the two.

Therefore, it may be surprising to find "Marxism" listed as the first chapter in a text about political science methodology. To many this will seem a contradiction in terms: Marxism as a political philosophy cannot be a method, or at least a valid method, of political science.

While Marxism is not equivalent to scientific social analysis, it is useful to consider how a Marxist orientation might be applied to analysis of political events. In spite of the resurgence of interest in Marxism in the last decade, very little literature deals directly with this topic. Nevertheless, Marxist analysis has become sufficiently common that its relevance to contemporary political science can be illustrated.

THE MARXIST PERSPECTIVE

Before turning to methodological aspects, what *is* the Marxist perspective in general?

Marx argued that man as a being is by nature productive, rather than evil (as Calvin), bellicose (as Hobbes), or rational-calculating (as Bentham). He saw man as alienated through idols of his own making—religion, the state, the market. "The social relations of individuals have become transformed," Marx wrote, "into the social connections of material things."[1] Whereas liberal man was a consumer and his image of politics was that of the free play of groups and ideas in the political marketplace, Marxist man was a producer, his political nature forged by his relationship to production. Marx was perhaps most romantic in his attacks on the division of labor, describing a day in the life of a socialist man as one in which he might hunt in the morning, farm in the afternoon, and write poetry in the evening.

In brief, Marx adopted an approach that divided history into epochs distinguished from one another by changed relationships of men to the means of production. He devoted his greatest attention to the most recent stage, capitalism. Under capitalism, citizens were divided into owners (and their agents—the intellectuals, the managers, the politicians) and workers (excluding the lumpen-proletariat subclass of criminals and riff-raff). Capitalism was seen to deny man his product and hence his natural fulfillment (his species-life) as a basically productive being. Marx argued that it was this capitalist relationship that had to be changed, not just inequality as implied by Proudhon and certain other utopian socialists. The socialists were not interested in "better pay for slaves." This issue was central to Marxists, since for them, unlike liberals, property relations were understood to relate directly to the inner essence of man.

Change in society was believed to occur through the natural development of the forces of technology, precipitated by the seeds of destruction harbored within each social stage in the form of internal contradictions. Each stage, such as feudalism, at first greatly facilitated the development of productive forces, but later impeded that development, at the same time generating the forces that would create the next stage. For example, the overthrow of feudalism was attributed to bourgeois needs to establish a liberal market in labor, goods, and capital, free of aristocratic and monarchic restraints. With regard to the capitalist stage, Marx predicted the growing immiseration of the masses, revolution, dictatorship of the proletariat, and abolition of exploitation by socialism. The "withering of the state" after socialism referred to the predicted demise of government as an agent of class rule, since class distinctions were abolished with the end of exploitation.

Criticisms

Most students of American political science have been exposed to numerous criticisms of Marxism, many of which were summarized by C. Wright Mills.[2] The concept of society constituted by an economic base and a political and cultural supersturcture, with the former determining the latter, was crucial to Marxist interpretations of political events. Yet, as Mills

[1]Karl Marx, *The Grundrisse*, ed. and trans. David McLellan (New York: Harper Row, 1971; written 1857–58) p. 66.
[2]C. Wright Mills, *The Marxists* (New York: Dell, 1962) ch. 6.

emphasized, this relationship and the mechanisms relating the "base" to the "superstructure" were never well specified.

Similarly, Marxist emphasis on property relationships (such as owner-worker relationships) in studying economic stratification came at the expense of underestimating the sometimes independent effects of status and income. Likewise, while it is possible to interpret all history as the history of class struggle, this can be done only if that struggle is seen as very intermittent and extremely multiformed. But using the concept of class struggle this loosely undermines its utility.

Mills also argued that in comparing bourgeois revolutions against feudalism with the anticipated proletarian revolution against capitalism, Marx made a bad analogy. If it were parallel bourgeois institutions growing within feudalism that led to its overthrow, so parallel socialist institutions growing within capitalism, not necessarily workers' organizations, should lead to the anticipated socialist revolution.

Mills also discussed the criticisms directed against Marx's economic predictions. The economic crises of capitalism are *not* clearly increasing. Unionism has proved to be a viable alternative to revolution, institutionally protecting workers' interests and, in general, growing immiseration has not occurred. Class structure does *not* seem to be becoming significantly more (or less) polarized. Wageworkers, a "class-in-itself," does *not* necessarily become the proletariat, a "class-for-itself," because men do not always act in terms of their ultimate interests. And lastly, the state is *not merely* the coercive instrument of the owning classes; political and military leaders have wide power in their own right.[3]

The student has no doubt already been exposed to these criticisms of Marxism on numerous occasions. Critics usually credit Marx with emphasizing the role of conflict at a time when there was much focus on harmony and equilibrium. Similarly, Marx's concept of class, although certainly not without precedent, stood in useful contrast to liberal emphasis on rational individuals as units of political action. These, however, are not the focal points of this discussion. Instead let us examine the theoretical issues faced by Marx that still concern researchers today.

CONTEMPORARY METHODOLOGICAL ISSUES

Nearly all political studies contain explicit or implicit theories of the nature of man, the structure of political life, and the way social change occurs. Failure to make these underlying assumptions explicit may lead the researcher to fail to consider all the relevant issues.

---

[3]For other criticism, see Ralf Dahrendorf, *Class and Class Conflict in Industrial Society* (Stanford: Stanford Univ. Press, 1959), esp. chs. 1 and 4; Jacques Barzun, *Darwin, Marx, Wagner: Critique of a Heritage* (New York: Doubleday, 1958; orig. pub. 1941); Murray Wolfson, *A Reappraisal of Marxian Economics* (Baltimore: Penguin, 1964).

Historical Epochs

Proof of various hypotheses is often sought by comparing similar phenomena across cultures in the same time period or by making comparisons over time. If the historical path is chosen, then as the length of time considered increases, the need to divide it grows. That is, history must be categorized to simplify analysis. What criteria are to be used? In one sense, all history is transitional and the process of dividing it into periods is arbitrary; however, simplification is necessary for analysis. Marx used the social relations of production as the criteria, establishing time periods such as feudalism and capitalism.

Other criteria might be used instead, such as great events, changes in forms of government, political boundaries, or intellectual currents. Of these alternatives, the great events approach has been the traditional mode, used even in primitive societies. Among the Buku islanders of the South Pacific, history is divided between "the time of fighting" and "the time of the white man," the great event that divides the two periods being the arrival of German imperialists. As with other approaches, there is nothing intrinsically wrong with using great events to distinguish time periods, but it is an approach that rarely served to clarify analysis. Preferable, the criterion should grow out of the historical process being described. Using wars to set off periods in the development of foreign policy might conceivably serve analysis in one instance, whereas the same criterion applied to the development of Supreme Court decisions would be meaningless. Rationale for the great events approach was given by the German sociologist Max Weber, who emphasized such events in history as instruments of widespread attitude changes; if used in this light, the approach may serve analysis in a nonarbitrary way.

The criterion of changes in political territory or government has been used by many political scientists. Machiavelli, for instance, developed a cyclical theory of the state, revolving from classic to despotic to republican form. This movement was based on the impulse to participate, which led to success and wealth, from this to corruption and decline, and was followed by the expectation of resurrection through great men. Generally, however, such divisions are characterized by little description of the dynamic by which one stage leads to the next; it is this issue that is at the heart of the problem of categorization of time periods.

The use of intellectual currents as a criterion raises a problem central to Marxism: are ideas to be considered products of material culture, or do ideas cause social change? All sides on this issue admit mutual causation, but primary emphasis is often given to one or the other. Seymour M. Lipset, for example, emphasizes ideal factors in his interpretation of American social-political history in *The First New Nation*. Emphasis on material factors might lead to divisions such as "the age of commercial capitalism," "the age of industrial capitalism," "the age of monopoly capitalism," and the like; whereas emphasis on ideal factors might lead to "the age of enlightenment," "the age of ideology," "the age of analysis." It is entirely possible to use ideal divisions and hold to a theory of material causation, but then the author may expect confusion in his readers. Usually criteria should be consistent with the underlying theory of development; if there is no such theory, this too should be made explicit.

The Marxist criterion of technology of production is explicitly related to a theory of change. As a criterion it has problems, but so do all the alternatives. Whether it is oversimplified for the student's own purposes is a question to be decided in each case, but the central issue of how to categorize time periods will continue to arise with insistent regularity.

Social Classes

The class concept is one that appears in a great variety of political works. One would do well, however, to keep firmly in mind Weber's distinction between class measures and status measures. Common measures of social status are income level, education, and occupational prestige. Class is a related but distinct concept, depending in the Marxist definition on relationships to the means of production.

Production classes are not the only possible type, of course. One might want to speak of "status classes," arguing that those with significantly higher status differ crucially on political matters from lower social status groups. Dahrendorf has argued for a class concept based on authority cleavages, with political behavior and attitudes related more to political status vis-à-vis authority than to socioeconomic status per se.

The concept of class contains many problems. The various measures of status may be discrepant; the same individual may have, for instance, a high education and a low income. Beyond this, people may objectively belong to certain classes, yet lack class consciousness or even identify with another class. In the United States, many wealthy people will identify themselves as middle class when queried on surveys. Moreover, as our economy has developed, property income has ceased to be a clear class criterion, and beyond this, economic conflict does not in the least exhaust the varieties of political conflict. T. B. Bottomore, in *Classes in Modern Society* (New York: Vintage, 1968; orig. pub. 1965), concludes that there is no clear evidence that inequality is changing relatively, that the vast majority of people do not shift in social class, and that most mobility is of the inter-generational type due to the changing occupational structure of the economy. He argues that while it is true in several countries that the correspondence between classes and specific ideologies has been weakened, ideological differentiation is still strong with regard to production relationships. He suggests that the real undermining of the Marxist class concept lies in the increasing importance of nonproduction relationships, which is related to increasing affluence. In a crisis, classes might again dominate political events even in countries now marked by status politics.

The central issue for the political scientist is how to conceive the general structure of political action. Classic liberals seemingly implied a system dominated by anomic individuals all acting rationally and individually, but somehow tending to the common good. More recently, political science has been dominated by the various group approaches, notably David Truman's work, *The Governmental Process*. The class approach is prepared to explain why the National Association of Manufacturers is more important than the National Association of Contract Bridge Players, however, and those who adopt the group approach must be prepared with their own explanations. That is, there is the danger of portraying politics as the result of the competition of many, more or less, equal groups, overlooking differentials in the power base of groups and in their institutionalized relationships to government.

The issue of social classes in Marxism thus raises the general methodological issue of how to describe the units of political action. As units, the individual, the group, and the class each have problems. Indeed, the whole literature on elitism and pluralism is largely devoted to this complex issue. Certainly the Marxist unit, social class, is not to be dismissed lightly until the student has formulated explicit alternatives.[4]

CLASS STRUGGLE

The political researcher must also consider whether he or she is assuming a system in equilibrium in which change is deviant (a view often ascribed to Talcott Parsons and other functionalist sociologists), or whether conflict is assumed to be a normal condition and stability exceptional (as in Marx's

[4]For more detailed discussion of issues in class analysis, see S. M. Lipset, "Issues in Social Class Analysis," in *Revolution and Counter-Revolution: Change and Persistence in Social Structures* (New York: Doubleday, 1968), ch. 5; John C. Leggett, *Class, Race, and Labor* (New York: Oxford University Press, 1968), ch. 2 and Appendixes A and D; Reinhard Bendix *Max Weber: An Intellecual Portrait* (New York: Doubleday, 1960), ch. 4, sec. A; Norman Birnbaum, *Toward Critical Sociology* (New York: Oxford University Press, 1971), pp. 101–109; Gerhard Lenski, *Power and Privilege* (New York: McGraw-Hill, 1966), ch. 4; essays in P. Blumberg, ed., *The Impact of Social Class* (New York: Crowell, 1972), esp. Parts I and II; and essays in G. Thielbar and S. Feldman, eds., *Issues in Social Inequality* (Boston: Little, Brown, 1972), esp. ch. 1.

[5]For more detailed discussion of equilibrium theory and conflict theory, see Dahrendorf, *Class and Class Conflict*; Lewis Coser, *The Functions of Social Conflict* (New York: Free Press, 1956); Georg Simmel, *Conflict and the Web of Group-Affiliations* (New York: Free Press, 1955; orig. pub. 1908); Richard Appelbaum, *Theories of Social-Change* (Chicago: Markham, 1970), chs. 3 and 4; Don Martindale, *The Nature and Types of Sociological Theory* (Boston: Houghton Mifflin, 1960), Part III.

characterization of the regime of Louis Bonaparte as a temporary balancing act).

Although most topics may be treated within the framework of either "equilibrium theory" or "conflict theory," the vocabulary of each carries certain connotations that should be recognized by the researcher. In general, more conservative theorists have felt more comfortable with equilibrium theory, while radical scholars such as Marx have usually pursued some variant of conflict theory.[5] This pattern does have many exceptions, notably the conservative doctrine of Social Darwinism, which incorporated conflict theory perspectives.

Dialectic of Change

Marx believed that social change occurs through a dialectic process, in which material forces are formed, generate their own antitheses, thereby causing a clash of forces, and resolve into a new synthesis more favorable to the next stage of development. This theory contrasts with that of Hegel, from which it derives. Hegel held that social change occurs as the result of the clash of ideal (intellectual) forces in a dialectic manner. Both of these theories are more complex than earlier theories of social change as simple progress (or decline) or as cycles. The theory that political relationships never change at all or do so at random may seem to be the implied view if issues such as this are not explicitly met.[6]

Scientific Method

Although Marx did not make politics a science, he did face and attempt to resolve many issues having a direct bearing on scientific method in political research. One of the earliest plans for a mass questionnaire survey was projected by Marx. More important, however, was his recognition of the need to make explicit the relevant variables and relationships leading up to his predictive hypotheses. As we shall see later, some modern methodologies, although more rigorously defining their variables, have undermined their own usefulness by failing to clarify a dynamic of social change. Marx did develop a predictive, empirically testable causal model bearing on substantively important matters. As Louis Hartz has noted, others have said that everything is related to everything else. That has been said before and will be said again. It more closely corresponds to reality, but it is not useful.

[6]For more detailed discussion of dialectical theory, see Kenneth Boulding, *A Primer on Social Dynamics: History as Dialectics and Development* (New York: Free Press, 1970); E. J. Hobsbawm, "Karl Marx's Contribution to Historiography," R. Blackburn, ed., *Ideology in Social Science: Readings in Critical Social Science* (New York: Vintage, 1973), ch. 12; Bertell Ollman, *Alienation: Marx's Conception of Man in Capitalist Society* (Cambridge, England: Cambridge Univ. Press, 1971), chs. 5 and 6.

When asked if a civil war will break out in India, for example, the Marxist can consult his or her theories, look at the known facts, and attempt an answer; many others will be so lost in complexity they will only be able to give the true but not very useful answer that it all depends on a hundred different factors. The job of political scientists interested in scientific method is not to accurately describe the overwhelmingly complex nature of political life; rather it is to develop workable simplifications more useful than Marxism and other contemporary explanatory theories.

Objectivity

Marx wrote, "The philosophers have only interpreted the world; the point, however, is to change it." Some have argued that an activist position undermines objectivity; others, like C. Wright Mills, argue that we all stand inside history and can never be truly objective. Many would agree that activism does not necessarily sacrifice objectivity, although it may pose a threat. Chester Barnard's work on organization theory or Schlesinger's work on the Kennedy administration are but two of many important works by authors active in the practical affairs they describe as objectively as authors not so involved. In fact, one could argue that the disengaged position breeds isolation from reality and hence encourages ideological distortion. Regardless, the issue of engaged observation and social relevance of research must also be faced by all political scientists.

Example   T. B. Bottomore distinguished between Marxian (pertaining to the man, Marx) and Marxist (in some manner taking off from Marxian writings) analyses. Here, concerned with the latter, our intent is not to determine what the orthodox Marxian approach would be. Rather, the student of political science must learn to think about a problem of analysis from a number of divergent points of view before attempting his own synthesis.

As a methodology, Marxism directs attention to certain considerations. In choosing issues to study, it focuses on conflict and class-related areas. In choosing groups to study, it looks at social classes. In terms of history, it emphasizes production epochs; its perspective is materialist and dialectic. The general method involves a historical model based on the tension between the dynamic of technology and the contradiction between the means of production and the social relationships of production. For example, Reconstruction in the United States might be interpreted as having ended because a victorious Northern business class traded rejection of radical reform interests for acceptance by the South of a tariff structure and other political arrangements favorable to the North.

Many variations of class analysis are possible. For example, one may specify many more classes than simply owners and workers, yet retain an emphasis on relationship to the means of production (intellectuals, managers, women, criminals are examples of possible additional classes). Alternatively, class may be defined in terms of one or more socioeconomic indicators, or Dahrendorf's suggestion about the use of authority cleavages may be pursued.

Following is a Marxist analysis of rioting:

Analysis	Example
1. Focus on an issue emphasizing conflict and change.	1. Why have riots occurred during the 1960s in American ghettos?
2. Specify the classes involved.	2. Primarily black lower class and white lower middle class (police).
3. Note historical changes in the relationship of each to the means of production.	3. Blacks: shifting from rural, peasant-like status into the marginal proletariat (as service workers), beginning shift into working class and to a much lesser extent to middle class status. Whites: shifting from working class into white collar and allied middle class positions.
4. Note changed interests resulting from altered relationships.	4. Blacks: new work relations forge greater responsibility and discipline, resulting in greater class consciousness. Whites: those remaining in working class and marginal middle class positions (as police) feel threatened.
5. Note direction of change suggested by changed interests.	5. Blacks: greater assertiveness of class issues, such as demands for equality and power for the poor. Whites: resist challenge to former class arrangements.
6. Note interaction with superstructure, including effect on the political event studied.	6. Black assertion of class demands leads to civil rights organizations and then to conflict with white working class and marginal middle class; norms of nonthreatened white upper classes invoked by blacks to gain legitimacy; assertiveness further encouraged. Failure of upper classes in control of government to meet demands in a tangible way (because major reallocation of resources not in their interest) leads to frustration and struggle through illegal means, and rioting.

One could no doubt elaborate greatly, perhaps emphasizing World War II in explaining the timing of changed race relationships to class structure, and hence explaining the timing of race conflict. The war, in turn, could be related to the international conflict of economic systems antithetical in nature.

One can challenge this interpretation of rioting, but it is used here to illustrate how Marxism might be adopted as a starting point to generate hypotheses about contemporary political phenomena. Later, explanations of rioting will be attempted from entirely different viewpoints. To repeat, the emphasis is not on searching for one "right" methodology, or even on working toward a unified political "science"; rather, these initial chapters are meant to jar the student out of preconceived solutions and stimulate him or her toward a creative, pluralistic approach in thinking about political issues prior to attempting a synthesis of the most nearly "correct" analysis.

A SELECTED INVENTORY
OF RESEARCH APPLICATIONS

The student beginning to apply Marxism or any other theoretical framework for political analysis usually starts with relatively simple mechanical versions, such as the one illustrated in the foregoing example. This is so much to the good: the student is on the way to acquiring intellectual literacy. That is, he or she is beginning to be able to look at a political phenomenon and ask, "How would a Marxist look at this?" "How would a systems theorist?" "How would a phenomenologist?" and so on, down to "How should *I* look at this?" Intellectual literacy means we have the capability of understanding what the range of contending interpretations is before we select or synthesize our own. It is certainly not raw empiricism—plunging into the data before we understand what is really at issue from each of a variety of perspectives.

That is why this methods book begins with theory, not with data-gathering techniques and statistics. This text can then direct the student beyond simplistic applications of Marxism toward political research and writings that do illustrate more sophisticated applications of Marxist and neo-Marxist concepts.

Much of this recent material falls within the realm of general political theory. Much has been sparked by the American publication in 1961 of Marx's *Economic and Philosophical Manuscripts of 1844*, translated by T. B. Bottomore and edited for the American public by Erich Fromm, a noted socialist psychoanalyst.[7] This publication renewed interest in the early works of Marx, with their neo-Hegelian emphasis on alienation and consciousness.

[7]Erich Fromm, *Marx's Concept of Man* (New York: Ungar, 1961); see also Lloyd Easton and Kurt Guddat, eds., *Writings of the Young Marx on Philosophy and Society* (Garden City, N. Y.: Doubleday, 1967).

The complex subject of socialization into "false consciousness" and the process by which one social class maintains ideational hegemony over another has led to great interest in the writings of such authors as Gramsci and Lukacs, both of whom build on the humanistic aspects of the early Marx.

Alan Wolfe has written an essay useful in orienting students to recent Marxist theory, comparing humanistic (e.g., Lukacs), Leninist (e.g., Moore), and other influential tendencies (e.g., Althusser, Poulantzas).[9] With the publication in English of the *Grundrisse*, (Marx's outline for a wider work than *Capital*, never completed), and Marx's three-volume *Theories of Surplus Value*, Marxist theory has undergone a reappraisal of its earlier humanistic appraisal.[10] Of critical importance here is the work of Shlomo Avineri, who has emphasized the fundamental continuity between the "early" and "older" Marx.[11]

Closely related to the recent theoretical literature, though more specific, are the studies of Ollman and others on the Marxist theory of alienation, commodity fetishism, roles, and masks.[12] Given the diffuse social discontents of contemporary America, this aspect of Marxist scholarship has received considerable attention. At a more empirical level, however, traditional subjects of Marxist study such as political economy, work relations, and imperialism have continued to be emphasized by Marxist and neo-Marxist scholars.[13]

[8] Antonio Bramsci, *Prison Notebooks* (New York: International Publishers, 1971); George Lukacs, *History and Class Consciousness: Studies in Marxist Dialectics* (Cambridge, Mass.: MIT Press, 1968; orig. pub. 1923). See also G. Lichtheim, *George Lukacs* (New York: Viking, 1970).

[9] Alan Wolfe, "New Directions in the Marxist Theory of the State" (Paper delivered at the Annual Meeting of the APSA, 1973); Stanley Moore, *The Critique of Capitalist Democracy* (New York: Augustus Kelley, 1968; orig. pub. 1957); Louis Althusser, *For Marx* (New York: Pantheon, 1970); Nicos Poulantzas, *Political Power and Social Classes* (London: New Left Books, 1973).

[10] Marx, *Grundrisse*; Karl Marx, *Theories of Surplus Value*, 3 vols. (Moscow: Foreign Languages Publishing House, n.d., 1969, 1972).

[11] Shlomo Avineri, *The Social and Political Thought of Karl Marx* (Cambridge, England: Cambridge Univ. Press, 1969). Such continuity is apparently evident in another major manuscript by Marx, now being published for the first time in English. Titled *Sixth Chapter: Results of the Immediate Process* (New York: Monthly Review, 1974), the work is a draft chapter originally intended for inclusion in *Capital*. Among other things, it discusses commodity fetishism, illustrating Marx's concern for this in his later as well as earlier life.

[12] Bertall Ollman, *Alienation*; see also essays by Igor Kon and Eduard Urbanek in P. L. Berger, ed., *Marxism and Sociology: Views from Eastern Europe* (New York: Appleton-Century-Crofts, 1969). A sympathetic non-Marxist commentary is provided in Joachim Israel, *Alienation: From Marx to Modern Sociology* (Boston: Allyn & Bacon, 1971). See W. Plasek, "Marxist and American Sociological Conceptions of Alienation," *Social Problems* 21, no. 3 (Winter 1974): 316–327.

[13] On political economy, see: James O'Connor, *The Fiscal Crisis of the State* (New York: St. Martin's, 1973); Charles H. Anderson, *The Political Economy of Social Class* (Englewood Cliffs, N.J.: Prentice-Hall, 1974); E. Hunt and J. Schwartz, eds., *A Critique of Economic Theory* (Baltimore: Penguin, 1972); and D. Horowitz, ed., *Marx and Modern Economics* (New York: Monthly Review, 1968).

A BRIEF SUMMARY

The purpose of political theory is to gain understanding of political phenomena. The crucial test of understanding is the ability to be able to predict political effects under varying conditions. To meet this test, political theory seeks to: (1) establish typologies or categories for classifying information; (2) indicate the relative causal importance of various factors as a criterion for sifting more important from less important information; and (3) establish the validity of interrelated sets of links between causes and effects thought to be important. Thus, political theory aids understanding by providing a mode of simplifying reality by losing information.

This is, perhaps, an unusual way of formulating what political theory is about, but it underscores the difference between description and analysis discussed in the introduction. Typology—a set of intellectual boxes into which to pigeonhole data—is not theory, useful as it is for purposes of description. Analytic theory, in contrast, deals with relationships among concepts and variables and with theories of how these relationships change. Such theories must identify factors thought to be of greatest causal importance.

Reality may be described accurately as a multidimensional web of causes and interactions. Theory seeks to establish a starting point for breaking into that web and a plan for understanding it. Marxism as political science methodology illustrates one such theoretical approach.

In Marxism, the point of departure is changes in the social relationships of production (not, as is thought in vernacular use, economic self-interest).

Anthologies on Marxist and radical interpretations of American politics include: R. Edwards, M. Reich, and T. Weisskopf, *The Capitalist System* (Englewood Cliffs, N.J.: Prentice-Hall, 1972); T. Christoffel, D. Finkelhor, and D. Gilbar, *Up Against the American Myth* (New York: Holt, Rinehart & Winston, 1970); M. Mankoff, *The Poverty of Progress* (New York: Holt, Rinehart & Winston, 1972); D. Mermelstein, *Economics: Mainstream Readings and Radical Critiques* (New York: Random House, 1970); M. Zeitlin, *American Society Inc.* (Chicago: Markham, 1970). Ralph Miliband's *The State in Capitalist Society* (New York: Basic Books, 1969) presents a Marxist overview in this area.

On work relations, see J.A. Banks, *Marxist Sociology in Action* (Harrisburg, Pa.: Stackpole Books, 1970); G. Hunnius, D. Garson and J. Case, eds., *Workers' Control: A Reader on Labor and Social Change* (New York: Random House, 1973).

On imperialism, see: I. Zeitlin, *Capitalism and Imperialism: An Introduction to Neo-Marxian Concepts* (Chicago: Markham, 1972); M.B. Brown, *After Imperialism*, rev. ed. (London: Merlin, 1970); H. Magdoff, *The Age of Imperialism* (New York: Monthly Review, 1969); and readings in K.T. Fann and D.C. Hodges, eds., *Readings in U. S. Imperialism* (Boston: Porter Sargent, 1971). The running commentary composing all issues of the British journal *Politics and Money* is useful as a starting point as well.

On Marxism and social science, see R. Blackburn, ed., *Ideology in Social Science: Readings in Critical Social Theory* (New York: Vintage, 1972).

On Marxism and political science, see Bertell Ollman, "Marxism and Political Science: Prolegemenon to a Debate on Marx's Method," *Politics and Society* 3, no. 4 (Summer 1973): 491–510.

Thus Marxism simplifies reality by assuming that : (1) changes in production apply to every aspect of substantial theoretical interest, from work roles to religion; and (2) the forms of consciousness forged at work override other forces of socialization (e.g., the family, school, church) in the long run.

Such simplifications are inherent in theory construction. To condemn them per se is to misunderstand the purpose of theory. The question is whether or not these simplifications serve understanding of what we deem to be important better than the simplifications in other theoretical approaches.

On this question I invite the reader to form his or her own conclusions. So that these conclusions can be based on empirical utility rather than on abstract considerations, each of the chapters in Part One ends with exercises that apply each approach to a given problem. At the end of the exercises the student should be in a position to understand more deeply the relative advantages of Marxism compared with other approaches. The value lies in the comparison, not in Marxism or any other specific framework.

EXERCISE

American political science has frequently emphasized the role of interest groups, notably business and labor groups, in the political process. It is therefore relevant to ask why people affiliate with such groups. Data on trade union membership follow (p. 24). As an exercise, hypothesize how a Marxist would explain the variations in this time series. Don't worry about what Marx "really meant"; simply try to put forward one clear line of reasoning on this subject that incorporates ideas discussed in this chapter.

Among the variables that might be discussed in such an exercise are: rise of industrial capitalism, concentration of industry, immigration, economic fluctuations and crises, decline of agriculture, urbanization, mass assembly techniques, government policies, composition of the workforce, and war.

To do this exercise, some background is necessary on the subject. The following are useful articles: A. Blum, "Why Unions Grow," *Labor History* 9, no. 19 (Winter 1968): 39–72; D. Bell, *The End of Ideology* (New York: Free Press, 1960), ch. 10, "The Capitalism of the Proletariat: A Theory of American Trade Unionism"; J. Leggett, *Class, Race and Labor* (New York: Oxford, 1968), chs. 1–3; A. Rees, *The Economics of Trade Unions* (Chicago: Univ. of Chicago, 1962), chs. 1 and 2; J. Dunlop, "The Development of Labor Organization: A Theoretical Framework," in R. Lester and J. Shister, eds.. *Insights into Labor Issues* (New York: Macmillan, 1948), pp. 163–193; David Prody, "The Expansion of the American Labor Movement," A. E. Ambrose, ed., *Institutions in Modern America* (Baltimore: Johns Hopkins, 1967), pp. 11–36.

Patterns of Trade Union Membership

Period	Membership as % of Non-Agricultural Employees	Change	
1897 – 1904	3.5 – 12.3%	+8.8%	(growth)
1905 – 1916	12.3 – 11.2%	– 1.1%	(stability)
1917 – 1920	11.2 – 19.5%	+8.3%	(growth)
1921 – 1929	19.5 – 11.0%	– 8.5%	(decline)
1930 – 1933	11.6 – 11.3%	– 0.3%	(stability)
1934 – 1939	11.9 – 28.6%	+16.7%	(growth)
1940 – 1945	26.9 – 35.5%	+8.6%	(growth)
1946 – 1958	34.5 – 33.2%	– 1.3%	(stability)
1959 – 1970	32.1 – 27.4%	– 4.7%	(moderate decline)

Psychological Approaches as Political Methodology

Marxism is, of course, one of many approaches to the study of politics. A second and even more influential set of methods has been associated with psychology, whose concepts have been important in political science since the 1920s. One enthusiastic scholar from that era concluded an essay with the remark, "So if political science is not psychology, what is it?" While we need not go that far, the vocabulary of psychology infuses the writings of many political scientists: displacement, repression, identification, regression, sublimation, catharsis, projection, internalization, etc. Political scientists speak of *identification* with a leader, *internalization* of an organization's goals, or the *cathartic effect* of collective violence—yet these are rarely explicit applications of psychology. In spite of this, the psychological heritage has been one of the most important for political scientists, altering their very image of man.

THE FREUDIAN PERSPECTIVE

If liberalism is understood in its nineteenth-century sense, Freud may be seen as a spokesman for a postliberal perspective. His concept of the unconscious constituted a fundamental challenge to the liberal concept of rationality, and through rationality to democracy. Once the importance of erotic and aggressive human tendencies became apparent, the possibilities of disinterested rational choice seemed much reduced. Political man came to be seen not as the logical calculator of possible pleasures and pains, but rather as a much more animal being whose needs for sex, aggression, power, and other selfish ends could be reconciled with "the greatest good for the greatest number" only in the most tenuous ways, and then with the aid of a considerable amount of civilized repression.

After Freud, and especially after World War I, a great pessimism developed because of man's aggressive instincts and the high cost of social repression of these instincts. Freud was seen by contemporaries as a reformer, perhaps primarily because of the attack on Victorian sexual morality that his writings represented. He also asserted the need to rid civilization of unnecessary repression (what Marcuse terms "surplus repression") and was sympathetic to the needs of the working class. Nevertheless, though a liberal, Freud still believed in the necessity of a ruling elite; his was a liberalism without the usual democratic underpinnings.

Freud's writings contain several different perspectives on history. In discussing religion, for example, Freud noted three epochs: the animistic, in which the self is seen as omnipotent; the religious, in which father figures are seen as omnipotent; and the scientific, in which omnipotence is no longer a necessary idea—libido is invested in other adults. In his famous letter to Albert Einstein, Freud saw the history of war as a progressive rejection of instinctive goals and a scaling down of instinctive reactions. He could even foresee the possibility that pacifism might become part of man's "instinctive nature," as he believed it might already be for himself and Einstein. In his essay on "Civilization and Its Discontents," Freud saw a continuing trend toward greater repression to overcome man's aggressive drives, as society's increasing complexity forced men into ever closer contact with one another.

Psychoanalytic writing presents four main developmental themes that may be used for political analysis: psychoanalytic stages, complexity-repression, dynamic normative orientation, and assimilation of experience.

The developmental sequence associated with the psychoanalytic stages (oral, anal, latent, genital) is perhaps the most familiar. According to Freud, the natural history of the human being from infancy to maturity involves a series of definite stages. The oral stage is passive in its early phase and aggressive, biting, and incorporative in its later phase. The anal stage that follows is also aggressive, selfish, and retentive. The latent stage, in which mental development is said to remain under the dominance of the pleasure principle, and the genital stage, in which the reality principle replaces the pleasure principle, complete the sequence.

The second theme involves the argument that civilization contains a drive toward complexity, which in turn results in an intensification of social interactions. This intensification, in view of man's aggressive impulses, endangers social organization unless civilization responds by heightening the general level of repression in society. The third developmental sequence, like the first, is a natural history of the individual, who develops from self-orientation through parent-orientation to peer-orientation. Finally, Freud sometimes expressed the view that just as past experiences forge present human nature, so current experiences forge the human nature to come. The difference in this last theme is between the way the city obliterates the town that preceded it, on the one hand, and the way, Freud believed, the child lies submerged but whole in the adult mind.[1]

Criticisms

Paul Roazen[2] has noted that Freud "was tempted to construct historical stages on scanty evidence." Indeed, psychoanalysis is today a minority tradition even within the field of psychology, in part because of the difficulty of documenting its theoretical constructs. Since Freud was *not* concerned with the development of political theory, he cannot be faulted for the shortcomings of some of his more politically minded followers. Nevertheless, it is useful to examine psychoanalytical approaches from the point of view of the methodological themes mentioned in the discussion on Marxism.

With regard to historical epochs, the psychoanalytic approach to politics might be criticized for ahistoricism. Lacking clear institutional or other tangible referents in history, the psychoanalytic developmental stages (self-parent-other orientations; oral-anal-latent-genital stages) are merely post facto analogies from what is controversially alleged to be the natural history of the individual. But even assuming that such stages are useful in analyzing individual development, it would be an ecological fallacy to assume relevance for political groupings. Although the organic analogy in politics (compare Hobbes' *Leviathan*) attests to the importance of this heritage, there is no reason to believe that what is true for the individual will be true for the group.

Regarding the unit of social or political action, the psychoanalytical approach tends to emphasize primarily the individual in isolation, and only secondarily the individual and his peers in collective relation to the leader, in contrast to Marx's use of social classes as the unit of action. The psychoanalytical approach, then, is most congenial to theories of "mass society," such as those advanced by Kornhauser, or theories that emphasize the translogical attachment of followers to leaders, such as Tucker's theory of communism as religion. A psychoanalytical approach would, for similar reasons, be less at home in a theory of interest groups.

---

[1] For terminology, the student is referred to the extensive glossary appended to John Rickman, ed., *A General Selection from the Works of Freud* (Garden City, N.Y.: Doubleday Anchor, 1957).

[2] Paul Roazen, *Freud: Political and Social Thought* (New York: Knopf, 1968).

As an overview of social change, Freud's views were contradictory. The pessimistic dominant theme, which points to increasing repression of civilization, is one of unilinear development toward an ultimate crisis. On the other hand, any of the other three development themes points to a more optimistic development. While a theory of social change is not stated with the self-assured finality of Marx's pronouncements on dialectic materialism, Freud's views on social change seem to assume a very simplified model that suffers by being made explicit.

A common criticism of writings in the political psychology tradition is that they use psychoanalytical concepts such as neurosis, paranoia, zenophobia, etc., to interpret historical figures (Stalin, Hitler, or Woodrow Wilson) on the slimmest factual evidence. In this way, the critics claim, psychoanalysis is used as a post facto slur on the character of the man studied, attributing his actions to something much less than rational decision. Such has been the general judgment of the book on Woodrow Wilson to which Freud himself contributed. The charge is that, as with the developmental themes, specific terms like "schizophrenia" or "paranoia" become mere metaphors when used in political analysis.

POST-FREUDIAN SOCIAL ANALYSIS

In the period immediately after Freud's major work, fascism constituted the central threat to traditional political institutions in the West. Not surprisingly, therefore, those who followed Freud in applying psychoanalytical concepts to social phenomena were drawn to the study of such topics as mass movements, authoritarianism, and the roots of aggression. In addition, the psychoanalytical tradition was extended to the study of charismatic leaders and their origins.

Mass Psychology

To Wilhelm Reich and others in this tradition, Freudian concepts seemed to provide a theoretical answer to questions that had confounded Marxist theorists. Why did German workers turn to fascism, against the radicalization predicted by Marx? "Owing to its lack of knowledge of mass psychology," Reich wrote, "Marxist sociology set 'bourgeois' against 'proletariat.' This is incorrect from a psychological viewpoint. The character structure is not restricted to the capitalists....There are liberal capitalists and reactionary workers....For that reason the purely economic concepts 'bourgeoisie' and 'proletariat' were replaced by the concepts 'reactionary' and 'revolutionary' or 'free-minded,' which relate to man's character and not to his social class. These changes were forced upon us by the fascist plague."[3]

Reich argued that politics cannot be understood as the conflict of economic interests grouped in social classes. The aspirations of political men are not reducible to economic or even socio-economic interests. To go beyond the level of understanding conventional to Marxism, Reich stated, it is necessary "to take into account the character structure of the masses and the social effect of mysticism.[4]   When this is taken into account, one can see that "the economic and ideologic situations of the masses need not necessarily coincide."[5] The economic situation is not directly and automatically translated into political consciousness, Reich believed. The hungry do not necessarily steal and the exploited do not necessarily go on strike—and in the depression of 1930, the masses did not necessarily turn to radical politics.

More generally, Reich asserted that any dominant political system produces in the masses the character structure that reinforces its dominance. Reich saw this as an extension of Marx's idea that "in every epoch the ideas of the ruling class are the ruling ideas." Psychology, he believed, rendered Marxism true to Marx; only vulgar Marxists sought to ignore psychological variables. What these vulgar Marxists failed to realize was that socioeconomic contradictions in society were reproduced in the consciousness of the individual worker!

This perception can be elaborated in a number of directions. For Reich, the key was to be found in sexual repression in an authoritarian society, such as that of Germany. Whereas economic oppression incites rebellion, Reich argued, sexual repression "anchors itself as a moral defense" involving the fear of sexual liberation and, more generally, "fear of freedom, in a word, reactionary thinking."[6] The conservative morality of the sexually repressed society not only reinforces this repression, but also prevents the expression of economic rebellion.

Fascists, who wished to reinforce this conservative character structure, did so through symbolism and mysticism. The symbolism of the uniform, the erotic aspect of rhythmic goose-stepping, and the implicit sexual release found in militarism were said to channel repressed energies in a direction reinforcing facism. Similarly, the mysticism of the facist ideology of racial purity is held by Reich to be based on asexuality, at once expressing a fear of sexuality and providing an acceptable outlet for the energy thereby suppressed. Antifascists, by contrast, could not assault fascism effectively by agitation around economic demands—that strategy was based on vulgar Marxism. Instead, the struggle for human freedom had to be based on liberating the young from sexual and political repression.

[3]Wilhelm Reich, *The Mass Psychology of Fascism* (New York: Farrar, Straus & Giroux, 1970; orig. pub. 1933), p. xxiv.
[4]*Ibid.*, p. 5.
[5]*Ibid.*, p. 19.
[6]*Ibid.*, p. 31.

The Authoritarian Personality

Erich Fromm, the German psychoanalyst who migrated to America in 1933, further developed the relation of authoritarian character structure to fascism. Isolation and powerlessness, rather than sexual repression, were the basis of his analysis in *Escape from Freedom* (1941). In his view, isolation and powerlessness are modern phenomena, reflecting both the effects of huge business and union organizations that dwarf the individual and the effects of political and commercial advertising that substitutes irrational for rational appeals, leaving the individual lost "in the vastness of cities."[7] The end result was the powerless man: "All he can do is to fall in step like a marching soldier or a worker on the endless belt. He can act; but the sense of independence, significance, has gone."[8]

Ironically, masochism and sadism "help the individual to escape his unbearable feeling of aloneness and powerlessness."[9] Through masochism, which is not simply sexual perversion, the individual can seek to belittle or annihilate his "self" in favor of identification with something larger and more powerful: a leader, a party, a nation. Sadism provides a symbiotically parallel means for escaping powerlessness. For Fromm, the sado-masochistic character was the authoritarian character.[10]

The authoritarian character prefers to submit himself to fate rather than to freedom; hence the importance of symbols involving "destiny" and "duty." As a subject, he prefers a dominating authority; as ruler, he seeks to dictate. He expects obedience from those below him, and obeys those above him. As long as modern society furthers the overshadowing of the individual by the economic machine, authoritarianism will continue to be prominent; its decline, Fromm believed, was contingent on providing the individual with active participation in social control.[11]

The Authoritarian Personality was published in 1950 by T. W. Adorno and his associates, popularizing this concept among American social scientists.[12] The Adorno study focused on anti-Semitism in the United States, finding anti-Semitism (measured by an "A-S Scale") related to authoritarianism (measured by an "F-Scale"), ethnocentrism ("E-Scale"), and economic conservatism ("PEC-Scale"). Although subject to sharp methodological criticism,[13] the authoritarian personality concept has persisted in

---

[7] Erich Fromm, *Escape from Freedom* (New York: Avon, 1965; orig. pub. 1941), p. 152.

[8] *Ibid.*, p. 153.

[9] *Ibid.*, p. 173.

[10] *Ibid.*, p. 186.

[11] *Ibid.*, p. 302.

[12] T. W. Adorno, Else Frenkel-Brunswik, D. J. Levinson, and R. N. Sanford, *The Authoritarian Personality* (New York: Harper & Row, 1950).

[13] Roger Brown, *Social Psychology* (New York: Free Press, 1965), pp. 509–523. See also Fred I. Greenstein, *Personality and Politics* (Chicago: Markham, 1969), pp. 114–118. Scaling is discussed in Chapter 9.

contemporary social science. Adorno and his associates rooted authoritarianism primarily in rigid child-rearing practices, rather than in sexual repression or powerlessness. Recent sholars have emphasized more rational factors, such as marginal social status, and the absence of information and little or no socialization toward the capacity to manipulate symbols.[14]

The Psychology of Aggression

Authoritarianism was linked to sadism and aggression by Fromm. Freud himself had made the connection between sadism and generalized aggression. LeBon's image of the crowd as impulsive, irritable, suggestible, intolerant, fickle, and sometimes violent[15] was accepted by Freud "because it fits so well with our own psychology in the emphasis which it lays on the unconscious mental life."[16] Freud saw "ruthless and hostile impulses" inhibited by libidinal ties to others in the group, with inhibited feelings finding expression in hostility toward out-groups.

These theorists believed the social order to be founded on renounced aggressive drives. The suppression of the level of aggression with too few outlets may lead to "the pressure of civilization" and a bursting forth of aggression. Civilization is thus seen as a tightrope between the indulgence of aggression and its oversuppression:

> Civilized society is perpetually menaced with disintegration through this primary hostility of men towards one another. Their interests in their common work would not hold them together; the passions of instinct are stronger than reasoned interests.[17]

In such a world, governments are run by ruling classes that seek to control the aggressiveness of the masses. However, as Freud wrote in his letter to Einstein, the governors themselves are driven by the selfsame needs and constantly seek to extend their own spheres, thereby fomenting wars and

---

[14]Herbert Hyman and Paul Sheatsley, "'The Authoritarian Personality'—A Methodological Critique," in R. Christie and M. Jahoda, eds., *Studies in the Scope and Method of 'The Authoritarian Personality'* (Glencoe: Free Press, 1954), pp. 50–122. See also Milton Rokeach, *The Open and Closed Mind* (New York: Basic Books, 1960); John Kirscht and Ronald Dillehay, *Dimensions of Authoritarianism: A Review of Research and Theory* (Lexington, Ky.: Univ. of Kentucky Press, 1967). For a striking experimental study suggesting the extent of acceptance of authority among diverse types of subjects, see Stanley Milgram, *Obedience To Authority* (New York: Harper & Row, 1974).

[15]Gustave LeBon, *The Crowd* (New York: Viking, 1960; orig. pub. 1895).

[16]Sigmund Freud, "Group Psychology and the Analysis of the Ego," in John Rickman, ed., *A General Selection from the Works of Sigmund Freud* (Garden City, N.Y.: Doubleday, 1957; orig. pub. 1921), p. 174.

[17]Sigmund Freud, *Civilization and Its Discontents* (1929), in J. Rickman, ed., *Civilization, War, and Death: Selections from Five Works by Sigmund Freud* (London: Hogarth, 1953), pp. 51–52.

insurrections.[18] Freud's pessimistic conclusion was that "there is no likelihood of our being able to suppress humanity's aggressive tendencies."

Freudian theorists saw aggression as an instinctual behavior, but one that was not constant over time because of variations in social control. The suppression of aggressive impulses occurs in a variety of ways, notable through group memberships involving mutual libidinal ties and submission to a fatherlike leader. The individual citizen is thus viewed as ambivalent toward authority: rebellious by instinct but dependent on paternalistic rulers.

Alfred Adler, on the other hand, viewed the antagonism toward authority as a striving for superiority and avoidance of threats of inferiority. This almost instinctual will to power as a path to self-esteem can be seen as an individual response to guilt, which is the central means of social control emphasized in Freudian writings.[19] C. G. Jung went further in asserting the existence of a collective (*racial*) unconscious, laying the basis for belief in innate hostile ideas quite apart from the repression Freud emphasized. Man's reason, Jung wrote, "has done violence to natural forces which seek their revenge and only await the moment when the partition falls to overwhelm the conscious life with destruction."[20]

In his later writings, Freud postulated the existence of a death instinct. This self-destructive drive, when projected outward, became aggression. The death instinct theory divided the infant discipline of psychoanalysis, with most contemporary Freudians preferring the earlier view of aggression as an independent instinct (or even Freud's initial view of aggression as a reaction to frustration, as in the influential work of Dollard and his associates).[21]

The concept of aggression as an instinct has been popularized in recent years by students of animal behavior, such as Lorenz, Ardery, and Morris.[22] Behaviorists, however, and other contemporary psychologists have denied the instinctual nature of aggression, instead relating it to social learning (e.g., peer group behavior), temperament (e.g., impatience), or other factors (e.g., as a compensation for feelings of rejection).[23] In spite of the proliferation of theories, all serve to suggest the psychological functions of

[18] Sigmund Freud, "Why War?" in Rickman, ed., *Civilization, War, and Death*, pp. 86–87.

[19] See J. A. C. Brown, *Freud and the Post-Freudians* (Baltimore: Penguin, 1961), pp. 40–41.

[20] C. G. Jung, *Modern Man in Search of a Soul* (New York: Harcourt, Brace and World, 33), p. 202. See also Brown, ed., *Freud and the Post-Freudians*, pp. 42–51.; and Roazen, *Freud: Political and Social Thought*, pp. 224–225.

[21] John Dollard, L. Doob, N. Miller, O. Mowrer, and R. Sears, *Frustration and Aggression* (New Haven: Yale Univ. Press, 1964; orig. pub. 1939). See also Aubrey Yates, ed., *Frustration and Conflict: Selected Readings* (Princeton, N.J.: D. Van Nostrand, 1965).

[22] Konrad Lorenz, *On Aggression* (New York: Bantam, 1966); Robert Ardrey, *African Genesis* (New York: Dell, 1967; orig. pub. 1961); Robert Ardrey, *The Territorial Imperative*

aggression, scapegoating, and hostility and call attention to underlying origins not attacked or solved by "better law-and-order legislation."

Human Needs

More recent psychologists have sometimes used the term "basic human needs" rather than "instincts." Abraham Maslow developed a need theory with five basic levels: survival, economic security, love and affiliation, status and self-esteem, and self-actualization. These needs constitute a hierarchy, and as lower needs like that for security become fulfilled by a society, the social order turns to concern for the next higher need. With this theory, one could predict that workers in affluent countries will gradually shift from strictly economic demands toward higher demands including self-actualization (e.g., participation and job control).[24]

The concept of a need hierarchy and a corresponding pattern of shifting central concerns of a social order over time has been sharply criticized. Chris Argyris, for example, has found less affluent, lower-level employees to value the "high" need of self-actualization as much as do managers.[25] The concept of human needs may be employed apart from the hierarchy relationship specified by Maslow, of course. Amitai Etzioni has set forth a theory of basic human needs by which to judge whether a society's structure is compatible with or contrary to human nature.[26] His theory seeks to find in psychological studies of human needs an empirical grounding for normative theory in social science. Robert Lane has also sought to detail the relationship between human needs and political theory at the level of the private individual.[27]

An important aspect of this dimension of political psychology has been the need theory of David McClelland and his associates. McClelland has analyzed socio-economic development in terms of "need-achievement," "need-power," and "need-affiliation." Through a content analysis (see

---

(New York: Dell, 1966); Desmond Morris, *The Naked Ape* (New York: McGraw-Hill, 1967). For criticism, see: Ashley Montague, *Man and Aggression* (New York: Oxford, 1968).

[23] For a survey of contemporary theories, see: Arnold Buss, *The Psychology of Aggression* (New York: John Wiley & Sons, 1961); Elton McNeil, ed., *The Nature of Human Conflict* (Englewood Cliffs, N.J.: Prentice-Hall, 1965); Ted Robert Gurr, "Psychological Factors in Civil Violence," *World Politics* 20 (January 1968): 245–278.

[24] Abraham Maslow, *Motivation and Personality* (New York: Harper & Row, 1954); *Toward a Psychology of Being* (Princeton, N.J.: D. Van Nostrand, 1962).

[25] Chris Argyris, *The Applicability of Organizational Sociology* (New York: Cambridge Univ. Press, 1972), pp. 64–67. For a theory of psychosocial development alternative to Maslow's, see Charles Hamden-Turner, *Radical Man: The Process of Psycho-Social Development* (Cambridge, Mass.: Schenkman, 1970).

[26] Amitai Etzioni, *The Active Society: A Theory of Societal and Political Processes* (New York: Free Press, 1968), pp. 622 ff.

[27] Robert E. Lane, *Political Thinking and Consciousness: The Private Mind* (Chicago: Markham, 1969), esp. ch. 2.

Chapter 7) of children's books and inference from cultural artifacts, McClelland has sought to demonstrate that societies with higher need-achievement are more likely to develop economically; development is not primarily rooted in investment, terms of trade, and other strictly economic factors.[28] Where Weber saw Western capitalism developing from the Protestant ethic, McClelland argues that the effect of Protestantism on capitalism is not direct. Instead, he contends, Protestantism is associated with early childhood independence and "mastery training" by parents, which leads to high achievement motivation in males, and only then to "the spirit of capitalism."[29]

Childhood and Leadership

The psychological effects of childhood are often traced in the lives of individual political actors. Sigmund Freud and William Bullitt interpreted Woodrow Wilson in this manner, as did Alexander and Juliette George.[30] These studies, particularly the former, have been strongly criticized for subjectivism and for their sweeping conclusions based on limited evidence. Skeptics question, for example, whether Wilson's firmness in defense of the League of Nations can really be interpreted as rigidity arising from subjection to a dominating father. Although a number of psychological studies have been made of individual leaders,[31] the work of Erik Erikson provides the most influential examples.

Erikson has emphasized the importance of the adolescent identity crisis in developing the individual's relationship with the social order. "It is necessary to understand the basic fact," he wrote, "that human childhood provides a most fundamental basis for human exploitation. The polarity Big-Small is the first in the inventory of existential oppositions such as Male and Female, Ruler and Ruled, Owner and Owned, Light Skin and Dark, over which emancipatory struggles are now raging both politically and psychologically."[32] Erikson has sought "to derive from such inquiries into man's conflicts a model of man....I have found myself studying in the lives of religious innovators that border area where neurotic and existential

---

[28] David McClelland, *The Achieving Society* (New York: Free Press, 1961).

[29] For a critical review of this and other aspects of McClelland's work, see Brown, *Freud and the Post-Freudians.* ch. 9.

[30] Sigmund Freud and William C. Bullitt, *Thomas Woodrow Wilson* (Boston: Houghton Mifflin, 1967; written 1938); Alexander George and Juliette George, *Woodrow Wilson and Colonel House* (New York: Dover, 1964). See also Erik Erikson and Richard Hofstadter, "The Strange Case of Freud, Bullitt, and Wilson," *New York Review of Books*, 9 February 1967, pp. 3–8.

[31] For a bibliographic review of such studies, see Greenstein, *Personality and Politics*, pp. 163–167.

[32] Erik Erikson, *Childhood and Society*, 2nd ed. (New York: Norton, 1963, 1 st ed., 1950), p. 418.

conflict meet and where the 'I' struggles for unencumbered awareness.... is it not in adolescent experience that the 'I' can first really perceive itself as separate?....in the long run, the 'I' transcends its limited identity and, sooner or later, faces the dilemma of existence versus politics which I have attempted to approach in my work on the Gandhian version of truth."[33]

In *Young Man Luther* (1958), Erikson undertook a psychohistorical work on the genesis of Protestantism and, more broadly, on the social ferment of an era, as distilled through the study of one man:

> Martin's reactions to his father's pressure are the beginnings of Luther's pre-occupation with matters of individual conscience . . . he incorporated his father's suspicious severity, his mother's fear of sorcery, and their mutual concern about catastrophes to be avoided and high goals to be met. Later he rebelled: first against his father, to join the monastery; then against the Church, to found his own church . . . . This biographical problem overlaps an historical one: Did Luther have a right to claim that his own fear and his feeling of being oppressed by the image of an avenging God, were shared by others?[34]

In Erikson's view, the series of childhood crises faced by Luther were indicative of the general crisis of the world image of the era in which he lived. In Erikson's later work, *Gandhi's Truth* (1969), he extends this way of looking at the world by arguing that religion and politics make "rituals out of man's basic need to confess the past in order to purge it."[35] By this, Erikson means that church and state institutionalize world images, whether through the Avenging God imagery of Luther's age or the caste imagery of Gandhi's. There is a close link between this imagery and the identity crisis of the maturing individual.

In normal times the institutionalized imagery prevails. Eventually, however, it becomes corrupted; it gains and loses in solidity and coherence; it fluctuates and may collapse. "Latent panic only waits for catastrophe—famines, pests, and depressions, overpopulation and migration, sudden shifts in technology or in leadership—to cause a shrinkage in the world image, a kind of chill attacking the sense of identity of large masses."[36]

Socialization, Roles, and Culture

Where Erikson has focused on the psychological roots of historical change, others have chosen to study the "normal process"—socialization to accept-

---

[33] Erik Erikson, "Autobiographic Notes on the Identity Crisis," in G. Holton, ed., *The Twentieth-Century Sciences* (New York: Norton, 1970). p. 30.

[34] Erik Erikson, *Young Man Luther* (New York: Norton, 1958), pp. 73–74.

[35] Erik Erikson, *Gandhi's Truth* (New York: Norton, 1969), p. 438.

[36] Erikson, *Young Man Luther*, p. 75. For a review of Erikson's work, see Robert Coles, *Erik H. Erikson: The Growth of His Work* (Boston: Little, Brown, 1970). For an alternative psychological theory of social change, see Everett E. Hagan, *On the Theory of Social Change* (Homewood, Ill.: Dorsey, 1962).

ance of prevailing role sets and cultural values. In the work of Easton and Dennis, for example, the central question deals with how socialization serves to accommodate stress and allow the political system to persist.[37] Political scientists like Easton have generally held a much broader conception of the possibilities of postchildhood social learning than have psychologists. The literature of political socialization covers the manner in which not only the family, but also the church, school, media, and peer group, orient the citizen.[38]

Nevertheless, much attention still focuses on childhood learning, even when this is not tied to a theory of personal development through psychoanalytic stages. Richard Merelman's application of learning theory to political science is illustrative. Merelman has argued that the legitimacy of political systems is based on reinforcements and sanctions. Through these, the citizen learns to support the system. Later, symbolic reinforcements may replace material ones in a mature and legitimate polity.[39] More recently, Merelman has called attention to the theory of stages of moral and cognitive development in the work of Piaget. To reach the higher stages, one must pass through the previous ones. Many, however, fail to make the passage and become fixated at a given level. Merelman has presented this version of learning theory as a framework for the analysis of political socialization.[40]

Empirical work by political scientists has tended to de-emphasize the role of the family in socialization. Jennings and Niemi, for example, used the facilities of the Survey Research Center of the University of Michigan to study a national sample of 1,669 seniors in nearly a hundred secondary schools across the nation. They failed to find family characteristics to be important determinants of the transmission rate of political values.[41] The transmission of party identification is an important exception to this, however. Another exception is indicated by Jaros, Hirsch, and Fleron, who found significant direct transmission of parental values among Appalachian

---

[37] David Easton and Jack Dennis, *Children in the Political System* (New York: McGraw-Hill, 1969). For a review of this literature, see R. Weissberg, *Political Learning, Political Choice, and Democratic Citizenship* (Englewood Cliffs, N.J.: Prentice-Hall, 1974).

[38] Lifelong learning is stressed in, for example, Richard Dawson and Kenneth Prewitt, *Political Socialization* (Boston: Little, Brown, 1969). See also an earlier work in the same series, Gabriel Almond and Sidney Verba, *The Civic Culture* (Boston, Little, Brown, 1963), ch. 11. For an additional survey of socialization literature in political science, see Jack Dennis, ed., *Socialization to Politics* (New York: John Wiley & Sons, 1973); and Dean Jaros, *Socialization to Politics* (New York: Praeger, 1973).

[39] Richard Merelman, "Learning and Legitimacy," *American Political Science Review* 60, no. 3 (September 1966): 548–561.

[40] Richard M. Merelman, "The Development of Political Ideology: A Framework for the Analysis of Political Socialization," *American Political Science Review* 63, no. 3 (September 1969): 750–767.

[41] M. Kent Jennings and Richard G. Niemi, "The Transmission of Political Values from Parent to Child," *American Political Science Review* 62, no. 1 (March 1968): 169–184.

children. Appalachian children were also found to deviate from national patterns by: (1) being much less favorably inclined toward authorities in general, and (2) not shifting these views with age. But no support was found for the theory of the image of the father extending to images of political authority.[42] Searing, Schwartz, and Lind have documented the more general tendency: little association between childhood orientations and the later learning of specific beliefs about important national issues.[43] Swanson, Kelleher, and English found in a study of delegates to a constitutional convention that, though pre-existing role orientations were important, "experience that contradicted the delegates' original perceptions acted as an important socializing agent in restructuring political attitudes."[44]

Role theory   The body of literature on "role theory" is generally compatible with political science emphasis on adult learning. Role theory links dispositions and opinions to position in the social system rather than to childhood experience or psychosocial stages. Correspondingly, much of the literature in role theory falls in sociology rather than psychology, emphasizing the means by which people's pre-existing views conform to the role set characteristic of their social positions. By focusing on the way social institutions and the social milieu change individual attitudes, role theory embodies an approach frequently contrary to the psychoanalytic orientation.

Among the most original and influential works in this field is Erving Goffman's *The Presentation of the Self in Everyday Life* (1956). Goffman uses the metaphor of the theater to analyze social behavior. Behavior is seen in terms of "performances" in which the "actor" arranges insofar as possible a "script" favorable to his own "role"; suitable "supporting actors" are chosen; critical events are "rehearsed backstage"; emphasis is placed on "the arts of impression management." Problems arise when the individual is forced to expose himself in "discrepant roles" or to "communicate out of character." This view assumes the importance of a given definition of the situation, and views behavior as dominated by a drive to sustain that definition in the face of social events.[45]

A somewhat different twist to role theory is given by Robert Bales, who pictures society as composed of "an irregular spiral web of interconnected group positions, with some breaks," constituting a sort of "social ladder."

[42] Dean Jaros, Herbert Hirsch, and Frederic Fleron, "The Malevolent Leader: Political Socialization in an American Sub-Culture," *American Political Science Review* 62, no. 2 (June 1968): 564–575.

[43] Donald D. Searing, Joel J. Schwartz, and Alden E. Lind, "The Structuring Principle: Political Socialization and Belief Systems," *American Political Science Review* 67, no. 2 (June 1973): 415–432.

[44] W. Swanson, S. Kelleher, and A. English, "Socialization of Constitution Makers," *Journal of Politics* 34, no. 1 (February 1972): 198.

[45] Erving Goffman, *The Presentation of the Self in Everyday Life* (New York: Doubleday, 1959: orig. pub. 1956).

The individual in this system does not simply carry out the role definitions associated with his given group position; individuals seeking to change their group role in favor of a more valued one will emulate those with proximate but superior positions on the ladder of social roles.[46]

The playing out of roles in which one is *not* incumbent creates empathy and reduces social distance. For this reason, role-playing is used in group retraining, to reduce prejudice, for example.[47]

In political science, the focus has been on role socialization and role conflict among political officeholders, notably legislators.[48] Donald Matthews, for example, has delineated the manner in which role consensus is maintained in the Senate through the socialization of freshman legislators to such institutional norms as deference to senior members and work specialization.[49] Role conflict arises when constituency and party have different expectations of the legislator or in conflict-of-interest situations.[50]

Political culture   The study of personal roles and role socialization is part of the study of culture. Culture, comprising the values and patterns of life of a society, conditions role definitions, role socialization, and change in roles. The study of culture is associated particularly with the discipline of anthropology, in which literature on the relation of culture to personality is becoming an established field.[51] The Social Darwinists and some earlier theorists were concerned with culture, but a greater focus was introduced to the discipline primarily through the work of the Social Science Research Council Committee on Political Behavior and Comparative Politics (which included Almond, Pye, and others).[52] As will be discussed in Chapter 3, this cultural perspective is closely associated with functionalist sociology.

[46] Robert F. Bales, *Personality and Interpersonal Behavior* (New York: Holt, Rinehart & Winston, 1970), p. 48. Compare Merton's concept of "anticipatory socialization" in Robert K. Merton,"Anticipatory Socialization," in B. Biddle and E. Thomas, eds., *Role Theory* (New York: John Wiley & Sons, 1966), pp. 347–349.

[47] Gordon Allport, *The Nature of Prejudice* (New York: Doubleday, 1954), p. 45.

[48] Compare John Wahlke et al., *The Legislative System* (New York: John Wiley & Sons, 1962). For a survey of political science socialization and role theory applications, see M. Conway and F. Feigert, *Political Analysis* (Boston: Allyn and Bacon, 1972), chs. 5 and 6.

[49] Donald Matthews, *U.S. Senators and their World* (Chapel Hill, N.C.: Univ. of North Carolina Press, 1960). For a discussion of possible biases of such approaches, see Fred Greenstein, "A Note on the Ambiguity of 'Political Socialization',"*The Journal of Politics* 32, no. 4 (November 1970): 969–978. For an empirical test of role theory as formulated in the volume by Wahlke *et al.*, *Legislative System*, see J. van der Slik, "Role Theory and the Behavior of Representatives," *Public Affairs Bulletin* 6, no. 2 (March–April, 1973): 1–7. Van der Slik is critical of the usefulness of these formulations.

[50] Compare Festinger's more general concept of "cognitive dissonance" in Leon Festinger, *Conflict, Decision, and Dissonance* (Stanford: Stanford Univ. Press, 1964).

[51] See Robert Hunt, ed., *Personalities and Cultures* (Garden City, N.Y.: Natural History Press, 1967).

[52] Gabriel Almond, "Comparative Political Systems," *Journal of Politics*, 18 (1956): 391–409; Almond and Verba, *Civic Culture*; Lucien Pye, *Politics, Personality, and Nation-Building* (New Haven: Yale Univ. Press, 1962). Almond distinguishes culture at cognitive, affective, and evaluative levels, using degree of civic competence to differentiate parochial, subject, and participant political cultures.

The concept of political culture has spread from its obvious application of comparing nations to other political science fields. Daniel Elazar, for example, has compared American states in terms of their relative associations with individualistic, moralistic, and traditional cultures.[53] Edgar Litt has compared factions within the state politics of Massachusetts on a similar basis.[54]   And a recent work by Donald Devine treats culture as a key "input" in a systems analysis (see Chapter 3) of American politics.[55]

PSYCHOLOGY AND POLITICAL SCIENCE

Psychological approaches to political phenomena have been important in American political science since the early years of the twentieth century. Among its earliest advocates was Graham Wallas, whose *Human Nature and Politics* sought to rescue the concept of human nature from the discredit into which it had fallen by the end of the nineteenth century.[56] Wallas attacked utilitarian rationalism for failing to recognize the importance of the irrational in politics. For Wallas, the art of politics revolved around the "creation of opinion by the deliberate exploitation of subconscious non-rational inference."[57] Given this fact perception, Wallas argued that the consent theory emphasized by democratic writers needed reformulation; elections were to be viewed as mechanisms for achieving "right decisions," not for effecting decisions already formed in the public mind.

Wallas was critical of the then-contemporary movement to extend democracy, but he believed human impulses (e.g., toward excellence) were served through political participation. If the citizen were not unduly burdened by reforms in representative government, the psychology of human nature might still be seen as consistent with democracy.[58] Nevertheless, the general thrust of these works was toward the control by the rational over the irrational. Though not elitist in political theory, works by later writers extended this theme. Ellwood, for example, emphasized the tendency of

[53]Daniel Elazar, *American Federalism: A View From the States* (New York: Crowell, 1966).

[54]Edgar Litt, *The Political Culture of Massachusetts* (Cambridge, Mass.: Harvard Univ. Press, 1965).

[55]Donald J. Devine, *The Political Culture of the United States* (Boston: Little, Brown, 1972). For additional reading, see L. Schneider and C. Bonjean, eds., *The Idea of Culture in the Social Sciences* (Cambridge, England: Cambridge University Press, 1973); William Bluhm, *Ideologies and Attitudes: Modern Political Culture* (Englewood Cliffs, N.J.: Prentice-Hall, 1974).

[56]See Martin Wiener, *Between Two Worlds: The Political Thought of Graham Wallas* (Oxford: Clarendon Press, 1971).

[57]Graham Wallas, *Human Nature in Politics*, 4th ed. (London: Constable, 1948; orig. pub. 1908), pp. 12—13.

[58] *Ibid.*, p. viii. In a later work, Wallas extended his treatment from political to general social organization. See *The Great Society* (New York: Macmillan, 1916).

intellect to play an increasing role in controlling group action as society advances.[59] MacIver emphasized the need for the state to play the role of coordinator and adjuster of the (irrational) special interests of society.[60] In this period, the debate over the basic characteristics of human nature was closely linked to debate over alternative conceptions of the good social order.[61]

By the 1920s, social psychology was widely employed in American political science writings.[62] Research led into the study of the political capacity of the electorate, the nature of bossism and party leadership, the extent of stereotyping and bias among voters, the causes of nonvoting, and the control of public opinion,[63] as well as the traditional inquiry into national characteristics. This research often supported the post-World War I disillusion expressed in the work of Walter Lippman and in similar essays attacking the perceptual, motivational, and psychological competence of the average voter.[64] Similar intellectual currents were fed by the psychological research leading to emphasis on propaganda and the new profession of public relations.[65]

During the 1930s and 1940s, the work of Harold Lasswell dominated writing on political psychology in America. In *Psychopathology and Politics* (1930), Lasswell used life histories (compare Erikson, discussed earlier) to relate personality growth to politics. Lasswell emphasized the displacement of private motives onto public objects, rationalizing this displacement as the public good.[66] From this theory, Lasswell derived three characteristic political types: the agitator (narcissistic), the administrator (affects displaced onto more immediate objects), and the theorist (remote displacement).[67] In this early work, Lasswell looked toward "preventive politics," which involved the use of psychological techniques to reduce tension in administrative work.

---

[59] Charles A. Ellwood, *An Introduction to Social Psychology* (New York: Appleton, 1917). See also Ellwood, *Sociology in its Psychological Aspects* (New York: Appleton, 1912); *The Psychology of Human Society* (New York: Appleton, 1924).

[60] R. M. MacIver, *Community: A Sociological Study* (New York: Macmillan, 1917).

[61] Horace M. Kallen, "Political Science as Psychology," *American Political Science Review* 17, no. 2 (May 1923): 181–203.

[62] Charles Merriam, "The Present State of the Study of Politics," *American Political Science Review* 15, no. 2 (May 1921): 180–181; Charles Merriam, "The Significance of Psychology for the Study of Politics," *American Political Science Review* 18 no. 3 (August 1924): 469–488.

[63] Floyd Allport, "The Psychological Nature of Politics," *American Political Science Review* 21, no. 3 (August 1927): 611–618.

[64] Walter Lippman, *The Phantom Public* (New York: Harcourt, Brace and Co., 1925).

[65] See Edward I. Bernays, *Crystallizing Public Opinion* (New York: Boni and Liveright, 1923) and *Propaganda* (New York: Horace Liveright, 1928); Harold Lasswell, *Propaganda Technique in the World War* (New York: Knopf, 1927); Leonard Doob, *Propaganda: Its Psychology and Technique* (New York: Holt, 1935).

[66] For a complete bibliography of Lasswell's works, see Arnold Rogow, ed., *Politics, Personality, and Social Science in the Twentieth Century: Essays in Honor of Harold Lasswell* (Chicago: Univ. of Chicago Press, 1969), pp. 407–446.

[67] Harold Lasswell, *Psychopathology and Politics* (Glencoe, Ill.: Free Press, 1951; orig. pub. 1930), 262–263.

In *World Politics and Personal Insecurity* (1935), Lasswell continued to call for a politics of prevention, but his method shifted from biography to what he termed "configurative analysis." Configurative analysis interprets politics in terms of elite symbols of identification, demand, and expectation.[68] Elite symbols eliciting cohesion clash with the diffusion of new social myths which are antithetical to the old order but which also appeal to the personal insecurities of individuals in societies in crisis. Social control through image manipulation is a central theme. Lasswell felt that the task of political leadership in America was "to stimulate effective class-consciousness among the middle income groups,"[69] while defending the system against new utopias asserted from below.

Lasswell extended this argument in *Politics: Who Gets What, When, How* (1936), asserting that "an established elite is usually so well situated in control of the goods, violence, and practices of a community that a challenging elite is constrained to rely chiefly upon symbols."[70] Lasswell attacked theories of revolution based on deprivation rather than on elite responses to surges in mass insecurity (e.g., how well the elite can induce catharsis through propaganda or violence). Although engendering much criticism of his methodology, Lasswell's work pioneered in the study of political elites and symbols.[71] His own later work returned, however, to the concepts of "political types" in relation to personality development.[72] Murray Edelman is a contemporary theorist in the Lasswell tradition; his work applies a more critical evaluation to the theme of social control through image manipulation.[73]

Since World War II, the most popularly known theorist concerned with psychological interpretations of politics has been Herbert Marcuse. Marcuse's work has centered on the subtle processes of "repressive tolerance" whereby modern society attenuates class struggle preserving the illusion of popular sovereignty while serving to validate socially dominant functions through mystification. Underlying this world view are an emphasis on "the historical nature of human needs" and the potential for emergence of liberating forces overthrowing the "surplus repression" inherent in present political culture.[74]

---

[68] Harold Lasswell, *World Politics and Personal Insecurity* (New York: Free Press, 1965; orig. pub. 1935), pp. 4—7.

[69] *Ibid.*, p. 177.

[70] Harold Lasswell, *Politics: Who Gets What, When, How* (Glencoe, Ill.: Free Press, 1951; orig. pub. 1936), p. 444.

[71] See essays in Rogow, ed., *Politics, Personality, and Social Science*, for example.

[72] See Harold Lasswell, *Power and Personality* (New York: Norton, 1948).

[73] See Murray Edelman, *The Symbolic Uses of Politics* (Urbana, Ill.: Illini Books, 1964) and *Politics as Symbolic Action* (Chicago: Markham, 1971).

[74] Herbert Marcuse, "Repressive Tolerance," in R.P. Wolff, B. Moore, Jr., and H. Marcuse, *A Critique of Pure Tolerance* (Boston: Beacon, 1965); *Eros and Civilization: A Philosophical Inquiry into Freud* (Boston, Beacon, 1955); *One-Dimensional Man* (Boston: Beacon, 1964); and *An Essay on Liberation* (Boston: Beacon, 1969).

Among political scientists, however, the work of Fred I. Greenstein is more representative. A student of Lasswell, Greenstein has been particularly concerned with the linkage between personality and political behavior, the relationship between psychological predispositions and role sets, and the correlation of censuses of psychological characteristics with system characteristics.[75]

A BRIEF SUMMARY

As methodology, the psychological approach directs attention toward irrational behavior, toward the personal stakes in public matters, and toward the development of relationships between the individual and the polity over time. It invites a wariness of surface appearances and watchfulness for and even expectation of hypocrisy or divergence of ideal and practice. It is a reminder to relate political analysis ultimately to the individual. That is, it is a warning against reification. Often, it emphasizes the ego defense of the individual against society. This defense involves numerous "irrational" mechanisms such as projection (ascribing one's own, unrecognized mental processes to others), negation (admission of a repressed thought to consciousness under the condition that it is denied), or regression (reversion to a less mature state, as in the face of unacceptable stress).[76]

Psychological approaches since Freud have become more and more diverse in nature.[77] It is therefore difficult to delineate a single clear"psychological method" for analyzing a given political problem.

An interpretation of black rioting in the 1960s that draws on Freud's interpretation in *Civilization and Its Discontents* might take the following outline:

Analysis	Example
1. Ask a question of the type "How has X developed?" where X would ordinarily involve a matter not explainable at the strictly rational level.	1. What is the developmental origin of riots?

[75] Many of Greenstein's journal articles are collected in his *Personality and Politics* (Chicago: Markham, 1969). Also influential has been the work of Robert E. Lane. See Lane, *Political Ideology* (New York: Free Press, 1962), for Lane's "theory of democratic personality." See also Lane's article on "political personality" in the *Encyclopedia of the Social Sciences* (New York: Macmillan, 1968).

[76] For a review of psychoanalytic terminology, see J. Rickman, ed., *A General Selection from the Works of Sigmund Freud* (Garden City, N.Y.: Doubleday, 1957; orig. pub. 1937) pp. 251—294.

[77] On neo-Freudian thought not reviewed here, see Else Frenkel-Brunswik, "Interaction of Psychological and Sociological Factors in Political Behavior," *American Political Science Review* 46, no. 1 (March 1952): 44—65. and Martin Birnbach, *Neo-Freudian Social Philosophy* (Stanford: Stanford Univ. Press, 1961).

2. Specify the groups involved, noting the individual's relation to the leader.

3. Note the relationship of complexity of civilization, social needs for repression, and changes in social spacing.

4. Note the relationship of groups involved to historical development.

2. Various black groups, often led by visionary, even messianic leader, usually with religious association.

3. Increasingly complex urban America requires proportionately greater repression in economic roles, which are quite rigid. Since black men are routinely assigned to lower, more rigid roles (for non-psychological reasons) they suffer relatively great repression.

4. As repression increases, falling disproportionately on blacks, aggressive energy is increasingly displaced into existing messianic groups traditionally sanctioning emotive behavior; riots result.

On the other hand, by drawing on other aspects of psychological theory (e.g., Dollard's frustration-aggression theory), we might come up with somewhat different analyses.

There is rarely a single "correct" interpretation of a political problem. Nor are the Marxist, psychoanalytic, or functionalist methods really reducible to simple formulae. They are more properly labelled "orientations," for that is their function: pointing us in a particular direction to uncover fruitful questions and suggestive answers. In psychological orientation, that direction is inward, toward ourselves as emotional beings rather than as rational calculators of political considerations.[78]

EXERCISE

Everett Hagen, in *On the Theory of Social Change*, set forth a psychologically based theory of sociopolitical change, focussing on the withdrawal

[78] For further reading on political and social science applications see the following: James Davies, *Human Nature in Politics* (New York: John Wiley & Sons, 1963); Jeanne Knutson, ed., *Handbook of Political Psychology* (San Francisco: Jossey-Bass, 1973); Donald McIntosh, "Weber and Freud: On the Nature and Sources of Authority," *American Sociological Review* 35, no. 5 (October 1970): 901–911; G. Di Palma and Herbert McClosky, "Personality and Conformity: The Learning of Political Attitudes," *American Political Science Review* 64, no. 4 (December 1970): 1054–1073; Arnold Rogow, "Psychiatry and Political Science: Some Reflections and Prospects," in S.M. Lipset, ed., *Politics and the Social Sciences* (New York: Oxford, 1969): 207–225; R. Schoenberger, "Conservatism, Personality, and Political Extremism," *American Political Science Review* 62, no. 3 (September 1968): 868–877; P. Sniderman and J. Citrin, "Psychological Sources of Political Belief: Self-Esteem and Isolationist Attitudes," *American Political Science Review* 65, no. 2 (June 1971): 401–417; and D. Thomas, D. Franks, and J. Calonica, "Role-Taking and Power in Social Psychology, *American Sociological Review* 37, no. 5 (October 1972): 605–614. A useful anthology is Gordon DiRenzo, ed., *Personality and Politics* (New York: Doubleday Anchor, 1974).

of status respect as the most important factor in social disintegration. The removal of this respect creates a social stress, Hagen argued, that may be resolved in one of several ways. The immediate reaction is apt to be one of resentment and anxiety, mixed with the degree of rage reflecting the severity of the withdrawal.

Beyond this reaction lie others, such as ritualism or retreat. The ritualist resolves his dilemma by scaling down his goals, going through the motions expected by dominant social groups without any real hope that this will enable him to attain cultural goals. Ritualism, common among colonial and neocolonial peoples, involves a degree of suppressed rage beneath an identification with an oppressing or dominant group. The retreatist adjusts to status withdrawal by repressing the fact of the denigration of his status. Unable to assert values and social purposes alternative to the prevailing ones, which degrade his status, the retreatist is characterized by high anomie, a listless social drift—an extreme example is the alcoholic or the vagabond.

Those who suffer status withdrawal in the first instance still retain their old values and may survive while hoping for the return of better days. Second and later generations will not react in this way. The father whose status is despised will vent his frustration on his family, the only socially acceptable outlet, adopting an authoritarian stance. The son, in turn, will perceive that the father's behavior results from the discrepancy between his belief in the value of his role and his belief in the attitudes of superior social groups.

The son is faced with a dilemma: an authoritarian childhood environment creates in him a high need for dependence, ordinarily involving acceptance of social hierarchy—yet to embrace either his father's status or the attitudes of superior social groups brings him pain. A few unusually creative sons may defy such groups and channel their need for dependence into some religious or social movement. But, more typically, the son will solve his problem by rejecting both his father's role and the beliefs of superiors. He will be reinforced in this by similar decisions of other sons. In this manner a distinctive youth culture appears, differentiated from the older generation by the ascendance of the retreatist personality, marked by suppressed rage and anomic lack of interest in prevailing work and values.

Change is thus intergenerational. After the withdrawal of status respect, retreatism deepens, paradoxically laying the basis for a more creative response. The first generation of sons, like their fathers, vents its frustration in adopting an authoritarian relation to the family. But there is this difference: they are not certain of the natural rightness of the authoritarian view of the world. As retreatism deepens in the second generation, the father's relation to his family becomes more erratic, alternatively dominant and withdrawn, continually decreasing his commitment to his social role.

At some point, often by the third or fourth generation, the father's retreatist rejection of prevailing values is generalized, the father conveying to his son his regret for his son's lot in life as well as his own. As the son comes to feel valued by his father, the pain of being at the bottom of an authoritarian hierarchy is blamed on sources higher than his father. In fact, the son may experience guilt and shame at not having come to his father's aid. Such sons become fathers who require their children to meet expectations that they themselves did not meet and about which they feel shame.

Under these circumstances, sons may acquire a drive to transcend the condition of the father. Retreatism yields to innovation and reform. This new personality orientation may manifest itself in economic and technological creativity, using nontraditional or even illegal means to economic gain, or it may be evident in political reformism. These creative energies will be channeled in whichever direction seems most promising. Writing at the start of the 1960s about the black movement, Hagen predicted: "It is likely that the next generation of the Negro population in many parts of the United States, losing its apathy, will go through this phase of attainment of social goals by unsanctioned means, and at one stage will support unscrupulous leaders."[79]

As an exercise, read Chapter 9 ("Disturbing Events and Reactions to Them") of Hagen's book; then write a short essay on whether this theory can be used to interpret changes in the black community and black social movements in the United States. In completing this exercise, the following readings may be helpful: Hanes Walton, *Black Politics* (Philadelphia: Lippincott, 1972); W. E. B. DuBois, *The Souls of Black Folk* (Greenwich, Conn.: Fawcett, 1961; orig. pub. 1953); E. Franklin Frazier, *Negro Youth at the Crossways: Their Personality Development in the Middle States* (New York: Schocken, 1967; orig. pub. 1940); William Grier and Price Cobbs, *Black Rage* (New York: Basic Books, 1968).

[79] Everett E. Hagen, *On the Theory of Social Change* (Homewood, Ill.: Dorsey, 1962) p. 243.

3 Functionalism and Systems Theory

Though each has assumed continued importance, neither Marxist nor psychological approaches have become dominant orientations within American political science. After World War II, new approaches such as "functionalism," "structural-functionalism," and "systems analysis" gained widespread support in social science and, eventually, in political science. Advocates of these approaches viewed Marxist and psychological methodologies as "monistic": that is, as concentrating on only one dimension, be it economic or psychological. In contrast, the functionalists and systems analysts viewed their methodologies as more powerful and multidimensional, subsuming the insights of the "monistic" approaches and providing a framework for integrating all previous social science knowledge. Amid this enthusiasm, at universities such as Harvard new departments of "social relations" were formed, based on the anticipated theoretical integration of social sciences.

Though that enthusiasm has now dwindled and such departments are being dismantled, functionalism and systems theory are useful contrasts to the orientations studied in the previous chapters. Both remain influential within our discipline in spite of the vigorous attacks on them in recent years.

Political scientists have borrowed so eclectically from these approaches, which themselves have undergone so many transformations, that it is difficult to state precisely the meaning of "functionalism," "Structural-functionalism," or "systems analysis." Many political scientists use the terms interchangeably and loosely, while others wish to make fine distinctions even if these are not generally accepted within political science. For purposes of this text we may begin discussion with the relatively "purer" original meanings of these terms and then work toward the looser formulations that have played a prominent role in political science applications.

FUNCTIONALISM

The concept of function became popular in late nineteenth-century sociology and social philosophy. Martindale has traced the origins of sociological functionalism to three sources: early sociology, functionalist psychology, and social anthropology.[1]

In early sociology, functionalism represented a break with social behaviorism. Where behaviorism focused on the behavior of the individual, implying an image of society as a constellation of social atoms, functionalism grew out of an organicist theory. That is, theorists such as Tonnies and Durkheim advanced a theory of society that emphasized the primacy of the system rather than the individual, and the interrelatedness of social units and individuals into the organic whole which is society.

Functionalism also drew from "configurationism" in psychology and in Gestalt theory. Functional psychologists, such as John Dewey, criticized the behavioral separation of "stimulus" and "response," instead insisting on examination of an operation as a whole reflex. Gestalt theorists such as Wolfgang Kohler and Kurt Koffka further developed these ideas, reacting against behavioral analysis (literally, separation into parts) in favor of emphasis on organic wholes as primary realities. In both functionalist sociology and functionalist psychology, the whole, be it the society or the personality, was not seen as a mere sum-of-the-parts; the whole was a dynamic configuration or system that conditioned behavior.

The third basis of functionalism lay in the social anthropology of A. R. Radcliffe-Brown and of Bronislaw Malinowski. Anthropological functionalists also emphasized the unity of culture as a system. Malinowski opposed the evolutionists' emphasis on survivals of the past and the diffusionists' emphasis on imitation of other cultures; instead culture was to be understood primarily in terms of its function of relating biological human needs to the environment.

At the core of nineteenth-century functionalism was the concept of the personality, the society, or the culture as an organic whole, not reducible to its parts. Each was conceived as a dynamic system fulfilling functions that enabled the entity to adapt and survive. In terms of methodology, functionalism opposed analysis of individuals or social structures. It instead emphasized evaluation of any social phenomenon in terms of its role in maintaining the system. In its extreme formulations, functionalism engendered a conservative philosophy: that every social form serves a vital function and that reform is misguided because it abrogates these functions. For example, corruption should not be the object of reform because it functions to allow vital flexibility and incentives in political systems.

---

[1] Don Martindale, *The Nature and Types of Sociological Theory* (Boston: Houghton Mifflin, 1960). The following discussion draws on this work.

PARSONSIAN STRUCTURAL-FUNCTIONALISM

Much of the contemporary importance of functionalism in political science derives from the field of sociology and the work of Talcott Parsons. In his first important work, *The Structure of Social Action* (1937), Parsons noted a convergence of social theories of that period toward a view of society that was neither Marxist nor atomistically behaviorist. This was a view of society as a system, not reducible to economic or psychological forces.[2] Parsons found in the work of Marshall, Pareto, Durkheim, and Weber a common, underlying concept of social organization describable as a means-ends "chain" or "hierarchy."

Contrasting atomistic behavioral theories, Parsons wrote, "Instead of single isolated unit acts it is necessary to think in terms of complicated webbed chains of means-ends relationships."[3] At the top of the chain is the system of coherently related ultimate ends. At the intermediate level there are technological considerations, considerations of choice under conditions of scarcity (the economic element), and considerations of coercion by others (the political element).

In this hierarchy, each level becomes "a condition of the attainment of the one before it."[4]   The technological considerations are subordinated to the economic, the economic to the political, and so on.

What is the intellectual significance of all this? Where the Marxists had pointed toward changes in the means of production as the engine of historical change, and the Freudians had cited the tensions between psychological drives and external realities, Parsonsian functionalism pointed to the ultimate importance of values in understanding social change. Referring to the second law of thermodynamics (systems tend toward entropy), Parsons wrote, "Rationality occupies a logical position in respect to action systems analogous to that of entropy in physical systems. . . . Effort energy is, in the processes of action, converted into realization of ends, or conformity with norms." Thus, the "law of increasing rationality" is that "a process of action can proceed only in the direction of increase in the value of the property rationality."[5]

By rejecting economic, psychological, and behaviorist determinism and by elevating rationality in relation to values to a crucial theoretical level, Parsons was justified in calling this the "*voluntaristic* theory of action." Parsons' feat was to avoid deterministic theories, particularly Marxism;

---

[2] For a discussion of this point and the Parsonsian theory generally, see W. J. M. Mackenzie, *Politics and Social Science* (Baltimore: Penguin, 1967), pp. 86 ff.

[3] Talcott Parsons, *The Structure of Social Action* (Glencoe, Ill.: Free Press, 1949; orig. pub. 1937), pp. 283–241.

[4] *Ibid.*, p. 240.

[5] *Ibid.*, pp. 751–752.

demonstrate the convergence of leading non-Marxist sociologists of that era; and lay the basis for a general set of concepts that promised to overcome the demoralization of sociology at that time[6] by uniting theoretically what others saw only as disparate fragments of knowledge.

Vocabulary of Structural-Functionalism

There are certain specific terms used in the structural-functionalism system, which are related in various ways. *Structures* are observable uniformities of action; it is the existence of these regularities that makes social science a possibility. *Functions* are the results of structures; they are not purposes or needs. Because the definition of function is tied to potentially observable results rather than imputed intent, that is, to actual behavior, this general method is compatible with behavioralism.

Institutions are defined as structures that, in their basic composition, are ideal (conform to social norms), actual (conform to reality), and enforced. A *tradition* is an institution whose perpetuation is institutionalized, even without regard for the functional implications of the tradition's operations. In this system of definitions, traditions are more stable than institutions, and institutions are more enduring than structures.

Functional requisites are results, usually generalized conditions, that are necessary to the maintenance of the unit with which they are associated. *Structural requisites* are patterns of actions necessary to fulfill functional requisites. *Equivalents* are structures that yield the same results (serve the same function). *Eufunctions* and *eustructures* are results or patterns leading to the maintenance or increase of adaptation, and hence to the persistence of the unit (where adaptation is any process that aids the survival, functioning, maintenance, or achievement of purpose of the unit considered). *Dysfunctions* and *dysstructures* are results or patterns leading to the lessening of adaptation and hence to failure of the unit to persist.

Functional prerequisites are results, usually generalized conditions, necessary for a unit to come into being. *Structural prerequisites* are structures leading to fulfillment of functional prerequisites. *Concrete structures* are capable of physical separation in time and/or space, whereas *analytic structures* are not.

Manifest functions are intended and recognized results, whereas results that are unintended and unrecognized are *latent* functions. Similarly *IUR* functions are intended and unrecognized, and *UIR* functions are unintended but recognized.

Example   Robert Merton's classic analysis of the role of the city political machine can be employed to illustrate the use of structural-functional

---

[6] *Ibid.*, p. 774.

vocabulary in the analysis of a political subject:[7]

The old city machine was a *structure* that served the *function* of adjusting immigrants to urban America. Its *functional prerequisites* included prior urbanization and immigration, the *structural prerequisites* for which included foremost the development of steam industry (Which in turn had the *functional prerequisite* of inexpensive labor). Continuation of immigration was a *structural requisite* of the urban political machine (presence of immigrants was the *functional requisite*). Decline of immigration and the growth of professionalization were among the *dysstructures* resulting in the *dysfunctions* (for the *unit* of the political machine subsystem) of fewer immigrants and fewer patronage jobs. Lacking these *structural-functional requisites*, the unit has failed to persist. The problem arises because only recently has the hitherto *latent function* of political machines in aiding the low-skilled to adjust to urban life become recognized. The poverty program is an effort to find a *structural equivalent* to fulfill that *eufunction* formerly fulfilled by the machines.

This example, though presented in an abbreviated and oversimplified form, suggests some of the strengths and weaknesses of structural-functional analysis.

Procedure

The following is a step outline of the procedure of structural-functional requisite analysis, showing specific applications to the previous example of the city political machine:

1. Identify the unit to be studied, e.g., the urban political machine, defined by party dominance of city politics and personal dominance of the party.
2. Identify the unit's setting. *Setting* refers to the set of factors limiting the range of variation of the unit. For the political machine, crucial aspects of the setting include the American constitutional framework and American capitalism.
3. Specify whether one is interested in why a structure persists or in how it came into being. If the former, discuss requisites; if the latter, discuss prerequisites.
4. Determine the functional (pre)requisites, e.g., urbanization, immigration.
5. Determine the structural (pre)requisites, e.g., steam industry.
6. Specify the eufunctional and dysfunctional structures affecting the unit at the time studied, e.g., professionalism, decline of immigration.
7. Identify possible structural equivalents for the eufunctions noted.
8. Throughout the analysis, try to recognize all types of functions, not just manifest (or latent) functions.
9. Finally, avoid *functional teleology*; that is, asserting that the presence of a structure is due to its being a functional requisite of the unit in which it is found. Being a necessity does not guarantee a structure's existence.

[7] See Robert K. Merton, *On Theoretical Sociology* (New York: Free Press, 1949), pp. 127–136.

Criticisms

Among the strengths of the structural-functional requisite method are rigorous definitions carefully interrelated, avoidance of a focus on governmental-institutional aspects alone, and systematic consideration of many possibly relevant types of variables. Weaknesses include definitions that are difficult to operationalize, absence of a criterion for determining which variables are more causally relevant than others, and hence a more retrospective than predictive usefulness. That is, structural-functional requisite analysis tends to be a typology, not a theory, and is better used to categorize variables than to predict relationships.

Structural-functional requisite analysis has been accused of a conservative bias because of its emphasis on equilibrating forces, often of a socially diffuse sort not amenable to intentional control, and for its emphasis on incremental change. It may lead researchers to overemphasize latent eufunctions to what are generally regarded as "social evils" (the city boss was good because he serviced immigrants; apathy is good because it prevents over-politicization of social life; corruption is good because it enables flexibly circumventing rigid rules) and not emphasize latent dysfunctions or, for that matter, manifest and other functions. (The attraction to latent eufunctions is that the political scientist often would like to assert something resulting from his research that is not "common sense."

On the other hand, structural-functional requisite analysis does have some potentially anticonservative aspects. If structural equivalents are emphasized, then the implication is that no existing political structure is necessary. Every structure must be examined to determine if it is more eufunctional than dysfunctional, and if there is a superior structural equivalent that might replace it.

LEVELS OF STRUCTURAL-FUNCTIONAL ANALYSIS

Beyond the structural-functional requisite analysis discussed above, there are three related types of analysis that fall within this tradition. These are *universal requisite analysis, pattern variable analysis,* and *AGIL system analysis.*

Universal Requisite Analysis

As a result of structural-functional requisite analysis, some scholars have attempted to delineate the functional requisites of any society in any place or time period. This list of "universal requisites" is sometimes used, often in abridged form, as a checklist procedure for studying society. This type of analysis is common in the study of comparative development in political science. Each of the ten functional requisites of any society may be used as a chapter in analyzing a society as a whole. These ten areas are:

1. Provision for adequate sexual *recruitment* and physiological relation to the environment. This functional requisite is so basic it is often assumed rather than discussed.

2. Provision for adequate *role differentiation* and role assignment. Roles are positions that are differentiated from one another in terms of a given social structure, and may be either *ideal* (normative definition of the role) or *actual* (role as defined by behavior). A particularly important part of role differentiation is differentiation by *status*, where status is the sum of the individual's ideal roles, as opposed to *social standing*, which is the sum of the individual's ideal and actual roles. If the same *role cluster* that exists in an individual also exists in a great many other individuals, the role cluster defines a *station* in life. A *stratum* is a mass of persons holding the same station, while *stratification* is role differentiation by higher or lower social standing.

3. Provision for adequate levels of *communication*. Here vocabulary is often borrowed from communications theory, and authors speak of a system composed of *input, transformation, output,* and *feedback* sectors.

4. Provision for adequate levels of *shared cognitive orientations*. That is, any society must provide for minimum levels of information common to all or most citizens if it is to function. *Basic* cognitive orientations are those that are functional requisites.

5. Provision for adequate levels of shared, articulated *goals*. This raises the possibility of tension among multiple goals or goals that entail dysfunctional aspects. The emphasis is usually on patterns resulting in adequate *consensus* about social goals.

6. Provision for the *regulation* of the choice of *means*.

7. Provision for adequate *regulation of affective expression* is also considered to be a functional requisite of any society, suggesting the importance of structures encouraging *conformity* in social behavior.

8. Provision for adequate *socialization* of individuals. Socialization is considered adequate if a sufficient number of socialized individuals exist to permit the structural requisites of society to operate. Socialization involves both the *education* and training of the young by the family, church, and school, and also the *assimilation* of outsiders into the dominant culture.

9. Provision for effective *control of disruptive behavior*. (Contrast 6, which deals with allocation problems.) The role of regulatory forces in maintaining *stability* is emphasized here.

10. Provision for adequate levels of *institutionalization*. Every society institutionalizes some of its basic structures, that is, assures that they be ideal, actual, and enforced. This involves eliciting adequate levels of *support* for and *commitment* to social institutions.

[8] See Marion J. Levy, *The Structure of Society* (Princeton: Princeton Univ. Press, 1952), ch. 4.

While Levy contains a lucid outline of structural-functionalism, Parsons' original formulations are found in T. Parsons and E. Shils, eds., *Toward a General Theory of Action* (New York: Harper & Row, 1951); T. Parsons, *The Social System* (New York: Free Press, 1951); T. Parsons, *Essays in Sociological Theory* (New York: Free Press, 1949; rev. ed. 1954); T.

Here again the strengths and weaknesses of structural-functionalism are revealed. The researcher has the advantage of a comprehensive set of categories in which to fit his data and which he may use as a mnemonic device. On the other hand, critics argue that all aspects of a society are not included and that there is a conservative bias involved in the focus on regulation, stability, conformity, assimilation, socialization, and the study of social stratification in its aspects as a functional requisite.

One might compensate for this bias by studying "provision for adequate levels of conflict" and "adequate institutionalization of innovation-generating structures." However, even with these adjustments, the researcher should be aware of the bias involved in the implicit posing of the question, "How have things come to be the way they are?" rather than the question raised by a focus on structural equivalents, "How might things be different?"

But even though structural-functionalism may be used to categorize noninstitutionally bound areas of study, for example, of a developing nation, and even if the biases of the method are kept in mind, the method of universal requisite analysis is much more a typology than a theory. There is here no dynamic element akin to Marxist dialectical materialism rooted in the evolution of technology, nor to the psychoanalytic development sequences rooted in the assumed relevance of biological and personality development. Hence there can be no "paradigm for analysis" equivalent to that given in the previous chapters for the case of rioting.

Nevertheless, it is not true that structural-functionalism is a mere typology, as is clear when the remaining two structural-functional methods of analysis are considered.

Pattern Variable Analysis

Universal requisite analysis is appropriate for studies undertaken at the level of societal units; pattern variable analysis is appropriate for study at the level of individual interactions. *Pattern variables* are ideal points marking the extremes of several continua used to represent dimensions of individual interactions. For example, self-orientation and collectivity-orientation mark the extremes of one of the pattern variable dimensions. The idea of the pattern variables may be traced back to Ferdinand Tonnies' work, *Community and Society*, and through Tonnies to Marx. The underlying conception is that traditional communities tend to be characterized by collectively oriented, functionally diffuse, hierarchic behavior patterns, whereas modern societies are more self-oriented, nonhierarchic, and universalistic. A look at each of the pattern variables will make this clearer:

Parsons, *Structure and Process in Modern Societies* (New York: Free Press, 1960); and works cited in other notes.

For a sympathetic interpretation by a political scientist, see William Mitchell, *Sociological Analysis and Politics* (Englewood Cliffs, N.J.: Prentice-Hall, 1967). Mitchell has also sought to apply this approach in his text, *The American Polity* (New York: Free Press, 1962).

1. *Universalistic v. particularistic:* Relationships are universalistic if admission to them is by germane criteria without social barriers. Relationships in modern organizations tend to be more universalistic than relationships in tribal organizations, for example.*

2. *Affective neutrality v. affectivity:* This is sometimes called the avoidant-intimate dimension. In more modern, impersonal organizations, relationships do not tend to elicit strong affective interactions; instead affective neutrality is the rule.

3. *Self-orientation v. collectivity-orientation:* This is also referred to as the individualistic-responsible dimension. Modern organizational relationships are often said to be self-oriented, where each individual is expected to calculate his own advantage in a given relationship.

4. *Functional specificity v. functional diffuseness:* Here, in modern relationships, rights and obligations are more often precisely defined. For example, one is treated specifically as a customer by the modern shopkeeper, whereas the traditional shopkeeper treated one not only as a customer, but also as a person of a particular religion, nationality, etc.

In addition to these four pattern variables, three others are occasionally used, although they are not always acknowledged to be universally applicable:

5. *Achievement v. ascription:* Modern societies are often seen as relying more on achievement as a criterion for relationships than on ascriptive factors like family background. Talcott Parsons used this pattern variable, but later substituted the term "performance-quality" as more descriptive. Others have rejected this pattern variable because it seemingly overlaps universalism-particularism.

6. *Rational-arational:* Marion Levy set forth this dimension, defining rational as the circumstance when objective and subjective ends are identical and the means are empirical. Irrational relationships occur when objective ends and subjective ends are not the same, although the means may be empirical. Arational behavior occurs when the means are not empirical, e.g., magic.

7. *Hierarchic-nonhierarchic:* Levy also set forth this dimension, noting that traditional relationships are more often hierarchic than are modern relationships.

Conceivably these pattern variables could be used as a dynamic part of structural-functional theory, based on a natural development sequence from traditional to modern pattern variable relationships. These assumptions sometimes underlie theories of personalism or clientelism in the administration of developing countries. Or one might attribute rioting to a period of anomie between the keeping of traditional pattern variables characteristic of the rural American South, and the holding of modern pattern variables characteristic of Northern city life.

Parsons himself, however, explicitly denies that he holds the conception of a shift from traditional to modern pattern variables. Instead of seeing the ideal points of the pattern variables grouped into two main sets, traditional

*See P. Blau, "Operationalizing a Conceptual Scheme: The Universalism-Particularism Pattern Variable," *American Sociological Review* 27, no. 2 (April 1962): 159–169.

and modern, Parsons asserts that the various dimensions may vary independently. He does, however, link universalism and specificity, particularism and diffuseness, achievement and neutrality, and ascription and affectivity. He refers to the first two of these pairs as orientation or attitudinal dimensions, and the second two pairs as modality or object-categorization dimensions. This more complex view tends to undercut severely the possibilities of a developmental sequence dynamic akin to the Freudian developmental themes that might be used to give structural-functionalism a predictive value.

AGIL System Analysis

The AGIL system is perhaps the best-known aspect of structural-functional analysis. It is a set of *functional analytic aspects hierarchically arranged* and associated with certain *general processes*.

TABLE 3.1   The AGIL System

ADAPTIVE   **GOAL-ATTAINING**

General Action Level: organism	personality	
cultural system	social systems	
	economy (industry)	polity (government)
	religion-family (church)	societal community (voluntary groups)

PATTERN MAINTAINING   **INTEGRATIVE**

Structural Components of Society

roles	collectivities
values	norms

The analytic aspects are used to describe the predominant functions of the parts of any system. There are four such aspects: *adaptive* (adjusts the system to environmental changes), *goal-attaining, integrative,* and *pattern maintaining* (protects basic structural patterns of a system). Originally the last aspect was termed "latent pattern maintaining" and together the beginning letters of the four aspects formed the acronym "AGIL." (Confusion is further compounded by the occasional use of the term "analytic aspects" to denote the pattern variables.)

Using these functional aspects, structural-functionalists may for purposes of analysis divide any system into four parts as illustrated by Table 3.1. For example, the action system is divided into the organism, personality, and social and cultural systems associated with the adaptive, goal-attaining, integrative, and pattern-maintaining aspects, respectively. The social system (Table 3.2) in turn is divided into the economy, polity, societal community (manifested, for example in voluntary groups), and the religion-family

TABLE 3.2 AGIL Subsystem Attributes of the Social System

Subsystem	General Symbolic Medium	Ultimate Base	Standard	Unit
Economy	Money	Gold	Utility	Dollar
Polity	Power	Physical Force	Effectiveness in goal-achievement	Vote
Societal Community	Influence	Ascriptive Membership	Solidarity	?
Religion-Family Complex	Commitment	?	Integrity	?

complex, each associated predominantly with the respective AGIL aspect. Any of these subsystems might in turn be divided into the *structural components* of any society—roles, collectivities, norms (rules specifying values), and values—associated with the AGIL aspect of the corresponding order.

Systems and subsystems are seen as related by a *cybernetic hierarchy*, a term drawn from information theory denoting the principle by which higher-information, lower-energy systems tend to "control" lower-information, higher-energy systems. For example, men control machines; collectivities control roles. In fact, the AGIL aspects stand in control hierarchy relationships to one another, with the pattern-maintaining aspect associated with the system or subsystem at the top of the control hierarchy. The implication would seem to be that components of the cultural system, primarily values, in some sense control the social system, of which the polity is a subsystem. Parsons speaks of the important role of the value of "instrumental activism"—using society as an instrument in asserting control over environment—in determining the course of American society. Similarly, Seymour M. Lipset in *The First New Nation* talks of changes of equality and achievement.

On the other hand, in spite of Lipset's praise of Parsons as "perhaps the foremost contemporary exponent of the importance of value systems as causal factors,"[9] Parsons himself does not equate cybernetic control with causation. He points to the role of "feedback" in information systems to show that causation flows both up and down the cybernetic hierarchy. Critics charge that cybernetic control is meaningless if it does not imply greater causation down the hierarchy than up.

Thus another conservative bias of structural-functionalism is revealed in the AGIL system. Parsons' thought, clearly in opposition to Marx, places material factors low in the control hierarchy. It places the economy under the control of the polity, and the polity ultimately under the control of the religion-family complex as mediated through a vaguely-defined "societal community."

An additional conservative bias is introduced into structural-functionalism in discussion of the *medium* and *base* of the four social subsystems. Here an analogy is built between the economic market and the political system, and a basis laid for a competitive market theory of politics. Besides the implications for predictive theory of the pattern variables, the cybernetic hierarchy, and the market analogy, Parsons and other structural-functionalists discuss at least four *general processes* of the social system: *differentiation, specification, inclusion,* and *upgrading.*

Processes   *Differentiation* is a process whereby a unit becomes divided into heterogeneous parts. An example at the social system level is the breaking up of the traditional family farm business into the modern, separate farm, family, and firm. Here one may contrast *segmentation*, whereby the family-farm-firm splits into the family-farm-firm of son #1 and the family-farm-firm of son #2. At the personality system level, the mother-child perception becomes differentiated into the mother-father-daughter-son perception, and is then further differentiated to take account of still others. At the cultural level, the church-state-school of traditional society becomes differentiated into separation of church, state and school.

[9] Seymour M. Lipset, *The First New Nation: The United States in Historical and Comparative Perspective* (Garden City, N.Y.: Doubleday Anchor, 1963), p. 4. For a critical view of the AGIL system, see R. Blain, "An Alternative to Parsons' Four-Function Paradigm," *American Sociological Review* 36, no. 4 (August 1971): 678–691.

Specification is the historical process in the social system whereby values (highly generalized goals) are translated into particular norms (heuristic rules for attaining values). *Inclusion* is another historical process whereby the societal community confers rights of community on new groups and imposes the obligation not to disrupt community solidarity. In this regard, one may contrast *assimilation*, whereby the included group members are dispersed throughout the system. *Upgrading* is the process whereby norms are improved to better fulfill values. Each of these four processes is predominantly associated with one of the AGIL aspects, in the usual order (differentiation with adaptation, specification with goal-attainment, etc.).

Examples

1. Changes in Black Status   The *value* of equality remains but *norms* have been *upgraded*. Blacks have been included in *collectivities* and their *roles* have become more *differentiated* (for instance, contrast the old, undifferentiated role of nonvoter, menial laborer, ghetto resident). Improvement in the *status* of blacks is attributed to the social system processes of *upgrading*, inclusion, and differentiation, a change in which the role of value changes as mediated by value specification is crucial. (Note that if one accepts the premise that specification, upgrading, etc., are natural social processes inherent in the social system, then changes in norms need not be explained in turn.)

2. Why Do Riots Happen?   The divergence of *ideal norms* and *actual norms* relating to the central *value* of equality became crucial when central *pattern-maintaining institutions* like the Supreme Court handed down authoritative decisions sanctioning *upgrading* of actual norms. Although whites recognized the need for *inclusion* of blacks by conferring community rights, this involved breaking the *obligation* of not disrupting community *solidarity*. That is, the process of inclusion in the course of its natural development was threatening the *functional requisite* of minimum levels of shared, articulated goals, or *consensus*. Out of this conflict a crisis was precipitated in which norms or goals bearing on inclusion became highly salient. Although the basic values of American society remained largely unchanged, the crisis reordered the hierarchy of conflicting norms specifying those values. In this reordering, adequate levels of consensus about the most salient goals were not reached, and the functional requisite of goal consensus was not met. Therefore, there was a disintegration of the *societal community* at the *boundary* where that subsystem was *articulated* with the group to be included. That disintegration took the form of rioting. Dissolution and regrouping enables a higher consensus to resolve friction.

Paradigm for AGIL System Analysis

1. Specify the unit to be studied. If the unit is societal, place it in the context of the universal requisites. If the unit is individual, place it in the context of the pattern variables.
2. Specify the relationship of the unit and its subsystems to the central values of the society and to norms assumed to be in the process of continuous specification and upgrading. Relate these normative changes to the social processes of inclusion and differentiation.
3. Assume the AGIL system cybernetic control hierarchy indicates the central flow of causation. This will ordinarily involve inputing high causal priority to normative factors.
4. Make explicit the biases noted elsewhere in this chapter.

Functionalism in Political Science

Parsonsian structural-functionalism embodies concepts central to the dominant paradigms in American political science in the 1950s and 1960s: the systems analysis of David Easton, the functional analysis of Gabriel Almond, the pluralist theory of Robert Dahl.[10] In each there is the image of power processes transcending government as part of a system of interrelated associations serving essential social functions. Each stands in contrast to the nineteenth-century tendency to restrict political science to law and government structures, as well as to Marxist emphasis on class considerations or Freudian focus on psychological drives and personality types.

Functionalist political imagery derives in important respects from the work of Emil Durkheim, with his conception of "organic solidarity."[11] Durkheim believed that, as the division of labor became more elaborate in modern society, functional interdependence increased, favoring stability without the need to rely on the coercive means prominent in more primitive or homogenous societies. In this sense, the differentiation of modern society is liberating.

In fact, one may argue that differentiation, the proliferation of associational life, and increasing interdependence are the social bases of democracy.[12] Emil Lederer, for example, analyzed totalitarianism in terms of the destruction of "all social associations," leading to a "dissolution of the whole

---

[10] Easton and Almond are discussed later in this chapter, Dahl in Chapter 4.

[11] For criticism of Parsons' interpretation of Durkheim, see W. Pope, "Classic on Classic: Parsons' Interpretation of Durkheim," *American Sociological Review* 38, no. 4 (August 1973): 399–415.

[12] T. Parsons, "On Building Social System Theory: A Personal History," in G. Holton, ed., *The Twentieth-Century Sciences: Studies in the Biography of Ideas* (New York: W. W. Norton & Co., 1970, pp. 128–129.

fabric of society."[13] In his most recent essays in political sociology,[14] Parsons emphasizes the analogy between money in the economy and power in the polity, again projecting the image of prolific and highly interdependent associations competing and cooperating in a system whose functions serve no single class or group.

Parsons' view of politics is thus a fundamentally optimistic one, embodying beliefs about the increasing realization of national values (e.g., the integration of blacks into American cluture, while still preserving their racial identity) in due course and about the possibilities for voluntary action not sharply defined by economic or other determinisms.

Gouldner has attributed this optimism to Parsons' personal development.

> Parsons was a mature man of twenty-seven when the stock market crash of 1929 heralded the coming of the Great Depression. His education had been completed (A.B., Amherst, and Ph.D., Heidelberg) two years before the economic crisis started. By 1929 Parsons had been married and on the faculty of Harvard for two years . . . . It was thus not simply that Parsons had witnessed the "success" of the American economy as an outsider, but that as an Instructor at Harvard and as the son of a college president he also participated in it. Much of Parsons' abiding optimism, I would suggest, is rooted in the fact that he viewed the Great Depression from a specific perspective: from the standpoint of a personal reality that had been formed by the experience of success.[15]

Whether or not one accepts this evaluation of Parsons, functionalism does appear to be linked to political optimism or, to put it another way, functionalist analyses of America and other Western democracies have been generally very favorable to "our way of life."[16] Not surprisingly, therefore, radical and critical social scientists who do not share this benign image of the capitalist countries have been quick to condemn functionalism for its conservative uses.[17]

---

[13] Emil Lederer, *State of the Masses* (New York: W. W. Norton & Co., 1940).

[14] T. Parsons, *Politics and Social Structure* (New York: Free Press, 1969). See reviews by William Gamson in *American Sociological Review* 36, no. 3 (June 1971): 523–524; and by J. D. Colfax in *American Journal of Sociology* (AJS) 76, no. 5 (March 1971): 932–936, with comment in *AJS* 77, no. 2 (September 1971): 306–309.

[15] Alvin W. Gouldner, *The Coming Crisis of Western Sociology* (New York: Basic Books, 1970), pp. 147–148.

[16] For an illustration, see T. Parsons, *The System of Modern Societies* (Englewood Cliffs, N.J.: Prentice-Hall, 1971), p. 114.

[17] In addition to Gouldner, see Max Black, ed., *The Social Theories of Talcott Parsons* (Englewood Cliffs, N.J.: Prentice-Hall, 1961); Daniel Foss, "The World View of Talcott Parsons," in M. Stein and A. Vidich, eds., *Sociology on Trial* (New York: Spectrum, 1963); B. Moore, "The New Scholasticism and the Study of Politics," in *Political Power and Social Theory* (New York: Harper & Row, 1958); and for a critique of another functionalist, Edward Shils, see Norman Birnbaum, *Toward a Critical Sociology* (New York: Oxford, 1971), pp. 57–80.

The Work of Gabriel Almond   Gabriel Almond is the American political scientist most closely associated with functionalism. Yet his application of it is far narrower than that of Parsons and earlier functionalists, thereby avoiding some of the charges of the critics of this approach.[18]

In *The Politics of Developing Areas* (1960), Almond set forth a variant of universal requisite analysis. But where the sociologists had concentrated on enumeration and investigation of functional requisites for the adaptation and survival of *social* systems, Almond was concerned with the following requisites of any adequately effective *political* system:[19]

1. Political socialization: perpetuation of political structures and cultures through patterned learning in childhood and early adulthood (e.g., in the family, church, school, work group, and voluntary association).
2. Political recruitment: this function follows up the general political socialization function, providing for induction of individuals into specialized political roles.
3. Interest articulation: the expression of collective interests, primarily through: (a) institutional interest groups (e.g., governmental agencies or bureaucracies); (b) nonassociational interest groups (e.g., ethnic or racial groups); (c) anomic interest groups (e.g., spontaneous demonstrations); and (d) associational interest groups (e.g., economic organizations).
4. Interest aggregation: the grouping of broad classes of interests (e.g., political parties).
5. Political communication: in some but not all societies, organized political communication (e.g., modern media) provides critical political input separate from communication by agencies of socialization, articulation, and aggregation.
6. Rule making: the legislative function as performed not only by Congress but also by the other branches of government.
7. Rule application: the executive function.
9. Rule adjudication: the judicial function.

While the student must refer to the literature for a more thorough review,[20] criticism of this framework has been threefold:

1. it is static, describing and categorizing political states but not addressing the question of change (i.e., there is no equivalent to the Marxian focus on tech-

[18] For a sympathetic review, see S. Rothman, "Functionalism and Its Critics: An Analysis of the Writings of Gabriel Almond," *Political Science Reviewer* 1 (Fall 1971): 236–276; and reply by Almond, *Political Science Reviewer* 3 (Fall 1973): 259–268.
[19] G. Almond, *The Politics of Developing Areas* (Princeton, N.J.: Princeton Univ. Press, 1960), pp. 26–57.
[20] L. Mayer, *Comparative Political Inquiry* (Homewood, Ill.: Dorsey, 1972), pp. 146–149. In chapter 8, Mayer also discusses the functionalist theory of Merton and Apter. See also R. Holt and J. Richardson, "Competing Paradigms in Comparative Politics," in R. Holt and J. Turner, eds., *The Methodology of Comparative Research* (New York: Free Press, 1970) pp. 33–37. The ambiguity of functionalist concepts is discussed in G. Sartori, "Concept Misformation in Comparative Politics," *American Political Science Review* 64, no. 4 (December 1970): 1033–1053.

nology and work relations as an engine of change, to the Freudian emphasis on psychological drives, or to the Parsonsian weight on rationalization and value causation: in sum, Almond advances a *typology* based on functionalism, not a functionalist *theory* of how systems operate and change);

2. it is ambigjous in terminology (e.g., the various functions are broadly overlapping: a single act may be considered part of several functions; the term "function" is sometimes equated with the term "process"; many terms are not defined in general, much less operationally); and

3. it is biased toward the status quo (the same charge discussed with regard to Parsonsian functionalism).

Almond's second work (*Comparative Politics*, 1966, written in conjunction with G. Bingham Powell), sought to answer some of these criticisms. In this work, political culture is emphasized as the setting for a political system characterized by certain system maintenance functions (socialization, recruitment), certain conversion functions (interest articulation, aggregation, communication, rule-making, rule-application, and rule-adjudication), and certain capabilities (extractive: ability to draw on human and material resources; regulative: ability to control the behavior of individuals and groups; distributive: ability to allocate goods, services, honors, statuses, and opportunities; and symbolic: ability to affirm values within the society and in the international environmeñt).[21]

In addition, *Comparative Politics* sought to lay the goundwork for a nonstatic theory of "political development." Development was defined by the degrees of differentiation, autonomy, and secularization within the system. Different futures were projected for varying combinations of these characteristics. Increasing development with these criteria is said to be associated with structural changes that alter system capabilities. For example, differentiation brings bureaucratic and economic structures of national scope, increasing system extractive capabilities.

Almond and Powell then developed typologies of political systems based on the levels of development. But this is not a theory of political development, as in Marxian theory of political-economic stages or McClelland's theory of need-achievement and growth—it is not a theory of how and why social change occurs. Rather, Almond and Powell presented a typology of levels of change. While addressed to the criticism that functionalism is static, the authors' developmental typologies ultimately fail to meet this problem, although they do serve to predict which combinations of system types and capabilities are unlikely to occur (e.g., highly differentiated systems with low subsystem autonomy require gigantic party-bureaucratic organizations in place of reliance on subsystem autonomy, hence such systems are not associated with high capacity for responsiveness).

[21] G. Almond and G. B. Powell, *Comparative Politics: A Developmental Approach* (Boston: Little, Brown, 1966), chaps. 2 and 8.

Because of this shortcoming in the works of Almond and other function-alists, A. James Gregor has concluded, "The major cognitive advantage provided by functionalist language is as a mnemonic convenience servicing the general storage and retrieval of information . . . . Whatever else it is, functionalism is not a theory, for as an analytic system it cannot, of itself, tender knowledge claims."[22] By this Gregor means that functionalism, as used by political scientists, provides convenient "check-lists" or typologies to categorize types of political systems, types of processes, and political data in general—but it does not ultimately embody a dynamic theory.

If Almond's use of functionalism moved away from causal theory toward typology, other political scientists have used functionalism even more loosely. It may refer to discussion of how the same purposes are fulfilled by alterna-tive structures—Hammond uses functional analysis to show how Kennedy-era program budgeting reforms in the Defense Department fulfilled the same social functions of rationalization, distribution of risks, and legitima-tion of institutions as the pre-reform arrangements.[23] Or it may refer to discussion of how a given purpose is fulfilled by multiple structures—Fenno discusses how the House Appropriations Committee achieves integration through such structures as articulated goal consensus and recruitment on the basis of conformity to norms.[24]

Finally, some political scientists use functionalist vocabulary to list the types of activities of a political actor or group. Thus Rossiter lists the func-tions of the President, Finer the functions of the legislator, and Sorauf those of political parties.[25] In this loose form, functionalism becomes simply one vocabulary among many by which the same ideas may be expressed. It can no longer be said to be a methodology.

SYSTEMS ANALYSIS

Systems analysis is one of the most abused concepts in political science, assuming almost as many meanings as there are political scientists! Func-tionalism, as we have seen, has at its core the concept of a highly interde-

[22] A.J. Gregor, "Political Science and the Uses of Functional Analysis," *American Political Science Review* 62, no. 2 (June 1968): 438.

[23] Paul Hammond, "A Functional Analysis of Defense Department Decision-Making in the McNamara Administration," *American Political Science Review* 62, no. 1 (March 1968): 57–69.

[24] Richard Fenno, "The Appropriations Committee as a Political System," *American Political Science Review* 56, no. 2 (June 1962): 310–324.

[25] Cited in Alan Isaak, *Scope and Methods of Political Science* (Homewood, Ill.: Dorsey, 1969), pp. 222–223. See Chapter 14 for a critical review of functionalism in political science. See also A. L. Stinchombe, "Functional Causal Imagery," in *Constructing Social Theories* (New York: Harcourt, Brace and World, 1968), pp. 80–101.

pendent, equilibriating system. Hence many writers equate the terms "functionalism" and "systems theory." But while all functionalism is a form of systems theory, not all systems theory is functionalist. Indeed, much of what is referred to as systems theory is not causal or social theory at all, but has to do with a form of program and budgetary analysis of a technical nature. (See Chapter 4 for a discussion of this subject.)

In the technical tradition of systems analysis, analogies are usually made to electronic systems composed of networks, flows, circuits, inputs, feedback, noise, channels, and the like. Social theorists using this approach are more likely to refer to the organism as an adaptive system, speaking of system boundaries, articulation with the environment, homeostasis, equilibrium, and regulation.

In most formulations the basic concept of a system is very simple: *inputs* are fed into some *conversion or transform* process, resulting in *outputs*, which are "fed back" as new inputs in the next system cycle. This image can be used to categorize almost any form of data. In political science, for example, one could write a "systems textbook" by organizing the material in three parts: inputs (e.g., a chapter on the Constitution to illustrate our political culture, chapters on parties, public opinion, socialization, voting behavior), conversion (Congress, President, judiciary, bureaucracy), and outputs (public policy). This hypothetical textbook could be a "functionalist systems textbook" if the author used Almond's universal political requisites as inputs (e.g., "interest aggregation" instead of "parties") and as conversion processes (e.g., "rule-adjudication" instead of "judiciary").

Of course, if this is all systems analysis comes to, then it is a trivial exercise in relabelling old concepts. At best, it is a convenient check-list to help the author (and reader) remember if all the inputs mentioned by Almond, Levy, or some other functionalist have actually been treated. Regrettable, this is the state of most systems-analysis applications in contemporary political science.

Information Systems

The concept of an information system is not antithetical to structural-functionalism; in fact, it is intimately bound to the concept of the cybernetic hierarchy that serves to relate the parts of the AGIL analytic system.

An *information system* is a set of interrelated structures that receives an *input* of *data* through *receptors* and *processes* this data by comparing it to *memory* and *values* and submitting it to *decision*. Decision leads to *storage* of data in memory and, if appropriate, to implementation of decisions through *effectors*. This affects the *environment* beyond the system *boundaries*, causing *feedback* as part of the data input of the next *phase* of the *input-transform-output* process.

Moreover, this information input may contain unneeded information or *noise*, as well as information at varying levels of importance. For this reason, the receptors must *scan* and *select* data received prior to processing. This selectivity introduces the possibility of *perceptual biases* and errors, especially as the *load* of data input increases. Load may also involve either *lag* in processing or reduction of *lead* in forecasting from received data.

Information systems are subject to certain patterned *distortions*. One of these is *amplification of positive feedback* in a spiral of implementations eliciting positive and negative feedbacks, of which only the positive are selected, leading to further implementations of the same sort. Of course, negative-only selectivity is also a possible distortion. Another is *channel drift*, where a system attuned to one channel of information input may gradually shift in frequency toward another channel with unintended system consequences. *Short-circuiting* is a distortion where data is not subject to all phases of the input-transform-output system; for example, implementation may occur without data being subjected to memory recall.[26]

The context of information systems is more limited than that of structural-functionalism, in that it is even less helpful in sorting out pertinent research data from the unimportant. Precisely because the categories of information systems are universalistic and all-encompassing, too much is taken in. By more closely reflecting reality, it is less helpful in making simplifications (theories). A positive way of saying this is to note that the approach requires greater creativity and less rote application.

Procedure Suppose the researcher asks, "Why was this decision made?" The information systems approach suggests a number of steps toward answering this question:

1. Examine relevant information inputs prior to the decision, including stored inputs, and place it in the context of a field of competing inputs.
2. Examine the structures that have been set up to receive, scan, and select information, noting the distortions introduced at this point.
3. Determine the formal and informal structures established for comparing received data with memory, determine the values of the system, and specify the manner in which processed data are evaluated.
4. Determine the procedures by which implementation outputs are assigned to evaluated data (e.g., is the procedure to work through a limited number of implementation strategies in a repertoire until a satisfactory one is found? are all strategies in a repertoire considered and then one selected by some criterion? etc.).

---

[26] For further discussion, see Oran R. Young, *Systems of Political Science* (Englewood Cliffs, N.J.: Prentice-Hall, 1968); and Walter Buckley, *Sociology and Modern Systems Theory* (Englewood Cliffs, N.J.: Prentice-Hall, 1967), especially ch. 2. Buckley illustrates the view of those who contrast functionalism and systems analysis.

5. Specify distortions involved in the implementation phase, after the decision is made but before implementation defines the decision in practice.

This is a very large order, precisely because it rightly suggests that in answering the original question above, all factors must be considered. Information theory gives no help in selecting relevant factors and, in fact, even points to the importance of competing noise. This task is not an altogether impossible one, however, and several respectable attempts to use this approach have been made.[27]

Sometimes information systems approaches do use certain criteria to narrow down the field of investigation, but these criteria are usually inconsistent with the general theory of information systems. One such criterion is *rationality*—there may be a tendency to treat information systems as rational systems processing relevant information in ways calculated to effect the desired result. In fact, there is no reason to assume that study may be confined to rational factors or to formal patterns of decision making. A second criterion sometimes used is the *quantifiableness* of inputs and outputs. There may be a tendency to look at inputs in terms of *quantities* of messages, with selective distortion being a function of load, without examining less quantifiable sources of distortion such as *cognitive dissonance*—the tendency to adjust one's perceptions and behavior to be consistent with those of positively valued others.

Neither criterion is consistent with information theory. In each case, all inputs, transforms, and outputs must be examined because all coexist in an interdependent field of mutual relationships. Not even the criterion of face relevance to the question is wholly valid, since information theory posits the relevance of even random noise to decision outcome.

Example   Using the five steps outlined above as a basis for information systems analysis, the question of rioting may be considered again.

1. *Memory and inputs.* Memory: Past violence against the black race, crime and violence of lower class life, past promises and hopes for future, repertoire of methods used in the past to settle grievances. Inputs: Marginal gains of civil rights movement; messages of legitimacy of protest, illegitimacy of status quo; plus competing inputs of changes in dress, music, work styles.
2. *Receptors and scanning and selecting.* Word-of-mouth inputs given priority; rumor distortion; selective accumulation of grievances; retention of inputs of dramatic, exciting, or shocking nature.
3. *Recall and evaluation.* Inputs related to grievances are selected, compared with past grievances, and assigned a negative value associated with slavery and later racial and class exploitation.

[27]See Roberta Wohlstetter, *Pearl Harbor: Warning and Decision* (Stanford: Stanford Univ. Press, 1962).

4. *Selection of implementation options.* Grievance inputs, although heavily weighted negatively, are ordinarily stored in memory, later to reinforce the negative value assigned to further grievance inputs. When the load of grievance inputs reaches a certain critical level, a repertoire of implementation options is searched. Violent crime is one of these options. Selection of lesser options, such as non-violent protest activity, generates an increasing load of grievance inputs. The store of grievance inputs in memory increases, more than compensating for the loss of similar information from memory through routine forgetfulness. As the store increases, the negative evaluation assigned incremental grievance inputs increases. Higher negative values are associated with stronger implementation options.

5. *Implementation.* An amplification spiral is thus established leading to escalating implementation options and ultimately the selection of the violent crime option. In a collective context, selection of this option appears as rioting, which is an adaptive response tending to preserve the structure of the black community.

Morphogenetic Systems

Walter Buckley has suggested that systems imagery be recast to take greater account of the capacity of systems not only to return to a previous state (*equilibrium*), or to move to a new state that preserves basic system structures when necessitated by changing environment (*homeostasis*), but also to change even basic structures when necessary to uphold cultural values (*morphogenesis*).

Morphogenesis involves a set of interrelated pattern-maintaining processes that tend to preserve a system's central values in the face of changing environment through structural elaboration. In contrast, homeostatic systems tend to preserve structure. Morphogenesis is said to be a better social model because society in fact does much more than preserve its central structures; it is continually in the process of elaborating and changing them so that institutions will serve central values even when conditions change.

In a morphogenetic system, if relevant variables exceed certain parameters, the system structure changes. In contrast, given the same situation in a homeostatic system like the organism, structure disintegrates. The importance of this difference for research orientation is that in morphogenetic systems such as society, deviance, conflict, and change are as integral to the system as structural maintenance. Where a homeostatic approach such as structural-functionalism or even information systems tends to focus on institutional persistence and maintenance of central structures of a society, the morphogenetic approach tends to focus on persistence of values through institutional and structural change.

Again, there is no clear distinction of this approach from structural-functionalism, and, indeed, the overlap with the idea of cultural values as controlling factors in system evolution is retained, with the concomitant biases mentioned in the previous chapter. The bias toward the analytic primacy of values may be removed by defining morphogenesis in an even more general way, as Buckley does, as a system characterized by a set of structure-elaborating processes not clearly tending toward anything. This definition, of course, comes at a price.

Such a definition usefully serves to deny any overriding importance of norms, values, roles, and institutions, and to upgrade the importance of informal processes, conflict, tension, and change. It removes the assumption that institutions are eufunctional and legitimate. On the other hand, such a definition also removes every dynamic from a system except the vague process of structural elaboration. At least in equilibrium theory one could posit that any given deviation from the normal state would be undercut by unintended consequences of the change, consequences tending to preserve the basic structures of the existing system. It is even further from the Marxist theories of social change as they relate to institutions and groups. That is, although systems analysis in the morphogenetic tradition is a truer description of reality, the price paid for this accuracy is a level of generality that fails to aid the researcher in selecting important factors from among the myriad unimportant ones.

The usefulness of the morphogenetic approach for the researcher depends on drawing upon the implications of structure-elaborating system. Buckley suggests that an ideal complex adaptive system of this sort would have five characteristics:

1. Sources for continuous introduction of "variety" into the system, where variety includes deviance as well as norm-conforming behavior.
2. Processes tending toward maintenance of both an optimum level of tension in society (e.g., cognitive dissonance, incongruent roles) and a relatively high level of individual satisfaction.
3. A full two-way communications system throughout the entire system.
4. A decision-making system sensitive to both external environment and its own internal state.
5. Mechanisms for preserving and propagating current information sets and symbolic meanings systems.

Followers of this approach need to accept the challenge of translating these and other criteria associated with morphogenetic systems into an operational paradigm for researchers. Until then, while this approach is helpful in understanding the shortcomings of other approaches, it may not serve the needs of the researcher attempting to devise useful theoretical simplifications of reality.

Systems Analysis in Political Science

In political science, the work of David Easton is most prominently associated with systems analysis. In *A Framework for Political Analysis* (1965), he sets forth his "Dynamic Response Model of a Political System."

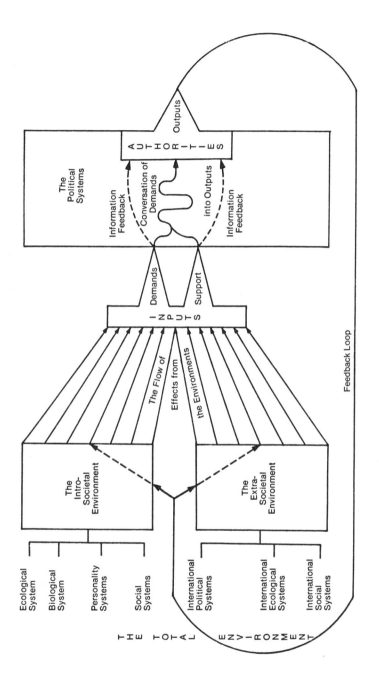

FIGURE 3.1   Easton's Dynamic Response Model of a Political System

This is, of course, a variant of the now-familiar "input-output" or "general systems" model. The "environment" includes the various functionalist AGIL action systems—biological, personality, social—but these are not embedded in a causal hierarchy as in Parsons' theory.

A most striking omission from the point of view of functionalism is lack of attention to the cultural system, which in Parsons was at the top of the "control hierarchy" conditioning the direction of the action and social systems. More weight was given to the role of values and culture in another of Easton's works, A *Systems Analysis of Political Life* (1965).[28] But even here Easton treats cultural mechanisms as only one of four types of system regulation, along with structural mechanisms, communication channel factors, and reduction (e.g., aggregation) processes.

Thus, "Eastonian analysis" does not commit the researcher to the idealist (i.e., value causation) social theory implicit in Parsons. It thereby achieves a higher level of generality, but does so by paying the price also paid by Almond: attainment of a useful typological concept set without well-developed causal theory.

There are, however, many respects in which functionalism and Eastonian systems analysis are similar. Both place a heavy emphasis on questions pertaining to system persistence and pattern maintenance (thereby opening themselves to the charge that each poses central questions most appropriate to conservative concerns). Both are systematic in orientation; that is, both emphasize analysis of whole systems and the danger of seeking to understand system elements in isolation from research on their relations to other system elements and the dynamic of the system itself.

But even in the terms "persistence" and "maintenance," differences from functionalism may be found. Where Parsons spoke of "pattern maintenance," evoking an image of an equilibrating system, Easton preferred to speak of "persistence" in order to suggest continuity *not* necessarily with equilibrium.[29] This also gives Eastonian analysis a greater degree of generality when compared with the customary functionalist emphasis on homeostatic equilibrium as a system characteristic. It is even more general than Buckley's concept of morphogenetic equilibrium. In fact, its very generality is a problem: it is difficult to find examples of failure to persist. Even after the Russian Revolution, there were tremendous systemic continuities in the bureaucracy, in factory organization, and among the peasantry.

---

[28] David Easton, A *Systems Analysis of Political Life* (New York: John Wiley & Sons, 1965), ch. 7.

[29] Easton, *Framework*, p. 88. For further reading, see E. F. Miller, "David Easton's Political Theory," *Political Science Reviewer* 1 (Fall 1971): 184–235; with reply by David Easton, *Political Science Review* 3 (Fall 1973): 268–301. See also J. S. Sorzano, "David Easton and the Invisible Hand," *American Political Science Review* 69, no. 1 (March 1975): 91–106. Sorzano critiques systems theory as analogous to Adam Smith's laissez-faire competitive markets economic theory, with the same biases but also with the same predictive powers.

Hence, if one really wishes to follow Easton's research focus on seeking "to reveal the conditions of persistence," one is faced immediately with the fact that system persistence is well-nigh universal under *all* conditions. The researcher will be strongly tempted to fall back on a discussion of degrees of persistence, thereby introducing by the back door the concepts of mechanical, homeostatic, and morphogenetic equilibrium. Which of these levels of persistence are associated with which social conditions is a more interesting and manageable problem, but Easton's analysis does not proceed along these lines.

Instead, at virtually every turn, Easton chose terms and concepts that preserve the high level of generality of the general systems model of input-transform-output-feedback. By avoiding specific theories of value causation or homeostatic equilibrium, Easton produced a vocabulary of wide appeal. With its concepts, a wide variety of empirical studies, hypotheses, and data may be ordered and understood. But it is difficult to say such studies support Easton's framework; rather, they simply fit within it. It is an ordering mechanism with greater potential than any other as a common basis for discussion among political scientists. But precisely because it does not commit itself to monistic and other strong theories of political change processes, it is unlikely to serve some of the most important needs of the researcher. Specifically, it is of only modest help in suggesting to the researcher alternative hypotheses that may be contrasted with Marxian, Freudian, Parsonian or other causal theories on the same subject.[30]

Thus systems analysis may be most useful at a late stage in research, when one may wish to present one's findings under a comprehensive theoretical framework accepted by most American political scientists. In the earlier stages of theory construction, the researcher may well find it more fruitful to avoid such frameworks in favor of comparing and synthesizing less inclusive but far stronger theories in relation to empirical evidence. In fact, a growing number of political scientists regard fitting one's findings into one of the boxes of the input-transform-output model as an unnecessary step, needlessly adding to the growth of jargon in our discipline.

EXERCISE

Complex organizations dominate political life. Organization theory is therefore widely relevant to political science in general, and is a mainstay of

---

[30] Similar pessimistic conclusions about the predictive and measurement utility of systems analysis are reached by S. Goldman in his useful review, "Systems Analysis and Judicial Systems: Potential and Limitations," *Polity* 3, no. 3 (Spring, 1971): 333–359. Similarly, see Mackenzie, *Politics and Social Science*, p. 110.

public administration in specific. In Part I of *Structure and Process in Modern Societies* (New York: Free Press, 1960), Talcott Parsons has advanced a general theory of formal organizations. As the first part of this exercise, read Parsons and then write a brief summary of his theory, emphasizing how it related to the AGIL system discussed in this chapter.

William Foote Whyte and Henry A. Landsberger, both well-known social scientists, have made numerous criticisms of Parsons' theory of organizations. These critiques are found in Max Black, ed., *The Social Theories of Talcott Parsons* (Englewood Cliffs, N.J.: Prentice-Hall, 1961). As a second part of this exercise, read these criticisms and write a summary of them. Then give your own evaluation of the value of functionalist theory for research and theory-construction about political and other formal organizations.

Contemporary Perspectives on Political Science

With the decline of postwar enthusiasm for functionalism and systems analysis has come, on the one hand, a demoralizing feeling that American political science has fallen apart into an unmanageable eclectic and disparate field with no unifying body of theory. On the other hand, numerous creative theories are continually being put forward to fill the supposed void. All the while, of course, the older approaches continue to hold their attraction, even if they cannot claim to constitute a basis for unity in the discipline. In fact, both Marxist and psychological approaches are enjoying something of a resurgence today.

It is impossible to do justice to the many newer approaches in a few pages. Only a few may be reviewed here. Presented in rough chronological order of their appearance in political science are group theory, decision-making theory and its relation to applied systems analysis and public choice theory, communications theory, phenomenology, and symbolic interactionism.

These perspectives are not necessarily new, for their expression in each case may be traced back several decades. What is new, however, is the reevaluation of these approaches in the search for theoretical unity in political science.

GROUP THEORY

The group approach has its origins in the very beginnings of American political science, but its popularity under the label of "group theory" dates from World War II. David Truman's *The Governmental Process* (1955) has become a modern classic for its integration of previous political science insights into a group framework. Group theory, like functionalism, stands in contrast to both the class analysis of the Marxists and the individualistic approach of the psychologists. In general, it is compatible with functionalism or systems analysis, though group theorists do not necessarily share the assumptions of the latter two orientations.

The Evolution of Group Theory

The history of interest group theory is one of the gradual encroachment of ideas rather than sequential building of scientific study on scientific study. Arthur Bentley's *The Process of Government* (1908) is customarily cited as the seminal work in group theory, marking the turn away from nineteenth-century preoccupation with jurisprudence and the legal structure of government institutions.

To understand the origins of group theory, one must understand this nineteenth-century approach. Jurisprudence was especially concerned with the "theory of sovereignty," which dealt with the problem of how the state assumed the power to coordinate the elements within it, discussing this in relation to the rights of citizens. Jurists wrestled, for example, with Locke's theory of the state based on the "social contract" and Rousseau's theory of the state's basis in "the general will." Group theory (though not called that) was represented, for example, by John Calhoun, who considered the community as "made up of different and conflicting interests" in which government "takes the sense of each through its appropriate organ, and the united sense of all as the sense of the entire community."[1] This theory of state sovereignty was opposed by most American students of government because it was believed to weaken the capacity of the state to act in the interests of all, over and above the narrow interests of the day. In its extreme form, of course, such "group theory" seemed a rationale for "states' rights" and the divisions underlying the Civil War.

Thus, although jurisprudential political science did focus on institutions and law, its real focus was the broad question of the role of government in coordinating individuals, associations, and public bodies within its jurisdiction. It was not rigidly confined to legal formalism, moreover, but gave considerable emphasis to the role of the family and church in what we would today call "political socialization," to the question of "national character," which we would today call "political culture," and to the relation of concrete historical changes to such forms of government as "representative democracy," "constitutional monarchy," and the like (that is, the relation of empirical evidence to ideal types in normative theory).

---

[1] Elisha Mulford, *The Nation: The Foundations of Civil Order and Political Life in the United States* (Boston: Houghton Mifflin, 1881; orig. pub. 1870), p. 212.

By the late nineteenth century, social and economic changes began to alter dramatically the American intellectual climate. With the consolidation of corporate capitalism and the rise of trusts in the decades after the Civil War, the *de facto*, if not the *de jure*, sovereignty of the state was brought into question. A wave of writing developed on the subject of "pressure politics," exemplified by Lincoln Steffens' *The Struggle for Self-Government* (1906). At the same time, historians such as Charles Beard paid much attention to the traditional importance of economic notables in America.[2]

The upshot of these changes was not Marxism, but rather a period of populism and progressivism in American life in general and in political analysis in particular. Textbooks changed. Young's 1915 text, *The New American Government and Its Work*, started its discussion not with the legal framework universal among earlier texts, but rather with a discussion of the influence of business on politics and the ensuing problems. In his presidential address to the 1916 meeting of the American Political Science Association, Jesse Macy called on political scientists to adopt the new "scientific spirit in politics."[3] By this he meant not behaviorism or empiricism, but rather the idea of applying the knowledge of political science to the urgent tasks of political reform.

Against this background, pluralism became popular in American political science. The early version of pluralism was associated with European writers such as Figgis, Maitland, Duguit, von Gierke and others, but American political scientists learned about it primarily through the work of Harold Laski:

> I would urge that you must place the individual at the center of things. You must regard him as linked to a variety of associations to which his personality attracts him. You must on this view admit that the State is only one of the associations to which he happens to belong.

On the surface, pluralism was a devastating rebuttal of traditional theory. Drawing on specific historical examples, Laski showed that, in practice, the state had abandoned its claim to complete sovereignty; for example, the English government formally recognized independence of religious groups after a struggle during the nineteenth century.

---

[2]Charles Beard, *An Economic Interpretation of the Constitution of the United States* (New York: Macmillan, 1913); *Economic Origins of Jeffersonian Democracy* (New York: Macmillan, 1915); *The Economic Basis of Politics* (New York: Vintage, 1957; orig. pub. 1922).

[3]Jesse Macy, "The Scientific Spirit in Politics," *American Political Science Review* 11, no. 1 (February 1917): 1–11.

[4]Harold Laski, in Waldo Browne, ed., *Leviathan in Crisis* (New York: Viking, 1946), p. 120. See Harold Laski, *Studies in the Problem of Sovereignty* (New Haven: Yale Univ. Press, 1917); H. Laski, *Authority in the Modern State* (New Haven: Yale Univ. Press, 1919); *The Foundations of Sovereignty* (New York: Harcourt, Brace and Co., 1921).

Laski's version of pluralism seemed to show that the jurists' legal theories about sovereignty were empirically false. Moreover, it presented a theoretical framework for the study of politics that could easily absorb the new thrusts of economic history and the study of pressure politics.

The jurists did not disappear without a fight. They pointed out that the theory of sovereignty was an ideal construct overarching other normative models such as constitutional monarchy or representative democracy. They said, in essence, that Laski was attacking a "straw man": no one was claiming that the state in fact was absolutely sovereign everywhere, at all times. They attacked Laski's pluralism for implying, if not anarchism, at least some form of associational rights of independence from the state, which would play havoc with social coordination and control.[5]

In this debate, most American political scientists eventually sided with the critics of Laski. Certainly the new associational groups were increasingly independent and powerful, but they saw no need to abandon the claims of ultimate state sovereignty over these new centers of power. Laski was originally concerned with defending labor union groups' independence against the claims of a hostile state; later, however, he became increasingly concerned with the state's right to regulate business. Thus he himself came to abandon pluralism in favor of a version of Marxist theory that provided for a high degree of social control over economic groups.[6]

Though classic pluralism was abandoned, jurisprudence was never revived. In the period of pessism after World War I, even the reform interest in pressure groups subsided. Instead there was an interest in "purifying" political science by stripping it of the normative-legal concerns of the jurists and the reform concerns of the progressives. In this search in the 1920s for a descriptive political science, many political scientists looked to the new field of psychology.

At this time, the psychologists were developing a different version of group theory. A leading political scientist of the day, Charles Merriam, wrote, "As social psychology develops, the whole study will be enriched by the addition of analysis of groups, of group relations, and individual-group relations."[7] The new psychological studies seemed to reinforce the pessimistic conclusions about the average citizen reached by Walter Lippman in *The Phantom Public* (1925). This version of group theory emphasized the role of limitation, emotion, and suggestibility of men and women in groups. It helped make understandable, for example, the role of demagogues and the rise of fascism.

---

[5] For a critique of Laski, see: Francis Coker, "The Technique of the Pluralist State," *American Political Science Review* 15, no. 2 (May 1921): 186–213; W. Y. Elliot, "The Pragmatic Politics of Mr. H. J. Laski," *American Political Science Review* 18, no. 2 (May 1924): 251–275.

[6] Harold Laski, *A Grammar of Politics* (New Haven: Yale Univ. Press, 1925): 488–508.

[7] Charles Merriam, "The Significance of Psychology for the Study of Politics," *American Political Science Review* 18, no. 3 (August 1924): 469–488.

Fascism affects the study of group behavior in a quite different way. Although fascism never had significant support within American political science, corporatism was not without its appeal in the period from 1925 to 1935. The basis for this had been laid by the descriptive political science of the 1920s, which documented the centrality of interests as part of processes of state. Corporatist theory, which envisioned the institutionalization of group interests in new "functional" parliaments, was hinted at in New Deal social planning. In the T.V.A., the Blue Eagle industrial code authorities, and the Agriculture Department's programs for "grass-roots democracy," among others, governmental authority was passed to interests, primarily economic, and institutionalized through formal representation on new organs of government.[8] Walter Shepard, in his presidential address to the 1934 meeting of the American Political Science Association, reflected this appeal of corporatist group theory in his observation that, "There is a large element of fascist doctrine and practice that we must appropriate," albeit with greater attention to civil liberties.[9]

At the same time, and increasing in the 1930s, other political scientists emphasized the dangers of centralism, prefiguring the later emphasis on pluralism: multiple centers of power in a system whose decentralization and fragmentation preserves freedom.[10] These writings took the corporatist emphasis on "functional self-government" of economic, educational, cultural, and other groups, but where the fascists sought coordination through new power centers institutionalizing these group interests, political scientists such as Lewis Rockow relied on the pluralist marketplace.[11]

During the 1930s, pluralist group theory was also prefigured by the use of group theory as a central part of the intellectual defense of democracy against the charges of fascism. After World War I, the defense of democracy had been seriously weakened by the credence given to Lippman's critique of public opinion, the psychologists' emphasis on group irrationality, and by the rise of the new "sciences" of propaganda and public relations conceived as means of social control. Where the pre-World War I reformers believed fervently in "direct democracy," by the 1930s few political scientists felt able to defend the "common man" as the repository of wisdom. Even among progressives, the tendency was toward social planning by experts, not toward direct democracy.

In this context, Francis Wilson and E. Pendleton Herring, among others, advanced a new, group theoretic basis for defending democracy that did not

[8] G. David Garson, "Research on Policy Alternatives for America During the 1930's," *Political Inquiry* 1, no. 1 (Fall 1973): 50–77.

[9] Walter Shepard, "Democracy in Transition," *American Political Science Review* 29, no. 1 (February 1935): 19.

[10] See, for example, Charles Beard and John Lewis, "Representative Government in Evolution," *American Political Science Review* 26, no. 2 (April 1932): 239.

[11] Lewis Rockow, "The Doctrine of the Sovereignty of the Constitution," *American Political Science Review* 25, no. 3 (August 1931): 573–578.

require an optimistic faith in the average citizen. Wilson argued that the individual vote or the individual response to a pollster's question might not be the best ways of understanding the American public. In fact, he noted, "Many new ways of making participation effective, especially by organized or conflicting groups or interests, have been developing."[12]

Herring carried this one step further, writing, "The public interest cannot be given concrete expression except through the compromise of special claims and demands finally effected. Special interests cannot then be banished from the picture, for they are the parts that make the whole."[13] Thus Herring argued for a conception of democracy as the sum of group interests, not of individual wills. This was a dramatic shift in democratic theory. While not original to Wilson or Herring, these writings set the basis for modern group theory.[14]   Through group theory, one could defend representative democracy as a system that affected the public interest through the accommodation of conflicting interests. This bordered on holding the public interest to reflect the might of groups that prevail in political competition, but might-makes-right theory was avoided by vague reference to the possibility of state direction and selection.[15]

The Work of David Truman and Earl Latham

Classic works frequently integrate a body of understanding that has evolved without previous systematic expression. Such is the work of David Truman. In part it relied on the almost forgotten work of Arthur Bentley, though it avoided Bentley's simplistic if strong mechanical model of politics as the physics of group forces.[16] It incorporated well-known studies of specific interest group cases, such as those by Odegard, Herring, Schattschneider,

---

[12] Francis Wilson, "Concepts of Public Opinion," *American Political Science Review* 27, no. 3 (June 1932): 375.

[13] E. Pendleton Herring, "Special Interests and the Interstate Commerce Commission," *American Political Science Review* 27, no. 6 (December 1933): 916–917.

[14] For criticism of this shift in democratic theory under the tutelage of modern political scientists, see Peter Bachrach, *The Theory of Democratic Elitism: A Critique* (Boston: Little, Brown, 1967); and Carole Pateman, *Participation and Democratic Theory* (Cambridge, England: Cambridge Univ. Press, 1970).

[15] For a review of this section, see G. David Garson, "The Evolution of Interest Group Theory: A Critique of the Process," *American Political Science Review* 68, no. 4 (December 1974): 1505–1519.

[16] Arthur Bentley, *The Process of Government* (Cambridge, Mass.: Harvard Univ. Press, 1967: orig. pub. 1908). For an excellent discussion of Bentley in comparison with Truman, see R. E. Dowling, "Pressure Group Theory: Its Methodological Range," *American Political Science Review* 54, no. 4 (December 1960): 944–954.

Though not without its ambiguity, Bentley's work cast politics as a decision-making process in which the sum of group forces determined the direction of outcomes. Later authors such as Latham disassociated themselves from this "inert cash-register" concept of the function of government.

and Garceau.[17] Although Truman did not treat this subject specifically, his work supported the postwar liberal counterattack on both Marxist interpretations of politics and revival of laissez-faire views.[18]

Like all theories of politics, group theory was not without its partisan implications. Against conservative argument, it could be used to defend the legitimacy of positive government. Against radical thinkers, it was part of an argument against social planning that overrides and reshapes private powers rather than reflecting them. It tottered on the brink of saying that current politics is the optimal result of the competition of many interest groups, none of which had the power to control the state. It stopped short of that brink, however, by leaving open the possibility (though not the likelihood) that other policy outcomes, from laissez faire to central planning, might conceivably emerge from the group process of politics.

Group theorists held that incremental change, rather than movement toward partisan extremes, was most likely, but cast that judgment as a "value-free" description of the political facts of life. A few, such as Charles Lindblom,[19] were frank in asserting the incrementalist, group-bargaining model as prescriptive as well descriptive, but most group theorists preferred normative ambiguity.

Major postwar group theorists, such as David Truman, maintained this ambiguity by leaving open the possibility that the group process was something more than the mechanistic physics of competing organized groups. Writers such as Truman and Latham are misrepresented when they are cast as either prescribing or describing politics as a system in which political outcomes are determined simply by the relative strengths of contending organized interests. Each added certain transcendant criteria to their models of political process.

Earlier writers would have made the public interest the key criteria affecting politics over and above specific pressures. The group theorists wished to avoid the public interest concept because they found it to be metaphysical, intrinsically normative, and opposed to their hope for a

[17] Peter Odegard, *Pressure Politics: The Story of the Anti-Saloon League* (New York: Columbia Univ. Press, 1928); E. Pendleton Herring, *Group Representation Before Congress* (Baltimore: John Hopkins Univ. Press, 1929); E. E. Schattschneider, *Politics, Pressures, and the Tariff* (New York: Prentice-Hall, 1935); and Oliver Garceau, *The Political Life of the American Medical Association* (Cambridge, Mass.: Harvard Univ. Press, 1941). It should be noted that none of these cases sought to apply group theory, and some contained antithetical implications. Schattschneider's study, for example, emphasized business hegemony, not interest group diversity.

[18] On the laissez-faire revival, see F. Hayek, *Road to Serfdom* (Chicago: Univ. of Chicago Press, 1944); L. von Mises, *Bureaucracy* (New Haven: Yale Univ. Press, 1944). On political science criticism, see for example, Herman Finer, *Road to Reaction* (Boston: Little, Brown, 1945). Numerous additional references exist on both sides of this debate.

[19] Charles Lindblom, "The Science of Muddling Through," *Public Administration Review* 19 (Spring 1959): 79–88; *The Intelligence of Democracy* (New York: Free Press, 1965); *The Policy-Making Process* (New York: Prentice-Hall, 1968).

value-free social science. Latham and Truman instead advanced the ostensibly empirical notion of "potential groups" as the factor making politics more than a sum of simple organized forces.

The idea of potential groups was implicit in Herring's distinction between "pressure politics" (in which relevant, countervailing interests are mobilized) and "compliance politics" (in which many potential interests remain latent, resulting in one-sided pressures). Herring implied that political decision makers might override interests of the moment in order to take potential but latent interests into account; Latham and Truman extended this idea.

Latham, for example, explicitly rejected the mechanistic model of the legislature as an "inert cash register, ringing up the additions and withdrawals of strength" of private interests. In addition to group interests, Latham argued, public bodies such as legislatures take into account their own institutional interests (e.g., in the executive branch, intragovernmental power and status rivalry) and the interests of their constituency.[20] By including constituency interest as a factor over and above group pressures, Latham introduced the idea of the legislator taking latent or diffuse interests into the decision-making process.

Though mentioned in the writings of such authors as Herring and Latham, the concept of the "potential group" was elaborated upon by David Truman.[21] Through this concept Truman emphasized the role of traditions, ideals, and other diffuse forces as important in determining political outcomes. For Truman, potential groups include "any mutual interest" and "any shared attitude."[22] This sweeping definition, coupled with the recognition potential as well as organized groups that play critical roles in politics, opens group theory to virtually any consideration or variable. That is, virtually all variables are "group variables," and it becomes difficult to avoid degeneration of group theory into the truism that all collective attributes affect politics.

Criticisms of the Group Approach

As advocated by Bentley, the group theory of politics was mechanistic: analogous to physics, the forces (group pressures) at work were measured and the resultant vector (the political outcome) computed. Latham and Truman advanced a far more complex theory, maintaining a focus on the group process, but admitting the importance of tradition, ideals, latent needs and desires, and politicians' perceptions thereof.

[20] Earl Latham, "The Group Basis of Politics: Notes for a Theory," *American Political Science Review* 46, no. 2 (June 1952): 391–392.
[21] David Truman, *The Governmental Process* (New York: Knopf, 1951). See Index, viii, "interest groups, potential."
[22] *Ibid.*, p. 511.

Dowling noted, however, that the use of the potential groups concept to circumvent the simplistic model of Bentley, was "a bit of very naive methodology." Truman did not see, Dowling wrote, "that the merit of a 'group interpretation' of politics would, if it were worked out, be precisely that it does 'leave something out.'"[23] By opening group theory to all things, Dowling felt, Truman sabotaged the utility of the theory. Instead of establishing a theoretical framework for determining whether or not the mechanistic model was descriptive or led to the desired outcomes, Truman helped turn group theory into a mere vocabulary, compatible with virtually any model of political process. Truman eventually disclaimed followers who interpreted his work as a group theory of politics, stating instead that his work had as its purpose simply to "examine interest groups and their role," not to invent a new theoretical approach to politics.[24]

As with classic pluralism after Laski had abandoned it, the importance of group theory *of* politics (as opposed to the simple study of the role of groups *in* politics) has declined in recent times. In addition to the basic criticism mentioned above, a number of other problems weakened group theory, a few of which are listed here:

1. *Conservative imagery:* In discussing consensual acceptance of the "rules of the game" in Western democracies, Truman asserted that "the great political task now as in the past is to perpetuate a viable system by maintaining the conditions under which such widespread understanding and appreciation can exist."[25] Many have found in the primacy given to "perpetuation" and "maintenance" of consensus the same sort of imagery that led to systems analysis and functionalism being labelled conservative.

2. *Equilibrium theory:* In discussing political behavior in courts and legislatures, Truman observed, "The institutionalized groups that exemplify these behavior patterns and the patterns themselves represent almost by definition an equilibrium among the interactions of the participants."[26] Critics have objected to these mentions of the equilibrium model of politics, finding them in tension with Truman's own acknowledgment that important political changes are due to more or less intense social disturbances that cannot be understood in terms of group influence patterns of an equilibriating sort.[27]

3. *Neglect of collective behavior:* Truman's work also invoked an orientation toward forms of collective behavior (such as social movements), which critics questioned. This is best illustrated by Truman's treatment of the process by which unorganized interests may coalesce in rebellion against the prevailing order under the heading of "morbific politics." "Morbific," meaning disease-causing, was a throwback to earlier imagery, such as the treatment of labor strikes as "social pathology" by Albion Small in the early years of group theory.[28]

[23] Dowling, "Pressure Group Theory," p. 953.
[24] David Truman, "On the Invention of 'Systems',"*American Political Science Review* 54, no. 2 (June 1960): 494–495.
[25] Truman, *Governmental Process*, p. 524.
[26] *Ibid.*, p. 27.
[27] *Ibid.*, p. 28.
[28] *Ibid.*, p. 516 ff.

4. *Avoidance of elite theory:* As with conflict theories of political process, Truman's work neglected any coverage of theories of politics in which elite dominance is projected. Although seemingly supporting a pluralist model rather than an elitist model of politics, Truman's discussion avoided dealing with contrast directly. For example, his section on "Difficulties in a Group Interpretation of Politics" confined itself to justifying a focus on the group (very broadly defined) rather than a focus on the individual in isolation or the society in abstract. Critics have felt the latter emphases to be straw-men, advocated by few if any contemporary political scientists. Instead, they argued, the real "difficulties" with the group approach were those being raised by C. Wright Mills and other "elite theorists."

Pluralism and the Work of Robert Dahl

Although Truman's group theory engendered initial excitement with its seeming promise of integrating many facets of political science research, its weaknesses soon became apparent. Many who were fundamentally sympathetic with Truman's approach sought to sharpen it by confronting issues not adequately dealt with by Truman. In particular, there was felt a need to deal with the arguments of elite theorists.

Group theory may be thought of as an overarching concept in which "pluralism" is a view that describes (and usually prescribes as well) American politics as relatively free from domination by any single group or coalition of groups representing any single social class. Specifically, business is seen as one group among many, in contrast to Marxist views, which hold it to be preeminent.

Dahl agreed with Latham and Truman that "we can only distinguish groups of various types and sizes, all seeking in various ways to advance their goals, usually at the expense, at least in part, of others."[30] Although Truman admitted that groups vary in influence, normally in the United States "there is a high probability that an active and legitimate group can make itself heard effectively at some crucial stage of the process of decision."[31] The result is that "the making of government decisions is not a majestic march of great majorities united upon certain matters of basic policy. It is the steady appeasement of relatively small groups."[32]

---

[29] *Ibid.*, p. 47 ff. Truman acknowledges that "it would be idle to deny that a large proportion of organized interest groups have a class character," (p. 165), but most of his discussion seems inconsistent with class analysis. For further criticism, see S. Rothman, "Systematic Political Theory: Observations on the Group Approach," *American Political Science Review* 54, no. 1 (February 1960): 15–33.

[30] Robert A. Dahl, *A Preface to Democratic Theory* (Chicago: Univ. of Chicago Press, 1956), p. 131.

[31] *Ibid.*, p. 145.

[32] *Ibid.*, p. 146.

On the basis of these views, Dahl described the American political system as one that appears "to be a relatively efficient system for reinforcing agreement, encouraging moderation, and maintaining social peace in a restless and immoderate people operating a gigantic, powerful, diversified, and incredibly complex society."[33] Dahl saw the political system as "efficient"—"reinforcing," "encouraging," and "maintaining"; the citizenry are "immoderate" and "restless." The work as a whole centers on the problem of majority tyranny (as opposed to elite dominance) and argues for the impossibility of the ideal of "majority rule." The value premises of such a view are easy to discern; they merely extend those found in group theory in general.

The elitism-pluralism debate is far too vast to be treated in depth here,[34] but elite theorists have generally opposed the pluralists on the following points:

1. Pluralists lack an adequate conception of the economic elite. Elite theorists argue that ownership, income, and economic position are highly stratified: that the upper strata share political orientations significantly different from the lower; and that divisions within the elite do not cancel out the effect of these shared orientations, which cannot be equated with the general interest of society.

2. Pluralists overlook central channels of economic elite influence on politics. Elite theorists emphasize the role of peak business associations, presidentially appointed task forces and commissions peopled by businessmen, advisory committees to administrative departments and agencies, the business background of many executive appointments, influence via campaign funds and lobbying, and more diffuse influence through control over information and hegemony over institutions of socialization. The many studies showing that economic groups neutralize or even dominate the regulatory agencies are cited as evidence by the elite theorists.

3. Pluralists concede the elite character of foreign policy, but they view popular influence as undesirable. Elite theorists tend to see the history of American foreign policy as one of imperialism and/or mistakes attributable to the closed, elite character of policymaking; the Vietnamese War is often cited as evidence against the desirability of elite, "expert" decision making in this area.

4. The pluralists view New Deal and other progressive social legislation as evidence that business loses as well as wins. Elite theorists usually attribute such legislation to economic elites rather than to popular pressure, and see it as cooptive in intent but merely symbolic in content, not redistributing power or benefits in any significant way.

---

[33] *Ibid.*, p. 151. See also Dahl's changing views in his text, *Pluralist Democracy in the United States* (Chicago: Rand McNally, 1967), and in his polemic, *After the Revolution?* (New Haven: Yale Univ. Press, 1970).

[34] A useful summary of the views sparked by the writings of C. Wright Mills is contained in G. William Domhoff and Hoyt Ballard, eds., *C. Wright Mills and "The Power Elite"* (Boston: Beacon, 1969). Useful anthologies include N. Crockett, ed., *The Power Elite in America* (Lexington, Mass: D. C. Heath, 1970); R. Gilliam, *Power in Postwar America* (Boston: Little, Brown, 1971). A bibliographic overview and interpretation are provided by Allen H. Barton, "Empirical Research on National Power Structures," Bureau of Applied Social Research, Columbia University (mimeo, 1973).

5. The pluralists see the economy as under the control of the government, at least ultimately. Elite theorists see these controls as generally insignificant in content, unenforced in practice, and overseen by officials heavily connected with the economic elite.

6. Pluralists focus on Congress and passing bills. Elite theorists see legislatures as existing at mere middle levels of power, serving symbolic and ritualistic purposes, and rarely challenging policy alternatives framed at higher levels. Congressional failure to challenge defense budgets is usually cited in this connection.

Group Theory: A Summary

Group theory can be used as an umbrella term to encompass much of American political science. While it is difficult to find defenders of the group theory of politics, the pluralist-elitist debate that is part of this tradition continues. Moreover, there is no shortage of studies of one or another aspect of various types of groups.[36]

Darryl Baskin has summarized the following five propositions today associated with pluralist group theory:[37]

1. The increasing complexity of modern society leads to higher government penetration of society, higher levels of cooperation between individuals through groups, and a greater likelihood that groups will seek government cooperation to obtain their ends.

2. Public policy is a function of the relative strengths of opposing group forces, *plus* the institutional interests and role perceptions of the political decision maker, *plus* the effect of traditions and potential groups (the decision maker may even play a leading role in initiating new groups or changing the rules of the game).

3. Group success is based on many factors, prime among which are number of adherents, intensity of their commitment, and mastery of technique (e.g., lobbying, public relations, etc.), combined with the level of resources (legitimacy, wealth, time, control over information).

4. Political stability rests on this complexity: the counterbalancing of opposing groups, overlapping memberships, consensual acceptance of the basic rules of the game, the incentive the system gives to accommodation and compromise, and the diffusion of power.

5. The "public interest" is a philosophical category, not a useful political science concept. The social interest can be assessed only through "summing" the often-conflicting interests of organized and potential groups. Perpetuation of the system is, in practice, the dominant characteristic of the political process.

[35] This listing is adapted from G. William Domhoff's critique of the late Arnold Rose's pluralist exposition, *The Power Structure* (New York: Oxford, 1967). See Domhoff, *The Higher Circles* (New York: Vintage, 1970), ch. 9. See also Domhoff's earlier work, *Who Rules America?* (Englewood Cliffs, N.J.: Prentice-Hall, 1967).

[36] A review of such studies is provided in M. Conway and F. Feigert, *Political Analysis* (Boston: Allyn & Bacon, 1972,), ch. 7.

[37] Darryl Baskin, "American Pluralism: Theory, Practice, and Ideology," *Journal of Politics* 32, no. 1 (February, 1970): 71–95.

In addition, Baskin notes, many pluralists adopt an explicitly prescriptive stance, to which the following additional point is relevant:

6. The group process more nearly approaches a social optimum (in terms of preserving individual liberty and satisfaction of needs) than any other political pattern. Specifically, the attempt to override group pressures through central social planning will lead to more problems than benefits. Thus rational central planning is a dangerous myth; in Lindblom's words, "muddling through" is better.

Baskin concludes that pluralism, like many ideologies, is self-reinforcing: the more that people believe that it *is* the way politics does and should work, the more they will operate in terms of its precepts and thereby validate the theory.

For each of these propositions, many elite theorists would draw counter-propositions:

1. Modernization leads to the merger of public and private elite interests.
2. Public policy is a function of elite bargaining.
3. Group success is based primarily on the correspondence between group goals and elite purposes.
4. Political stability rests on elite manipulation of symbols, control of socialization processes, and control over agencies of force and means of livelihood. Groups are not countervailing, but rather one set of groups—business—is dominant. Dissensus is as common as consensus, and consensus is frequently shallowly held and manipulated from above.
5. Normative concerns must be the core of political studies, and system perpetuation as a value has a conservative bias.
6. "Muddling through" by reliance on group conflict increases inequities and avoids solution to problems, thereby allowing them to mount to eventual crisis proportions: in this sense acceptance of group process is the basis of instability.

---

[38] For further criticism of pluralist group theory, see Michael Parenti, "Power and Pluralism," *Journal of Politics* 32, no. 3 (August 1970): 501–530; Robert Ross, "Relations Among National Interest Groups," *Journal of Politics* 32, no. 1 (February 1970): 96–114; D. Ricci, *Community Power and Democratic Theory* (New York: Random House, 1971), chs. 8–10. Literature on the pluralism-elitism debate at the community level is annotated in C. Press, *Main Street Politics* (East Lansing: Michigan State Univ. Press, 1962); and W. Hawley and J. Svara, *The Study of Community Power: A Bibliographic Review* (Santa Barbara: ABC-Clio, 1972). An illustrative anthology is M. Aiken and P. Mott, eds., *The Structure of Community Power* (New York: Random House, 1970). A useful overview and analysis is T. Clark, *Community Structure and Decision-Making* (San Francisco: Chandler, 1968). A defense of pluralism is found in R. Merelman, "On the New-Elitists Critique of Community Power," *American Political Science Review* 62, no. 2 (June 1968): 451–460, with related correspondence in *American Political Science Review* 62, no. 4: 1268–1269. See also R. Wolfinger, "Nondecisions and the Study of Local Politics," *American Political Science Review* 65, no. 4 (December 1971): 1063–1080, with commentary by Frey (1081–1101) and rejoinder by Wolfinger (1102–1104). A review is provided in Conway and Feigert, *Political Analysis*, ch. 8. After community studies, the study of comparative politics is the second arena in which group theory is most in use. See C. Lande, "Networks and Groups in Southeast Asia: Some

DECISION-MAKING THEORY, APPLIED
SYSTEMS ANALYSIS, AND PUBLIC CHOICE

Examination of group theory and pluralism overlaps the area often labelled "decision-making theory." Pluralist critics of elite theorists often charged the latter with inferring (wrongly, it was alleged) the structure of power from the distribution of wealth and income, from leaders' reputation for power, from the social background of officials—in short, from virtually anything but the actual examination of how decisions are made, by whom, and with what effect. Group theorists preferred to understand power through the study of the mechanics of specific decisions.

The literature cited (see note 38) with reference to community power studies illustrates fully the debate that ensued. Elite theorists charged that the most important aspects of politics are not embodied in decisions, much less routine decisions, but rather emerge through the indirect and diffuse manner in which ruling institutions define the issues and alternatives. This manner, they asserted, was better characterized as "nondecisions" than as "decisions." Pluralist defenders replied that the concept of nondecision was ambiguous and did not serve as a useful operational research tool. Elite theorists in turn responded by reasserting the necessity of examining indirect measures of power such as the distribution of benefits, rather than trying to "measure" power in various decisions and nondecisions.

While this debate was proceeding, however, those who were concerned with developing an operational research paradigm for the study of decisions —whether they were pluralists or not—began developing some insightful literature on the basic nature of decision-making. In some ways this literature rested on a formalized and artificial analytic separation of the "internal" aspects of decision making from the study of the larger sociopolitical environment that so dominated the elitist-pluralist debate. Nevertheless, many found in this emerging "decision theory" a possible new key to the study of politics.

Decision-Making Theory

It should be noted at the outset that "decision-making theory," like most terms in political science, lacks a commonly accepted meaning. Some equate

---

Observations on the Group Theory of Politics," *American Political Science Review* 67, no. 1 (March 1973): 103–127; Robert Lieber, "Interest Groups and Political Integration: British Entry into Europe," *American Political Science Review* 66, no. 1 (March 1972): 53–67; Donald Kelley, "Interest Groups in the USSR," *Journal of Politics* 34, no. 3 (August 1972): 860–888; and J. Schwartz and W. Keech, "Group Influence and Policy Process in the Soviet Union," *American Political Science Review* 62, no. 3 (September 1968): 840–851. These studies contain both support and criticism of group theory.

it with the elitist-pluralist debate over the distribution of power. Others equate it with mathematical game theory (see below). All these areas of study overlap highly, but for our purposes "decision-making theory" is used here to mean the conceptualization of formal models of rational decisions, together with empirical studies testing the degree to which these models approximate reality. Game theory, applied systems analysis, and public choice theory are specific variants of decision-making theory. The elitist-pluralist literature raises many of the same issues, but is organized around questions of power distribution, whereas decision-making theory is organized around rational decisional models.

Decision-making theory is not part of the tradition of group theory. If anything, it represents a step back towards the individualistic focus of the psychological approaches discussed in Chapter 2. Harold Lasswell, who was cited as a leading figure in the study of psychological approaches to politics, figures prominently in decision-making theory as well. In *The Future of Political Science* (1963), Lasswell set forth what might be called an "anatomy of a decision"—the subprocesses of which it is composed.

Every decision, Lasswell wrote, is composed of seven phases:

1. an intelligence phase, involving an influx of information;
2. a recommending phase, involving activities designed to influence the outcome;
3. a prescribing phrase, involving the articulation of norms;
4. an invoking phase, involving establishing correspondence between prescriptions and concrete circumstances;
5. an application phase, in which the prescription is executed;
6. an appraisal phase, assessing intent in relation to effect; and
7. a terminating phase, treating expectations ("rights") established while the prescription was in force.

This breakdown bears some resemblance to the input-transform-output systems model and to typologies of administrative functions in classic public administration literature.[40] Of these two, Lasswell's views were closer to the latter, sharing the administrationists' concern for responsible and rational decision making in government. Lasswell saw this concern as part of the social responsibility of political scientists,[41] and detailed how this responsibility might be assumed through "micromodelling" and "decision seminars."[42]

These orientations of Lasswell may be traced back to the enthusiasm for "policy science" in the early 1950s.[43] In the late 1950s Richard C. Snyder

[39] Harold Lasswell, *The Future of Political Science* (New York: Atherton, 1963), ch. 1.
[40] On the systems model, see the section in Chapter 3 of this text. On administrationist typologies, see, for example, the review in J. Miner, *Management Theory* (New York: Macmillan, 1971), ch. 6.
[41] Lasswell, *Future of Political Science*, p. 26.
[42] *Ibid.*, ch. 60.
[43] See Daniel Lerner and Harold D. Lasswell, eds., *The Policy Sciences* (Stanford, Cal.: Stanford Univ. Press, 1951).

emerged as the leading advocate of a "decision-making approach." Snyder saw this approach as an alternative to functionalism and other equilibrium theories which seemed "static," describing a system at a given point in time. A focus on decision making, in contrast, seemed to build an emphasis on a dynamic process of change over time.

"The key to political action," Snyder wrote, "lies in the way decision-makers as actors define their situation."[44] This definition was cast in four dimensions: (1) discriminating and grouping phenomena; (2) perception and establishment of goals; (3) estimation of the consequences of courses of action with regard to the phenomenon; and (4) application of "standards of acceptability" to narrow perceptions, goals, and alternatives. This formulation could have been a point of departure into phenomenology and other approaches to be discussed below. For Snyder, however, "defining the situation" was not explored through a focus on subjective perceptions of the actor, but rather through the general intrinsic logic of the decision-making process as a sequence of predecisional, choice, and implementation activities. [45]

For further discussion of Snyder's theoretical framework the student must refer to the original. The point here is simply that in Snyder's work one may find a reasoned and systematic presentation of decision making as an approach to all political events. [46] It sheds the normative concerns of Lasswell (the social responsibility of political scientists) and adopts a generalized perspective compatible both with modelling of rational decisions and with behavioral examination of real-life deviations from such models.

Snyder's optimistic expectations of the decision-making approach had specific reference to certain emerging bodies of literature. First, there were rational models of voting and other political decisions, based primarily on analogies to economics and that discipline's assumptions about man as a rational consumer; Anthony Downs' work was crucial here. [47] Second, there was mention of the then-new "organization theory" emphasis on decision making introduced by Herbert Simon and others in the field of public administration. [48] And third, there was growing interest in game theory[49]

[44]Richard C. Snyder, "A Decision-Making Approach to the Study of Political Phenomena," in Roland Young, ed., *Approaches to the Study of Politics* (Evanston, Ill.: Northwestern Univ. Press, 1958), p. 17.

[45]*Ibid.*, p. 20.

[46]See also Richard C. Snyder and James A. Robinson, *National and International Decision-Making* (New York: Institute for International Order, 1961); R. Snyder, H. Bruck, and B. Sapin, *Decision-Making as an Approach to the Study of International Politics* (Princeton: Princeton Univ. Press, 1954) Foreign Policy Analysis Series, no. 3.

[47]Anthony Downs, *An Economic Theory of Democracy* (New York: Harper & Row, 1957), and "Why the Government Budget is Too Small in a Democracy," *World Politics* 12 (July 1960): 541–563.

[48]Herbert Simon, "Some Strategic Considerations in the Construction of Social Science Models," in P. Lazarsfeld, ed., *Mathematical Thinking in the Social Sciences* (Glencoe, Ill.:

and experimental tests of theories about decision making.[50] Each of these areas of research has continued to grow, forming the core of what is loosely called "decision-making theory."

The Rational Voter Downs' *Economic Theory of Democracy* (1957) was based on assumptions of (1) self-interest as the basis of political motivation (specifically, the interest of the politician in holding office), leading to (2) political parties in a democracy as formulators of policy strictly as a means of gaining votes. Thus, government is seen as "an entrepreneur selling policies for votes instead of products for money."[51] Voters, in turn, vote according to changes in their "utility incomes" from government activity in comparison with what may be expected from the opposition. This model led Downs to twenty-five testable propositions about politics.[52] These include, among others, the propositions that party members are chiefly motivated by the intrinsic benefits of holding office, not ideals; that in order to maximize votes, parties compete for the middle, thereby causing their programs to be relatively similar; and that democratic governments seek to maximize votes by tending to redistribute income from the rich to the poor.

Downs' work has received both praise and criticism. It has the merit of presenting a systematic model of politics against which reality may be measured. Moreover, that model may be used to make predictions about expected behavior. It avoids the problem of much of group theory by *not* seeking to be "closer to reality" by employing all-embracing concepts that exclude few, if any, factors from consideration. Instead, Downs' theory is a strong one, projecting a clear image of political decisions based on premises of rationality.

Free Press, 1954), pp. 388–416; H. Simon, "Rational Choice and the Structure of the Environments," *Psychological Review* 63 (1956): 129–138; H. Simon, *Administrative Behavior*, 2nd ed. (New York: Macmillan, 1957; orig. pub. 1948); H. Simon, *Models of Man* (New York: John Wiley & Sons, 1957); H. Simon, *The New Sciences of Management Decision* (New York: Harper & Row, 1960).

[49]Richard Snyder, "Game Theory and the Analysis of Political Behavior," in Stephen K. Bailey, ed., *Research Frontiers in Politics and Government* (Washington, D. C.: Brookings Institution, 1955), pp. 70–104. See also J. von Neumann and O. Morgenstern, *Theory of Games and Economic Behavior* (Princeton: Princeton Univ. Press, 1944); D. Blackwell and M. Girshick, *Theory of Games and Statistical Decisions* (New York: John Wiley & Sons, 1954); J. Williams, *The Compleat Strategyst* (New York: McGraw-Hill, 1954); M. Shubik, ed., *Readings in Game Theory and Political Behavior* (New York: Doubleday, 1954); T. Schelling, *The Strategy of Conflict* (New York: Oxford, 1963; orig. pub. 1960); and M. Shubik, "Bibliography on Simulation, Gaming, Artificial Intelligence, and Related Topics," *Journal of the American Statistical Association* 65, no. 292 (1960): 736–751; D. Luce and H. Raiffa, *Games and Decisions* (New York: John Wiley & Sons, 1957).

[50]D. Davidson and P. Suppes, *Decision-Making—An Experimental Approach* (Stanford: Stanford Univ. Press, 1957).

[51]Anthony Downs, "An Economic Theory of Political Action in a Democracy," *Journal of Political Economy* 65, no. 2 (April 1957): 135–150. This journal gives continuing coverage to this area of research.

[52]Downs, *Economic Theory of Democracy*, ch. 16.

Criticism of Downs has focused on the fact that the assumptions of his model are not always descriptive of reality: politicians are sometimes motivated by ideals, voters do not necessarily weigh "utilities," the assumption of complete voter information is improbable, etc. Downs' axiomatic reasoning has seemed to some to channel political science toward philosophy. These critics note that Downs' work is not based on empirical evidence, which must come before the use of the deductive method.[53] In particular, Downs' model hinges in a very important way on the belief that vote maximization figures as large for parties as profit maximization does for business enterprises. As James Q. Wilson and others have noted, it is more reasonable to believe that vote maximization is only one of several, indeed of a variety of goals, of political organizations.[54] If one admits that, Downs' model stands in need of severe reformulation.[55]

A second, closely related line of analysis stems from the work of Kenneth Arrow. Arrow and others showed that if one has a binary choice among three alternatives, a summation of votes will lead to paradoxes. For example, in a choice among three candidates, it is possible for voters' preferences to be such that a majority will oppose any given candidate. Similarly, a majority may oppose any given policy alternative, making "rational" government action impossible.[56] Downs had recognized this dilemma, but felt its manifestations in practice were limited in significance.[57] This problem of democratic decision making has continued to be a focus for developing rational models of political choice.[58] The body of research emerging from this aspect

[53]W. H. Rogers, "Some Methodological Difficulties in Anthony Downs's 'An Economic Theory of Democracy'," *American Political Science Review* 53, no. 2 (June 1959): 483–485.

[54]James Q. Wilson, "The Economy of Patronage," *Journal of Political Economy* 69, no. 4 (August 1961): 369–380.

[55]Reformulation has tended toward increasing mathematical formalization of Downs' concepts. See G. Tullock, *Toward a Mathematics of Politics* (Ann Arbor: Univ. of Michigan Press, 1968), ch. 7; W. Riker and P. Ordeshook, "A Theory of the Calculus of Voting," *American Political Science Review* 62, no. 1 (March 1968): 25–42; T. Casstevens, "A Theorem About Voting," *American Political Science Review* 62, no. 1 (March 1968): 205–207; S. Brams and M. O'Leary, "An Axiomatic Model of Voting Bodies," *American Political Science Review* 64, no. 2 (June 1970): 449–470; P. Ordeshook, "Extensions to a Mathematical Model of the Electoral Process and Implications for the Theory of Responsible Parties," *Midwest Journal of Political Science* (February 1970); M. Hinich and P. Ordeshook, "Plurality Maximization vs. Vote Maximization," *American Political Science Review* 64, no. 3 (September 1970): 772–791.

[56]Kenneth Arrow, *Social Choice and Individual Values* (New York: John Wiley & Sons, 1951), esp. chs. 1 and 2.

[57]Downs, *An Economic Theory of Democracy*, ch. 4.

[58]See Duncan Black, *The Theory of Committees and Elections* (Cambridge, England: Cambridge Univ. Press, 1958); Richard Niemi, "Majority Decision-Making with Partial Unidimensionality," *American Political Science Review* 63, no. 2 (June 1969): 488–497; Douglas Rae, "Decision Rules and Individual Values in Constitutional Choice," *American Political Science Review* 63, no. 1 (March 1969): 40–56; Richard Zeckhauser, "Voting Systems, Honest Preferences, and Pareto Optimality," *American Political Science Review* 67, no. 3 (September 1973): 934-946; James Coleman, *Mathematics of Collective Action* (Chicago: Aldine, 1973).

of decision-making theory is highly formal, mathematical, and esoteric in that it has relatively little influence on the rest of political science compared to previously discussed approaches. Nonetheless, they are not simply "useless abstractions"; decision-making research leads into a practical discussion of the relative advantages of different systems of ascertaining "what the majority wants." One of these systems concerns reliance on the (private) economic marketplace for provision of public goods, an idea that underlies "public choice theory," to be discussed below.

The Rational Administrator   Before turning to public choice theory, another aspect of decision-making theory merits notice. Simon and the administrationists also developed a rational decision-making model. But where Downs' model, like game theory, assumed maximization of utilities ("economic man"), Simon assumed rational decision makers in general and administrators in particular simply sought the first satisfactory solution ("satisficing" by "administrative man").[59] Amitai Etzioni has agreed that the "rational-comprehensive" approach of the economic model is impossible in practice, but has asserted administrators can do better in the way of planning than simply "satisficing." Etzioni's model is one based on what he terms "mixed scanning," a process which combines the two.[60] These distinctions illustrate the point that "rationality" has different meanings. Paul Diesing has usefully provided categories:

1. Technical Rationality: continual solution of technical problems: order as utility.
2. Economic Reality: continual comparison of values (competition): order as efficiency.
3. Legal Rationality: continual application of rules (precedents): order as law.
4. Social Rationality: continual resolution of conflicts: order as integration.
5. Substantive Rationality: different kinds of order call for different kinds of reason.[61]

In addition to examination of the generalized nature of governmental decision making, organization theorists have also been concerned with the relatively technical application of decision-making theory to specific problems such as the classic debate over centralization versus decentralization.[62]

[59]Herbert A. Simon, *Models of Man*, pp. 198 ff.
[60]Amitai Etzioni, *The Active Society* (New York: Free Press, 1968), ch. 12.
[61]Paul Diesing, *Reason in Society* (Urbana: Univ. of Illinois Press, 1962).
[62]M. Kochen and K. Deutsch, "Toward a Rational Theory of Decentralization," *American Political Science Review* 63, no. 3 (September 1969): 734–749; F. Levy and E. Truman, "Toward a Rational Theory of Decentralization: Another View," *American Political Science Review* 65, no. 1 (March 1971): 172–179.
 For a defense of utility maximization assumptions, see W. Riker and W. Zavoina, "Rational Behavior in Politics," *American Political Science Review* 64, no. 1 (March 1970): 48–60.

Theory of Public Goods
and Applied Systems Analysis

Decision-making theory can lead easily into questions of optimal allocation of public goods. Literature on public finance and political economy has involved economists more and more in the traditional domain of political science.[63] William C. Mitchell, who played an important role in popularizing functionalism in political science, has sought to do the same for the theory of public goods. He has usefully summarized many of the propositions that emerge from this literature, among which the following are representative: the public sector tends to increase; interest groups prefer added benefits to decreased burdens; budgeting agencies seek short-run, incremental gains.[64] The proposition that public goods are more efficiently allocated by the economic marketplace than by government is undoubtedly the most controversial aspect of this theory.[65] Overall, these propositions, though all growing from a common interest in the allocation of public goods, do not form a unified theory. Rather, they constitute a body of research, sometimes contradictory in its assertions, and, like much of political science, in need of empirical testing.

On the other hand, a well-developed literature on the *techniques* of managerial decision making emerged during the 1960s, even though no *general* theory of political behavior serves to integrate them, unless one counts systems analysis. These techniques include operations research,[66] "managing by objectives,"[67] and program-planning-budgeting systems (PPBS).[68] All are variants of what is often called "applied systems analysis,"

For an overview of decision-making theory from an administrationist perspective, see J. Pfiffner and R. Presthus, *Public Administration*, 5th. ed. (New York: Ronald Press, 1967), ch. 6; and F. Nigro, *Modern Public Administration* 2nd. ed. (New York: Harper & Row, 1970), ch. 8.

[63]See J. Buchanan, *The Demand and Supply of Public Goods* (Chicago: Rand McNally, 1968); M. Olson, *The Logic of Collective Action: Public Goods and the Theory of Groups* (New York: Schocken, 1968; rev. ed. 1971).

[64]William C. Mitchell, "The Shape of Political Theory to Come: From Political Sociology to Political Economy," in S. M. Lipset, ed., *Politics and the Social Sciences* (New York: Oxford, 1969), ch. 5.

[65]This proposition is advanced, for example, by Martin Shubik, in "Voting, or a Price System in a Competitive Market Structure," *American Political Science Review* 64, no. 1 (March 1970): 179–181. For a rebuttal, see John Ferejohn and Talbot Page, "A Note on 'Voting, or a Price System in a Competitive Market Structure'," *American Political Science Review* 67, no. 1 (March 1973): 157–160.

[66]See F. Hillier and G. Lieberman, *Introduction to Operations Research* (San Francisco: Holden-Day, 1967); D. Plane and G. Kochenberger, *Operations Research for Managerial Decisions* (Homewood, Ill.: Irwin, 1972).

[67]See S. Carroll and H. Tosi, *Management by Objectives* (New York: Macmillan, 1973).

[68]See H. Hovey, *The Planning-Programming-Budgeting Approach to Government Decision-Making* (New York: Praeger, 1968); F. Lyden and E. Miller, eds., *Planning Programming Budgeting: A Systems Approach to Government* (Chicago: Markham, 1967); J. Davis, ed.,

interest in which intensified with the attempt to introduce such methods of decision making into the Defense Department under Kennedy[69] and in all federal departments under Johnson.[70]

Evaluating Service Programs in Applied Systems Analysis   The problems involved in quantifying and comparing hardware are formidable. When the subject to be evaluated is a service or a package of services and hardware, evaluation becomes extremely difficult. Direct measurement of each cost and benefit becomes impossible, and instead cost-benefit analysis focuses on a search for useful indices of costs and benefits as indirect measures.

For example, in measuring the benefits of urban renewal, *one* of the indices might be increase in area tax revenue adjusted for increases in comparable areas not renewed. An indirect measure of the benefits of a national health program might be years increase in life expectancy, or changes in a certain disease rate, adjusting for trends predating the program. Every such index may be challenged, and ordinarily many indices are used in a given evaluation. The indices need not be quantitative. For example, in evaluating to what extent an experimental school is satisfying parents' needs, in the absence of objective measures of satisfaction, subjective satisfaction increases might be measured by opinion surveys.

Procedure   The paradigms for cost-benefit analysis vary, but the following two are prominent:[72]

Cost/gain ratio approach

1. Evaluate the package directly or, if necessary, indirectly, in terms of gains minus cost.

Politics, Programs, and Budgets (Englewood Cliffs, N.J.: Prentice-Hall, 1969); and R. Lee and R. Johnson, *Public Budgeting Systems* (Baltimore: University Park Press, 1973), especially ch. 6.

For a case illustration, see H. Hatry, R. Winnie, and D. Fisk, *Practical Program Evaluation for State and Local Government Officials* (Washington, D. C.: Urban Institute, 1973).

[69]See Charles Hitch and Roland McKean, *The Economics of Defense in The Nuclear Age* (New York: Atheneum, 1965).

[70]This effort, generally deemed a failure, is reviewed in F. Mosher and J. Harr, *Programming Systems and Foreign Affairs Leadership* (New York: Oxford, 1970); L. Merewitz and S. Sosnick, *The Budget's New Clothes* (Chicago: Markham, 1971); in symposia in the *Public Administration Review* 26, no. 6 (December 1966), 29, no. 2 (March–April 1969), and 34, no. 4 (July–August 1974); A Rivlin, *Systematic Thinking for Social Action* (Washington, D. C.: Brookings Institution, 1971); and I. Hoos, *Systems Analysis in Public Policy: A Critique* (Berkeley: Univ. of California Press, 1972).

[71]See H. Hinrichs and G. Taylor, *Program Budgeting and Benefit-Cost Analysis* (Pacific Palisades, Cal.: Goodyear, 1969); and for an alternative approach, see D. Gil, *Unravelling Social Policy* (Cambridge, Mass.: Schenkman, 1973).

2. If gains and cost are not expressable in terms of common units, either (a) determine the least cost for a specified gain, or (b) determine the maximum gain for a specified cost.

3. When gain is intangible, use 2(a); when costs are intangible, use 2(b) above.

4. Examine the consistency of the gain criterion with higher-level values.

5. Be careful to include in gains any spillover effects, and exclude from costs historical sunk costs.

Paired cost/gain ratio approach

1. Enumerate the "producers" of the services studied and pair them with the "consumers" of the services.

2. Itemize the costs and benefits of the present "without services" situation and the future "without" situation.

3. Itemize the costs and benefits of service under alternative "with services" situations.

4. Compare the net differences between step 3 and step 2 situations.

The fact that extreme creativity and effort are required to implement these steps does not alter the fact that full evaluation requires such procedures. In practical political analyses, the general procedure is often followed in a nonrigorous way. For example, in considering the suggestion that the United States propose to China that the two countries exchange newsmen, the political scientist may follow cost-benefit procedures. He will list, for each country, the costs and benefits of both accepting and not accepting the proposal. If he is sufficiently thorough he may do this for the present period and some projected future period. Among the costs to China in accepting, for example, is the perceived threat of additional foreign agents. Benefits include a greater likelihood that the U.S. will be responsive to later Chinese initiatives. Among the costs to the U.S. would be poorer relations with Taiwan; among the gains would be perceived better relations with China. The researcher could then go on to distinguish among costs and benefits in the short and long run.

In sum, cost-benefit analysis can vary from value engineering precision about hardware to a simple checklist summary of costs and gains. Although not demanded by the approach, there is often a certain bias toward quantifiable variables and the present period. It may tend to underemphasize important but intangible benefits and avoid making projective evaluations needed for future-oriented planning.

Management Systems   Much of applied systems analysis was developed for business purposes, growing out of the industrial engineering tradition of Frederick Taylor. This tradition covers such matters as organization hierarchy charts, product flowcharts, benchmark time-and-motion studies, data processing, and inventory control.[72] The business management systems approach is also a checklist-oriented paradigm, focusing on the following criteria:

1. *Purpose*. Have conditions changed since the operation was instituted? Are other operations equivalent in function but superior in performance?
2. *Equipment*. Does volume justify investment in data processing systems?
3. *Organization*. Is there a functional write-up of organizational units? Are goals set for various jobs and units?
4. *Procedures*. How adequate are manuals of training of personnel in various job descriptions?
5. *Measurement*. Can management evaluate performance?
6. *Schedule*. What is the lag in processing? Is the most efficient flow sequence used?
7. *Facilities*. Is the assigned area adequate?
8. *Records*. What is the memory capacity and recall rate of files?
9. *Budgeting*. In addition to performance measures, are there functionally itemized cost measures?

The management analyst covers these and similar points prior to designing existing and ideal operations flowcharts. While the approach takes the form of a checklist, the systems management analyst seeks to understand the relationships of all factors taken as a whole. This is often epitomized by the operations control plan. Again, although not logically inseparable from the approach, management analysis tends to emphasize quantifiable variables, formal relationships (as opposed, for example, to effects of informal work groups), and economic-tangible product criteria.

Program Planning Systems   Program planning and budgeting systems (PPBS) has been established in many branches of the federal government as an attempt at systems analysis of government decision making.* It is an effort to rationalize decision making, facilitate more comprehensive planning, and provide government officials with better information and clearer criteria with which to make judgments.

If a policy package is conceived as a set of inputs that have *costs* and yield outputs that have *benefits*, the *program planning budget* presents benefits in cost terms. That is, instead of a military budget listing expenditures for airplanes, tanks, pay of personnel, etc., the program planning budget groups costs by benefits—cost of the Vietnam war, cost of Latin

---

[72] A good introduction is Stanford L. Optner, *Systems Analysis for Business Management* (Englewood Cliffs: Prentice-Hall, 1968). See also, C. McMillan and R. Gonzalez, *Systems Analysis*, 3rd ed. (Homewood, Ill.: Irwin, 1973).
  *By OMB Circular A-11 and Memorandum 38 of June, 1971, much of the PPB system was made nonmandatory for federal agencies, after which many of them dropped experimentation with the system.

American military support, cost of European military presence, etc. By presenting a budget in the latter manner, the decision maker is in a better position to judge the worth of various programs. The point may seem trivial, but the former materials budget has been the standard approach until recently and has greatly thwarted evaluation of benefit costs.

Procedure   The program budget is the end result of systems analysis, the plan for expenditures for the next fiscal year, and for usually the next five years to follow. The problems involved are great, if only because of the question of allocating such things as overhead costs to various specific program benefits. Leaving this aside, what is the procedure by which the systems analyst arrives at a program budget?

1. The first step involves specifying the *goals* of the organization, the long-run states of accomplishment toward which programs are directed. Sometimes this is part of an explicit legislative mandate; more often it emerges, if at all, from arduous discussions between planners and administrators. (In practice, goals may be determined as a result of later steps.)

2. For each goal, planners consult with agency staff and others to determine a set of program *objectives*. Objectives are measured, and specific kinds of progress showing movement toward a goal in a stated time period are identified.

3. For each objective, various *indicators*, usually of a quantitative nature, are devised as measures of progress toward objectives. Sometimes these indicators are combined into a single objective *index*.

4. After the planner has clarified goals as best he can, specified objectives, and determined one or more indicators for each, he then goes through an analogous process for organization activities. The activities of the organization are separated into *general activity areas*, each of which is divided into *program categories*, which in turn are composed of *program elements*.

    For example, in Public Health Service planning, the *service* areas are considered to be normal development, repair, containment, and basic research. Activity areas for each of these are direct operations, facilities, research, and training. Then, for instance, the direct operations activity area of the normal development health service contains the program category of "public education in health," of which one of the program elements is "technical information services."

5. The service areas and their components down to the program element level may be coded. The code for the above example is 110105, where the first digit stands for the service area, the second digit stands for the general activity, the next two digits represent the program category, and the last two the program element.

6. A coded list of all output measures for each of the program elements (i.e., one master code for all elements) then is prepared. For example, code 041 corresponds to the output measure "number of community sources inspected," code 049 corresponds to "number of insulin samples tested." Over time, codes tend to become standardized.

7. The program element measures are then related to the indicators of objectives. This involves not only finding which measures are equivalent to or indices of which objectives indicators, but also translating the units used in element mea-

sures into units used in the indicators of objectives. It also entails setting up special procedures for handling nonquantitative measures and indicators.

8. *Performance accounting* (program budgeting) procedures are then used to allocate organization costs to the various program elements. This completes the planning process of establishing an *information system*, ordinarily geared to data processing, that relates costs to programs to goals to benefits.

Program planning systems involve many problems, but the procedures described above (much simplified) leave the planner in a better position to evaluate the activities of his or her agency. It enables the formulation and review of performance (program) budgets.

The systems analyst ordinarily will do more than establish an information system, however. Other tasks involve establishing a *liaison* between the program planning office and various relevant departments and agencies. Sometimes various advisory committees and consultants must be integrated into the liaison network. In addition, the data processing deparment itself must be organized, including bodies responsible for establishing *standardized* budget, program element measurement, and other forms, the manuals and *training facilities* to teach administrators the use of the new evaluative planning system, and even writers and designers to aid in presentation of information system results.

Also in addition to the basic information system, an office of *program analysis* may be established to do cost-benefit studies of programs alternative to the existing ones, so that a constant review of proposals occurs, phrased in terms comparable to the terms used in the basic information system. Working closely with this office would ordinarily be an office of *finance planning*, seeking to uncover new sources of funding for the organization and capable of both writing grant proposals and detailing how proposed grants would be integrated into the organization's total activities. Other groups must be charged with the all too unscientific tasks of coordinating public participation and political or other institutional interests in the organization. These activities involve great discretion and value choices, and are therefore ordinarily carried on by, or closely subordinated to, the organization's higher leadership.

Criticisms   The main *strength* of program planning systems is provision of more and better information for decision makers, which forces administrators at all levels to keep goals and objectives in mind, compels cost evaluation of each program element, facilitates the systematic study of possible alternatives, and does all this across traditional organizational lines. It enables political decisions to be made on a more reasoned basis.

Weaknesses of PPBS include its sometimes erroneous assumption of the absence of frequent politically originated, unplanned interruptions, delays, and changes; the belief that planners can get administrators and legislators to articulate their goals and specify objectives; its further assumption that finances can be counted on for a year or more in advance; and for that matter, its conclusion that it is possible to plan for the future in some specific way.

It provides the decision maker with no value criteria, although there is a certain presumption that the cost criterion will predominate. Like other applied systems approaches, there is a certain tendency to neglect unmeasurable, intangible factors. In practice, outputs of programs are extremely difficult to define and costs are not easily allocated to program elements. Although PPBS sometimes claims to represent comprehensive planning, it tends in practice to be aggregative planning—that is, total activities are rarely evaluated as more than the sum of the parts. There is a bias against risky experimentation of evaluation by criteria of political or social rather than economic efficiency. Finally, by the very fact of enabling decision makers to make better judgments, it may have a centralizing effect on the organization.

Game Theory   The most highly quantified and formal dimension of decision-making theory is termed "game theory."[73] Game theory has many variants, but it is most frequently used to analyze conflicts between specified opponents (usually few in number) who operate through discrete strategies (again, usually few in number) resulting in gains or losses of a known quantity. Thus game theory assumes that the *players* can be identified, their *strategies* separated, and the results of any pair of strategies given a numeric value. In addition, game theory *usually* assumes players of *conservative rationality* (i.e., who choose strategies that assure maximum average gains or minimum average losses) operating under conditions of full information. These and other assumptions are rarely met in the "real world," but game theorists respond that their results only need to improve on political intuition and reasoning, not perfect it. Moreover, experiments can be designed to test how well game theory results approximate reality.

In game theory, a two-person game is a game with two interests, such as man versus man, man versus nature, or team versus fate. A *strategy* is a plan of action that cannot be upset by an opponent or nature; in the long run it will result in the most favorable *game value*. One's own particular strategy waged against a given opposing strategy will result in a particular *payoff*. A *game matrix* represents the payoffs for all combinations of strategies. *Pure strategy* means always pursuing the same strategy. *Mixed strategy* means choosing randomly among one's best strategies according to some proportion

[73]See note 49. Game theory is here distinguished from simulation, which includes both role-playing of political situations and computer modelling. See J. Raser, *Simulation and Society* (Boston: Allyn and Bacon, 1969); P. Smoker, "International Relations Simulations: A Summary," in H. Alker, K. Deutsch, and A. Stoetzel, eds., *Mathematical Approaches to Politics* (San Francisco: Jossey Bass, 1973), pp. 417-464.

or mix. The part of a proportion (such as the 3 in the proportion 1:3) corresponding to a particular strategy is called the *oddment* of that strategy. Tables 4.1 and 4.2 are examples of game matrices.

TABLE 4.1

		Person A	
		#1	#2
Person B	#1	−1	−25
	#2	0	−20

TABLE 4.2

		Person A		
		#1	#2	#3
Person B	#1	7	6	4
	#2	3	2	5

In these matrices, payoffs are to Person B (this is a convention). Thus, in Table 4.1, when Person A pursues strategy #2 and Person B strategy #1, the payoff to B is − 25 units. Using conservative reasoning, Person B will select the strategy where the least he will gain is highest (or the most he will lose is lowest). The row containing the highest minimum (the maximum row minimum, or *maximin*) for Person B in Table 4.1 is the row for Strategy #2; there the maximin is − 20. Person A, also using conservative rationality, will seek the column containing the lowest maximum (the minimum column maximum, or *minimax*); in Table 4.1 the minimax is the same cell, − 20. When the same cell is both the maximin and the minimax, it is called the *saddle point*. Any saddle point is also the *solution* to the game in the sense that it will be the payoff which results when the game is played by opponents using conservative rationality.

Table 4.2 represents a more complex game. Here Person A will always prefer strategy #2 over strategy #1. This is because if Person B chooses strategy #1, Person A will lose only 6 units (remember payoffs are to B) with his strategy #2 as compared with 7 units for A's strategy #1. Similarly, Person A will lose less with his strategy 2 when Person B chooses his strategy #2. When a given column or row always yields better results, cell for cell, than a second column or row, the first is said to *dominate* the second. Rows or columns that are dominated may be ignored, for they do not affect the solution of the game. In Table 4.2, the column for strategy #1 may be ignored because it is dominated by column 2.

In the *reduced game* that results from ignoring column 1 in Table 4.2, there is no saddle point. The maximin is 4 but the minimax is 5. Person B will prefer strategy #1 because he will win at least 4 and possibly 6, whereas with strategy #2 he would win only 2 or possibly 5. Person A will prefer strategy #3 because he will lose no more than 5, and possibly only 4, whereas with strategy #2 he might lose 6. But Person A might want to play strategy #2 once in a while if Person A is consistently playing his strategy #1 because then Person B will lose only 2. Person A can't do this consistently, however,

because then Person B will move to his strategy #2 and Person A will lose 5. Person A wants to usually play his strategy #3, but every once in a while "sneak in" a strategy #2. The question is, how often? How often should A play strategy #3 in proportion to randomly dispersed use of strategy #2, assuming the game is being played repeatedly? Game theory can answer this question.

TABLE 4.3   Reduced Version of Table 4.2

Person A

		Strategy #2	Strategy #3		
Person B	Strategy #1	6	4	3	B's odds
	Strategy #2	2	5	2	
		1	4		

A's odds

To solve this game, the proportions (the *odds*) can be found by: (1) subtracting the cells within each column or row (for columns, $6 - 2 = 4$; $4 - 5 = -1$); (2) ignoring minus signs in the results; and (3) listing the results in the column (or row) *opposite* to the one in which the corresponding subtraction was performed. The answers are indicated in Table 4.3. Person A should randomly use his strategy #2 once for every four times he uses his strategy #3. Person B should use strategies #1 and #2 in the ratio of 3:2.

The *value* of this game equals either person's odds played against any single strategy of the opponent. Thus,

$$\frac{(3 \times 6) + (2 \times 2)}{3 + 2} = 4.4$$

the value of this game is 4.4 (i.e., B wins 4.4 units and A loses that amount). Since a *fair game* has a value of 0, B should make a *side payment* of 4.4 units to A before each game if it is to be fair.

Such games are elementary, but space prevents further illustration of complicated games. The student must refer to more extended treatments for illustrations of more complex games.[74] Games may include other assump-

---

[74]In addition to Williams, *Compleat Strategyst*, a simple introduction to game theory is provided in Dennis Palumbo, *Statistics in Political and Behavioral Science* (New York: Appleton-Century-Crofts, 1969), ch. 14; and in A. Rapoport, *Two-Person Game Theory* (Ann Arbor: Univ. of Michigan, 1966). More extended treatment is found in M. Dresher, *Games of Strategy: Theory and Applications* (Englewood Cliffs, N. J.: Prentice-Hall, 1961).

tions on rationality, may be *cooperative* rather than *zero-sum* (zero-sum means gains to one are losses to another, such that the sum of all gains and losses is zero), or may be based on ordinal rather than interval payoff data.[75] Political scientists have been particularly interested in testing game theory's assumptions about rational behavior in political bargaining and conflict through behavioral experiments.[76]

COMMUNICATIONS THEORY

In some ways, communications theory is simply an extension of the information systems variant discussed with respect to systems analysis.[77] Adequate levels of communication are also one of the universal requisites of any social system emphasized in functionalist theory.[78] Nonetheless, communications theory is usually presented as a distinct approach to political science, associated with the work of Karl Deutsch, even though it is conceptually similar to both these methodologies.

Communications theory draws its inspiration from cybernetics, the science that studies systems that communicate with the environment and, by receiving feedback, are self-controlling.[79] For this reason, communications theory has the benefits and biases of an analogy between political systems and machines. The image is of the political system as a mechanism that achieves goals by processing information, adjusting for feedback, and coming to decisions. This imagery directs attention to such questions as openness or blockage of channels of communication (e.g., are a president's mistakes due to his staff overinsulating him by blocking unfavorable feedback?) or problems of information overload (e.g., Nader has suggested that the FTC fails to tackle serious matters because of the felt need to communicate a response on all matters, of which there are too many). These questions may lead logically to the view that the essential element in overcoming system problems is better communications. This may be contrasted with the Marxist view that most problems of the political system are based on different class

[75]Levels of data are explained in Chapter 7.
[76]See William Riker, "Bargaining in a Three-Person Game," *American Political Science Review* 61, no. 3 (September 1967): 642–656; W. Riker and W. Zavoina, "Rational Behavior" (see note 62); David Sankoff and Koula Mellos, "The Swing Ratio and Game Theory," *American Political Science Review* 66, no. 2 (June 1972): 551–554; and David Burhans, "Coalition Game Research: A Reexamination," *American Journal of Sociology* 79, no. 2 (September 1973): 389–408.
[77]See pp. 92–98 in this text.
[78]See pp. 51–53 in this text.
[79]The seminal work is Norbert Wiener, *Cybernetics* (Cambridge, Mass.: MIT Press, 1948; 2nd ed., 1961). See also N. Wiener, *The Human Use of Human Beings: Cybernetics and Society* (Garden City, N. Y.: Doubleday, 1954).

interests; improved communications are largely irrelevant, unless such improvement heightens class consciousness, thereby intensifying conflict (for example, bringing poor people into city poverty agency boards often intensified conflict).

Since most of the essential concepts of communications theory have already been discussed with reference to information systems, it is appropriate to concentrate specifically on the ideas of Karl Deutsch. Deutsch felt that communications processes constituted the core of Eastonian systems analysis.[80] Moreover, communications seemed a key factor in understanding processes of political integration and disintegration in developing countries, one of Deutsch's major research interests.[81] Finally, it had the advantage of a good data base: information on communications patterns was much more accessible than that on interest group activity or most other political variables. Since Deutsch was intensely committed to the development of systematic quantitative research in political science, this aspect was critical. It made it possible, for example, to see more easily the integration of communications theory with game theory, which required a high level of quantification.[82]

More than most information theorists, Deutsch emphasized change. He termed the communications system a "learning net." Although he used machine analogies (e.g., radar tracking systems), his work is suffused with a strong humanistic emphasis on change through learning and creativity. History was cast in terms of the combination or disintegration of "subassemblies," "pathways," and routines embodying learning. Thus, the Dark Ages in Europe, or the American colonies between 1730 and 1850, were seen as periods of partial disintegration that represented decline in one sense but served to diffuse knowledge and technology, making possible new and wider combinations at a later stage.[83]

Such later stages involve the temporary fixing of new combinations of learning. These stages seem stable and conservative, marked by a different form of learning, expanding the possibilities existing within the framework of the relatively stable combination of the times. Deutsch called this "adult learning," and considered it in some ways subordinate to the "child learning" of periods of partial disintegration, when there is a creative reconsideration of the fundamental nature of the old combinations and the possibility of new ones.

[80]Karl W. Deutsch, *The Nerves of Government: Models of Political Communication and Control* (New York: Free Press, 1966, with new introduction; orig. pub. 1963), p. viii.
[81]See K. Deutsch, *Nationalism and Social Communications* (New York: John Wiley & Sons, 1953). Quantitative analysis of communications flows became an important technique in the study of comparative development generally and regionalism specifically. See P. Jacob and J. Toscano, eds., *The Integration of Political Communities* (Philadelphia: Lippincott, 1964), especially pp. 46–97; and L. Lindberg and S. Scheingold, eds., *Regional Integration: Theory and Research* (Cambridge, Mass.: Harvard Univ. Press, 1970).
[82]Deutsch, *Nerves*, ch. 4.
[83]*Ibid.*, pp. 170–171.

The major point of Deutsch's theories that concerns us here is that in his writings one may find a general and dynamic theory of political processes that is absent from the narrow perspectives of "communications flow analysts" who have come to dominate communications theory research. As with Lasswell and decision-making theory, more recent political scientists have largely ignored Deutsch's humanistic premises and general theory of political process in favor of a quite technical and conceptually limited form of research. As a consequence, they lack the stature and influence of their mentors, be it Lasswell or Deutsch.

Data used in transaction flow analysis may be indicators such as value of trade, number of diplomats exchanged, or number of shared memberships in intergovernmental organizations. Brams, for example, has used this data to develop criteria for grouping nations according to their mutual communications patterns. One finds, for instance, that diplomatic transactions are more stable than trade transactions. Brams suggests that by grouping ("mapping") nations by communications patterns over time, one may gain clearer insights into the evolution of the international system. But where communications theory in Deutsch is tied to a particular theory of history, with authors such as Brams it is more a technique for measuring a particular aspect of change.[84] While there is an underlying compatibility with systems analysis and decision-making approaches, Deutsch's humanistic premises and general theory is largely ignored. In no small part this is because Deutsch himself has not emphasized these aspects, instead focusing on problems of measurement and the construction of quantitative systems models which represent applications of, not innovations upon, information systems concepts.[85]

Other communications theorists do continue to place change and theories of change at the center of their research. Such theorists may see the rise of mass communications as the engine of development and not a mere corollary or consequence. McCrone and Cnudde, for example, have empirically tested the following theory:[86]

1. Democratic political development occurs when mass communications permeate society. Education affects democratic political development by contributing to the growth of mass communications, therefore:

2. Mass communications occur when literacy and educational levels rise in society. Urbanization affects democratic political development primarily by increasing education levels, which then increase mass communications, therefore:

[84]Steven J. Brams, "Transaction Flows in the International System," *American Political Science Review* 60, no. 4 (December 1966): 880–898.

[85]For a representative discussion, see Robert North, "The Analytical Prospects of Communications Theory," in J. Charlesworth, ed., *Contemporary Political Analysis* (New York: Free Press, 1967), pp. 300–316.

[86]Donald McCrone and Charles Cnudde, "Toward a Communications Theory of Democratic Political Development: A Causal Model," *American Political Science Review* 61, no. 1 (March 1967): 72–79.

3. Education and literacy development occur in urbanizing societies.

McCrone and Cnudde found political instability associated with imbalanced development of mass communications in relation to democratic institutions.

Although the examples above all pertain to international comparisons, communications theorists have also studied community-level patterns. Orbell, for example, found that information flows had the least influence on highly participative community members (their views resist change by new information) and on low participative members (they tend not to receive information cues in the first place). Information flows had the greatest effect on community members of moderate information; high and low partici-pators were therefore less likely to conform to the objective political structure of their districts than were moderate participators.[87]

PHENOMENOLOGY AND
SYMBOLIC INTERACTIONISM

Political science is sometimes characterized as a split between empiricists preoccupied with statistics and relatively limited and technical questions on the one hand, and traditionalists who avoid quantification and prefer discussion of wider questions on the other. Although this caricature mis-represents both tendencies (empiricists often ask broad questions; tradition-alists often use quantitative data), it is enough of a reality to constitute a source of some polarization and fraction within the discipline.

Communications theory provides a bridge between the congeries of overlapping ideas of systems analysis, group theory, and decision-making theory which have provided a supportive environment for empirical theory and the newer approaches sharply critical of "narrow empiricism." While communications theory has most often been applied through highly quanti-tative techniques, a focus on communication inevitably brings attention to its highly subjective nature. As Orbell showed, the effect of information flows depends critically on the environment, background, and perceptions of the receiver.

Adherents to phenomenology and symbolic interactionism hold these subjective factors of perception rather than the "objective logic" of the communications network as a decision-making system to be the critical key to understanding political process. It is not surprising, therefore, that both

[87]John M. Orbell, "An Information-Flow Theory of Community Influence," *Journal of Politics* 32, no. 1 (February 1970): 322–338. For further reading on communications theory, see Ithiel de Sola Pool *et al.*, eds., *Handbook of Communications* (Chicago: Rand McNally, 1973).

orientations are connected with social psychology and are extensions of approaches to politics discussed in Chapter 2.

Phenomenology

Political scientists of a phenomenological persuasion criticize the approaches discussed in this chapter for attempting to "reorder the body politic into an instrumental system of technical problem-solving," conceptualizing "political phenomena in terms of economical models of replicability at the expense of their historicity."[88] This criticism raises basic issues about scientific method. By charging much of empirical social science with "ahistoricity," phenomenologists are raising the questions about data relativism discussed at the very outset of this volume (see page 7).[89]

Edmund Husserl, the founder of phenomenology, held a view of perception fundamentally alien to most contemporary political scientists.[90] The self-evident relation between data and theory customarily asserted by social scientists was not "self-evident" at all to Husserl:

> Men believed that they knew in advance what self-evidence is. They believed that they could measure every other item of cognition against ideal, absolute, apodictally certain knowledge. They did not suspect that this ideal of knowledge (and with it the cognitions of the logician, which imply a claim of apodicticity for themselves) could for its part also require a justification and originary foundation.[91]

That is, Husserl argued that the rationale for conventional forms of inquiry was in error.

The conventional social scientist, for example, may wish to determine if a particular segment of the population is "alienated." He or she will devise a definition of "alienation," develop empirical indicators (e.g., questionnaire items), gather data, and infer conclusions. The phenomenologist, however, believes this approach is misleading, due to the "pregivenness of objects,"

[88]Herbert Reid, "American Social Science in the Politics of Time and the Crisis of Techno-corporate Society: Toward a Critical Phenomenology," *Politics and Society* 3, no. 2 (Winter 1973): 215–216, 219.

[89]See Hwa Yol Jung, "A Critique of the Behavioral Persuasion in Politics: A Phenom-enological View," in M. Natanson, ed., *Phenomenology and the Social Sciences* (Evanston, Ill.: Northwestern Univ. Press, 1973), 2: 133–174.

[90]This aspect is the theme of Carl Friedrich, "Phenomenology and Political Science," in Natanson, ed., *Phenomenology*, pp. 175–196.

[91]Edmund Husserl, *Experience and Judgement* (Evanston, Ill.: Northwestern Univ. Press, 1973; orig. pub. 1948), p. 18. See also by Husserl, *The Idea of Phenomenology* (The Hague: Nijhoff, 1964; orig. pub. 1907); *Ideas: General Introduction to Pure Phenomenology* (New York: Macmillan, 1931; orig. pub. 1913); *The Phenomenology of Internal Time Consciousness* (Bloomington: Indiana Univ. Press, 1964); and *The Crisis of European Sciences and Transcendental Phenomenology* (Evanston: Northwestern Univ. Press, 1970; orig. pub. 1936).

intersubjectivity, and the "horizon structure of experience"—none of which is taken into account by the empiricist. Explanation of each of these will give a flavor of phenomenology.

First, meaning is not based on the self-evidence of a given state alone, but also on the richly complex modes of evolution ("pregivenness") whereby what is given has come to be. Thus, "I am not only what I am, but also what I have been"; no aspect of me (e.g., my "level of alienation") is definable by the self-evidence of my present without being wedded to even greater emphasis on the self-evidence of my past.[92] *Second*, because any perceived object reminds the perceiver "of something past that is similar or like even though temporally separated,"[93] we may say that every object is defined by a subjectively organized "horizon" which gives the objective world unity. Thus, any object I experience (e.g., a questionnaire item) takes meaning from both the "internal" horizon of the intuitive constructs I use to organize and unify perceptions, and the "external" horizon of other objects that are anticipated together with the given one.[94] These horizons are not determined by the "objective" (e.g., social, economic, cultural) factors of my past. *Third*, meaning is intersubjective; every experience is connected with every other experience of the same ego, "a connection which produces the association of everything that is experienced in one time."[95] Thus I belong to a "community of egos" who are related to a single time and through empathy I am aware that this common time is an intersubjectively shared basis for orienting myself. The pregiven factors of perception organized by intuitive horizons are subjective. They may be in tension with intersubjective meanings and, indeed, to the extent such tension exists I will experience anguish. This, too, will condition how I present what I perceive.

If one shares these views, Husserl's philosophy represents a fundamental attack on empirical research in general and survey research and other "shallow" ways of tapping subjective meaning in specific. Insofar as political science hinges critically on subjective factors such as "influence," "efficacy," "loyalty," etc., phenomenology suggests that our conventional methods of research may have led us to mistake the "given" for the "real," ignoring the pregiven, its horizon context, and its intersubjective nature.

The reader should refer to the following for discussion on the evolution of this theoretical orientation: Alfred Vierkandt, and particularly his work

---

[92]This, of course, relates to the existentialist differentiation of "being" and "becoming"; existential phenomenology is thus an important branch of this approach. While not explicitly employing a phenomenological approach, a study that rejects conventional survey methodology in favor of in-depth approaches amenable to phenomenological interpretation is that by Richard Sennett and John Cobb, *The Hidden Injuries of Class* (New York: Random House, 1972).

[93]Husserl, *Experience and Judgment*, p. 162.

[94]*Ibid.*, pp. 32–33.

[95]*Ibid.*, pp. 162–167.

on the subjective elements of domination and submission;[96] Max Scheler, expecially his work on the nature of sympathy;[97] Maurice Merleau-Ponty and his phenomenological critique of conventional psychology and physiology;[98] Georges Gurvitch and his development of the radical implications of phenomenology;[99] and Alfred Schutz, particularly his elaboration of the theory of intersubjectivity.[100] In addition, several commentaries exist to guide the reader to further study.[101]

Before passing to a new subject, we must consider what the methodological procedures of phenomenology are. Severyn Bruyn is among the phenomenologists who address this question most concretely. "Phenomenology," Bruyn writes,"serves as the rationale behind efforts to understand individuals by entering into their field of perception in order to see life as these individuals see it."[102] Participant observation (discussed further in Chapter 7) is considered an appropriate technique because of its capacity to provide in-depth, vivid data on the subjects of study.

Participant data is thought by phenomenologists to better reveal the "essence" of relationships than empirical observation of the survey or behavioral sort. Scheler's study of sympathy, for example, distinguishes "fellow feeling" from "emotional infection" (in which there is no *community* of feeling). Bruyn suggests that these two states bear similar outward behavior and appearance for the empirical observer, but the participant observer who experiences each of these states will understand that they are quite different in essence. Phenomenologists believe that it is through examination of inward states (essences) rather than outward behavior (appearances) that we may gain greatest understanding.[103] Bruyn has summarized the following differences between the phenomenological and empirical approaches:[104]

[96]Vierkandt's major works are not yet available in English. See T. F. Abel, *Systematic Sociology in Germany* (New York: Columbia Univ. Press, 1929).

[97]Max Scheler, *The Nature of Sympathy* (New Haven: Yale Univ. Press, 1954; orig. pub. 1923), and *Philosophical Perspectives* (Boston: Beacon, 1958; orig. pub. 1929).

[98]Maurice Merleau-Ponty, *The Phenomenology of Perception* (New York: Humanities Press, 1962; orig. pub. 1945), and *Structure of Behavior* (Boston: Beacon, 1963).

[99]Georges Gurvitch, *The Social Frameworks of Knowledge* (New York: Harper & Row, 1971; orig. pub. 1966), and *The Spectrum of Social Time* (Dordrecht: D. Reidel, 1964).

[100]Alfred Schutz, *Reflections on the Problem of Relevance* (New Haven: Yale Univ. Press, 1970), and *The Phenomenology of the Social World* (Evanston, Ill.: Northwestern Univ. Press, 1967).

[101]For a view defending scientific value relativism against phenomenology, see Arnold Brecht, *Political Theory* (Princeton: Princeton Univ. Press, 1959), ch. 9. For a defense of phenomenology, see John Gunnell, "Political Inquiry and the Concept of Action: A Phenomenological Analysis," in Natanson, ed., *Phenomenology*, pp. 197–275. See also Martindale, *op. cit.*, ch. 11.

[102]Severyn Bruyn, *The Human Perspective in Sociology: The Methodology of Participant Observation* (Englewood Cliffs, N. J.: Prentice-Hall, 1966), p. 90.

[103]*Ibid.*, pp. 89–96, 271–281.

[104]*Ibid.*, p. 277.

Observing Phenomenologically	Observing Empirically
1. Investigate particular phenomena without definitive preconceptions of their nature.	1. Investigate particular phenomena with definitive preconceptions (hypotheses) of their nature.
2. Observe in phenomena that which appears immediately to consciousness.	2. Observe in phenomena that which appears immediately to the senses.
3. Look for similarities in phenomena as given to consciousness; distinguish their essences and essential relations intuitively.	3. Look for similarities and differences between what is observed and what is operationally defined; distinguish correlations statistically.
4. Explore how the phenomena constitute themselves in consciousness while continuing to suspend prior conceptions of their nature.	4. Explore how the phenomena constitute themselves in reason relative to social typologies.
5. Examine what concealed meanings may be discovered through application of ontological conceptions of reality.	5. Examine what concealed meanings may be discovered through the application of theoretical conceptions of social action.

Phenomenologists need not employ participant observation. The core idea is intuitive, in-depth investigation of subjective factors as perceived by the subjects being considered. Each of several different subject viewpoints with regard to the same objective reality may be investigated in turn, to reveal the varying subjective and intersubjective aspects of a complex social relationship.[105]

Phenomenology has not been without its critics.[106] Just as phenomenologists charged the empiricists with "ahistoricism," so radical social scientists have brought the same charge against phenomenology. Phenomenology is "historical" in the sense of emphasizing the "becoming" as well as the "being" aspects of a given state, but it does not focus on the socioeconomic factors traced by Marxists, leading to the charge that "their focus is really abstract man and not a concrete historical subject . . . . They abstractly discuss the formal organization and intentionality of experience, but neglect its socioeconomic foundation and hence its content."[107] This criticism brings

[105]Though not intended as an example of phenomenology, one is reminded of Kurosawa's famous film, *Rashomon*, in which an incident is investigated from each of three viewpoints in turn: that of the attacker, that of the woman, and that of the husband. Each viewpoint is different; together they constitute a whole.

[106]For a critique of Bruyn and others, see James Heap and Phillip Roth, "On Phenomenological Sociology," *American Sociological Review* 38, no. 3 (June 1973): 354–366.

[107]Carl Ratner, "Review of Schutz' *Reflections on the Problem of Relevance* and Berger and Luckman's *The Social Construction of Reality*," *The Insurgent Sociologist* 4, no. 1 (Fall 1973): 90.

us back full circle to the Marxist views discussed in Chapter 1![108]

Symbolic Interactionism

In the array of social science approaches, symbolic interactionism is conceptually close to phenomenology. It derives from the work of George Mead.[109] Norman Denzin has summarized conveniently five methodological assumptions of interactionism:[110]

1. Work from overt behaviors back to the meaning attached to those behaviors; relate overt patterns of interaction with covert symbolic behavior; note changing phases of interpretation as meaning changes during the interaction studied.
2. Examine behavior from the perspective of those being studied; indicate shifting meanings and statuses attached to the self, which is the central object of study.
3. Link the subject's symbols and meanings to relevant social circles and relationships.
4. Note that differences in behavior may be due to: (a) different self-definitions; (b) different definitions of other objects in the setting (e.g., lighting); (c) different definitions of action held before the interaction occurs; or (d) different temporal sequencing of action.
5. Operationalization of concepts is delayed until the situated meanings of concepts are discovered; use multiple methods of observation; continual reciprocation exists between observation and hypothesis-formation; the goal is seeking universal propositions about human interactions.

Denzin has also noted criticisms of symbolic interactionism analogous to those of phenomenology: vagueness of concepts, a focus on individual meanings at the expense of examination of the concrete sociohistoric setting and larger social organization, and overemphasis on support of the self as the guiding motivation in all interactions. Others, such as Huber, charge symbolic interactionism with allowing "the perspectives of the researcher and the people in interactive situations to bias the research."[111] Huber defends prior theoretical formulations and scientific selection of subjects as

---

[108]For further reading, see: Peter Berger and Thomas Luckman, *The Social Construction of Reality* (New York: Doubleday, 1966); Edward Tiryakian, "Existential Phenomenology and Sociology," *American Sociological Review* 30, (October 1965): 674–688. See also: E. Shmueli, "Can Phenomenology Accomodate Marxism?" *Telos* 17 (Fall 1973): 169–180.

[109]George H. Mead, *Mind, Self, and Society* (Chicago: Univ. of Chicago Press, 1934); G. Mead, *The Philosophy of the Act* (Chicago: Univ. of Chicago Press, 1938); Anselm Strauss, ed., *On Social Psychology: Selected Papers of George Herbert Mead* (Chicago: Univ. of Chicago Press, 1964).

[110]Norman Denzin, "Symbolic Interactionism and Ethnomethodology: A Proposed Synthesis," *American Sociological Review* 34, no. 6 (December 1969); 925–926.

[111]Joan Huber, "Symbolic Interaction as a Pragmatic Perspective: The Bias of Emergent Theory," *American Sociological Review* 38, no. 2 (April 1973): 274–284.

essential to maintaining "objectivity," a concept disputed by symbolic interactionists.[112]

A BRIEF SUMMARY

After the war there was great hope that systems theory, and later, group theory and decision-making theory, might provide the vehicle for a dramatic breakthrough in social science theory. Today, with that "behavioral revolution" nearly a quarter-century old, we can no longer speak of such empirical orientations as new. Indeed, with the faltering of behavioral approaches has come a revival of neo-Marxist and psychological approaches to the study of politics, along with the beginnings of methodologies such as phenomenology that attack the foundations of current, leading attempts to make "political *science*" more than an empty metaphor.

In Part One we have been able to present only the bare outlines of the various methodologies that shape political science. The necessarily brief treatment of each has inevitably failed to convey the rich complexity—and ambiguity—that is associated with a deeper understanding of these approaches; the reader should turn to the original sources and commentaries cited extensively in the footnotes for an in-depth study. The outline in Part One and the footnoted bibliography together constitute a guide for further study, not a full explanation.

Recognizing that a little knowledge is a dangerous thing, nonetheless, it is hoped that Part One conveyed to the reader some insight into the historical development of our highly eclectic discipline. That development is not one of scientific study logically founded upon scientific study. Rather, political science has been swept with many, often inconsistent, intellectual currents. As with the tides of immigrants to America, the result of these succeeding waves has not been the prevalence of any one nor the emergence of some homogenous synthesis. Instead each tendency has remained, taken root, and developed its own body of research and theory.

Therefore it is not surprising that today many confess their inability to "make sense," much less find an underlying unity in political science. Some

---

[112]For further reading, see George Cronk, "Symbolic Interactionism: A 'Left-Meadian' Interpretation," *Social Theory and Practice* 2, no. 3 (Spring 1973): 313–334; Peter Singelmann, "Exchange as Symbolic Interaction," *American Sociological Review* 37, no. 4 (August 1972): 414–424, with comments in *American Sociological Review* 38, no. 4: 504–508. See also Arnold Rose, "A Systematic Summary of Symbolic Interaction Theory," in Arnold Rose, ed., *Human Behavior and Social Processes* (Boston: Houghton Mifflin, 1962), pp. 3–19. *Catalyst* 7 (Winter 1973) contains a symposium by seven authors on symbolic interactionism. Finally, though not explicitly in the symbolic interactionist framework, a work by a prominent political scientist showing a strong influence by Mead is Henry S. Kariel, *Saving Appearances: The Reestablishment of Political Science* (North Scituate, Mass.: Duxbury Press, 1972).

have despaired of this seeming methodological confusion and have retreated to focus solely on specific techniques to be discussed in Parts Two and Three—but this retreat from theory has involved *implicit*, usually empiricist, theoretical assumptions. The question is not one of whether or not to adopt a methodological framework; it is simply whether this framework is to be explicit and reasoned, or whether it is to remain implicit and unexamined.

Although the history of political science is in some ways the history of a faddish search for "the one right framework," there is no reason why only *one* methodology need be selected. Most political scientists do not fall conveniently under the label of any one of the methodologies discussed here. Rather than despairing at the multiplicity of approaches to political science (far more numerous than outlined), we may count it to our advantage. We may suspend the search for the "one best framework" while we examine research problems from the methodologies of several orientations in turn, prior to formulating our final views.

EXERCISE

Identify some political problem about which you might wish to write a term paper. Outline what thoughts an advocate of each of three different methodologies might have about this subject (e.g., a Marxist, a group theorist, and a phenomenologist). Then try to make a list of what facts and observations might support or undermine each of these perspectives.

In simplified form, this exercise involves the elements of a good "research design," which is the topic of the following chapters.

two

Basic Concepts and Techniques

5 Explanatory Models

An explanatory model is the core of a political analysis. A model is composed of some phenomenon to be explained, together with the variables said to bring about this phenomenon, and the relationships among these variables. That is, political analysis has to do with thinking in terms of "cause and effect." The researcher must go beyond talking about a given phenomenon, such as labor rioting, and, instead, identify in detail *how* such rioting comes about, under what conditions, and at what times. Nor is it enough merely to list all the variables, such as unemployment, inflation, labor union competition, legislation, political trends, etc., that in one way or another affect labor rioting. In political analysis, the researcher is called upon to explain *how* each variable relates to the others. Rather than simply *listing* the causes of the given phenomenon, the political analyst must identify a *set of inter- relationships* among the causes and effects.

It is readily apparent that political analysis must be a matter of degree. It is never possible to fully establish *all* the relationships among a set of variables. Most researchers consider themselves lucky if the explanatory model they employ can explain at least half of the variance in the phenomenon under study (for example, accounting for half of the ups and downs of the frequency of labor rioting over the years). Among the reasons why an explanatory model is never fully satisfactory are measurement errors, inability to measure intangible variables adequately (e.g., alienation, dignity), inability to include all the relevant variables without making the model unmanageably complex, the importance of idiosyncratic traits of individuals, and "free will" in social relationships.

If it *were* possible to devise fully satisfactory explanatory models for a wide range of political phenomena, then one could speak of a deterministic political science. Rather than determinism, however, political science is oriented toward *probabilistic* models. That is, ordinarily it is not possible to establish relationships of the "if X, then Y" sort. Instead, most findings in political analysis take the form "if X under conditions a, b, and c, then Y will follow n percent of the time." Often even this probabilistic version will prove unobtainable, and the researcher will have to fall back on sets of interrelated hypotheses, each demonstrable individually but too complex to integrate.

One may be able to demonstrate, for example, that "the more unemployment, the more labor rioting"; "the more union competition, the more labor rioting"; "the stronger the Communist Party, the more union competition"; etc. Yet though each of these individual hypotheses may be "true," each indicates only a certain *direction* of a relationship. It may prove impossible to determine the exact *strength* of the relationship under specific conditions (e.g., *How* strong does the Communist Party have to be to bring about a specified level of union competition? How would "strength" be measured in the first place? Even if it were measured, could one specify the conditions under which the relationship would hold at the observed strength?) Yet unless these extremely difficult questions can be answered, and answered with some precision, one cannot satisfactorily integrate the individual hypotheses to determine the *net* effect.

Even though fully satisfactory explanatory models are rare, an understanding of what they are provides an ideal or standard toward which the researcher can work and by which he or she can evaluate the success of work done. Moreover, by understanding what would constitute an explanation, the researcher is already well on his or her way to knowing how to undertake political analysis.

PSEUDO-QUESTIONS VERSUS REAL QUESTIONS

The first step in political analysis is to select a "real question." Unless this is done it will be impossible to develop an explanatory model. By a "real question" is meant one phrased with sufficient precision that it can be answered. A "pseudo-question," in contrast, is one that merely indicates a type of phenomenon to be discussed in a relatively general and open-ended way. The vagueness of a pseudo-question allows it to be interpreted in many different ways. In other words, a pseudo-question encompasses many implicit real questions but does not specify which are to be dealt with.

A few examples will make this clear. A pseudo-question would be "How does XYZ government agency work?" or "What is the nature of labor rioting?" To answer a question such as "How does XYZ agency work?" the researcher must break the question down into a series of concrete questions, a few of which might be "What criteria determine personnel recruitment?" "What is the ratio of costs to benefits?" or "What is the incentive effect of staff payment on work content?" Similarly, the question "What is the nature of labor rioting?" must be broken down into questions such as "To what extent is rioting a function of economic adversity?" "Do generalized personality traits differentiate labor rioters from nonrioters?" or "Do wartime patriotism and mobilization inhibit labor conflict, including labor violence?" These more concrete questions are but a few of a great many that might be chosen by the researcher to bring a pseudo-question "down to earth."

A real question, then, goes beyond identifying an area for discussion and specifies a relationship to be investigated. The question, "What criteria determine personnel recruitment?" for example, calls on the researcher to establish a list of criteria (age, training, sex, sociability, status, etc.) and then to investigate the relative weight given to each in the process of selecting the staff of XYZ agency. The question "Does wartime patriotism inhibit labor conflict?" calls on the researcher to find some method of measuring patriotism (as through content analysis of newspapers) and then to establish the correlation or lack of it between this measure and the indices of labor conflict. (After establishing that there is a relationship, the researcher must then see if this relationship is spurious when control variables are introduced—this will be dealt with in a later chapter.)

DEPENDENT AND INDEPENDENT VARIABLES

The dependent variable is the variable that the researcher is trying to understand and explain. The variance in the dependent variable is thought to depend upon the independent (causal) variables. Thus, in the previous example, labor conflict is the dependent variable and wartime patriotism is the independent variable. The variance in labor conflict (the extent to which there is more or less conflict in any given year, state, industry, or other unit) may at least in part be accounted for by the variance in wartime patriotism.

A variable can be defined as any quality or quantity of a material condition or an abstraction identified for study by the researcher. A variable need not "vary," however. In studying labor rioting, for example, the unemployment rate may be used as one variable, and it would be so considered even if it remained constant for the period under study. Those variables that are the subject of study and are to be explained are the *dependent variables*, while the variables that do the explaining are the *independent variables*.

Therefore, whether a variable is dependent or independent is relative to the research context. An independent variable in one context may be a dependent variable in another. Labor rioting may be a dependent variable with respect to the unemployment rate, but may be an independent variable when political stability is the object of study. In the former situation, labor rioting is seen as caused *by* unemployment, while in the latter context it is seen as the *cause of* political instability.

Traditionally, only quantifiable traits were considered variables, while qualities (race, nationality, religion) were considered attributes. Today this distinction is no longer made, though it is occasionally encountered in older books. Two other distinctions are made, however, and these deserve note. An *intervening variable* is a variable that mediates between a prior independent variable and a subsequent variable. Hence all intervening variables are also independent variables. For example, one might hypothesize that unemployment causes perceptions of status loss, which in turn causes frustration, which then causes labor rioting. Here both "perception of status loss" and "frustration" are intervening variables. Intervening variables are thus those independent variables that form the middle part or parts of a chain of causation.

A *constant* is another type of independent variable. (Theoretically it could be a dependent variable, but in practice researchers rarely focus on unchanging variables as the objects of political investigation.) A constant is a variable that does not change in quantity or quality during the study for any of the individuals, governmental bodies, or other units under examination. Thus a constant is also relative to the study being done. What is a constant in one study may not be one in another. For example, sex would be a constant in a study of rioting at a male prison, but would not be in a study of prisoner rioting within an entire state penal jurisdiction.

QUESTIONS VERSUS HYPOTHESES

In order to clarify the purposes of the study, the researcher ordinarily will not stop with the formulation of a specific question and identification or relevant independent variables. Rather than identify such a question, collect data on it, and then find out what answers the data support, the researcher will set out the answers he or she expects *before* gathering the data (except in phenomenological or symbolic interactionist approaches). For any given question, the data will usually support several "answers" rather than just one. Hence to work from the data back to an answer lends itself to rationalizing one's information (that is, the researcher is tempted to accept one interpretation as supported by the data when others may apply as well, including the interpretation that the source of the distribution of the data is chance or measurement error). Although this retrospective approach (collect data, then formulate interpretations) is a reasonable and often used one, it is considered more in accord with scientific method to formulate one's expected answers first, then *test* these by the data.

Expected answers are usually phrased as *hypotheses*. A hypothesis is a statement that specifies two or more variables and the direction of the relationship between or among them. For example, each of the following are hypotheses: "The more the external threat to a group, the greater the internal solidarity of the group"; "The greater the amount of conflict a group engages in, the more defined are group boundaries"; and "The greater the unemployment, the more labor rioting." Usually hypotheses specify the relationship between just two variables.

A *positive relationship* between two variables occurs when both rise or both drop at the same time. Thus each of the following hypotheses specify positive relationships: "The more unemployment, the more rioting"; "The weaker the legitimacy of the government, the weaker the political stability of the government." *Negative relationships* take the form "The more the one, the less the other" or "The less the one, the more the other." Examples of negative relationships include the following: "The more unemployment, the less job security" or "The smaller the turnout in primary elections, the greater the chance of renomination of the incumbent."

THESES AND MODELS

Political analysis starts with the formulation of a specific question which involves a *thesis*, which in turn can be further specified by a set of *hypotheses*. A thesis is a generalized proposition based on any set of hypotheses. A few examples may clarify this distinction:

QUESTION: Why have third parties been unsuccessful in American politics?

THESIS: American political structure creates prohibitive social costs to the potential third-party voter.

HYPOTHESES: *H1* In electoral districts providing for election of a single candidate receiving the most votes, the voter will perceive voting for third party candidates as "throwing away" one's vote.

H2 The more decentralized and undisciplined the leading political parties within a society, the better able leading party candidates will be to adopt positions that co-opt potential third-party votes.

H3 The more numerous the differentiated ethnic and racial groups within a society, the greater the emphasis on patriotism as the defining characteristic of citizenship.

H4 The greater the emphasis on patriotism within a society, the greater the social inhibitions against supporting irregular political parties.

A full analysis would require investigating *alternative theses* and hypotheses. In this example, however, the argument is made that the absence of strong third parties in America is due to the absence of proportional representation (H1), to loose party structure which allows local candidates to repudiate national party positions in order to ward off local challenges (H2), and to "melting pot" social history which has fostered great emphasis on consensus (H3 and H4). A second example follows:

QUESTION: Why do labor riots occur more in some years than in others?

THESIS: Labor riots are a function of economic factors.

HYPOTHESES: *H1* The more unemployment, the more labor rioting.

H2 The sharper the reverse in the trend of real wages, the greater the rioting.

H3 The lower the profit rate, the greater the employer intransigence.

H4 The greater the employer intransigence, the greater the frustration of labor goals.

H5 The greater the frustration, the more likely labor rioting.

A complete set of explanatory hypotheses may constitute a *model*. A model is a set of independent variables and one or more dependent variables, and the relationships among them. It is perhaps easiest to think about a model in its diagrammatic form: each variable is represented by a circle, lines between circles represent relationships, arrows denote the direction of relationships, and plus or minus signs indicate whether the relationship is positive or negative (for simplicity, it is usual to print only negative signs and assume positive relationships elsewhere). Figure 5.1 represents the diagrammatic form of the preceding hypotheses.

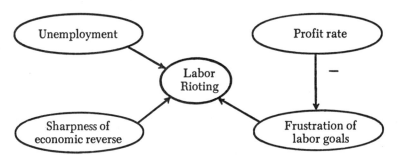

FIGURE 5.1   Diagrammatic Model for Labor Rioting as a
Dependent Variable

The explanatory model in Figure 5.1 is a simple one; it conveys to the reader only the information contained in the set of hypotheses cited. Yet, particularly in more complex explanations, drawing such a model may help the researcher clarify the thesis with which he or she is concerned.

When looking at such a model, the researcher should ask a number of questions:

1. What is the dependent variable? Is it clearly defined? (In the example, the dependent variable is labor rioting, but it is not clear how it is operationally defined—in terms of annual frequency of riots, number of people involved, amount of damage, etc.—nor is what constitutes a "riot" defined.)

2. What are the independent or explaining variables? Are there others that should be included? (Here the independent variables are primarily economic, but perhaps other variables should be included, such as factors relating to attributes of union leadership or to characteristics of particular groups of workers.)
3. Is there evidence presented to support the plausibility of each arrow in the diagrammatic model? (Consideration of each arrow helps focus the researcher's attention on the specific types of evidence appropriate to each study.)

Every explanation of some political phenomenon that the researcher encounters in a book, magazine, journal, or newspaper contains an implicit model that can also be portrayed in diagrammatic form. While it is not customary in political writing to present one's explanation in diagram form, it *is* ordinarily useful for the exploratory phases of research.

THE NULL HYPOTHESIS

The most common hypothesis in social science research is the null hypothesis: the hypothesis that no relationship exists between the researcher's independent and dependent variables. The null hypothesis is important in social science methods because it raises the question of significance. A relationship is said to be *significant* if there is less than an arbitrarily specified chance of wrongly rejecting a true null hypothesis. (Political scientists commonly specify less than one chance in twenty, or less than .05 probability.) In later chapters (especially Chapter 10, where the null hypothesis is treated more fully) we shall focus on particular techniques of determining when there is less than, say, a .05 chance that we believe a relationship exists when, in fact, the null hypothesis (that it does not exist) is true.

FROM WORDS TO MODELS: AN EXAMPLE

By drawing the diagrammatic model implicit in any written explanation, the researcher is in a better position to compare one explanation with another, to consider which variables are included and which are not, and to evaluate the extent to which evidence is cited to support the relationships represented by arrows in the diagram. This procedure is particularly useful when it is necessary to compare a large number of explanations of the same phenomenon and when explanations are complex and involve many variables and relationships. Diagrammatic modeling helps the researcher to systematically go about his or her analysis with a maximum of clarity and ease.

The process of deriving models from written explanations is illustrated below. First, however, the student should read the following passage,

"Slaughter East and West," from Louis Adamic's account of the "Ludlow Massacre" of 1914:[1]

The capitalists and industrialists of the United States took advantage of the public's intense reaction to the exposure of the A.F. of L.'s dynamiting operations and once more tightened up their lines against further efforts of labor to improve its conditions. Encouraged by General Otis's shining victory for the open shop in Los Angeles, they took up the battle for the "American Plan" against the "Mafia-like unions," and in not a few instances they were highly successful. On the other hand, excepting the Lawrence strike of 1912, led by the Wobblies, there was no great labor victory between the end of the McNamara case and 1917, when the United States entered the World War.

The climax of the employers' war for the open shop was reached in the spring of 1914, in the so-called Ludlow Massacre.

In the coal-fields of southern Colorado several thousand miners had been "out" since September 1913. They were loosely organized, but motivated by bitterness born of ill treatment. The mines in which they worked when they were employed were for the most part controlled by the Rockefeller interests. Their demands included the eight-hour day, pay for "narrow and dead work," a check weighman without interference of company officials, the right to trade in any store they pleased, the abolition of the criminal guard system, ten percent advance in wages, and recognition of the union. Of these demands five were guaranteed under severe penalty by the laws of the State of Colorado. They were, however, not enforced, for the mining interests, interlocked with other interests in the state, controlled and ran the state government through politicians they had installed in office.

And so the miners were compelled to resort to a strike in order to put into effect a series of laws which it was the obligation of the employers to obey and the state to enforce! But the demand that the operators opposed most strenuously was that for the recognition of the union. They, with John D. Rockefeller, Jr., as their leader, were determined to keep down any effort which might endanger the lofty open-shop "principle." John D. spoke eloquently of his devotion to "principles." He said:

> We would rather that the unfortunate conditions should continue, and that we should lose all the millions invested, than American workmen should be deprived of their right, under the Constitution, to work for whom they please. That is the great principle at stake. It is a national issue.

The strike dragged into the spring of 1914. Mines were being operated by nonunion men, most of them foreigners. To protect the properties and the nonunion miners, the Rockefellers and other operators engaged hundreds of "guards" or gunmen, while the State called out considerable bodies of militia. Martial law was declared long before there were any shots; then strikers were beaten up and shot at, and disturbances occurred. The striking miners, to protect themselves, began to procure arms and ammunition. They moved off the companies' grounds and camped in tents. They dug trenches around the camps and holes inside the tents, into which women and children might crawl in the event of attack.

---

[1]From pp. 257–260 in *Dynamite: The Story of Class Violence in America* by Louis Adamic. Copyright 1931, 1934 by Louis Adamic; renewed 1958 by Stella Adamic. By permission of Harper & Row, Publishers, Inc.

On April 20, 1914, either a striker shot a non-union miner or a soldier fired at a striker near the camp outside Ludlow, whereupon a battle started and soon spread over an area of three miles. About 500 miners were opposed by approximately 200 militia, but the soldiers, many of whom were but recently sworn-in gunmen, were equipped with machine-guns and other superior weapons, which made the strikers' numbers count for nothing.

Machine-gun bullets riddled the tents; then the camp took fire. "In the holes which had been dug for their protection against the rifles' fire," says one contemporary account of the battle, "the women and children died like trapped rats when the flames swept over them."

Thirty-three people were either shot or burned to death. More than half of these were women and children. Over a hundred others were wounded or badly burned.

The Ludlow battle lasted fourteen hours, after which the camp was abandoned and most of the women and children, dead and alive, were taken to Trinidad, while the strikers began organizing military companies, taking up positions on the hills. Several mine-shafts were attacked and burned. More battles occurred. The Denver *Express*, which, though not a labor paper, favored the strike, printed a vivid characterization of the Ludlow slaughter:

> Mothers and babies were crucified on the cross of human liberty. Their crucifixion was effected by the operators' paid gunmen who have worn militia uniforms less than a week. The dead will go down in history as the hero victims of the burned offering laid on the altar of Rockefeller's Great God Greed.

President Wilson ordered out Federal troops, but, before they arrived in southern Colorado and disarmed both the strikers and the gunmen wearing militia uniforms, about a dozen more miners had been killed. Ultimately Rockefeller won; he did not recognize the union. His great passion for "principles" was gratified.

It is possible to find an implicit explanation or model of some political or social phenomenon even in an account as dramatic as this. If one looks back over this passage, one will find various factors (variables) identified as important, and a causal relationship suggested among them. In the first paragraph, for example, it is stated that labor sabotage ("the A.F. of L's dynamiting operations") led to lower public support for labor ("public's intense reaction"), which in turn led to increased management intransigence to labor demands ("they took up the battle for the American Plan").

Similarly, the third paragraph contains another portion of the model. Here it is noted that a number of variables, especially "ill treatment" and lack of labor law enforcement ("of these demands five...were, however, not enforced") led to "bitterness" and eventually support for a strike.

When reading such a passage, much of the researcher's job lies in rejection of extraneous material, not just identification of what is important. By keeping clearly in mind what is being sought the researcher can sharply cut down on the amount of note taking in the early stages of analysis.

In considering the model implicit in Adamic's account, the amount of detail will vary according to the researcher's interests. Usually there is no one "right" model that will accurately reflect a given piece of writing. This is because: (1) the writing may be vague, ambiguous, or self-contradicting, and (2) the researcher may find it appropriate to simplify by omitting some of the less important or more particularistic factors mentioned by the writer. Figure 5.2 presents one model based on Adamic's description of the Ludlow Massacre.

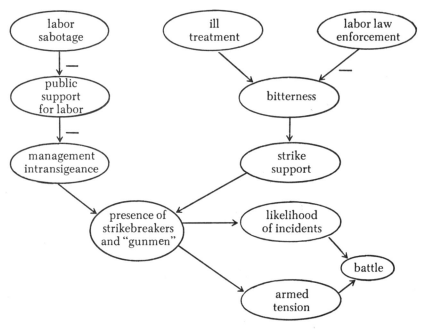

FIGURE 5.2   Diagrammatic Model for Adamic's Account of the Ludlow Massacre

Adamic's interpretation of the Ludlow Massacre is obviously not the only one. By modelling other explanations of the same event, specific differences of interpretation would be highlighted for further investigation. While this is the central purpose of modelling, this procedure also helps identify a set of hypothesized relationships for which evidence must be presented. Was management intransigence really rooted in public opinion relating to labor violence, or does the evidence show some other source of motivation to be more important? Perhaps, for example, the management's behavior was based on strictly economic factors. At each point in the model one must also consider the meaning of the variables. What exactly is "ill treatment?" Perhaps some other, more specific factor should be substituted, such as "rise followed by a drop in wages."

Knowledge of the process of forming theses, hypotheses, and models enables the researcher to begin empirical research in a systematic way.[2] The

[2]For further reading, see Hubert M. Blalock, *Theory Construction: From Verbal to Mathematical Formulations* (Englewood Cliffs, N. J.: Prentice-Hall, 1969), chs. 1 and 2;

first step is usually to survey what has already been written about the subject. This is the topic of the next chapter.

EXERCISE

Find a magazine or journal article that attempts to explain some aspect of the topic you discussed in the exercise for Chapter Four. Clarify the question the writer is addressing and the thesis and supporting hypotheses. Present these in a diagrammatic model. In doing this exercise you should make a list of the independent and dependent variables, note whether each variable is well defined, and evaluate the sufficiency of the evidence to support each arrow in your explanatory diagram of the writer's explicit or implicit model. Discuss what variables not mentioned in the article could be also included, and, finally, try to suggest a different thesis at least as consistent with the evidence as is the author's.

David Everson and Joann Paine, *An Introduction to Systemic Political Science* (Homewood, Ill.: Dorsey, 1973), ch. 7; Wayne Francis, *Formal Models of American Politics* (New York: Harper & Row, 1972), ch. 1.

6 | Surveying the Literature

In almost any political science journal one will find that virtually all the articles begin with a section surveying what else has been written about the question under study. Surveying the literature is useful not only in giving the researcher ideas and insights in general, but also in helping him or her specifically identify the contending explanatory models.

While it may seem at first that the body of relevant literature is enormous, the researcher will usually find that very little has been written about the *specific* hypotheses he or she is interested in. There will usually be a few articles directly relevant, then a large number of nonanalytic case studies or histories that describe related events or processes, and a large number of studies dealing with the hypotheses in different contexts or in a more general way or using differently defined concepts. Thus there may be a few articles seeking to explain why labor rioting has varied by year in the United States, a large number of articles which simply describe specific riots (such as Adamic's description of the Ludlow Massacre), and a large number of studies that deal with the question in other contexts (black-related rioting, for example), in more general ways (studies of the causes of wars, or studies of aggression in social psychology), or using differently defined concepts (studies of labor conflict, conflict defined to include strikes as well as violence). The general lament of the researcher is that nothing has been written on the topic, yet everything printed is somehow or other relevant.

The bibliographic search is actually a circular process. That is, though the researcher starts with certain theories and hypotheses for investigation and then looks for studies related to these subjects, once such studies are found they often lead to reformulation of the original theories and hypotheses. Further investigation may generate further cycles of research and conceptualization. Approaching the bibliographic task as one step in a chronological sequence is too rigid an approach. A good researcher will repeatedly review the relation between his or her writing and the available literature.

With literally thousands of social science journals and millions of books of varying relevance to social science, surveying the literature might at first seem an impossible task. And in the full sense it is. If taken too seriously, the research would grind to a halt under a mountain of notes. Fortunately, however, there are now available many research aids which greatly speed this task. These indexes of journal articles, bibliographies, and directories of statistical sources constitute a sort of "instant research assistance" providing conveniently what would otherwise be discouragingly difficult-to-obtain information on a wide range of relatively specialized topics.

Books have been written on the nature and extent of bibliographic sources useful for political scientists. This chapter presents illustrative material on some of the leading sources. Following this, the process of note-taking and its relation to analytic modelling is discussed.

JOURNALS

There are today so many journals relevant to political science that the student who wishes to seek out what "the literature" has to offer with regard to his or her research must use the abstracts, indexes, and other guides discussed later in this chapter. For information purposes, however, below are listed some of the relevant journals:

Field and Title	Date Established
Political Science	
American Journal of Political Science	1973
American Political Science Review	1903
American Politics Quarterly	1973
Annals of the American Academy of Political and Social Science	1889
Comparative Political Studies	1968
European Journal of Political Research	1973
Foreign Affairs	1921
Journal of Black Studies	1970
Journal of Conflict Resolution	1957
Journal of Politics	1938
International Studies Quarterly	1957
Midwest Review of Public Administration	1967
Modern Government	1960
Policy Sciences	1970
Policy Studies Journal	1973
Political Communication Bulletin	1966
Political Science Quarterly	1886
Political Theory	1973

Politics and Society	1970
Polity	1968
Public Administration-Journal of the Royal	
Institute of Public Administration	1922
Public Adminstration Review	1940
Public Finance Quarterly	1973
Public Interest	1965
Public Opinion Quarterly	1937
Public Policy	1950
Public Productivity Review	1975
Theory and Society	1974
Urban Affairs Quarterly	1965
Western Political Quarterly	1948
World Politics	1948

Psychology

American Behavioral Scientist	1957
Journal of Applied Behavioral Research	1965
Journal of Applied Psychology	1917
Journal of Applied Social Psychology	1971
Personnel Psychology	1948
Psychometrica	1946

Sociology

American Journal of Sociology	1895
American Sociological Review	1936
Human Organization	1941
Human Relations	1947
International Journal of Comparative Sociology	1960
International Journal of Contemporary Sociology	1963
International Journal of Sociology	1970
Journal of Mathematical Sociology	1971
Journal of Social Issues	1936
Pacific Sociological Review	1958
Social Forces	1922
Social Problems	1953
Society: Social Science & Modern Society	1963
Sociometry	1937

Administration and Management

Academy of Management Journal	1958
Administrative Management	1940
Administrative Science Quarterly	1956
Advanced Management Journal	1935
California Management Review	1959
Decision Sciences	1970
Evaluation	1972
Harvard Business Review	1922
Journal of Communication	1951
Journal of Comparative Administration	1969
Management Science	1953
Omega: Int. Journal of Management Science	1973
Personnel	1919
Personnel Administration	1938

Public Administration Review   1940
Sloan Management Review   1960

Economics and Business

American Economic Review   1911
Bell Journal of Economics and Management Science   1970
Columbia Journal of World Business   1965
Econometrica   1933
Economic Journal   1891
Fortune   1930
Journal of Business   1928
Journal of Political Economy   1892
Quarterly Journal of Economics   1886
Review of Economics & Statistics   1919
Socio-Economic Planning Sciences   1968
Southern Economic Journal   1934

ABSTRACTS: A GOOD STARTING POINT

A periodical that cumulatively indexes and abstracts political or social science articles and books is one of the best places to begin in a survey of the literature. An abstract is a brief summary of the central points of a given piece of writing, and a citation of its source. Where an index will merely list the author, title, and source, an abstract will give a much better idea of what the article or book says and hence whether it would be worth searching the item out in the library stacks or through interlibrary loan.

The most comprehensive and relevant abstract index for the political scientist is that edited by Alfred de Grazia, *The Universal Reference System: Political Science, Government and Public Policy Series* (Princeton, N.J.: Princeton Publishing Co., 1967). This is a ten-volume set, arranged by broad topics (e.g., "Public Opinion, Mass Behavior, and Political Psychology"), and updated through annual supplements.

Continuing with our example, let us say that we are interested in finding out if anyone else has written an article on why labor rioting occurs more in some years than in others, under some conditions rather than others. We would first look over the set to find the volumes most related to our subject. Since none of the volumes deals with "labor," we may settle on *Volume VIII: Economic Regulation, Business and Government.*

Within this volume we find that the first few pages contain a "Dictionary of Descriptors," which is jargon for a list of key words. Looking down this list we see that there are 426 listings beginning on page 665 for the key word "labor." There is no key word for "violence," "rioting," or even "conflict," so we turn to the "Topical Index," also at the beginning of the volume. Here we find that violence is listed under the key word "coerce," with 62 listings beginning on page 283 of the volume.

Starting with the labor listings at page 665, we find that they begin with a list of other bibliographies. If we don't find what we need in *The Universal Reference System*, these other bibliographies may help. For example, reproduced below is a listing for one such bibliography:

RAND SCHOOL OF SOCIAL SCIENCE, INDEX TO LABOR ARTICLES. ECO/DEV INT/ORG LEGIS DIPLOM GP/REL . . . NAT/COMP 20. PAGE 109. F 2143.

This means that a publication titled "Index to Labor Articles," published by the Rand School of Social Science, deals with topics of economic development (ECO/DEV), international organizations, legislation, diplomacy, group relations, and comparison of nations as these relate to labor. These abbreviations, such as "'ECO/DEV," are the same as the key words listed in the "Dictionary of Descriptors." The term "F 2143" tells the location of the actual abstract that describes this work at greater length. These abstracts are printed at the beginning of the book, in alphabetical order by the author, with corresponding index numbers like "F 2143."

Turning to abstract number F 2143, on page 109, we find the following full abstract:

2143   RAND SCHOOL OF SOCIAL SCIENCE
       INDEX TO LABOR ARTICLES
       LONDON: MAYER LONDON MEMORIAL LIBRARY

       MONTHLY UNANNOTATED GUIDE TO ARTICLES CURRENTLY APPEARING IN SELECTED PERIODICALS. COVERS BUSINESS AND LABOR CONDITIONS, TRADE UNIONISM, LABOR LEGISLATION, DISPUTES AND ARBITRATION, AND INTERNATIONAL ORGANIZATIONS. FIRST ISSUED IN 1926.

We may set aside a list of such bibliographic reference sources in case we need them later.

Looking through the list of labor abstract listings for an article on labor violence, we find that only one is directly on the subject. This one is listed:

SOREL G. REFLECTIONS ON VIOLENCE (1908) (TRANS BY T E HULME AND J ROTH). UNIV SOCIETY LABOR UTOPIA MORAL SOCIALISM . . . ANARCH SOCIALIST CONCPT 20. PAGE 124. F 2445.

While we may make note of this, this listing shows the article is not an empirical study of labor rioting but is an essay written in 1908 on anarchist theory. We may wish to refer to it in the introduction to our eventual research paper, but it probably won't be quite what we want.

Having exhausted the "labor" listings, we now look in the same volume under our other relevant key word, "coerce." Here we find 62 listings on force, coercion, and violence. While many of them do not relate specifically to labor, they all fall under the category indicated in the title of the volume: "Economic Regulation, Business and Government." In this section the most relevant article seems to be one by F. C. Lane, listed as abstract number 1472 on page 75. Turning to this page we find the following abstract:

1472 LANE, FC
"ECONOMIC CONSEQUENCES OF ORGANIZED VIOLENCE"
J ECON HIST, 18 (DEC 58), 401–17

ENTERPRISES USING AND CONTROLLING VIOLENCE AFFECT AMOUNT AND DISTRIBUTION OF MATERIAL WEALTH BY IN-CURRING COSTS AND EXACTING LARGE SUMS. AS NATURAL MONOPOLIES, AFFECT MONOPOLIES IN OTHER FIELDS. THESE RELATIONSHIPS HAVE REPERCUSSIONS ON ENTIRE ECONOMIC ORGANIZATION.

Again, we find that the article may be somewhat relevant but is not quite what we want either. It seems to deal with the effects rather than the causes of violence. Even so, it may be suggestive and we should take note of it and, if time permits, check it out.

Having exhausted *Volume VIII* with only limited success, we should consider if our topic might also be listed under another volume. Perhaps group violence falls under *Volume VI; Public Opinion, Mass Behavior, and Political Psychology*. In this volume we can look under the same two key words, "labor" and "coerce" and find different listings. Under "labor" we find reference to a possible case study, N. O'Connor's *Revolution in Seattle*, described under abstract number 2400. Under "coerce" we find a general theory which may be relevant, J. Dollard and N. E. Miller et al., *Frustration and Aggression*, described under abstract number 0831.

Nevertheless, to this point we have still not found an empirical study of labor rioting. Our next step is to look in the annual supplements to *The Universal Reference System*. Here we find references to the following abstracts:

R 2255 HUNTER, R
VIOLENCE AND THE LABOR MOVEMENT (1914 REPRINT)
NEW YORK: ARNO PRESS, 1969, 388 pp

DISCUSSES OPPOSING POINTS OF VIEW TOWARD THE USE OF VIOLENCE DEBATED BY THE LABOR MOVEMENT AT VARIOUS POINTS IN ITS HISTORY. ATTEMPTS TO PRESENT BOTH SIDES OF THE ARGUMENT. TOPICS INCLUDE TER-RORISM IN WESTERN EUROPE, THE BIRTH OF MODERN SOCIALISM, THE BATTLE BETWEEN MARX AND BAKUNIN AND A DISCUSSION OF OLD AND NEW STYLE ANARCHISM.

R 3501 OBERSCHALL, A
"GROUP VIOLENCE: SOME HYPOTHESES AND EMPIRICAL UNIFORMITIES"
LAW AND SOCIETY REVIEW, 5(1) AUG 1970, 61-92

DISCUSSES HYPOTHESES AND EMPIRICAL UNIFORMITIES OF GROUP VIOLENCE TO LINK THEM TOGETHER IN A MORE SYSTEMATIC FASHION THAN IS PRESENTLY AVAILABLE. EXAMINES THE LIKELIHOOD OF VIOLENCE, ECONOMIC FACTORS AND THE STRUCTURAL LOCATION OF GROUP CONFLICT AND VIOLENCE IN THE US IN THE FORM OF STRIKES FROM 1870's TO 1930's.

These listings are found in the 1971 annual supplement. Other supplements contain other helpful references. Of course, once an article is located that seems directly on the subject, further bibliography can be obtained from consulting the notes to that article.

The *Universal Reference System* is only one among many collections of abstracts. Others that may be helpful include the following:

ABS Guide to Recent Publications in the Social and Behavioral Sciences (since 1965, covering since 1957)

Abstracts of the APSA Annual Meeting (since 1968)

African Abstracts (since 1950)

America: History and Life (since 1964)

American Politics and Elections: Selected Abstracts (Garrison, 1968)

Arms Control and Disarmament: Bibliography with Abstracts (since 1965)

Book Review Digest (since 1905)

Bulletin Analytique de Documentation Politique (since 1946)

CIS Index to Publications of the U.S. Congress (by subject, author, witness, and subcommittee)

CVS-VOLINFLO Bibliography and Abstracts File (continuously updated computer print-out on voluntary associations, since 1972)

Current Thought on Peace and War (since 1960)

Dissertation Abstracts International (since 1938; microfilm)

Historical Abstracts (since 1955)

International Political Science Abstracts (since 1951)

Journal of Economic Abstracts (since 1963)

Masters Abstracts (since 1962; microfilm)

Peace Research Abstracts Journal (since 1964)

Political Science Reviewer (since 1972; reviews recent and classic studies)

Political Science Thesaurus (since 1975; an APSA publication)

Psychological Abstracts (since 1927)

Public Administration Abstracts (since 1957)

Race Relations Abstracts (since 1968)

SAGE Urban Studies Abstracts (since 1973)

SAGE Public Administration Abstracts (since 1974)

Social Science Abstracts (1929–1932)

Sociological Abstracts (since 1953)

Women Studies Abstracts (since 1972)

INDEXES: THE SECOND STEP

Indexes are already familiar to most college students. You have probably used the *Readers' Guide to Periodical Literature*, which indexes, by subject, articles from such magazines as *Time, Newsweek, Life, Commentary, New Republic*, and other popular periodicals. Students are generally less familiar with the more specialized and more helpful indexes available to aid social science research. These indexes are generally arranged in a manner similar to that found in the abstracts mentioned above, but no summary of the material is presented and the researcher must decide what is relevant on the basis of the title (or author or source) of the article or book alone. However, indexes are frequently more comprehensive or more specialized than abstracts, and they often cover listings for years prior to the proliferation of abstracts in the 1960s.

Perhaps the best index to begin with in political science is the *International Bibliography of Political Science*, published by the United Nations Educational, Social, and Cultural Organization since 1952. This work is produced in annual volumes which organize subjects into broad topic areas, such as "Pressure Groups," "Political Ideas: Antiquity," or "Labor Influences." A subject index in the back of each volume provides references to more specific topics such as "violence."

One of the frequently used indexes which goes back to the 1930s is the *Social Sciences and Humanities Index* which, from its founding in 1916 until 1966 was called the *International Index to Periodicals*. Here, too, some creativity is called for. Using *Volume VIII* as an example (July 1937 – March 1940), we may look under the word "violence." Here we are told "see force." Looking under "force" we find three listings, all irrelevant. We try "riots" and are told to see "mob violence," which in turn has one listing, also irrelevant. We then look under "labor" and find many sublistings, such as "labor, casual," "labor and laboring classes," etc. Under one of these sublistings, "labor and laboring classes: history," we find the following possibly useful reference:

Was the West a Safety Valve for Labor? J Schafer, bibliog f Miss Val Hist R 24: 299-314 D 37.

Thus the December 1937 issue of the *Mississippi Valley Historical Review* contains an article on the proposition that emigration to the West relieved social pressure and hence may have lowered the likelihood of labor rioting among (Eastern) laborers.

In addition to the *Social Sciences Index and Humanities Index,* a second common source dating back some years is the *Public Affairs Information Service Bulletin* (since 1915). Other indexes include:

ABC Pol Sci (since 1972; indexes advance tables of contents of academic journals)

American Political Science Review, Index (in the December issue of the *APSR* each year; see also Kenneth Janda, ed., *Cumulative Index to the APSR, 1906 – 1968.*)

Atlantic Studies (since 1964)

Australian Public Affairs Information Service (since 1945)

Bibliographie de Sozialwissenschaften (since 1905)

British Humanities Index (since 1915; includes social science)

Biography Index (since 1947)

Book Review Index (since 1965)

Bulletin analytique de documentation politique, economique et sociale contemporaine (since 1946)

Catalogue of the Public Documents of Congress & All Depts of The Government 1893 – 1940 (1896 – 1945)

Canadian Periodical Index (since 1948)

Comprehensive Dissertation Index, 1861 – 1972 (since 1973; 37 vols. with annual supplements)

Contemporary Authors (quarterly since 1962; bibliographic biographies)

Cumulative Book Index (since 1898)

Cumulative Index to the Proceedings of the (APSA) Annual Meetings (1904 – 1912, 1956 – 1970)

Current Contents: Behavioral, Social and Management Sciences (since 1969; lists tables of contents)

Current Issues (since 1965; U.N. –related)

Education Index (since 1929)

Guide to the Study of the United States of America (Library of Congress, 1960)

Guide to United States Government Serials & Periodicals (Andriot, 1962)

Housing and Planning References (from HUD)

Index to Current Urban Documents (quarterly; since 1973)

Index of Economic Journals (since 1961, covering since 1886)

Index to Foreign Legal Periodicals (since 1960)

Index to Latin American Periodicals (since 1961)

Index to Legal Periodicals (since 1908)

Index to Post-1944 Periodical Articles on Political, Economic and Social Problems (since 1968; not annual but periodically updated)

Index to Selected Periodicals (since 1950; black affairs)

International Bibliography of Book Reviews of Scholarly Literature (since 1971)

International Bibliography of Economics (since 1952)

International Bibliography Periodical Literature Covering All Fields of Knowledge (since 1965)

International Bibliography and Reference Guide on Urban Affairs (since 1966)

International Bibliography of Social and Cultural Anthropology (since 1955)

International Bibliography of Sociology (since 1955)

International Information Service (since 1963)

Literature-Verzeichnis der politishen Wissenschaften (since 1952)

Michigan Index to Labor Union Periodicals (since 1960)

Monthly Catalogue of United States Government Publications (since 1895)

National Union Catalog of Manuscript Collections

Publications of the United Nations System (Winton, 1972)

Serial Bibliographies in the Humanities and Social Sciences (Richard Gray, 1969)

Social Sciences Citation Index (since 1973; enables the researcher to determine which works have cited specified other works)

UN Documents Index (since 1950)

U.S. Government Publications in the Social Sciences: an Annotated Guide (Lv, 1975)

Witness Index to U.S. Congressional Hearings (since 1839)

In addition to these indexes to books and periodicals, some newspapers are also indexed. The most helpful of these is the *New York Times Index,* which goes back to 1851. This index is not simply a listing of topics and corresponding pages; it is a readable book in itself. Under any topic, such as "Elections, presidential, 1972" one will find brief one-sentence summaries of pertinent news articles, ordered chronologically, helpful in establishing sequences of events, key names, and basic facts even without using the page listings to go back to the original newspaper accounts (usually stored on microfilm in most college libraries).

To continue our example on labor rioting, the newspaper index may be used as a last resort to find out basic facts about what we want to study. If it turns out that no one else has collected the basic data about labor riots—the how many? when? where? what type?—we can always obtain a rough estimate by going through these newspaper accounts to develop our own data. Although such use must go along with gauging possible reporting bias (does the *New York Times* under-report West Coast events, for example?), reliance on newspaper accounts may be the *only* feasible way of obtaining data. It is particularly appropriate when the subject of research is especially newsworthy, as is violence, and when the object is to determine basic facts (e.g., did a labor riot happen or not? on what date? in which industry?) rather than to uncover more abstract or detailed information (e.g., what caused the riot? how many people were injured seriously?).

In addition to the *New York Times Index,* other important newspaper sources are:

Alternative Press Index (since 1969)

Canadian News Index (since 1966)

Christian Science Monitor, Subject Index to (since 1960)

Times, Index to the (London, since 1906; for 1790–1905, see *Palmer's Index to the Times Newspaper*)

Le Monde, Index (since 1967, covering since 1965)
Le Temps, Table du Journal (since 1966, covering since 1861)
Wall Street Journal Index (since 1958)

Many newspapers also keep unpublished indexes or clipping files at the newspaper headquarters, which may be used with permission by researchers.

Finally, there are also a number of news summary services which serve as news digests:

Africa Diary (since 1961)
Africa Research Bulletin (since 1964)
Annual Register of World Events (since 1785)
Asian Recorder (since 1955)
Atlas (since 1961; covers foreign newspapers and periodicals)
Bureau of National Affairs (since 1933; over three dozen daily, weekly, or bi-weekly reports on economic affairs, labor, taxation, environment, housing, regulatory agencies, government employees, antitrust, federal contracts, and energy use)
Canadian News Facts (since 1967)
Congressional Quarterly Weekly Report (since 1946; also appears as an annual report; also has an editorial research series)
Current Digest of the Soviet Press (since 1949)
Deadline Data on World Affairs (since 1956)
Digest of the Soviet Ukrainian Press (since 1957)
Facts-on-File (since 1940; also *Editorials-on-File*)
From the State Capitals (since 1930)
Historic Documents (since 1972; from Congressional Quarterly)
International Yearbook (since 1953)
Keesing's Contemporary Archives (since 1931)
National Technical Information Services (administration, transportation, environment, urban technology and other specialized reports)
Political Handbook and Atlas of the World (since 1953)
Survey of China Mainland Press (since 1952)
UN Monthly Chronicle

STATISTICAL SOURCES: THE THIRD STEP

Statistical sources are listed as a later step to emphasize the primacy of conceptualization over data gathering. Collecting empirical date, whether statistical or otherwise, is fruitful only after the researcher has clearly determined what contending theories are to be examined and at what points empirical data will help to support one or another theory. Unless this conceptual task receives precedence, it is almost inevitable that the researcher will waste a great deal of time gathering unneeded data, or having to go back for needed data.

Some may have heard of a supposed debate between behaviorists and antibehaviorists, characterizing the former as statistically oriented and narrow. While there is such a debate, the equation of statistics with any one school of thought is mistaken. A mass-based questionnaire was used by Karl Marx as well as by conservatives, and arguing against the use of statistics per se is like arguing against the utility of evidence.

The real question has to do with the proper *use* of statistics. In particular, the researcher should not subordinate his or her analysis to the availability of data. Available data will ordinarily be biased toward the concrete rather than the abstract; hence it will be easier to find data on the number of people voting in an election than on their attitudes toward the voting process. Data will also be easier to find on matters relating to economics (our "business civilization" requires and generates a huge amount of data) than on psychology. The number of dollars spent will be readily obtainable information, but the results achieved will not. In general, available information of a statistical sort will correspond only in a rough way to the concepts and relationships posited in any given theory. For example, instead of data on "alienation from politics" we are likely to have statistics on "nonvoting rates in elections." Therefore it is usually necessary to inquire into the relationship between what we actually wish to learn and what concrete evidence is available.[1]

Three works stand out as the most likely to be used sources of statistical data for American political scientists. The first of these, cited in the previous section, is the *Congressional Quarterly*, appearing as a *Weekly Report* and an annual *Almanac*. In addition, a related summary title, *Congress and Nation, Vol. I* (1945—1964), *Vol. II* (1965—1968) and *Vol. III* (1969—1972); *America Votes* (nine volumes covering national elections since 1954); *Guide to Congress, 1789—1970* and *Historical Review of Presidential Candidates, 1788—1968* are available from the same publisher. Although functioning primarily as news digests, these sources provide general statistics on national-level elections, Congressional votes, and the federal budget, as well as political biographies, presidential speeches, and topical studies. The publishers of *Congressional Quarterly* also issue *Historic Documents* (annual, since 1972) and the *Washington Information Directory 1975*.

A second valuable source, *The Almanac of American Politics* (Gambit Press), edited by Michael Barone, Grant Ujifusa, and Douglas Matthews,

---

[1]For further treatment of the problem of inference from statistical data see the following: Hubert N. Blalock, *Causal Inference in Non-Experimental Research* (Chapel Hill: Univ. of North Carolina Press 1961), Abraham Kaplan, *The Conduct of Inquiry* (San Francisco: Chandler, 1964); Barrington Moore, Jr., "A Note on Statistics and Conservative Historiography," in B. Moore, *Social Origins of Dictatorship and Democracy* (Boston: Beacon, 1966), pp. 508–523; Hubert M. Blalock, *Theory Construction: From Verbal to Mathematical Formulations* (Englewood Cliffs, N. J.: Prentice-Hall, 1969); G. David Garson, *Handbook of Political Science Methods* (Boston: Holbrook, 1971); Ted Robert Gurr, *Politimetrics: An Introduction to Quantitative Macropolitics* (Englewood Cliffs, N. J.: Prentice-Hall, 1972).

was first published in 1972. To be updated by volumes on each succeeding Congress, the *Almanac* provides information broken down by states on:

political history, by state and by electoral district

number of electoral votes

census data, by state and electoral district

share of federal tax burden

share of federal expenditures, by government agency

economic base

voter profile (registration, employment, ethnic groups)

past presidential votes

profile of senators and representatives (biography, committees, interest group ratings, key votes, election results, military-industrial commitments)

In addition, appendixes to the *Almanac* provide congressional committee memberships, state electoral district maps, federal outlays by agency, defense contractors, and a list of administrative assistants to Congressmen.

The third prominent source of statistical data is the set available from the United States government. A general guide is that from the Office of Statistical Standards, Bureau of the Budget, titled *Statistical Services of the United States Government* (revised edition, 1968). This guide describes the operation of the federal statistical system and lists sources broken down by program (demographic, social, labor, price, production, distribution, transportation/communication, construction, financial, research, consumer, government, foreign) and by agency (Office of the President, Department of Agriculture, Department of Commerce, etc.).

Most students are somewhat familiar with another government publication, the *US Census*. What is less well known is that in addition to the decennial population census, others are taken every year. A guide to these materials from the U.S. Bureau of the Census is the *Catalog of US Census Publications, 1790–1945* (1950), supplemented by a monthly *Catalog of US Census Publications* covering the postwar period. The census data covering various "tracts" can be obtained—data are broken down by city blocks or equivalent units; virtually all other statistical data are available only for much larger units such as cities, counties, states, and the nation.

Depending on the unit involved in the particular study, one of the following government sources may also be useful: *Statistical Abstract of the United States* (since 1878), *Congressional District Data Book and Supplements* (since 1961), and the *County and City Data Book* (since 1949). In addition, the Council of State Governments has published the *Book of the States* since 1935.

Since political scientists are often concerned with *trends* over time, yet another government publication is particularly useful. Also from the Bureau of the Census is *Historical Statistics of the United States*, in two volumes (*Colonial Times to 1957* and *Continuation to 1962*). Historical data are provided on population, vital statistics, health, migration, labor, prices, national income and wealth, consumers, social statistics, environment, agriculture, various areas of enterprise, foreign trade, government, and colonial statistics. "Social statistics" includes welfare, education, crime, recreation, and religion. Under "government" one finds coverage of electoral votes, party affiliation, government employment, taxation and finance, and the armed forces.

In writing a political analysis of labor rioting, *Historical Statistics of the United States* would be quite valuable. While it does not contain specific data on rioting (as mentioned, we would have had to cull this from newspaper indexes as a rough gauge of frequency by year, region, and industry), historical data are presented on a number of unrelated variables such as:

unemployment	we can check to see if the years with highest unemployment also had the most labor rioting
work stoppages	is rioting a direct function of strike frequency...the more strikes, the more riots? If so, analysis should focus on explaining strike frequency rather than riot frequency per se.
immigration	is riot frequency associated with the influx of foreign-born workers in general, or of any particular nationality?
work stoppages over issue of union organization	is rioting associated with periods of increase of union membership, when unionism is first introduced (often against bitter employer opposition)?
occupational distribution of the work force	is rioting associated with changing job structure, declining as the proportion of blue-collar jobs does?

If we *do* find that the years of highest unemployment are the years of highest rioting, we may then wish to see if this relationship checks out within each industry. Are the industries with the highest unemployment the ones with the highest rate of labor rioting? For this we must get employment rate breakdowns by industry, which are not available in *Historical Statistics of the United States.*

The researcher should then consult the Bureau of the Budget's book *Statistical Services*, cited above. If this does not direct the student to the needed source, he or she can write to the relevant department of government (see chart in the back of *Statistical Services*). Alternatively, the Superintendent of Documents now has regional offices as well as the Washington office, and these are helpful in locating needed government-related information sources. Information from a Federal Archives Center may also be relevant in some cases; for these materials, consult *Prologue: The Journal of the National Archives* (Fall 1970 and subsequent issues). In our case, seeking unemployment figures by industry and year, the relevant volume would be from the U.S.Department of Labor, *Employment and Earnings Statistics for the United States, 1909—1968.*

Other guides to statistical and related forms of data are these:

"Guide to Sources of Statistics," appendix to *Statistical Abstract of the United States* (mentioned above)

Directory of Federal Statistics for Local Areas (1966)

Directory of Federal Statistics for States (1967)

Council of Social Science Data Archives (since 1965; survey data)

Encyclopedia of Information Systems and Services (since 1971)

Foreign Statistical Documents: A Bibliography (Ball, 1967)

Guide to Recurrent & Special Governmental Statistics (Dept. of Commerce, 1972)

Statistical Sources: A Subject Guide (1965, by Wasserman *et al.*)

"Student's Guide to American Federal Government Statistics" (*Journal of Economic Literature* 10, no. 2, June 1972, 371–397)

Survey Data for Trend Analysis: An Index to Repeated Questions (Roper, 1974)

Further sources include:

African Encyclopedia (Kajubi, Lewis, and Taiwo, 1974)

Almanach de Gotha: Annuaire diplomatique et statistique (since 1763, with lapses)

America at the Polls: A Handbook of American Presidential Election Statistics, 1920–1964 (Scammon, 1965)

American Statistics Index (U.S. Government)

Annuaire européen (since 1965)

Asian Annual (since 1954)

Black Africa: A Comparative Handbook (Morrison *et al.*, 1972)

California Poll (periodical)

California Statistical Abstract (annual; note that most states have yearbooks)

Census of Governments (1972 and every 5 years)

Comparative International Almanac (since 1967)

Convention Decisions and Voting Records, 1832–1956 (Bain, 1960)

Convention Decisions and Voting Records, 2nd ed. (Bain & Parris, 1973)

Cross-Cultural Summary, A (Textor, 1967)

Cross-Polity Time Series Data (Banks, 1971)

Cross-Polity Survey, A (Banks and Textor, 1963)

Current Opinion (Roper Center, since 1973)

Demographic Yearbook (UN, since 1948)

Dimensions of Nations: A Factor Analysis of 236 Social, Political and Economic Characteristics (Rummel, 1971)

Economic Almanac (since 1940)

Economic Bulletin for Africa (since 1961)

Economic Developments in the Middle East (since 1949)

Ethnographic Atlas (Murdock, 1967)

Europe Yearbook (since 1926)

Federal Reserve Bulletin (best source on current American economic data)

Foreign Statistical Publications: Accessions (U.S. Dept. of Commerce)

Gallup Opinion Index (since 1965); see also *Gallup Political Almanac, 1936 – 1945* (1952); *Gallup Political Index* (Great Britain, periodical); *Gallup Poll Public Opinion Reports, Reference Guide to, 1935 – 1968* (1970); and *The Gallup Report* (Canada, periodical)

Geography of Social Well-Being in the US (Smith, 1973)

Guide to U.S. Elections 1789 – 1974 (*Congressional Quarterly*, 1975)

Handbook of Soviet Social Science Data (Mickiewicz, 1973)

How Wisconsin Voted, 1848 – 1960 (Donoghue, 1962)

Illinois Votes, 1900 – 1958 (Gove, 1959); *Supplement* (1964)

Middle East Record (since 1960)

Minnesota Poll (covering since 1944)

Monthly Labor Review (U.S. Dept. of Labor, periodical); see also *Handbook of Labor Statistics* (annual)

Monthly Public Opinion Surveys (India, since 1956)

Municipal Yearbook, The (since 1934)

National Opinion Polls Bulletin (London)

National Technical Information Service Directory of Computerized Federal Data Files (U.S. Dept. of Commerce; since 1974)

Politogramm (German polls, since 1966)

Perspective Canada (Ottawa: Information Canada, 1974)

Polls: International Review (since 1965)

Population and Vital Statistics Report (UN, since 1949)

Population Studies (UN, since 1948, monograph series)

Presidential Ballots, 1836 – 1892 (Burnham, 1955)

Presidential Vote, The (Robinson, 1934); see also *The Presidential Vote* (1936), *They Voted for Roosevelt, The Presidential Vote 1932 – 1944* (1947)

Public Opinion, 1935 – 1946 (Cantril, 1951)

Public Opinion Quarterly (periodical)

Public Opinion Surveys (New Delhi)

Review of Elections of the World (since 1954)

Review of Public Data Use (since 1973)

Roper Public Opinion Research Center Newsletter (since 1965)

Social Indicators Newsletter (since 1973)

Social Indicators, 1973 (Office of Management and Budget, 1973)

Society, Politics and Economic Development (Adelman & Morris, 1967)

Sondages: Revue Française de l'opinion publique (since 1945)

Sources and Uses of Social and Economic Data: A Manual for Lawyers (Goodman, 1973)

Statistical History of American Presidential Elections, A (Petersen, 1963)

Statistical Yearbook (UN, since 1948)

Statesman's Yearbook (since 1864)

Texas Poll (periodical)

Wages of War, 1816–1965: A Statistical Handbook (Singer & Small, 1972)

Who's Who in American Politics; (4th ed., 1974); see also *International Who's Who, Who's Who in America,* etc.

World Communications (UNESCO, every few years)

World Economic Survey (UN periodical)

World Handbook of Economic and Social Indicators (Russett, Alker, Deutsch, and Lasswell, 1964); (2nd ed., Taylor & Hudson, 1972)

World Population: An Analysis of Vital Data (Keyfits and Fleiger, 1968)

World Survey of Education (UNESCO, every few years, since 1955)

Yearbook of Human Rights (UN, since 1946)

Yearbook of International Trade Statistics (UN, since 1950)

Yearbook of Labor Statistics (International Labor Office, since 1935)

Yearbook of National Accounts Statistics (UN, since 1954)

Among the most useful other sources are:

Ascatopics, 325 Chestnut St., Philadelphia, Pa. 19106 (weekly specialized indexing of 3,700 journals)

Human Relations Area Files (a carefully indexed card-file system based primarily on anthropological studies; through it one can uncover data on a topic such as "violence" for virtually any cultural group; oriented to study of traditional cultures), available through many participating universities

Inter-University Consortium for Political Research, P.O. Box 1248, University of Michigan, Ann Arbor, Mich. 48106 (a clearinghouse and distributor of survey and other data on "IBM" cards or computer tape)

International Data Library and Reference Service University of California, Berkeley, Cal.

Machine-Readable Archives Branch, National Archives Service, General Services Administration, Washington, D.C. 20408 (gov't data sets)

Nexus Information Services, Bldg. 3, Suite 201, 3001 Red Hill Ave., Costa Mesa, Cal. 92626. (a computerized citation retrieval system for sociology, political science, and history)

New York Times Information Bank (a computerized information retrieval system, especially for economic, legal, business-related research)

Roper Public Opinion Center, Williams College, Williamstown, Mass. 02167 (data from the Roper Surveys and many other sources may be purchased in card or tape form, or as computer printout of requested tables)

SSRC Center for Social Indicators, 1785 Mass. Ave. NW, Washington, D.C. 20036 (information on social indicators, especially as pertaining to the United States)

Xerox University Microfilms, "Datrix II Search Service," 300 N. Zeeb Road, Ann Arbor, Michigan 58106 (a computer service providing complete bibliographies of doctoral dissertations on requested topics, for a fee of approximately $15 per request)

GOVERNMENT DOCUMENTS

In addition to the government sources cited in the discussion of indexes and statistical sources above, the researcher may be interested in obtaining specific government documents. Most are available through the Superintendent of Documents, Washington, D.C. 20402. House documents are available through the House Documents Room, H226, U.S. Capitol, Washington, D.C. 20515. The address for Senate documents is Senate Documents Room, S325, U.S. Capitol, Washington, D.C. 20510. The U.S. Department of Commerce's National Technical Information Service (5281 Port Royal Rd., Springfield, Va. 22151) will, for a fee of approximately fifty dollars, search out government reports customized to the researcher's specific questions. In addition, NTIS functions as a central source for sale of government-sponsored research reports. For reference, see Laurence Schmeckebier, *Government Publications and Their Use*, 2nd ed. (Washington, D.C.: Brookings Institution, 1969); and John Andriot, *Guide to U.S. Publications*, 3 vols. (McLean, Va.: Documents Index, 1973).

Xerox University Microfilms (300 N. Zeeb Road, Ann Arbor, Mich. 58106) has made available commercially Congressional hearings dating back to the 41st Congress (1869) and records of state constitutional conventions. Grossman Publishers (625 Madison Avenue, NYC 10022) distributes the reports of the Ralph Nader Congress Project, profiling most U.S. Congressmen in detail.

Also helpful is Alexander Body, *Annotated Bibliography of Bibliographies on Selected Government Publications* (Kalamazoo, Mich.: Western Michigan Univ., 1967; 4th Supplement, 1974).

Finally, the researcher may find himself or herself denied access to needed information. Under the Freedom of Information Act, which became effective July 4, 1967, each government department was required to designate an official to receive requests for information and documents. If access is not granted by this official, a suit may be filed under the act.

INFORMATION GUIDES IN POLITICAL SCIENCE

In one chapter it is impossible to do more than skim the surface of the types of reference works available to the researcher. Whole books have been devoted to this task alone. Among those most useful to the beginning student is that by Frederick Holler, *The Information Sources of Political Science* (Santa Barbara, Cal.: ABC*Clio Press, 1971; paperback). This book is a good starting point for building a reference library.

Among other helpful general guides to the literature are:

American Library Association, *Guide to Reference Books* (Chicago; intermittently since 1902)

T.B. Bottomore, *Sociology: A Guide to Problems and Literature, Second Edition* (1971; 1st ed. 1962)

Clifton Brock, *The Literature of Political Science* (1969)

Laverne Burchfield, *Students' Guide to Materials in Political Science* (1935)

Ted Gurr, *Polimetrics*, pp. 67–81 (1972)

Robert B. Harmon, *Political Science: A Bibliographical Guide to the Literature* (1965)

Berthol Hoselitz, *A Reader's Guide to the Social Sciences* (1970)

Carl Kalvelage, Morley Segal, and Peter Anderson, *Research Guide for Undergraduates in Political Science* (Morristown, N.J.: General Learning Press, 1972)

Peter R. Lewis, *The Literature of the Social Sciences* (London, 1960)

John Brown Mason, *Research Sources: Annotated Guide to the Social Sciences* (two volumes, 1968)

Richard L. Merritt and Gloria J. Pyszka, *The Student Political Scientist's Handbook* (Cambridge, Mass.: Schenkman Publishers, 1969)

U.S. Library of Congress, *A Directory of Information Resources in the United States: Social Sciences* (1965)

Clement Vose, *A Guide to Library Sources in Political Science* (1975); and "Political Dictionaries," *APSR*, 68, no. 4 (Dec., 1974): 1696–1705.

Carl M. White, *Sources of Information in the Social Sciences* (1964)

Lubomyr Roman Wynar, *Guide to Reference Materials in Political Science* (1966)

THE ART OF NOTE TAKING

The art of taking notes should be the same process as the process of writing the paper itself, rather than a time-consuming mechanical chore done before thinking seriously about the paper. Note taking can be divided into a number of considerations.

When to Take Notes

When to take notes depends upon your topic—an obvious truth, which is nevertheless often ignored. If the researcher has only identified a topic without specifying a question with a thesis and supporting hypotheses (perhaps together with alternative theses and their hypotheses), as discussed in Chapter 5, then it is likely that he or she will not really know what to look for specifically. Instead, such a researcher is likely to take notes on anything in any way related to the topic and will not be able to limit note taking to material on the research at hand.

Many students think they will take notes on everything related to the topic, *then* think of a question, and *then* write the paper. Not only is this wasting time, but it tends not to work. Actually, notes will *not* be taken on "everything relevant to the topic"—there is too much of it, and much has to be overlooked. When a specific question is finally formulated, it is extremely likely that the notes taken will include much that is unneeded and not include much that is essential.

Of course, for the beginning student a certain amount of reading and research is necessary before he or she feels able to decide upon a good question. In addition to sources that may be located through abstracts, indexes, and guides, some more general sources of basic ideas and concepts are worth citing. The *Encyclopedia of the Social Sciences* (1933) and the *International Encyclopedia of the Social Sciences* (1968) contain short articles by leading social scientists on such broad topics as "revolution," "interest groups," and "organizations." In addition to definitions of these terms, a brief history of research illuminating each topic is presented—these brief essays are often helpful in gaining a basic orientation to a given subject. Although much briefer, a number of social science dictionaries also exist, serving similar purposes.[2] Also useful for exploratory purposes is the review of social science literature by Bernard Berelsom and Gary Steiner, *Human Behavior: An Inventory of Scientific Findings* (1964).

For term papers, the period of exploratory reading must be brief. But, though a question with its related thesis and hypotheses must be formed early, research is actually circular and the question can be clarified as work

---

[2]With regard to dictionaries, I recommend emphasis on that compiled under the auspices of UNESCO with the purpose of providing a common international vocabulary in social sciences: Julius Gould and William L. Kolb, eds., *A Dictionary of the Social Sciences* (New York: Free Press, 1964). Next in order of helpfulness I have found Harold D. Lasswell and Abraham Kaplan, *Power and Society: A Framework for Political Inquiry* (New Haven: Yale Univ. Press, 1950; in spite of its title, can be used as a dictionary); and George A Theodorson and Achilles G. Theodorson, *Modern Dictionary of Sociology* (New York: Crowell, 1969). See also: Jack C. Plano and Milton Greenberg, *The American Political Dictionary* (New York: Holt, Rinehart & Winston, 1st ed. 1962, 2nd ed. 1967); Thomas Ford Hoult, *Dictionary of Modern Sociology* (Totowa, N. J.: Littlefield, Adams, 1969). Primarily for proper names, see: Joseph Dunner, *Dictionary of Political Science* (Totowa, N. J.: Littlefield, Adams, 1970); and Florence Elliot, *A Dictionary of Politics* (Baltimore: Penguin Books, 1st ed. 1957, 6th ed. 1969). A list of other relevant dictionaries is given in Carl Kalvelage et al., *Research Guide for Undergraduates in Political Science* (Morristown, N.J.: General Learning Press; 1972), p. 59. C. O. Kernig, ed., *Marxism, Communism & Western Society: A Comparative Encyclopedia* (New York: McGraw-Hill, 1973) alphabetically treats major research topics as viewed in Communist nations.

See also Maurice Cranston and Sanford Lakoff, eds., *A Glossary of Political Ideas* (New York: Basic Books, 1969); Walter Lacquer, *A Dictionary of Politics* (New York: Free Press, 1971); Geoffrey Roberts, *A Dictionary of Political Analysis* (New York: St. Martin's Press, 1971); William Safire, *The New Language of Politics* (New York: Collier Books, 1972); Edward Smith and Arnold Zurcher, *Dictionary of American Politics*, 2nd ed. (New York: Barnes and Noble, 1968).

proceeds. Clear formulation of the objectives of the research helps answer the question, "When should notes be taken?" As the following example shows, it is customary for the researcher to work from clarification of the topic to specification of alternative theses of the subject, and from there to identification of the points at which each of the theses can be supported or disproved. Specification of the question, possible answers (theses), definition of terms, identification of needed evidence, and a plan to get that evidence and present it—all this constitutes the *research design* of the paper. Although discussed more fully in a later chapter, this process can be illustrated by the example below.

The general framework includes selecting a question, framing two or more theses for comparison, specifying their supporting hypotheses, and listing the evidence that upholds or disproves each hypothesis. This list will be the list of what the researcher should take notes on:

Question: Why do labor riots occur more in some years than in others?
Thesis: Labor riots are a function of economic factors.

Supporting Hypotheses	**Corresponding Evidence Needed**
H1 The more unemployment, the greater the labor rioting.	Unemployment and riot data by year, area, industry. Were the years, areas, and industries with the most rioting the ones with the most unemployment?
H2 The sharper the reverse in the trend of real wages, the more rioting.	Adjusted (real) wage income by year, area, industry, Is the change of adjusted income associated with higher riot years, areas, or industries?
H3 The lower the profit rate, the more employer intransigeance.	Data on profits and intransigeance by year, area, industry; the latter from content analysis of trade association publications.
H4 The more employer intransigeance, the greater the frustration of labor goals.	The above data on intransigeance plus similar data on frustration of labor goals; the latter from content analysis of union periodicals plus sampling of newspaper accounts of union demands and outcomes.
H5 The more the frustration, the more likely labor rioting.	Above data on frustration and on rioting by year, area, industry.

Alternate Thesis: Labor riots are a function of the breakdown of a system of moral legitimation.

H1 When the state, church, and media uphold and legitimate prevailing business practices, violent revolt against them is unlikely.	Content analysis of presidential messages, church pronouncements, and newspaper editorials by year (area and industry not applicable); riot data by year.

H2 When the above institutions cease to legitimate prevailing business practices, and instead, legitimate labor grievances, then (a) hitherto illegitimate grievances will be pressed (e.g., nonunionized firms) and (b) grievances will be intensified by left-wing activists (the importance of which is also augmented by changed legitimation patterns).

Same as above; information on whether riots occurred primarily at nonunionized firms; data on whether riots involved left-wing agitation, based on use of newspaper indexes.

H3 Changes in legitimation patterns are not a direct function of economic trends.

Data from previous thesis correlated with H1, above; this hypothesis rules out the possibility that *both* the thesis and alternative thesis are supported by the available evidence.

The right-hand column constitutes a list of the kinds of data that are essential to investigating the given thesis and alternative thesis. It is the core of what notes should be taken. Such a list can be composed only if a clear question, competing thesis, and their respective specific supporting hypotheses are established; conceptualization must precede note taking if note taking is to be efficient and appropriate to the research. Of course, some amount of "background reading" is needed before the student can conceptualize a good question and possible answers (theses). And some notes should also be taken on the historical and theoretical background of the subject, definition of terms, and supporting case illustrations. But, the evidence needed for each hypothesis is primarily toward what note taking is directed.

How to Take Notes

Beyond the more important problem of *when* to take notes lies the mechanical problem of *how* to take notes. Here, too, considerable time can be saved by systematic approach. There are several ways *not* to take notes:

Avoid these Methods of Note Taking

Method	Its Problem
Outline each source on a sheet of paper as you read it.	This results in notes arranged by source; you want them arranged by order of use in your research paper.
In order to take notes on as many sources as possible, just take notes on the author's conclusions.	Nothing can be proved by toting up authorities on one side or the other; take notes on each author's evidence, not his or her opinions and conclusions only.

Of the more suitable approaches to taking notes, the one most familiar to students is using 3-x-5 cards. On one or more cards, a master list of sources consulted is established and each book or article given a code number. Cards are listed by key idea or type of evidence, with just one specific type of information on a card. The master code number on each information card indicates the source to which page numbers refer. At the end of the research process, the cards are ordered along the lines of the projected paper outline. (Of course one should make sure information cards are set up for each of the kinds of evidence needed, as indicated in the previous section on "when to take notes.") This system has the advantage of enabling the researcher to order notes by their use in the paper (rather than arbitrarily by book, by author) *and* to change this order as research suggests.

When there is a great deal of statistical data, the library card system is inefficient. If one wishes to know, for example, how many coal mining firms suffered labor riots involving fatalities in a study of such matters, one would have to go back to the appropriate cards and tote up the information by hand. This is all right if there are not a great many such questions—but often there are. The solution is the "Hollerith" or IBM card.

Most colleges now have data centers open to students. Even students with no computer experience can still use these in the following way. First, arrange the data by columns (graph or accounting paper helps) on a piece of paper. Then go to the data center and obtain (usually free on an open rack) some blank IBM cards. The color or what is printed on them doesn't matter as long as they are not punched. After this, find a *keypunch machine* and insert the cards in the right-hand slot. This is a very simple machine not much different from a typewriter; it punches numbers on cards instead of letters on a piece of paper. A data center attendant or fellow student can easily show you how to operate it in a few minutes.

Use the keypunch machine to type up your data cards: in the first three (or more) columns punch an identification number on each card (i.e., 001 for data pertaining to the first year, Senator, state, or other unit; 002 for the second card on the second unit; 003 for the third; etc.). Then type the rest of the data on your data sheet onto the card, with one (or more if needed) card per unit (i.e., per year, state, industry, Senator, or whatever the desired unit of analysis). You can get 80 digits of information on each card; there is no need to skip spaces between columns of data.

Finally, use the *counter-sorter* to tabulate your data. (Again, an attendant or fellow student can show you how in a few minutes.) Let us say that in a study of labor riots you have listed the variable "industry" as column 32, with coal mining as a "6" under this column, and that columns 62 and 63 list the number of fatalities ranging from 00 = none to 99 = 99 or more. Turn the counter-sorter column pointer to column 32 and run the machine. All the cards in slot 6 will represent riots in the coal mining industry, assuming data is listed by the unit riot. (The researcher may need to list data by other units used as bases.) Now take these cards labelled "6" in column 32 and set the others aside. For this smaller set, representing the coal industry, run the machine for columns 62 and 63. The number of cards sorted out by this step will give the breakdown of coal mining labor riots by number of fatalities. Use of the counter-sorter is much easier if all the data varies between 0 and 9, and hence each variable corresponds to only one column on an IBM card.)

One can also obtain *data punch cards* at most stationery stores. These are rectangular cards with numbers around all four edges, along with a hole-punch and a skewer. Data can be punched on the cards so that a skewer, when inserted through the holes corresponding to a certain type of information, will lift out only those cards punched in a certain way. In essence, it is a manual form of counter-sorting, but is more limited in the amount of data contained on each card. Statistical data processing is not difficult, and a good self-instruction manual on this subject is Kenneth Janda's *Data Processing: Application to Political Research*, 2nd ed. (Evanston, Ill.: Northwestern Univ. Press, 1969).[3]

Finally, a word on footnoting. There are many styles of footnotes, but the "Chicago style" (from the University of Chicago Press) is still the most widely used among political scientists. A standard handbook is Kate Turabian's *A Manual for Writers of Term Papers, Theses, and Dissertations* (1955). In addition, most journals and publishing houses will make available upon request style sheets or booklets reflecting their own tastes in this matter. The main principles underlying any style of footnoting should be consistency of usage and provision of information sufficient to enable other researchers to check one's work.

EXERCISE

Using the bibliographic aids discussed in this chapter, compile an annotated list of a dozen references relating to the topic you dealt with in the previous two exercises. Choose one statistical reference, if possible. Use your library to obtain a few of these references, including articles in professional journals. As mentioned earlier, such journal articles usually begin by placing the problem in the context of other literature. Seek out and read a few such introductions in the references you have found. Then write a short preliminary introduction to a term paper yourself, incorporating the literature you have found to be relevant to your topic.

[3]The handbook series of which the Janda volume is a part is a very valuable addition to a student research library. See Charles H. Backstrom and Gerald D. Hursh, *Survey Research* (Evanston, Ill.: Northwestern Univ. Press, 1963); Robert North *et al.*, *Content Analysis* (1963); Lee F. Anderson et. al., *Legislative Roll-Call Analysis* (1966); Thomas W. Madron, *Small Group Methods and the Study of Politics* (1969); Lewis A. Dexter, *Elite and Specialized Interviewing* (1970).

7 | Conceptualizing and Measuring

The most important variables in political science are abstractions: power, influence, trust, efficacy, loyalty, alienation, status, and so on. Only a few, such as votes, campaign expenses, and government budgets, are measurable through direct counting. Even with these few, the researcher is frequently interested in the abstractions that lie beyond the raw numbers: in partisanship rather than simply votes, in political corruption rather than simply expenses, in policy orientations rather than simply budget figures.

Not only are political variables often abstract, they are also frequently nonunitary. That is, the word that we use to label an abstraction commonly represents a general category of phenomenon, subsuming many different aspects of the same phenomenon. For example, the word "peasant" seems at first to refer to something concrete and directly measurable. Students of peasant politics quickly realize, however, that there is an almost endless variety of relations between people and the land systems they work. The word "peasant" is an abstraction representing a general category of such relations. "Peasant" subsumes several distinct types of relations: peasant workers, peasant family farmers, wealthy peasants (kulaks), estate laborers, etc.[1]

In addition to the abstract, nonunitary nature of the variables with which political scientists deal, there is also the problem of operationalization. "Operationalization of concepts" refers to the process of linking those concepts with observable indicators. We may have a general concept such as "political development," and we may break it down into "democratic development" and "authoritarian development." But how do we know "democratic development" when we see it? What, specifically, do we look for? Such specifics are the "indicators" of our concepts.

Conceptualization thus typically involves three stages. First, we develop

---

[1]John Powell, "On Defining Peasants and Peasant Society," *Peasant Studies Newsletter* 1, no. 3 (July 1972): 94–99.

general or *categorical definitions*. Second, we develop a set of *typological definitions* subsumed by the categorical definition. Third, we identify indicators by which we can empirically measure each of our types; the set of indicators that distinguish a given type constitutes its *operational definition*. If our categorical definition may be considered unitary for purposes of our research, typological definitions are omitted and operational definitions pertain to the general definition directly.

For example, in analyzing the meaning of *alienation*, Melvin Seeman cited Nathan Glazer's categorical definition: "a sense of the splitting asunder of what was once held together, the breaking of the seamless mold in which values, behavior, and expectations were once cast into interlocking forms." Five meanings or typological definitions are subsumed within the word "alienation": (1) *powerlessness* ("the expectancy by an individual that his own behavior cannot determine the occurrence of the outcomes or reinforcements he seeks"); (2) *meaninglessness* (perception by the individual that his "minimal standards for clarity in decision making are not met"); (3) *normlessness* ("high expectancy that socially unapproved behaviors are required to achieve given goals"); (4) *isolation* (assignment of "low reward value to goals and beliefs that are typically highly valued in the given society"); and (5) *self-estrangement* ("the degree of dependence of the given behavior upon anticipated future rewards that lie outside the activity itself").[2] Although Seeman did not present operational definitions for each of these dimensions of alienation, the set of indicators operationalizing "powerlessness," for example, might well be responses to a scale of questionnaire items (e.g., responses of agree, disagree, etc., to the item, "People like me have no influence on national government").

Validity is the extent to which (1) operational definitions adequately measure typological definitions; (2) typological definitions adequately set forth the dimensions of the categorical definition; and (3) the categorical definitions adequately correspond to the meaning of the given word (e.g., "alienation") in the relevant body of usage (usually the relevant body of professional literature within the discipline).[3] In evaluating political analysis it is important to establish validity at each of these three levels of conceptualization.

Validation of a concept involves establishing the internal consistency of the definitions and establishing the fit of the concept with some outside reference point already assumed valid itself. *Internal consistency* refers to the first two points listed in the preceding paragraph, and will be discussed further in the section on typologies later in this chapter. *Validation* of fit with regard to reference points is discussed in Chapter 11. For now, however, a few points may be suggested. A measure of power, as an example,

[2] Melvin Seeman, 'On the Meaning of Alienation," in Paul Lazarsfeld, Ann Pasanella, and Morris Rosenberg, eds., *Continuities in the Language of Social Research* (New York: Free Press, 1972), pp. 25–34.
[3] Validity is discussed in greater detail in Chapter 11.

may be partially validated if it intuitively seems to measure power (face validity). Such intuitive validation may be undertaken by a panel of experts.[4] Or a measure of power may be partly validated by showing that it also measures as powerful the persons who are already measured as powerful by an accepted indicator. Or validation may involve showing that one's measure indicates as powerful the persons who have other attributes known to correlate highly with power. If, for example, one knows that power is highly correlated with membership in many groups, then one's measure of power should show that powerful persons hold multiple group memberships. Thus, a measure may be validated only by reference to some other factor assumed to be valid, such as intuition, by reference to other measures of the same concept, or by correlation with other variables known to be related.

PROPERTY SPACE, CODING, AND TYPOLOGIES

Property Space

Property space is simply one of two basic forms of data representation. Ordinarily it is equated with tabular property space, whereby one property (e.g., family income) of *n* levels (low, medium, high) is cross-tabulated against another property (e.g., party identification of *m* levels (Republican or Democrat), resulting in an *n*-by-*m* table (in this case 3 by 2).

Property space may also refer to graphic property space, where one property is represented as an *x*-axis (usually the dependent variable) and the other as a *y*-axis. Any given data observation then has a set of *x* and *y* property space coordinates. This form of property space thus results in a *scatter diagram* of the data points.

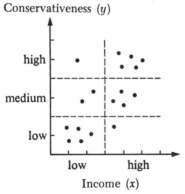

FIGURE 7.1   Graphic Representation of Property Space

---

[4]Point three in the preceding paragraph may involve "face validity" from the point of view of a panel of experts. Such "experts" range from nationally known authorities in relevant fields to samples of average individuals from relevant constituencies.

Coding

Coding is the classifying of properties. That is, any property or variable (e.g., income) may be classed or coded into a number of classes or ranges (high, medium, and low incomes) for purposes of analysis. These ranges then become the rows and columns of tabular property space, that is, of tables. All of this is extremely elementary in conception, but in practice becomes problematic. It is easy to set ranges to properties—to code variables—but it is difficult to do this well.

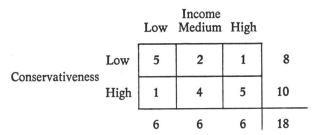

FIGURE 7.2   Tabular Representation of Property Space

There are several general criteria for good coding. The first is that the code must serve the purposes of the researcher; this criterion overrides the others. But beyond this, generally speaking, coded variables should have ranges that:

1. Avoid having too large a proportion of the observations fall in any one class.
2. Are comprehensive, so that all observations will fall into some class.
3. Have classes that do not overlap, so that any observation will fall into only one class.

In addition, provision must be made for the handling of all data, including "no response," "no data," "refused to answer," and ambiguous or irrelevant responses or observations. As the number of variables and the number of observations increase, there is greater need to handle data in quantitative ways through data processing machines; here the problems of coding become paramount.

Examples   Some examples of coding problems may clarify this point. First, to code income one might set three ranges: below $8000, $8,000-15,000, and $15,000 and above. This would meet the distribution-of-respondents criterion above in the case of an average suburb, but for a slum neighborhood it would not, since the great majority of respondents would fall in the first category. Thus some *prior knowledge* of the distribution of the variable is essential to setting good ranges. Second, it is often difficult to get *comprehensive* ranges. One item used in coding newspaper riot reports might be "predominant mode of dispersal of crowd," divided into eight ranges: police force, troops force, appeal, negotiation, spontaneous, other, not reported or uncertain, and not dispersed. Even this formulation results in many events being classed as "other," and it is not always easy to determine which mode is "predominant," resulting in "ambiguous" (uncertain) responses. Third, avoiding *overlap* is also difficult. For example, the variable, "type of police action in a particular riot sequence," may require over two dozen ranges. To take another example, the variable, "physical setting of first violence," cannot be broken into mutually exclusive categories (a riot might simultaneously be in "a street outside a school" and in "a street in a predominantly shopping area")—yet to have mutually exclusive variables would mean having not one variable (physical setting), but a great many, one for each setting. Thus, especially for nominal data, coding becomes difficult; often it is impossible to meet the criteria for a good code given above.

Typologies

A typology consists of two or more ideal types constituting the poles of one or more continua, together with other ideal types ranged along these continua. *Ideal types* are hypothetically concrete units (such as role types, personality types, social classes, types of buildings) constructed by the researcher from relevant associated traits. They are thus a special form of classification, intended not to be exhaustive or even descriptive of reality, but rather to aid analysis by enabling strong contrasts. Ideal types may be thought of as poles of a continuum along which reality lies. Ideal types may then be used as standards against which observed cases may be measured and compared.

For example, Weber distinguished traditional, charismatic, and rational-legal types of organization. Amitai Etzioni, a well known organization theorist, has typed organizations according to their mode of control—coercive, utilitarian, or normative. In any particular case, the researcher would have to choose which organization typology is most useful for his purposes. And in any particular case he would probably find that coercive, utilitarian, and normative elements were all present, although he would presumably class the organization by its dominant trait.

To return to the example of riots, one could employ a set of ideal-typical explanations of riots: human drives, cultural character, social conditions, and pragmatic goals. Human drives explanations of rioting may be broken into three types—biogenetic, medical, and psychological; e.g., riots are caused by man's instinct toward aggression. Cultural character explanations can be separated into racial, class, age, sex, and cultural conjunction types; e.g., riots are caused by youthfulness. Social conditions explanations divide into absolute, relative, and changing deprivation; e.g., riots are caused by economic reversals. Finally, the pragmatic goals explanations are divided into economic and political goals, and these into popular and conspiratorial theories; e.g., riots are caused by subversives.

The very fact that various authors writing on why riots happen use a great many sometimes conflicting, often ambiguous explanations hinders consideration of the issue. By constructing ideal-type explanations one is able to avoid the problem of "What did Smith *really* mean?" and instead focus first on the simply ideal-typical explanations, and then upon various combinations of them, until a sufficiently sophisticated theoretical explanation is elaborated.

Typology as Reduction of Attribute Space It was stated above that ideal types were constructed by the researcher from relevant associated traits. But how is this done? While the development of typologies is often intuitive and haphazard, a more systematic approach involves performing the following steps:

1. Identify the focus of the typology: Paul Lazarsfeld, for example, has focused on types of people according to their probability of being subject to discrimination[5].
2. List the relevant attributes: Lazarsfeld listed only three attributes as relevant— race, nativity, and education. Listing many attributes will lead to unwieldy typologies, as the next step demonstrates.
3. List the combinations of attributes: this listing constitutes the "attribute space." The most common methods are tabular or tree-diagram presentation, as demonstrated in Figure 7.3.

Tabular Presentation

	Black		White	
	Foreign	Native	Foreign	Native
College	comb. 1	comb. 3	comb. 5	comb. 7
Noncollege	comb. 2	comb. 4	comb. 6	comb. 8

FIGURE 7.3 (cont. on p. 156)

[5]Paul Lazarsfeld, "Some Remarks on Typological Procedures in Social Research," in Lazarsfeld et al., *Continuities in the Language of Social Research*, pp. 99–106.

Tree Diagram

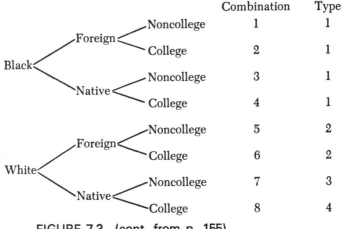

FIGURE 7.3   (cont. from p. 155)

In this example, there are only three attributes, each of which assumes only two values (black or white, for example). The number of combinations in such a schema will equal the number of values assumed by the first attribute times the number assumed by the second attribute times the number of the third, and so on down to the last attribute. Here the number of combinations is 2 x 2 x 2 = 8.

Listing many attributes and/or many values per attribute will yield a great many combinations. Parsonsian functionalism has been criticized by Dubin, for example, for generating unwieldy typologies of as many as 1,024 combinations.[6] Therefore, a fourth step is often necessary—

4. Reduce the combinations to a smaller number of types: in Lazarsfeld's example, the eight combinations are reduced to four types. Lazarsfeld reasoned that being black is such a disadvantage in terms of discrimination that education and nativity made little difference. Therefore combinations 1 through 4 were all classed as type 1. He also asserted that being foreign born elicited discrimination even among college-educated people. Therefore combinations 5 and 6 were both classed as type 2. Finally, Lazarsfeld considered that among native whites, the noncollege-educated would be more likely to suffer discrimination. Hence noncollege native whites were categorized as type 3 and college-educated native whites as type 4.

Typology as Idealization   Lazarsfeld's approach to typologies is appropriate for empirical, descriptive work. Sometimes, however, the researcher may wish to construct ideal models that represent combinations of attributes

[6]R. Dubin, "Parsons' Actor: Continuities in Social Theory," *American Sociological Review* 25, no. 4 (August 1960): 457–466.

never fully attained in real life. Weber's ideal-typical bureaucracy, for example, was defined by full attair.ment of such attributes as rationality, formalization of organization, and hierarchical ordering of the chain of command. While no government agency is actually fully rational, without any significant informal processes or lateral lines of influence, organization theorists have found that the fully bureaucratic ideal type is a useful construct. It provides a standard by which to assess the degree of bureaucracy of various organizations, *none* of which attain all the attributes of the bureaucratic ideal type.

Similarly, if we restrict a typology of "democracy" to existing combinations of democratic attributes, we would not consider the possibility of a hypothetical combination (ideal type) representing democracy. While a complete democracy might be impossible to attain, as an intellectual construct it might be useful as a standard by which to assess existing democracies. In fact, Peter Bachrach has cited the failure to apply just such a democratic ideal type as the central problem of the voting studies literature in political science.[7]

CONTENT ANALYSIS

Content analysis is used as a way of coding and thereby quantifying written material such as newspapers and speeches or other communications such as broadcasts. A simple form of content analysis might be to count the number of newspaper editorials for or against a particular policy, or for or against the president's position as an index of policy of presidential support. One researcher used fiction stories to classify characters by ethnicity and treatment; by this method he showed that Anglo-Saxons appear in more socially approved character roles.

A better-known example is Frederick Mosteller's work on the identification of the *Federalist Papers*. Mosteller started with four sets of papers: those known to have been written by Hamilton, those known to have been written by Madison, those that were thought to have been written by one or the other, and those thought to have been written by both. One of the initial steps was to feed into a computer the text of the known sets of papers, programming it to tabulate word frequencies and select out words that differentiated between the two men. Table 7.1 shows that the word "enough" was usually used by Hamilton but not by Madison. The key differentiating words were then used in combination to attribute authorship of the disputed papers.

---

[7]Peter Bachrach, *The Theory of Democratic Elitism: A Critique* (Boston: Little, Brown, 1967). For further reading on typologies, see John C. McKinney, *Constructive Typology and Social Theory* (New York: Appleton, 1966).

TABLE 7.1   Example of Content Analysis on the Federalist Papers

Key Word Rate per 1000 Words

Key Word	enough	while	whilst	upon	Total words included (1000's)
Hamilton known set	0.59	0.26	0.00	2.94	45.7
Madison known set	0.00	0.00	0.47	0.16	51.1
Disputed set	0.00	0.00	0.34	0.08	23.8
Both set	0.18	0.00	0.36	0.36	5.6

A non-mathematical solution of the authorship problem would be to attribute papers with "whiles" and no "whilsts" to Hamilton, and the reverse to Madison. This would be checked by a high or low rate of "enoughs" and "upons." In social science the solution is somewhat more complex, involving the application of tests of significance. Since this requires an understanding of materials to be treated in later chapters, detailed content analysis tests are not discussed here. The texts listed in the notes, however, may be consulted once the student has gained a deeper knowledge of statistics.[8]

A content analyst would not attempt to code a newspaper article or a speech as a whole. Instead the analyst would break the article or speech down into "meaning units," which might be only sentences, phrases, or words. Each meaning unit (e.g., a reference to the housewife role in a discussion of women) would be classified and counted, enabling the researcher to make a judgment about the relative salience of that dimension of meaning to its originator (e.g., to assess the extent to which a politician casts women in traditional roles).

INTERACTION ANALYSIS

Interaction analysis is to behavior what content analysis is to communications. That is, interaction analysis is a way of classifying types of behavior. It was designed for the general study of the small group by Robert Bales, who developed a typology with twelve ranges to classify observed behavior:

Bales then used these categories, which have since become somewhat

[8]For further reading, see Robert North, Ole Holsti, George Aninovich, and Dina Zinnes, *Content Analysis: A Handbook* (Evanston, Ill.: Northwestern Univ. Press, 1963); Ole Holsti, *Content Analysis for the Social Sciences and Humanities* (Reading, Mass.: Addison-Wesley, 1969). A more concise treatment is found in W. Goode and P. Hatt, *Methods in Social Research* (New York: McGraw-Hill, 1952), ch. 19. See also: Frederick Mosteller and D. Wallace, *Inference and Disputed Authorship: The Federalist Papers* (Reading, Mass.: Addison-Wesley, 1964).

Observation Categories in Bales' Typology[9]

I. Positive Reactions: expressive-integrative social-emotional area
   A. Shows solidarity; raises status of others, gives help
   B. Shows tension release; laughs, shows satisfaction
   C. Agrees; shows passive acceptance, understands, complies

II. Attempted Answers: instrumental-adaptive task area
   A. Gives suggestions; direction, implies autonomy for other
   B. Gives opinion; evaluation, expresses feeling, wish
   C. Gives orientation; information, repeats, clarifies

III. Questions: instrumental-adaptive task area
   A. Asks for orientation; information, repetition, confirmation
   B. Asks for opinion; evaluation, analysis, expression of feeling
   C. Asks for suggestion; direction, possible ways to act

IV. Negative Reactions: expressive-integrations, social-emotional area
   A. Disagrees; shows passive rejection, withholds help
   B. Shows tension; asks for help, withdraws from field
   C. Shows antagonism; deflates status of others, defends or asserts self.

standard, to observe the behavior of an experimental group that was given an artificial task. He observed, for example, that groups of three or four tend to have more even distribution of participation, whereas in larger groups, participation is more often confined to a "number one man." In examining the Borgatta and Crowther text mentioned in the notes, however, it is apparent there are many alternatives to Bales' exact typology.[10] Which typology is chosen depends upon the purposes of the researcher. Such analyses are often confined to experimental small group situations, but in general the researcher may develop his own set of categories to classify any type of observable behavior, just as he can devise any set of categories to classify words or concepts in content analysis. These observation categories may be used to note the pattern of interactions at one point in time (*static analysis*) or over several points in time (*dynamic analysis*), both to focus on general patterns of interaction of particular *individuals* in a variety of contexts, and on differences in such *patterns* when contexts vary.[11]

PARTICIPANT OBSERVATION

Participant observation raises the methodological issue of objectivity discussed in the chapter on Marxism. Ostensibly this is a straightforward

[9]Robert F. Bales, *Interaction Process Analysis: A Method for the Study of Small Groups* (Reading, Mass.: Addison-Wesley, 1950), p. 486.

[10]E. Borgatta and B. Crowther, *Workbook for the Study of Social Interaction Processes* (Chicago: Rand McNally, 1965).

[11]A handbook providing detailed instructions and numerous examples of interaction analysis is Thomas William Madron, *Small Group Methods and the Study of Politics* (Evanston, Ill.: Northwestern Univ. Press, 1969), especially chs. 6 and 7. Madron's Chapter 9 also treats content analysis.

technique—by immersing himself or herself in the subject being studied, the researcher is presumed to gain the greatest understanding. Arguments in its favor are the reliance on first hand information, its ability to convey a vast wealth of data to the researcher, the avoidance of sophisticated but data-losing transformation techniques (such as factor analysis), its "face validity" as a procedure for gathering information, and its relatively simple and inexpensive research procedures.

Arguments opposing participant observation usually mention its tendency to gather data unsystematically, the relative lack of procedures for assuring "value-free" information collection, reliance on subjective rather than objective measures, and the involvement of an observer effect (the observer's presence may affect the behavior of the observed). In addition, the emphasis on myriad details and intimacies may lead the researcher to present his findings in a journalistic or novelistic fashion without proper regard for underlying premises and theories. For example, one study of life in Mexico City selects quotes suggesting the theory that absolute deprivation leads to alienation from government. At the same time, alternative theories (relative or changing deprivation, characteristics of leaders) are not explicitly considered, nor is the underlying absolute deprivation theory itself explicitly defended. That is, participant observation may tempt the researcher into anecdotal writing rather than theory testing.

On the other hand, as we have seen, phenomenologists have defended participant observation precisely because of its unstructured and subjective aspects—they find bias not in the impressionistic and subjective nature of participant observation but rather in the imposition of an externally conceived "scientific" measuring device (e.g., a questionnaire) on individuals who do not perceive reality according to that external conception.[12]

Procedure

Procedure in participant observation is quite different for phenomenologists than for empiricists, both of whom may use this method.

Severyn Bruyn has outlined some of the steps in the phenomenological approach to participant observation:[13]

1. *Awareness of time:* Record the temporal phases of research according to the sequence of experience of the observer in relation to the milieu (e.g., newcomer, provisional member, categorical member, personalized rapport, and imminent migrant—i.e., the researcher is about to leave the community).

2. *Awareness of the physical environment:* Record the relations of people to their

---

[12]Severyn Bruyn, *The Human Perspective in Sociology: The Methodology of Participant Observation* (Englewood Cliffs, N. J.: Prentice-Hall, 1966).
   [13]*Ibid.*, ch. 7.

physical environment as they perceive it, not as you, the researcher, experience or conceptualize it.

3. *Awareness of contrasting experiences:* Record the experiences of people under contrasting social circumstances; meanings cannot be assessed under one set of circumstances, for they are relative to the setting.

4. *Awareness of social openings and barriers:* Meaning changes as the participant is admitted to narrower social regions (e.g., strangers, members, and insiders).

While other steps could be mentioned, the general approach of the phenomenologist is to seek out the meaning of the experiences of the group being studied from each of many different perspectives within it.

Participant observation does require considerable skill and creativity, its simplicity of approach notwithstanding. William Foote Whyte, in his classic study, *Street Corner Society* (University of Chicago, 1955), presented several methodological considerations. First, he urged users of this method to make their initial expectations clear (he himself expected to find lower class organization, not disorganization). Second, he stressed real participation, not just observation (he learned Italian, took local girls to dances, campaigned for a local politician, and lived with a local family). Third, he recommended that determining vocabulary concepts be an explicit process (Whyte sought to define the concepts of role, hierarchy, social distance). Fourth, it is necessary to secure clearance. That is, the participant observer's entry into the community or other research context must seem legitimate to the actors studied. Sometimes official sanction will be necessary or appropriate; at other times disguise and infiltration may be required. More typical, however, was the approach of Herbert Gans,[14] who presented himself as a researcher seeking to record the history of the organizations and groups of an area, and was accepted on this basis.

Empiricists look at participant observation as an opportunity for in-depth systematic study of a particular incident or situation. Morris Zelditch, for example, has urged researchers to think in terms of field studies using multiple measurement methods. The participant observer, in this view, employs at least three techniques: enumeration of frequencies (as in interaction analysis); informant interviewing (to establish social rules and statuses); and participant observation (to detail illustrative incidents).[15]

In participant observation, phenomenologists emphasize the participant's experiencing meanings through empathy, whereas empiricists stress systematic observation and recording of the milieu. Although this is more a

---

[14]Herbert J. Gans, *Urban Villagers* (New York: The Free Press, 1962). For further reading, see John Bollens and Dale Marshall, *A Guide to Participation Field Work, Role-Playing Cases, and other Forms* (Englewood Cliffs, N. J.: Prentice-Hall, 1973). This work also covers simulation techniques, discussed later in this chapter.

[15]Morris Zelditch, "Some Methodological Problems of Field Studies," *American Journal of Sociology* 67, no. 5 (March 1962): 566–576.

difference in emphasis than a dichotomy, the empirical approach is much more likely to be tied to an explicit schedule of observation geared to theses and hypotheses framed in advance of participation. Participation may yield new information requiring an alteration of the schedule of observation, or may suggest new hypotheses requiring additional types of observation, but the attempt to observe systematically is retained throughout.[16] This may involve systematic sampling of informants to be interviewed, interaction analysis techniques, content analysis of written materials encountered, and recording observations in structured question-and-answer form.

Definitional mapping is an interesting specific technique consistent with either approach to participant observation. The labels people use for the types of individuals who affect them are often illuminating indicators of the nature of the group being studied. Gresham Sykes and Sheldon Messinger, for example, investigated inmate social structure by starting with an inventory of prison argot for different types of convicts: rats, peddlars, toughs, weak sisters, fags, innocents, square Johns, right guys, and suckers.[17] A further step would be to trace such labels and distinctions as perceived from each of several points of view. An early study of class structure in the American South, summarized in Table 7.2, illustrates this more complex approach. Although definitional mapping is not limited to participant observation, it is a technique well suited for it.

TABLE 7.2 Perceived Status Distinctions by Social Class

Upper-Upper Class		Lower-Upper Class
"Old aristocracy"	UU	"Old aristocracy"
"Aristocracy," but not "old"	LU	**"Aristocracy," but not "old"**
"Nice, respectable people"	UM	"Nice, respectable people"
"Good people, but 'nobody'"	LM	"Good people, but 'nobody'"
"Po' whites"	UL / LL	"Po' whites"

Upper-Middle Class		Lower-Middle Class
"Society" — "Old families"	UU	—
"Society" but not "old families"	LU	"Old aristocracy" (older) — "Broken-down aristocracy" (younger)
"People who should be upper class"	UM	"People who think they are somebody"
"People who don't have much money"	LM	**"We poor folk"**
—	UL	"People poorer than us"
"No 'count lot"	LL	"No 'count lot"

---

[16]Albert Reiss, "Systematic Observation of Natural Social Phenomena," in Herbert Costner, ed., *Sociological Methodology 1971* (San Francisco: Jossey-Bass, 1971), pp. 3–33.

[17]Gresham Sykes and Sheldon Messinger, "The Inmate Social System," in *Theoretical Studies in the Social Organization of the Prison* (New York: Social Science Research Council, 1960), pp. 9–11.

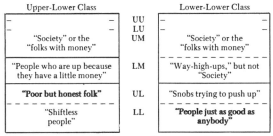

Upper-Lower Class		Lower-Lower Class
	UU	
	LU	
"Society" or the "folks with money"	UM	"Society" or the "folks with money"
"People who are up because they have a little money"	LM	"Way-high-ups," but not "Society"
"Poor but honest folk"	UL	"Snobs trying to push up"
"Shiftless people"	LL	**"People just as good as anybody"**

Source: Allison Davis, Burleigh Gardner, and Mary Gardner, *Deep South* (Chicago: Univ. of Chicago Press, 1941), p. 65. Reprinted by permission.

In summary, participant observation can be a valuable approach to gathering data. It is especially appropriate for community or group studies (as opposed, for example, to policy studies), and in this area is frequently used as an exploratory technique, uncovering in detail many hidden or latent patterns in their natural context. Because of the strong possibility of personal biases and observer effects, the researcher must take great pains to define and relate terms, make systematic observations, and relate observations to existing political or social science theories. This requires considerable methodological preparation on the part of the would-be participant observer if the study is to be of theoretical value.

CASE STUDIES

Case studies carry many of the same disadvantages and advantages that participant observer studies do. At one time the case study method dominated certain sectors of political science, particularly the area of public administration, partly because of the success of the case method of teaching pioneered by the Harvard Business School.[18] Today, however, the case study approach, like participant observation, tends to be favored primarily as a valuable exploratory tool in the earlier stages of research.

The case study is limited in a number of ways. It is difficult to research more than a few cases in depth (case studies commonly take up to a year or more per case because of the necessity of gathering documents, interviewing relevant actors, processing and coding information and data, etc.); yet it is logically invalid to generalize on the basis of one or even several cases. Second, case studies are frequently static, examining a situation at only one point in time. Political scientists do not desire to emulate the anthropologists, who may live for many years totally immersed in their study of some cultural group. Empiricists often add the objection that case studies usually cannot be replicated, therefore preventing scientific confirmation of findings.

[18]The best-known approach to case studies is represented by the Inter-University Case Program (ICP). Over one hundred ICP cases are available from ICP, Box 229, Syracuse, N. Y. 13210. An ICP companion text is Edwin A. Bock, ed., *Essays on the Case Method in Public Administration and Political Sciences* (Chicago: Public Administration Service, 1965).

Example

The drawbacks of the case study can be made more explicit by considering some problems involved in studying decision making to determine "Who has power?" If power is defined as control over the distribution of benefits, the case study researcher must seek to measure three factors: he must assess the value of the decision outcome for the participants whose power he wishes to determine; he must assess the value of the opposition to these participants; and he must assess the value of the supports received. That is, the amount of power of a particular decision maker is a function of how much the outcome is worth, increased by the strength of the opposition he must overcome, and diminished by the value of the supports he received to accomplish this. Even then, the researcher has only estimated the decision maker's power exercised in a particular matter, as opposed to potential power or power over time.

The study of decisions to find out who has power thus involves not only problems of definition and conceptualization, but also formidable difficulties in measurement if the case study is done systematically. Consider the problem of assessing the value of a decision maker's opposition, for example. This might involve not only the strengths of opponents in the decision-making body, but also the worth of opponents (such as hostile newspapers) outside the decision-making body, and even indirect factors such as the values instilled in all the actors by the society's educational system. Non-decisions as well as decisions must be considered. In explaining the "givens" in any case, it is necessary to explain the historical development of the case setting. For example, urban renewal laws, and for that matter, the capitalist system, were presented in Robert Dahl's study of New Haven politics of urban renewal.[19] Ultimately, the explanation of any case tends to require an explanation of history itself. What starts out as a study of power in a particular decision is apt to become the study of a total power system as an entity.

The case study approach therefore raises again the need for *multiple approaches* to any given political topic, such as rioting or power. Because the mind cannot directly comprehend a tremendously complex reality, researchers are influenced toward selecting a small bit they can grasp, perhaps by the case approach. However, because any case is intricately related to the whole and cannot be understood in isolation, the researcher is then influenced back toward grand theory. Political scientists need not choose between grand theory and case studies; both of these approaches and points in between are necessary to the development of political theory. These are contrasts only if methodology is understood narrowly; for political science as a whole they are complements.

[19]Robert Dahl, *Who Governs: Democracy and Power in an American City* (New Haven: Yale Univ. Press, 1961).

In conclusion, the case study approach is justified on several grounds, which the researcher should keep clearly in mind:

1. as an exploratory phase of research, not supporting generalizations, but providing insights useful in later undertaking more comprehensive approaches;

2. as a method of obtaining information or concrete illustrations that make vivid the generalizations supported by other sorts of data (e.g., statistical data may show the correlation of strikes with a period of rising and then falling wages, but case examples showing concrete instances of this allow a more complete understanding of the phenomenon); or

3. as a method when the number of theoretically important or unique cases is small (e.g., while there are thousands of business associations, four or five stand out from the rest in terms of their continuing political importance on a broad range of issues; in such instances, the case approach is also an in-depth survey of most or all important cases and does not suffer from unrepresentative sampling of relevant instances).

SOCIOMETRY

In its broadest definition, sociometry can be equated with all research involving quantitative scales. However, it is ordinarily equated with sociography, which was devised as a system for examining group behavior as a totality. The focus, as in interaction analysis, is ordinarily on the small group, although it has been applied to national studies as well (as in Hunter's *Top Leadership, U.S.A.*). This method provides a pictorial means of presenting data about complex individual relationships.

For example, if individuals are thought of as points on a piece of paper, we might employ certain conventions of sociometry, as shown in Figure 7.4, to illustrate various typical relationships. Thus, the "star" is made up of several lines pointing toward or away from a central point, representing an individual who becomes involved with many relationships and who in turn reciprocates, ignores, or rejects them. Other typical formations are the "chain," a series of unreciprocated relationships; and the "power behind the throne"—the object of attraction of a few very attractive individuals. Finally, of course, there is the "isolate," not chosen by anyone.

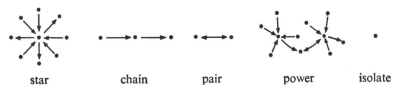

star   chain   pair   power   isolate

FIGURE 7.4   Some Typical Sociometric Representations

Sociometry is a method used to map informal groups. Sociometric *tests* are administered to the participants to determine direction of relationships, although sometimes this is determined by *observation*. For example, a socio-metric test might ask members of a political group which other members they like best and least in personal relationships, whom they like best and least as someone to work with, or whom they hold in highest or lowest esteem. Using responses to such questions, relationships among group members could be mapped, as shown in Figure 7.5.

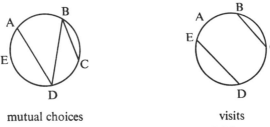

mutual choices   visits

FIGURE 7.5   Sociometrically Mapped Diagrams

Sociometric diagrams may represent either *attitudinally* based or *obser-vationally* based relationships, such as mutual choices or mutual visits, respectively. Attitudinally based measures may rely on *ideal* (who do you want to work with?) or *actual* (who do you in fact work with?) subject orientations. Thus, the question of reputation for power—"Who do you think has the most power in this group, if anyone?"—could be an attitudinal-actual criterion in a sociometric test of a power relationship.

Criticisms

This method, like any other, has several problems: it tends not to record illicit or subconscious relationships; it is apt to record attractions more than dislikes because respondents are more willing to reveal their attractions; and it is a static measure for one point in time. Sociometry is difficult to apply to larger, more complex groups. Also, it is liable not to record or compensate for subjects' tendencies to confine choices to their own general class range and it usually (but not inevitably) relies on subjective data.

On the other hand, sociometric testing and presentation can be much more varied and complex than it is possible to present here. Not only are objective as well as subjective measures of relationships possible, and affective as well as instrumental, but sociometry can also be applied at several points in time and for more than dichotomous relationships (such as attraction and repulsion). In more complex treatments, presentation of data becomes elaborate, sometimes necessitating representation of data in a *sociometric matrix* rather than a pictorial diagram. The matrix is an *n-by-n* table (square table) representing individuals across the top and the same individuals in the same order down the side. For each possible pair the range of the criterion is shown; for example, for the criterion "Whom do you like most?" the ranges might be: attraction = plus one, indifference = zero, repulsion = minus one. Moreover, such sociometric information may be used as an index of abstract relationship variables. For instance, the general level of popularity in one group might be compared with the level in a second group by comparing the proportion of members chosen as "liked" in the former with the proportion in the latter.

Some generality may be attained by securing data for many incumbents of each of several roles or positions and using the averages to map relationships between positions rather than between individuals. Thus, if analogous political groups exist, the researcher may use averaged sociometric data to indicate general relationships between, for example, a group's president and his executive secretary. This general procedure may be used to relate occupational categories, social classes, age cohorts, and the like. The researcher must be aware, however, that this procedure involves transforming the data by classifying, measuring, and averaging; like any indirect method of measurement, information is lost at each step. Furthermore, there is the general question of validity, the question of whether the indices really do measure the variables they are supposed to.[20]

SIMULATION

Participant observation and case studies involve research on real-life situations. Sociometry may be applied either to existing groups or to ones created "in the laboratory" for experimental research purposes. Simulation, at the other end of this spectrum, always involves artificially created situations.

Simulation refers to two distinctly different techniques: gaming and computer simulation. Gaming is the simulation of real-life situations through role playing, while computer simulation involves reduction of some real-life process to a set of quantifiable relationships which may be used to trace the eventual effect of many iterations of the process.

Gaming is used extensively in education, industry, and the military as a method of gaining deeper understanding of some dynamic process. Increasingly, such games are used in college courses. War games are perhaps the oldest and best known simulation examples, but many social science examples exist as well. An earlier chapter referred to some of these with regard to

[20]For further reading, see Jacob L. Moreno, ed., *The Sociometry Reader* (Glencoe, Ill.: Free Press, 1960). Moreno's *Who Shall Survive?* (Washington: Nervous and Mental Disorders Publishing Company, 1934) was the seminal study popularizing this technique.

Sociometric data can be processed quantitatively through use of matrix algebra, enabling rapid determination of the net effect of a series of sociometric matrices representing different conditions. See: John P. van der Geer, *Introduction to Multivariate Analysis for the Social Sciences* (San Francisco: Freeman, 1971), ch. 2, especially ex. 11.

For an illustrative application, see M. Becker, "Sociometric Location and Innovativeness: Reformulation and Extension to the Diffusion Model," *American Sociological Review* 35, no. 2 (April 1970): 267–282.

experiments to see whether real people, under laboratory conditions, would play games the way mathematical game theory predicts. The case studies of the Harvard Business School, also mentioned earlier, were acted out by students playing the different roles of the cases they were dealing with.

John Raser has put forward several of the purposes of gaming:

1. *confrontation:* gaming forces the researcher to make explicit the assumptions, parameters, and expected relationships of the subject of study;

2. *explication:* gaming also forces the researcher to clarify his or her concepts more rigorously than would otherwise be necessary;

3. *expansion:* gaming helps offset overspecialization by the researcher; it necessitates dealing with all the aspects of the whole system under study;

4. *communication and involvement:* gaming makes the relationships of the process vivid and motivates the researcher to find out more about them.[21] As one illustration, Drabek and Haas have used gaming to study the effects of stress, using police communications personnel as game players.[22]

Perhaps the best-known example of computer simulation is the work of Ithiel de Sola Pool and his colleagues at M.I.T. at the time of the Kennedy campaign for the Presidency in 1960. Pool developed a model of voting which predicted election results with greater accuracy than previously possible. Moreover, the same technique could have been used to predict different election results had the candidates employed different issues.[23] Shaffer has also applied computer simulations to voting behavior in order to test Downs' model, discussed in Chapter 4.[24]

PANEL STUDIES AND COHORT ANALYSIS

In several of the methods discussed above it is possible to apply static measures such as sociometric tests at various intervals in time to the same subjects in order to gain a "dynamic" perspective. The *panel method* involves the problem of possible *sensitization* of subjects. That is, persons given a test may react differently to a later similar test simply due to the experience of the first test itself. Checking for sensitization effects involves administering

[21]John R. Raser, *Simulation and Society* (Boston: Allyn and Bacon, 1969), ch. 4.

[22]Thomas Drabek and Eugene Haas, "Laboratory Simulation of Organizational Stress," *American Sociological Review* 34, no. 2 (April 1969): 223–238. Gaming in education is discussed in Clark Abt, *Serious Games* (New York: Viking, 1970).

[23]Ithiel de Sola Pool, R. Abelson, and S. Popkin, *Candidates, Issues, and Strategies: A Computer Simulation of the 1960 and 1964 Presidential Elections* (Cambridge, Mass.: M.I.T. Press, 1965).

[24]William R. Shaffer, *Computer Simulations of Voting Behavior* (New York: Oxford, 1972). For further reading, see Harold Guetzkow, ed., *Simulation in Social Science: Readings* (Englewood Cliffs, N. J.: Prentice-Hall, 1962).

the test to a control group (one chosen in the same way and apparently similar to the test group) as well as the retesting the test group to see if both groups respond similarly. Sensitization may occur not only in testing and questionnaires but also in studies involving observation.[25]

Cohort analysis is similar to panel study analysis. It traces changes in attitudes of the same group over time, although not for the same individuals. Age cohorts (age groups) from different time periods on similar survey questions can be used to simulate panel studies. For example, if survey question X is asked in both 1945 and 1965, and if in both cases data are available by age groups, then the researcher can look at the age 20—29 cohort in 1945 and compare responses with the age 40—49 cohort for 1965. Conceivably one could look at both age groups at the same point in time, but only if all other relevant variables except age could be held constant (which can rarely, if ever, be done).

QUANTITATIVE MEASUREMENT METHODS

Levels of Data

Levels of data include the nominal, ordinal, interval, and ratio. *Ratio scale* data have a true zero point and equal intervals; they can be used for any arithmetic operation. Data on income are ratio data—having a measurement of zero income really means no income, and the distance from $0 to $1000 is the same as the distance from $1000 to $2000. *Interval data* lack a true zero point but have equal intervals; addition and subtraction are possible, but not multiplication or division. For example, degrees Fahrenheit is an interval measure—the distance from zero degrees to 10 degrees is the same as from 10 to 20 degrees, but 20 degrees is *not* twice as hot as 10 degrees because there is no true zero point (zero degrees is not really "no temperature").

Ordinal data lack both a true zero point and equal intervals; adding, dividing, multiplying, and subtracting are not possible. For example, the class rank of students is of this type. Assuming class rank is supposed to measure achievement validly (a debatable proposition!), it is still not possible in a class of 100 to say that rank 50 represents twice the achievement of rank 25; intervals may well be not equal. Nor does any adding or substracting operation make sense with ordinal data. The only possible operations involve less than, equal to, and more than concepts. *Nominal data* do not even meet the requirement of order met by all "higher" forms of data. For

[25]For further reading, see Paul Lazarsfeld, Ann Pasanella, and Morris Rosenberg, eds., *Continuities in the Language of Social Research* (New York: Free Press, 1972), sec. IV; Herbert Hyman, *Secondary Analysis of Sample Surveys* (New York: John Wiley & Sons, 1972), ch. 7.

example, the various physical settings discussed under coding are nominal data—even though the settings may be numbered 1 through 35, these numbers are arbitrary; a particular setting might just as well be numbered 6 as 22, for example. There is no logical basis for adding or multiplying such numbers.

Most of the statistical techniques to be discussed in later chapters require adding, subtracting, multiplying, and dividing, and therefore are appropriate only for interval or ratio data. Since most social science data is ordinal at best (e.g., judgment scales range from "strongly disagree" to "strongly agree"), it is tempting to ignore the level-of-data requirement so as to be able to employ "sophisticated" quantitative techniques. While most statisticians (and this author) assert that low-level data must be explored through simple techniques such as multivariate table analysis (to be discussed below), it must be noted that much that is published in political science violates that data requirement. Such violations are justified by the unproved assertion that the "power" of the more "sophisticated" techniques more than compensates for problems of misrepresentation that may arise from violating the mathematical assumptions of the given statistics. The student is urged not to follow this practice unless the assertion justifying the violation of normal requirements can be proved.[26] A compromise position is advocated by Wilson, who urges that when "sophisticated" techniques are applied to ordinal data, the results be taken as heuristic (suggestive, not conclusive), since "the ordinal level of measurement prohibits all but the weakest inferences concerning the fit between data and a theoretical model formulated in terms of interval variables.[27]

Data Transformation

When we have interval or ratio data it is often convenient, in computation of many statistics, to simplify the data by transforming it. For such data we may add or subtract a constant, or multiply or divide by a constant, without changing the statistic. For example, correlation measures the extent two variables go up and down in quantity together. Since what counts in correlation is this mutual variation, it does not matter if we simplify our calcu-

---

[26]For a contrary view, see: Ted Gurr, *Polimetrics* (Englewood Cliffs, N. J.: Prentice-Hall, 1972), pp. 62–63.

[27]Thomas Wilson, "Critique of Ordinal Variables," in H. M. Blalock, ed., *Causal Models in the Social Sciences* (Chicago: Aldine, 1971), ch. 24.

The debate over using interval statistics with ordinal data and the question of assessing the magnitude of the likely resulting error is debated in Sanford Labovitz, "The Assignment of Numbers to Bank Order Categories," *American Sociological Review* 35, no. 3 (June 1970): 515–524. Labovitz favored use of interval statistics with ordinal data, but was sharply criticised by L. S. Mayer (35, no. 5: 916–917; and 36, no. 3: 519–520), L. G. Vargo (36, no. 3: 517–518), and S. Schweitzer and D. G. Schweitzer (36, no. 3: 518–519). See also Labovitz's reply (36, no. 3: 521–522).

lations by subtracting a constant from each value so as to make the numbers we deal with smaller.

A second purpose of data transformation is to make linear statistics applicable to nonlinear relationships. A linear relationship between two variables forms a straight line when plotted on two axes, as in Figure 7.6a. A nonlinear relation forms a curve, as illustrated in Figure 7.6b.

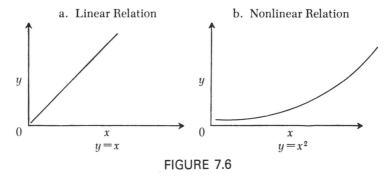

FIGURE 7.6

Linear relations occur when one variable, y, is an arithmetic function of another variable, x. Arithmetic functions take the general form, $y = bx + c$, where b determines the slope of the line and c is a constant determining where the line intercepts the y-axis. Nonlinear relations occur when one variable, y, is an exponential function of another variable, x. Exponential functions take the general form, $y = ax^n + bx^{n-1} + \ldots + zx + c$. For example, the following is an exponential function: $y = 2x^3 + 0x^2 + 14x \div 5$.

Many statistics, such as the most common form of correlation (Pearsonian product-moment correlation, r, discussed in Chapter 12), assume that the variables under study are linearly related. In order to employ statistics that assume linearity, it is sometimes necessary to transform the data from nonlinear to linear form. This is often done through logarithmic transformations. A set of points forming a curve on arithmetic graph paper will frequently form a straight line when plotted on semi-log graph paper.

Semi-log Transformation   The most common form of logarithmic transformation is called semi-log transformation. In this method each y value is replaced by its corresponding logarithmic equivalent. Suppose y is 694, for example, and we wish to find its logarithm. We look in a table of logarithms and find that 694 corresponds to a logarithm of 8414. Actually, a logarithm has two parts: a *mantissa* and a *characteristic*. The number we just found (8414) is the mantissa. The characteristic tells us where the decimal place should go. For example, the logarithm 1.8414 corresponds to the number 69.4. The logarithm 3.8414 corresponds to the number 6,940. The logarithm 2.8414 corresponds to the number 694. Similarly, the logarithm $\bar{2}.8414$ corresponds to the number .0694. Thus, when the characteristic is zero, there is only one integer before the decimal. A characteristic of 1 corresponds to two integers before the decimal. A characteristic of 2 corresponds to three integers before the decimal, and so on. A characteristic of minus 1 (written $\bar{1}$) means no integers come before the decimal. A characteristic of minus 2 (written $\bar{2}$) means the decimal is moved one more place to the left, as in the number .0694. Regardless of the decimal place, the mantissa remains the same. Once the y values are replaced by their logarithmic equivalents, the statistic is computed as it would have been in the first place.

Double-log Transformation   Double-log transformation involves converting *both* the x and the y values to logarithms. Sometimes this is necessary to create a more linear relationship than semi-log transformation can give. Thus *semi-log graph paper* contains evenly spaced columns (the x-axis) and logarithmically spaced rows (the y-axis), whereas *double-log graph paper* contains logarithmically spaced columns *and* rows. By plotting points directly onto logarithmic graph paper, the researcher avoids having to consult the logarithmic tables. Beginning researchers frequently find logarithmic graph paper easier to use than the tables, but a little practice will demonstrate the basic simplicity of such transformations.[28]

When to Use Log Transformations   Relationships are linear and require no logarithmic transformation if they take the form $y = bx + c$; for example, $y = 2x + 3$. Such relationships will form straight lines when plotted on ordinary graph paper. A change in the size of the constant ($c = 3$, in the illustration) will shift the y-intercept; a change in the size of the multiplier ($b = 2$) will change the slope of the line—but the line will be straight.

Relationships are nonlinear and require a double-log transformation when they are of the general form $y = bx^{n}$; for example, $y = 1x^2$. Such relationships will form straight lines when plotted on double-log paper. A change in the exponent ($n = 2$, in the illustration) will shift the slope of the line, but it will still be straight. A change in the multiplier ($b = 1$, in the illustration) will shift the y-intercept, but, again, the line will be straight, paralleling the previous slope. Addition of a constant remainder (e.g., $y = 1x^2 + 1$) will shift the y-intercept, *but* the double-log transform will not lead to a straight line since this constant remainder will have a larger effect on y for small values of x than for large values. Such constants must be subtracted from y prior to applying a double-log transform.

Relationships are nonlinear and require a semi-log transformation when they are of the general form, $y = bn^{x}$; for example, $y = 1(2^x) = 2^x$. Such

---

[28]For further reading, see Karl Schuessler, *Analyzing Social Data* (Boston: Houghton Mifflin, 1971), ch. 9; K. A. Yeomans, *Applied Statistics* (Baltimore: Penguin, 1968), 1: 25–27, 62–65; 2: 167–172, 237–242.

relationships will form straight lines when plotted on semi-log paper. A change in the multiplier ($b = 1$, in the illustration) will shift the y-intercept, but the slope will be the same and the line will be parallel to the original straight line [e.g., $y = 3(2^x)$]. A constant multiplier of x will shift the slope, but the line will still be straight (e.g., $y = 2^{2x}$). A larger base (n) will also change the slope (e.g., $y = 3^x$). Addition of a constant remainder (e.g., $y = 2^x + 1$; will shift the y-intercept, *but* the semi-log transform will not lead to a straight line for the same reasons as in double-log transformations; again, such constants must be subtracted from y prior to applying a semi-log transformation.

Many other forms of transformation exist. These include transformations by taking roots, logistic transformations (used for S-shaped curves), and arcsin transformations, all discussed by Schuessler (as noted). Trigonometric functions are frequently used for relationships that, when drawn on ordinary graph paper, form a cyclical wavy line. Most political scientists do not use anything more complex than log transforms, however. For now, we simply wish to make the point that data must sometimes be transformed in order to apply the relevant statistics. Failure to transform the data will yield misleading results. For example, Pearsonian correlation of curvilinearly related data will indicate less correlation (mutual variation up and down) than actually exists. After the data is properly transformed, a higher (and more accurate) measure of correlation will be obtained.

Averages and Quotients

Interval data is summarized by a particular form of average, the *mean*. The mean is the mathematical average computed by adding a list of n numbers and dividing by n. Ordinal data is summarized by the *median*. After a list is ordered by rank (e.g., rank in class), the median item is the one exactly halfway down the list. Nominal data is summarized by the *mode*. After items are placed into the various nominal categories, the category with the most items is the mode. However, when the data are highly skewed (i.e., when most values fail to cluster toward the middle of the distribution), the mean is misleading, necessitating its supplementation or replacement by the median or mode.[29]

A *quotient* or *ratio* is an amount expressed relative to some base. Percentages are the most familiar form of ratios. Other ratios include intelligence quotients (which are a measure of "mental age" expressed relative to chronological age), automobile speedometer readings (distance in miles divided by time in hours), and cost efficiency figures in political campaigns

[29]For further reading, see: John Mueller and Karl Schuessler, *Statistical Reasoning in Sociology* (Boston: Houghton Mifflin, 1961), pp. 143–150.

(dollars expended per vote received). By expressing amounts relative to a base, settings involving differing magnitudes can be compared. For example, in comparing the 1972 presidential vote by states it is difficult to interpret Massachusetts' 1,067,000 votes for Nixon as compared with Alabama's 692,000 votes for Nixon. One might make the mistake of thinking Alabama gave less support to Nixon. The relevant comparison, of course, is the ratio of votes for Nixon as a percentage of all votes for President in that state. On this basis we find Massachusetts gave only 45 percent of its votes to Nixon as compared with Alabama's 76 percent.

While most percentages are easy to interpret, two errors are common in discussions of ratios. The first error is to assume that the line representing the relation of the numerator to the denominator in a ratio passes through the origin when these are plotted on a scatter diagram. In Figure 7.7, for example, we may find that 4,000 votes corresponded to an expenditure of $3000, representing a cost efficiency ratio of 4,000 divided by 3,000, or 1.3. We might be tempted to think that this means that every dollar expended will result in 1.3 votes on the average. This would be an erroneous interpretation. The error arises because the line representing the relationship does not pass through the origin. Actually, Figure 7.7 shows that an expenditure of zero dollars results in 2,000 votes; an expenditure of $1000 results in 2,800 votes (a ratio of 2.8); an expenditure of $2000 results in 3,500 votes (a ratio of 1.75); etc. Thus, ratios can be used as standards for all levels of y (all vote levels in this case) only when this relationship passes through the origin, and when a second condition is fulfilled. This second condition, which also embodies the second problem of interpreting ratios, occurs when the relation is linear. Only when the relation passes through the origin and is linear can ratios be used as standards for all magnitudes of y.

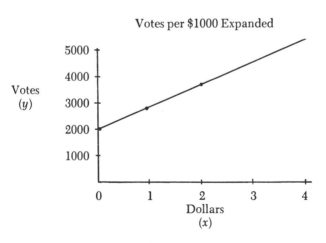

FIGURE 7.7

Indexes

An index is a composite measure created through the combination of two or more indicators.[30] For example, socioeconomic status (SES) is a common index created by the combination of three indicators: income, education, and occupational status. Often the indicators are combined through simple addition, but depending on the researcher's purpose, they may be multiplied, differently weighted by adding to or multiplying indicators by constants, or otherwise transformed during combination.

For example, Austin Ranney was interested in developing an "index of competitiveness" in state-level party politics.[31] To compute this index he took the average of three indicators: the percentage of specified state offices occupied by Democrats, the percentage of Democratic votes in the two-party gubernatorial vote, and the percentage of Democrats among state legislators. Thus, this index varies from 0 to 100, with maximum competitiveness at the middle, 50.

As Paul David has pointed out, Ranney's measure illustrated some of the problems of constructing indexes. First, it is better to construct one that varies from 0 to 100, with 100 as the maximum. (This could be done by forming a new index equal to twice the absolute difference between Ranney's index and 50, subtracted from 100: New Index $= 100 - 2|$ Ranney's Index $- 50|$.) Second, every index uses some indicators rather than others, thereby opening the door to disagreement. In Ranney's case, some later researchers objected to the restriction of looking only at the two-party vote, while others wished to ignore the office-holding indicators and concentrate solely on competitiveness in voting.[32]

EXERCISE

Social class is one of the most common variables in political analysis, yet it is also one of the most controversial and difficult to conceptualize. After reading some of the literature cited below, formulate categorical, typological (if appropriate), and operational definitions of social class. Contrast

---

[30]Note that some authors use the term index as synonymous with indicator, and use the term composite index to refer to what is here termed simply an index.

[31]Austin Ranney, "Parties in State Politics," in H. Jacobs and K. Vines, eds., *Politics in the American States* (Boston: Little, Brown, 1965), p. 64.

[32]Paul David, "How Can an Index of Party Competition Best be Derived?" *Journal of Politics* 34, no. 2 (May 1972): 632–638. David urged the use of a simple ratio of runner-up's vote as a percent of one-half the sum of the runner-up's and the winner's votes. Stern has suggested a measure based on respondents' perceptions of chances of success rather than on voting data. See Mark Stern, "Measuring Interparty Competition: A Proposal and a Test of a Method," *Journal of Politics* 34, no. 3 (August 1972): 889–904.

your definitions with those of others and justify the differences. Make a list of indicators proposed by various authors and discuss which indicators seem most useful to an operational definition. If appropriate, construct an index of social class; if inappropriate, explain why. The following readings may be helpful in doing this exercise:

Robert Alford, *Party and Society* (Chicago: Rand McNally, 1963), pp. 73–86.

Charles Anderson, *The Political Economy of Social Class* (Englewood Cliffs, N.J.: Prentice-Hall, 1974), pp. 49–51.

August Hollingshead and Fredrick Redlich, "The Index of Social Position," in Lazarsfeld *et al.*, eds., *Continuities*, pp. 66–72.

Joseph Kahl, *The American Class Structure* (New York: Holt, Rinehart & Winston, 1967), pp. 1–14.

Seymour Martin Lipset, "Issues in Social Class Analysis," in Lipset, *Revolution and Counter-revolution* (Garden City, N.Y.: Doubleday, rev. ed. 1970; orig. pub. 1968), ch. 5.

In addition, the following provide more extended or more advanced treatments:

T. B. Bottomore, *Classes in Modern Society* (New York: Vintage, 1966).

Elton Jackson and Richard Curtis, "Conceptualization and Measurement in the Study of Social Stratification," in Hubert Blalock and Ann Blalock, eds., *Methodology in Social Research* (New York: McGraw-Hill, 1968), ch. 4.

Bryan Jones and Richard Shorter, "The Ratio Measurement of Social Status: Some Cross-Cultural Comparisons," *Social Forces* 50, no. 4 (June 1972): 499–511.

Lawrence Hazelrigg, "Class, Property and Authority: Dahrendorf's Critique of Marx's Theory of Class," *Social Forces* 50, no. 4 (June 1972): 473–486.

Kaare Svalastoga, *Social Differentiation* (New York: McKay, 1965).

W. Lloyd Warner, *Social Class in America* (New York: Harper & Row, 1960; orig. pub. 1949).

J. H. Westergaard, "Sociology: The Myth of Classlessness," in R. Blackburn, ed., *Ideology in Social Science* (New York: Vintage, 1973).

8 | Survey Research and Sampling Statistics

Though it was developed earlier, the sample survey has become a common means of gathering data in political science especially since World War II. Vast amounts of opinion data (see Chapter 6), useful for purposes ranging from student term papers to government reports are now available. To use this information or to undertake similar studies of one's own necessitates an understanding of the basic processes of framing interview and questionnaire schedules (survey design), selection of subjects (sampling), and appraisal of the significance of the results (sampling statistics). This last factor, sampling statistics, is also important because it raises the concept of the "normal distribution," which, as later chapters discuss, is the basis of several other political science techniques.

SURVEY DESIGN

Interviews (oral) and questionnaires (written) are often used in the social sciences to gain attitudinal or factual data. Despite the great time and expense usually involved in this method, its advocates justify it on the ground of its greater breadth. Thus, while the participant observer may become more deeply immersed in the subject matter, the sample surveyor makes shallower but more representative observations. Survey researchers argue that it is better to generalize on the basis of less information which is nonetheless representative than on the basis of more information on cases of unknown representativeness.

Writing the question

Survey research is perhaps the most common method used by political scientists in obtaining the data needed to test their ideas, hypotheses, and explanatory models. Questionnaires and interviews may be used to elicit information about people's attitudes, social characteristics, and life experiences—in short, about many of the variables that go into an explanatory model. Recalling Chapter 5, the researcher potentially needs such information as evidence to support or refute the existence of each hypothesized relationship (i.e., each arrow in the diagrammatic model) being examined. This in turn means survey researchers must take care to ask questions which measure each variable in the theoretical model. In fact, these questions *operationally define* such variables.

The following general procedure is often used: (1) clear formulation of a thesis and its alternatives, together with their supporting hypotheses; (2) listing of the variables contained in any of these theses and hypotheses, together with categorical, typological (optional), and operational definitions of each variable; (3) formulation of survey questions pertaining to all operational definitions. (In addition, the researcher usually includes questions on background traits such as age, sex, income, occupation, nationality, and education).

A review of the literature not only aids in suggesting alternative theses and hypotheses for analysis, but it also frequently brings to light similar social surveys that have been conducted. Often the researcher will want to include the exact questions asked in previous surveys so as to better enable the comparison of one's own results with previous research.*

The interview or questionnaire usually starts off with the simple identification questions. Part of the identification can be done by a trained interviewer without asking questions. Sometimes, for example, the interviewer rates "life style" by the nature of living room furnishings (the Chapin Social Status Scale). Identification can also include matters relating to the respondent's *role* (club and religious affiliations, friendship patterns, leadership positions) and *level of information* (sources of information, frequency of exposure). *Entrapment questions* (such as asking if the respondent has recently read a nonexistent magazine) may be used to weed out unreliable respondents.

In formulating the *attitude questions*, including questions involving *self-evaluation* (e.g., Are you very/average/not very popular?), a whole series of considerations arises:

1. Are all terms well defined and unambiguous? In the above example, for instance, popular with whom? In the question "Do you know anyone who participated in the riot?" the word "participate" is ambiguous; it could apply only to those who actually engaged in violence or could also include onlookers who followed the crowds.

2. Are emotionally toned words and leading questions avoided? For example, the researcher should never put words into the respondent's mouth, as by asking,

---

*It is often desirable to ask questions used previously by other researchers so as to make one's data comparable. See *Survey Data for Trend Analysis: An Index to Repeated Questions in U.S. National Surveys* (Williamstown, Mass.: Roper Center, 1975).

"You weren't involved in the riot, were you?" A variant is to give the respondent unfair alternatives, or simply failing to inform him of the alternatives. The respondent who favors policy A, even knowing that alternative B is available, gives a quite different response from one who favors A when not given any alternative.

3. Are all terms specific? For example, in the question "Do you approve of government policy?" does "government" refer to local, state, or federal levels? Is the time period about which the question is asked clear? If value judgments are called for, is the value comparison made clear? That is, if the respondent is asked to rank town officials' performances as "above average/average/below average," is the criterion of comparison—what is considered "average performance"—made clear?

4. Is enough information provided in a readily understandable way? Complicated terms like "sovereignty" should not be used, nor should technical social science jargon. Enough background information should be provided to assure that the respondent understands the context of the question, yet not so much that he may fail to follow it. For example, if a respondent's attitudes toward the Voting Rights Act of 1965 are called for, a brief explanation of the provisions of the act is necessary.

5. Other considerations: Is the question too "folksy?" Does the question involve just one point, or does it call for several possible responses to different parts of the question? Are double negatives used? If the question is answered by multiple choice, are the questions mutually exclusive or is more than one response permitted?

Structuring the Interview

One of the first decisions is that of *format*. Is direct interview possible, or do cost and time considerations force resort to the less reliable mail or telephone formats? Is the interview going to be intensive, covering a subject in depth, or extensive, covering a broader range of topics? Will it be long or short? Mail questionnaires call for shorter schedules. The impersonality of the telephone format makes intensive interviewing difficult.

A second consideration is that of *response structure*. Will the respondent be allowed to frame his answer in his own words ("open-ended responses") or must he select from among predetermined alternatives ("structured responses," such as multiple choice or ranking scales). Or is a combination to be used, with the interviewer asking a structured question and then following it up with an open-ended question for greater depth? The researcher should not assume that open-ended questions are a substitute for "depth" studies used in motivational psychology, for example. The psychological techniques include various "projective" items, such as having the respondent interpret ink blots or give a short story about an ambiguous picture; their purpose is to get around the psychological inhibitions that may affect answers to even open-ended questions.

A third consideration relates to the *sequence* of items on the questionnaire or interview schedule. The interviewer should begin with a brief, natural introduction identifying the auspices under which the study is conducted. Assurance of anonymity should be given, and the initial questions should be neutral and nonthreatening, including, if possible, questions that rouse the respondents' interest. Entrapment or filter questions may be used to get rid of undesirable respondents (e.g., noncitizens or nonvoters, in some studies). Then questions of a general nature about the subject of the study may be asked, and eventually the more specific and more controversial questions.

Finally, internal and external *checks* must be considered. Items should be scattered throughout the interview, enabling the researcher to check the consistency of responses. Internal checks spot the consistency of one response with another; for example, age asked directly on one item and compared with date of graduation from high school asked on another would be an internal check. Structured responses may be compared with follow-up or open-ended responses. Or the same respondent may be interviewed again at a later date and responses compared. External checks involve comparison of responses with interviewer's observations or with answers in previous surveys, archival data, or interviews with related others. For instance, a man's responses may be compared with his wife's. Or a split-form interview—two similar interviews with corresponding questions differing slightly in wording—may be used to check whether specific wording is having an effect.

Mechanics of Interviewing

The survey researcher exists at the mercy of the interviewers. Therefore, careful selection and instruction of interviewers is essential. Mature women have been found to be the best interviewers, eliciting highest response rates. The interviewer should be instructed in the importance of objectivity, should understand the purpose of each question, never suggest answers, should interview alone, be friendly and naturally sociable yet firm and neutral, and have a neat, not formidable, appearance. Interviewers should be paid by the hour, not by the interview, as this might give incentive for quick, slipshod techniques. Preparation of interviewers should include role-playing and, if possible, supervised field experience. In addition, the interviewer must be provided with the paraphernalia of his or her trade.

Sources of error include faults in coding, tabulating, and processing data, or errors of judgment in interpreting the data, including those due to interviewer or researcher bias. In addition, error can occur because of bad timing: a sample of rainy-day bus riders will be different from fair-weather riders, for example. Or the sample itself may be nonrandom, unrepresentative of the target universe (the population group relevant to the hypotheses).

Pretesting the interview or questionnaire is also an essential step. No matter how careful the advance preparation, the initial interview usually contains words people do not understand, has confusing terms and phrases, asks for information too bluntly, or contains some other problem. Pretesting is simply trying out the interview in draft form on a population group in the field, preferably a small random sample taken in the manner projected for the final sample. Respondents' reactions to the questions and difficulties encountered by the interviewer provide an invaluable guide to revising the draft interview.[1]

Special Problems

In recent years, survey methodology has come under heavy attack for its allegedly superficial level of information gathering. While the phenomenologists present the strongest criticism of methodology on this score, social scientists of all methodological persuasions have become increasingly sensitized to this issue. The issue, moreover, has three dimensions: the ability of questions to tap the underlying attitudes, the ability of the interviewers to tap the underlying attitudes, and the assumptions about the relation of attitudes to behavior. Each of these problems will be treated briefly.

First, survey research is sometimes charged with lack of depth. By asking only a few questions in an artificial situation, the survey researcher seeks to elicit very complex attitudes which may be difficult or impossible to discover by this method. People may have many contradictory attitudes, one or another dimension of which may become salient depending on the context; these attitudes differ in intensity, duration and experiential meaning among individuals; and articulate responses are filtered through the effects of various socializing agencies which, some analysts claim, superimpose a "false consciousness" on "authentic consciousness." Survey researchers have tended to discount these charges, but their effect is discernible in the trends toward: (1) inclusion of open-ended questions paralleling the subjects treated by structured (e.g., multiple choice) questions; (2) conceptual explication and confirmation through feedback of interview results to discussion groups of respondents assembled at a later stage; and (3) research designs in which survey research is only one of several methods of inquiry.

Second, especially in the highly politicized 1960s and early 1970s, strong questions have been raised about the meaningfulness of questions asked by

---

[1]For further reading, see Herbert Hyman, *Survey Design and Analysis* (New York: Free Press, 1955). This is still considered the standard work on the subject. See also more recent treatments such as A. N. Oppenheim, *Questionnaire Design and Attitude Measurement* (New York: Basic Books, 1966); Raymond Gorden, *Interviewing: Strategy, Techniques, and Tactics* (Homewood, Ill.: Dorsey, 1969); and Lewis Dexter, *Elite and Specialized Interviewing* (Evanston, Ill.: Northwestern Univ. Press, 1970). Two handbooks at a more how-to-do-it level are Charles Backstrom and Gerald Hursh, *Survey Research* (Evanston, Ill.: Northwestern Univ. Press, 1963); and Survey Research Center, *Interviewer's Manual* (Ann Arbor: Institute for Social Research, Univ. of Michigan, 1969).

On problems of coding, see K. Crittenden and R. Hill, "Coding Reliability and Validity of Interview Data," *American Sociological Review* 36, no. 6 (December 1971): 1073–1079.

"outside" survey groups in black and other non-middle-class settings. As Eric Josephson's attempted health survey in Harlem demonstrated, a tendency exists for survey researchers in such settings to be associated with the government, "the Man," or with other images drawn from the previous experiences of working- and lower-class residents with people who come to the door to ask questions.[2] This problem has led survey researchers to seek a screening of proposed community surveys to reduce their number and avoid "saturation." Far more preliminary work is now done to establish the credentials and entry into the community of the researcher with both formal and informal community leaders. Greater provisions are made for protection of privacy, for the involvement of community people in the formulation of the research, and for proof that the research will benefit the community. In addition, there has been an increasing trend toward paying respondents, to avoid the charge of "exploitation." Nevertheless, these solutions still leave open the basic question of whether the respondents would give different answers to their friends than to interviewers. Survey researchers have tried to compensate for this possibility by training community residents as interviewers.

Third, survey researchers often assume that the attitudes they tap are predispositions to behavior. The high accuracy of Gallup-poll predictions of actual electoral vote outcomes seems to confirm this supposition. One may question, however, whether this example is generalizable to all attitude surveys. In a study of extreme pro- and antiblack attitudes, for example, Donald Tarter found that 65 percent of the respondents changed their behavior away from measured attitudes when confronted with situational opposition.[3] Nor is this exceptional. As Ehrlich noted, "Studies on the relation of attitudes and behavior have almost consistently resulted in the conclusion that attitudes are a poor predictor of behavior."[4] In addition to discussing problems of multiple attitudes in the same individual and of different meanings according to the situational context, Ehrlich outlined seven considerations that intervene between an attitude and its expression in actual behavior:

1. There must be a clear way for the attitude to be expressed in behavior;
2. Attitudes may be expressed in fantasy or sublimation rather than in actual behavior;

[2]Eric Josephson, "Resistance to Community Surveys," *Social Problems* 18, no. 1 (Summer 1970): 117–129.
[3]Donald Tarter, "Toward Prediction of Attitude-Action Discrepancy," *Social Forces* 47, no. 4 (June 1969): 398–404; D. Tarter, "Attitude: The Mental Myth," *American Sociologist* 5, no. 3 (August 1970): 276–278.
[4]Howard Ehrlich, "Attitudes, Behavior, and the Intervening Variables," *American Sociologist* 4, no. 1 (February 1969): 29–34. A partial exception is illustrated in R. Brannon et al., "Attitude and Action: A Field Experiment," *American Sociological Review* 38, no. 5 (October 1973): 625–636.

3. The individual must be willing to disclose this aspect of himself or herself;

4. Attitudes may be expressed by inaction or in ways contrary to what would be predicted because the individual defines reality differently (e.g., anachronistically orients behavior to a former time) or rationalizes it;

5. The individual may never have learned how to act in a manner consistent with his attitudes;

6. The individual may lack the opportunity or access to act;

7. The individual may lack the competence or sense of efficacy to do so.

SAMPLING METHODS

Ideally, researchers would not take samples at all; instead they would take *enumerations*—information from everybody. The idea behind sampling is simply that because it is too expensive in time and money to interview everyone concerned, it is the second-best thing to interview a number of representative people. Sampling methods have been devised to help the researcher find representative people to interview.

Nonrandom Sampling

Most sampling is *probability* or *random sampling*, but other kinds of samples are sometimes used. Newspapers often use *haphazard samples* in their man-on-the-street interview columns. This is one foim of *availability sample*, in which the researcher selects his sample from among those who volunteer or are otherwise available. Naturally, such a sample cannot be presumed to be representative. The well-known *Kinsey Report* on sexual behavior of females has often been criticized for including a large number of female prison inmates in the sample simply because they were available for interview.

Other forms of nonrandom sampling methods include the *judgment sample*, in which the researcher asks an arbitrary list of "experts" to select representative men. Or a *chain sample* may be used, starting with one respondent selected by any means who meets some basic criterion (in a sample of draft resisters, for example, someone who had turned in his draft card); this respondent is then asked to name other individuals like himself with regards to the criterion. These reference individuals are then interviewed and further references acquired in a snowballing or chain process. The nonrandom sampling methods have the advantage of being quicker and cheaper, but it cannot be assumed that they result in a representative sample. In fact, many researchers believe it is best to assume that a sample selected by any nonrandom method will be significantly different from a random sample.

Random Sampling

The basic idea behind *simple random sampling* is to make a list of all members of the target population and then select respondents from this list in a way such that every member has an equal chance of being selected. This is usually done by using a table of random numbers generated by a computer. For example, the researcher might arbitrarily determine in advance that he will start with the first page, fifth row, second column of the table of random numbers. He finds this number and selects that individual from the list of all members. He may continue in this manner or may use *interval sampling;* that is, the researcher may start with the individual selected above and then take every fifth, every ninth, or whatever interval is appropriate to generate the desired number of respondents.

Although these methods may be used on small populations, such as the universe of students at a college, it is impossible to list all the residents of a country or even of a large city. Sometimes surrogate lists are used, such as telephone and city directories, police, utility company, voter registration, school census, auto owners, or marriage-divorce lists, or some combination. None of these surrogates can be considered highly reliable. Telephone directories, for example, are biased against inclusion of the poor, who cannot afford telephones or share them among several families, and the well-to-do, who often have unlisted numbers.

For larger population groups some form of *multistage sampling* is generally used—either *cluster sampling* (sample of groups) or *area sampling* (sample of territorial units). Here the researcher makes a list of all states, takes a simple random sample of states, then for these states makes a list of all counties, takes a random sample of counties, then a sample of census tracts, then a sample of tract blocks (or the equivalent units for rural areas). Next a list is made, in the field or from city directories, of the dwelling units in the final sample blocks—or of all families or even all individuals living on the block—and finally a random interval sample is taken of these families or individuals. This is an extremely laborious and complicated procedure dealt with at length in the Backstrom and Hursh reading. Large national samples, when desired by political scientists, are usually taken by professional polling companies such as the Gallup or Harris poll groups.

Figure 8.1 illustrates this sampling process as practiced by the Survey Research Center of the University of Michigan. By dividing the United States into a great many Primary Sampling Units (PSUs), the Survey Research Center is then in a position to randomly select a certain number (seventy-four) according to certain desired attributes, such as urbanism, region of the country, and so on. This is called "stratified sampling," and applies to the first stages of sampling steps in Figure 8.1.

Random sampling alone does not guarantee representativeness of the sample. Therefore, some researchers use *stratified sampling* to assure that all

FIGURE 8.1   SRC Sampling Method

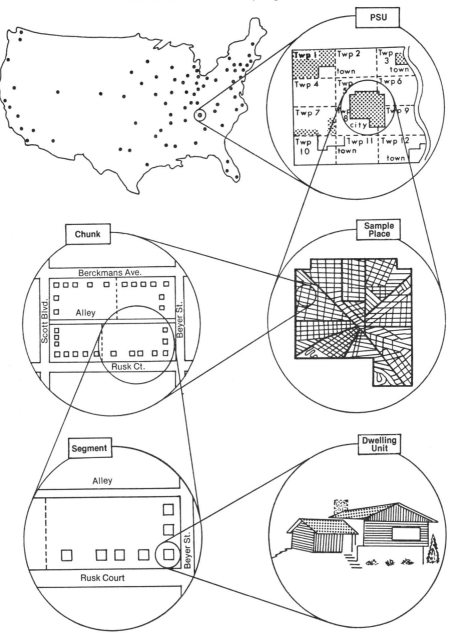

Source: Survey Research Center, *Interviewer's Manual* (Ann Arbor: Institute for Social Research), p. 8–2. Copyright 1969 by the University of Michigan; reprinted by permission of the publisher, the Survey Research Center of the Institute for Social Research.

important groups will be represented according to their known proportion in the population. This method, often used in conjunction with area sampling, simply breaks the overall sample into several samples. For example, an overall sample of 2000 might be divided into two subsamples: 1000 men and 1000 women. These subsamples might in turn be broken down several times by such criteria as age, region, city size, socioeconomic status, and race. These are then used as the target populations of random sampling methods such as cluster or area sampling.

Sampling Error

There is always the danger of unexpected sampling error. Interviewer bias, bad timing, or poorly worded interviews have already been mentioned. In addition there is the danger of "systematic sampling"; the researcher may use the random interval method without realizing that the list from which he is sampling is not haphazard but instead has a systematic pattern. For example, sampling every other U.S. senator on the *Congressional Quarterly* list will result in either all senior or all junior senators, since there are two per state and senators are listed by state with the senior senator first. Or a sample that always starts with the corner house in a block would oversample corner houses, which usually are more valuable and have occupants with above average income. Samples during the day are likely to oversample women and the unemployed. All samples tend to undersample transient members of the population. Persons living in institutions such as nursing homes or prisons are not always considered. Interviewing more than one person in the same household will exaggerate any sampling bias that exists.

The greatest problem for the survey researcher is dealing with those who are not at home or refuse to answer. He or she must plan in advance that a certain proportion of his sample will be in this category. It is therefore necessary to take a sample some percentage higher (ordinarily 10%, sometimes more in neighborhoods with high transiency and many vacancies) than would otherwise be taken. In a random sample, substitutions should never be made. If a selected house is vacant, the interview is so marked and is processed as such; it is not thrown out since it does represent real information. This is even more true of persons refusing to answer questions or who are not locatable. The researcher must assume that nonrespondents are significantly different from first responders. Nonrespondents are never thrown out of the sample, but like vacancies are processed along with the rest of the sample. Nonrespondents may be handled by setting aside those interviews secured initially and then making *call-backs* to again try to interview those not contacted the first time. Interviews obtained the second time are set aside, as are those obtained the third time. By comparing answers to a given item among the initial, second, and third sets, some extrapolation estimate may be made about the nature of the responses of the final nonresponse set.

In cases where the respondent has answered some but not all of the items, the researcher must decide what to do about missing data. If a great many items have missing data, the researcher may wish to delete the respondent, thereby lowering the response rate in the study. Most computer programs are set up to delete respondents when data for them are missing in a particular table, correlation, or other application (though such respondents arc included in other tables using items to which they *did* respond). In time-series or other ordered data, extrapolated estimates are sometimes plugged in to the slots missing data. Even in attitude surveys, average responses are sometimes used as estimates when the actual response is missing. Ted Gurr suggests that the researcher conduct two analyses: one for the smaller number of respondents with complete data, and a second for all respondents including those for whom missing data has been estimated. If the smaller group has the same range of responses but stronger relationships, this suggests that the estimates of missing data in the larger group contain "more error than information."[5]

SAMPLING STATISTICS

Once we have collected data through a sample survey, coded the responses, and put the information on data cards, we are in a position to begin to interpret what we have found. One of the central problems of interpretation has to do with *significance*. A relationship between two variables is said to be significant if there is only a low probability (one chance out of twenty is often used as an arbitrary cut-off) that it is due to a bad sample and in actuality no such relationship exists at all. Tests of significance help answer such questions as, "Is this relationship due to chance?" "How far apart do the averages of two sampled groups have to be before I can say they are definitely different by this given criterion?" or "If the percentage of those voting Democratic in one sampled city is slightly higher than in another, can we definitely be sure the first city is more strongly Democratic?" Before answering these questions, however, it is necessary to look at the basic ideas of sampling statistics.

[5]Ted Gurr, *Polimetrics* (Englewood Cliffs, N. J.: Prentice-Hall, 1972), p. 87. For further reading see Morris Slonim, *Sampling in a Nutshell* (New York: Simon and Schuster, 1966); K. A. Yeomans, *Applied Statistics* (Baltimore: Penguin, 1968), 2: ch. 3. A standard work sponsored by the Social Science Research Council is F. Stephan and P. McCarthy, *Sampling Opinions* (New York: John Wiley & Sons, 1958).

Probability

All of the above questions ask whether the sampling results are different enough from chance results to be accurate, and not due to a misleading survey. To answer this sort of question it is obviously necessary to know what chance results would be expected. This has to do with probability.

Probability begins with *counting*. Counting "how many" can refer to two things: how many *permutations* (how many different arrangement sequences of a given number of things) and how many *combinations* (how many sets of things, without considering order or sequence). In mathematical notation, $_nP_n$ is the number of permutations of all n things out of a set of n things; $_nP_r$ is the number of permutations of r things out of a set of n things. Similarly, $_nC_n$ is the number of combinations of n things out of a set of size n; $_nC_r$ is the number of combinations of r things out of a set of n things.[6]

TABLE 8.1   Counting Formulas for a Set of n Things,
Each of Them Different from the Other

$$_nP_n = n!$$
$$_nP_r = n!/(n-r)!$$
$$_nC_n = 1$$
$$_nC_r = \binom{n}{r} = n!/(n-r)!\, r!$$

Let's try some examples. Suppose we want to know how many slates are possible given ten candidates for four positions. If the four positions are all the same, then we are interested in combinations (since a slate of four people for four identical offices can be listed in any order or sequence). Thus we want $_{10}C_4$:

$$_{10}C_4 = \frac{10!}{(10-4)!4!} = 210$$

We see that given ten possible candidates for four positions, it is possible to have 210 slates of four candidates each. Suppose that four close friends among the ten want to know what the chances are for them all to be the ones put on the slate by random selection. Since they are only one out of 210 combinations of four, their chances are 1/210, or less than one-half percent.

---

[6]The exclamation point expression (!) in mathematics is called a "factorial". It instructs the researcher to multiply 1 times 2 times 3, etc., all the way up to the number in question. For example, 6! = 1 x 2 x 3 x 4 x 5 x 6 = 720.

If the four positions are all different, then it *does* make a difference in what order or sequence the four candidates on the slate are listed. Even among the same four people, different orders of listing would pair each of the four with a different office, resulting in different slates. Thus, if the positions are all different, we are interested in permutations, and specifically in $_{10}P_4$:

$$_{10}P_4 = \frac{10!}{(10-4)!} = 5040$$

By using the permutation formula, we find that there are 5,040 arrangements of four candidates out of a possible ten.

TABLE 8.2 Computing Formulas for a Set of n Things, Not All of
Them Different from the Other

$_nP_{n_1,n_2,\ldots,n_k}$	$=$	$n!/\,n_1!\,n_2!\cdots n_k!$
$_nC_{n_1,n_2,\ldots,n_k}$	$=$	1

When the set of n things are not all different, and instead include subsets $n_1, n_2, \ldots, n_k$, each of which contains the same things, then the number of permutations will be less than $n!$ (The number of combinations of n out of n things, similar or different, will remain 1, of course.) Thus, for example, we might want to know how many seating arrangements by party affiliation there are of four people, two of them Democrats and two Republicans. The answer is $_1P_{2,2}$:

$$_4P_{2,2} = \frac{4!}{2!\,2!} = 6$$

There are six seating arrangements by party for four individuals, two of each party.

TABLE 8.3 Computing Formula for Permutations When
Recurrences Are Permitted

$_nP_r$ with recurrences permitted $= n^r$

Sometimes we face a situation in which we are interested in the number of arrangements of n things, when any of the things can be used more than once. Seven-digit telephone numbers are such an example, since any digit can be repeated at any place in the sequence. Since there are ten possible digits, and we might be interested in obtaining the number of seven-digit sequences allowing recurrences of numbers, we would wish to know 10^7. Thus, there are 10,000,000 such seven-digit sequences.

TABLE 8.4   Formula for Computing the Number of Combinations of any Size from Among n Things

$$_nC_{0,1,\ldots,n} = 2^n$$

Finally, we are sometimes interested in the number of combinations *of any size* from among n things. If there are four possible committee members, and the committee can be any size, then there are $2^4 = 16$ possible committees, including the null committee of no members.

We are now ready to consider how probabilities are computed. First, read the following list of probability terms:

$P(A)$	the probability of condition A occurring, where probability varies from .00 = no chance to 1.00 = certainty.
$P(A \cup B)$	the probability of A *or* B occurring
$P(A \cap B)$	the probability of A *and* B occurring
$P(A \mid B)$	the probability of A occurring, given the occurrence of B
independent events	two or more events such that a given outcome of the first does not change the outcome chances of the second or later events (e.g., throws of dice)
dependent events	two or more events such that the given outcome of the first alters the outcome chances of the second and later events (e.g., the chances of being picked for a team are different on the second pick because the first pick eliminated one person)

Now let us suppose that four people have been chosen for a committee, two Democrats (Ds) and two Republicans (Rs). Suppose further that some random process is to be used to arrange these four individuals in order, with the first individual picked to serve as chairperson and the last to be merely an alternate member of the committee. This involves *dependent* events, since the first pick eliminates a person, altering the chances for the remaining people on later picks. For comparison purposes we may also consider a similar situation involving *independent* events: four, repeated, random dips into a bag containing one chip marked D and one chip marked R, replacing the chosen chip after each dip.

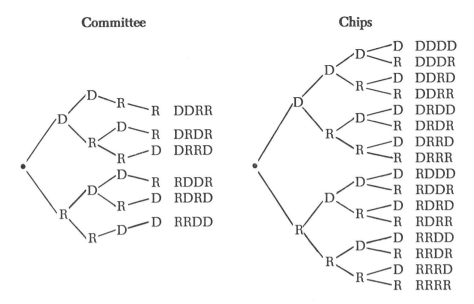

FIGURE 8.2   Probability Trees for Committee and Chips Examples

With the committee, we have $_4P_{2,2}$ = six possible arrangements, and with the chips, we have $_2P_4$ with recurrences = 2^4 = 16 possible arrangements. These arrangements of Rs and Ds are shown in the *probability trees* in Figure 8.2. The chips assume a larger property space (have more permutations) because they are not restricted to two Ds and two Rs only.

TABLE 8.5   Probability Rules for Independent and Dependent Events

Independent Events (chips)		Dependent Events (the committee)
$P(A)$ $=$	$\dfrac{\text{number of events corresponding to A}}{\text{total number of events}}$	same
$P(A \cap B) = P(A) \cdot P(B)$		$P(A \cap B) = P(A) \cdot P(B\|A)$
$P(A \cup B) = P(A) + P(B) - P(A \cap B)$		same
$P(A\|B)$ $= P(A)$		$P(A\|B) = \dfrac{P(A \cap B)}{P(B)}$

Now let A equal picking a Democrat or a D-chip first, and B equal picking a Republican or R-chip last. What is the chance of getting a Democrat or D-chip first? Of getting a Republican or R-chip last? Of getting *both* a Democrat first and a Republican last? Of getting both a D-chip first and an R-chip last? Of getting a Democrat first *or* a Republican last? Of getting a D-chip first or an R-chip last? Of getting a Democrat first, given a Republican is last? Of getting a D-chip first, given an R-chip last? These questions can be answered using the probability rules in Table 8.6, as illustrated for our particular example in Table 8.6.

TABLE 8.6   Probabilities in the Committees and Chips Examples

Chips Example (independent events)	Committee Example (dependent events)
$P(A) = \dfrac{\text{number of events corresponding to } A}{\text{total number of events}}$	$P(A) =$ same formula
$= \dfrac{_2P_3 \text{ with recurrences}}{_2P_4 \text{ with recurrences}}$	$= \dfrac{_3P_{2,1}}{_4P_{2,2}}$
$= \dfrac{8}{16} = \dfrac{1}{2}$	$= \dfrac{3}{6} = \dfrac{1}{2}$
$P(B) =$ same formula, same result as above	$P(B) =$ same formula, same result as above
$= \dfrac{1}{2}$	$= \dfrac{1}{2}$
$P(A \cap B) = P(A) \cdot P(B)$	$P(A \cap B) = P(A) \cdot P(B/A)$
$= \dfrac{1}{2} \cdot \dfrac{1}{2} = \dfrac{1}{4}$	$= \dfrac{1}{2} \cdot \dfrac{_2P_{1,1}}{_3P_{2,1}}$
	$= \dfrac{1}{2} \cdot \dfrac{2}{3} = \dfrac{1}{3}$
$P(A \cup B) = P(A) + P(B) - P(A \cap B)$	$P(A \cup B) =$ same formula
$= \dfrac{1}{2} + \dfrac{1}{2} - \dfrac{1}{4} = \dfrac{3}{4}$	$= \dfrac{1}{2} + \dfrac{1}{2} - \dfrac{1}{3} = \dfrac{2}{3}$
$P(A \mid B) = P(A)$	$P(A \mid B) = \dfrac{P(A \cap B)}{P(B)}$
$= \dfrac{1}{2}$	$= \dfrac{1/3}{1/2} = \dfrac{2}{3}$

To take the chips example first, since there are only two chips, it is obvious that the chance of getting a D-chip on the first (or any) draw is ½. More complex examples cannot be so easily intuited, so it is worth understanding the full reasoning process. The chance of getting a D-chip first equals the number of permutations on the last three draws (after the first draw is set aside as a D-chip), divided by the number of permutations on all four draws. This gives us 8/16, or a probability of .5. The remaining steps simply apply the probability rules. If the chance of getting a D-chip first is .5 and the chance of getting an R-chip last is .5, the probability of getting both is .5 times .5 or .25. (Thus, *the joint probability of two independent events is the product of their individual probabilities.*) When we subtract this joint probability from the sum of their individual probabilities we get the chance of getting one *or* the other, which in this case is .75. Since independence of events means that the outcome of one event doesn't affect another, it is unimportant to find out that the probability of getting a D-chip first given an R-chip last is just the same as the probability of getting a D-chip in the first place, or .5 in this example.

Somewhat similar reasoning but different rules apply in the case of the committee, because we must adjust for the fact that once an individual is chosen, he or she is out of consideration. The probability of getting a Democratic chairperson (i.e., a Democratic picked first) is the number of permutations among the three remaining slots (for which there are two Republicans and one Democrat) once we set aside the first slot for a Democrat, divided by the total number of permutations of four people, two of each of two types. That probability, as worked out in Table 8.6, is .5. There is a 50 percent chance of getting a Democratic chairperson. The chance of getting a Democratic chairperson and a Republican alternate is the chance of the former, .5, times the chance of getting a Republican alternate, given a Democrat as chairperson. This chance is the number of permutations among the two individuals who remain after we set aside the chairperson slot for a Democrat and the alternate slot for a Republican divided by the permutations among the three people who remain after the chairperson slot is set aside for a Democrat. Again, as worked out in Table 8.6, the answer is one-third. Simple application of the probability rules results in the last two findings: that the chance of getting a Democratic chairperson *or* a Republican alternate is two-thirds, and the chance of getting a Democratic chairperson given a Republican as alternate is also two-thirds.[7]

Measures of Variation

In addition to measures of central tendency or averages, discussed earlier, another convenient statistic for summarizing one's data is the measure of how much spread there is around the central tendency. For example, in measuring age in a sample survey we might wish to know if most people are very close to the average age—is the group homogeneous? Or is there a wide spread from young to old, with only a few within a year of the average age? *Variance*, the measure of this spread around the central tendency, is based on how much each unit (each person's age, for example) deviates from the

[7]For further reading, see Frederick Mosteller, Robert Rourke, and George Thomas, *Probability with Statistical Applications* (Reading, Mass.: Addison-Wesley, 1961); Bernard Gelbaum and James March, *Mathematics for the Social and Behavioral Sciences* (Philadelphia: Saunders, 1969), chs. 3 and 4.

mean (the mean age in this example). Since this involves subtracting, *deviation measures of variance can only be used with interval, or ratio, data.* Although often ignored in political science, this rule is especially important since a great amount of survey data are nominal or ordinal. *Q* dispersion, discussed in Chapter 9, measures ordinal variance.

The difference between the unit score *x* (a given person's age), and the average score $\bar{x}$ (the mean age for a list of people), is called a *deviation*. The mean deviation is derived from the absolute values of all the *x* scores on a list added up and divided by the number of items in the list, *n*. Absolute value means ignoring the plus or minus sign; if raw values of the deviations were added, the sum would be zero by definition of the mean. Unfortunately, taking absolute values interferes with later statistical inferences one may want to make. However, it is possible to get rid of the signs by squaring the *x* values, then adjusting by dividing through by *n*. That gives the formula for the *variance*, σ^2. (See footnote 8.)

$$\sigma^2 = \frac{\Sigma(x - \bar{x})^2}{n}$$

The *standard deviation*, σ, is simply the square root of the variance.

When dealing with samples rather than complete enumerations, the researcher divides by $(n - 1)$ rather than *n*. This modification for *sample variance*, s^2, and *sample standard deviation*, *s*, serves to give a conservative estimate preferred by statisticians when dealing with samples.

There is one further statistic of variation that should be mentioned. In one sample of people's ages, the researcher could compute the mean age as a measure of central tendency, and also compute the standard deviation of age as a measure of the spread of sample ages around the mean. But if several samples were taken, then the researcher could compute several means; in fact, he could compute the mean of all the sample means, the *grand mean*, and also compute the spread of sample means around the grand mean. This measure of the variations of sample means from the grand mean of many samples (from the same population universe) is called the *standard error* (SE), and is approximated by dividing the sample standard deviation *s* by the square root of the sample size minus 1, or $\sqrt{n - 1}$. This means that the standard error is always smaller than the standard deviation; the variation of the sample mean from a hypothetical grand mean will be less than the variation of sample scores from the sample mean.

Example Begin with a list, in this case a list of labor riot frequencies by year for the 1930s in America.

For ten observations (years; $n = 10$) a sum of 200 riots were recorded ($\Sigma x = 200$). This is an enumeration, not a sample. The *x* scores (riot frequencies) are metric data.

---

[8]Note that "Σ" means "the sum of." The Greek letter "σ," sigma, is used in connection with population data. For sample data the letter "*s*" is used.

The sum of the squared deviations is 1322. To get the standard deviation this is divided by n (not $n - 1$ as would be the case with a sample) and the square root is taken.*

Standard error is computed by dividing the standard deviation by the square root of n (square root of 10 in this case). But note that since this is an enumeration and not a sample, standard error has no meaning in this case. The mean of an enumeration *is* the true mean; hence it makes no sense to talk about deviations of the computed mean from some grand mean.

TABLE 8.7   Labor Riot Frequencies

Year	x	$(x-\bar{x})^2$
1930	3	289
1931	28	64
1932	21	1
1933	17	9
1934	37	289
1935	30	100
1936	31	121
1937	22	4
1938	2	324
1939	9	121
$n=10$	$\Sigma x=200$	1322

$\bar{x} = 200/10 = 20$

$\sigma = \sqrt{1322/10} = 11.50$

$SE = 11.50/\sqrt{10} = 3.64$

$\sigma = \dfrac{\Sigma x^2}{n} - \bar{x}^2$

The Normal Distribution

The rules of probability and the measures of variation are both important in the concept of the normal distribution, the key to assessing the significance of sample survey results. Look back at the chips example in the probability tree shown in Figure 8.2. There you will find that there were sixteen permutations of two things taken four at a time with recurrences allowed (P with recurrences $= 16$): one permutation of all Ds, four permutations of three Ds and one R, six permutations of two Ds and two Rs, four permutations of one D and three Rs, and one permutation of all Rs. This distribution is shown in the bar graph in Figure 8.3.

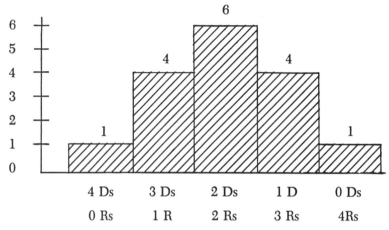

FIGURE 8.3   Distribution of Two Things, Each with a 0.5 Probability of Occurrence, Taken Four at a Time with Recurrences Allowed

This distribution is called a *binomial distribution*. In the chips example we had two outcomes: R and D. Actually, most situations can be thought of in terms of two outcomes: success (with a probability p of occurring) or failure (with a probability of occurring of $q = 1 - p$). The binomial distribution is a function of the probability of success, the probability of failure, and the number of trials. If we arbitrarily consider getting a D-chip to be success, then $p = \frac{1}{2}$ in our example; $q = 1 - \frac{1}{2} = \frac{1}{2}$; and the number of trials is four.

The formula for the binomial expansion, which gives us the distribution such as that shown in Figure 8.3, is shown in Table 8.8.

TABLE 8.8   Formula for the Binomial Expansion, with Example

General formula: $(p + q)^n$

Example: $(p + q)^4 = 1p^4 + 4p^3q + 6p^2q^2 + 4pq^3 + 1q^4$

$$(\frac{1}{2} + \frac{1}{2})^4 = \frac{1}{16} + \frac{4}{16} + \frac{6}{16} + \frac{4}{16} + \frac{1}{16}$$

Thus when p is $\frac{1}{2}$, q is $\frac{1}{2}$, and the number of trials, n, is 4, one-sixteenth of the permutations will be four successes (four of what p corresponds to); four-sixteenths will be three successes and one failure; six-sixteenths will be two successes and two failures; four-sixteenths will be one success and three failures; and one-sixteenth will be four failures. Since we know the number of permutations is sixteen, we know that by the rules of chance that out of those possible outcomes, 1 should be all successes, 4 should be three successes and one failure, etc. In other words, we can compute the distribution in Figure 8.3 without having to draw the tree diagram in Figure 8.2.

Now let us notice something else. In Table 8.8, the n in the formula for the binomial expansion is 4 for our example. When expanded, this gave five components in the equation (p^4 is one component, $4p^3q$ is a second component, etc.). These five components corresponded to the five bars in the bar graph in Figure 8.3 If the n were higher, the number of bars in the bar graph would be more. With only five bars in the graph, the steps from one bar to the next are very distinct; the curve formed by these bars is not smooth. If we had more bars, the steps between bars would be smaller and the curve would be smoother. In fact, mathematicians have proved that when n is reasonably large (say, 20 or more) in a binomial expansion, the binomial curve comes very close to what we call the *normal curve.*

The standard normal curve occurs when the distribution represented by the normal curve has a mean of zero and when one standard deviation equals one measurement unit. For example, to express the riot frequencies in *standard scores* (z scores) rather than raw scores (x scores), one simply subtracts the mean, 20 in the previous example—this gives the distribution a mean of zero—and divides by the standard deviation, 11.5—this gives the distribution a standard deviation of one.

The standard normal curve, illustrated in Figure 8.4, has certain useful properties. If the distribution is normally distributed—and many political science variables are *not*, including dichotomous variables like sex and party, nominal variables like region—then a certain proportion of the universe will lie within one standard deviation of the mean (namely, 34.13 percent on one side or roughly ⅔ on both sides. Approximately 95 percent of

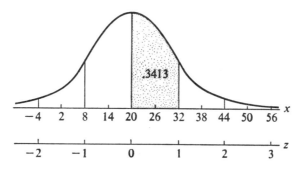

FIGURE 8.4   Standard Normal Curve

the universe will lie within two standard deviations either way of the mean. About 99 percent will lie within three. The exact proportions can be read easily from Table 3 in the Appendix.

Applications to Sampling   Suppose one has taken a sample and computed the sample mean and sample standard deviation as 12 and 1.1, respectively. The normal table enables us to say that we can be about 95 percent sure that any given sample measurement will lie within two (actually 1.96) standard deviations of the mean; or any given sample measurement will lie within plus or minus 1.96 times 1.1 of the mean, 12.

More important, if the standard error in this sample is .20, then we can say that the sample mean (in this case 12) lies within plus or minus 1.96 (the number of standard errors one way or the other from the mean that mark off 95 percent of the area under the normal curve) times .20 of the real mean, with 95 percent confidence. These plus or minus limits are called *confidence limits*. The 95 percent confidence level is often considered the minimum acceptable level, meaning that in 100 samples from the same universe, in 95 percent of these the sample mean will fall within the stated confidence limits of the real mean. The 98 percent, 99 percent, and 99.9 percent levels are also used in more rigorous studies.

Tests of Hypotheses   These same sorts of inferences can be used to test *hypotheses about means*. A hypothesis of this type would be as follows:

> Someone claims the average age of U. S. senators is fifty-five, but you think it is higher. You take a sample of senators' ages and find the sample mean age is sixty-one—but is sixty-one significantly different from fifty-five? Or could this just be due to a chance sample when the real mean age was fifty-five?

We could ask the same question this way: If we hypothesize a normal distribution around mean age of 55 and take samples from this distribution, what percentage of the time would we get a sample mean age of 61 or higher? The shaded area to the right of the normal curve in Figure 8.5 represents that chance. The chance of getting a sample mean 6 units (years,

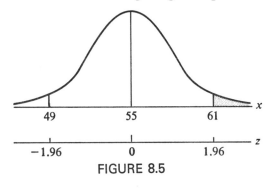

FIGURE 8.5

in this case) away from the hypothesized real mean, 55, is equal to the area to the right of 61 and to the left of 49 on the normal curve. This would be a *two-tailed test* because it looks at both sides of the normal distribution.

Note that 1.96 z units (normal standard deviations or normal standard errors) corresponds to .4750 of the area under the normal curve.[9] Thus, if the distance from 55 to 61 and from 55 to 49 is equal to 1.96 or more, then the proportion under both tails would be .05 or less. This means that only .05 of the time would such a difference occur by chance.[10]

On the other hand, our original question calls for a *one-tailed test*, because we are not interested in the chance of getting a sample mean age 6 years *different* (greater or less, referring to both tails of the curve), but only the chance of getting a sample mean 6 years *greater* (referring to the right-side tail only) by chance. If 61 were 1.96 standard errors away from 55, then the proportion under *one tail* would be .025 (computed exactly as above), meaning that a sample mean 6 years higher or more would occur by chance only 2.5 percent of the time.

An easy formula for testing hypotheses about means involves simply taking the difference between the sample mean and the hypothesized real mean, between 61 and 55, and dividing by the standard error of the sample. But when the z score is computed this way, the researcher must be careful to decide whether he is interested in greater-or-less relationships (two tails) or only greater or only less relationships (one tail). The following examples show sample formulas for hypothesis testing.

One Sample Formula for z Values in Testing Hypotheses About Means

$$z = \frac{\bar{x} - \mu_0}{s/\sqrt{n-1}}$$

Where $\bar{x}$ = the sample mean

μ_o = the hypothesized real mean

s = the sample standard deviation (logically should be the real but unknown standard deviation)

n = the sample size

After z is computed, consult the normal table to see if the number of z units obtained mark off enough area under the normal curve, as in Figure 8.5. For instance, 1.96 z units either way mark off 95 percent of the area; if the sample mean is more than 1.96 z units away from the hypothesized real

---

[9]This fraction can be read directly from Table III.

[10]Note that .05 is obtained by subtracting the proportion 1.96 from the mean, namely .4750, from half the curve, .5000, thus getting .025; the same is done for the other half of the curve, also getting .025—added together this gives .050.

mean, then we can be 95 percent confident it is different from the hypothesized mean, and 97.5 percent confident it is more than the hypothesized mean (two- and one-tailed tests, respectively).

Note: Since the normal tables assume a relatively large n for this test, when any sample is under 30, the t test should be used. Computation is identical to the z test for larger samples, except that the t tables (Table 4) are used instead of the z tables. To read the t table you need to know "degrees of freedom," which is equal to $n - 1$ in this case. This note applies to the next five formulas as "degrees of freedom" equal $(n_1 + n_2 - 2)$.[11]

One Sample Formula For Testing Hypotheses About Proportions

$$z = \frac{P_o - P_u}{\sqrt{P_u Q_u / n}}$$

Where P_o = the observed sample proportion

P_u = the hypothesized real proportion

Q_u = $1 - P_u$

It frequently happens that we are interested in testing whether or not two samples are significantly different. For example, we may test to see if there are significant differences between means (e.g., to see if the average age of people sampled from City 1 differs from that sampled from City 2), between proportions (e.g., to see if the percentage of Democrats differs between two sampled cities), and between variances (e.g., to see if the spread around the mean is the same for men as for women in two samples, even if the means are the same).

How we test these differences depends on whether our data are correlated or uncorrelated. Here we are *not* talking about whether variables in our sample are correlated (e.g., we are *not* concerned with whether we find income is correlated with political attitude). Instead we are concerned with whether person number 1 in sample number one tends to give the same responses as person number 1 in sample number 2, person 2 in sample 1 the same as person 2 in sample 2, and so on. This happens when our two samples are *before-after tests* of the same individuals, or *matched-pair tests* where

---

[11]The t test assumes (1) normal distribution underlying the data, and (2) equal variances in the two-sample tests, as does the z test. The assumption of normal distribution is checked by the chi-square goodness-of-fit test discussed in Chapter 10. The assumption of equal variance is checked by the F-ratio, discussed later in this chapter. Non-normal distributions are associated with the use of nonparametric tests of significance, discussed in Chapter 10.

NOTE: in comparing two samples in the t test, *when sample size is small*, "degrees of freedom" should *not* equal $(n_1 + n_2 - 2)$; instead the number of degrees of freedom is computed as below:

$$df = \frac{[s_1^2/(n_1 - 1)] + [s_2^2/(n_2 - 1)]^2}{\left[[s_1^2/(n_1 - 1)]^2 \ [1/(n_1 + 1)] \ [s_2^2/(n_2 - 1)]^2 \ [1/(n_2 + 1)] \right]} - 2$$

TABLE 8.9

Test of	Uncorrelated Data	Correlated Data
Means	$$z = \dfrac{\bar{x}_1 - \bar{x}_2}{\sqrt{\left(\dfrac{s_1^2}{n_1-1}\right) + \left(\dfrac{s_2^2}{n_2-1}\right)}}$$	$$z = \dfrac{\bar{x}_1 - \bar{x}_2}{\sqrt{\left(\dfrac{s_1^2}{n_1-1}\right) + \left(\dfrac{s_2^2}{n_2-1}\right) - 2r_{12}\left(\dfrac{s_1}{\sqrt{n_1-1}}\right)\left(\dfrac{s_2}{\sqrt{n_2-1}}\right)}}$$
Proportions	$$z = \dfrac{P_1 - P_2}{\sqrt{\left(\dfrac{P_1Q_1}{n_1}\right) + \left(\dfrac{P_2Q_2}{n_2}\right)}}$$	$$z = \dfrac{P_1 - P_2}{\sqrt{\left(\dfrac{P_1Q_1}{n_1}\right) + \left(\dfrac{P_2Q_2}{n_2}\right) - 2r_{12}\left(\sqrt{\dfrac{P_1Q_1}{n_1}}\right)\left(\sqrt{\dfrac{P_2Q_2}{n_2}}\right)}}$$
Variances	$$F = \dfrac{s_1^2}{s_2^2}$$ Where the larger of the two is the numerator.	$$t = \dfrac{(s_1^2 - s_2^2)\,(\sqrt{n-2}\,)}{\sqrt{4\,s_1^2\,s_2^2\,(1 - r_{12}^2)}}$$

Where $\bar{x}$ = the mean for sample 1 or 2, depending on the subscript
$\quad\;\; s^2$ = the variance of sample 1 or 2
$\quad\;\; s$ = the standard deviation of sample 1 or 2
$\quad\;\; p$ = the proportion in sample 1 or 2
$\quad\;\; q$ = $1 - p$
$\quad\;\; r_{12}$ = the Pearsonian correlation between samples 1 and 2, discussed in Chapter 12
$\quad\;\; n$ = the sample size of sample 1 or 2

we make sure that for each person in sample 1 there is a similar (e.g., in respect to age, race, income) person in sample 2. The correlation between the individuals in sample 1 and the individuals in sample 2 is the Pearsonian correlation, r_{12}. Look at the tests of differences between two samples given in Table 8.9. The tests for correlated data all contain an adjustment for this correlation, r_{12}. How to compute correlations is discussed in Chapter 12. For now we only need to know that we cannot use the same formulas for correlated data as for uncorrelated data. Fortunately, most political science samples are uncorrelated and therefore involve the simpler formulas given on the lefthand side of the table.

Since the formulas for tests of differences between means and between proportions are computed in the same way as in one-sample test examples already discussed, here we will look only at tests of differences between variances. The *F-ratio* test to see if the variance of one sample is different from that of another sample is very easy. It is simply the larger of the variances divided by the smaller. (Recall the formula for a variance.) After we divide, we look in the *F* table (Table 6). The *F* table requires that we know the number of "degrees of freedom." For the *F* ratio, the first such number is $(n - 1)$ for the larger sample; the second is $(n - 1)$ for the smaller sample. If our computed *F* is as large or larger than the number found in the *F* table we can reject the null hypothesis that the variances of the two samples are not different. For correlated data a more complicated formula using the *t* statistic is employed, but the same reasoning is involved.[12]

Other Distributions

Normal distribution is appropriate when the units involved are normally distributed. A later chapter will give a way of testing to see if a variable is normally distributed; for now we should recognize that there are other distributions, such as those illustrated in Figure 8.6.

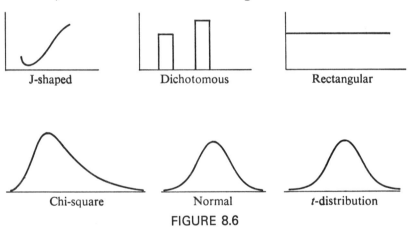

FIGURE 8.6

In the example just mentioned, one might think that the variable used (political party, divided into Democratic and non-Democratic) is a dichotomous variable and hence cannot be used in *parametric tests*—tests that assume a particular distribution as *z* tests assume a normal distribution. An

[12]For further discussion, see: D. Adkins, *Statistics* (Columbus, Ohio: Merrill, 1964), ch. 15; V. Senders, *Measurement and Statistics* (New York: Oxford, 1958), ch. 14; and N. Downie and R. Heath, *Basic Statistical Methods*, 2nd ed. (New York: Harper and Row, 1965), chs. 11 and 12.

important distinction must be made here. If we were working with the distribution of *parties* per se, then the z test could not be used. However, in the example, we were working with the distribution of *voters*, which is quite a different matter. Similarly, party is a nominal-level variable and cannot be meaningfully added. Letting Democrat=1 and non-Democrat=2, it makes no sense to add to get 3. But voters is a metric-level variable and hence the arithmetic operations involved in z tests are permissible.

The beginning researcher should understand that although an impressive array of statistics is built on the normal distribution as a parameter, there is nothing sacred about the normal distribution. Variables used in political analysis may very well *not* be normally distributed. It is even conceivable to make up one's own "ideal" distribution and work out a statistics based on that! The *t distribution* is a distribution similar but not identical to the normal distribution, and is used when sample size n is less than 30. The researcher simply uses a table of the t distribution instead of tables of the normal (z) distribution in an analogous manner. Finally, the *chi-square distribution* (X^2), where

$$X^2 = \frac{(n-1)s^2}{\sigma^2},$$

based on sample and real standard deviations, is used in nonparametric tests of significance of tables (normal distribution not assumed), to be discussed in a later chapter.

Computing Sample Size

"How do we know in advance how large a sample we need to take?" *We need to take a sample big enough so that the variable with the largest ratio of standard deviation to tolerance limits will still have a sample mean that falls within a tolerated limit of the real but unknown mean, the desired percentage of the time.* For example, suppose the variable with the largest such ratio is age. We then want a sample large enough so that some high percentage of the time (say 95 percent of the time), the sample mean age would be within plus or minus the limit chosen, e.g., ± 2 years of the real (population) mean age.

The formula for sample size is given below, where σ is the standard deviation of the variable with the largest variance, z is the number of normal standard deviations (z units) corresponding to the desired percentage of the area under the normal curve (1.96 z units to get 95 percent of the area either side of the mean, in this example), and T is the tolerated variation of the sample (2 in this case):

$$ss = (\sigma z/T)^2$$

Thus the bigger the standard deviation (the more variation), the larger the sample size. The higher the confidence level desired (the bigger the z), the larger the sample size needed. And the smaller the confidence limits desired (the smaller the T), the larger the sample size needed.

How does the survey researcher get the values to "plug into" this formula? He or she makes an educated guess. The z and T values are arbitrary, chosen by the researcher according to how rigorous the study is to be. The σ value (sigma, the standard deviation) is the hard part; σ is not known at all, and the sample standard deviation s is not known either, prior to taking the sample. The best that can be done is to take a small pretest sample, mentioned earlier, and compute the pretest sample standard deviations for each variable. The largest pretest s is increased by some arbitrary amount (say 10 percent) to be on the conservative side and is used as an educated guess of σ in the sample size equation.

Note that, if a sample is truly random, the size of the real universe is irrelevant. Given the expected deviations, the desired confidence level, and limits, the same sample size would be appropriate whether the universe were a thousand or a million. Second, if the researcher plans on breaking the survey data down into subtables, each of which he or she hopes will be sensitive to (significant for) small relationships, the sample size must be even larger. This is dealt with by a chi-square method discussed in Chapter 10.

Extrapolating from a Sample to a Population Estimate

Suppose a sample of 20 out of the 120 months in a decade is taken and the number of riots for those sample months is determined to be 25. One might then want to estimate how many riots occurred during the whole decade, not just in the sample months. Since 120 months is six times 20 months, one could estimate that the entire decade had six times as many riots as the sample 20 months, 6 x 25 = 150 riots for the decade. This is called the simple *blow-up estimate*.

Having just one sample, the blow-up estimate is the only possible one. However, in a situation where a series of samples are taken, different methods may be used. Suppose a researcher stood outside a polling place, asked a random sample of people how they voted, and made a blow-up estimate of the total vote for a particular party at that place. Later he or she might find out the actual vote and what his error was. The next time this survey is taken, knowledge of past error can be used to improve his estimate.

One way is to assume that the same percent of *error* will occur the second time. Thus, if the percent voting Democratic was overestimated by 10 percent the first time, compute the second simple blow-up and decrease it by 10 percent to get the *ratio estimate*. Or it could be assumed that the same absolute error will be made the second time. Thus, if the number voting

Democratic is underestimated the first time by 800, then add 800 to the second blow-up to get the *difference estimate.* Or, a fraction of the absolute error could be added, that fraction being the regression coefficient, discussed in a later chapter, for the *regression estimate.* [13]

Review: Taking a Sample of Legislators' Ages

Step 1.   Estimate sample size. Set arbitrary desired confidence level (e.g., 95 percent level, z equals 1.96) and arbitrary limits (e.g., $T = 6$). Take a small sample of, say, 10 legislators and compute the standard deviation as shown in Table 8.10.

TABLE 8.10

Pretest sample ages, x	$(x-\bar{x})^2$
49	27.0
38	262.4
59	23.0
81	718.2
44	104.0
64	96.0
59	23.0
49	27.0
38	262.4
61	46.2
$\Sigma x = 542$	$\Sigma (x-\bar{x})^2 = 1589.2$
$n = 10$	
$\bar{x} = 54.2$	

$$s = \sqrt{\frac{\Sigma (x-\bar{x})^2}{n-1}} = \sqrt{\frac{1589.2}{9}} = \sqrt{176.6} = 13.3$$

$$s' = 13.3 + .10 (13.3) = 14.6$$

$$\text{sample size} = (\sigma z/T)^2 = 14.6 \times 1.96/6)^2 \cong 23$$

If we randomly sample 23 legislators from a real population of any number of normally distributed (by age) legislators, then 95 percent of the time our sample mean age would be within 6 years of the real mean age.

---

[13]See: Slonim, *Sampling in a Nutshell.*

Note that multi-stage sampling requires some refinements as compared with simple random samples. These are discussed in K. Schuessler, *Analyzing Social Data* (Boston: Houghton Mifflin, 1971), ch. 6; and B. Lazerwitz, "Sampling Theory and Procedures," in Hubert Blalock and Ann Blalock, eds., *Methodology in Social Research* (New York: McGraw-Hill, 1968), ch. 8. Such complex probability samples generate wider confidence limits for the same sample size.

General discussion of topics in this chapter is contained in B. Lieberman, ed., *Contemporary Problems in Statistics* (New York: Oxford, 1971), sec. 2; R. Kirk, *Statistical Issues* (Monterey, Cal.: Brooks-Cole, 1972).

Step 2. Select the sample of 23 from a list of all legislators using a table of random numbers. Compute the measure of central tendency, mean, measure of variation, sample standard deviation, and standard error. (See Table 8.11.)

TABLE 8.11

sample	$(x-\bar{x})$	$(x-\bar{x})^2$
57	5	25
53	1	1
50	−2	4
58	6	36
66	14	196
45	−7	49
48	−4	16
51	−1	1
53	1	1
61	9	81
60	8	64
44	−8	64
42	−10	100
69	17	289
42	−10	100
45	−7	49
54	2	4
46	−6	36
51	−1	1
50	−2	4
65	13	169
48	−4	16
45	−7	49
$\Sigma x = \overline{1203}$		$\overline{1355} = \Sigma (x-\bar{x})^2$

$$\text{mean} = 1203/93 \cong 52$$

$$\text{standard deviation} = s = \sqrt{\frac{\Sigma (x-\bar{x})^2}{n-1}}$$

$$= \sqrt{\frac{1355}{22}} = \sqrt{61.6} \cong 7.8$$

$$\text{standard error} = s/\sqrt{n-1}$$

$$= 7.8/\sqrt{22}$$

$$\cong 1.7$$

EXERCISE

It is frequently asserted that Defense Department spending on domestic military installations favors the South. This is attributed to the tendency of Congressional committees dealing with defense to be chaired by Southerners (because of their high seniority due to the relative noncompetitiveness of their districts). Table 8.12 below lists defense Department payrolls by state for fiscal year 1972; these figures can be used to check this assertion.

Use Table VII (Random Numbers) to select a random sample of fifteen states, stratified by region. Have two regions: the South (for this example, the following ten states: Alabama, Arkansas, Florida, Georgia, Louisiana, Mississippi, North and South Carolina, Texas, and Virginia) and the non-South. To stratify, make separate lists of the states in each region (e.g., the Southern states numbered 01 through 10, and the non-Southern states numbered 01 through 40). To use the random number table, set each number of the list of states for the South equal to a set of two-digit random numbers, such that each state will be equally likely to be chosen. (E.g., let state number 01 equal random digits 01 through 10, state 02 equal to 11 through 20, etc.) Do the same for the forty non-Southern states, setting each equal to a set of three-digit random numbers (e.g., let state 01 equal random numbers 001 through 025, state 02 equal to random numbers 026 through 050, and so on).

Since the number of Southern states is ten out of fifty states, under stratified sampling we want one-fifth of our sample of fifteen to be Southern states and four-fifths to be non-Southern. Using these proportions, select randomly the appropriate number of Southern and non-Southern states for analysis.

Is the mean personnel payroll higher for the South than the non-South? Is the difference in means between the two groups significant at the .05 level? Do the variances of the two samples differ?

Now use the population figures in Table 8.12 to compute data for defense payroll per 1,000 population. Is the same difference in means found? The same difference in variances? What do you conclude about the assertion outlined in the first paragraph? (Be careful: outline the explanatory model in the first paragraph in this exercise; list the asserted relationships; identify which of the several relationships the data you just computed bear on; and discuss whether this data supports that particular asserted relationship; then try to imagine if any other hypothetical relationship would *both* be consistent with your data *and* inconsistent with the explanatory model of the first paragraph.)

TABLE 8.12

State	Defense Department Payroll (in 1,000,000's)	Population (in 1,000's)
Alabama	457	3,444
Alaska	259	300
Arizona	335	1,771
Arkansas	129	1,923
California	3,506	19,953
Colorado	514	2,207
Connecticut	72	3,032
Delaware	70	548

TABLE 8.12   (continued)

State	Defense Department Payroll (in 1,000,000's)	Population (in 1,000's)
Florida	877	6,789
Georgia	788	4,590
Hawaii	520	769
Idaho	52	713
Illinois	584	11,114
Indiana	230	5,194
Iowa	20	2,824
Kansas	305	2,247
Kentucky	419	3,219
Louisiana	295	3,641
Maine	75	992
Maryland	899	3,922
Massachusetts	366	5,689
Michigan	241	8,875
Minnesota	58	3,805
Mississippi	262	2,217
Missouri	441	4,677
Montana	68	694
Nebraska	155	1,483
Nevada	100	489
New Hampshire	126	738
New Jersey	605	7,168
New Mexico	240	1,016
New York	442	18,237
North Carolina	754	5,082
North Dakota	129	618
Ohio	574	10,652
Oklahoma	552	2,559
Oregon	50	2,091
Pennsylvania	769	11,794
Rhode Island	199	947
South Carolina	574	2,591
South Dakota	67	666
Tennessee	164	3,924
Texas	1,993	11,197
Utah	325	1,059
Vermont	7	444
Virginia	1,806	4,648
Washington	554	3,409
West Virginia	19	1,744
Wisconsin	47	4,418
Wyoming	41	332

9 | Scaling

Scaling is a measuring technique. Many concepts in political science cannot be measured by counting "natural" units such as votes. For example, power, welfare, and alienation are important concepts in political theory that cannot be easily quantified. Scales are a means of measuring important variables that cannot simply be counted in natural units. Figure 9.1 shows that the abstract variable "happiness," which lies along a continuum with no natural dividing points, can be measured by a scale made up of *items* (eleven in this case) assumed to represent arbitrary points on the true continuum.

True Happiness   True Unhappiness
in extreme   in extreme
                    True Underlying Continuum
_____

                              Scale
_____
   1   2   3   4   5   6   7   8   9   10   11
Measured   Measured
Happiness   Unhappiness
in extreme   in extreme

FIGURE 9.1 "Happiness Scale"

An individual who agrees with the statement, "I am truly happy" (item 1), might be ranked 1 on the happiness scale. Item 6 might be agreement with the statement, "I don't know if I'm happy or unhappy," while item 11 might be agreement with the statement, "I am truly unhappy." While this is not a "scientific" scale, it does bring out some of the important characteristics of scaling:

1. A scale is a series of ordered items. These items might be answers to questions, votes in a legislative body, or Supreme Court Decisions—used to indicate some unmeasurable abstract variable, such as "conservativeness."

2. The items constitute an ordinal level of measurement. Point 2 on the happiness scale represents more happiness than point 3, but we cannot assume that the distance between points is equal in each case. Some researchers have sought to develop near-interval level scales. In better social science scales, intervals are less than equal but more than randomly unequal; such scales are somewhere between the ordinal and interval level of measurement.

3. The true underlying continuum assumed to be measured by the scale is represented by a single line. This is because the underlying continuum is presumed to be *unidimensional.* That is, happiness is assumed to be a single concept and not an umbrella term encompassing many sometimes inconsistent subconcpets. Related to this, the scale is obviously assumed to measure the underlying continuum. Whether or not the "happiness scale" really measures true happiness is the question of *validity.* The ways of testing validity are discussed in Chapter 1.

4. It is also assumed that the scale is *reproducible,* that it could be reliably applied twice and get the same results, all other things equal.

There are many examples of simple, untested scales—scales with unknown validity and reproducibility. For example, one might ask a respondent directly, "From 1 equaling most liberal to 8 equaling least liberal, how liberal are you?" The respondent's answer would be his scale score. Of course such a direct method is too blunt a research instrument. Respondents would have difficulty, for example, in agreeing on the meaning of intermediate scale values like 6—is 6 "somewhat liberal" or "fairly liberal" or "rather liberal?"

Such direct "self-scaling" is not used in political science; instead, some more indirect measurement is used. For instance, in the sociometric tests discussed in Chapter 7, the number of times an individual is chosen by others can be used as a scale of popularity. Another example is the widely used "Bogardus Social Distance Scale," used to measure the "social distance" between groups.

The Bogardus Scale uses seven items, ranging from 1 = "Would admit blacks (or the name of some other group) to close kinship by marriage," through 4 = "Would admit blacks to employment in my occupation," to 7 = "Would exclude blacks from my country." The respondent's score is the lowest item he endorses. This scale might be administered to a cross-section of Americans, their scores averaged, and a "racial distance quotient" between blacks and the general population could be computed. Alternatively, this scale could be administered to a cross-section of blacks, asking them to respond to the scale for each of a number of other ethnic groups (English, Poles, Italians, etc.); this would be a second measure of "racial distance" between blacks and others, this time from the point of view of the black citizen. The Bogardus measure can be used in testing such hypotheses as "Groups characterized by higher social distance from others are more likely to be involved in rioting," or "Groups characterized by low social distance from others tend to occupy higher status roles."

THE CLUSTER BLOC TECHNIQUE

The cluster bloc was a technique commonly used before modern scaling techniques were developed, and is still widely used in legislative roll-call analysis, following procedures specified by Stuart Rice and Herman Beyle in the 1920s and early 1930s. Like modern scales, cluster bloc analysis enables the researcher to rank individuals according to some criterion and to group together those who are most alike by this criterion. For example, U.S. senators can be ranked according to their agreements on a set of votes and blocs of like-voting senators can be identified.

1.   Selecting the Set of Votes

The first step is simply to decide which votes are relevant to the researcher's particular study. One study by David Truman looked at issues that divided political parties; "low cohesion" votes were selected by use of the Rice Index of Cohesion (R.I.C.) which equals the percent of Democrats (or some other party) for an issue minus the percent against. Thus it varies from 0 (when 50 percent are for and 50 percent are opposed) to 100 (when 100 percent are for and none are opposed, or vice versa). R.I.C. takes absolute values, ignoring minus signs. A list of low cohesion votes could be those with a Rice Index below some arbitrary level, such as 0.40.[1]

2.   Computing Indices of Agreement

The second step, computing the indices of agreement, requires determining how much any given senator agrees with every other senator for the set of votes selected in the first step. A *simple* index of agreement would be the percent of times the aye votes of a given Senator match the aye votes of each other senator, but this has the unfortunate effect of treating absences as non-agreements. There are two ways of treating absences. First, in any pair if

---

[1]For further discussion of the Rice Index of Cohesion, see: S. Rice, "Measuring Cohesion in Legislative Groups," in J. Wahlke and H. Eulau, eds., *Legislative Behavior* (Glencoe, Ill.: Free Press, 1959), pp. 372–377; T. Casstevens and O. Porterfield, "The Index of Likeness as a Mathematical Function of the Indices of Cohesion for Roll Call Voting," *Behavioral Science* 13, no. 3 (May 1968): 234–237; T. Casstevens, "Linear Algebra and Legislative Voting Behavior: Rice's Indices," *Journal of Politics* 32, no. 4 (November 1970): 769–783. Casstevens presents a method of adjusting the Rice index for abstentions and nonvoting.

one or both senators were absent, that vote could be ignored; thus the index of agreement would be simply the percent of pairs of agreeing votes for those votes when both were present and voting. Alternatively, if the researcher believes absences or abstentions are not random but actually reflect "partial agreement" (because one senator may not agree, but may deliberately not oppose, by not voting), then the index of agreement could be the number of pairs of agreeing votes (full agreements) plus half, or some other arbitrary fraction, the number of votes where one senator did not vote (partial agreements) as a percentage of total number of pairs of votes.

In any given voting group the number of possible pairs is $n(n-1)/2$, where n is the size of the voting group. For 100 senators there thus could be 4,950 pairs. For a voting group of any considerable size, the data must be processed by a computer, as discussed in the Anderson, Watts, and Wilcox handbook.[2]

3. Establishing Nonarbitrary Cutoff Points

Once we have computed the indices of agreement, we must ask ourselves, "How strong must agreement be?" While we can pick some arbitrary level of strength such as .4 or .8, it is better to establish a nonarbitrary cutoff. Peter Willetts has suggested that a desirable nonarbitrary cutoff would be the lowest level that would be significantly unlikely to occur by chance alone. Willetts has presented a procedure and tables for determining that lowest significant level.[3]

The reason for doing this is simple. Suppose we had taken an arbitrarily chosen cutoff of .5 and identified clusters or voting blocs of senators all of whom had an interagreement of .5 or more. Then suppose we found out that in fact, there was a 60 percent chance of getting 50 percent (.5) agreement between any two senators by chance alone. Given this, we would be forced to admit that our cluster blocs of senators may be based as much on chance agreement as on some greater tendency to agree over and beyond chance agreements.

To avoid this problem, we want to pick a level of agreement that is high enough so that the chance of getting that agreement by chance is very low. Political scientists, by arbitrary custom, usually say that that chance must be only one chance out of twenty (.05) or lower. (Of course, we could pick an even more stringent significance requirement, such as one out of a hundred, or .01, and this is sometimes done; political scientists almost never pick a

[2]Lee Anderson, Meredith Watts, and Allen Wilcox, *Legislative Roll-Call Analysis* (Evanston, Ill.: Northwestern Univ. Press, 1966).

[3]Peter Willetts, "Cluster-Bloc Analysis and Statistical Inference," *American Political Science Review* 66, no. 2 (June 1972): 569–582. Further refinements are reflected in Peter Willetts, "Non-Alignment and African Voting in the United Nations," paper, Canadian Association of African Studies, February 1974.

significant requirement more lenient than one in ten, or .10 level of significance.)

But how do we know which agreement level corresponds to only one chance in twenty, or the .05 significance level? As Willetts has pointed out, this can be determined by simple application of the probability rules discussed earlier:

1. To take a simple example, imagine two senators who vote either "Aye" or "Nay" on a random basis for any given vote. The chance of voting "Aye" is thus .5 and the chance of voting "Nay" is also .5. The chance of getting two "Ayes" (agreement) equals the chance of senator number one voting Aye (.5) times the chance of senator number two voting Aye also (.5), or .25. Similarly, the chances of two Nays is .25. Adding these, the chance of agreement is .5.

2. Let the chance of agreement .5, equal p. Let the chance of disagreement, $1 - .5 = .5$, equal q.

3. The number of ways of getting a specific number of agreements, r, in a given number of roll-call votes, n, equals $_nC_r$ (recall Table 8.1). For example, the number of ways of getting eight agreements out of eight votes equals $_8C_8$, which equals one: the one and only way is to have an agreement on each of the eight votes. Similarly, the number of ways of getting seven agreements out of eight votes is equal to $_8C_7$, which equals eight: allowing one disagreement on any of the eight votes provides eight ways to have seven agreements out of eight votes.

4. The probability of r agreements out of n votes equals the number of ways of getting r agreements out of n votes times the probability of agreement times itself r times, times the probability of disagreement times itself $(n - r)$ times:

$$P = {_nC_r} \cdot p^r \cdot q^{n-r}$$

In our example, the probability of 100 percent agreement on eight votes equals $_8C_8 \cdot .5^8 \cdot .5^0$, which equals .004. The probability of 87.5 percent agreement (seven out of eight) equals $_8C_7 \cdot .5^7 \cdot .5^1$, which equals .031. Thus, the probability of seven agreements *or more* out of eight equals the sum of these two probabilities: $.004 + .031 = .035$. The chance of six agreements out of eight is .109; hence the chance of six *or more* is .144.

Thus, if our cutoff is .875 we stay below the probability or significance level .05. If we moved to the next lower cutoff level of agreement, six out of eight, or the .75 cutoff level, we go above the .10 significance level—more than one chance in ten our agreement is due to chance alone, far too high for customary political science standards. Therefore, the lowest still significant (at the .05 level or better) agreement index cutoff is .875.

Since this is somewhat tedious to compute, Willetts has provided a table for reading the appropriate cutoff level for any given number of roll calls and for any of four significance levels: .05, .025, .01, and .001. This table, applicable when $p = .5$ and $q = .5$, is Table XII in the Appendix. (When p and q are not .5, the formula for P in item 4 of the preceding list must be applied.)

4. Forming the Cluster Bloc Matrix

The cluster bloc matrix in Figure 9.2 is a square table showing the index of agreement for each senator with every other senator. It lists senators down the side and also across the top, in the same order; the intersection of these columns and rows contains the indices of agreement.

Figure 9.2 shows all indices of agreement of 0.4 or higher. If this table is based on eighty roll calls, and if we assume p and q both equal .5 (a reasonable assumption if we could eliminate nonvoters by accurately estimating their vote intentions; alternatively, Willetts suggests we may set a different cutoff level for pairs of senators differing in number of votes attended; thus Table XII suggests that a .60 cutoff level for a pair mutually voting on 80 issues is comparable to a cutoff level of .61 for a pair mutually voting on only 70 issues), Table XII tells us that only indices of .60 or higher are significant at the .05 level. Figure 9.1 thus identifies two main clusters of voters, but some of the levels of interagreement among pairs within the clusters are not significant.

Senator

		1	2	3	4	5	6	7	8	9	10	11	12	13	14
Senator	1		81	59	62	43	44					40			
	2	81		78	54	54		41							
	3	59	78		60		40								
	4	62	54	60		40									
	5	43	54		40										
	6	44		40											
	7		41							68					
	8							68							
	9										40				
	10									40		51	58	50	
	11	40									51		68	63	71
	12										58	68		80	
	13										50	63	80		42
	14											71		42	

FIGURE 9.2   A Cluster Bloc Matrix, Showing Two Blocs in Which the Index of Agreement is 5.4 or Higher for Any Pair

Once indices of agreement are computed (step 2), formation of a cluster bloc matrix is relatively simple. The main problem is ordering the senators (in this case) in such a way that the largest number of blocs and the most inclusive blocs will be apparent. If in the example, senators 1, 2, 3, and 4 were instead listed as numbers 1, 5, 10, and 14, the bloc that appears in the upper left corner would not be readily apparent in the matrix.

The following procedure is used to order the members of a voting group in cluster bloc analysis:

1. Find the pair with the highest agreement score and list it first.
2. Find the next highest agreement score that includes a member of the first pair; the other member of this second pair is listed third.
3. Find the highest agreement score that includes one of the first three members and a fourth member, who is then listed fourth in the matrix. This process is continued until the matrix is complete.

Agreement scores that are above an arbitrarily picked level (e.g., .4 in Figure 9.2) or, preferably, above a significant level (e.g., .6 in our previous example) are then entered on the matrix.

Thus, the cluster bloc technique results in an ordering of senators according to their agreement on a set of votes of one type or another. The blocs that are identified for one set of votes can be compared to blocs existing for another set. For example, the bloc structure of Congress for race-related bills could be compared to the bloc structure for social security-related bills to test the extent to which civil rights policy is related to domestic welfare policy. On the other hand, one must be careful not to assume that agreement is due to similar thinking—agreement can also be born of constituency pressures, bargaining ("log-rolling"), or party discipline.

THURSTONE EQUAL-APPEARING INTERVAL SCALES

The general idea of scaling, then, is to rank individuals or groups of individuals according to some criterion. The Thurstone technique was developed to do this in such a way that the intervals between the rankings assigned by the scales would approximate equal intervals. This was considered important because interval-level statistical techniques (involving arithmetic manipulation of the data) could then be applied. Recent evidence suggests that less rigorous or less time-consuming scaling techniques may be sufficient in this regard. That is, deviation from normal distribution and interval-level data assumptions may not be as important as formerly assumed. Nevertheless, Thurstone scales are still in use and it is instructive to understand their construction.

The general procedure of the Thurstone technique is to have "judges" rank opinion statements into piles. The researcher then selects from these piles some statements to form the scale. Statements are selected from each of the ordered piles, giving preference to those statements the judges agreed on in ranking.

1. Compiling Possible Scale Items

As the first step, the researcher writes on slips a large number (perhaps 100) of statements about the subject, such as attitudes toward rioting. For example, these could include: "Rioting does more good than harm. Rioting encourages crime. Rioting helps focus needed attention on city problems." Each statement should:

1. Express only one idea (*not* "Rioting costs too much in moral and economic terms").
2. Avoid extremes that only a *small* minority could endorse (e.g., "Nearly all rioters are Communists").
3. Refer to the present, not the past (*not* "Riots have never done this country any good"). Referring to the past tends to ask the respondent for two responses, past effect of riots and effect of present riots.
4. Avoid unclear, ambiguous, or slang words (e.g., any of the examples listed in Chapter 8 under "Writing the Questions").
5. Avoid *biasing response sets*. Biased response sets include the *agreeing response set*—since people tend to agree with statements regardless of content, statements should be worded positively and negatively in equal numbers—and *response sets related to format*—people tend to endorse items listed first more than last.

These comments apply to other types of scales and, for that matter, to questionnaire and interview items.

2.   Having Judges Order the Possible Items

The second step is to have judges rank the researcher's statements into a number of piles according to how favorable or unfavorable the items are *to the variable* being studied. Judges are *not* asked, and in fact are instructed *not* to rank the items according to how favorable or unfavorable their own feelings are. The researcher must assemble a large number of judges and give them each a set of the paper slips with the possible statements written on them. In our example each judge would have a set of 100 slips. Thurstone used 300 judges to rank 130 items. Theoretically, the best judges would be selected by a random sample of the population to be scaled. Empirical studies have shown, however, that even white Southerners do not rank civil rights items much differently from blacks. The judges, usually college students because of their availability, rank the slips according to favorableness of the statement on each slip to the subject, on a "scale" from one to eleven (or some other arbitrary scale). Thus the statement "Rioting does more good than harm" might be ranked in the ninth pile by one judge, in the seventh pile by another, and in the tenth pile by a third (where the eleventh pile represents the most favorable).

3.   Computing the Average Value
for Each Statement

Each judge thus has made eleven piles; these are combined into one master set of eleven piles. Each slip receives the number of its pile.

Once this is done, the slips are regrouped by *statement*. Suppose the statement "Rioting does more good than harm" had slips in piles 7, 9, 10, and perhaps others; all of the slips corresponding to this statement are collected and put aside, and this is done for each statement. Each statement will then have a pile of slips corresponding to the number of judges. For each statement the *median* value is found; median, as discussed earlier, is the measure of central tendency appropriate for ordinal data.

To complete step 3, all statements with a median of 1 are placed in the 1 pile, all those with a median of 2 are placed in the 2 pile, and so on up to 11.

4. Selecting the Specific Scale Items

Two criteria are used to select which specific statements (items) out of the 100 possible items are to be used in the final scale. First, the full range of the scale should be represented. This is accomplished by making sure that at least one item (statement) is selected from each of the final eleven piles in step three. Second, in each pile, items are selected according to how much agreement there was among judges that the item belonged in that pile; the items thus chosen are characterized by having the least *dispersion*—where judges' placements are spread out the least.

One could identify the items with the least dispersion as those with the lowest standard deviation, but this would require treating the item rank numbers (one to eleven) as if they were interval-level data, which they are not. Therefore, Thurstone used the *Q value* method. *Q* values are measures of dispersion, akin to standard deviations in their general purpose, but suitable for ordinal data. They are based on computing *graphic medians* and *ogive values* (cumulative percentage values) as shown in Figure 9.3.

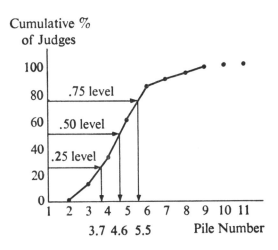

FIGURE 9.3   Graph of *Q* Values for One Item

4a. *Computing Q Values* To compute Q values, first a graph is constructed, with the cumulative percentage of judges in the y-axis and pile number on the x-axis; such a graph is constructed for each statement. Sample data for this graph are given in Table 9.1

TABLE 9.1   Sample Data for Graph of Figure 9.3

Pile Number	Number of Judges	Cumulative %
1	0	0%
2	3	2.5
3	12	12.5
4	21	30.0
5	36	60.0
6	24	80.0
7	12	90.0
8	9	97.5
9	3	100.0
10	0	100.0
11	0	100.0
	$n = 120$	

Thus, Figure 9.3 shows that 60 percent of the judges ranked this particular item in pile 5 or lower; 97.5 percent ranked it in pile 8 or lower. The .60, .975, etc. levels are the *ogive* levels. The *graphic median* can be determined by reading the pile number that corresponds to the .50 level (4.6 in this example).

Q dispersion is the difference between the pile number corresponding to the .75 level and the .25 level (Q thus stands for quartile). In this case, Q dispersion equals 5.5 minus 3.7 or 1.8. The Q value for this item is 1.8. If that is the lowest Q value for any statement in that particular pile (reflecting highest judges' agreement), it will be selected for the final scale.[4]

5.   Testing the Reliability of the Thurstone Scale

The four previous steps should result in a set of scale items that can be used to rank subjects into eleven groups according to their feelings toward rioting. Note that unlike the judges, subjects are asked to rank items according to how favorable their *own feelings* are toward the statement, *not* how favor-

---

[4]Note that the 0.75 and 0.25 levels are arbitrary and could be changed to suit particular research needs. Similarly, when dispersion is "low enough" is an arbitrary choice.

For a more advanced discussion of variants of the conventional technique described here, see Sam Webb, "Studies of Scale and Ambiguity Values Obtained by the Method of Equal-Appearing Intervals," *Psychological Monographs* 69, no. 3 (1955): 1–20.

able the statement is toward the variable being studied. The subject's *scale score* is the average (usually the mean, sometimes the median) of the scale values of the items (statements) he or she endorses.

The scale is said to be *reliable* if the same individuals would get the same scores for similar Thurstone scales. To test reliability, enough items are selected in step 4 to form two scales from the same group of possible items (devised in step 1). The two similar scales are administered to the same individuals and the average percent difference in scale scores is taken as a measure of unreliability; reliability is 1 minus this average. Thus, if for a group of fifty subjects, the scale scores on the first test were on an average 8.2 percent different from the scale scores on a second similar test, then the *split-halves reliability* (i.e., reliability measured by using two similar tests) would be 91.8 percent. How high reliability must be before the scale is "good enough" is arbitrary, although the 90 percent level is ordinarily considered acceptable.

LIKERT SCALES

Likert scales are much simpler than Thurstone scales, and although in Likert scales there is no specific attempt to attain a near-interval level of measurement, it has not been proved that Thurstone scales are much different in this regard. In the Likert method judges are asked to score statement items according to the degree to which they themselves agree or disagree with the statement. Ordinarily there are five choices for each statement: strongly agree/agree/uncertain/disagree/strongly disagree. Items are selected according to the degree to which they reflect differences in the judges' feelings about the variable being examined. Sometimes seven choices are provided rather than five, so as to avoid having the first (e.g., "strongly agree") and fifth (e.g., "strongly disagree") in a five-choice format seem to be the "extremes."

1. Compiling Possible Scale Items

This step is the same as step 1 in the Thurstone method.

2. Having Judges Rank the Possible Items

Each judge is given a list of all the possible statement items compiled in the first step. Each is then asked to strongly agree, agree, etc., and assign point values to each choice (e.g., strongly agree = 1, agree = 2, and so on).

3. Computing the Average Value
   for Each Statement

Each statement item is then given a score equal to the average response, 1 to 5, given by the judges.[5] The standard deviation of these item scores can then be computed, ignoring the fact that the data are ordinal, not interval, and normal tables can be used to weight the statement items according to how far they deviate from the average item score for all items. Thus these weights constitute criteria for weighting a 1 ("strongly agree") response on an extreme item *more* than a 1 response on a less extreme item. However, it has been found that this refinement gives results only 1 percent or 2 percent different than if no weights are computed; therefore, *this step is usually omitted.*

4. Selecting the Scale Items

Each judge is given a score equal to the average, 1 to 5, of all his responses— again, after items have been reordered so that a 1 response always represents strong favorability toward the variable, even when the statement is negatively worded. Judges are then ranked by this score and the top and bottom 25 percent (or some other arbitrary fraction) of the judges are identified. The top 25 percent represents those judges least favorable toward the variable being studied and the bottom 25 percent the most favorable (in this case, those who tended to give 1 and 2 responses to statements such as "Riots help focus needed attention on city problems"). The items to select are those that best distinguish between the top 25 percent of judges and the bottom 25 percent.

Items that meet this criterion are identified by the *discriminative power* (*DP*) *method.* For any given statement, the DP measure is the weighted mean response of the top 25 percent minus the weighted mean response of the bottom 25 percent of the judges, as illustrated in Table 9.2.

The DP index must be computed for each of the possible scale items, and those items with the largest DP indices will be selected. These are the items that best discriminate among judges holding differing attitudes toward the test variable. The *number of items* in a "good" scale is arbitrary, most Likert scales ranging between fifty and a few hundred statement items. The number should be large enough to give stability to the scale yet not so great that the respondent becomes bored or tired with the study; these factors will be different according to the research task. Note also that there is nothing absolute about having five responses, although this is common. Often the

---

[5]Statements are first renumbered, of course, so that a 1 response is always favorable to the variable being studied, whether that statement is worded positively or negatively; this involves making "strongly disagree" equal 1 for items worded negatively.

TABLE 9.2 DP Computing Table for One Scale Item

(1) Group	(2) Number in Group	(3) Item Responses 1 2 3 4 5	(4) Weighted Total (response value times frequency)	(5) Weighted Mean (4) / (2)
Top 25%	30	0 2 10 9 9	$0+4+30+$ $36+45=115$	$115/30=3.83$
Low 25%	30	6 24 0 0 0	$6+48+0+$ $0+0=54$	$54/30 = 1.80$

(6) Discriminative Power of a particular item	$DP=3.83-1.80=2.03$

"uncertain" category is left out, forcing respondents to take a position, on the assumption that "true neutrals" will be forced one direction or the other at random. Few Likert scales contain less than four or more than seven response categories, however.

Factor analysis (to be discussed in Chapter 16) is an alternative (or supplementary) method of selecting Likert scale items. In this technique, items are retained that have high factor loadings on the general factor score. Moreover, the relative importance of the factor loadings can be used as criteria for differentially weighting each item selected, as an alternative procedure to step 3 above. This technique works best when inter-item correlations are not greatly a function of skewed item marginals (i.e., when chance factors are not likely to generate high inter-item correlations).

5. Testing the Reliability of the Scale

When a Likert test is administered, by asking a respondent to rank 50 or more statement items from 1 = strongly agree to 5 = strongly disagree, the respondent's *scale score* is simply the average score, 1 to 5, for his responses to all the items, again after negatively worded statements have been renumbered. The Likert scale thus provides a mechanism for ranking individuals according to their position on a test variable.

Reliability of the scale can be tested in much the same manner as in the Thurstone method, simply by selecting enough items for two scales (usually at least one hundred) and randomly dividing them into two sets, constituting two scales. The test of *split-halves reliability* is administered as described for the Thurstone technique.

The Likert scale, finally, involves several additional features. First, unlike the Thurstone method, no attempt is made by the judges (or anyone) to evaluate the meaning or affective content of the items. Although the items do differentiate quite clearly between high- and low-scoring judges, there is no guarantee that the scale items selected will be representative of statements (items) about the test variable in general. Hence there may be some danger, as Harry Upshaw has noted, that the items appropriate to one set of judges may not be appropriate to another. Upshaw suggests a precautionary measure of selecting judges at random from the population eventually to be tested. Moreover, the Likert method tends toward selection of items reflecting extreme statements, since the criterion for item selection is ability to differentiate between judges in the extreme quartiles, and may be less sensitive in distinguishing among "moderate" respondents. When the research objective is the latter, it is preferable to select Likert items by the factor analytic technique discussed above, or by selecting items whose individual scores correlate most highly with the total score for all items.

GUTTMAN SCALES (SCALOGRAM ANALYSIS)

The Guttman scale, often used in more rigorous social science research, aims for *unidimensionality*. That is, it attempts to assure that the scale measures only one underlying dimension—in the "happiness" example given initially, that only one of the many meanings of happiness is measured. It does this not simply by evaluating a number of scale item responses, but by looking at each response in relation to every other response. Specifically, the items on a Guttman scale may be arranged so that an endorsement of one implies endorsement of all previous items. In a Guttman scale, if a respondent agrees with statement 3, he will also agree with statements 2 and 1; if a senator votes for bill 3, he will also vote for bills 2 and 1; if a city experiences riot behavior type 3, it will have also experienced types 2 and 1.

1.   Selecting the Scale Items

As implied in the preceding paragraph, the items scaled can be statement items, calling for agreement or disagreement; legislative votes, aye or nay; or even political events—what happened or did not happen. Although more complex Guttman scaling may be undertaken, this section will deal only with the case in which each item has two response values.

2.   Forming the Initial Guttman Table

Once selected according to the particular researcher's needs, possible scale items are then presented to a large number of judges for their evaluation. Thus a table could be made listing judges down the side and items across the top, with Xs in the appropriate spaces to indicate agreement with the item.

A perfect Guttman scale would look like Table 9.3, resembling a right

TABLE 9.3 Perfect Guttman Scale

		Item									
		1	2	3	4	5	6	7	8	9	10
	1	X	X								
	2	X	X	X							
	3	X	X	X	X	X					
Judge	4	X	X	X	X	X	X	X			
	5	X	X	X	X	X	X	X	X		
	6	X	X	X	X	X	X	X	X	X	
	7	X	X	X	X	X	X	X	X	X	X

triangle with no blanks (non-agreements) inside the triangle and no Xs outside it; if blanks or deviant Xs occur they would be *scale errors*.

The problem of how to know which item to put first, second, etc., and the parallel problem of which judge to put first, second, etc., is the problem of *arrangement*. First, relying on his own judgment, the researcher orders the items according to their extremism. Then the respondent who endorsed the fewest items is placed first, and so on down to the last person, who endorsed the most items.

3. Selecting the Final Scale Items

The initial table may be refined by inspection or by applying Yule's Q test. By *inspection* of the initial table, judges may be rearranged to reduce scale errors. For example, in Table 9.3, if the third judge responded "X, X, blank, blank, X," the number of errors (2, for the two internal blanks) could be reduced to 1 by making him the second judge (1 error for the 1 external X). Also by inspection, items may be rearranged to form a more perfect triangle. Similarly, items in whose columns appear many errors may be omitted entirely. Finally, redundant items may also be omitted. Redundant items are those whose presence does not lead to greater differentiation among the judges. In Table 9.3, items 1 or 2, 4 or 5, and 6 or 7 are redundant.

By the Q test, scalable items may be identified and nonscalable items thrown out. This will not refine the table for redundant items, nor will it deal with minimizing scale errors due to poor ordering of judges, however. Research on legislative roll-call analysis by Duncan MacRea has shown that items having a Yule's Q of 0.80 or higher with each other are scalable. Yule's Q is equal to the main diagonal product, minus the off diagonal product, divided by the sum of both, for the 2-by-2 table formed by any two items. (See Table 9.4.) It is a measure of "association" further discussed in Chapter 11. Each item in the scale should have a Q of 0.80 or higher when paired with any item before it on the scale. For instance, in Table 9.3, item 5 should be associated at the 0.80 level or better with items 4, 3, 2, and 1. Item 10 should be associated with all the other items, since all precede it on the

TABLE 9.4   Yule's Q

Item A

		+	−
Item B	+	a	b
	−	c	d

$$Q = \frac{ad-bc}{ad+bc}$$

scale. This method will lead to omitting items like 1 and 2 in the example—items on which *all* judges agree. This is because in the 2-by-2 table formed by items 1 or 2 with any of the others, the b and d boxes will be zero, so that Yule's Q will be zero as well. The main reason for emphasis on the Q test is that the inspection method becomes extremely unwieldy when the number of judges and items is large. The Q test method can be used on computer programs in these situations.

4. Testing the Scale

Once final scale items have been selected in step 3, the test scale can be administered to the population (people or events) to be studied, and a Guttman table ("scalogram") constructed. Unlike Table 9.3, this table will undoubtedly have errors (interior blanks and exterior Xs). How many errors are permissible before a scale is regarded as inadequate for the population under study? Two tests have been devised to answer this question: the test of reproducibility and the test of scalability. (In some studies the judges *are* the population to be studied, so step 4 proceeds immediately to these tests).

   The coefficient of reproducibility method has been a standard test. It is equal to 1 minus the number of errors divided by the number of choices:

$$C_r = 1 - e/n$$

where e = number of errors = either interior blanks
or exterior Xs,

and n = number of choices = number of items times
the number of judges or subjects.

A scale is arbitrarily but commonly considered adequate if the coefficient of reproducibility is .90 or higher.

   Unfortunately, the coefficient of reproducibility has some problems as a statistic. If Xs and blanks are considered response categories, then by definition the number of errors for any item cannot be greater than the number of responses in the least numerous category. If the percent of responses in the most numerous category is 90 percent, then the coefficient of reproducibility *must* be at least .90! C_r is never below .50.[6]

---

[6]If the number of errors for any item *were* larger than the number of responses in the least numerous category for that item, the item could be rearranged on the scale so that the number of errors would be no more than the number of responses in the least numerous category.

Thus the percent of responses in the most numerous category is the *minimum marginal reproducibility*. (In the notation cited below for the coefficient of scalability, mmr $= T_n /n$.) The *percent improvement* is the difference between the coefficient of reproducibility and the minimum marginal reproducibility.

The coefficient of scalability is a statistic that varies between zero and one and is not affected by response category (Xs or blanks) frequencies. It is equal to 1 minus the number of errors divided by the number of errors expected by chance:

$$C_s = 1 - e/x$$

where $e =$ number of errors $=$ interior blanks plus exterior Xs,

$x =$ errors expected by chance $= c(n - T_n)$,

$c =$ chance of getting any choice right by chance alone (0.5 if there are only two response categories),

$n =$ number of choices of any type,

and $T_n =$ number of choices in the most numerous response category for each item.

While this seems complex, the following examples will illustrate its simplicity.

Example 1   A Guttman scale such as that shown in Table 9.5 might be developed for fifteen senators on a committee, voting on ten issues (Xs denote aye votes, blanks denote nay). Is this scale good enough? By counting interior blanks and exterior Xs we see there are sixteen errors, but is this too many?

TABLE 9.5

		1	2	3	4	5	6	7	8	9	10
	1	X	X				X				
	2		X	X							
	3	X	X	X							
	4	X	X	X							
	5	X	X		X					X	
	6	X	X	X	X			X		X	
	7	X	X		X						
Senator	8		X	X	X	X				X	
	9	X		X	X	X					
	10	X	X				X	X	X		
	11	X	X	X	X	X	X	X			
	12	X	X	X	X	X	X	X	X		
	13	X			X	X		X	X	X	X
	14	X	X	X			X	X	X	X	X
	15	X			X	X	X	X	X	X	X
$e=$		2	3	3	2	1	1	1	0	3	0= 16
$T_n=$		13	12	11	9	8	8	8	11	9	14= 103
$n=15\times10=150$											c= .5

The answer depends on how many errors we would expect by chance, given the total aye and nay count for each vote. Knowing that thirteen senators out of fifteen voted aye on vote 1, for example, tells us that there could not possibly be more than 15 − 13 = 2 errors. Knowing that nine of fifteen senators voted nay (unlike vote 1, here the nay votes are the most numerous response category) on vote 9 tells us that there could not be more than 15 − 9 = 6 errors.

That is, the most errors there could be, given the total count for each vote, is the number of choices ($n = 150$) minus the total in the most numerous category of each item ($T_n = 103$). In this case the maximum possible errors would be 150 − 103 = 47. Since in this example a senator could vote two ways (aye or nay), the number of errors expected by chance is $\frac{1}{2}(47) = 23.5$

The question now becomes, "Is a scale that reduces chance errors from 23.5 to observed errors of 16 good enough?" The coefficient of scalability is an index used to answer this question; the scale is commonly but arbitrarily judged "good enough" if C_s is .60 or better. C_s is 1 minus observed errors divided by errors by chance. In this example, $C_s = 1 - (16/23.5) = 1 - .68 = .32$; hence the scale is judged an inadequate tool for ranking senators.

Example 2 Guttman scales need not be limited to ranking people by attitudes or votes; they may also be used to rank events. Jules Wanderer[7] for example, recently developed an eight-item scale of riot severity which met Guttman criteria and had a C_r of .92.

TABLE 9.6 Wanderer's Guttman Scale of Riot Severity

Scale Type	% Cities ($n=75$)	Items Reported	Scale Errors
8	4	No scale items	2
7	19	"Vandalism"	10
6	13	All of the above & "interference with firemen"	3
5	16	All of the above & "looting"	3
4	13	All of the above & "sniping"	7
3	7	All of the above & "called state police"	4
2	17	All of the above & "called National Guard"	11
1	11	All of the above & "law officer or civilian killed"	2
Total	100%		42

Source: Jules J. Wanderer, "An Index of Riot Severity and Some Correlates," *American Journal of Sociology* 74:5 (March, 1969), Table 1, page 503. Copyright © The University of Chicago Press, by permission of the author and publisher.

[7]Jules J. Wanderer, "An Index of Riot Severity and Some Correlates," *American Journal of Sociology* 74, no. 5 (March 1969): 503.

Additional Considerations

Since Guttman scales were developed, many refinements and criticisms have been made. *Stouffer's H technique*, for example, is a proposal to give greater stability to Guttman scales by basing each scale item on three or more sub-items. Thus item 1 might reflect sub-items 1(a), 1(b), and 1(c); if a respondent endorsed at least two out of the three sub-items he would be listed on item 1 as endorsing item 1. That is, the *H* technique is a method that reduces the effect of random errors on the Guttman scale by making each item a summary of three or more similar sub-items.

It is somewhat misleading simply to present a coefficient of reproducibility without indicating the level of confidence one may have in it. Guttman therefore suggested computing the *standard error of reproducibility* when scale data are based on a sample. Recall from the previous chapter that when data are based on enumeration rather than sample, the coefficient of reproducibility is the true one and there is no point in computing standard error. The formula

$$\text{SE Rep} \approx \sqrt{(1 - C_r)(C_r)/n}$$

gives a close approximation to standard error of reproducibility, which in Example 1 would equal the square root of $[(1 - .89)(.89)]/150$, or .026. Since two standard errors corresponds to roughly 95 percent of a normal distribution, one may be 95 percent confident that the real coefficient of reproducibility lies within plus or minus $2(.026) = .052$ of the scale coefficient of .89.[8]

Karl Schuessler has suggested a *chi-square test of scale significance*. Using this method, the researcher would first determine his observed Guttman-scale data in the usual manner, noting the proportion of respondents endorsing each item. In Example 1, for instance, item 1 was endorsed by 13 out of 15, or about 87 percent of respondents; item 2 by 80 percent, etc. Then, using a table of random numbers, the researcher can generate a hypothetical chance scale. For item 1, if the first two random numbers encountered (found in a random number table) are 87 or less, the first respondent is listed as endorsing item 1; if the first two random numbers are from 88 to 00, then he is listed as not endorsing item 1. The same procedure is applied to respondents 2 through 15 for each item. For item 2, 01 through 80 correspond to endorsements and 81 through 00 correspond to nonendorsements, etc. In this way, a hypothetical chance table can be constructed. Finally, a list can be made for number of respondents with no errors, number with one error, number with two errors, etc. This list can be made

---

[8]For more advanced tests of scale significance, see: Roland Chilton, "A Review and Comparison of Simple Statistical Tests for Scalogram Analysis," *American Sociological Review* 34, no. 2 (April 1969): 237.

for both the observed data and the expected (hypothetical, chance) data. Chi-square, discussed in the next chapter, is a measure of the significance of the difference between observed and expected (chance) data.

Finally, it must be emphasized that Guttman scales do not guarantee unidimensionality; however, any scale not meeting Guttman criteria is very probably multidimensional. That is, Guttman scaling is not a foolproof test of the claim that a particular scale measures only one underlying continuum. Even if the reproducibility of the scale is significantly better than chance, some of the scale items may still measure underlying dimensions. In a fully homogeneous scale there will be no cases in which a respondent does not endorse one item but nevertheless endorses another less frequently endorsed item. That is, for every pair of items (arranged in a 2-by-2 table with the more endorsed item to the side and the less endorsed on top, as shown in Table 9.7) the c cell will tend to be zero except for random errors.

TABLE 9.7

Less Endorsed Item

		Aye	Nay
More Endorsed Item	Aye	a	b
	Nay	c	d

Thus in a perfect scale—one that is fully homogeneous—every pair of items will have $Q = 1.0$. The Q test must be used as a check on the full unidimensionality of Guttman scales.[9]

PROXIMITY SCALES

A perfect Guttman scale is one in which a respondent who endorses a given item will also endorse each of the less extreme items. If on a four-item scale, for example, the fourth item is, "I don't like Eskimos to shop where I shop," and this is endorsed by a respondent, then that respondent would also en-

[9]A review of the problem of checking unidimensionality is contained in Carmi Schooler, "A Note of Extreme Caution in the Use of Guttman Scales," *American Journal of Sociology* 74 no. 3 (November 1968): 296. See also replies to Schooler in *American Journal of Sociology* 75 no. 2 (September 1969): 278–280.

For further reading on Thurstone, Likert, and Guttman scaling, see Karl Schuessler, *Analyzing Social Data* (Boston: Houghton Mifflin, 1971), ch. 6; Harry Upshaw, "Attitude Measurement," in Hubert Blalock and Ann Blalock, eds., *Methodology in Social Research* (New York: McGraw-Hill, 1968), ch. 3; and Warren Torgerson, *Theory and Methods of Scaling* (New York: John Wiley & Sons, 1958).

dorse the less extreme items such as the third ("I don't like Eskimos where I work"), second ("I don't like Eskimos to live on my street"), and first ("I don't want an Eskimo to marry into my family."). For a set of people, the fewest will endorse the most extremely prejudiced item, item four, and the most will endorse the least extreme item, number one.

But now suppose the items do not range from least extreme to most extreme. Suppose instead that they range from the most extreme in one direction (e.g., the "far right") through moderate items and on out to items most extreme in the other direction (e.g., the "far left"). Here we might expect that respondents would select adjacent items, rejecting those more extreme in *either* direction. If the items are positions on political issues, then the further the item from the respondent's preferred item (position), the less likely it is to be endorsed.

As Herbert Weisberg has pointed out, Guttman scaling is appropriate under two conditions.[10] First, Guttman scales are legitimate when there is consensus on one end of the spectrum but there is progressively less consensus as items toward the other end of the spectrum are chosen. For example, all senators would agree that "some government intervention in the economy is necessary," but as items proposing more and more extensive forms of intervention were considered, the consensus of agreement would decline. Second, Guttman scales are useful when the items are legislative votes and legislators can be ranked from those who prefer the status quo (and who will vote "nay" on the proposal) to those who strongly prefer passage of the bill.

In contrast, Weisberg noted, proximity scales are appropriate "when a motion is supported by the moderates but is opposed by both extremes."[11] This also applies to situations in which the Guttman scale conditions above are *not* met: lack of consensus on goals and a situation where respondents cannot be ranked along a continuum of status quo to anti-status quo. Such a situation would be exemplified by a European legislature in the 1930s, with both fascist and Communist delegates, in which the Communists often voted against anti-status quo reforms of the socialists because these were considered bourgeois attempts to co-opt the working class. Thus a further implication of proximity voting, as noted by Weisberg, is that the particular vote not be seen as crucial (i.e., in the above example, the socialist reform proposal must seem not critical; if the Communists were forced to view it as crucial, the situation would revert to the status quo – anti-status quo continuum and be Guttman scalable). A special case of this occurs when anti-status quo proposals are perceived by a group of legislators to be insufficient and the group feels that by voting against the reform (and hence allying with pro-status quo legislators) they will make it more likely that a more extensive reform

---

[10] Herbert Weisberg, "Scaling Models for Legislative Roll-Call Analysis," *American Political Science Review* 66, no. 4 (December 1972): 1307.
[11] *Ibid.*, p. 1308.

proposal will be voted on later (hence, the vote on the insufficient reform must seem not critical in the long run). Weisberg gave the example of Senator Morse (Dem., Ore.), who voted against the Civil Rights Bill of 1957 because it was inadequate.

More generally, Weisberg noted, Guttman voting occurs when the issue is one of expansion (how much in a consensual direction); proximity voting occurs when the issue is one of basic direction. Further, Guttman scaling is more likely to be appropriate to voting in tranquil times, while proximity scaling may be more important in times of crisis, when basic directions are brought into question. Weisberg's article demonstrated that proximity voting was a better model for Congress at the time of the Compromise of 1850, for example, than was the Guttman scale model, which in turn worked well for the more consensual era of the 1950s and early 1960s.

Weisberg's findings are presented in Tables 9.8 and 9.9. Tables 9.8 and 9.9 show that for voting in the Compromise of 1850, Guttman scaling provides an acceptable scale, but proximity scaling provides even better results. It will be noticed that where the general form of the Guttman scale is a triangle, the pattern of the proximity scale is a diagonal track of "Yes" votes with small triangles of "No" votes in the upper left and lower right corners. An error in Guttman scaling is, as before, a "Pro" vote in the triangle of "Anti's," or an "Anti" vote in the triangle of "Pro's." An error in proximity scaling is a "No" vote with the "Yes's" on either side (that is, proximity analysis assumes that no legislator will vote for both extremes and against the middle). Once errors are counted, the coefficient of reproducibility is computed the same in proximity as in Guttman scaling. The coefficient of scalability, though not used by Weisberg, is also computed in a similar manner.

LATENT STRUCTURE ANALYSIS

In Chapter 16 we shall see that factor analysis is a method usually used with interval data to reduce a large number of items (e.g., a large number of political measures) to a smaller number of underlying types or sets (factors) of items (e.g., a socioeconomic set, a psychological set, an ideological set—each set being one dimension of the grand set of all the items), using data for a given number of respondents. In scaling, we are doing something similar: we are using ordinal or dichotomous data to group (reduce) a large number of respondents (e.g., 100 senators) to a smaller number of underlying types or sets (scale types) of respondents (e.g., a proslavery set, an antislavery set, etc.), using data for a given number of items (votes).

In fact, if we have interval data, a given set of individuals (e.g., Congressmen) can be grouped into underlying blocs through Q-technique factor

TABLE 9.8 Proximity Scale of House Voting on the Compromise of 1850*

Fugitive slaves	Utah territory	Texas/ N. Mex.	Calif. statehood	D. C. slavery	Total	Northern			Southern	
						Free Soil	Whig	Dem.	Whig	Dem.
No	No	No	Yes	Yes	48	7	32	9	—	—
No	No	Yes	Yes	Yes	6	—	5	1	—	—
No	Yes	Yes	Yes	Yes	5	—	3	2	—	1
Yes	Yes	Yes	Yes	Yes	28	—	1	24	2	3
Yes	Yes	Yes	Yes	No	9	—	—	—	6	11
Yes	Yes	Yes	No	No	15	—	—	—	4	5
Yes	Yes	No	No	No	5	—	—	—	—	12
Yes	No	No	No	No	13	—	1	—	1	—
Yes	No	Yes	Yes	Yes	1**	—	—	—	—	1
Yes	Yes	Yes	No	Yes	1**	—	—	—	—	—
Total					131	7	42	36	13	33

Coefficient of reproducibility   = 0.996
Percentage of perfect scale patterns = 98% (N = 131, based on those legislators without any missing data)

*Only those legislators who voted on all five items are shown.
**These are error patterns under the proximity model.

Source: Herbert Weisberg, "Scaling Models for Legislative Roll-Call Analysis," *American Political Science Review* 66 no. 4 (December 1972): 1310. Reprinted by permission.

TABLE 9.9 Guttman Scale of Support for Abolitionist Positions in House Voting on the Compromise of 1850*

Texas/ N. Mex.	Utah territory	Fugitive slaves	D. C. slavery	Calif. statehood	Frequency	Northerners	Southerners
Pro**	Pro**	Pro**	Pro**	Pro**	48	48	0
Anti	Pro	Pro	Pro	Pro	6	6	0
Anti	Anti	Pro	Pro	Pro	5	5	0
Anti	Anti	Anti	Pro	Pro	28	25	3
Anti	Anti	Anti	Anti	Pro	9	0	9
Anti	Anti	Anti	Anti	Anti	15	0	15
Anti	Anti	Pro	Anti	Anti	5***	0	5
Anti	Pro	Pro	Anti	Anti	13***	0	13
Anti	Pro	Anti	Pro	Pro	1***	1	0
Anti	Anti	Anti	Pro	Anti	1***	0	1
Total					131	85	46

Coefficient of reproducibility   = 0.960
Percentage of perfect scale patterns = 85% (N = 113, based on those legislators without any missing data)

*Only those legislators who voted on all five items are shown.
**Pro-abolition: Votes *against* the Texas-New Mexico bill, the Utah territory bill, and the fugitive slave bill are treated as Pro-abolition as are votes *for* the District of Columbia slave trade bill and the California statehood bill.
***These are error patterns under the Guttman scale.
Source: Ibid.

analysis (discussed in Chapter 16), thus using factor analysis for the same purpose to which scaling techniques are directed.

Latent structure analysis can be thought of as analogous to factor analysis, but is appropriate for data below the interval level. To explain the principle behind latent structure analysis, it is necessary to give a hint of how multivariate table analysis works (which will be discussed more fully in Chapter 13).

TABLE 9.10   Example of Multivariate Analysis

Original Table

Education

		High	Low	Total
	Protestant	55	35	90
Religion	Catholic	35	55	90
	Total	90	90	180

"Upper Half" Class Subtable

	High	Low	Total
Protestant	50	10	60
Catholic	25	5	30
Total	75	15	90

"Lower Half" Class Subtable

	High	Low	Total
Protestant	5	25	30
Catholic	10	50	60
Total	15	75	90

In Table 9.10, we see an original table that shows a tendency for Protestants to be highly educated and Catholics to be poorly educated. But when we divide this original table into a similar subtable for upper-income respondents and another for lower-income respondents, the relationship disappears! That is, in each subtable Protestants and Catholics have the same ratio of highly educated to poorly educated. We conclude from this that the criterion of subgrouping (income) is really responsible for the apparent original relationship of religion and education.

Latent structure analysis assumes that we have N respondents who answer m items, all of which reflect some underlying dimension X. The latent group structure of X is a set of subgroups of N such that the inter-item correlation between any pair of the m items *within any given subgroup* approaches zero. We will know that we have grouped the N respondents according to the latent group structure of X, the underlying dimension, if the inter-item association of pairs of items is not statistically significant when the data is taken subgroup by subgroup. This is because this subgrouping controls for the effect of different levels of X, the criterion variable. Since the effect of the underlying dimension X, which all m items relate to, is the cause of inter-item correlations, those correlations will disappear when X is controlled by appropriate subgroupings.

This logic of latent structure analysis is simpler than the actual computations necessary to identify what these "appropriate subgroupings" are. In fact, the computation is too complex to be discussed here, and the reader must refer to more specialized texts.[12] Because of this complexity of computation and the fact that methods of computation of latent groups have been worked out only for special cases (no general solution for finding the latent group structure of any group has yet been found), latent structure analysis is not widely used in political science.

MULTIDIMENSIONAL SCALING

The scaling techniques discussed up to this point assume unidimensionality. In constructing a Guttman scale, for instance, we strive to make sure that each item contains only one basic dimension (e.g., prejudice dimension) and that all the items contain that same dimension. If we find an item that seems to contain two dimensions, it will usually create many errors when it is included in a Guttman-type scale, and we will discard it. To illustrate, the item, "I would not want blacks to work with me because they are pushy," contains two dimensions: (1) whether or not the respondent would want to work with blacks, and (2) whether or not the respondent thinks blacks are pushy. Some respondents will answer primarily in terms of their attitude on the first dimension, and some on the second dimension—leaving the researcher unsure which meaning was attached to this item by various respondents.

When we are constructing questionnaire items to be scaled, it is relatively easy to throw out items that seem multidimensional and to confine our attention to the remainder. Even when the items are legislative votes, it may be possible to restrict our consideration to a small subset of apparently unidimensional votes from among the universe of all votes. But sometimes we are committed to looking at a set of items or votes that are multidimensional

[12]Paul Lazarsfeld and Neil Henry, *Latent Structure Analysis* (Boston: Houghton Mifflin, 1968). A brief introduction is provided in Schuessler, *Analyzing Social Data*, pp. 332–340. See also Torgerson, *Theory and Methods of Scaling*, pp. 361–364, 374–385; and Samuel Stouffer, "Comparison of Guttman and Latent Structure Scales," in P. Lazarsfeld *et al.*, eds., *Continuities in the Language of Social Research* (New York: Free Press, 1972), pp. 48–57.

Schuessler (p. 340) cites the following additional techniques of attitude measurement: semantic differential [C. Osgood *et al.*, *The Measurement of Meaning* (Urbana: Univ. of Illinois Press, 1957)], Stephenson's Q technique [W. Stephenson, *The Study of Behavior* (Chicago: Univ. of Chicago, 1953)], the ratio method [S. Stevens, "Measurement, Psychophysics, and Utility," in C. Churchman and P. Ratoosh, eds., *Measurement* (New York: John Wiley & Sons, 1959), pp. 18–63], and the unfolding technique [C. Coombs, *A Theory of Data* (New York: John Wiley & Sons, 1964)].

(e.g., a set of votes that reflect *both* a conservativeness dimension and a presidential support dimension) and we are not willing to disregard any of them. If we always confined our attention to discrete exposures to unidimensional stimuli, we would unduly narrow the scope of political science research. Consequently, it may be useful to develop techniques of scaling that allow for multidimensionality.

If we have a set of votes reflecting more than one dimension, a reasonable first question is to ask what is the smallest number of dimensions by which the data on the votes may be interpreted. Determining the underlying dimensions of a set of measures (votes) for a population of persons (senators) where each measure (vote) is taken on only one occasion is the conventional method of factor analysis—the R-technique, to be discussed in Chapter 16.

Factor analysis has several problems, however. Among these are the large number of underlying dimensions often uncovered, the complexity of interpreting the final factor matrix even after it is computed and the attending difficulty of explaining the results clearly, and the assumptions of interval-level, linearly related data which it ordinarily postulates. Multidimensional scaling consists of a set of techniques that are meant to accomplish much the same purposes as R-technique factor analysis, while avoiding the problems (just as latent structure analysis is designed as an alternative to Q-technique factor analysis).

The computational techniques involved in multidimensional scaling are too advanced for the level of knowledge thus far developed in this book.[13] Again, advanced students must be referred to specialized texts, while this volume proceeds to coverage of other more basic techniques in political science.[14]

EXERCISE

Table 9.11 contains roll-call vote information on nineteen military-related votes for twenty-nine randomly selected senators.

Using the data in Table 9.11, find out if some or all of these nineteen military-related votes constitute a good Guttman scale by which the sampled senators may be ranked according to their degree of promilitary stance. Rearrange the senators and votes to minimize scale errors; combine votes

[13]See: Roger Shepard, Kimball Romney and Sara Nerlove, eds., *Multidimensional Scaling* (New York: Seminar Press, 1972), vol. I (*Theory*) and vol. II (*Applications*).

[14]For a survey of specific attitude scales useful in political science, see: John Robinson, Jerrold Rusk, and Kendra Head, *Measures of Political Attitudes* (Ann Arbor: Survey Research Center, Univ. of Michigan, 1968); and Delbert Miller, *Handbook of Research Design and Social Measurement* (New York: McKay, 1964). See also: John Robinson and Philip Shaver, eds., *Measures of Social Psychological Attitudes* (Ann Arbor: Institute for Social Research, 1968).

TABLE 9.11

Senators	Votes																			Total Xs
	1	2	3	4	5	6	7	8	9	10	11	12	13	14	15	16	17	18	19	
Allen	x	x	x	x	x	x	x		x	x	x	x			x	x	x	x	x	16
Stevens	x	x	x	x	x	x	x	x	x	x	x	x		x	x			x	x	16
Fulbright										s										0
Cranston				x																1
Allott	x	x	x	x	x	x	x	x	x	x	x	x	x	x	x			x	x	17
Boggs	x	x	x	x	x	x	x	x	x	x	x	x	x	x	x		x	x	x	18
Gurney	x	x	x	x	x	x	x	x	x	x	x	x	x	x	x	x	x	x	x	19
Talmadge	x		x	x	x	x	x		x		x	x		x				x	x	12
Church		?	?	?	x				x						x			x		4
Percy		x	x	x	x	x	x	x	x		x	x	x	x	x			x		14
Hartke		?	?	?	?	?	?		?		?	?	?	x						1
Miller	x				x	x	x	x	x	x	x	x	x	x	x			x	x	14
Ellender	x		x	x	x	x			x	x					x			x	x	10
Beall	x	x	?	x	x	x	x	x	x	x	x	x	x	x	x			x	x	16

Senators	\#1	2	3	4	5	6	7	8	9	10	11	12	13	14	15	16	17	18	19	Total Xs
Brooke		×	×	×	×	×		×					×					×		8
Griffin	×	×	×	×	×	×	×	×	×	×	×	×	×	×	×			×	×	17
Mansfield												×								1
Curtis	×	×	×	×	×	×	×	×	×	×	×	×	×	×	×	×	×	×	×	19
Bible	×		×	×	×	×	×	×	×	×	×	×			×			×		13
Case		×		×	×			×					×		×			×		7
Buckley	×	×	×	×	×	×	×	×	×	×	×	×		×	×	×	×	×	×	18
Young	×		×	×	×	×	×	×	×	×	×	×	×	×	×		×			15
Schweiker			×	×	×	×	×	×	×		×	×	×					×		11
Tower		×	×	×	×	×	×	×	×	×	×	×	×	×	×	×	×	×	×	18
Bennett	×	×	×	×	×	×	×	×	×	×	×	×	×	×	×			×	×	17
Stafford	?	×	×	×	×	×	×	×	?	×	?	?	?	×	×			×	×	12
Jackson	×		×	×	×	×	×	×	×	×	×	×	×	×	×			×	×	16
Nelson				×																1
McGee	×	×	×	×	×	×	×	×	?	×	?	?	?	×	×			×	×	13
Total Xs	18	18	21	25	23	21	19	20	20	17	17	19	15	17	22	6	7	23	16	

Votes

that do not differentiate among senators to give greater item stability, using the H technique (in combining, list the aggregate item as a vote in the direction of the majority of items; if the component items are evenly split, assign the vote by use of the random number table); and compute the coefficients of reproducibility and scalability.

Note: In Table 9.11, the "Xs" indicate a promilitary vote, and blanks indicate an antimilitary vote. The "s" for Senator Fulbright is a special case where a promilitary vote was cast only so as to make the Senator eligible to move to reconsider; hence the "s" should be treated as a blank. The "?" entries are votes where there was no indication stated of the given senator's voting intention. In such cases of missing data, one of four procedures is customary:

1. the vote is assigned by use of the random number table (this procedure is best when there is no other relevant knowledge about the vote intention);
2. the vote is assigned by use of the random number table, using the row proportion of "Xs" to blanks (this is appropriate when the senator's disposition is deemed relevant, but not the nature of the vote);
3. the vote is assigned by use of the random number table, using the column proportions of "Xs" to blanks (appropriate when the nature of the vote is deemed relevant, but not the senator's disposition); and
4. the vote is assigned using the random number table, using the sum of column and row proportions of "Xs" to blanks (when both qualities are deemed relevant).

This exercise can be extended by computing a proximity scale for the same data to determine if this method gives better results. Similarly, a cluster bloc analysis can be computed for comparison purposes.

10 | Significance

After the researcher's hypotheses have been formulated and the data collected, perhaps by survey or scaling techniques previously discussed, there still remain four central methodological questions:

1. Do the data show any relationship at all?
2. Is the relationship strong?
3. Is the relationship really what the researcher thinks it is?
4. Does it matter?

The first three questions relate to *significance, association,* and *validity,* respectively. The fourth question, the *substantive importance of the research,* while absolutely essential, relates to creativity and a sensitivity for relevant scholarship, which cannot be taught by a methods textbook.

Significance deals with the question of whether or not the observed results are very likely to be different from chance. If in a sample of 6 we found that the 3 men were Democrats and the 3 women were Republicans, we might think this was just chance. But if the sample were of 600 and the same proportions held, all men being Democrats and all women Republicans, we would not attribute this to mere chance.

Association, in contrast, deals with the strength of the relationship. The above examples both have the same strength, because the proportion of men being Democratic and women being Republican is the same, whether the sample size is 6 or 600.

Validity is the question of whether the researcher is truly measuring party affiliation or whether he is really measuring something else; whether the data were gathered properly; whether the relationship would hold for a future set of data; whether the relationship would hold if other variables were controlled.

SIGNIFICANCE VERSUS POWER

In Chapter 8, in discussing the z, t, and F tests, the concept of significance was raised. These tests, which required interval data, sought to determine whether or not there was "too much" chance that the results found by the researcher were just due to chance (i.e., to a "bad sample"). It was observed that most political scientists felt that one chance in twenty (the .05 level of significance) should be the cutoff, with anything greater being "too much." It was also noted that some researchers used cutoff significance levels varying from one chance in ten (the .10 significance level) to one chance in a thousand (the .001 level).

Thus, the *significance level* equals the chance that we would think our results really showed a relationship, when in fact the relationship was just due to chance. More technically, significance is the chance of wrongly rejecting a true null hypothesis (the null hypothesis says that no relationship exists). Wrongly rejecting a true null hypothesis (i.e., thinking we have a relationship when we don't) is what significance levels are all about. The error we make when we do wrongly reject a true null hypothesis is commonly known as a *Type I error*.

A *Type II error* is the chance of wrongly accepting a false null hypothesis (thinking we don't have anything when in fact we do). Type II errors may happen when we pick a given significance level (say the .05 level) and the relationship in our data tends toward significance (is below the .50 level) but doesn't meet the given cutoff level (e.g., when the significance level of a relationship based on our data turns out to be .12; in this situation it is still our *best guess* that this relationship is significant, because .12 is below the .50 level, but we *cannot conclude* that the relationship is significant because there is still too much chance this relationship is due to chance alone, since .12 is above the given cutoff significance level, .05). In such a situation we may make a Type II error by accepting the null hypothesis that there is no relationship, when in reality there is. *Power* has to do with the chance that we would make a Type II error. It is defined as 1.0 minus this chance. Hence a *low* chance of Type II error corresponds to a *high* power level.

If the researcher wishes to avoid mistakes, he or she must be concerned about *both* significance levels *and* power levels. The researcher wants little chance of making either type of error: he or she wants the significance level to be *low* and the power level to be *high*. But there is an inverse relationship between significance levels and power levels. When we pick a very low significance level (e.g., .001) in order to minimize the chance of getting a Type I error, we thereby get a quite high chance of making a Type II error (i.e., we get a low power level). Thus, it is *not* necessarily true that "the lower the significance level, the better," because a very low significance level (.001) may mean we are making a lot of Type II errors.

When we apply a test of significance and we decide there *is* a real relationship not due to chance, then there is a possibility we have made a

Type I error. In this situation, the lower the significance level that can be established the better. When we decide the relationship is *not* real but is due to chance, then there is the possibility we have made a Type II error. In this situation, the higher the power level that can be established, the better.[1]

WHEN SIGNIFICANCE TESTS ARE APPROPRIATE

In Chapter 8 we noted that significance tests are *not* appropriate when we do not have a sample. If we have data on the entire universe (*all* the relevant cases), then any relationship we find based on our data, no matter how weak, is a relationship. Since we did not take a sample, there can be no question that our results cannot be due to chance in the sense of a "bad sample."Moreover, the tests of significance we will be discussing assume a *random* sample. The significance of relationships based on a nonrandom sample would be nice to know, but there is no way of statistically determining the likelihood that such a relationship is based on chance alone.[2]

The significance tests discussed in Chapter 8 (the *z* tests based on the normal distribution tables, the *t* test based on the *t* distribution, and the *F* test based on the *F* distribution) are called *parametric* tests of significance. That is, they assume that the researcher's data has certain parameters or characteristics. These assumptions are that the data are: (1) normally distributed; (2) interval or ratio in level; and (3) in the case of two or more samples, are derived from populations with the same variance (this last assumption does not apply to tests of differences of variances between samples).

Moderate violations of these assumptions appear to have small effect in most cases,[3] but the difficulty of generalizing about this frequently prevents the researcher from knowing whether or not moderate violations would be all right in each particular case.[4] Some situations in which the meaningfulness of statistical significance tests of a parametric nature may be undermined are the following: (1) when the parametric assumptions above are met, but the sample is nonrandom or is small; (2) when the data are

---

[1]Most political scientists use the term "significance tests" to cover both levels of significance and levels of power. We will accept that usage in the following pages, but the student should keep in mind the distinction between these two aspects of significance. Power level tables for many significance tests are contained in Jacob Cohen, *Statistical Power Analysis for the Behavioral Sciences* (New York: Academic Press, 1969).

[2]It is relevant to note that many political scientists nonetheless use significance tests on nonrandom data and even on enumerations. However, as Bradley has noted, "Both distribution-free and parametric tests generally require the 'sampling assumptions' that sample observations have been drawn randomly and independently from their parent populations, and both are highly vulnerable to violation of this type of assumption." James Bradley, *Distribution-Free Statistical Tests* (Englewood Cliffs, N. J.: Prentice-Hall, 1968), p. 23.

[3]Cohen, *Statistical Power Analysis*, pp. 266–267.

[4]See Bradley, *Distribution-Free Statistical Tests*, pp. 23–43.

normally distributed in general, but the tails (extremes) are not (often because there are too many extreme cases), especially when the research emphasizes the importance of looking at cases that are the exception rather than the rule; (3) when data are nominal in level, or when ordinal data are not near-interval (e.g., Guttman scale data, though ordinal, frequently approaches interval level characteristics); (4) when more than one assumption is violated and each violation reinforces the error in the same direction; and (5) when the normal distribution assumption is violated a great deal, a frequent research situation. Moreover, even when *none* of these five conditions are present, parametric statistics may *still* be distorted by violations of assumptions. The only certain way for a researcher to justify violation of the assumptions of parametric tests is to find a particular empirical study of what happens to the statistic used when the same assumptions are violated to the same degree or more under similar conditions, or to conduct such a study.

Usually, when the researcher has data that do not meet the assumptions of the parametric tests discussed in Chapter 8, he or she should use the distribution-free statistics discussed in this chapter. These do not in most cases make any of the assumptions of the parametric tests, and they usually are better for small samples, although they too are undermined by non-random selection of data. Distribution-free tests can be used with data of any underlying distribution, including a normal distribution; hence they can be applied to any situation a parametric test can, and many more besides. (Parametric tests are, however, more efficient when the assumptions are met and the sample is random and sufficiently large.)

Before turning to specific tests of significance, however, it is necessary to call attention to several abuses of such statistics:

1. Mistaking statistical significance for substantive significance—if a relationship is found to be statistically significant, it can still be so weak as to be inconsequential; and, of course, even if it is strong *and* significant, it may not be important for political science as a discipline, for public policy, or for any other criterion.[5]

2. A *posteriori* application of significance tests—one famous political science researcher, having data on very large sample surveys, routinely crosstabulates (makes tables of) each variable with each other variable, and then conducts significance tests on each table; but if, say, the .05 significance level is taken as a cutoff, then just by chance 5 percent of the "significant" tables this researcher uncovers are going to be Type I errors. A *posteriori* selection of tables because they are found to be significant (rather than selection because they test hypotheses and can be selected *a priori* on this basis) is appropriate only in exploratory research when the researcher is not seeking to reach a definite conclusion about his or her data.[6]

3. Applying strong tests of significance for exploratory research purposes—since

[5]See K. W. Taylor and James Frideres, "Issues versus Controversies: Substantive and Statistical Significance," *American Sociological Review* 37, no. 4 (August 1972): 464–472.
[6]See Leslie Kish, "Some Statistical Problems in Research Design," *American Sociological Review* 24, no. 3 (June 1959): 328–338.

strong significance tests involve weak power levels, it is not advisable to apply strong tests when research is for purposes of exploration rather than as proof of the existence or nonexistence of a given relationship.

4. Assuming that significance tests establish the significance of any portion of a contingency table—if a given contingency table is found to be significant at the .05 level, we cannot assume that each cell in the table contributed equally to this finding; for example, the significance level may be due to a very strong relationship in say the upper-left corner of the table, while no relationship exists in the remainder of the table. In such situations, the general relationship of x and y is found to be significant, but we cannot assume that this relationship holds for all values of the two variables.

5. Confusing random sampling with experimental randomization—experimental randomization involves assignment of subjects to an experimental and a control group on a random basis, thereby randomizing uncontrolled variables; random sampling, in contrast, does not prevent uncontrolled variables from having a nonrandom net effect. In fact, correlation of uncontrolled variables may well lead to cumulative bias. This can be compensated by taking measures of all important uncontrolled variables and applying multivariate table analysis (recall Table 9.10), applying tests of significance to the given relationship only for the controlled subtables. When such controls are relevant but cannot be applied (e.g., because of failure to measure possible variables which might confound the given relationship, as class is a confounding variable in the relationship of religion and education in Table 9.10; or because small sample size precludes subtabling), then the significance of the overall given table may be spurious. That is, when possible confounding variables are controlled, it may be found that the overall relationship is not significant at all. It is in this sense that Selvin and others hold significance tests to be technically appropriate only for the subtables that result when all important possible confounding variables are dealt with. (This topic is treated further in Chapter 13).[7]

6. Applying chi-square to inappropriate measures of association—the significance level determined by chi-square is based on sample size, table size, and strength of relationship in the table. The strength of relationship is defined in terms of deviation from statistical independence. Some measures of association (discussed in Chapter 11) such as lambda do not define strength of association in this manner, and hence the usual form of chi-square test is inappropriate. That is, the researcher should employ the same definition of strength of association in tests of significance as in measures of association or correlation.

THE CHI-SQUARE TEST OF
STATISTICAL SIGNIFICANCE

To facilitate easy communication, social scientists use certain (arbitrary) standard ways of presenting data in tables. First, when data are presented in

[7]Hanan Selvin, "A Critique of Tests of Significance in Survey Research," *American Sociological Review* 22, no. 5 (October 1957): 519–527. Selvin's essay and numerous related articles are reprinted in D. Morrison and R. Henkel, eds., *The Significance Test Controversy* (Chicago: Aldine, 1970). Morrison and Henkel note that "significance tests have severe restrictions and difficult requirements for use in any research endeavor" (p. 310). Since the full assumptions of these tests are only rarely met, findings of statistical significance must usually be treated as exploratory evidence rather than definitive proof with regard to the relationship under research.

percentages, the researcher must also present the sample size on which the percentages are based. Second, the independent variable is usually placed at the top of the table, the dependent variable to the side, and percentages are computed down the columns. For example, in Table 10.1, political party is the independent (causal) variable presumed to "cause" voting or nonvoting.

TABLE 10.1

	Democrat	Republican	
Voted	72%	58%	
Didn't Vote	28%	42%	
	100%	100%	$n = 150$

Hence it is placed at the top of the table. Having percentages add to 100 percent by columns rather than rows enables the researcher to see quickly what he is most interested in, the differential effect of the independent variable on the dependent variable. The sample size, 150, is stated at the side to indicate that this relationship is based on 150 individuals.

Using Chi-Square for Significance Tests

A table is considered significant if it is "sufficiently" different from what would occur by chance. This implies that two tables are needed for comparison: a table of observed (real) data and a table of expected (chance) data.

1. Computing the Expected Frequencies If Table 10.2 were the result of a sample survey, for example, the next step would be to compute the expected cell frequencies, *given* the marginals, that is, given that half of the

TABLE 10.2   Observed Data

	Male	Female	row marginals
Republican	15	10	25
Democrat	5	20	25
column marginals	20	30	$n = 50$

sample is Republican and half Democrat, and that its male-female ratio is 2:3. The expected frequency for any cell is the product of its row marginal times its column marginal divided by n, the sample size. Thus by chance, given the marginals, one would expect the number of male Republicans to be not 15 (the observed frequency), but rather the marginal of the cell's row (25), times the marginal of the cell's column (20), divided by n (50), which equals 10. [To check: the marginal products divided by n should be the same as the proportion of Republicans (1/2) times the proportion of males (2/5) times *n*. Both give the expected frequency given the marginals.] Note that this procedure necessarily results in an "expected" table that has marginals identical to the "observed" table.

TABLE 10.3 Expected Data

	Male	Female	row marginals
Republican	10	15	25
Democrat	10	15	25
column marginals	20	30	50

2. Computing Chi-square [X^2] Chi-square is a statistic designed to summarize the extent of difference of observed data from expected data. The expected data need *not* be normally distributed; therefore chi-square, unlike the normal *z* tests discussed in Chapter 8 is *nonparametric*. The data need not conform to any particular distribution parameters, such as the normal distribution, for chi-square to be used. Chi-square,

$$X^2 = \sum \frac{(0 - E)^2}{E}$$

is the sum equal to the square of the *observed* first cell frequency minus the *expected* first cell frequency, divided by the expected first cell frequency, plus the same for the second cell, and so on for as many cells as the table contains.

From Tables 10.2 and 10.3 in the example, chi-square equals 8.33:

$$X^2 = \sum \frac{(15 - 10)^2}{10} + \frac{(10 - 15)^2}{15} + \frac{(5 - 10)^2}{10} + \frac{(20 - 15)^2}{15}$$

$$= 2.5 + 1.67 + 2.5 + 1.67$$

$$= 8.33$$

3. Computing Degrees of Freedom One more step is necessary before the researcher can use a chi-square statistics table to determine if his observed table is significant. The more cells there are in a table, the bigger the chi-square value has to be for the same level of significance. For example, a chi-square of 8.33 is significant at the .05 level for a 2-by-2 table, but would not be for a 3-by-3 table.

Degrees of freedom equals number of rows minus 1, times number of columns minus 1:

$$d.f. = (r - 1)(c - 1)$$

Thus a 2-by-2 table has 1 degree of freedom. This refers to the fact that given the marginals and the frequency of one cell in a 2-by-2 table, the rest of the cells may be filled out. Similarly, the last row and last column in a 3-by-3 (or any size) table can be filled out if the marginals and the other row and column entries are known.

4. Using the Chi-square Table   Once the researcher has presented his or her observed table, computed the expected table and the chi-square value, and determined the number of degrees of freedom associated with that size table, he or she then simply looks at a table of chi-square values such as that shown in Table 10.4.

TABLE 10.4   Table of Distribution of X^2

	Probability			
d.f.	.99	.98	.95	.90
1	.000157	.000628	.00393	.0158
2	.0201	.0404	.103	.211
3	.115	.185	.352	.584
4	.297	.429	.711	1.064
30	14.053	16.306	18.493	20.599

d.f.	.10	.05	.02	.01	.001
1	2.706	3.841	5.412	6.635	10.827
2	4.605	5.991	7.824	9.210	13.815
3	6.251	7.815	9.837	11.345	16.268
4	7.779	9.488	11.668	13.277	18.465
30	40.256	43.773	47.962	50.892	59.703

Thus, for 1 d.f. the researcher finds that the chi-square value, 8.33, lies between the .01 and .001 probability levels. This means that a table as or more different from the expected table would occur by chance, given the marginal distribution of the variables, only one time in a hundred to one time in a thousand. The .05 level is usually considered the minimum level of acceptable significance—even then the researcher will be wrong five times out of a hundred in thinking the table is significant when it is not. Similarly, the computed chi-square value must be higher than the .95 level for the researcher to conclude that the table is significantly *not* different from chance. Actually, the researcher should determine *in advance* what level of significance (e.g., .05, .02, .01, .001) is appropriate to the needs of his or her research; he or she should *not*, for example, start with the decision that the

.01 level is required and then make "exceptions" for relationships that only meet the .05 level.[8]

Assumptions of the Chi-Square Test

1. Data must be randomly sampled.
2. The hypothesis being tested should be nondirectional (chi-square tests are insensitive to the direction of deviation of observed from expected values; consequently a chi-square or any nondirectional test of a directional hypothesis will involve a higher rate of Type I errors than the same test for the same data for a nondirectional hypothesis).
3. Observations must be independent (dependent observations would arise, for example, when the same individual is counted more than once in a table of n observations, and where that individual's contribution to the count in one cell is tied to his or her contribution to the count in another cell; conversely, observations are usually independent when n observations are made of n different individuals).
4. The sum of expected frequencies must equal the sum of observed frequencies (this assumption is not a problem when expected frequencies are computed as illustrated earlier. Sometimes, however, expected frequencies are based on other lines of reasoning, such as assertions based on past experience without regard to the marginal distribution of observed data).
5. The deviations must be normally distributed in the population (this assumption is mentioned because some texts assert that the variables must be normally distributed, which is misleading; although the chi-square distribution *is* a function of the normal distribution, there is no assumption that the underlying distribution of the variables be normal, in contrast to the z test discussed in Chapter 8; rather, chi-square procedures assume that the deviations of the observed values are from a true central value and are normally distributed around it; since the true central value is unknown, this assumption is generally neglected although it may be noted that sometimes the true central value is known, in which case the appropriateness of the chi-square test may be checked; moreover, when assumption 4 is not met, assumption 5 will not be met).

---

[8]Computing the power level is more complex, and the student is referred to Cohen, *Statistical Power Analysis*, ch. 7. In brief, however, the power level depends upon the sample size ($n = 50$ in Table 10.2, for example); the number of degrees of freedom (d.f. $= 1$ in this example; degrees of freedom is labelled "u" in Cohen's tables); the chosen cutoff significance level (.05 in the example; this is labelled "a" in Cohen's tables); and the effect size index (labelled "e" in Cohen's tables; effect size is the degree of discrepancy of the actually observed or hypothetically observed results from chance; for chi-square tests, e is computed by the same formula as chi-square, except cell and marginal frequencies are expressed as percentages of n, and n is replaced by 1.0; thus, for Table 10.2, $e \cong .17$). Taking Table 10.2 as an example, the appropriate power table in Cohen is Table 7.3.15 at p. 228; here we find that the chi-square test in this example assumes a power level of somewhere between .61 ($e = .10$) and .89 ($e = .20$). Extrapolating, we estimate the power level to be .81 ($e = .17$). Accepting Cohen's suggestion of .80 power level as an arbitrary cutoff for acceptable minimum power, we conclude that the chi-square test is adequately powerful for this example. Most political scientists, it should be noted, ignore computation of power levels.

6. Sample size must be sufficiently large (some authors set 50 as the cutoff, while others allow as few as 20, provided conditions listed below are met).[9]

7. All expected cell frequencies should be 5 or more in a 2-by-2 table (assumption 5 is violated when an expected frequency is, say, 2; this is because deviations below this value are restricted to the narrow range of 0 or 1, while deviations above have a broad range of 3 or more; in such an instance deviations cannot be assumed to be normally distributed).[10]

8. Eighty percent or more of all expected cell frequencies should be 5 or more in larger tables.[11] No cell in any size table may be zero in frequency.

9. Percentages may not be substituted for frequencies (percentage data, in effect, sets n equal to 100; since chi-square is sensitive to sample size, allowing smaller deviations to be found significant at a given level for larger samples, the use of percentage data would result in the same findings as if frequency data had been used only when sample size was 100).

10. Finally, it may be noted that no assumptions are made about level of data. Some texts misleadingly assert that nominal-level data are assumed. It would be more correct to say that chi-square is not as efficient as other significance tests designed for higher-level (ordinal and interval) data when one has such data and meets the assumptions of the tests involved (e.g., the t test). Nonetheless, chi-square tests may be performed on data of any level.[12]

Yates' Correction for Continuity

If sample size is 20 or more in a 2-by-2 table but a cell frequency is less than 5, then Yates' Correction may be used. This is done by simply replacing the regular chi-square formula in step 2 above with the following formula:

$$\chi^2 = \sum \frac{(|0 - E| - .5)^2}{E}$$

That is, for each cell, .5 is subtracted from the difference of observed frequencies minus expected frequencies before squaring and dividing by E. The other steps remain the same.

It should be noted that the effect of Yates' correction is to reduce the computed chi-square value, thereby making it more difficult to find a relationship to be significant at a given level of significance. Some authors

---

[9]In 2-by-2 tables with small sample size, the Fisher exact test is used, as discussed later in this chapter. For exact tests for larger tables, see W. L. Hays, ed., *Statistics for Psychologists* (New York: Holt, Rinehart & Winston, 1963): 155–156, 598–601.

[10]Some authors specify more than 5, while others insist on 10 or more. If this assumption is not met and if no cell is zero, Yates' correction for chi-square is used, discussed later in this chapter.

[11]Again, some authors specify more than 5, while others insist on 10 or more. If this assumption is not met and if no cell is zero, rows and/or columns must be omitted and/or combined to obtain a table that satisfies this condition.

[12]For further reading on assumptions of chi-square procedures, see Bernhardt Lieberman, ed., *Contemporary Problems in Statistics* (New York: Oxford, 1971), sec. 5.

apply Yates' correction in *all* 2-by-2 tables regardless of sample size, and others in *all* 2-by-2 tables *over sample size 40.* Yet other authors apply Yates' correction in all 2-by-2 tables having a cell frequency of *less than 10.* Such more stringent requirements operate in the same direction, reducing the likelihood of finding significant relationships in one's data. Some even require sample size to be 50 or more before either chi-square or corrected chi-square may be used. In this writer's estimate, however, the conventional sample size of 20 and cutoff of 5 are the most commonly used in political science. Adoption of the more stringent conventions would decrease the likelihood of Type I errors but increase the likelihood of Type II errors. Regardless of the convention adopted, when the stipulated assumptions are *not* met, the researcher must turn to an exact test such as Fisher's, discussed later in this chapter; in some cases, some of the distribution-free tests discussed later in this chapter may also be appropriate. In spite of all these stipulations and requirements, chi-square tests remain far and away the most common tests of significance in political science.

Other Applications of Chi-Square Tests

Chi-Square and Scale Significance   At the end of Chapter 9, Schuessler's method of testing Guttman scales was mentioned. In this method, the researcher constructs the observed scale in the usual way and then constructs a chance, expected scale using random numbers. Two lists are then made, one for the observed and one for the expected data, listing the number of respondents with no scale errors, with one error, and so on, up to n respondents. These observed and expected frequencies can then be substituted in the regular chi-square formula (step 2) and the resulting chi-square statistic can be used to check significance levels. Degrees of freedom in this test is $n-1$. This enables the researcher to present a Guttman scale, and to state that it is scalable at least at the .60 level and is significant at least at the .05 level, for example.

Chi-square and Sample Size   Chi-square can also help the researcher determine sample size needed. He or she needs a sample big enough to reasonably assure that specified differences from chance will be found significant, as the following example illustrates.

1. Determining Desired Significance and Difference Levels   The researcher simply specifies the level of significance he or she feels appropriate for the study (.05 for most social science research, .001 for medical research, for example), and what is the *least* difference he or she wants to be detected as significant. For example, in the simple example of sex and political party affiliation cited earlier, the researcher might specify that he or she wants a

10 percent difference found significant at the .05 level. This step is purely arbitrary, depending on research needs.

2. Specifying Expected and Least-difference Tables To specify the expected table, the researcher must have some way of estimating the marginal frequencies. That is, through some method—census data, small sample, expert opinion, sheer guess—he or she must make an estimate; once this is done the expected cell frequencies are computed as discussed earlier—marginal products divided by N, or as in Table 10.5, expressed in terms of percentages.

TABLE 10.5

	Male	Female	
Republican	.20N	.30N	.50N
Democrat	.20N	.30N	.50N
	.40N	.60N	1.00N

(a) Expected Table

	Male	Female	
Republican	.25N	.25N	.50N
Democrat	.15N	.35N	.50N
	.40N	.60N	1.00N

(b) Least-difference Table

If the researcher knows that half the population is Democrat and half Republican, and also knows 40 percent is male and 60 percent female, he or she can construct an expected table as shown in Table 10.5 (a). By placing 10 percent more of the relationship on the diagonal that he or she expects to show a relationship—here, the Male-Republican, Female-Democrat diagonal—and 10 percent less on the other diagonal, the researcher can specify the 10-percent-difference table chosen in step 1.[13]

3. Solve for N The researcher then substitutes the least-difference proportions (using them as the observed frequencies) and also the expected frequencies in the chi-square formula and solves for N, first setting X^2 equal to 3.841, which is the chi-square value for 1 d.f. at the .05 level:

$$X^2 = 3.841 = \sum \frac{(.25N - .20N)^2}{.20N} + \frac{(.25N - .30N)^2}{.30N}$$
$$+ \frac{(.15N - .20N)^2}{.20N} + \frac{(.35N - .30N)^2}{.30N}$$
$$= \frac{.0025N^2}{.20N} + \frac{.0025N^2}{.30N} + \frac{.0025N^2}{.20N} + \frac{.0025N^2}{.30N}$$
$$= .0125N + .0083N + .0125N + .0083N$$
$$3.841 = .0416N$$
$$N = 3.841/.0416 = 92.3$$

[13]The least-difference table is arbitrary and may be specified in any manner the researcher desires, as long as that is the least-strong difference to be detected.

Thus the researcher needs to take a sample of at least 93 individuals to be 95 percent sure of detecting a 10 percent difference from chance. Note that this is for one table only. If the table is to be subtabled, as in multivariate analysis discussed earlier, an even larger sample will be needed to detect a 10-percent difference in the subtables. If the subtable divides the main table into two equal subtables, then twice as large a sample will be needed; if it splits the main table 3/4 in one subtable and 1/4 the other, then a sample four times as large is needed. For subtables, the computed sample size is multiplied by the reciprocal of the smallest fraction of the main table received by any subtable, in this case by 4, the reciprocal of 1/4.

This method does not eliminate the need to compute sample size by the binomial (normal table) method presented earlier. Whichever method results in the *higher* sample size is used.[14]

Chi-square and Goodness of Fit   The researcher often desires to know if the frequencies associated with a particular variable conform to his expectations. For example, a researcher dealing with the Guttman scale of riot severity may wish to know if the distribution of numbers of riots (frequencies) on this scale of severity (the variable) is normally distributed (a hypothesized expectation). The chi-square goodness-of-fit test is used to determine if results for a particular variable are normally distributed, are the same as another known distribution of data, or conform to any other particular distribution specified in advance.

Chi-square, as mentioned earlier, is a nonparametric statistic because it can be used to test whether *any* observed distribution is significantly different from any given hypothetical distribution. Most often the hypothetical (expected) distribution is the normal distribution; the researcher wishes to see if it is technically valid to use *parametric tests*—tests that assume the variable is normally distributed in the "real world," although not *necessarily* in a given sample.

The previous chapter presented an index of riot severity; Table 10.6 shows a way of testing to see if the index is normally distributed. The scale in Chapter 9 had 8 scale types (column 1). In addition, data were presented showing the number of cities in each scale category (column 2). The question is, "Is the distribution shown in column 2 what would be expected if riot severity were normally distributed?"

To answer this we must compute the normally expected frequencies for each scale category (columns 3—7). In columns 3 and 4 we find the normalized frequency of riot scale intervals; this is obtained by subtracting the weighted mean frequency $f(\bar{x})$ from the scale intervals in column 1 (this gives column 3), and then by dividing the result in column 3 by the standard

---

[14]Compute sample size for the smallest subtable; *then* estimate sample size needed overall.

Cohen, *Statistical Power Analysis*, outlines a different procedure of this general type for computing sample size, and presents corresponding power level tables (see pp. 262–265 and Table 7.4.1).

deviation of the observed frequencies s (this yields column 4).

By subtracting the mean and dividing by the standard deviation we get a normal z distribution, as discussed in Chapter 8 on sampling. Simply by looking in a table of values for the normal curve found in any statistics text, we can derive the figures in column 5. Column 5 is the percent of cases which, in the normal table case, would fall in a particular category or lower. For example, 78 percent of the cases should fall to the left of $z = .76$ on a normal curve.

Column 6 shows the percentage of cases falling within a particular scale category. For the lowest case, scale category 1, the percent is the same as in column 5, 24 percent. Note that the lowest and highest category percentages include cases which, if the variable were truly normally distributed and if the normal case had the same mean and standard deviation as the observed data, would be in the extreme tails of the normal curve (would be outside the scale categories entirely). Often these "tails" make little difference since the percent of cases in them is so small; here, the standard deviation, 4.7 on an 8-point scale, is so large that the tails have a large effect. Thus, if riot severity were normally distributed, fully 24 percent of the cases would lie in category 1 or lower. The amount in category 2 is this proportion, .24, subtracted from the proportion listed in column 5 for category 2, .07. This subtracting process is continued on up the scale to the highest category, where the expected frequency is the other extreme "tail," in this case .29.

Expected frequency equals the proportions in column 6 times the total number of cases (100 in this case), rounded to whole numbers. The expected frequencies, shown in column 7, are subtracted from the observed frequencies (column 2) to give column 8. Column 9 is the chi-square formula for the observed minus expected frequencies squared and divided by the expected frequencies. The sum of column 9 is the *chi-square value* for the observed distribution of riot severity. The number of *degrees of freedom* is the number of categories (8), minus the number of restrictions on the data (3; normal distribution with observed mean, standard deviation, and sample size specified in advance), or 5 in this case.[15]

Finally, we take the computed chi-square value, 70.2, and refer to the chi-square table found in the Appendix. For 5 d.f., the .95 level indicates how *small* chi-square must be for us to be 95 percent sure that the observed distribution is *not* significantly different from the normal distribution. The .05 level tells how large chi-square must be for us to be 95 percent sure the

---

[15]For a helpful discussion of degrees of freedom in goodness-of-fit and other tests, see Helen Walker, "Degrees of Freedom," in A. Haber, R. Runyon, and P. Badia, eds., *Readings in Statistics* (Reading, Mass.: Addison-Wesley, 1970), ch. 12.

Note that the use of normal probability graph paper is an alternative method of assessing goodness-of-fit to normal distribution. If a variable, x, is plotted on normal probability paper, using the y-axis as the cumulative percent of units of x and the x-axis as units of x, a straight line will result when x is normally distributed.

TABLE 10.6 Chi-square Goodness-of-Fit Test for the Riot Severity Scale

(1) category interval	(2) observed frequency	(3) $(1) - f(\bar{x})$	(4) $(3)/s$ normalized frequency	(5) percent below	(6) percent within	(7) $(6) \times \Sigma(2)$ expected frequency	(8) $\lvert (2) - (7) \rvert$ absolute observed minus expected frequency	(9) $[(2) - (7)]^2/(7)$
8	4	3.6	.76	.78	.29	29	25	21.5
7	19	2.6	.55	.71	.08	8	11	15.1
6	13	1.6	.34	.63	.07	7	6	5.1
5	16	.6	.14	.56	.09	9	7	5.4
4	13	-.4	-.08	.47	.09	9	4	1.8
3	7	-1.4	-.30	.38	.07	7	0	0
2	17	-2.4	-.51	.31	.07	7	10	14.3
1	11	-3.4	-.72	.24	.24	24	13	7.0
	100							$\chi^2 = 70.2$

$$\Sigma x = 100$$
$$\bar{x} = 100/8$$
$$= 12.5$$

$$\Sigma f(x) = \Sigma (1)(2)$$
$$= 441$$
$$f(\bar{x}) = 441/100$$
$$= 4.41$$

$$s = \sqrt{\frac{\Sigma [(2) - \bar{x}]^2}{8}}$$
$$= \sqrt{180/8}$$
$$= 4.74$$

observed distribution *is* significantly different from chance. Since the chi-square value here of 70.2 is much larger than even the .001 level, we therefore conclude that the index of riot severity can *not* be treated as a normally distributed variable.

Note that in this example the test item—riot severity—is an ordinal-level scale. While the goodness-of-fit test shows whether or not we can assume normality for this variable when we treat it as interval in level, it does *not* justify the assumption of interval level in the first place. Note also that Column 1 in Table 10.6 may range from 0 to 7 rather than 1 to 8 without affecting the results. More generally, Column 1 may contain any ordered set of item values. When ranges are used in Column 1 (e.g., ages 0–9.9 years, 10.0–19.9, 20.0–29.9, etc.) the upper limits are used (i.e., 9.9, 19.9, 29.9, etc.).

Other Considerations   The chi-square goodness-of-fit test can also be used to check the extent to which a set of data approximates any given distribution, not only the normal distribution. Although neglected in political science, the *Poisson distribution* is a likely alternative. The normal distribution works best in significance testing when the probability of success (p) and of failure (q) are both .5. As the probability of one of these outcomes becomes very low, the resulting distribution will not approximate a normal distribution, even when the sample size is quite large. In such cases the Poisson distribution may be more appropriate. A typical instance involves the distribution of arrivals of customers or demands for a service; hence the Poisson distribution is commonly used in operations research.[16]

When sample size is too small for use of the chi-square goodness-of-fit test, the Kolmogorov-Smirnov goodness-of-fit test (to be discussed later in the chapter) may be used.

Finally, it should be remarked that chi-square is additive. By partitioning it is possible to make finer comparison of cells within a given table.[17] Additivity does not apply to corrected chi-square, however, as Yates' correction is justified only when the number of degrees of freedom is one.

FISHER EXACT TEST OF SIGNIFICANCE

When sample size is less than 20 for a 2-by-2 table, the Fisher exact test should be used. This method gives the exact chance of getting a particular table, given the marginals.

---

[16]For illustration, see F. Hillier and G. Lieberman, *Introduction to Operations Research* (San Francisco: Holden Day, 1967), pp. 38, 287 ff., and Appendix Five, Table A.5.4. See also D. Plane and G. Kochenberger, *Operations Research for Managerial Decisions* (Homewood, Ill.: Irwin-Dorsey, 1972): 177–180, 192–198.

[17]Jean Bresnahan and Martin Shapiro, "A General Equation and Technique for the Exact Partitioning of Chi-Square Contingency Tables," in Haber, Runyon, and Badia, eds., *Read-*

TABLE 10.7   General Case

a	b	r_1
c	d	r_2
c_1	c_2	n

$$p = \frac{r_1! r_2! c_1! c_2!}{n! a! b! c! d!}$$

1. Specify the Observed Table and All Stronger Tables

First the given table is presented, along with all stronger tables, as shown in Table 10.8. The stronger tables are specified by reducing the cell with the lowest count (the upper-right cell, 2, in this case) successively down to zero—since the marginals are known, the other cell frequencies follow automatically. The researcher must then compute p for each of these tables.

TABLE 10.8

7	2	9
5	6	11
12	8	20

observed table

8	1	9
4	7	11
12	8	20

next stronger

9	0	9
3	8	11
12	8	20

strongest table

2. Computing p

The probability of a table of a given strength is equal to the product of the marginal factorials divided by sample size factorial times the cell factorials,[18] as shown in the following equation:

$$p_{\text{observed}} = \frac{9! 11! 12! 8!}{20! 7! 2! 5! 6!} = .132$$

$$p_{\text{next stronger}} = \frac{9! 11! 12! 8!}{20! 8! 1! 4! 7!} = .024$$

$$p_{\text{strongest}} = \frac{9! 11! 12! 8!}{20! 9! 0! 3! 8!} = .001$$

$$p_{\text{total}} = .157$$

---

ings in Statistics, ch. 15. Bresnahan and Shapiro advocate a partitioning procedure as superior to omitting and/or combining rows and/or columns when less than 80 percent of all expected cell frequencies are 5 or more in a table larger than 2-by-2 (recall the assumptions of the chi-square test).

[18]Factorial (!) is an arithmetic operation in which 1 is multiplied by 2, and this product by 3, and the resulting product by 4, and so on up to n. For example, $5! = 1 \times 2 \times 3 \times 4 \times 5 = 120$. Zero factorial (0!) equals 1.

The result indicates that there is a 15.7-percent chance that, given the observed marginals, a table as strong or stronger than the observed table would occur by chance alone. Ordinarily, social scientists consider a 5-percent chance the maximum acceptable level, so this observed table would not be considered significant.

Assumptions of the Fisher Exact Test

1. *Random sampling.*
2. *Directional hypothesis.* A directional hypothesis is involved in the example cited (the researcher is interested in a relationship as strong or stronger than the observed relationship). To use the Fisher exact test for a nondirectional hypothesis (for a relationship as strong or stronger as the observed relationship in *either* direction), then p_{total} in step 2 must be doubled.
3. *Independent observations.* While no assumption is made about *sample* size, it is assumed that the *population* size from which the sample was drawn was sufficiently large that the sampling of the first (or any) individual does not alter the remaining distribution of the population; in such a situation observations would not be independent, unless sampling was the replacement of sampled individuals in the population.
4. *Mutually exclusive* (any given individual or unit can fall into only one category) *and exhaustive* (no individual or unit in the population fails to fall into one of the two categories) *dichotomies in the 2-by-2 table* (to which this test is restricted).
5. *No assumption made about level of data.* As with chi-square tests, however, the Fisher exact test is especially appropriate to nominal-level data. With ordinal data, the sign or runs tests are more efficient, and with interval data, the t or F tests are more efficient, for example, provided the other assumptions of these tests are met.

Finally, it should be noted that some authors apply the Fisher exact text for sample sizes up to 50 in preference to the chi-square test (rather than up to 20, as suggested earlier). While the difficulty of computing the exact test for larger samples has meant that most political scientists have chosen cutoffs lower than 50, it is true that the exact test is more accurate than the chi-square test for any size sample. All political scientists seem to agree that the exact test must be used for samples under 20, and that the difference of chi-square from exact test results is negligible for samples over 50. As computer routines make computation of the exact test no burden to the researcher, we can expect a sample size of 50 to become the conventional cutoff.

Tocher's Modification

Tocher has proposed a modification of the Fisher exact test that increases its power for a given level of significance.[19] Tocher's modification is appro-

---

[19] Sidney Siegel, *Nonparametric Statistics for the Behavioral Sciences* (New York: McGraw-Hill, 1956), 101–103. This work is a standard reference for many of the tests discussed in this chapter.

priate when (1) we have chosen a given level of significance as our test criterion (the .05 level is commonly chosen) and (2) we find (as in the example for the Fisher exact test) that p_{total} is greater than .05, but p_{total} *minus* $p_{observed}$ is less than .05.

Look at the example for the Fisher exact test. In this example, the probability of getting tables stronger than that observed was .024 plus .001, which equals .025; we observe that .025 is below the .05 significance level. When we add in the probability of the observed table, .132, the total probability zooms way up to .157, far above the .05 cutoff level, so we fail to reject the null hypothesis.

Consider this more closely, however. The probability of getting the observed table is .132. Part of this probability *is* below the cutoff level of .05. Specifically, .05 minus .025 (the probability of getting tables stronger than the observed), or .025 of the .132 lies below the cutoff level of .05; the remaining .107 of the .132 lies above this level. It is relevant to ask whether our *particular* observed distribution should be counted as the part under the .05 level (in which case we would reject the null hypothesis) or the part over the .05 level (in which case we would fail to reject the null hypothesis). To decide which way we should count our particular observed distribution, we use the random number table: .025 divided by .132 equals .189; we take a 3-digit number from the table at random; if it is 189 or less, we count our case as falling below the .05 level; otherwise we count it as falling above, and make our inference accordingly.

OTHER NOMINAL-LEVEL
DISTRIBUTION-FREE TESTS

The chi-square and Fisher exact tests are the most commonly used tests of significance for nominal data. The former is used for large samples and the latter for small samples. Neither assume that the variables are distributed in a particular way (e.g., the normal distribution is not assumed). In addition to these tests there are others also designed for nominal-level data, free from any distribution requirement. These include the *binomial test*, the *McNemar test*, and *Cochran's Q test*.

The Binomial Test

The binomial test is based on the probability rules studied in Chapter 8. It is similar to the Fisher exact test (the binomial test also yields exact probabilities—whereas the chi-square test is an approximation to an exact test), but where the Fisher exact test deals with the joint distribution of *two* dichotomies (i.e., with 2-by-2 tables), the binomial test deals with the distribution of *one* dichotomy.

In the binomial test, for example, we may determine the probability of getting r observations in one category and $n-r$ observations in the other, given the chance, p, of getting an observation of the first type and the chance, q, of not getting it. (Recall $q = 1 - p$):

$$p(r)_{\text{binomial}} \quad = \quad {}_nC_r \cdot p^r \cdot q^{n-r} \quad = \quad \frac{n!p^r q^{n-r}}{r!(n-r)!}$$

Thus, if we know that a particular city is 60 percent Democratic ($p = .60$) and 40 percent non-Democratic ($q = .40$), and we sample a particular fraternal organization and find 70 Democrats ($r = 70$) in a sample of 100 persons sampled from a population split 60/40:

$$p(70)_{\text{binomial}} \quad = \quad \frac{100! \;.60^{70}\;.40^{30}}{70!\;30!}$$

To get the chance of getting 70 Democrats *or more* we would, as we did in the Fisher exact test, compute the exact probability of *each* stronger case. In this example, we would have to compute $p(71), p(72), \ldots, p(100)$, and sum these along with $p(70)$ to get the exact chance of getting 70 Democrats or more. Tocher's modification could also be applied to the binomial test to give it greater power at the same significance level.

It can be seen that when n is large, as in this example, its computation requires a computer. Tables have also been published giving binomial probabilities for various levels of n, r, and p.[20] Another alternative is possible when n is large.

When n is greater than 25 and p is near .5 and the product npq is at least 9, then the binomial distribution approximates the normal distribution and the normal tables may be used to determine binomial probabilities:

$$z \quad = \quad \frac{(r\pm.5)-np}{\sqrt{npq}} \quad = \quad \frac{69.5-60}{\sqrt{24}} \quad = \quad 1.94$$

Note that when r is smaller than np, .5 is added to r; when r is larger than np, .5 is subtracted from r. Since 70 (r) is larger than 60 (np) in our example, .5 is subtracted from 70 in the illustration above. After z is computed, a normal table may be consulted. Here we find that the area under a normal curve as or more extreme than 1.94 is .0264. That is, just by chance we would expect 2.64 percent of samples to result in 70 or more Democrats out of 100, when the true split in the whole population is 60/40. Therefore, we can say that the hypothesis that the fraternal organization has *more* Democrats than would be expected for that city is significant at the .026 level. (This is a one-tailed test; for the two-tailed hypothesis, that the

[20]See Table II for the case of $p = .5$ and $n \le 25$.

organization is *different* from what would be expected, the significance level is doubled, .052).

The binomial test assumes that the sample was taken at random, the observations were independent, and that the dichotomy (to which this test is restricted) is mutually exclusive and exhaustive.

The McNemar Test

We may use the chi-square or Fisher exact tests for nominal-level, two-sample cases when both samples are taken *independently*. For example, we can use these tests when we want to see if one sample (e.g., the percentage of Democrats in sample city A) is different from another independent sample (e.g., the percentage of Democrats in sample city B). But when the two samples are related (*dependent*), then the McNemar test is used.

Two samples are dependent if:

1. They are matched pairs, where every member of the first sample has a "partner" in the second sample, known in advance to have the same age, sex, educational level, or other relevant control-variable characteristics, or
2. The two samples are of the "before" and "after" type, where each individual serves as his own partner.

For example, the McNemar method might be used to test whether or not a television broadcast affected a group's political views. The McNemar method uses a variation of chi-square, emphasizing the difference between cells a and d (See Table 10.9).

TABLE 10.9

		After Broadcast		
		oppose	favor	
Before	favor	$a=6$	$b=20$	26
	oppose	$c=10$	$d=14$	24
		16	34	50

$$X^2 = \frac{(|a - d| - 1)^2}{a + d} = \frac{49}{20} = 2.45$$

Looking up this chi-square value in a chi-square table, we find that a 2.45 value with d.f. = 1 (determined as before, $r-1$ times $c-1$) is not significant. Note that chi-square tables list significance levels for nondirectional hypotheses; for a directional hypothesis such as "broadcast affects opinion," the significance found must be doubled—the .01 level becomes the .02 level, the .05 level becomes the .1 level, etc. Second, if the expected frequency of $\frac{1}{2}(a + d)$ is less than 5, the binomial test should be used instead of the McNemar test. To do this, the binomial formula is used, with $n = a + d$

and $r = a$ or d, whichever is smaller. Third, while the McNemar test *may* be used with any level data, it is designed for nominal-level data; if ordinal data are available, then the sign test (discussed later) is used.[21]

Neither the McNemar nor the sign test assume that the two samples come from the same population. The McNemar test assumes random sampling, mutually exclusive and exhaustive dichotomies, and that $.5(a + d)$ is 5 or more. Although the samples may be correlated, observations within either sample are assumed to be independent.

Cochran's Q Test

The Cochran Q test is an extension of the McNemar test, adapting the McNemar test for the case of *more than two dependent samples*. (Chi-square may be used for the case of more than two *independent* samples; for r independent samples that assume c values for a given variable, construct an r-by-c table and compute chi-square as previously indicated.) Though no data level is assumed, Cochran's Q is designed for use with nominal variables or dichotomized ordinal variables. (For *ordinal* data and more than two dependent samples, Friedman two-way analysis of variance is preferred; for ordinal data and more than two independent samples, either the extension of the median test or the Kruskal-Wallis one-way analysis of variance is preferred.) For these relatively specialized tests, the student is referred to Siegel.[22]

ORDINAL-LEVEL DISTRIBUTION-FREE TESTS

While all the nominal-level tests just described may be applied to ordinal-level data, it is preferable to employ test statistics designed specifically for the ordinal level, provided the relevant assumptions can be met. These tests include the runs tests, Kolmogorov-Smirnov tests, the median test, the Mann-Whitney U test, the sign test, the Wilcoxon test, and others.

Runs Tests

The *one-sample runs test* is frequently used as a one-sample, nonparametric test of significance, appropriate when the population is divided into just two classes (male-female, Republican-Democrat, etc.). It is often used as a *test of randomness* of a sample. The idea is that a random sample will have at least

---

[21]Recall Table 8.10 for treatment of interval-level, parametric, correlated data.

[22]Computation of these statistics is treated in Siegel, *Nonparametric Statistics*, pp. 161–172, 179–193.

a certain number of "runs." A run is a series of similar responses; in Figure 10.1, the first two R responses (indicating that the first two persons sampled

| R | R | D | D | D | D | R | D | D | R | R | R | D | R | D |

FIGURE 10.1 Party Affiliations in Sample of 15

were Republican) constitute a run, the four Ds are a second run, etc., for 8 runs. Thus the number of runs, r, is 8; the number in the first category, n_1, is 7, and the number in the second category, n_2, is 8 (7 Rs and 8 Ds). Looking in a table of critical values for r in the runs test, for $n_1 = 7$ and $n_2 = 8$ we find that the number of runs, r, must be 4 or less, or 13 or more, for us to conclude that the sample is significantly different from random. Since our runs total, 8, is between 4 and 13, we fail to reject the null hypothesis that Republicans and Democrats were samples by chance. That is, at the .05 level we may be confident that ours was not a nonrandom sample.

For a series of responses larger than 20, the normal z distribution approximates the r distribution:

$$z = \frac{r - \left(\dfrac{2n_1 n_2}{n_1 + n_2} + 1\right)}{\sqrt{\dfrac{2n_1 n_2 (2n_1 n_2 - n_1 - n_2)}{(n_1 + n_2)^2 (n_1 + n_2 - 1)}}}$$

where the critical z value equals r reduced by a mean (the term after the minus sign in the numerator) and divided by a specified standard deviation (the term in the denominator).[23]

This one-sample runs test tests the *number* of observed runs compared with the number that would be obtained at random (by chance), assuming independent observations. A similar one-sample runs test tests the *length* of observed runs compared to the length that would be expected by chance.[24] Both tests may be applied in assessing the randomness of responses, though the former is more commonly used. Both assume that responses fall into a mutually exclusive and exhaustive dichotomy. There is some evidence that the number-of-runs test is more powerful than the length-of-runs test for the same level of significance.

The *Wald-Wolfowitz two-sample runs test* tests whether or not two samples significantly differ in the size (rank level) of some ordinal criterion variable. It assumes that data are at least ordinal, sampling is random, observations are independent, and samples are independent. For ordinal

[23]When the number of observations in both categories is small, this formula is adjusted for continuity by subtracting .5 from the absolute value of the numerator.
[24]This test is described in Bradley, *Distribution-Free Statistical Tests*, pp. 255–259.

data, it also assumes that the range of possible rank values is the same for the two samples (e.g., that possible rank levels range from 1 through 25 for both samples, whether or not the samples or populations are of the same size). The test is most meaningful when sample sizes are the same, and should not be used when one sample is much greater than the other, even if other assumptions are met.

When the necessary conditions are met, the Wald-Wolfowitz test is computed as follows. First, let there be two samples of size n_1 and n_2, respectively (e.g., a sample of 25 persons from City A and 25 persons from City B); let the criterion variable range in rank from a to k (e.g., an "authoritarianism" scale score ranging from 1 to 20). Second, list the $n_1 + n_2$ persons (50, in our example) in order by their rank level, combining both samples.[25] In the *same* order, list whether the person was from sample A or sample B. This string of As and Bs may then be tested for significant deviation from the null hypotheses of independence (no relation; the criterion variable does not differentiate the two populations sampled) in the same manner as for the one-sample runs test.[26]

Kolmogorov-Smirnov Tests

For the one-sample ordinal case, the *Kolmogorov-Smirnov D test* is used; as will be discussed, this can be extended to the two-sample ordinal case as well. Like chi-square, the D test is a goodness-of-fit significance test (one sample), but is considered a more powerful test and may be used when data are ordinal. Although chi-square may also be used on ordinal data for goodness of fit, the D test is preferred. To take the riot severity scale again, we might want to use the D test to see if the data are significantly different from the null hypothesis that riots are equally distributed by severity.

The D *value* is the largest absolute difference between the cumulative observed proportion and the cumulative expected proportion; when this is found (here .085), the researcher looks in a table of critical values of D to find the corresponding level of significance. By inspecting such a table we find that for $N = 75$ (the number of riot cities) at the .05 level (usually

---

[25]Tied scores will not affect this statistic if ties are between persons within the same sample. When ties are between persons in different samples, one of two procedures may be used: (1) as an approximation, assign the order by use of the random number table; (2) a better but more tedious method is to determine the significance level for each possible combination of ordering of ties, then basing inference on the most probable significance finding. When such ties are numerous, this test should not be used.

[26]Note that the Wald-Wolfowitz test of differences in rank level encompasses tests of other differences. For example, a difference in median values would lead to clustering of A runs and B runs at different portions of the rank order continuum; hence this is also a test for differences in median values.

TABLE 10.10   **D** Value Computing Table for Riot Severity

Rank Interval	1	2	3	4	5	6	7	8
$f(x)$ = number in category	8	13	5	10	12	10	14	3
$f_{cum}(x)$ = cumulative %	11	28	35	48	64	77	96	100
$f_{exp.\ cum}(x)$ = expected cumulative %	12.5	25	37.5	50	62.5	75	87.5	100
difference		1.5	3	2.5	2	1.5	2	8.5	—
D value								.085	

arbitrarily considered the minimum acceptable level), D must be at least .157. Since .085 is considerably less than that, we fail to reject the null hypothesis that riots are equally distributed by severity—this assumes, of course, that the data are based on good samples. The D test may be used even on small samples, unlike the chi-square test.

The Kolmogorov-Smirnov test assumes random sampling. Whether the observations are independent or dependent will affect how the expected cumulative proportions are derived, but this is not a test assumption. In the two-sample Kolmogorov-Smirnov test discussed below, samples are assumed to be independent. Note that this test compares whether or not an observed distribution conforms to an expected distribution not only *in general* (as in chi-square goodness-of-fit tests) but also *even for the most deviant value* of the ordinal criterion variable. Thus it is a more stringent test.

The *Kolmogorov-Smirnov two-sample test*, K_D, follows the same logic as the Kolmogorov-Smirnov one-sample D test, except instead of subtracting expected cumulative percentages from observed cumulative percentages, the observed cumulative percentages in one sample (e.g., cumulative percentage of cities in 1967 ranked by riot severity) are subtracted from the cumulative percentages for a second independent sample (e.g., the cumulative percentage of cities in 1969 ranked by riot severity). The D value is the largest difference in cumulative percentages for any given ordinal rank; its significance is checked by looking in a table of critical values of K_D, where $K_D = ND$, N is no more than 40, and when $n_1 = n_2 = N$. This table will give significance values of both two-tailed (different from) or one-tailed, (greater than *or* less than specified) hypotheses.

If n_1 and n_2 are both over 40 it is not necessary that $n_1 = n_2$, and in this case the significance of D (not K_D) can be checked in a table of critical values of D in the Kolmogorov-Smirnov two-sample test; this table will give significance levels for a two-tailed test. For a one-tailed test (where the researcher is interested in greater than relationships rather than different from) when both n_1 and n_2 are over 40, the significance of D is tested by looking at a table of chi-square values for d.f. = 2; this method approximates the desired result when n_1 and n_2 are large. When they are small it may be used, but the test is apt to be "conservative"—tending to find results not significant when they are.

Other Two-Sample Tests for Independent Studies

In addition to the Wald-Wolfowitz two-sample runs test and the Kolmogorov-Smirnov two-sample maximum deviation test, both for ordinal data or better, there are three other common tests for comparing two independent samples: the median test, the Mann-Whitney U test, and the Moses test.

The *median test* is a variant of chi-square tests. In this procedure, as in the Wald-Wolfowitz test, we may test the hypothesis that there is no difference between two samples with respect to their median values on some criterion variable. The same assumptions apply as in the Wald-Wolfowitz test, except the relative size of the two samples need not approach equality. As in the Wald-Wolfowitz test, a high number of ties precludes use of this test. Since it is a chi-square test, chi-square assumptions apply as well.

In the median test, the two samples are combined temporarily in order to find the median value. Then a 2-by-2 table can be constructed in which the columns tell whether the observation is from Sample A or Sample B, and in which the rows tell whether the observation is at or above the combined mean on the one hand or below the combined mean on the other. The significance level of this 2-by-2 table can then be tested by chi-square, corrected chi-square, or Fisher's exact test according to the previously discussed considerations applying to any 2-by-2 table.[27] This test is sometimes termed the Westenberg-Mood median test.[28]

The *Mann-Whitney U test* is also used for ordinal-level, two-sample significance tests. In this technique, the two samples are combined exactly as in the Wald-Wolfowitz runs test. U^a equals the number of A-scores preceding the first B, plus the number preceding the second B, etc., where A is the smaller sample and B is the larger sample. Table 10.11 provides an example.

TABLE 10.11

Score	1	1	2	3	4	5	5	6	7	8	9	9	10	11	12	14
Group	A	B	B	A	B	A	A	A	B	A	A	B	A	B	B	B

[27]Some authors present a formula for the median test that is the chi-square formula for the 2-by-2 case with a correction for continuity. This usage follows Siegel, who never applies uncorrected chi-square to any 2-by-2 table. As previously noted, this usage varies, and would vary in the same way for the median test as for any chi-square test.

[28]For additional median tests, see Bradley, *Distribution-Free Statistical Tests*, ch. 8. Bradley also treats additional runs tests in chs. 11 and 12.

Let the As and Bs be sampled cities, A and B, with each column corresponding to a sampled individual, ordered according to some ordinal score (e.g., rank on a scale of "conservativeness"). (For simplicity, ties are assigned by use of the random number table; see footnote 25). Given this data, U^a equals:

$$U^a = 1+1+2+5+7+8+8+8 = 40$$

This is a way of measuring the likelihood that one sample gets consistently higher scores than the other; if so, then we conclude that the two populations are significantly different. A companion statistic, U^b, equals the product of the sample sizes minus U^a:

$$U^b = n_A n_B - U^a = 8 \times 8 - 40 = 24$$

U is either U^a or U^b, whichever is smaller.

To check the significance of two samples by the U test, different methods are used according to the sample size:

1. If both samples are 8 or less, a table of probabilities for U may be consulted. In the example for $n_1 = 8$, $n_2 = 8$, and $U = 24$, the corresponding value is .221. This means that the difference measured by the U statistics would occur by chance alone 22.1 percent of the time; since this is far above the 5-percent level, we do *not* conclude that the two samples are different. Note that n_1 applies to the smaller group, n_2 to the larger. Use Table X in the Appendix.

2. If the larger sample is between 9 and 20, a table of critical values of U is consulted in an analogous manner, either for one- or two-tailed tests. Use Table XI in the Appendix.

3. For larger samples, consult the normal distribution table (Table III), where the appropriate z value is

$$z = \frac{U - \dfrac{n_1 n_2}{2}}{\sqrt{\dfrac{(n_1 n_2)(n_1 + n_2 + 1)}{12}}}$$

Again, this a formula that transforms U into a normal z value by subtracting a specified mean and dividing by a specified standard deviation.

The *Moses test of extreme reactions* is yet another ordinal-level, two-sample significance test for independent samples. But where the median test and the Mann-Whitney test are both oriented toward detecting differences between two samples with regard to central tendency (the median in the median test; mean rank in the Mann-Whitney test), the Moses test seeks to detect differences between two samples with regard to extreme tendencies.

That is, we could imagine two samples, one normally distributed and the other polarized at the two extremes; in such a situation it is possible that both samples would have the *same* "central tendency." For the polarized sample, however, a measure of "central tendency" is misleading because the units are clustered at the poles, not at the center, even though an average of the two extremes *is* in the center.

Therefore, the Moses test should be used whenever the researcher thinks his or her two samples may differ in their respective extreme distributions rather than in their central tendencies. For example, opinions in a crisis situation may be extremely polarized compared to opinions in a routine situation, yet the "average" opinion may be similar.

The Moses test assumes random sampling, independent observations, independent samples, data of at least ordinal level, and a negligible number of ties between samples. While it may be used to test differences in central tendency it is less efficient for this purpose than the median or Mann-Whitney tests.

To compute the Moses test probability, first arrange the data as in the Mann-Whitney test, obtaining a table such as Table 10.12.

TABLE 10.12

Score	1	2	3	4	5	6	7	8	9	10	11	12	13	14
Group	B	A	B	B	B	A	A	A	A	B	A	A	B	B

The Moses test focuses on the sample thought *not* to be characterized by extreme reactions—sample A in our example. *Second,* for this sample, a small number of cases, h, are ignored at either extreme; h is set by the researcher in advance, at some low level such as 2. Ignoring unusually extreme cases helps stabilize the test, especially when sample size, n_A, is large. For small samples, this step may be omitted, though for purposes of our example we will let $h = 1$.

Third, determine the span, s_A, of sample A; the span equals its highest rank minus its lowest rank, plus one (for our example, $s_{mA} = 11 - 6 + 1 = 6$, after omitting the one observation of A at either extreme). *Fourth,* determine the minimum span, s_{mA}, of sample A. The minimum span equals the sample size, n_A, minus the 2h cases we ignored (in the example, $s_{mA} = 7 - 2(1) = 5$. *Fifth,* we want to find the probability of getting an observed span, s_A, this much greater or less so that the minimum span, s_{mA} (in the example, a difference of $6 - 5 = 1$); we will label this difference g.

Sixth, the formula for the probability of getting exactly a difference of g is:[29]

$$p(g) = \frac{{}_{(g+s_{mA}-2)}C_g \cdot {}_{(n_B+2h+1-g)}C_{n_B-g}}{{}_{(n_A+n_B)}C_{n_A}}$$

$$= \frac{{}_4C_1 \cdot {}_9C_6}{{}_{14}C_7} = .098$$

[29]Recall that C is the probability operation of combination: ${}_nC_r = n!/(n-r)!r!$.

Thus there is a 9.8 percent chance of getting a difference of just 1. The *seventh step* would be to compute this formula for g equal to each lesser value down to zero. In our example, since the observed g equals 1; we would only have to compute the formula once more, for g equal to zero. We would then add the two individual probabilities to get the probability of getting the observed difference *or smaller*. However, since a 9.8 percent chance is already too much (i.e., is over the 5 percent or .05 significance level conventionally required), there is no real purpose served by the seventh step in this example. This is because in either case we would fail to reject the null hypothesis. That is, we would *not conclude* that there was a difference between sample A and sample B by the Moses extreme reaction test. (However, since the probability is still well below the .05 level, it is still our *best guess* that there is a difference, even though a conclusion is not statistically justified.)

Tests for Dependent Samples

The tests just discussed assume independent samples (*not* matched pairs or before-after samples). When samples are dependent, the McNemar or Cochran Q tests *may* be used, as previously discussed, but these are designed for nominal data. For ordinal data in related samples, it is better to use the sign or Wilcoxon tests (two samples) or Friedman two-way analysis of variance (more than two samples).

The *sign test* focuses on pairs of matched observations in two correlated samples, A and B. For each pair in which B has a lower rank than A, a minus ($-$) is entered; when B is greater than A, a plus ($+$) is entered; ties are assigned a plus or minus by use of the random number tables (or tied pairs are deleted). For the null hypothesis that there is no difference between A and B, we would expect the same number of pluses and minuses.

After data is arranged in this manner, the sign test becomes the binomial test, discussed earlier, in which $p = q = .5$, $n =$ the number of paired observations (not counting any ties discarded), and $r =$ the number of pluses *or* the number of minuses, whichever is fewer. Computation is the same (note the usefulness of Table II for the case of $n \leq 25$). Similarly, the assumptions are the same.[30]

The *Wilcoxon matched-pairs signed-ranks test* (T) is a sign test sensitive to *size* as well as to direction (plus or minus) of differences between pairs. But since size of difference between one pair must be compared with size of difference between another pair, the Wilcoxon test requires not only that the data on the criterion variable used in the comparison be ordinal, but also that the differences between pairs be susceptible to ordinal ranking. That is,

---

[30]For power level tables for the sign test (or the binomial test when $p = q = .5$), see Cohen, *Statistical Power Analysis*, ch. 5.

the ordinal data must be near-interval (this is often the case with Guttman scale data, for example). The Wilcoxon test also assumes random sampling, and that there are no zeros among the differences. When the assumptions are met, it is more powerful than the sign test.

To compute Wilcoxon's T, *first* list the pair scores in two columns, A and B, corresponding to the two samples. *Second*, for each pair subtract the value of B from the value of A, resulting in a column of differences. *Third*, delete pairs with zero difference. *Fourth*, rank these differences from one to n (both A and B samples have the same n since observations are paired) according to the size of their absolute values; assign the average of the ranks which would otherwise have been assigned in the cases of tied pairs.

Fifth, compute T_p and T_n. T_p is the sum of the ranks assigned in the fourth step for the differences that were positive in the second step. Similarly, T_n is the sum of ranks for negative difference pairs. *Sixth*, let T equal T_p or T_n, whichever is smaller.

When n is equal or less than 25, a table of critical values of T may be consulted (see Table XIV). The researcher cannot conclude that sample A is different from sample B unless T is equal to or less than the value in this table for a given significance level (e.g., the .05 level). When n is more than 25, the normal tables may be consulted, using z equal to:

$$z = \frac{T - \left(\dfrac{n(n+1)}{4}\right)}{\sqrt{\dfrac{n(n+1)(2n+1)}{24}}}$$

Table III gives test probabilities for z values. If the z value computed by the formula above is 1.96 or higher, we can conclude at the .05 significance level that the two samples are different (a two-tailed test). The significance level corresponding to the computed z is derived from Table III in the same manner as was discussed for other z tests in Chapter 8.

DISTRIBUTION-FREE TESTS FOR MORE THAN TWO SAMPLES

When we have three or more *uncorrelated* (independent) *samples*, we may use the chi-square test, but this is designed for nominal data. When we have *ordinal* data and other assumptions are met, we may wish to use the extension of the median test. The *median test extension* involves the same steps as the median test itself, except one constructs a 2-by-k table, with columns corresponding to samples $a, b, \ldots, k$. As in the median test, chi-square is applied to the table as a test, provided the assumptions of chi-square are met (note that corrected chi-square and Fisher's exact tests cannot be substituted for chi-square since these apply only to 2-by-2 tables).

The *Kruskal-Wallis H test*, like the median test extension, tests three or more independent samples for differences in central tendency (mean rank in the *H* test; median in the median test). Because it takes rank size into account rather than just an above-below dichotomy, the Kruskal-Wallis *H* test is more powerful than, and should be used in preference to, the median test extension, provided its assumptions are met.

The *H* test assumes random sampling, independent observations, independent samples, ordinal data or better, and that data have a continuous distribution in the population from which the samples were taken. (Although it involves summation of ranks, as in the Wilcoxon test, the *H* test does *not* involve an assumption that rank differences can be arranged ordinally.)

$$H = \frac{12}{N(N+1)} \sum \frac{R^2}{n} - 3(N+1)$$
$$\text{d.f.} = k - 1$$

The *H* statistic is computed by the above formula, where *N* is the number of observations in all samples together, *n* is the number of observations in any particular sample, *R* is the number of ranks in any particular sample, and *k* is the number of samples. *First*, data from all samples are ordered as in the Wald-Wolfowitz or Mann-Whitney tests. *Second*, the data scores are renumbered from 1 to *N*, with 1 corresponding to the lowest score, 2 to the next-lowest, and on up to *N*, the highest score—1 to *N* are the "ranks." *Third*, using these rank scores, data for each sample are listed by rank. *Fourth*, these rank scores are added up for each sample; these sums are the *R* scores. *Fifth*, the *H* value is determined by the formula above. If there are many ties, *H* is divided by the quantity

$$1 - \frac{\sum (t^3 - t)}{N^3 - N}$$

where *t* is the number of ties in any sample (the numerator is a sum for all samples), and *N* is, as before, the total number of observations in all samples together. Finally, if *all* samples are of size 5 or less, a table of probabilities associated with *H* may be consulted. If the samples are larger, a standard chi-square table may be consulted, using *H* as the chi-square value and degrees of freedom as the number of samples minus one; if the corresponding chi-square value is equal to or less than the *H* value, then the difference is significant at the level indicated by the table.

Finally, when we have three or more *correlated* (dependent) *samples*, we may use the Cochran *Q* test as previously discussed in relation to treatment of nominal data. When we have more than two dependent samples and *ordinal* data, we may use the Friedman two-way analysis of variance. Since this situation arises so rarely in political science (because political scientists rarely use matched pairs or before-after experimental designs for more than two groups), its computation is not treated here.[31]

REVIEW: WHICH TEST OF SIGNIFICANCE?

The following chart may be helpful in keeping track of the many tests discussed in this chapter:[32]

Which Test of Significance?

Test Statistic When the Data Are:

I. Nominal in Level, and one is testing:
    A. One Sample; then one uses the:
        1. Chi-Square Test: an approximation to an exact test (p. 243).
        2. Binomial Test: an exact test, but tedious to compute (p. 257).
    B. Two Samples, and the samples are:
        1. Independent; then one uses the
            a. Chi-Square Test: large samples (p. 243).
            b. Fisher Exact Test: small samples (p. 254).
        2. Dependent; then one uses the
            a. McNemar Test (p. 259).
    C. Multiple Samples, and the samples are:
        1. Independent; then one uses the
            a. Chi-Square Test (p. 243).
        2. Dependent; then one uses the
            a. Cochran Q Test (p. 260).

II. Ordinal in Level,[33] and one is testing:
    A. One Sample; then one uses the:
        1. Runs Test: tests randomness (p. 260).
        2. Kolmogorov-Smirnov D Test: tests goodness-of-fit of the most deviant value (p. 262).
    B. Two Samples, and the samples are:
        1. Independent; then one uses the
            a. Wald-Wolfowitz Test: compares rank levels (p. 261).

[31]Siegel, *Nonparametric Statistics*, pp. 166–172; Bradley, *Distribution-Free Statistical Tests*, pp. 123–129, 134–141; Virginia Senders, *Measurement and Statistics* (New York: Oxford, 1958), pp. 450–452.

[32]For additional reading, see also Siegel, *Nonparametric Statistics*; and Bradley, *Distribution-Free Statistical Tests*; these, together with Cohen, *Statistical Power Analysis*, provide good discussions of the assumptions and power of the various tests. See also E. Edgington, *Statistical Inference: The Distribution-Free Approach* (New York: McGraw-Hill, 1969).

[33]Remember that higher-level data *may* be used on lower-level tests.

    b. Kolmogorov-Smirnov K_D Test: compares the most deviant values (p. 263).

    c. Median Test: compares medians (p. 264).

    d. Mann-Whitney U Test: compares ranks (p. 264).

    e. Moses Test: compares extreme distributions (p. 265).

  2. Dependent; then one uses the

    a. Sign Test: compares direction of paired differences (p. 267).

    b. Wilcoxon T Test: compares direction and size of paired differences (p. 267).

 C. Multiple Samples, and the samples are:

  1. Independent; then one uses the

    a. Median Test Extension: compares medians (p. 268).

    b. Kruskal-Wallis H Test: compares mean ranks (p. 269).

  2. Dependent; then one uses the

    a. Friedman Test (p. 270).

III. Interval or Ratio in Level; and one is testing:

 A. One Sample, and the data are:

  1. Normally Distributed;[34] then one uses the

    a. Normal (z) Tests: large samples (pp. 198–202).

    b. Student's t Test: small samples (p. 200).

  2. Not Normally Distributed; then one may use the

    a. Tchebychev's Inequality Test.[35]

 B. Two Samples, and the samples are:

  1. Independent, and the data are

    a. Normally Distributed; then one may use the

     i. Normal (z) Test: large samples—see Table 8.10.

     ii. Student's t Test: small samples—see Table 8.10.

     iii. F Test: for differences of variances—see Table 8.10.

    b. Not Normally Distributed; then one may use the

     i. Randomization Test for Independent Samples.[36]

  2. Dependent, and the data are

    a. Normally Distributed; then one may use the

     i. Normal (z) Test: large samples—see Table 8.10.

     ii. Student's t Test: small samples—see Table 8.10.

    b. Not Normally Distributed; then one may use the

     i. Randomization Test for Matched Pairs.[37]

     ii. Wilcoxon Test for Paired Replicates.[38]

     iii. Walsh Test.[39]

 C. Multiple Samples (see Chapter 14, Analysis of Variance).

---

[34]Tests for goodness-of-fit to the normal distribution are the chi-square test and the Kolmogorov-Smirnov D test. See also Senders, *Measurement and Statistics*, pp. 461–464.

[35]Tchebychev's Inequality Test is very weak, and an ordinal test is often preferred even when data is interval. The one-tailed probability of getting a value k standard deviations away from the mean is less than $1/k^2$ for *any* distribution. Thus, Tchebychev's Inequality implies, for example, that the chance of getting a value two standard deviations from the mean is less than 25 percent. See: Senders, *Measurement and Statistics*, pp. 464–465.

[36]See Siegel, *Nonparametric Statistics*, pp. 152–156, for computation.

[37]See Siegel, *Nonparametric Statistics*, pp. 88–92, for computation.

[38]See Senders, *Measurement and Statistics*, pp. 489–491, for computation.

[39]See Siegel, *Nonparametric Statistics*, pp. 83–87, for computation.

EXERCISE

1.   During the Watergate crisis of the Nixon Administration, the Gallup Poll organization took monthly polls, asking 1,600 citizens sampled randomly from across the country, "Do you approve or disapprove of the way Nixon is handling his job as President?" Figures from January and February of 1974, prior to Nixon's resignation, showed only a small decline in approval Was this decline significant at the .05 level?

	Jan. 4-7, 1974	Feb. 4-7, 1974
Approve	27%	26%
Disapprove	63%	64%
No Opinion	10%	10%

2.   The following data were computed for the "presidential support" (PS) scores of Congressional committee chairpeople. Do these frequencies justify our treating this variable as normally distributed for research on committee chairpeople? PS is based on an index of votes.

Score Category	Number
00—09	0
10—19	0
20—29	0
30—39	3
40—49	9
50—59	5
60—69	14
70—79	6
80—89	5
90—99	1

3.   In a sample of a college class the following distribution is found. Is this relationship significant?

	Blacks	Whites
Liberals	3	2
Conservatives	1	4

4.   Thirty U. S. Senators are picked for a sample, with their party identification given as R = Republican and D = Democrat, in the following order:

DRRRRDRDRDDDRRDRDRDRRRRDRRDDDR

Does this seem to have been a randomly picked sample?

5.   A randomly selected group of ten individuals is given a test of "authoritarianism" and their respective scale scores (from 00 to 99) are computed. They are then exposed to a film on tolerance and, at a later time, retested for "authoritarianism." Does the film seem to have made a difference? How would a control group (one being tested, but *not* seeing the film) be used in this experiment?

Individual	First Test Score	Second Test Score
1	44	34
2	81	80
3	69	75
4	40	22
5	55	55
6	10	8
7	97	85
8	70	71
9	35	29
10	59	32

11 | Validity and Association

The researcher faces four basic questions in empirical research:

1. Is the relationship that is observed real or due to chance? (The question of *significance*, treated in Chapter 10.)
2. Is the relationship spurious due to uncontrolled variables, misconceptualization, or various fallacies? (The question of *validity*, discussed below.)
3. Is the relationship strong? (The question of *association*, involving measures of association discussed below and measures of correlation discussed in Chapter 12.)
4. Is the relationship important in terms of the concerns of the discipline, of policy, or some other criterion? (The question of *substance*.)

VALIDITY

After asking whether or not a relationship exists at all (significance), the researcher must be careful to ask if the relationship is *valid*. Social scientists have distinguished four types of validity: predictive, concurrent, content, and construct validity. In addition, the technique of factor analysis (to be discussed in Chapter 16) has led many to add a fifth type, factor validity.

Predicitive Validity

For predictive validity, the researcher is concerned with whether or not the relationship found for one set of data will hold for a future set of data. If it worked once, will it work again? Two dimensions must be considered here: time and group. How much or how little may we validly say? Is the relationship the same for all time periods, or just recent times, or perhaps only for a particular month? Is the relationship the same for all groups everywhere in the world, only for American groups, or perhaps only true for a particular group in a particular city? In assessing this type of validity, the political scientist correlates results for his research group with similar studies for other groups and other time periods.

The correlation coefficient[1] between the observed results and the results in a second set of data is sometimes called the "validity coefficient." When the second set is a restudy, the coefficient is sometimes called a "coefficient of stability." When the second set is a parallel study conducted concurrently, the coefficient is called a "coefficient of equivalence." If the second set is really a subset of the original study, as when every other observation is considered part of a "second" study, the coefficient of correlation between the two is called the "coefficient of internal consistency."

Concurrent Validity

This brings us to concurrent validity, the question of whether the relation will hold for a control set of data. The coefficient of internal consistency (also called the split-halves test) is of this type. *Reliability* by the Spearman-Brown measure[2] for split halves equals twice the coefficient of internal consistency divided by 1 plus that coefficient:

$$r_t = \frac{2r_{ic}}{1+r_{ic}}$$

These coefficients require an interval level of data, and are used primarily in assessing the validity of *measures* (scales, tests) rather than *relationships*. Such scales and tests are ordinarily expected to have a reliability of .90 or higher to be accepted.

In testing the concurrent validity of a relationship, the more common problem in political science, the control set of data may consist of paired individuals with characteristics matched by age, sex, education, social class or other control variables. Or the control set may consist of a group of random individuals (or groups, cities, etc.) not "exposed" in a before-after study—for example, not exposed to a political campaign technique in a study of the relation between a candidate's issue stand and his popularity. Or the members of the control group may be selected by a random split-halves method.

Criterion Validity

Predictive and concurrent validity are categories of a more general type, criterion validity. This raises the question of whether all the relevant variables have been controlled for, as by multivariate analysis, partial correlation, or some other technique. One may find a strong relationship between

---

[1] Correlation is a type of measure of association, discussed in the next chapter.
[2] The study is arbitrarily divided into two by random process.

religion and political identification, for example, but find that this relationship "disappears" when social class is introduced as a control variable. This question of possible control variables is called the question of *spuriousness*, and can be met only by creativity on the part of the researcher in anticipating the relevance of possible control variables not present in the initial relationship.

Another area of concern relating to criterion validity is that of *logical fallacy*, raising again the question, "For which group or groups the relationship is valid?" Religion may be related to party preference in some groups

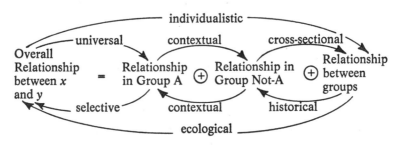

FIGURE 11.1   Types of Fallacies

but not in others. Moreover, it may be related between groups but not within any particular group. For example, it could happen that predominantly Catholic states vote Democratic and predominantly Protestant states vote Republican, yet within any particular state Protestants and Catholics vote the same; this would occur if Protestants voted Democratic in predominantly Catholic states, and Catholics voted Republican in Protestant states.

Thus there are three types of relationships: relationship within a particular group, relationship between groups, and the overall relationship that combines these two. Logical fallacies occur by confusing these three types. What is true overall is not necessarily true within any particular group (universal fallacy) or between groups (individualistic fallacy). What is true in a particular group is not necessarily true overall (selective fallacy), or in another group (contextual fallacy), or between groups (cross-sectional fallacy). What is true between groups need not be true within any particular group (historical fallacy) or true overall (ecological fallacy). Some writers refer to all of these logical fallacies as *ecological fallacies*.

The problem of fallacy is a serious one, since the political scientist very often has only group data[3] such as number of Catholics by state and number of Democrats by state. One cannot logically reason from group data to individual relationships. The fact that Catholic states have many Democrats suggests but *does not* logically prove that individual Catholics tend to be Democrats.

[3]Group data are sometimes referred to as "ecological data," in contrast to "individual data."

Fallacies Pertaining to Aggregated Data Aggregated data are data which are grouped, such as, for example, data on family income grouped by state and presented as state averages. *When the criterion variable for grouping* (usually geographic area) *is itself a variable correlated with the dependent variable, aggregated data leads to spuriously high measures of association.* For example, if data on individual income and individual political information levels are grouped by state, and if "state" is a variable correlated with information level, grouping by state will artificially (and misleadingly) lead to a higher measure of association (e.g., a higher Pearsonian correlation coefficient, r, discussed in Chapter 12; r varies from a low of 0—no association—to a high of 1.0—perfect association: the two variables vary together).

Let X be individual income and Y be political information level of individuals. The researcher may hypothesize that X causes Y, as in Figure 11.2:

FIGURE 11.2

Now let the available data on X and Y be grouped by state, which we shall call variable Z. Let us further assume that Z (state) affects the dependent variable (information level, Y) through two variables which the researcher has not measured: uncontrolled variables of education (U_1) and sense of political efficacy (U_2), as in Figure 11.3.

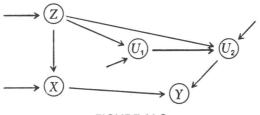

FIGURE 11.3

Because of their common cause, Z, variables U_1 and U_2 will be correlated with variable X (income). Variables U_1 and U_2 will also have other causes (represented by side arrows in Figure 11.2) not correlated with Z; the overall effect of these other causes is zero, since that is what "not correlated" implies. That is, grouping by state wipes out the effect of these other causes, *but* they are nonetheless real causes: if we had individual-level data and had not grouped the data by state, these other causes would still have an observable effect on the dependent variable Y. With grouped data such as that in this example, the correlation of these other variables with the dependent variable, Y, artifically increases the correlations between the unmeasured variables, U_1 and U_2, with X. Moreover, the researcher may be tempted to spuriously attribute to X the causation of Y due to the unmeasured variables, U_1 and U_2.

Thus, the more unmeasured variables, the stronger their correlation with the grouping variable (Z in the example), and the larger the grouping involved in this variable, the higher the correlation between X and Y is spuriously raised. Aggregation (grouping of data) has *no* effect on measures of association or correlation when the units (e.g., individuals) are grouped on a basis which is random (independent of the correlated variables). It follows that the only way to know if aggregation of data is spuriously increasing the strength (association) of one's findings is to find out if the grouping criterion (e.g., state) is itself an important causal variable. Or the whole problem may be avoided by obtaining individual-level data in the first place, if possible.[4]

Note that this fallacy is different from the ecological fallacy, which may operate *either* to increase or decrease group-level correlations compared to individual-level correlations. The aggregation fallacy operates to increase group-level correlations relative to individual-level correlations. Thus it is possible to have an ecological fallacy artifically depressing the correlation observed, while an aggregation fallacy is artificially increasing it (if these contrary tendencies balance out, one could theoretically come up with correct answers on the basis of fallacious reasoning!). For example, the researcher may be interested in the correlation of individual income with participation in rioting. State-level data may generate a low correlation of income and rioting, artificially low because of the ecological fallacy. On the other hand, a third, unmeasured variable such as "urbanism" may be correlated with income by state and rioting; through the fallacy of aggregation, this will tend to artificially increase the state-level correlation of income with rioting compared to what one would obtain with individual-level data.

Content Validity

Content validity is also called *face validity*, and refers more to the validity of measures than of relationships. Social scientists usually insist that measures seem, on the face, to measure what they claim to. First, questions should seem to relate to the subject and cover the full range that is relevant. A test of tolerance levels composed of items dealing only with racial issues would not have *content validity*, since the content of the test fails to deal with nonracial aspects of tolerance. Second, the method of gathering data must, on the face, seem to be proper. Generally, random sampling or full enu-

[4]See Michael T. Hannan, "Problems of Aggregation and Disaggregation in Sociological Research," *Working Papers in Methodology*, no. 4 (Chapel Hill, N. C.: University of North Carolina Press, 1970); Hubert M. Blalock, "Aggregation and Measurement Error," *Social Forces* 50, no. 2 (December 1971): 151–165. See also G. Iverson, "Recovering Individual Data in the Presence of Group and Individual Effects," *American Journal of Sociology* 79, no. 2 (September 1973): 420–434; W. P. Shively, "'Ecological' Inference: The Use of Aggregate Data to Study Individuals," *American Political Science Review* 63, no. 4 (December 1969): 1183–1196.

meration are considered necessary in a valid study, although less rigorous standards are applied to exploratory studies.

Construct Validity

Construct validity also relates to validity of measures, asking if the researcher is truly measuring what he or she thinks is being measured. If the researcher is using a measure of racial tolerance, even though its content *seems* valid, is he or she really measuring racial tolerance or is he or she measuring something else? This question cannot be answered unless the measure of racial tolerance can be assessed against some other standard considered accepted and nondebatable. The researcher can only see if the measure works in the expected direction for groups that, for whatever reasons, are *assumed* to be tolerant. Or the measure can be tested to see if it works in the expected direction with regard to other standardized tests; for example, the index of intolerance should correlate, one might *assume*, with the widely used measure of "authoritarian personality."

Multi-Method, Multi-Trait Methods of Validation   An increasingly popular approach to construct validity is to explain the dependent variable through a number of different methods and criteria. That is, rather than using just one measurement of a trait and relating it to the dependent variable through one method, many social scientists recommend a multi-faceted approach.

This approach is illustrated in the work of Johannes Pennings on organizational structure.[5] Surveying ten organizations, Pennings focused on two concepts, centralization (variable A) and formalization (B). Each concept had several measures [centralization, for example, was based on a measure of autonomy or participation (a), a measure of span of control or job specificity (b), and a measure of worker-supervisor ratio or job strictness (c)]; and each measure was taken in two ways (method 1 was based on institutional reports and method 2 was based on a questionnaire survey of employees). This data results in the multi-method, multi-trait matrix shown in Table 11.1.

Althauser and Heberlein have outlined the inferences about validity that may be made on the basis of such a matrix:[6]

1. *"Convergent validity"* Correlations of a given concept (e.g., Concept A, by any of the three measures) should be high with data for the same concept by a different method. Thus, in the example, the A variables with subscript 1 should be highly correlated with the A variables with subscript 2. Since, in the example,

[5]Johannes Pennings, "Measures of Organizational Structure," *American Journal of Sociology* 79, no. 3 (November 1973): 686–704.

[6]Robert Althauser and Thomas Heberlein, "Validity and the Multitrait-Multimethod Matrix," in E. Borgatta, ed., *Sociological Methodology 1970* (San Francisco: Jossey-Bass, 1970), 151–169.

TABLE 11.1   Multi-Method, Multi-Trait Matrix of Organizational Structure

	Method 1					Method 2				
	A_{1a}	A_{1b}	A_{1c}	B_{1a}	B_{1b}	A_{2a}	A_{2b}	A_{2c}	B_{2a}	B_{2b}
Method 1: Institutional										
Concept A: Centralization										
Measure a: Autonomy (A_{1a})										
Measure b: Control Span (A_{1b})	.58									
Measure c: Worker-Supervisor ratio (A_{1c})	.16	.25								
Concept B: Formalization										
Measure a: specialization (B_{1a})	.30	−.17	.16							
Measure b: role definition (B_{1b})	−.59	−.67	.10	.24						
Method 2: Questionnaire										
Concept A: Centralization										
Measure a: Participation (A_{2a})	−.73	−.53	−.25	−.53	.45	.96				
Measure b: Hierarchy (A_{2b})	−.39	−.41	.05	−.24	.50	.59	.72			
Measure c: Departmental participation (A_{2c})	−.41	−.52	.09	−.15	.55	.71	.93	.83		
Concept B: Formalization										
Measure a: Codification (B_{2a})	−.05	−.09	.49	−.43	−.05	.45	.50	.61	.78	
Measure b: Job specificity (B_{2b})	−.02	−.15	−.29	−.71	−.05	.53	.43	.40	.47	.75

*Only coefficients .57 or higher are significant at the .05 level.

Source: Adapted from Johannes Pennings, "Measures of Organizational Structure," *American Journal of Sociology* 79, no. 3 (November 1973): 693. By permission of the author and publisher.

many of these correlations are low or negative, we cannot assume convergent validity: we cannot assume that these measures by two methods all validly measure Concept A.

2. *"Discriminant validity"*

a. The correlations of a given concept (Concept A) by two methods (Methods 1 and 2) should be higher than the correlations of a given concept by one method (Concept A on Method 1) with the correlations of another concept by another method (Concept B on Method 2). Thus, in the example, the correlation of A_{1a} with A_{2n} should be higher than the correlation of A_{1a} with B_{2a}, for example. This particular comparison holds up, but validity is not sustained for Measure c of Concept A; nor are the relevant correlations for Concept B validated.

When different concepts by different methods correlate more highly than the same concept by different methods, we may suspect that the "same concept" is actually different in the two methods, either because the researcher has unrecognizingly used different conceptualizations in the two methods or because measurement error or some other aspect of the general methods is different for different concepts. This is called *general methods bias*.

b. Similarly, measures of the same concept using different methods should correlate more highly than measures of different concepts using the same method. When this is not so, one has reason to suspect that the latter correlations are due to the same method, not similarity in substance. This is called *common methods bias*.

c. The ratio of correlations within one method should equal the ratio of correlations with any other method, and each of these should equal the ratio of correlations between methods. (Take three variables, A, B, and C, measured through two methods, 1 and 2. The ratio of the correlation of A with B, r_{AB}, to the correlation of B with C, r_{BC}, should be the same for data based on method 1 as for data based on method 2, and each the same as for data for each variable by method 1 correlated with data on each variable by method 2. That is, the ratio of r_{AB} to r_{BC} occurs three times: once for method 1 with method 1, once for method 2 with method 2, and once for method 1 with method 2; the ratio should be the same in all three cases.)

Factor Validity

Factor validity is a special topic, with a statistical meaning for validity. Validity is sometimes arbitrarily defined as "factor communality," or the percent of variance in the dependent (y) variable explained by all the factors in factor analysis. This communality is called h^2, and equals the sum of the squares of the factor loadings. Factor validity thus measures validity solely in terms of predictability: do the independent variables or factors predict the variance of the dependent variable? Because of this special, limited meaning of validity, other approaches to validity should normally be employed.[7]

[7]For further reading, see Hubert Blalock, "The Measurement Problem: The Gap Between the Languages of Theory and Research," in Hubert Blalock and Ann Blalock, eds., *Methodology in Social Research* (New York: McGraw-Hill, 1968). See also G. Summers, L. Seiler; and G. Wiley, "Validation of Reputational Leadership by the Multitrait-Multimethod Matrix," in Borgatta, ed., *Sociological Methodology 1970*, pp. 170–181.

ASSOCIATION

After discussing how the validity of research findings about the seeming strength of relationships can be undermined in various ways, and learning to be on guard against spuriousness and fallacies, we must return to the question of how to measure the strength of association in the first place. How do we put a number on the association of variable X with variable Y? This is the topic of the remainder of this chapter and all of the next.

Percent Difference and the Concept of Pairs

Percent difference (%d) is a simple, traditional measure of association in 2-by-2 tables. It is computed by subtracting the difference, measured in percent, between the first and second columns in either row, as in Table 11.2. In this example, %d equals 25% minus 0%, or 0.25; if we had

TABLE 11.2

City Size

	1	2	r_i
Riot Intensity 1	1(25%)	0(0%)	1
Riot Intensity 2	3(75%)	4(100%)	7
c_i	4	4	8=n

selected the other row, we would get 75% minus 100%, again equaling .25. (Note that %d is expressed in terms of its absolute value.) Thus, city size is associated with riot intensity at the level of 25% difference.

The *concept of pairs* can be illustrated by generalizing about a 2-by-2 table, as shown in Table 11.3. A *strong* relationship occurs when most of the

TABLE 11.3

Variable x

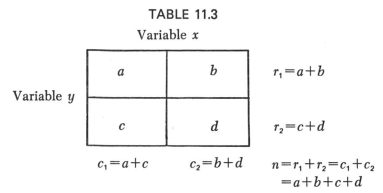

Variable y	a	b	$r_1 = a+b$
	c	d	$r_2 = c+d$
	$c_1 = a+c$	$c_2 = b+d$	$n = r_1 + r_2 = c_1 + c_2$ $= a+b+c+d$

cases are on one diagonal $(a-d)$ *or* the other $(b-c)$. Correspondingly, a *weak* relationship occurs when there are relatively even numbers of cases on *both* diagonals. Percent difference measures the extent to which cases fall on one diagonal (a or d cells) and *not* on the corresponding cell of the other diagonal (b or c cells):

$$\% d = \frac{a}{(a+c)} - \frac{c}{(b+d)} = \frac{c}{(a+c)} - \frac{d}{(b+d)}$$

A pair is the same in mathematics as in popular speech. *The number of pairs of a certain type equals the product of the cells of that certain type.* There are four basic types of pairs:

1. *Concordant pairs*, which fall on the main (right-sloping) diagonal.
2. *Discordant pairs*, which fall on the off diagonal (slopes down to the left).
3. *Pairs tied on* x, the independent variable.
4. *Pairs tied on* y, the dependent variable.

In Table 11.3, for instance, the number of concordant pairs (P) equals ad (a times d). The number of discordant pairs (Q) equals bc; pairs tied on x (X_o) equals $ac + bd$; pairs tied on y (Y_o) equals $ab + cd$.

Similar reasoning applies in the case of larger tables, as illustrated in Table 11.4.

TABLE 11.4

		Variable x			
		1	2	3	r_i
	1	a	b	c	r_1
Variable y	2	d	e	f	r_2
	c_i	c_1	c_2	c_3	N

Type of Pair	Number of Pairs	Symbol
Concordant	$a(e+f)+b(f)$	P
Discordant	$c(d+e)+b(d)$	Q
Tied on x	$ad+be+cf$	X_o
Tied on y	$a(b+c)+bc+d(e+f)+ef$	Y_o
Tied on both	$\frac{1}{2}[a(a-1)+b(b-1)+ \ldots +f(f-1)]$	Z

Total number of pairs $= N(N-1)/2$

As the example shows, a pair is concordant, consistent with a relation on the main diagonal, if it is on one of the main diagonals ($a-e$, $a-ef$, or $b-f$). A pair is discordant if it is associated with one of the off diagonals ($c-e$, $c-ed$, or $b-d$), making it inconsistent with a main diagonal relationship. In addition a pair could be merely tied on x if it is in a column ($a-d$, $b-e$, or $c-f$), while in a row it is tied on y ($a-b$, $a-c$, $b-c$, $d-e$, $d-f$, or $e-f$). Finally, the entries within any cell may constitute pairs tied on both x and y. The symbols for these different types of pairs will be used in many of the measures of association discussed later.

In larger tables, one obtains P by multiplying the upper-left cell entry by the sum of all entries below and to the right; then adding this product to the top-row, second-from-the-left cell times all entries below and to the right of it; then adding this, in turn, to each other cell's product with the sum of entries below and to the right. After all the cells in the top row are used, one proceeds to the second row, and so on. The cells in the right-most column and bottom row, of course, have no entries below and to the right. The number of discordant pairs, Q, is computed in the same manner, except starting with the upper-right cell and multiplying by all entries below and to the left.

Perfect Association and the Concept of Pairs

The measure of association we choose depends in large part on what we mean by "association." There are five types.

1.   *Strict Monotonic Association* is "perfect" if (1) when the independent variable x increases, then y increases, *and* if (2) each value of x corresponds to only one y value. (Note that these two conditions necessarily imply that when y increases, x must also increase, and each y value corresponds to only one x value). In strict monotonic association, there are no ties on x (X_o) *and* no ties on y (Y_o):

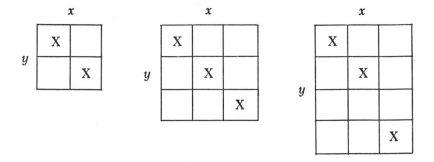

Examples of Perfect Strict Monotonic Association

Thus, association defined in terms of strict monotonic correlation is *high* not only when discordant pairs (Q) are low (this is the criterion used by weak association) but also when ties (X_o and Y_o) are low. That is, for high strict monotonic association, Q, X_o, and Y_o must *all* approach zero.

2.   *Ordered Monotonic Association* is "perfect" (1) when as x increases, y increases, *and* (2) if every y value corresponds to just one x value. That is, ordered monotonic association is high when discordant pairs (Q) are low and, at the same time, ties on y (Y_o) are also low.

Examples of Perfect Ordered Monotonic Association

Note that all cases of perfect strict monotonic association are also cases of perfect dered monotonic association, although the reverse is *not* true.

3. *Predictive Monotonic Association* is "perfect" (1) when as x increases, y increases *or* remains the same, *and* (2) if each x value corresponds to only one value of y. That is, predictive monotonic association is high when discordant pairs (Q) are low and, at the same time, ties on x (X_o) are also low.

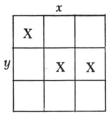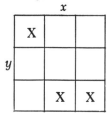

Examples of Perfect Predictive Monotonic Association

All cases of strict monotonic correlation (association) are also cases of perfect predictive monotonic association, though the reverse is *not* true. This form of association is called "predictive" because the dependent variable can be uniquely predicted from the independent variable (this is because each independent or x value corresponds to only one dependent or y value when association is "perfect").

4. *Weak Monotonic Association* is "perfect" if, when the independent (x) variable increases, the dependent (y) variable remains the same or changes in the same direction for all pairs of observations. Note that this condition corresponds to the presence of a zero cell in a 2-by-2 table or in any 2-by-2 subsection of a larger table.

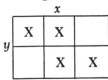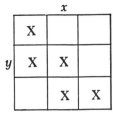

Examples of Perfect Weak Monotonic Association

5. *Curvilinear association* is "perfect" when every x value corresponds to only one y value.

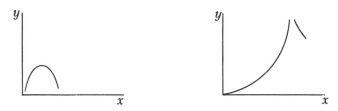

Examples of Perfect Curvilinear Correlation

Note that the curves need not be continuous lines to meet this criterion. Most applications of curvilinear association involve "curve-fitting," which adds the additional criterion that the curve be *continuous*. Some applications also require that the curve be describable as a mathematical function (e.g., $y = x^3 - 4$); that is, that a perfectly fitting curve be found. These additional criteria are not included in the basic definition above since they do not conform to the most common definition of curvilinear correlation in political science, that implicit in the eta coefficient. For hypotheses in which y is the independent variable, of course, curvilinear association is "perfect" when every y value corresponds to only one x value.

Weisberg's Framework for Models of Association   Herbert Weisberg recently published an important article in the *American Political Science Review*[8] which is relevant to the foregoing discussion. Weisberg made the essential point that the researcher must select a measure of association to an important degree on the basis of his or her definition of "perfectly strong" and "perfectly null" relationship. In Weisberg's terminology, "strong monotonicity" corresponds to what is here called "strict monotonicity," "moderate monotonicity" corresponds to ordered *or* to predictive monotonicity, and "weak monotonicity" remains essentially the same in meaning. These alternatives constitute the criteria by which one may define a measure of association to be "perfectly strong" and hence to assume a value of 1.0. Note that all strict monotonic perfect relationships are also perfect by ordered, predictive, or weak monotonic criteria; similarly, ordered or predictive monotonic perfect relationships are also perfect by weak monotonic criteria.

While the level of monotonicity defines the definition of maximum or perfect relationship, there are also four types of minimum or null relationship definitions:

Independence: when cell entries are what would be expected on the basis of the marginals (i.e., the values of the "expected" table in chi-square);

[8]Herbert F. Weisberg, "Models of Statistical Relationship," *American Political Science Review* 68, no. 4 (December 1974): 1638–1655.

Accord: assuming the independent variable is placed at the top of the table, when column maxima are all in the same row (i.e., when the largest cell entries for the independent variable all have the same value for the dependent variable);

Balance: when the number of cases (*not* number of pairs) on the right-sloping diagonal(s) equals the number on the left-sloping diagonal(s); and

Cleavage: when the number of cases associated with each independent variable category is split evenly among the dependent variable categories.

Independence and accord are by far the most common criteria used. Choice of definition of maximum and null conditions depends upon the researcher's purpose. If the purpose emphasizes prediction, then the criteria of predictive monotonicity and accord would be indicated. Strict monotonicity and independence are the traditional criteria. These criteria are carefully indicated in the table of alternative measures of association at the close of this chapter.

Measures of Association Based on Chi-Square

Chi-square, as discussed in Chapter 10, is a test of significance that assumes a larger value as (1) the strength of the relationship is greater (i.e., the greater the deviation of observed from expected values); (2) sample size is greater (larger sample size means greater absolute deviation of observed from expected scores for the same proportionate deviation in a smaller sample); and (3) the table size is larger (more table cells mean more deviations to be summed). If we could figure out a way to "subtract" the last two characteristics from chi-square, we would be left with a measure of association (strength of relationship). That is the purpose of the statistics discussed in this section.

Phi (ϕ) In the discussion of percent difference we were referring to percent difference across columns (i.e., two cells in the same row but different columns). It would also be possible to discuss percent difference across rows. The phi coefficient (ϕ) is the geometric mean of the percent differences across rows and across columns.[9]

Phi is often used as a measure of association when one has a 2-by-2 table and the variables are true dichotomies. That is, the variables should be natural dichotomies such as male-female or white-nonwhite, not compressed continuous variables such as high and low income. Although phi *may* be used with dichotomized continuous data, tetrachoric correlation (discussed in Chapter 12) is preferred.

---

[9]Gudmund Hernes, "A Markovian Approach to Measures of Association," *American Journal of Sociology* 75, no. 6 (May 1970):997. The *geometric mean* is a measure of central tendency computed by multiplying *n* values and taking the *n*th root of their product.

Phi-square equals chi-square divided by n. (Division by n "subtracts" sample size from chi-square; the chi-square table itself adjusts for table size; this converts chi-square into a measure of association). Yates' correction is *not* used in computing phi. Phi is, of course, the square root of phi-square, computed by the formula shown in Table 11.5. It thus measures the strength of the relationship—number of cases on the main diagonal minus number not on main diagonal—adjusting for the given marginal distribution of the variables.

TABLE 11.5

	Male	Female	
Voted	$a = 140$	$b = 10$	$r_1 = 150$
Didn't Vote	$c = 10$	$d = 40$	$r_2 = 50$
	$c_1 = 150$	$c_2 = 50$	$N = 200$

$$\phi = \frac{ad - bc}{\sqrt{r_1 r_2 c_1 c_2}}$$

$$= \frac{5600 - 100}{\sqrt{56,250,000}} \qquad = \frac{P - Q}{\sqrt{r_1 r_2 c_1 c_2}} \qquad = \sqrt{\frac{X^2}{n}}$$

$$= .73$$

Only when both variables in a 2-by-2 table have the same marginals $(r_1 = c_1; r_2 = c_2)$ does phi vary between 0 and 1. In Table 11.5 the variables have the same marginals, but if they were different, we would have to compute the maximum value of phi (ϕ_{max}):

$$\varphi_{max} = \sqrt{\frac{s_i}{l_i} \times \frac{l_i}{s_j}}$$

Where s_i is the smallest row or column marginal

s_j is the smallest row marginal if s_i is a column marginal, or the smallest column marginal if s_i is a row marginal

l_i and l_j are the same for the largest row or column marginals

Tables with differing marginals will have differing maximum phi values, and hence comparability among a series of phi values for these tables would be very difficult. Even when phi values are comparable, they, like all chi-square measures, (a) are comparable only among themselves, (b) tend to understate one-way relationships, and (c) are very sensitive to shifts in marginal distributions.

Pearson's C   Several statistics have been developed to extend a chi-square measure of association to tables larger than 2-by-2. These include Pearson's C, Tschuprow's T, and Cramer's V. *Pearson's C*, also called the *contingency coefficient* and the coefficient of mean square contingency, is a traditional measure equal to the square root of chi-square divided by chi-square plus n:

$$C = \sqrt{\frac{X^2}{X^2 + n}}$$

Its upper limit is .71 in the 2-by-2 case and approaches 1 as the number of rows and columns increases. Moreover, C tends to underestimate the level of association, often resulting in an association of less than 1.0, even though all the observations are on the main diagonal (or, alternatively, on the off diagonal) of a table.[10] Some social scientists recommend computing C only for tables of at least 5-by-5 size, since only in these tables does maximum C approach 1.0. For normally distributed, linearly related variables, Pearson believed C was an approximation of product-moment correlation, r, used with interval data and discussed in the next chapter.

Tschuprow's **T**   Tschuprow's T is a similar statistic equal to the square root of the quantity chi-square divided by n (the number of observations in the table) times the square root of the number of degrees of freedom (rows minus one times columns minus one):

$$T = \sqrt{\frac{X^2}{n\sqrt{(r-1)(c-1)}}}$$

T has a limit of 1.0 in square tables, even those below the 5-by-5 size, when row marginals are identical to column marginals. (Note that Tschuprow's T is unrelated to Wilcoxon's T test of significance.)

Cramer's **V**   *Cramer's* V is a chi-square measure of association for r-by-c tables and gives better norming—variation between zero and one—than does C or T, although until recently it has not been as widely used:

$$V = \sqrt{\frac{X^2}{mn}} \qquad \text{where } m = (r-1) \text{ or } (c-1), \text{ whichever is smaller}$$

Social scientists now generally prefer V over C or T, since it varies between 0 and 1 even in the case of tables that are not square—although, like C and T, its maximum value is less than 1.0 when row marginals are not identical to column marginals. Like T, V is the same as phi in the 2-by-2 case.

The effect of marginal distributions in these statistics is illustrated in Table 11.6. Table A is a hypothetical distribution for a particular group, showing that in this group there is a certain tendency for males to be Republican and females to be Democratic. The strength of this relationship is $V = .408$; since this is a 2-by-2 table, this same figure holds for phi and T. This figure, .408, has no intrinsic meaning; .408 V is simply .408 V, and the strength of this can only be assessed by comparing it to Vs computed for other tables. Moreover, given the marginals which are unequal, the strongest possible relationship is illustrated in Table B, for which $V = .817$. Thus Table A is strong at the .408 V level, where V has a maximum of .817.

---

[10]In square tables, $C_{max} = \sqrt{(r-1)/r}$, where r = number of rows.

Similarly, Table C illustrates the case where row marginals (30, 20) are identical to column marginals (30, 20), and where the relationship is strong at the $V = .583$ level. The marginals in Table C are such that it would be possible to have all the observations on one diagonal, as is illustrated in Table B. In that case the maximum V would be 1.0. Thus Table C is associated at the $V = .583$ level, where $V_{max} = 1.0$. Note that the maximum will be 1.0 when row marginals equal column marginals, and this happens when all of the observations are on just *one* of the diagonals. Failure to norm to one when row and column marginals differ is not necessarily a fault; many times a researcher will want such a situation to correspond to less than perfect association.

TABLE 11.6

Table A

	Male	Female	r_i
Republican	15	10	25
Democrat	5	20	25
c_i	20	30	$N=50$

chi-square$=8.33$
$V = \sqrt{8.33/50} = .408$

Table C

	Male	Female	r_i
Republican	25	5	30
Democrat	5	15	20
c_i	30	20	$N=50$

chi-square$=17.02$
$V = \sqrt{17.02/50} = .583$

Table B

	Male	Female	r_i
Republican	20	5	25
Democrat	0	25	25
c_i	20	30	$N=50$

chi-square$=33.33$
$V = \sqrt{33.33/50} = .817$

Table D

	Male	Female	r_i
Republican	30	0	30
Democrat	0	20	20
c_i	30	20	$N=50$

chi-square$=50.00$
$V = \sqrt{50/50} = 1.00$

Measures Based on the Difference of Concordant and Discordant Pairs

As we have seen, phi is both a chi-square-based measure and a ratio of the surplus of concordant over discordant pairs $(P - Q)$ to the geometric mean of row and column marginals. In Table 11.6, for example, if we hypothesize that males are Republican and females are Democratic in a given sample, then the concordant pairs (P) represent pairs consistent with our hypothesis; discordant pairs (Q) represent pairs inconsistent with our hypothesis. The surplus of concordant over discordant pairs $(P - Q)$ represents the extent to which our hypothesis is supported. But this surplus $(P - Q)$ means little as an absolute number. We must ask whether this surplus is large in comparison with something else as, for example, the maximum possible surplus. That is, we must express the surplus $(P - Q)$ as a ratio of something. In the case of phi, we expressed the surplus of consistent pairs as a percent of the geometric mean of the marginals. The problem with this was twofold: phi's range was not always 0 to 1, and this percentage does not have much readily understandable intrinsic meaning to most political scientists. Kendall's tau-*b* and tau-*c* are somewhat similar in this respect.

Kendall's tau-b (τ_b)   Most often used for 2-by-2 tables, *Kendall's tau-b* may also be used for other size arrays as well. It is equal to the excess of concordant over discordant pairs $(P - Q)$,[11] divided by a term representing the geometric mean between the number of pairs not tied on *x* and the number of pairs not tied on *y*:

$$\text{tau-}b = \frac{P - Q}{\sqrt{(P + Q + Y_0)(P + Q + X_0)}}$$

As will be seen in the discussion on Somer's *d*, it is this averaging of pairs tied to the dependent variable with pairs tied to the independent variable that makes tau a nondirectional (symmetric) statistic.

TABLE 11.7

		City Size		r_i
		1	2	
Riot Intensity	1	1	0	1
	2	3	4	7
	c_i	4	4	8

$$\text{tau-}b = \frac{4-0}{\sqrt{(4+0+12)(4+0+3)}}$$
$$= 4/\sqrt{112} = .37$$

Tau-*b* reaches a maximum of 1.0 only when $r = c$—only in square tables—*and* when the row marginals are the same as the column marginals, and when all entries are on one diagonal.

Kendall's tau-c (τ_c)   *Kendall's tau-c* is a variant of tau-*b* for larger tables. It equals the excess of concordant over discordant pairs times another term representing an adjustment for the size of the table:

$$\text{tau-}c = (P - Q)\left[\frac{(2m)}{n^2(m - 1)}\right]$$

where m = the number of rows *or* the number of columns, whichever is smaller. (Note that this differs from the m used in Cramer's *V*).

TABLE 11.8

		City Size			r_i
		1	2	3	
Riot Intensity	1	4	2	0	6
	2	2	3	4	9
	c_i	6	5	4	15

$$\text{tau-}c = (36-4)(4/15^2[1])$$
$$= 32(4/225)$$
$$= 128/225 = .57$$

[11]If the main relationship is on the off diagonal, this will be negative.

Kendall's tau is used in preference to Cramer's V or other nominal-level statistics when dealing with ordinal-level data because it measures strength of deviation from statistical independence toward monotonic correlation, whereas the nominal-level statistics measure any deviation from statistical independence—that is, from the "expected" value, given the marginal distribution. Tau-c has the advantage of reaching a maximum of 1.0 even for rectangular tables, whereas tau-b reaches 1.0 only for square tables. The main problem with these measures is that they lack an operational meaning, tau-bs being comparable only with other tau-bs, for instance, with no clear meanings attached to values between 0 (statistical independence) and 1 (perfect monotonic association).

Ordinarily tau-c is used as a substitute for tau-b when tables are not square. But while both are similar in that both assume statistical independence as the null value condition, it should be noted that they differ on the definition of maximum association: tau-b is strict monotonic while tau-c is maximum under moderate monotonicity with a uniform distribution of cases on the variable with fewer categories.

There are four measures that are related to Kendall's tau but that have an intrinsic meaning enabling comparison outside their own internal framework. These are Goodman and Kruskal's gamma, Yule's Q, Yule's Y, and Somers' d:

Goodman and Kruskal's Gamma (γ) and Yule's Q   Goodman and *Kruskal's* gamma is a symmetric measure based on the difference between concordant and discordant pairs. It equals this difference $(P - Q)$ as a percentage of both consistent and discordant pairs $(P + Q)$:

$$\gamma = \frac{P - Q}{P + Q}$$

In Table 11.7, for instance gamma $= 4 - 0/4 + 0 = 1.0$, since *all* larger communities had more severe riots. In Example C, gamma $= (36 - 4)/(36 + 4)$, or 0.80; this reflects the fact that in this example there were very few discordant pairs (the off-diagonal products totaled $Q = 4$) and many consistent (concordant) pairs $(P = 36)$. *Yule's* Q is simply gamma for 2-by-2 tables:

$$Q = \frac{ad - bc}{ad + bc} = \gamma$$

Thus gamma is the surplus of consistent pairs as a percentage of all consistent and inconsistent pairs. Gamma and Yule's Q both represent the probability that, when we draw two units (a pair) from our population excluding ties $(P + Q)$, that pair will be consistent with our hypothesis. [This is assuming our hypothesis expects the units to fall on the main diagonal (or diagonals in the case of gamma), and that the off-diagonal products will be zero or low; if our hypothesis expects the opposite pattern, Q and gamma are the probability that such a random pair will be inconsistent with our hypothesis—in such cases, Q and gamma are negative.]

James Davis has listed five comparisons of Q and gamma:[12]

1. If one does not dichotomize one's data, one must use gamma since Q is gamma for the 2-by-2 case; it is much easier to compute Q than gamma.
2. Gamma uses more of your data if your data is not a natural dichotomy.
3. Gamma will be more sensitive to how the relationship operates at the extremes, whereas unnecessary dichotomization washes out these effects.
4. *Gamma requires the data be ordinal or better* for both variables.
5. Q will ordinarily be higher than gamma for the same data (that is, unnecessary dichotomization will wash out many of the small differences between variables, and these are often more inconsistent than the gross differences tapped by dichotomization).

Finally, we may note that gamma and Q reach a maximum of 1.0 (perfect association) under weak monotonicity. If our concept of "perfect relationship" is strict monotonicity, then we must use Somers' d, which is discussed later. Note that the significance level of gamma can be approximated by the z test (normal distribution), where

$$z = (\gamma) \left[\sqrt{2(P + Q) / (2n) (1 - \gamma^2)} \right]$$

The z statistic for gamma is compared with the normal tables in the usual manner.

Yule's Y   *Yule's Y* is sometimes called the coefficient of colligation. It is the same as Q, except all terms are expressed as square roots:

$$Y = \frac{\sqrt{P} - \sqrt{Q}}{\sqrt{P} + \sqrt{Q}}$$

In effect, Y uses the geometric mean of diagonal and off-diagonal entries ($\sqrt{P}$ and $\sqrt{Q}$) rather than the number of pairs in each diagonal (P and Q). Like Q, Y is restricted to use in 2-by-2 tables. Like Q, it assumes a value of 1.0 either for all entries on the diagonal, or for weak monotonicity (i.e., a zero entry in an off-diagonal cell; it assumes a value of −1.0 for a zero in a diagonal cell). When these conditions are not met perfectly, it assumes a

[12]James A. Davis, *Elementary Survey Analysis* (Englewood Cliffs, N. J.: Prentice-Hall, 1971), p. 75. This is an excellent, in-depth basic text on the use of Q (and gamma) in analysis of tables. See Davis, pp. 51−58, for a discussion of setting confidence limits on Q.

lower value than Q. In particular, as Table 11.9 indicates, Y approaches Somers' d in penalizing for near-weak monotonic arrangements, whereas Q gives high values for this. Although Y has this characteristic, Somers' d is used far more commonly because of its more readily intuited meaning.

TABLE 11.9

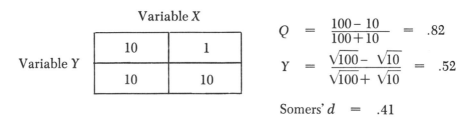

Variable X

Variable Y	10	1
	10	10

$$Q = \frac{100 - 10}{100 + 10} = .82$$

$$Y = \frac{\sqrt{100} - \sqrt{10}}{\sqrt{100} + \sqrt{10}} = .52$$

$$\text{Somers' } d = .41$$

Somers' d   *Somers' d* is gamma modified to penalize for pairs tied on x only, in directional (asymmetric) hypotheses in which x causes or predicts y; and to penalize for pairs tied on y only, in hypotheses in which y causes or predicts x:

$$d_{yx} = P - Q/P + Q + Y_0 \qquad \text{for the hypothesis that}$$
$$x \text{ causes or predicts } y$$

$$d_{xy} = P - Q/P + Q + X_0 \qquad \text{for the hypothesis that}$$
$$y \text{ causes or predicts } x$$

It is thus an *asymmetric statistic*, its value depending on the direction of the researcher's hypothesis.

Somers' d reaches a maximum of 1.0 for perfect strict monotonic association *or* for perfect ordered monotonic relationships. As Somers has noted, *interchanging the formulas* for d_{yx} and d_{xy} *may well be preferred* when the researcher wishes a maximum of 1.0 to correspond to perfect strict monotonic association *or* perfect predictive monotonic association. In Table 11.10,

TABLE 11.10

City Size (x)

		1	2	3	r_i
Riot	1	6	0	0	6
Intensity	2	0	5	4	9
(y)	c_i	6	5	4	15

$d_{yx} = 54 - 0/54 + 0 + 20 = .73$
$d_{xy} = 54 - 0/54 + 0 + 0 = 1.0$
tau-$c = 54 (4/15^2) = .96$

for instance, is perfect ordered monotonic for d_{xy} but not for d_{yx}. This example also illustrates how Somers' d takes on different values according to the direction of the hypothesis—in Table 11.10, only d_{yx} is relevant, since one would not predict that city size is caused by riot intensity; similarly, the symmetric statistic tau-c also overstates the strength of the relationship since it is not restricted to relationships in just one direction. For square tables, tau-b is the geometric mean between d_{xy} and d_{yx}. In 2-by-2 tables, d_{ux} equals $\%d$, as indicated in Table 11.11.

TABLE 11.11

		City Size		
		1	2	r_i
Riot	1	1 (25%)	0 (0%)	1
Intensity	2	3 (75%)	4 (100%)	7
	c_i	4 (100%)	4 (100%)	8

$\%d = .25-0 = .25$
$= 1.0-.75 = .25$
$d_{yx} = 4/4+0+12 = .25$
$d_{xy} = 4/4+0+3 = .57$
tau-b = .38 gamma = 1.0

If one has a symmetric (nondirectional) hypothesis, it is possible to compute Somers' symmetric d by the following formula:

$$ d = \frac{P-Q}{.5(Y_0 + X_0) + P + Q} $$

Thus Somers' symmetric d is based on the arithmetic mean of ties, whereas Kendall's tau-b is based on the geometric mean. The measures are quite similar in most cases. Somers' symmetric d is 1.0 only when X and Y are *both* monotonic functions of the other.[13]

Measures Based on the Proportionate Reduction of Error (PRE)

Robert K. Leik and Walter R. Gove have recently demonstrated how the logic of chi-square measures of association can be combined with the logic of measures based on the surplus of concordant pairs, to result in a measure that is the percentage by which knowing one variable reduces errors in guessing the value of the other variable. Lambda has been the traditional proportionate-reduction-of-error measure used until now, but Leik and Gove's d_n may well eclipse it as its superior qualities become better known in political science.

[13]For further reading on Somers' d, see Jae-On Kim, "Predictive measures of Ordinal Association," *American Journal of Sociology* 76 no. 5 (March 1971): 891–907. Note that Somers' d *is* percent difference ($\%d$) in the 2-by-2 case.

Leik and Gove's d_N Leik and Gove's d_N enables us to make a statement like the following: In the relation of city size to riot intensity in Table 11.6, 19 percent of the pairs are constrained by the marginal distribution, but of the remaining 81 percent, knowing city size will reduce our errors in predicting riot intensity by about 22 percent compared to the number of errors that would have occurred under statistical independence between the two variables. (Lambda, in contrast, does not correct for marginal distribution, and expresses reduction of error in comparison with the number of errors that would have occurred knowing only the marginals of the variable being predicted.)

1. Imagine two individuals, i and j. Let the term X_{ij} equal the score of both individuals on variable X. When the scores are the same, let $X_{ij} = 0$; when they are not the same, let $X_{ij} = 1$.

2. Given this, we would have perfect monotonic association if, when a pair of individuals score the same on X, they also score the same on Y. That is, perfect association would occur when $X_{ij} - Y_{ij} = 0$.

3. It follows that an error (a deviation from perfect monotonic association) occurs when X_{ij} differs from Y_{ij}; in such cases $X_{ij} - Y_{ij}$ will equal 1 or -1.

4. From this it may be seen that the total number of errors in a table will equal the number of pairs in which X differs from Y_{ij}. This can be expressed as $(X_{ij} = Y_{ij})$. But when doex X_{ij} differ from Y_{ij}? Only in the case of ties because only then do two individuals score the same on one variable but not the other. Thus the number of errors, E_{ij} equals ties on X plus ties on Y:

$$E_{ij} = X_0 + Y_0$$

5. Naturally, all this reasoning applies equally well to the table of expected values (as was computed in chi-square). We can distinguish ties in the expected table from ties in the observed table by adding a prime (') to these values: X_0', Y_0', etc.

6. Thus, a PRE measure of association would be:

$$\frac{\text{errors under no association} - \text{observed errors}}{\text{errors under no association}} = \frac{(X_0' + Y_0') - (X_0 + Y_0)}{(X_0' + Y_0')}$$

This formula is Leik-Gove's d_N, uncorrected for marginals, for symmetric (nondirectional) hypotheses. For the asymmetric hypothesis that X causes Y, d_N equals $(Y_0' - Y_0)/Y_0'$; for the hypothesis that Y causes X, d_N equals $(X_0' - X_0)/X_0'$. Note that by the asymmetric measures it is an error if the dependent variable is different between members of a pair when the independent variable is the same (that is, pairs tied on the dependent variable are errors); *but* it is *not* an error if the independent variable is different between members of a pair when the dependent variable is the same (that is, pairs tied on the independent variable are not errors). For d_N symmetric, both types of pairs are considered errors. For any of these three d_N formulas, d_N reaches 1.0 (perfect association) when there are no errors in the observed table.

7. However, d_N is not a good measure because it can never attain 1.0 (i.e., there *must* be errors) if the number of rows is different from the number of columns, *or* if row marginals do not equal column marginals. Therefore it is necessary to correct d_N for marginal constraints on the minimum number of errors; corrected

d_N is labelled d_N^c.

8. The correction for marginal constraint is made by subtracting the minimum number of errors (Y_o and/or X_o) from the denominator of the equations for d_N:

$$\text{symmetric } d_N^c = \frac{(X_0' + Y_0') - (X_0 + Y_0)}{(X_0' + Y_0' - Y_{0\,(min)} - X_{0\,(min)})}$$

$$\text{asymmetric } d_N^c \text{ for } x \text{ causes } y = \frac{(Y_0' - Y_0)}{(Y_0' - Y_{0\,(min)})}$$

$$\text{asymmetric } d_N^c \text{ for } y \text{ causes } x = \frac{(X_0' - X_0)}{(X_0' - X_{0\,(min)})}$$

9. It turns out that it is easier to compute Z, pairs tied on both X and Y, than it is to compute the minimum number of errors—and Z is related to the minimum number of errors according to the following equalities:

$$Z_{max} - Z = X_0 - X_{0\,(min)} = Y_0 - Y_{0\,(min)}$$

$$Z'_{max} - Z' = X_0' - X_{0\,(min)}' = Y_0' - Y_{0\,(min)}'$$

$$Z = \tfrac{1}{2}([a^2 + b^2 + \bullet \bullet \bullet + f^2] - n)$$

Note that the formula for Z given above is the same as for Z', and is mathematically equivalent to the formula for Z in Table 11.4, but is easier to compute by hand.

10. Z_{max} is computed by the following procedure:
   a. Create a set, $s(r,c)$.
   b. Look at the marginals in your table; if a row marginal equals a column marginal, enter it in set $s(r,c)$ and make both the row and column marginal equal to zero. Keep doing this till you run out of equal pairs.
   c. Find the largest row and largest column marginal; of these two, enter the smaller in set $s(r,c)$ and reduce that marginal to zero; at the same time, reduce the larger of the two by subtracting the smaller from it.
   d. Return to step b and keep repeating the cycle until all marginals are zero.
   e. Z_{max} equals the sum of squares of each number in set $s(r,c)$ minus n, this whole quantity divided by two:

$$Z_{max} = .5(\Sigma s_{rc}^2 - n)$$

Z_{max} is the same formula, of course, computed for the expected rather than the observed table.

11. Finally, the percentage of pairs that is constrained by the marginals in a table can be obtained by the following formula:

$$\% \text{ of constrained pairs} = \frac{2(X_{0\,(min)} + Y_{0\,(min)})}{n(n-1)}$$

From the formulas in step 9, we note that:

$$X_{0\,(min)} = Z - Z_{max} + Y_0$$

$$Y_{0\,(min)} = Z - Z_{max} + X_0$$

Exercise on Leik-Gove d_N^c   Consider Table 11.8 again, together with the corresponding table of expected values (computed as in the discussion on chi-square in Chapter 10).

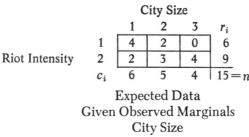

TABLE 11.8 (11.12)

City Size

		1	2	3	r_i
	1	4	2	0	6
Riot Intensity	2	2	3	4	9
	c_i	6	5	4	$15 = n$

Expected Data
Given Observed Marginals
City Size

		1	2	3	
Riot Intensity	1	2.4	2.0	1.6	
	2	3.6	3.0	2.4	
		6	5	4	$15 = n$

From the formulas discussed earlier in this chapter, the following quantities can be computed directly (remember that a prime indicates the statistic is based on the expected table):

$$X_0 = 4(2) + 2(3) + 0(4) = 14$$

$$Y_0 = 4(2) + 2(0) + 2(7) + 3(4) = 34$$

$$Z = .5([4^2 + 2^2 + 0^2 + 2^2 + 3^2 + 4^2] - 15) = 17$$

$$X_0' = 2.4(3.6) + 2(3) + 1.6(2.4) \cong 26$$

$$Y_0' = 2.4(3.6) + 2(1.6) + 3.6(5.4) + 3(2.4) \cong 38$$

$$Z' = .5([2.4^2 + 2^2 + 1.6^2 + 3.6^2 + 3^2 + 2.4^2] - 15) \cong 13$$

To compute Z_{max}

a. Create a set; the column on the
   right: Consider marginals $X(6, 5, 4)$;
   $Y(6, 9)$

b. Find any common row and column
   marginal and enter it: 6   36

c. Largest remaining marginals are
   $X(9)$ and $Y(5)$; enter the smaller
   of the two: 5   25
   Reduce to $X(0, 4)$; $Y(0, 0, 4)$

d. Look for more row and column
   marginals which are equal; in this
   example, 4, which is entered: 4   16

e. Compute the sum of squares of
   values in the set: * (See note p. 299.) $\Sigma s_{rc}^2 = 77$

$$Z_{max} = \tfrac{1}{2}(77 - 15) = 31$$

To compute d_N^c for the hypothesis that city size (X) causes riot intensity (Y):

$$d_N^c = \frac{Y_0' - Y_0}{Y_0' - Y_{0\,(min)}} = \frac{Y_0' - Y_0}{Z_{max} - Z'}$$

$$= \frac{38 - 34}{31 - 13} = .22$$

To compute the proportion constrained:

$$\% \text{ of constrained pairs} = \frac{2(X_{0\,(min)} + Y_{0\,(min)})}{n(n - 1)}$$

where . . .

$$X_{0\,(min)} = Z - Z_{max} + Y_0 = 17 - 31 + 14 = 0$$

$$Y_{0\,(min)} = Z - Z_{max} + X_0 = 17 - 31 + 34 = 20$$

Therefore . . .

$$\% \text{ of constrained pairs} = \frac{2(0 + 20)}{15(14)} = .19$$

On this basis we may say that 19 percent of the pairs in Table 11.8 are constrained by the marginals, but of the remaining 81 percent, knowing city size will reduce our errors of prediction by about 22 percent compared to errors assuming independence of the two variables.

Thus, Leik and Gove's d_N^c is a proportionate-reduction-of-error (PRE) measure of association, suitable for nominal data (or better), which can be cast in symmetric or asymmetric form, can be applied to tables of any size, and does not require marginals to be equal to reach a maximum of 1.0. It does assume, however, that the researcher defines "perfect association" as strict monotonic association. Since these characteristics cover a wide range of research settings in political science, d_N^c may well replace many of the previously discussed measures of association that are now more popular.[14]

Leik and Gove's d_o Although space limitations prevent full discussion, it may be noted that Leik and Gove have also adapted their PRE measure to

---

*Note that this set maximizes the number of cells with zero entries, while maintaining the marginals. This leads to Z_{max} because Z is pairs tied on a cell; the sum of all Z-type pairs is maximized by concentrating observations in as few cells as possible.

[14]See Robert Leik and Walter Gove, "Integrated Approach to Measuring Association," in H. Costner, ed., *Sociological Methodology 1971* (San Francisco: Jossey-Bass, 1971) ch. 10.

the cases of ordinal and interval data. Leik and Gove's d_o is the corresponding measure of association for ordinal data. In d_o, perfect association occurs when, for any shift in X, the shift in Y is concordant (a P pair). Where gamma counts ties (Y_o pairs) as acceptable and Somers' d_{yx} treats them as half right and half wrong, Leik and Gove's d_o introduces a variable factor, k, which allows the researcher to choose his or her own error criterion for ties. When, as in gamma, ties are to be considered acceptable, k equals 0; when, as in Somers' d, ties are to be considered half acceptable and half not, k equals 1; when ties are to be considered errors, k equals 2:

$$d_o = \frac{(P-Q) + (k-1)(Y_0' - Y_0)}{(P+Q) + k\left(\frac{Y_0 + X_0}{2}\right) + (k-1)(Y_0' - Y_0)}$$

The maximum value assumed by d_o is

$$d_{o\,(max)} = \frac{2P' + k[(Y_0' - Y_{0\,(min)})]}{2P' + k[(Y_0' + X_0')/2]}$$

Corrected d_o equals

$$d_o^c = \frac{d_o}{d_{o\,(max)}}$$

For the ordinal case, Z_{max} is computed differently:

1. List the marginals of X and Y in their ordinal sequence.
2. Create an index, i, and set it equal to 1.
3. Create a set, s_{rc}.
4. Look at the first row marginal that is not zero, and the first column marginal that is not zero; place the smaller in set s, and also subtract it from each of the two marginals.
5. Keep repeating step 4 until all marginals equal zero.
6. Compute Z_{max} as before.

With these adjustments, we can compute Leik and Gove's corrected d_n^c for the case of *symmetric* hypotheses.[15]

   What of the case when one variable is ordinal and the other nominal? When the nominal variable is the *dependent* variable, d_n^c must be used. When the nominal variable is the *independent* variable, d_o^c may be used with one alteration: the columns of the nominal variable (remember that

---

[15]Leik and Gove, "Integrated Approach," in Costner, *Sociological Methodology 1971*, pp. 292–297; Leik and Gove also indicate implications for ordinal asymmetric hypotheses.

independent variables are placed at the top of the table) should be placed in whatever order maximizes d_o.

Leik and Gove's d_o^c will ordinarily give values close to Somers' d. Its principle advantage, then, lies in its incorporation of a measure of deviation from statistical independence along the lines of chi-square based statistics.

***Leik and Gove's* d_i *and Corrected* r^2**   Finally, in the case of interval-level data, Leik and Gove's variant is d_i, which is mathematically equivalent to Pearson's coefficient of determination, r^2, to be discussed in the next chapter. Leik and Gove's d_i, like r^2, cannot attain a value of 1.0 (perfect association) unless the two variables in question contain marginal distributions which are identical to or are linear transformations of each other.

To correct for marginal constraints, one simply divides d_i (or r^2) by the maximum possible d_i (or r^2) given the marginal distribution of the variables. (Note that this is a general form of correction applicable, for example, to marginal constraints on phi or C; divide the observed statistic by the maximum possible value of that statistic for the given marginals.) To obtain the maximum possible value of $d_i = r_{max}^2$, arrange the data in two columns: one for X and one for Y. Within each column, order the values from highest to lowest. The correlation of these reordered pairs (e.g., highest X with highest Y, etc.) will be the maximum possible given the marginals. With this correction, d_i or r^2 will vary from $+1$ to -1, indicating the extent of correlation *for those pairs not constrained by the marginals*.

***Lambda* (λ)**   Gamma was the surplus of concordant pairs as a percentage of concordant and discordant pairs. Somers' d was the surplus of concordant pairs as a percentage of concordant, discordant, and relevant tied pairs. Leik and Gove's d_N^c was the surplus of errors expected under independence over observed errors as a percentage of errors under independence not counting (minus) the marginally constrained minimum number of observed errors. *Lambda*, in comparison, is the surplus of errors made when the marginals of the dependent variable are known over errors made when the dependent variable frequencies within each class of the independent variable are known, expressed as a percentage of errors of the first type.

Lambda asymmetric equals the number of errors of prediction made when only the marginals of the dependent variable are known, minus the number when the marginals of the independent variable are known, as a proportion of the number of errors when only the dependent is known. *Lambda*$_{se}$ is the standard statistic,

$$\text{lambda}_{se} = \frac{(\Sigma f_i) - F_d}{N - F_d}$$

where f_i = the largest frequency for each class of the independent (x) variable
F_d = the largest marginal value of the dependent variable

but it has three companions. *Lambda* sp is based on probable improvement of prediction, not reduction of error:

$$\text{lambda}_{sp} = \frac{(\Sigma f_i) - F_d}{F_d}$$

Lambda pe and *lambda* pp are statistics for reduction of error and improvement of prediction measures respectively, where the table is expressed in terms of percentages (p), not scores (s).

Lambda cannot be computed if all the entries lie in just one column of the independent variable, but otherwise it varies between 0 and 1. It is 0 when knowing the independent variable is of no help in prediction; it may be 0 even though there is not complete statistical independence. It is 1 only if a unit's *y* (independent variable) classification completely determines its *x* (dependent) classification. Lambda is unaffected by the ordering of columns or rows, and hence may be used with nominal-level data.

TABLE 11.13

		City Size (y)			r_i	
		1	2	3		
Riot Severity (x)	1	80 (67%)	9 (90%)	1 (10%)	90	(167)
	2	40 (33%)	1 (10%)	9 (90%)	50	(133)
	c_i	120 (100%)	10 (100%)	10 (100%)	140	(300)

$$\text{lambda}_{se} = \frac{(80+9+9) - 90}{140-90} = .160$$

$$\text{lambda}_{pe} = \frac{(67+90+90) - 167}{300-167} = .600$$

$$\text{lambda}_{sp} = \frac{(80+9+9) - 90}{90} = .089$$

$$\text{lambda}_{pp} = \frac{(67+90+90) - 167}{167} = .479$$

Table 11.13 illustrates the great difference in results obtained for the same table, depending on which version of lambda is applied. Lambda$_{se}$, suggested by Guttman and developed by Goodman and Kruskal, equals .160 for this table. Knowing the independent variable, city size, reduces by 16 percent the number of errors in predicting riot severity. On the other hand, lambda$_{sp}$ tells us that the number of correct predictions is improved only 8.9 percent. Others have argued that when the independent (*y*) marginals are highly unequal, as they are in this example, it is better to express the table in percentages and then act *as if* the percentages were scores. This has the effect of giving the reduction of error or improvement of prediction for the case which *would* (but actually does not) exist if each class of the independent variable had the same number of cases—for example, if city sizes 2 and 3 had as many cases as does city size 1, which actually has 120 in comparison with 10 each for 2 and 3. *If* independent variable classes were equal, then errors of prediction would be reduced 60 percent and correct predictions increased 47.9 percent.

Which lambda should be used in a particular case? The researcher must first decide if he is interested in reduction of error or improvement of prediction; often both kinds of statistics will be desired. If only one is used and the researcher is indifferent, lambda $_{se}$ is usually used. If the independent (y) variable margins are highly unequal, the researcher should consider computing lambda $_{pe}$ or lambda $_{pp}$—otherwise, strong relationships in independent variable classes with small numbers of cases (as with city sizes 2 and 3 in the example) may be obscured. If the largest dependent marginal is a very large proportion of N, then the researcher should consider computing lambda $_{sp}$ or lambda $_{pp}$, since otherwise, the small denominator that would occur in the lambda $_{se}$ and lambda $_{pe}$ formulas would lead to misleadingly large measures of association. Since each of the four statistics provides a distinct bit of information, it may often be useful to present all four lambda measures in each case. Note, however, that lambda is an asymmetric measure whose value would usually be different if the dependent and independent variables were switched; by switching, computing lambda both ways, and averaging, *lambda symmetric* may be derived.[16] Lambda symmetric is sometimes written λ_{ab}.

REVIEW: WHICH MEASURE OF ASSOCIATION?

Two considerations enter into the choice of a measure of association: validity and assumptions about data made by the statistic. Very little has been written on validation of measures of association, but A. A. Hunter has explored the special but common case of 2-by-2 tables and nominal data. Hunter found that %d and lambda correlated much more closely (.98 for %d; .68 – .86 for lambda, depending on whether a symmetric or asymmetric version was considered) with social scientists' intuitive estimate of degree of association than did chi-square based measures such as C, Q, and phi (these correlated .59, .59, and .56 respectively with the intuitive estimates).[17] That is, percent difference and proportionate-reduction-of-error measures may correspond more closely to social scientists' "common sense" impressions of what they mean by association than do more complicated measures such as those based on chi-square. If this is so, then, as

[16]For a method of assessing the statistical significance of lambda coefficients, see F. Hartwig, "Statistical Significance of the Lambda Coefficients," *Behavioral Science* 18, no.4 (July 1973):307–319.

[17]A. A. Hunter, "On the Validity of Measures of Association: The Nominal-Nominal, Two-by-Two Case," *American Journal of Sociology*, 79, no. 1 (July 1973): 99–109.

Hunter points out, a statistic designed for the nominal-level 2-by-2 case, such as phi, may deviate more from what social scientists intuitively perceive as association than statistics, such as lambda, that are not designed for such cases specifically.

With this qualification in mind, it must be admitted that most political scientists select measures of association according to their respective mathematical assumptions and purposes. In this regard, the outline in Table 11.14 may be helpful.[18]

EXERCISE

In a study of economic development and various forms of political instability, made as part of a report to the National Commission on the Causes and Prevention of Violence, Table 11.15 was presented. First, make a "gut estimate," from 0 through 1.0, of how strong the relationship between economic development and political instability is in this table. Then group the data into a second table by combining columns I through IV (resulting in a 2-by-2 table). Give your estimate from 0 to 1.0 of how strong the relationship is in this second table. Now compute all possible appropriate statistics mentioned in this chapter for both of these tables. Remember that nominal statistics may be used on ordinal data. Write up your findings in a brief (two- or three-page) paper, coming to some conclusion about the relative merits and problems of the various measures of association for this data.

---

[18] For further reading, see Leo Goodman and William Kruskal, "Measures of Association for Cross Classification," (Indianapolis: Bobbs-Merrill Reprints, Nos. S405-6); and Weisberg, "Models or Statistical Relationship." Weisberg cites a number of lesser-known measures of association that have the unusual null value conditions of balance and cleavage. These include:

$$x$$

For the table y

	a	b	r_1
	c	d	r_2

c_1 c_2 n

where a, b, c, and d are the cell entries expressed as *percentages* of n; where r_1, r_2, c_1, and c_2 are the row and column marginals expressed as *percentages* of n; and where n is the number of observations.

Average cohesion $= (|a - c|/c_1 + |b - d|/c_2)/2$
based on moderate monotonicity and cleavage

Maximum cohesion $= (|a - c|/c_1)$ or $(|b - d|/c_2)$, whichever is larger
based on weak monotonicity and cleavage

Koppa $= |a + d - b - c|$
based on strong monotonicity and balance (note this formula is for the case of dichotomous nominal variable relationships; signs have been deleted)

Note that accord and balance are always associated with strong monotonicity, whereas cleavage never is

TABLE 11.4   Which Measure of Association?

Consideration	% d (p. 282)	phi (φ) (p. 287)	C (p. 288)	T (p. 289)
minimum level of data	nominal	nominal	nominal	nominal
table size	2-by-2 only	2-by-2 only; natural dichotomy preferred	any size	any size
symmetric?	no	yes	yes	yes
meaning of "perfect" association	strict monotonic	strict monotonic	strict monotonic	strict monotonic
meaning of "null relation"	independence	independence	independence	independence
is maximum value less than 1.0 due to marginal constraints?	no	yes, when row marginals don't equal column marginals; but correction available (p. 000)	same as phi, or in nonsquare tables, or in tables smaller than 5-by-5	same as phi, or in nonsquare tables
nearest intuitive meaning	indentical to Somers' d for the 2-by-2 case	geometric mean of % d's across rows and across columns	an approximation to phi	an approximation to phi

TABLE 11.14   (cont.)

Consideration	V (p. 289)	tau-b (τ_b) (p. 291)	tau-c (τ_c) (p. 291)	gamma (V) (p. 292)
minimum level of data	nominal	ordinal	ordinal	ordinal
table size	any size	any size, but usually 2-by-2	any size	any size
symmetric?	yes	yes, but can be adapted by dropping the radical and one parenthetical expression in the denominator, giving Somers' d	yes	yes
meaning of "perfect" association	strict monotonic	strict monotonic	moderate monotonic	weak monotonic
meaning of "null relation"	independence	independence	independence	independence
is maximum value less than 1.0 due to marginal constraints?	yes, when row marginals do not equal column marginals	yes, when row marginals don't equal column marginals; or in nonsquare tables	yes, when row marginals don't equal column marginals	no

Consideration	Q (p. 292)	Y (p. 293)	d_{yx} (p. 294)	d_N^c (p. 295)	lambda (λ) (p. 301)
nearest intuitive meaning	an approximation to phi	surplus of concordant pairs as a percentage of concordant, discordant, and approximately one half of tied pairs	an approximation to tau-*b*		surplus of concordant pairs as a percentage of concordant and discordant pairs
minimum level of data	nominal	nominal	ordinal	nominal (ordinal variant available)	nominal
table size	2-by-2 only	2-by-2 only	any size	any size	any size
symmetric?	yes	yes	no, but asymmetric variant available	yes, but symmetric variants available	no, but symmetric variant available
meaning of "perfect" association	weak monotonic	weak monotonic	strict *or* ordered monotonic; strict *or* predictive monotonic variants; symmetric form is strict monotonic	same as d_{yx} but ties adjusted for marginals and errors under independence (but see p. 300)	strict monotonic *or* predictive monotonic
meaning of "null relation"	independence	independence	independence	independence	accord

TABLE 11.14   (cont.)

Consideration	Q	Y	d_{yx}	d_N^c	lambda (λ)
is maximum value less than 1.0 due to marginal constraints?	no	no	no	no	no
nearest intuitive meaning	same as gamma	difference between geometric means of concordant and discordant pairs as a percentage of both	surplus of concordant pairs as a percentage of concordant, discordant, and relevant tied pairs	surplus of errors under independence over observed errors as a percentage of errors under independence	surplus of errors on basis of dependent variable marginals over errors when dependent variable frequencies are known within each class of the independent variable, as a percentage of errors of the first type

TABLE 11.15 Relationship Between Economic Development and Political Instability, 1948-65

	I. Traditional Primitive	II. Traditional Civilization	III. Transitional	IV. Industrial Revolution	V. High Mass Consumption
Unstable (5:105-6:445)	Burma Laos Sudan 3	Bolivia China (mainland) Haiti India Thailand 5	Dominican Republic Ecuador Egypt Guatemala Honduras Indonesia Iraq Jordan Korea Morocco Paraguay Peru Philippines Portugal Syria Tunisia Turkey 17	Argentina Brazil Colombia Costa Rica Cuba Cyprus Czechoslovakia East Germany Greece Hungary Lebanon Malaya Panama Poland Union of South Africa Venezuela 16	France 1	42
Stable (1:012-5-096)	Afghanistan Ethiopia Libya 3	Cambodia Liberia Pakistan 3	Albania Ceylon China (Taiwan) El Salvador Ghana Iran Nicaragua Saudi Arabia 8	Austria Japan Bulgaria Mexico Chile Romania Finland Spain Iceland Uruguay Ireland U.S.S.R. Israel Yugoslavia Italy 15	Australia Norway Belgium Sudan Canada Switzerland Denmark United Luxembourg Kingdom Netherlands United States New Zealand West Germany 13	42
	6	8	25	31	14	84

Source: Ivo Feierabend, Rosalind Feierabend, and Betty Nesvold, "Social Change and Political Violence: Cross-National Patterns," in H. Graham and T. Gurr, eds., *The History of Violence in America* (New York: Bantam Books, 1969), p. 656.

12 | Correlation

Correlation coefficients and measures of association are both measures of the strength of a relationship. The distinction between correlation and association is arbitrary. In fact, some measures of association, such as phi or C, are sometimes also called correlation coefficients. Although this book follows conventional usage in treating correlation separately from association, the student should think of correlation as part of the question of association: how strong is a relationship between two variables?

INTERVAL-LEVEL CORRELATION

Pearsonian Product-moment Correlation, *r*

Pearsonian correlation, r, varies from 0 to 1, or 0 to -1 for negative relationships, as the points representing x and y on a scatter diagram move from a random arrangement to a straight line. Thus Pearsonian correlation assumes

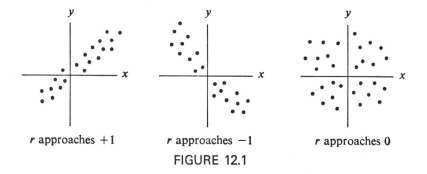

r approaches $+1$ r approaches -1 r approaches 0

FIGURE 12.1

that the relationship between x and y is *linear*. If the relationship is on a curve (*curvilinear*), then r will be misleadingly low. Furthermore, these techniques assume *homoscedasticity* of the variables. The x variable must

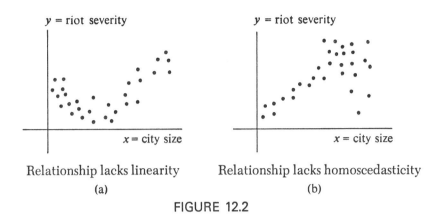

Relationship lacks linearity   Relationship lacks homoscedasticity

(a)   (b)

FIGURE 12.2

not have a low variance for some values of y and a high variance for other values of y. That is, not only must a straight line rather than a curved line be drawn through the paired (x,y) points (linearity), but the spread of points around the line should be about the same all along the line (homoscedasticity).

For example, the relationship shown in Figure 12.2 (a) is curvilinear; there is a clear pattern of covariation, but it cannot be summarized by one straight line. Figure 12.2(b) lacks homoscedasticity even though a straight line could be drawn through the points because the relationship is much stronger for smaller cities (x) than larger. If the relationship is nonlinear, lacks homoscedasticity, or is below the interval level of measurement, the assumptions involved in Pearsonian correlation are not met. Linearity and homoscedasticity are most easily checked by visual inspection of a scatter diagram. Finally, Pearsonian r will vary between 0 and ± 1 only if both variables being correlated have the same underlying (usually normal) distribution.[1]

Pearsonian correlation is called *product-moment* correlation, the term "product-moment" being a mathematical term referring to the mean of a product, which is what r is based on. Pearsonian r equals the sum of the product of x and y deviations from their respective means divided by the value that sum would have if the observations fell perfectly on a straight line.

[1]See the discussion in Chapter 11 of the effect of the marginal distribution on r.

The definitional formula for r follows:

$$r = \frac{\Sigma(x - \bar{x})(y - \bar{y})}{\sqrt{\Sigma(x - \bar{x})^2 \, \Sigma(y - \bar{y})^2}}$$

The computational formula:

$$r = \frac{n\Sigma(xy) - (\Sigma x)(\Sigma y)}{\sqrt{[n\Sigma x^2 - (\Sigma x)^2] \, [n\Sigma y^2 - (\Sigma y)^2]}}$$

In the *definitional formula* for r, the numerator measures the deviation of the x and y scores from mean x and mean y (see Figure 12.3). When the data form a straight line, points with high x deviations (high $x - \bar{x}$) will also have high y deviations; those with low x deviations will have low y deviations. In Table 12.1, a list of x values is paired in a perfect linear relationship with a list of y values. As a result, low x deviations are matched by low y deviations, medium by medium, high by high. When each x deviation is multiplied by its respective y deviation, a list of deviation products is derived that adds up to 20. The student may experiment by rearranging the y column to see that

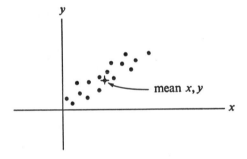

FIGURE 12.3

no other arrangement would result in a sum as high as 20; any deviation from perfect linearity reduces the sum of deviation products.

TABLE 12.1   A Table of Deviation Products

x	y	$x - \bar{x}$	$y - \bar{y}$	$(x - \bar{x})(y - \bar{y})$
1	2	−2	−4	8
2	4	−1	−2	2
3	6	0	0	0
4	8	1	2	2
5	10	2	4	8
$\bar{x} = 3$	$\bar{y} = 6$			20

The denominator in the definitional formula of r states the maximum value that the numerator can take. Since in the example the relationship is perfect, the denominator equals 20 also. The student may again experiment by rearranging the original y column to show that while any rearrangement of the column from its illustrated perfect linear relationship diminishes the numerator, it does not affect the denominator.

Pearson's r thus uses the product-moment method of measuring degree of linearity as a criterion for correlation. Perfect correlation is perfect linearity, and the correlation coefficient itself is a ratio of observed linearity to perfect

TABLE 12.2 Computing the Maximum Deviation Product

$x-\bar{x}$	$y-\bar{y}$	$(x-\bar{x})^2$	$(y-\bar{y})^2$
-2	-4	4	16
-1	-2	1	4
0	0	0	0
1	2	1	4
2	4	4	16
		10	40

$\Sigma(x-\bar{x})^2 \Sigma(y-\bar{y})^2 = 10(40) = 400$

$\text{m.d.p.} = \sqrt{\Sigma(x-\bar{x})^2 \Sigma(y-\bar{y})^2} = \sqrt{400} = 20$

linearity. In computing r in practice, however, the *computational formula* is used, which is the mathematical equivalent of the definitional formula, but which avoids the need to compute deviations from the mean for each pair of observations. Also as a means of simplifying computation, certain *data transformation rules* are available: x or y scores may be added to, subtracted from, divided or multiplied by any constant without affecting the correlation coefficient, since none of these operations affect the linearity of the relationship between x and y; roots or power functions would affect r, however. Moreover, transformations applied to x need not be applied to y.

Taking the simple example shown in Table 12.3, suppose we sampled five small communities whose voting population had not changed over these four years, and found the number voting for Nixon in 1968 and 1972, labelling these votes x and y respectively. These may be simplified, first by subtracting 100 from x to get x', then transforming y by subtracting 100 and dividing by 10 to get y'. These transformations enable us to work with small numbers in the computational formula, eventually arriving at $r = -.45$. This shows that there is a moderate negative correlation between voting for Nixon in 1968 and voting for Nixon in 1972 for these five towns. It would be an historical fallacy, discussed in the last chapter, to conclude that this necessarily means that individuals who voted for Nixon in 1968 did not do so in 1972; what is true between groups is not necessarily true at the individual level within groups.

One way of transforming the data would be to take both x and y, subtract from each their respective means, and divide each by their respective

TABLE 12.3

Town	1968 votes (x)	1972 votes (y)	x'	y'	x'^2	y'^2	$x'y'$
1	100	130	0	3	0	9	0
2	102	120	2	2	4	4	4
3	105	110	5	1	25	1	5
4	103	150	3	5	9	25	15
5	100	140	0	4	0	16	0
			10	15	38	55	24

$$r = \frac{n\Sigma(xy) - (\Sigma x)(\Sigma y)}{\sqrt{[n\Sigma x^2 - (\Sigma x)^2][n\Sigma y^2 - (\Sigma y)^2]}}$$

$$= \frac{5(24) - 10(15)}{\sqrt{[5(38) - 100][5(55) - 225]}}$$

$$= \frac{120 - 150}{\sqrt{(190 - 100)(275 - 225)}} = \frac{-30}{\sqrt{90(50)}}$$

$$= \frac{-30}{\sqrt{4500}} = \frac{-30}{10\sqrt{45}} = \frac{-3}{\sqrt{45}} = \frac{-3}{6.71}$$

$$= -.45$$

standard deviations. Note that this is the way to transform *raw scores* into *normal scores*: subtract the mean and divide by the standard deviation. If the scores are in normal form, then r equals the sum of the products of the normal (standard) scores divided by n:

$$r = \Sigma z_x z_y / n$$

That is, Pearson's r can be thought of as the average crossproduct of standard scores between two variables. The sum of squares of standard scores equals the number of units ($\Sigma z_x^2 = n$). But the sum of crossproducts will equal n (and hence r will equal 1.0) only when low x normal scores are paired with low y normal scores, medium with medium, and high with high. This formula is mathematically equivalent to the definitional and computational formulas for r.

Coefficient of Determination, r^2

The square of the correlation coefficient, r^2, is considered to be the proportion of the variance in the dependent variable "explained" by the independent variable. If the correlation between income and an index of "sense of political efficacy" is .60, then the square of this, .36, is the fraction of the variance in political efficacy explained by income. This implies that a correlation of .60 is not twice as strong as one of .30, since .36 is more than twice .09.

Significance of the Correlation Coefficient Like any measure of association, a strong correlation does not assure significance.[2] The smaller the sample size, the higher r must be to be significant. The significance of r may be read directly from a table of coefficients of correlation and t ratios, where degrees of freedom equals sample size minus 2. If our sample included only 5 observations, then sample size $5 - 2 = 3$ would be the number of degrees of freedom. For 3 degrees of freedom, the table tells us that r must be .878 or higher to be significant at the .05 level, and .959 or higher to be significant at the .01 level. At the .05 level, for a sample size of 25, r must be .396; for 100, .195; for 1000, .062.

If such a table is unavailable, critical values of r may be determined from a t table by the formula:

$$r_{crit} = \sqrt{t^2 / [t^2 + (n - 2)]}$$

For a certain number of degrees of freedom (the researcher's sample size minus 2) and the desired level of significance (.05, .01, or whatever), a value of t may be read and placed in the formula. For sample size 25 and significance level .05, $t = 2.069$; the student may use this in the r_{crit} formula to see if the minimum significant value of r is .396 as stated above. Note that the t (and z and F) test *assumes* both variables are normally distributed and have the same variance.

If one wishes to test whether or not a specific r is significant, the formula above may be transformed to:

$$t = \sqrt{\frac{r^2 (n - 2)}{1 - r^2}}$$

In this procedure, one places the observed r in the formula, computes t, and reads the significance level of the computed t from a t table such as Table IV in the Appendix, using degrees of freedom equal to $(n - 2)$.

The significance of r can also be tested by the F table, in which . . .

$$F = \frac{r^2 (n - 2)}{1 - r^2}$$

using the same procedure as in the t test, except degrees of freedom equal to 1 (d.f.$_1 = 1$) and sample size minus 2 (d.f.$_2 = n - 2$).

[2]Significance is relevant only for random samples.

The above-mentioned procedures for assessing the significance of r are best suited for low values of r (below .40 or .50). A better, more generally applicable procedure for testing the significance of r is Fisher's z_r transformation. This involves two steps:

1. Convert r to z_r.
   a. Use a table of conversion for z_r to read directly the z_r that corresponds to one's computed r, (See footnote 3.)
   b. Or use the following conversion formula:

$$z_r = .5 \log_e(1 + r) - .5 \log_e(1 - r)$$

   c. Or use the following formula:

$$z_r = 1.1513 \log_{10} \left(\frac{1 + r}{1 - r} \right)$$

2. Test the significance of z_r.
   a. Compute the standard error of z_r:

$$\sigma z_r = 1/\sqrt{n - 3}$$

   b. Then compute the confidence limits of z_r. This is done in the same manner as discussed in the section on sampling statistics. For example, the .95 confidence limits equal $(z_r + 1.96 \sigma \, t_r)$ for the upper limit and $(z_r - 1.96 \sigma \, t_r)$ for the lower limit. If the lower limit is zero or less, we cannot be 95 percent confident that z_r is different from zero; or to put it another way, z_r is not significant at the .05 level.
   c. Lastly, the upper and lower confidence limit z_r is reconverted to r through the procedures of step 1.

Fisher's z_r can also be used in testing *the significance of the difference between two rs based on uncorrelated samples.* (Recall similar tests given in Table 8.9.) The steps for this procedure are as follows:

1. Convert r to z_r.
2. Compute the z test statistic:

$$z = \frac{z_{r1} - z_{r2}}{\sqrt{\sigma_{z_{r1}}^2 + \sigma_{z_{r2}}^2}}$$

3. Interpret z as discussed earlier (in the section on sampling statistics).

For *the significance of the difference between two rs based on the same sample,* the t test is used:

$$t = \frac{(r_{12} - r_{13}) \sqrt{(n - 3)(1 + r_{23})}}{\sqrt{2(1 - r_{12}^2 - r_{13}^2 - r_{23}^2 + 2r_{12}r_{13}r_{23})}}$$

[3]These tables are given in numerous sources, including Q. McNemar, *Psychological Statistics*, 3rd ed. (New York: John Wiley & Sons, 1962), pp. 426–427.

For this application, degrees of freedom equals $(n - 3)$, and the correlations refer to variables 1, 2, and 3. Note that other correlation statistics may *not* be substituted for r in these formulas, which refer solely to Pearson's r.

Finally, Fisher's z_r may be used when one wants to *average Pearsonian correlations*:

1. Convert r to $_r z$.
2. Compute the average z_r:

$$z_r \text{ (ave)} = \frac{(n_1 - 3)z_{r1} + (n_2 - 3)z_{r2} + \cdots + (n_k - 3)z_{rk}}{(n_1 - 3) + (n_2 - 3) + \cdots + (n_k - 3)}$$

For this application, k equals the number of rs to be averaged, and the n refers to the sample sizes of z_r.

3. Compute the significance of $z_{r \text{ (ave)}}$ by the z test:

$$z = \frac{z_{r \text{ (ave)}}}{\sqrt{(n_1 - 3) + (n_2 - 3) + \cdots + (n_k - 3)}}$$

4. Reconvert $z_{r \text{(ave)}}$ to an average r in the same manner one would reconvert a z_r back to an r.

Pearsonian correlations should always be averaged in this manner when the values of r to be averaged either are not fairly equal, or are fairly large (e.g., above .25 in conservative tests, and in any event when rs are above .40).

Other Considerations Relating to Pearson's r   In testing the significance of r, the researcher must keep in mind that the magnitude of r is "artificially" low when the *range* of the data is narrow. For example, the correlation between unemployment and labor rioting is .77 for the years 1927–1963, but only .34 for the years 1930–1939. This is not primarily because there was some strong correlation after the 1930s, but rather because low unemployment and low rates of labor rioting after 1939 served to increase the range of both variables. When the variables being correlated do not vary greatly, the correlation coefficient is unlikely to be large. Because this is so, social scientists increasingly report the variance along with the correlation coefficients.[4] Similarly, it may be better to leave extreme cases out of the correlation when they are few in number, since their inclusion will lead to a misleadingly large r. (Or better yet, r may be presented for all cases, and again for all cases but the extremes.)

Similarly, when r is based on a small sample size, r *overstates* the actual degree of correlation. In the extreme case of two observations, there will always be a perfect linear relation between variables. For small samples (100

---

[4]Some authors have developed "corrections" for range of data; see J. P. Guilford, *Psychometric Methods* (New York: McGraw-Hill, 1954).

or less) Ezekiel and Fox have developed an adjustment for *r* (and for partial *r* and multiple *R*, to be discussed later)[5]. Since this adjustment for sample size requires the use of regression techniques to be discussed later in this book, it is not treated here. Ezekiel and Fox's adjusted *r*, which they term $\bar{r}$, is not yet commonly used in political science.

Inducing a Model from a Correlation Matrix   In a later chapter we will deal with the use of Pearson's *r* to infer causality in the sort of explanatory models discussed in Chapter 5. It sometimes happens, however, that for exploratory purposes we may want to have some heuristic method of uncovering what sort of explanatory model may be embedded in a correlations matrix.

Table 12.4 contains a matrix of correlation coefficients computed by Raoul Naroll in a study of the factors underlying deterrence in international relations.[6] When one is confronted with a matrix with hundreds of correlation coefficients it is natural to feel confused about what explanatory models it is meant to support. The following "rule-of-thumb" procedure may be used to help overcome this confusion:

1. Decide upon an arbitrary level of correlation sufficient to be interesting. If the data are based on a random sample, this level should be at least the critical value of *r*. For example, the .5 level "explains" 25 percent of the variance in a dependent variable and might be picked as an arbitrary cutoff. This is used as a criterion for ignoring many of the coefficients in the matrix.
2. Decide upon an arbitrary "starting variable" for the model. Starting variables may be natural or historical phenomena which could not be conceived of as dependent variables in the research context. For example, in Table 12.4, "presence of natural barriers" is a natural phenomenon that could not have been caused by the other military and political variables. Similarly, presence of a "civil war tradition" is a historical factor that could not be caused by variables pertaining to the present.
3. Consider all correlations above the cutting point between the starting variable(s) and other variables. Enter these variables in a model, using intuition as a guide for the direction of causality (the direction of the arrow in a diagrammatic model).
4. Continue this process for the second variable entered, and so on, until all entered variables are considered and no correlations below the cutting point are omitted.
5. Some causal arrows may be erased because indirect causation is indicated. This may be checked by partial correlation. For example, in Table 12.4, though centralization is correlated with war, this arrow may be omitted if the partial correlation of centralization and war, controlling for quality of the military, tends toward zero. (This procedure is discussed more fully in Chapter 18).

[5]Moredecai Ezekiel and Karl Fox, *Methods of Correlation and Regression Analysis*, 3rd ed. (New York: John Wiley & Sons, 1967), pp. 300–304.
[6]The source for Table 12.4 is R. Naroll, "Deterrence in History," in D. Pruitt and R. Snyder, eds., *Theory and Research on The Causes of War* (Englewood Cliffs, N. J.: Prentice-Hall, 1969), pp. 156–157. Reprinted by permission.

TABLE 12.4   Correlations and Significance Levels

	Months of War A732	Territorial Gain A730	Territorial Instability A731	Defensive Stance 718	Strength, S.I. A701	Strength, D.S. B701	Mobility, S.I. A702	Mobility, D.S. B702	Quality, S.I. A703	Quality, D.S. B703	Fortifications, S.I. A704	Fortifications, D.S. B704	Propinquity 712	Prestige 713
Months of War A732		.08	-.25	-.03	.07	.12	.13	.26	.36	.14	.32	-.18	.21	-.09
Territorial Gain A730	.08		.21	-.35	.27	-.09	.00	-.22	.39	-.04	.21	-.03	.08	.00
Territorial Instability A731		.05		-.13	.12	-.10	.01	-.22	.08	-.01	.30	-.29	-.31	-.14
Defensive Stance 718			.09		.30	-.39	-.10	.12	-.03	-.39	-.06	.40	.03	.05
Strength, S.I. A701				.053		.20	-.14	.05	-.13	-.10	.25	.37	.07	.15
Strength, D.S. B701							-.13	-.01	.04	.29	-.12	.05	-.13	.21
Mobility, S.I. A702								.47	.09	.18	-.06	-.17	.06	.00
Mobility, D.S. B702									-.01	.32	-.10	-.01	-.04	.13
Quality, S.I. A703							.018			.30	.12	-.02	.07	.15
Quality, D.S. B703							.074				.11	.15	.13	.33
Fortifications, S.I. A704					.088				.058			.33	-.02	-.23
Fortifications, D.S. B704					.057								.05	.03
Propinquity 712														-.12
Prestige 713														
Previous Conflict 714			.09		.088								.032	
Natural Barriers 715			.04									.051		
Capital City 716			.03										.051	
Announcements A705														
Surprise B705														
Alliances A706				.003		.036				.036		.027		
Active Diplomacy A707		.004	.025	.043										
Intense Diplomacy B707			.015	.044										
Benefits A709			.08				.08							
Cultural Exchange A708		.10		.045										
Trade B708					.017					.067				
General Exchange C708	.05		.04		.054									
Experience of Ruler A710			.005		.092									
Youth of Ruler B710								.095				.036	.036	
Unbridled Ruler C710				.044						.020				
Hereditary Monarchy D710														
Civil War 711	.08	.06	.10		.017					.020				
Centralization 717	.08		.10				.068		.017	.060				

The upper right half of this table show coefficients of correlations. The first three columns and lines are of quantitative variables (see Table 1); the remaining columns and lines are of qualitative variables. The coefficients of correlation between two quantitative variable are product moment coefficients; between one quantitative and one qualitative variable are point biserial coefficients; between two qualitative variables are phi coefficients. Phi coefficients marked with asterisks were computed from contingency tables in which one empty cell occurred by adding unity to each of the four cells.

The lower left half of this table shows one-tailed probabilities. That is to say, the table shows the probability of obtaining this unlikely a relationship in one direction (plus or minus) only. Each of these then gives the probability of obtaining the particular result actually obtained, or one even less likely, if in fact the two variables are not related and the result is a mere chance freak or sampling or other random factor. Needless to say, since many of these

TABLE 12.4 Correlations and Significance Levels (cont.)

Previous Conflict 714	Natural Barriers 715	Capital City 716	Announcements A705	Surprise B705	Alliances A706	Active Diplomacy A707	Intense Diplomacy B707	Benefits A709	Cultural Exchange A708	Trade B708	General Exchange C708	Experience of Ruler A710	Youth of Ruler B710	Unbridled Ruler C710	Heriditary Monarchy D710	Civil War 711	Centralization 717
.15	.18	−.10	.33	−.07	−.11	.29	−.21	.11	−.27	−.17	−.40	.14	−.29	.17	.30	.25	.34
−.22	.02	−.34	−.33	.03	.03	−.58	−.22	−.07	.31	−.33	.10	.22	.20	−.26	−.26	−.44	.29
−.04	−.24	.31	.69	−.52	−.33	−.15	−.45	−.52	.37	−.20	.42	.62	.07	−.17	−.19	−.10	.18
−.10	−.08	.25	−.12	•.53	.41	.41	−.03	.00	•.39	.00	.25	−.14	−.41	−.13	.30	.30	−.05
−.02	.30	•−.25	.12	−.10	−.12	−.17	−.15	−.04	−.07	−.33	•−.29	•.29	.05	•.38	.14	−.14	−.07
−.05	.08	−.12	.04	−.17	.45	.08	.03	.07	−.12	.11	−.03	−.05	.10	.11	.10	−.08
.11	−.10	−.12	−.10	•.04	.08	−.16	.05	•.27	.03	.04	−.14	.08	−.13	.14	•.12	•.12	•.29
.00	•.02	.14	−.20	•.02	•.26	•.02	−.13	•.11	−.12	−.15	.12	−.10	•−.30	•−.08	•−.03	•.10	•.21
−.02	.07	−.15	.04	•.02	−.14	−.10	.15	−.07	−.04	−.11	.03	.02	−.04	−.04	.02	•.38
−.10	.07	−.09	.02	.02	.45	.07	−.04	.10	.08	.45	.19	−.07	−.12	•−.39	−.30	.16	.38
−.02	−.11	.05	•.18	.00	−.05	.05	.05	.05	.14	.09	−.31	.11	−.05	.01	.12	.05
•.05	−.15	•.33	−.11	−.05	•.42	.03	.19	−.02	−.03	•.45	.11	•−.23	−.23	−.19	.14	.30	−.30
.43	.03	.05	•.15	−.12	−.12	.03	.08	.02	−.21	•.30	−.05	•.38	−.18	.05	−.05	.12	.03
.00	.00	−.01	−.43	.07	−.07	.00	.20	−.05	.28	.02	.15	.03	−.14	.06	.06	.08	.08
	−.06	.05	−.16	.15	.00	−.06	−.06	.16	−.21	•.30	−.05	•−.38	.18	.15	.10	•.17	−.12
		•−.42	.00	−.02	.10	.01	−.07	−.08	−.22	−.27	•−.38	.10	−.05	.10	−.10	−.03	.06
	.011		−.06	.01	−.05	.20	.24	.05	.37	.26	.44	−.37	.05	−.05	−.08	.19	.01
				•−.38	.17	.00	−.30	−.23	−.14	−.18	.00	.08	.04	.06	.08	.13	−.14
			.035		.17	−.02	.02	.22	.07	.20	−.02	•−.27	•.24	−.01	.12	−.04	−.07
						.20	.13	−.03	.05	.37	−.05	−.12	−.46	−.39	−.14	.10	−.03
							•.47	.04	−.12	.19	−.10	−.17	−.05	−.12	−.10	•.34	.06
								.06	.03	.27	.19	−.13	.05	−.06	−.03	.35	−.02
									−.09	−.08	−.23	.05	.02	.37	.56	.33	.18
		.057								.02	•.52	.33	−.14	.01	−.18	−.02	.03
.070											.20	•−.43	.12	•−.36	−.06	.12	−.14
	.017	.031										.03	−.14	−.32	−.14	.02	−.03
.036									.092	.027			−.14	.08	.03	−.18	.13
				.052										.33	−.14	−.18	−.05
				.059				.045		.049	.088				•.50	.10	−.10
								.008								•.31	.10
					.042	.084									.063		−.03

results were not predicted in advance, since many of the relationships predicted in advance were not in fact found, and since most of the correlations observed did not attain statistical significance, these particular probabilities cannot be taken at face value. The probabilities of product moment coefficients were computed by using the standard error of these coefficients and entering a normal distribution table; of point biserial coefficients, by using Student's *t* distribution; and of phi coefficients, by obtaining the exact probabilities (Fisher's exact test) from the tables of Lieberman and Owen (1961). Two kinds of probabilities were omitted: (1) those greater than 0.10; (2) those between two variables whose relationship was an artifact of coding definitions, e.g., between Strength, Defensive Stance (B701) and Defensive Stance (718) in general. D.S. means Defensive Stance, and S.I. means Stance Immaterial.

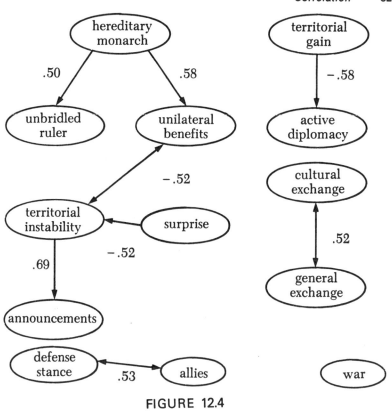

FIGURE 12.4

This process may generate a diagrammatic model such as Figure 12.4, which is based on Table 12.4. Once such a model is drawn, several further steps may be taken:

6. The model generated may be compared with the explanatory model discussed by the author within the article.
7. One should consider whether or not some important variables may be missing altogether.
8. A more complex, but weaker, model may be constructed by lowering the cutting point for r, and this second induced model can also be compared with that of the author.

It is not infrequent to find that authors assert models that seem, on the surface, to differ from the model that may be induced from the correlation matrix of their own data. Since this heuristic procedure does not generate a unique explanatory model, such differences are not necessarily "errors of interpretation" by authors of their own data, but these differences do direct the critical reader to specific aspects of the author's explanation that should be examined with special care for possible erroneous inference.

Reliability Coefficients   *Reliability coefficients* refer to another use of Pearson's *r*. A reliability coefficient is a Pearson *r* that is: (1) between responses to two forms of the same questionnaire administered to a group randomly split into two subgroups; (2) between responses to two forms of the same questionnaire administered to one group on one occasion; or (3) between responses to a questionnaire administered to one group on two occasions. When two forms of a questionnaire are used, both are designed to measure the same thing(s). A good questionnaire should have high reliability coefficients ("high" commonly means "above .90").

The second type of reliability coefficient refers to the "parallel forms method," and in this situation Pearson's *r* is called a *"coefficient of equivalence."* When, in the second method, the two forms are interspersed (e.g., the first form refers to the even-numbered items and the second form to the odd-numbered items) rather than sequential, it is called the "split-halves method" and Pearson's *r* is called the *"coefficient of internal consistency."*

The third type of reliability coefficient refers to the "test-retest method," and in this situation Pearson's *r* is called a *"coefficient of stability."*

Since the purpose of reliability coefficients is to check the validity of one's questionnaire, these are sometimes called *validity coefficients.*[7]

Partial Correlation   Partial correlation means correlation between two variables controlling for one or more other variables, as between income and sense of political efficacy, controlling for educational level. When education is held constant, does the correlation of .60 between income and efficacy diminish or disappear? This question is answered by using the partial correlation coefficient with education as a control.

First-order partial (one control):

$$r_{ij.k} = \frac{r_{ij} - (r_{ik})(r_{jk})}{\sqrt{1 - (r_{ik})^2} \times \sqrt{1 - (r_{jk})^2}}$$

As many control variables as desired may be used at the same time, although ordinarily measurement error and intercorrelation of control variables makes controlling for more than three variables at the same time unlikely to be meaningful. Note that each higher-order partial correlation equation requires computation of all lower orders of partial correlation:

---

[7]For certain research purposes, Pearson's *r* may be adjusted for such factors as length of the questionnaire. See McNemar, *Psychological Statistics*, pp. 145–154; N. Downie and R. Heath, *Basic Statistical Methods*, 2nd ed. (New York: Harper & Row, 1965), pp. 215–221.

S ond-order partial (two controls):[8]

$$r_{ij.kl} = \frac{r_{ij.k} - (r_{jl.k})(r_{il.k})}{\sqrt{1 - (r_{il.k})^2} \times \sqrt{1 - (r_{jl.k})^2}}$$

Third-order partial (three controls):

$$r_{ij.klm} = \frac{r_{ij.kl} - (r_{im.kl})(r_{jm.kl})}{\sqrt{1 - (r_{im.kl})^2} \times \sqrt{1 - (r_{jm.kl})^2}}$$

As will be seen in a later chapter, partial correlation coefficients are important in "causal modeling," building and testing mathematical models of political reality. Significance of partial correlation is tested by the *F* test, where:

$$F = (r_{ij.k}^2 / 1 - r_{ij.k}^2)(n - v - 1)$$

In this formula, v equals the number of independent and control variables. After computing the *F* value by this formula, the student may determine whether the partial correlation coefficient is significant by consulting the *F* distribution table in the Appendix, for 1 and $(n - v - 1)$ degrees of freedom.

For small samples, partial correlation can be tested for significance by use of the *t* tables:

$$t = \frac{r_{ij.k}}{\sqrt{\dfrac{1 - r_{ij.k}^2}{n - 3}}}$$

In this test, the *t* tables are used in the conventional way, with degrees of freedom equal to $(n - 3)$.

Part Correlation   Partial correlation "removes" the effect of the control variable(s) on *both* the dependent (*i* in the formulas above) and the independent (*j* in the formulas above) variables. *Part correlation*, in contrast,

---

[8]When multiple correlation, *R* (discussed in Chapter 15), is known, the following formula may simplify calculations:

$$r_{ij.kl} = \sqrt{\frac{(1 - R_{i.kl}^2) - (1 - R_{i.jkl}^2)}{(1 - R_{i.kl}^2)}}$$

"removes" the effect of the control variable(s) on the independent variable *alone*. Part correlation is used when one hypothesizes that the control variable affects the independent variable but not the dependent variable, and when one wants to assess the unique effect of the independent variable on the dependent variable.

That is, partial correlation is the correlation of an independent variable with the variance in the dependent variable *remaining* after the effect of a control variable is taken into account. Part correlation is the correlation of an independent variable with the *full* variance in the dependent variable.

The formula for part correlation is:

$$r_{i(j.k)} = \frac{r_{ij} - r_{ik}r_{jk}}{\sqrt{1 - r_{jk}^2}}$$

The Correlation Ratio, Eta (η), for Nonlinear Relationships

Pearson's r measures *linear* relationships. When relationships are *curvilinear*, r understates the amount of correlation. The correlation ratio, eta, is sometimes termed the "coefficient of curvilinear correlation." When a relationship is linear, r equals eta; in curvilinear relationships, the degree to which r is less than eta is a measure of the extent to which curvilinearity exists. Even a perfect curvilinear relationship (eta = 1.0) might have an r of zero.

Eta may be computed:

1. *if* the dependent variable data are interval or ratio in level;
2. *if* the frequencies in each class of the independent variable (x, corresponding to columns in Table 12.5) are large enough to give statistical stability to the means of these classes (columns). (Note that this is *not* the case in Table 12.5, which uses low frequencies for simplicity of illustration);
3. *if* there are enough classes of the independent variable to give the grand mean of column means stability.

Note also that eta will be different for the hypothesis that x is independent and y dependent, and for the hypothesis that y causes x. Hence we must specify whether we wish the former (eta_{yx}) or the latter (eta_{xy}).

As indicated in Table 12.5, eta $_{yx}$ (η_{yx}) equals the square root of the sum of squares for y between columns (x classes) divided by the total sum of squares. (Sums of squares will be discussed more fully in Chapter 14.) The numerator and denominator in this formula for eta serve similar parts to their counterparts in the correlation equation: to the extent x and y are related, linearly *or* curvilinearly, the numerator will be as large as the denominator and eta will approach 1.0. Eta varies from 0 to 1.0, and has no sign since it measures extent but not direction of relationship.

In the example in Table 12.5, data are given for x and y. Usually such data will have to be grouped into ranges and classes in order to give an adequate number of y values for each value of x. (As noted, eta would require larger frequencies than in Table 12.5, but small values are used for simplicity). The grouped data are ranged in numbered classes from 0 to k, where k is the number of ranges minus one. Such data are relabelled x' and y'. A table of x' and y' is called a table of joint frequencies. Visual inspection of Table 12.5 reveals that these values are, literally, curvilinearly related. That is, the entries in the table form a curve. This suggests that r will underestimate the degree of correlation.

The chart in Table 12.5 can be used to compute eta, which can be used as a measure of the curvilinear relation between x and y:

1. Column A lists f_y, the number of units in each range of y.
2. Column B lists y', the grouped values of y, from 0 to the number of ranges minus one (6).
3. Column C is obtained by multiplying the values in column B by the values in column A.
4. Column D is obtained by multiplying the values in column C by the values in column B.
5. Column E lists x', the grouped values of x, from 0 to the number of ranges minus 1 (9).
6. Column F lists f_x, the number of units in each range of x.
7. Column G lists, for each value of x' (0 through 9), the sum of y'; the sum of y' equals the sum of y' values times the corresponding number of units in that class (column) of x'; for example, this sum for column 9 equals $2(1)+1(0)=2$.
8. Column H is obtained by squaring the values in column G.
9. Column I is obtained by dividing the values in column H by the values in column F.

Eta-squared may be computed by using the sums of columns A, C, D, G, and I in the appropriate places in the formulas in Table 12.5.

In Table 12.5, eta$_{yx}$ is .47, which shows considerably more relationship between x and y than did Pearson's r, which was .11 for the grouped data in this example. Eta-squared can be interpreted in the same manner as the coefficient of determination, r^2.

As for r, there is a way of *testing the significance of eta*—the F test. Using the formula

$$F = \frac{\Sigma y_b^2/(c-1)}{\Sigma y_t - \Sigma y_b^2/(n-c)}$$

where Σy_b^2 is the numerator of eta,
Σy_t^2 is the denominator of eta,
c is the number of columns, and
n is the number of entries in the table

TABLE 12.5

x	y
11	14
24	46
31	35
42	39
81	46
74	41
66	37
98	09
50	51
25	32
08	04
51	61
86	15
90	14
92	25
38	34
61	55
28	27
15	04
50	44

joint frequencies

y range	y'	x range: 0–9	10–9	20–9	30–9	40–9	50–9	60–9	70–9	80–9	90–9	f_y
	x'	0	1	2	3	4	5	6	7	8	9	
60–69	6						1					1
50–59	5						1	1				2
40–49	4			1			1		1	1		4
30–39	3			1	2	1		1				5
20–29	2			1							1	2
10–19	1		1							1	1	3
0–9	0	1	1								1	3
f_x		1	2	3	2	1	3	2	1	2	3	
$\Sigma y'$		0	1	9	6	3	15	8	4	5	3	

Eta Computing Chart

A f_y	B y'	C $f_y(y')$	D $f_y(y')^2$
1	6	6	36
2	5	10	50
4	4	16	64
5	3	15	45
1	2	2	4
4	1	4	4
3	0	0	0
$n = 20$		$\Sigma f_y(y') = 53$	$\Sigma f_y(y')^2 = 203$

E x'	F f_x	G $\Sigma y'$	H $(\Sigma y')^2$	I $(\Sigma y')^2/f_x$
0	1	0	0	0
1	2	1	1	.5
2	3	9	81	27
3	2	6	36	18
4	1	3	9	9
5	3	15	225	75
6	2	8	64	36
7	1	4	16	16
8	2	5	25	12.5
9	3	2	4	1.3
	$n = 20$	$\Sigma(\Sigma y') = 53$		$\Sigma(\Sigma y')^2/f_x = 195.3$

$$\text{Eta}^2_{yx} = \frac{\text{sum of squares between groups,}}{\text{total sum of squares}}$$

$$\text{Eta}^2_{yx} \cong 44.8/200 = .224$$

$$\text{Eta}_{yx} \cong \sqrt{.224} = .47$$

where the sum of squares between groups

$$= \sum\left[\frac{(\Sigma y')^2}{f_x}\right] - \frac{[\Sigma(\Sigma y')]^2}{n}$$

$$= 195.3 - 53^2/20 \cong 44.8$$

total sum of squares

$$= \Sigma f_y(y')^2 - [\Sigma f_y(y')]^2/n$$

$$= 203 - 53^2/20 \cong 200$$

the F ratio is computed. The researcher uses a table of the distribution of F, seeing whether the computed value of F is as large as that in the table, for the level of significance he desires (usually .05 or .01) and for degrees of freedom equal to $c - 1$ *and* to $n - c$.[9] If the computed F value is as large as that in the table, eta is considered significant. In any perfect relationship, the denominator of the F ratio is 0 and therefore significance is indeterminate (not computable) as it is when $n \leq c$.

In concluding the discussion of eta, the user must be warned that this statistic is not sensitive to the order of the ranges in the *independent* variable. Therefore, a high eta would result from *both* relations shown in Figure 12.5. Eta$_{yx}$, however, would not be high for the diagram on the

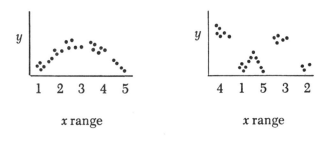

FIGURE 12.5

right. Eta is computed in the same manner as for eta$_{yx}$, with xs and ys interchanged in the computing chart.

Because of the interchangeability of ranges (columns) of the independent variable in computing eta, only the dependent variable must be interval or ratio in level of data. *The independent variable may be data of any level, even nominal.*

ORDINAL-LEVEL CORRELATION

Kendall's Rank Correlation, tau (τ)

Tau is a correlation measure used in association of two sets of rank-ordered data. For example, we might want to correlate students ordered by their class rank (x, the independent variable) with students ranked by their scores on an index of level of political information (y, the dependent variable).

---

[9]Recall that the F table requires use of two degrees-of-freedom measures.

First, the *x* scores, the ordinal data for the independent variable, are listed by their rank order from lowest to highest. Second, the *y* scores, the ordinal data for the dependent variable, are listed as pairs of the *x* scores. In Table

TABLE 12.6

x	1	2	3.5	3.5	5	6	7	8	9	10	11	12	
y	4	2	2	5	6	7.5	2	7.5	9	11.5	10	11.5	$n = 12$

12.6, the student with the highest class rank, 1, has a political information level that ranks 4th; that is this student had the fourth highest score—the score itself was not necessarily 4. The 2nd, 3.5th, and 7th students by class rank were in a three-way tie for first place by information level.

Third, *S*, a measure of the consistency of the *y* ranks with the *x* ranks, is computed. If when the data have been arranged as in steps 1 and 2 there is a perfect rank correlation, then all values in the *y* row to the right of any given *y* value will be as large or larger (smaller if correlation is negative) than that value. *S* is thus the sum of the number of higher minus lower *y* values to the right of each *y* value. For example, the first *y* value in Table 12.6 is 4, which has 8 higher and 3 lower values to the right. The next *y* value is 2, which has 8 higher and none lower, ignoring values equal to it. The third *y* value is also 2, which is paired with an *x* value (3.5) that is itself tied (equal to) with another *x* value. In the case of these *x* ties, the *y* values paired with each of the tied *x* values are ignored. Thus, ignoring the *y* value of 5, the third *y* value has 7 higher and zero lower *y* values to the right. *S* is the sum of all these differences:

$$S = (8 - 3) + (8 - 0) + (7 - 0) + (7 - 1) + (6 - 1) + (5 - 1)$$
$$+ (5 - 0) + (4 - 0) + (3 - 0) + (0 - 1) + (1 - 0)$$
$$= 47$$

$$\text{tau} = 2S/n(n - 1) = 2(47)/12(12 - 1) = 94/132$$
$$= .712$$

Although tau is not directly comparable to Pearson's *r* (.712 tau is *not* equivalent to .712 *r*), it does tend to be significant at the same level for the same data. For random sample data, the *significance* of tau may be tested through the normal (*z*) tables:

$$z_{tau} = \text{tau}/\sqrt{2(2n + 5)/9n(n - 1)}$$
$$= .712/\sqrt{2(24 + 5)/9(12)11} = .712/\sqrt{58/1188}$$
$$= 3.32.$$

This z value is applied in the customary way, resulting in this instance in a finding of very high significance (i.e., a very low significance value).[10]

In conclusion, we may note that the formula for tau is sometimes written

$$tau = S/.5n(n - 1)$$

In this version, it is easier to see that tau equals the actual score (S) as a percentage of the maximum possible score $[(.5\,n(n-1)]$ when there is perfect correlation by order. Thus, when correlation is perfect, S will equal

$$S = (n - 1) + (n - 2) + (n - 3) + \bullet\bullet\bullet + (n - n)$$

The student may check for him- or herself to see why this equals $[.5n(n-1)]$.

Spearman's rho (ρ)

Rho (ρ) is an older measure than tau, simple to compute—it is sometimes used as a quick but rough approximation of r and often used when data are rank-order in form but are assumed to be based on an underlying interval level of measurement. For example, states ranked 1 to 50 in terms of unemployment rates (x) might be correlated with states ranked 1 to 50 by number of riots experienced during the year.* Rho is sometimes called *rank difference correlation* and is a product-moment correlation coefficient for ranked data, interpreted like r:

1. The x and y data are arranged by rank orders as in steps 1 and 2 of the tau procedure, from lowest to highest unemployment rates, and the paired values for number of riots.
2. Each y value is subtracted from its corresponding x value.
3. This difference is squared.
4. The squared difference (D^2) is used in the *computational formula for rho*:

$$\rho = 1 - [6\,\Sigma\,D^2/n(n^2 - 1)]$$

---

[10]Kendall has developed a *partial rank correlation coefficient* control variables. See M. Kendall, *Rank Correlation Methods* (New York: Hafner, 1962), ch. 8; and S. Siegel, *Nonparametric Statistics* (New York: McGraw-Hill, 1956), pp. 223–229. Siegel also presents a table for the significance of tau when $n \leqslant 10$. Partial tau employs a formula equivalent to that for partial r, substituting taus for rs. For a discussion of partial tau and partial Somer's d, see also R. Hawkes, "The Multivariate Analysis of Ordinal Measures," *American Journal of Sociology* 76, no. 5 (March 1971): 908–926.

Note that tau may be thought of as the surplus of possible pairs in which higher y values could be paired with the given x value over pairs in which lower y values could be paired with the given x value, this quantity as a percentage of both types of pairs. More generally, tau is a measure of the extent properly ordered pairs are greater than improperly ordered pairs.

*Note: For rho, unlike tau, ranking must be in terms of the same universe (e.g., 50 states) for both variables.

TABLE 12.7

x	1	2	3.5	3.5	5	6	7	8	9	10	11	12
y	4	2	2	5	6	7.5	2	17.5	9	11.5	10	11.5
D	−3	0	1.5	−1.5	−1	−1.5	5	.5	0	−1.5	1	.5
D^2	9	0	2.25	2.25	1	2.25	25	.25	0	2.25	1	.25

$\Sigma D^2 = 45.5$ $n = 12$

$$\text{rho} = \rho = 1 - [6\,(45.5)/12\,(144-1)]$$
$$= 1 - (273/1716) = 1 - .159$$
$$= .841$$

The definitional formula for rho is the same as that for r; the derivation for the computational formula when x and y are ranks is given in Siegel, page 203 (see note 10).

The *significance of rho* is computed by the use of t tables when n is over 10. Using Table 12.7, t equals 4.93 and degrees of freedom equals 10. For

$$t = (\rho/\sqrt{1-\rho^2})\,(\sqrt{n-2})$$
$$= (.841/\sqrt{1-.841^2})\,(\sqrt{12-2})$$
$$= (.841/.540)\,(3.16) = 4.93$$
$$\text{d.f.} = n - 2 = 12 - 2 = 10$$

d.f. $= 10$ at the .01 level, the t table shows that the computed t value must be 3.17 or greater. Since the computed value (4.93) is greater, we may conclude that rho is significant at the .01 level. However, when n is 10 or less, the t test is not appropriate and a table of critical values of rho should be consulted. [11]

Rho is easier to compute than tau. Pearson's r is preferred when data are interval, but even then, if simplicity and/or time of computation is a factor and n is less than 30, rho may be used as an approximation to r. Rho and r are similar but not identical in magnitude for the same level of association when the number of ties is negligible. [12] Tau, which is not a product-moment

[11] Such a table is presented in Siegel, *Nonparametric Statistics*, p. 284.
[12] When more than five units are tied for the same rank value, corrected rank values are assigned to the tied values by the following formula:

$$\text{corrected rank} = \sqrt{A^2 + [(N^2 - 1)/12]}$$

where N is the number of scores tied for the given rank value, and A is the average of rank values that would have been assigned if no ties existed (in the case of five ties or fewer, A is the rank value assigned to ties).

correlation as are rho and r, is not comparable in magnitude to either for the same level of association. Except for extreme values (near 0 or 1.0), rho tends to be higher in magnitude than tau for the same association. Rho may also be thought of as the slope of the best-fitting straight line through the points on a scatter diagram relating two ordinal variables.[13]

DICHOTOMOUS CORRELATION

Dichotomous Correlation for Continuous Independent Variables

Pearson's r is addressed to the correlation of two interval-level variables that have the same (usually normally distributed) underlying distribution. Kendall's tau and Spearman's rho deal with the correlation of two ordinal variables, or the correlation of an interval with an ordinal variable. But what if the dependent variable is not continuous, but is instead a dichotomy [a variable which assumes two values, such as sex = male, female (a true dichotomy); or income = high, low (a forced dichotomy)]?

Point-biserial correlation is used for continuous variables when the other variable is a true dichotomy. Although the formula is different from that of r, it is derived from that of Pearson's r, and point-biserial correlation *is*, literally, Pearson's r when the dependent (y) variable assumes the values of 0 and 1 only, and it is interpreted in a similar manner. When x is the independent variable (e.g., political information level) and y is the dichotomous dependent variable (e.g., voting or not voting), r_{pb} equals the x mean for one dichotomous class, minus the x mean for the total, divided by the standard deviation of x, and multiplied by the root of the dividend of the proportions of cases in each class of the dichotomous y variable, as shown in Table 12.8

Point-biserial correlation is most often used in *item analysis*, testing to see if test or index items discriminate well between individuals who score high by some criterion and those who score low. For example, the criterion, the continuous x variable, might be scores on a standardized scale of authoritarianism, and the item, the dichotomous y variable, might be endorsing or not endorsing the statement "Communists should be allowed to teach at the

---

[13]For further discussion, see V. Senders, *Measurement and Statistics* (New York: Oxford, 1958), pp. 133–143. Note that rho[2] (or tau[2]) may *not* be interpreted as a coefficient of determination (i.e., may *not* be interpreted like Pearson's r^2). Tau is superior to rho in that it is generalizable to partial tau, one may test for significance for smaller sample size, and it may be computed even when the number of ties is large.

TABLE 12.8

Person	Information Level (x)	Vote (y)
1	84	1
2	73	1
3	69	0
4	65	1
5	60	0
6	51	1
7	42	1
8	38	0
9	33	0
10	20	0
	$\overline{535}$	$\overline{5}$

$$\bar{x} = 535/10 = 53.5$$
$$\bar{x}_y = (84+73+65+51+42)/5 = 63$$
$$s_x = \sqrt{\Sigma(x-\bar{x})^2/n}$$
or for a sample,
$$= \sqrt{\Sigma(x-\bar{x})^2/n-1}$$
$$= 19.1$$

$$r_{pb} = [(\bar{x}_y-\bar{x})/s_x](\sqrt{p/q}), \text{ where}$$

$\bar{x}$ is the mean of the continuous variable
$\bar{x}_y$ is the mean of the x values for the cases where the y value is 1
s_x the standard deviation of x; for samples, the sample standard deviation of x
p the proportion of cases in y having a value of 1
$q = 1-p$

$$r_{pb} = [(63-53.5)/19.1](\sqrt{\frac{1}{2}/\frac{1}{2}})$$
$$= .49$$
$$d.f. = n-2 = 8$$

state university." Items with a high point-biserial correlation with the authoritarianism scale discriminate well between persons with high and low measured authoritarianism, and would presumably be used in a survey or test on this subject.

In Table 12.8, point-biserial correlation is computed easily:

1. Units of data are listed in the first column (units may be persons, cities, years, etc.); the corresponding x score (information level in the example) listed in a

second column; and the y score (vote, in the example, where $1=$ voted and $0=$ didn't vote) in a third.

2. The mean of the x column and its standard deviation are computed, along with the x mean for those units whose y value was 1. Also computed are p and q, the proportions voting and not voting.

3. These values are placed in the formula for r_{pb}, generating a coefficient of .49.

Significance of r_{pb} is computed by use of a t table, as with rho, for degrees of freedom equal to $n - 2$:

$$t = r_{pb} \sqrt{n-2} / \sqrt{1 - r_{pb}^2}$$
$$= .49\sqrt{8} / \sqrt{1 - .49^2}$$
$$= 1.60$$

Note that point-biserial correlation may have a maximum *lower* than 1.0 because of marginal constraints (i.e., the proportion of units in the two categories of the dichotomy). While this is true of r as well, it is more likely to be a problem when the correlated variable is a dichotomy, as in r_{pb}. See the index for reference to corrected r^2 (a correction that applies to r_{pb} as well). Another problem of interpretation of r_{pb} arises when, as is possible, r_{pb} is computed to be *greater* than 1.0. This may occur when the continuous variable is platykurtic or bimodal in distribution.[14] Point-biserial correlation may be substituted for r in techniques based on correlation, such as multiple regression and factor analysis, to be discussed in later chapters.

Biserial correlation is used for continuous variables when the other variable is a forced dichotomy. The formula for biserial correlation, r_b,

$$r_b = ([\bar{x}_y - \bar{x}]/s_x)(p/y)$$

is identical to that for point-biserial correlation, except that p/y is substituted for $\sqrt{p/q}$. The term y represents the ordinate on a normal curve where the pth unit of x would fall. This ordinate is read from the normal tables. Suppose p equalled .30. Then by definition the proportion between this and the mean would be .20. Looking in the normal tables, we find that 20 percent of the area lies between $z = .524$ and the mean, and when this is so, the ordinate is .347 as illustrated in Figure 12.6. Otherwise, the computation is the same as for point-biserial correlation. Both are parametric statistics used in item analysis, and the *significance of biserial correlation* is also

[14]See McNemar, *Psychological Statistics*, p. 193. This may also occur when the dichotomized variable is not normally distributed. A platykurtic distribution is one with a flatter curve than the normal distribution. A bimodal distribution is one whose curve forms two peaks, in comparison with the one peak of a normal distribution (which is thus unimodal).

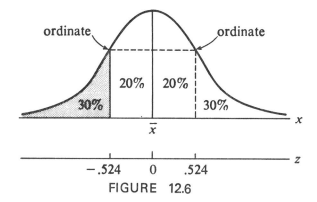

FIGURE 12.6

tested by the t table, where $t = r_b/(\sqrt{pq}/y\sqrt{n}\,)$, with notation as before. [15]

Biserial correlation assumes that the underlying distributions of both variables are normally distributed and linearly related. Like point-biserial correlation, it may be greater than 1.0 for certain nonnormal distributions, but (unlike point-biserial correlation) the dichotomy need not be split 50-50 for the coefficient to reach its maximum. In most cases, biserial correlation will be higher than point-biserial correlation for the same level of association. Unlike point-biserial correlation, biserial correlation is an approximation to, rather than a mathematical derivative of, Pearson's r; consequently it is not technically interchangeable with r in techniques employing r. The significance of high biserial coefficients cannot be adequately assessed because no transformation procedure exists equivalent to Fisher's z_r for high r coefficients.

Triserial correlation is a variant for the case when a continuous variable is correlated with a trichotomized variable. The trichotomy must be ordinal in level (e.g., low, medium, and high riot severity):

$$r_{\text{tri}} = \frac{y_h(\bar{x}_h) + (y_m - y_h)\bar{x}_m - y_m\bar{x}_l}{s_t[y_h^2/p_h + (y_m - y_h)^2/p_m + y_m^2/p_l]}$$

where y_h, y_m, y_l are normal curve ordinates, as in biserial correlation, related to

         p_h, p_m, p_l which are the proportions of observations in the three classes of the trichotomous variable.

[15]Note that if p were larger than .5, say .66, then the proportion between p and the mean would equal $p - .5$, or .16. One would then compute as indicated above, first finding the z value from Table III in the Appendix that corresponds to an area of .16, then using a table of ordinates of the normal curve (e.g., McNemar, *Psychological Statistics*, p. 424) to find the ordinate, y, that corresponds to that z value.

$\bar{x}_h, \bar{x}_m, \bar{x}_l$ are the x means (the means of the continuous variable) for those observations falling into the three classes of the trichotomous (y) variable, and

s_t is the standard deviation of all the x values combined.

Triserial correlation appears formidable, but it is in fact a logical extension of the biserial coefficient and is computed in a similar manner.

Dichotomous Correlation for True Dichotomous Independent Variables

The foregoing coefficients (point-biserial, biserial, triserial) were discussed with regard to a continuous independent variable. We should also discuss the case of a true dichotomous independent variable. In such a case, point-biserial correlation may be used if the dependent variable is continuous. When the dependent variable is also a true dichotomy, percent difference or phi are appropriate, as discussed in the previous chapter. When true dichotomies are to be correlated with forced dichotomies, Pearson's C is often used as an approximation to r.

Dichotomous Correlation for Forced Dichotomous Independent Variables

When a forced dichotomy is to be correlated with a continuous variable, biserial correlation may be used. If the correlation is to be with a true dichotomy, Pearson's C may be used. For the correlation of forced dichotomies with other forced dichotomies, tetrachoric correlation is appropriate.[16]

Tetrachoric correlation, r_t, is used when both variables are assumed to be forced dichotomies—continuous variables condensed into dichotomies—and when the marginals are 70:30, or less extremely split. The computation of r_t is extremely complicated and therefore, tables have been developed. Tetrachoric correlation is a function of the dividend of the marginal products in a 2-by-2 table, and is read from a table of estimates of r_t for values of ad/bc after the dividend has been computed. In Table 12.9 the

---

[16]Note that this discussion follows the conventional but arbitrary custom of discussing measures of "correlation" separately from measures of "association." As previously emphasized, both are measures of strength and in selecting a statistic to measure strength of relation, many of the measures discussed in the previous chapter are *also* appropriate for dichotomous data, under conditions outlined at the end of Chapter 11.

TABLE 12.9

	Class Rank (x)		
	Top Half	Bottom Half	r_i
Information Level (y) — High	140	10	150
Low	10	40	50
c_i	150	50	200

$r_t = f \ (ad/bc)$ if ad is larger (correlation is positive)
  or $f(bc/ad)$ if ad is less (correlation is negative)

$= f(56)$

dividend is 56; looking this up in a table of r , we find it corresponds to $r_t = .93.$[17]

Tetrachoric correlation can be understood as an approximation to Pearson's r. However, r_t, like gamma and Q, does *not* define strength of relationship in terms of monotonic correlation alone. Tetrachoric correlation will signify unity either when all entries are on the diagonal (monotonic correlation for symmetric statistical purposes) *or* when any cell is zero (weak monotonicity). Like biserial correlation, no equivalent to Fisher's z_r transformation for r exists that is adequate to assess the significance of high tetrachoric coefficients.

REVIEW: WHICH MEASURE OF CORRELATION?

Since correlation coefficients are measures of association, a summary of their characteristics is presented in Table 12.11, paralleling the one for measures of association in the previous chapter. For all coefficients below, a maximum value less than 1.0 may result from marginal constraints. The correction for Pearson's r has already been mentioned and the other coefficients may be corrected in a directly analogous manner. Note, however, that the researcher may *want* the coefficient to be less than 1.0 in such a situation. A corrected value is desirable if perfect association means the best matching of x and y values possible given the observed values which each actually assume. Table 12.10 is perfectly correlated in this sense, and a corrected correlation coefficient will be 1.0 for this joint distribution. If, however, the researcher assumes that, in Table 12.10, y *could* have increased to correspond to x values of 4 and 5, but didn't, then uncorrected coefficients are appropriate.

[17]A table of r_t is contained, for example, in A. Edwards, *Statistical Methods for the Behavioral Sciences* (New York: Rinehart, 1956), p. 510.

Table 12.10

x	1	2	3	4	5
y	1	2	3	3	3

TABLE 12.11   Which Measure of Correlation?

Consideration	r, $r_{ij.k}$, or $r_{i(j.k)}$ (p. 310)	eta (η) (p. 324)	tau (τ) (p. 326)	rho (ρ) (p. 330)
level of data	interval	interval dependent; any independent	ordinal	ordinal
appropriate distribution	same for x and y^* (usually normal)	same for x and y^* (usually normal)	any	any
data format	two lists of grouped or ungrouped data; three or more for partial and part r	two lists of grouped data	two rank lists	two rank lists
is the coefficient symmetric?	yes	no	yes	yes
meaning of "perfect" association	strict monotonic	curvilinear *or* strict monotonic	strict monotonic	strict monotonic
nearest intuitive meaning	r^2 is the percentage of the variance in one variable explained by its linear relation to another variable	eta^2 is same as r^2 except for linear *and* curvilinear relation of independent to dependent variable	surplus of properly- over improperly- ordered pairs as a percentage of both	ordinal equivalent of r when ties are few

Consideration	r_{pb} (p. 332)	r_b (p. 334)	r_{tri} (p. 335)	r_t (p. 336)
level of data	one interval, other a nominal-level dichotomy	one interval, other an ordinal- or interval-level dichotomy	one interval, other an ordinal- or interval-level trichotomy	dichotomized interval
appropriate distribution	same for x and y^* (usually normal)	normal	normal	normal
data format	r-by-2 or 2-by-c	r-by-2 or 2-by-c	r-by-3 or 3-by-c	2-by-2
is the coefficient symmetric?	yes	yes	yes	yes
meaning of "perfect" association	strict monotonic	strict monotonic	strict monotonic	weak monotonic
nearest intuitive meaning	a derivative of r, interpreted the same way	an approximation to r; similar to r_{pb} but higher in magnitude	an approximation to r	an approximation to r

EXERCISE

1.   Below are data on a measure of "authoritarianism" and on a measure of "conservatism" for a random sample of business leaders. Assume the data are interval in level. How related are these two variables? Is this relation significant?

Authoritarianism Score	Conservatism Score
82	76
73	83
95	89
66	76
84	79
89	73
51	62
82	89
75	77
90	85
60	48
81	69
34	51
49	25
87	74

*While only the same underlying distribution of x and y is necessary to compute the coefficient, some authors specify normal distribution since significance levels cannot be computed when the same distribution is not also normal.

2.   Assume that the variable "socioeconomic status" has been measured in the sample above, and its correlation with "authoritarianism" is found to be .84 and with "conservatism," .86. What is the correlation between "authoritarianism" and "conservatism" when "socioeconomic status" is used as a control variable? Compare this with the results of step 1. What is the unique contribution of "authoritarianism" to the total variance in "conservatism?" Compare this with the coefficients you have already computed.

3.   Convert the data in step 1 to ranks. Compute the appropriate coefficients of correlation for these rank values. Compare them with the coefficients computed already. How does rho compare to r? What meaning can be attached to tau?

4.   Dichotomize both variables in step 1 at their respective means. Compute phi and tetrachoric correlation, and compare each with r. Which seems better to use in the case of forced dichotomies?

three

Complex Analysis

<table>
<tr><td>**13**</td><td>## Introduction to Multivariate Analysis</td></tr>
</table>

The preceding sections of this book have dealt with general conceptual orientations to political analysis and with statistical or logical methods of assessing the significance, strength of association, and validity of relationships between political variables. With this chapter we begin the consideration of empirical analyses of relationships among a set of more than two variables. In other words, this chapter begins the discussion of multivariate techniques appropriate for use in connection with the sort of multivariable models discussed in Chapter 5.

We have already referred to the simplest of these techniques: the use of control variables to divide an "original" table into two or more subtables. Another alternative already mentioned is partial correlation. Both will be discussed further in this chapter, but first it is necessary to take a closer look at the relationship between two variables as presented in a simple r-by-c table.

GOODMAN'S METHOD OF ANALYZING INTERACTIONS WITHIN TABLES

When we have a 2-by-2 table, it is relatively easy to assess whether or not two variables are related in a way that is significant (Chapter 10) and strong (Chapters 11 and 12). While measures of significance or strength of association (correlation) may be computed for larger tables, it may well happen that the magnitude of the measure is caused more by one part of the table than another. For Example, in Table 13.1, most of the apparent relationship is due to a small part of the table in the upper-left corner. That is, the relation of certain ranges of x (e.g., $x = 1$, 2) to

TABLE 13.1

x

	1	2	3	4	5	6
1	82	2	1	2	0	3
2	4	69	1	0	1	3
3	2	40	4	2	0	1
4	0	5	0	1	3	2
5	3	2	2	0	1	0
6	1	1	0	1	3	1

(y labels the rows)

certain ranges of y (e.g., $y = 1, 2, 3$) is probably stronger and more significant than the relation of other ranges of x and y.

Leo Goodman has developed a systematic method for assessing the effect of such intratable differences, which are called *interaction effects*.[1] A simplified outline of this method is presented below.

First, Goodman presents some basic definitions for a 2-by-2 table.

TABLE 13.2

	x				x	
	1	2			1	2
1	f_{11}	f_{12}		1	6	2
2	f_{21}	f_{22}		2	1	10
	(a)				(b)	

(y labels the rows in both)

The *frequencies*, f_{ij}, are the cell entries, where i is the row and j is the column; thus f_{21} of Table 13.2(b) is 1. The *odds* of getting x_2 given y_1 equal

---

[1] Leo A. Goodman, "How to Ransack Social Mobility Tables and Other Kinds of Cross-Classification Tables," *American Journal of Sociology* 75, no. 1 (July 1969): 1–40.

f_{12}/f_{11}; for Table 13.2(b) the odds of getting x_2 given y_1 equal 2/6 or 1/3. Similarly, the odds of getting x_2 given y_2 equal f_{22}/f_{21}; for Table 13.2(b) these odds equal 10/1, or 10. The *odds ratio* is simply the ratio of these odds:

$$\text{odds ratio} = \frac{f_{22}/f_{21}}{f_{12}/f_{11}} = \frac{f_{11}f_{22}}{f_{21}f_{12}}$$

$$\text{odds ratio [Table 13.2(b)]} = \frac{10/1}{2/6} = \frac{6(10)}{1(2)} = 30$$

The *interaction* of a 2-by-2 table is the natural logarithm of the odds ratio, and is labelled "G":

$$G = \ln \log \left(\frac{f_{11}f_{22}}{f_{21}f_{12}}\right) = \ln \log f_{11} + \ln \log f_{22} - \ln \log f_{21} - \ln \log f_{12}$$

Thus, the odds ratio is a measure of the strength of the relationship in the table. When the distribution of x is the same for both categories of y, then the odds will be identical and the odds ratio will be 1. The odds ratio can also be thought of in terms used in Chapter 11 as equal to ad/bc, or as P/Q. That is, the odds ratio is the ratio of pairs on the main diagonal to pairs on the off diagonal in a 2-by-2 table. The interaction is simply a logarithmic function of this measure. The purpose of logarithmic functions, as discussed earlier (Chapter 7), is to take account of curvilinear relationships as well as linear ones. The interaction in Table 13.2(b) is computed as follows:

$$\begin{aligned}
\text{[Table 13.2(b)] } G &= \ln \log 6 + \ln \log 10 - \ln \log 1 - \ln \log 2 \\
&= 1.792 + 2.303 - 0.000 - 0.693 \\
&= 3.402
\end{aligned}$$

[Recall the discussion of logarithms in Chapter 7; note that $\ln \log (n) = 2.302585 \log_{10}(n)$, and $\log_{10}(n) = .434294 \ln \log (n)$; or natural log values may be read from a table of natural logarithms.] The *standard error* of the interaction, labelled S, equals:

$$S = \sqrt{1/f_{11} + 1/f_{12} + 1/f_{21} + 1/f_{22}}$$

$$\text{[Table 13.2(b)] } S = \sqrt{1/6 + 1/2 + 1/1 + 1/10}$$

$$= \sqrt{1.77} = 1.33$$

The *standardized value* of the interaction, labelled Z_G, equals:

$$Z_G = G/S$$

[Table 13.2(b)] $Z_G = 3.402/1.33 = 2.56$

This value may be interpreted by the usual z test, with values above 1.96 being interpreted as significant at the .05 level in two-tailed tests of the null hypothesis (that the observed interaction is not different from what would be expected by chance in a random sample).

Second, Goodman points out that larger, r-by-c tables (r rows, c columns) may be broken down into a number of 2-by-2 tables. Specifically, an r-by-c table contains $r(r-1)c(c-1)/4$ subtables. For example, a 3-by-3 table contains nine 2-by-2 subtables, as shown in Table 13.3. For each of the nine

TABLE 13.3

		Party (X)					Party (X)				
		1	2	3			X_1,X_2		X_1,X_3		X_2,X_3
	1	9	2	1		Y_1,Y_2	9	2	9	1	2	1
							1	9	1	3	9	3
Vote (Y)	2	1	9	3			9	2	9	1	2	1
	3	2	1	4	Vote (Y)	Y_1,Y_3	2	1	2	4	1	4
							1	9	1	3	9	3
						Y_2,Y_3	2	1	2	4	1	4

subtables, G and Z_G are computed in Table 13.4. The absolute and relative

TABLE 13.4   Absolute and Standardized Values of
Interaction Effects in Table 13.3

	G	Z_G
Parties 1 and 2 with votes 1 and 2	3.71	2.83
Parties 1 and 3 with votes 1 and 2	3.30	2.12
Parties 2 and 3 with votes 1 and 2	−0.41	−0.29
Parties 1 and 2 with votes 1 and 3	0.82	0.57
Parties 1 and 3 with votes 1 and 3	2.90	2.13
Parties 2 and 3 with votes 1 and 3	2.08	1.25
Parties 1 and 2 with votes 2 and 3	−2.89	−1.78
Parties 1 and 3 with votes 2 and 3	−0.40	−0.28
Parties 2 and 3 with votes 2 and 3	2.49	1.92

(standardized) levels of interaction indicated in Table 13.4 enable us to identify quickly which portions of a table contribute the most to its level of relationship, and which interactions are actually opposite to the general relationship (e.g., in Tables 13.3 and 13.4, the interaction of Parties 1 and 2 with Votes 1 and 2 contributes the most to the relationship, while the interaction of Parties 1 and 2 with Votes 2 and 3 is opposite to the general relationship).

The significance levels of the z values in larger tables depends upon the number of degrees of freedom in the table and the number of interactions we wish to test. (Note that Goodman discusses eleven other types of interaction in a 3-by-3 table; we present only the elements of his analysis here, centering on the 2-by-2 subtables of a larger table.) Goodman has presented a table of critical values of Z_G, reproduced in Table 13.5. If we specify the

TABLE 13.5 Critical Constants for Set of Multiple Tests at The 5% Level of Significance

Degrees of Freedom (a) or Number of Tests of Possible Interest (b)	Critical Constants (a)*	(b)†	Degrees of Freedom (a) or Number of Tests of Possible Interest (b)	Critical Constants (a)*	(b)†
1	1.960	1.960	19	5.490	3.008
2	2.448	2.241	20	5.605	3.023
3	2.795	2.394	21	5.716	3.038
4	3.080	2.498	22	5.824	3.052
5	3.327	2.576	23	5.931	3.065
6	3.548	2.638	24	6.034	3.078
7	3.751	2.690	25	6.136	3.091
8	3.938	2.734	26	6.236	3.102
9	4.113	2.773	27	6.334	3.113
10	4.279	2.807	28	6.429	3.124
11	4.436	2.838	29	6.523	3.134
12	4.585	2.865	30	6.616	3.144
13	4.729	2.891	31	6.707	3.154
14	4.867	2.914	32	6.797	3.163
15	5.000	2.935	33	6.885	3.172
16	5.128	2.955	34	6.972	3.180
17	5.252	2.974	35	7.057	3.189
18	5.373	2.991			

*Appropriate when an unlimited number of tests about interactions might be made in a cross-classification table having a specified number of degrees of freedom.
†Appropriate when the number of tests of possible interest is specified.

Source: Leo A. Goodman, "How to Ransack Social Mobility Tables and Other Kinds of Cross-Classification Tables," *American Journal of Sociology* 75, no. 1 (July 1969): 11, Table 3. Reprinted by permission.

number of tests of interest *in advance* of our investigation, we use column (b) of Table 13.5; if we do not (if, for example, we seek to test the significance of an interaction that, upon inspection of the table, appears to be significant in a contrary direction; that is, a subtable selected *after* looking at the data in Table 13.3), we use column (a). For the data in Table 13.4, assuming we specified nine tests of interest in advance, the critical value of

Z_C is 2.77. Except for the largest interaction, no interaction can be judged significant at the .05 level since all the Z_C values are below the critical value.

Note that Goodman's method may be used with data of any level, even nominal. We shall return to its application in the analysis of more than two variables shortly, but first it is necessary to recall the basic idea of multivariate analysis of tables.

Simple Controls in Multivariate Analysis of Tables

In analysis of tables, it often happens that the initial table conceals "hidden" relationships which become apparent when the table is broken down into subtables. In this breakdown procedure, an initial table (e.g., between education and party) is constructed for each value assumed by a control variable (e.g., class). In Table 13.6, for example, the control variable is "income" and it assumes two values: above the mean and equal to or below the mean. Therefore there are two subtables of the original relationship, in this case between education and political party.

In Table 13.6 we find a moderately strong relationship (48 percent difference) between going to private school and being Republican. But someone might challenge this by saying that it isn't *private school* that makes for Republicanism, but rather *higher income*, saying that the apparent (initial) result is *spurious* due to the presence of a *prior variable* (income) which causes both variables in the initial table. To check this we may divide the initial table, Table A, into two subtables: one for lower income, and another for higher income.

Tables B and C illustrate one possible outcome of the use of a control variable. In these two subtables, each representing 500 of the 1000 people in the initial table, we find that the relationship between education and party is identical: 48 percent difference. That is, regardless of whether one receives higher or lower income, there is the same level of relationship between going to private school and being Republican. This being so, it is unlikely that income is a prior variable, and we conclude that our relationship in Table A was *not* spurious. (A finer test might use more income levels than just two; moreover, additional control variables might also be tested.)

Tables D and E illustrate a quite different outcome. Here we find that the relationship between education and party disappears for *both* higher and lower-income groups. Percent difference drops to zero, because for each group there is the same ratio of Republicans to Democrats regardless of type of education (i.e., a ratio of 1:9 for lower income and 9:1 for higher income). This suggests that income *is* a prior causal variable and that education is only apparently (spuriously) related to political party. Therefore we note that the relationship in Table A is misleading because it fails to show the critical effect of income as a control variable.

Finally, Tables F and G illustrate a third sort of outcome. In Table F, for lower-income subjects, we find that the strength of the relationship between education and party *increases* to 100 percent difference. For Table G, however, we find that there is practically no relationship (4 percent difference) and even that is in the opposite direction (the off diagonal) from what Table A would lead us to expect. Since Table A is the sum of Tables F

TABLE 13.6

		Education		
		Private	Public	
Party	Rep.	370	130	%d = .48
	Dem.	130	370	

Table A (Initial)

	Education	
	Private	Public
Rep.	185	65
Dem.	65	185

% d = .48

Table B (Below Mean Income)

	Education	
	Private	Public
Rep.	185	65
Dem.	65	185

% d = .48

Table C (Above Mean Income)

	Education	
	Private	Public
Rep.	10	40
Dem.	90	360

% d = 0

Table D (Below Mean Income)

	Education	
	Private	Public
Rep.	360	90
Dem.	40	10

% d = 0

Table E (Above Mean Income)

	Education	
	Private	Public
Rep.	250	0
Dem.	0	250

% d = 1.00

Table F (Below Mean Income)

	Education	
	Private	Public
Rep.	120	130
Dem.	130	120

% d = .04 (-)

Table G (Above Mean Income)

and G, we see that it understates the relation in Table F and overstates the relation in Table G.

In general, we must realize that an initial table may be the sum of two or more subtables, each representing a subgroup of the population sampled. The relationship between two variables which we observe in the initial tables may be the same as in the subtables but it also may not. The relationship of the two variables in the subtables may be the same, more, or less, or even in the opposite direction! This is why *multivariate* analysis of tables is essential.

Goodman's Method Applied to Multivariate Analysis of Tables

The methods just described enable us to estimate the degree to which a control variable influences a relationship between two variables. This estimate, in turn, is based on some measure of association such as percent difference (%d) for the initial table compared to those for the control subtables. Goodman's method enables us to compare *association of each interaction* in the initial tables with those in the subtables. It allows us to make much finer distinctions about exactly how a control variable does or does not affect the relationship observed initially.

TABLE 13.7

		Party		
		1	2	3
Vote	1	90	20	10
	2	10	90	30
	3	20	10	40

Table A (Initial)

		Party		
		1	2	3
Vote	1	30	10	5
	2	5	10	10
	3	10	5	30

Table B (East Region)

		Party		
		1	2	3
Vote	1	60	10	5
	2	5	80	20
	3	10	5	10

Table C (West Region)

Table 13.7 contains a table similar to Table 13.3, but with cell frequencies ten times as large. For each table we may compute Goodman's measure of absolute interaction, G, and the measure of standardized interaction, Z_G. We may compare the subtables with each other by dividing the difference, D, between the absolute interactions, G, by the standard error of the difference:

$$I, J \quad = \text{ the sets of interactions in Tables I and J}$$

$$G_I, G_J \quad = \text{ the absolute level of interactions in set I and set } J, \text{ respectively}$$

$$Z_{G_I}, Z_{G_J} \quad = \text{ the standardized level of interactions in set } I \text{ and set } J, \text{ respectively}$$

$$D_{I-J} \quad = G_I - G_J \quad \text{(the difference between subtable interactions)}$$

$$S_{I-J} \quad = \sqrt{S_I^2 + S_J^2} \quad \text{(the standard error of difference)}$$

$$Z_{I-J} \quad = D_{I-J}/S_{I-J}$$

Table 13.8 gives the absolute and standardized interactions for Tables 13.7 A, 13.7 B, and 13.7 C, along with the absolute and standardized differences between comparable interactions in different tables.

First, note that the level of absolute interaction, G, is the same for Table 13.7 A as for Table 13.3, even though the cell frequencies are ten times as large in the former as in the latter. Thus, the same relationship will have the same size absolute interaction (G) even when the magnitude (sum of cell frequencies, n) differs. To compare interaction levels, we compare G values. But to test the significance of these G levels, we must take magnitude (size of cell frequencies) into account; this is done in the Z_G statistic, which is used in testing the significance of interactions when data are based on a random sample.

Second, following from the above assumption, in comparing interactions in any pair of tables, the corresponding G levels are used. (We do *not* use the corresponding Z_G levels. The standardized difference in Z_G levels is *not* the difference in Z_G levels; instead, the standardized difference is found by dividing by the term S_{I-J}.)

Note: When an initial table, such as Table A, is a marginal table obtained by summing subtables (such as Tables B and C), then that table is not sampled independently from the others. Consequently, it is not appropriate to test the significance of differences between it and the subtables. Only the difference of interactions between pairs of subtables is tested. If the control variable (the criterion for subtabling) explains the relationship between the independent and dependent variables, no difference of interaction between a pair of subtables (there is only one such pair in our example) should be significant. However, while we cannot test for significance of differences between an initial table and a subtable, we can still compare magnitudes (differences in G levels).

TABLE 13.8   Absolute and Standardized Interactions in and between Tables 13.7A, 13.7B, and 13.7C

Interaction	Table A		Table B		Table C		G Difference			Standardized Difference
	G	Z_G	G	Z_G	G	Z_G	D_{A-B}	D_{A-C}	D_{B-C}	Z_{B-C}
$P_1,P_2, + V_1,V_2$	3.70	8.92	1.79	2.72	4.56	7.95	1.91	-.86	-2.77	-3.17
$P_1,P_2, + V_1,V_3$	.81	1.76	.41	.62	1.10	1.70	.40	-.29	-.69	-.75
$P_1,P_2, + V_2,V_3$	-2.89	-5.66	-1.39	-1.79	-3.47	-4.85	-1.50	-6.36	2.08	1.97
$P_1,P_3, + V_1,V_2$	3.30	6.67	2.48	3.40	3.87	5.67	.82	-.57	-1.39	-1.39
$P_1,P_3, + V_1,V_3$	2.89	6.70	2.89	4.77	2.48	3.84	0	.41	.41	.46
$P_1,P_3, + V_2,V_3$	-.41	-.90	.41	.62	4.13	6.16	-.82	-4.54	-3.72	-3.96
$P_2,P_3, + V_1,V_2$	-.41	-.93	.69	.98	-.69	-1.15	-1.10	-1.10	1.38	1.49
$P_2,P_3, + V_1,V_3$	1.39	2.65	2.48	3.40	1.39	1.79	-1.09	0	1.09	1.02
$P_2,P_3, + V_2,V_3$	2.48	6.02	1.79	2.72	2.08	3.45	.69	.40	-.29	-.33
		d.f.=4		d.f.=4		d.f.=4				d.f.=4

Key: $P_{1,2,3}$ = Parties listed in Table 13.7; $V_{1,2,3}$ = Votes listed in Table 13.7. Table A is the initial table; Tables B and C are the "East and West" subtables respectively when the initial relationship is controlled for region. D stands for the difference in absolute interactions (Gs) between subtables.

Third, note that Table 13.8 contains nine tests of difference of inter-actions. If our data are based on a random sample, we may wish to test the differences for significance. If we specified these nine tests as being the ones of interest to us in advance of computing the values in Table 13.8, then we now use row 9, column (*b*) of Table 13.5 to find a critical Z_G level of 2.77. [If we did not specify the number of tests of interest, then we use degrees of freedom and column (*a*) of Table 13.5. In comparing differences among a set of *k* *r*-by-*c* tables, the number of degrees of freedom equals $\overline{(r-1)}$ times $(c-1)$ times $(k-1)$. For our example, this equals $(3-1)(3-1)(2-1)$, or 4, which corresponds to a critical value of 3.08].[2]

Assuming we had specified nine tests of difference as the ones of interest, only two interactions are significant at the .05 level. These are (1) the inter-action for Parties 1 and 2 with Votes 1 and 2, and (2) the interaction for Parties 1 and 3 with Votes 2 and 3, for the difference between East and West Regions. No other difference is significant. (As mentioned, the significance of the differences between the initial table and a subtable cannot be tested, as the samples are not independent.) Thus Goodman's method helps to pinpoint the effect of a control variable (region in this case) on each possible interaction. Moreover, we may compare absolute levels of interaction (*G*) or absolute differences of corresponding interactions between pairs of tables $(D_{1 \ j})$ to understand which interactions contribute the most, the least, or in a negative way to the overall relationship or the overall difference.

STRUCTURAL, CONTEXTUAL, AND COMPOSITIONAL FORMS OF MULTIVARIATE ANALYSIS

Up to this point we have been discussing *structural analysis*.[3] By structural analysis we mean analysis of how an initially observed relationship (e.g., Table 13.7 A) changes or does not change when it is structured (grouped) according to some control variable. *Contextual analysis* involves analysis of how an initially observed relationship changes or does not change when it is grouped according to degrees of the independent variable. *Compositional analysis* is the simultaneous use of both structural and contextual analysis.

Table 13.9 illustrates these types of analyses. In this table, the right-hand column ("All Contexts") corresponds to structural analysis, in which the

---

[2]For critical values in the (*a*) column of Table 13.5 corresponding to degrees of freedom larger than 35, take the square root of the .05 level chi-square value corresponding to that number of degrees of freedom. For critical values in the (*b*) column of Table 13.5 correspond-ing to tests of interest larger than 35, take the *z* value in a table of normal distribution that corresponds to a percent of the area under a normal curve equal to .025 divided by the number of tests of interest.

[3]Not to be confused with structural-functional analysis, discussed in Chapter 3.

TABLE 13.9 Compositional Effects of Party on Vote by Region

	Context by party			
Structured by Region	Individuals in predominantly Republican municipalities	Individuals in mixed municipalities	Individuals in predominantly Democratic municipalities	All Contexts
South Region	Party R / D V_1: 50 / 0 V_2: 5 / 73 %d = .91	Party R / D V_1: 60 / 18 V_2: 16 / 40 %d = .48	Party R / D V_1: 20 / 30 V_2: 20 / 20 %d = .10(−)	Party R / D V_1: 130 / 48 V_2: 41 / 133 %d = .45
West Region	Party R / D V_1: 50 / 10 V_2: 10 / 2 %d = 0	Party R / D V_1: 60 / 16 V_2: 17 / 40 %d = .49	Party R / D V_1: 20 / 40 V_2: 20 / 30 %d = .07(−)	Party R / D V_1: 130 / 66 V_2: 47 / 72 %d = .26
East Region	Party R / D V_1: 100 / 15 V_2: 10 / 75 %d = .75	Party R / D V_1: 60 / 16 V_2: 17 / 40 %d = .49	Party R / D V_1: 35 / 80 V_2: 50 / 35 %d = .26(−)	Party R / D V_1: 195 / 111 V_2: 77 / 150 %d = .29

TABLE 13.9 (cont.)

	Party			Party			Party			Party	
	R	D		R	D		R	D		R	D
V_1	200	25	V_1	180	50	V_1	75	150	V_1	455	225
V_2	25	150	V_2	50	120	V_2	90	85	V_2	165	355

All Regions

$\%d = .75$ $\%d = .49$ $\%d = .18(-)$ $\%\dot{d} = .35$

(V_1 and V_2 refer to vote choices 1 and 2, as between candidates)

bottom table is the "initial" table and the three upper tables are the subtables for the control variable "region." The bottom row ("All Regions") corresponds to contextual analysis, in which the right-most table is the "initial" table and the three tables to the left are the subtables for the contextual variable, "predominant party of municipality." The entire Table 13.9, combining both structural and contextual dimensions, constitutes a compositional analysis of the effect of party on vote by region.

Contextual analysis may be thought of as a special type of structural analysis—one in which the control variable is the independent variable measured at the group level. (Recall the discussion of aggregate versus individual data at the beginning of Chapter 11.) Structural analysis focuses on the effect of control variables. Contextual analysis focuses on the effect of measurement of the independent variable at the group level as compared to the individual level (i.e., with the relationship "between groups" and "within groups"). Compositional analysis is simply the analysis of the joint effect of a control variable and measurement level on an initially observed relationship.

Regardless of the approach employed, multivariate analysis of tables frequently shows that what initially appear to be general or universal relationships (e.g., between party and vote) are in fact *conditional relationships*. That is, multivariate analysis often demonstrates that the strength and even direction of the given relationship differs according to the condition (e.g., different control variable subgroups, different contexts of the independent variable). More generally, multivariate analysis reveals that, under different conditions, different independent (predictor) variables must be used to explain the dependent (criterion) variable—different explanatory models (recall Chapter 5) may be necessary for different conditions (e.g., different models may be necessary to explain voting patterns in different regions).

Morris Rosenberg has pointed out that many social scientists are uneasy about conditional relationships.[4] To some, a conditional relationship may seem analogous to the idea of a physicist finding that gravity works differently in Kansas than in Missouri. Rosenberg emphasizes, however, that conditional relationships play an important role in the development of political theory. First, they call attention to the oversimplified nature of initial generalizations (e.g., the generalization that party always determines vote). Second, the variable used to create structural or contextual subgroups of the initial population provides clues about the nature of other variables that must be included in the generalization (e.g., the generalization that the individual's party influences the vote, but does so more strongly as that party is also the municipal party for Republicans, and more weakly as that

[4]Morris Rosenberg, "Conditional Relationships," in P. Lazarsfeld, A. Pasanella, and M. Rosenberg, eds., *Continuities in the Language of Social Research* (New York: Free Press, 1972), pp. 133–146.

party is also the municipal party for Democrats). That is, conditional relationships pinpoint ways in which simple bivariate generalizations must be transformed into more complex, multivariate generalizations.

PARTIAL CORRELATION AND PARTIAL ASSOCIATION IN MULTIVARIATE ANALYSIS

Multivariate analysis of tables has one central defect: because it involves decomposing an original table into subtables, the number of cases in the original table must be quite large to assure that the number of cases in the subtables will be statistically interesting. Moreover, the very fact that it employs tables means that the data must be grouped into a relatively small number of ranges; but when a continuous variable (e.g., income) is grouped into ranges (e.g., high, middle, low), information is lost. When the number of cases is not large or when variables are continuous, an alternative method of multivariate analysis is preferable. This alternative involves the use of partial correlation and partial association. This alternative may only be used if the data are interval (partial correlation) or ordinal (partial association) in level, except for the case of nominal-level dichotomies.

Causal Inference in Multivariate Analysis by Partial Correlation

Suppose we have a correlation coefficient between i and j, and we seek to determine the effect of a control variable, k. When we compare r_{ij} with $r_{ij.k}$, there are three possible results: (1) the partial correlation will be the same as the zero-order (initial, r_{ij}) correlation; (2) the partial correlation will be lower; or (3) the partial will be higher. If the partial correlation is the same, we say the control variable has *no effect*. If the partial correlation is lower, we say the control variable *explains* the relationship between i and j (that is, we regard the zero-order correlation, r_{ij}, as *spurious*). If the partial correlation is higher, we say the control variable *suppresses* the relationship between i and j. Before passing to the fuller discussion that follows, the reader is encouraged to stop and think why these three inferences are so.

No Effect   A finding of no effect occurs for the model in Figure 13.1.

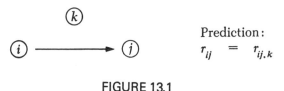

FIGURE 13.1

This model is so simple as to be trivial. If k is not causally connected to i and j, then its use as a control variable in partial correlation will have no effect on the zero-order correlation. For example, let i be income, j be party, and k be class. If we find a correlation $(r_{ij} = .7)$ between income and party, we might test to see whether class (defined on some basis other than income) was a cause of both, or was an intervening variable. If our model in Figure 13.1 is correct, then the partial correlation will be the same $(r_{ij.k} = .7)$.

Explanation   When a significant zero-order correlation is reduced to a nonsignificant (e.g., zero) partial correlation, one of the models in Figure 13.2 holds. For the model in which the control variable, k, is a prior

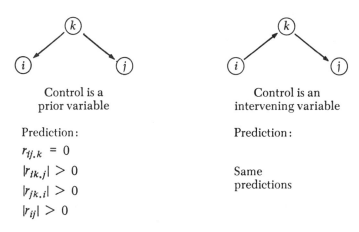

Control is a
prior variable

Prediction:

$r_{ij.k} = 0$

$|r_{ik.j}| > 0$

$|r_{jk.i}| > 0$

$|r_{ij}| > 0$

Control is an
intervening variable

Prediction:

Same
predictions

FIGURE 13.2

variable, i and j *seem* correlated, but this correlation is not due to any causal relation between i and j; rather, the correlation is a consequence of both i and j being caused by the same variable, k. For the model in which the control variable is an intervening variable, the apparent correlation between i and j must operate through k; therefore, when k is held constant (controlled), the zero-order correlation (r_{ij}) will disappear $(r_{ij.k} = 0)$.

Partial Explanation   When a significant zero-order correlation is lowered to a lesser but still significant partial correlation, one of the models in Figure 13.3 may hold. That is, the magnitude (disregarding the sign) of the partial will be lower than the magnitude of the original correlation. Note that other models are possible for the same predictions (e.g., the minus signs on the second and fourth models might be changed in position, though there must be two). In these models, there is a direct relationship between i and j.

Prediction:

$$|r_{ij}| > |r_{ij.k}| > 0$$
$$|r_{ij}|, |r_{ik}|, \text{ and } |r_{jk}| > 0$$
$$|r_{ik.j}|, |r_{jk.i}| > 0$$

Prediction:

Same predictions

FIGURE 13.3

When we control for the relationship of i and j, we control only the indirect relationship (i.e., that due to k). Hence the partial correlation does not disappear—because there *is* some direct causal relationship between i and j—though it will drop in magnitude.

Unfortunately, however, such a partial drop in magnitude may have other interpretations as well: (1) k *is* a control but so is a fourth variable, m; since m is not also controlled in the partial correlation $r_{ij.k}$, that partial does not drop all the way to zero; (2) k *is* a control and the only control, but because of measurement error in k, the partial does not drop all the way to zero; or (3) k is an antecedent variable for i but not j (i.e., the model: $K \to I \to J$).

Spurious Suppression   In the case of a model in which the control variable is a consequent variable, partial correlations will be spurious. In Figure 13.4, k is a consequence of i and j. Assuming, as the model does, that

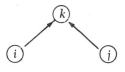

Prediction:

$$r_{ij} = 0$$
$$|r_{ik}|, |r_{jk}| > 0$$

FIGURE 13.4

i and j are not related by some fourth variable, r_{ij} should be not significantly different from zero. When this is so, however, the partial correlation will be larger in magnitude (positive in sign when r_{ik} and r_{jk} have different signs; negative in sign when they have the same signs, whether both positive or both negative). Although the partial will be greater in magnitude than the zero-order correlation, we cannot treat this as a case where the control variable suppresses (lowers) the initial correlation. That is, the partial correlation, $r_{ij.k}$, is spurious, reflecting not a causal relation (k tends to cause i and j) but rather a consequential relation (k tends to have been caused by i and j). Since we are interested in causal inference and not consequential inference, we regard $r_{ij.k}$ as spurious (for consequential analysis, of course, the finding is "real" rather than spurious).

Suppression   Nonspurious suppression occurs when, in the models in Figure 13.5, *below*, partial correlation is greater than the zero-order correlation. That is, the magnitude (disregarding the sign) of the partial will

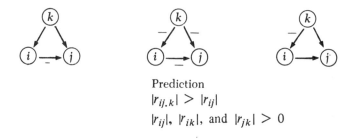

Prediction

$|r_{ij.k}| > |r_{ij}|$

$|r_{ij}|,\ |r_{ik}|,\ \text{and}\ |r_{jk}| > 0$

FIGURE 13.5

be higher than the magnitude of the original correlation. Note that other models are available for the same predictions (e.g., a minus sign on any one and only one of the causal arrows). In these models, the control variable operates on the dependent variable (j) directly in a manner opposite to the way it works on the dependent variable indirectly [through the independent variable (i)]. The effect is to suppress the zero-order correlation, r_{ij}. That is, r_{ij} *understates* the actual degree of correlation of i and j. (Just as, correspondingly, r_{ij} *overstates* the actual degree of correlation of i and j in Figures 13.2 and 13.3).

Analysis of 4-variable and larger models follows the same principles of inference. Often, larger models are decomposed into 3-variable submodels for purposes of analysis. Alternatively, second-order partial correlation may be used. That is, when there are two control variables, as in Figure 13.6, the second-order partial ($r_{ij.kl}$) is used in a manner analogous to what has already been discussed with regard to (first-order) partial correlations. Causal inference in larger models is discussed further in Chapter 18.

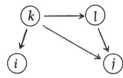

Prediction:
$$r_{ij \cdot kl} = 0$$

Four-Variable Model: Controls
are prior variables

$$\left| \begin{array}{l} \text{all zero-order} \\ \text{correlations} \end{array} \right| > 0$$

$$r_{il \cdot k} = 0$$

$$\eta_{ij \cdot l} > 0$$

FIGURE 13.6

Causal Inference in Multivariate Analysis by Partial Association

In the foregoing section we discussed a method of multivariate analysis using Pearson's partial correlation coefficient. This coefficient, among other things, assumes that data are interval or ratio in level. What if we have a small sample, inappropriate for multivariate table analysis, with data that are not interval or ratio? If the data are nominal in level and not dichotomized, partial association will not help us. For other situations, partial association may be appropriate.

Dichotomies, Nominal or Higher   James Davis has detailed how partial Q, noted earlier, may be constructed. Since causal inference is the same for partial measures of association as for partial correlation, we shall confine our attention to how partial Q is computed. The process of computing partial Q is directly analogous to the method for computing most partial measures of association.[5]

Recall that for any 2-by-2 table, such as the upper half of Table 13.10, Q equals $(ad-bc)/(ad + bc)$. Partial Q is simply Q for those pairs of i and j

[5]See James Davis, *Elementary Survey Analysis* (Englewood Cliffs, N. J.: Prentice-Hall, 1971). Davis bases his method on G. Yule and M. Kendall, *An Introduction to the Theory of Statistics* (New York: Hafner, 1950).

For a discussion of partial Somer's d and partial tau, see R. Hawkes, "The Multivariate Analysis of Ordinal Measures," *American Journal of Sociology* 76, no. 5 (March 1971): 908–926.

TABLE 13.10

| | | Variable j | |
		0	1
$k=0$	$i=0$	a	b
	$i=1$	c	d
$k=1$	$i=0$	a'	b'
	$i=1$	c'	d'

that are tied (have the same value) on the control variable, k. The formula for partial Q is directly analogous to that for Q:

$$Q_{ij.k} = \frac{(ad - bc) + (a'd' - b'c')}{(ad + bc) + (a'd' + b'c')}$$

When Q has the same strength in the upper half of Table 13.10 as in the lower half [i.e., when $(ad-bc) = (a'd-b'c')$ and when $(ad + bc) = (a'd' + b'c')$], then Q_{ij} will equal $Q_{ij.k}$. Second-order partial Q's (e.g., $Q_{ij.kl}$) are constructed according to a directly analogous procedure and formula.

For second-order partial Q, a table corresponding to Table 13.10 would have four 2-by-2 tables stacked atop one another, two corresponding to the second control, 1, equal to 0; two corresponding to 1 equal to 1. Frequencies in the first two subtables would be a, a', etc., as in Table 13.10; frequencies in the bottom two subtables would be a'', a''', etc.). Thus the formula would be:

$$Q_{ij.kl} = \frac{(ad - bc) + (a'd' - b'c') + (a''d'' - b''c'') + (a'''d''' - b'''c''')}{(ad + bc) + (a'd' + b'c') + (a''d'' + b''c'') + (a'''d''' + b'''c''')}$$

Davis also makes the following useful observation about causal inference, whether by partial correlation or by partial association. In the previous section we treated the situation in which the researcher wishes to test whether the predictions implied in a given model correspond to the data. Davis notes we may be in the opposite situation: we have no model, but want to select a control variable that either explains or suppresses a given relationship. How do we know a likely control variable when we see one? Davis gives the following suggestions:

1. Obtain a matrix of r or Q coefficients for each variable with every other.
2. If $|r_{ik}|$ (or a corresponding coefficient) and $|r_{jk}|$ are both greater than the given relationship, $|r_{ij}|$, and if r_{ik} and r_{jk} have the same sign as each other, then $r_{ij.k}$ will be less positive or more negative than r_{ij}.
   a. if r_{ij} is positive, k is an explanatory (control) variable
   b. if r_{ij} is negative, k is a suppressor variable
3. If $|r_{ij}|$ and $|r_{jk}|$ are both greater than r_{ij}, but r_{ik} and r_{jk} have different signs from each other, then $r_{ij.k}$ will be more positive or less negative than r_{ij}
   a. if r_{ij} is positive, k is a suppressor variable
   b. if r_{ij} is negative, k is an explanatory (control) variable

The only great difference of interpretation with partial r as compared to partial Q arises in the case of partial explanation (see Figure 13.3). In partial explanation, we recall, the partial coefficient drops toward zero but does not reach it; it does not reach zero because for these models, there is some direct relationship of i and j. In interpreting partial Q we may observe the same drop for the same reason *or* for another reason. Partial Q may drop toward zero but not become zero because the dichotomous categories of the control variable, k, are too gross to adequately control the relationship. We may need finer categories of k (e.g., five categories rather than two, as in Q). That is, if we need finer categories of the control variable, k, the full explanation models (Figure 13.2) will generate partials that spuriously appear to support partial explanation models (Figure 13.3).

Ordinal Data   When data are ordinal, Kendall's tau and partial tau may be used in the same manner as for r and partial r, (substituting tau for r).[6] There is no test of significance yet devised for partial tau. When an asymmetric statistic is desired, partial Somers' d is another alternative.[7]

SUMMARY

Multivariate causal inference is based on a comparison of the empirical effect of various control variables on an initially observed relationship, and, in particular, on whether each effect is what would be predicted by the researcher's explanatory model. Sometimes multivariate techniques are used to "work backwards": to search for a set of controls that explain, partially explain, or suppress a given relationship, using these qualifiers of the original relationship as guides to constructing an explanatory model. No empirical analysis in political science can be considered even minimally complete until such an analysis of the effect of control variables is undertaken.

[6]M. G. Kendall, *Rank Correlation Methods* (New York: Hafner, 1962), p. 121. Note that there is no partial rho for ordinal data.
[7]See R. Smith, "Neighborhood Context and College Plans: An Ordinal Path Analysis," in *Social Forces* 51, no. 2 (December 1972): 202– 203. See Chap. 18, however.

Multivariate causal inference is essential because zero-order (initial) correlations are often misleading. The correlation between two variables may remain the same, increase, drop to zero, or even change sign when the effect of a control variable is taken into account. At the same time, however, we must call attention to an important warning. Partial correlation and partial association can also be misleading under certain circumstances.

Partial correlation or partial association is best used when the control variable is conceptually distinct from the initial variables. This does *not* mean that the control variable should not be correlated with the independent and dependent variables—it frequently will be. By "conceptually distinct" we mean that the control variable should not overlap the initial variables. For example, when we control the correlation of party and vote for region, the definition of "region" does not enter into the definitions of "party" and "vote." A famous example of variables that are *not* conceptually distinct arises in education research. If we control the correlation of reading and arithmetic scores for IQ, we *will* find IQ explains the initial relationship (i.e., $r_{ij\cdot}$ will be much lower than r_{ij}, where i = reading, j = arithmetic, and k = IQ). *But* since reading and arithmetic conceptually overlap IQ (i.e., since reading and arithmetic enter into the definition of IQ as it is operationalized in IQ tests), this drop in the partial correlation coefficient is difficult to interpret. The idea of "controlling" reading and arithmetic scores for a variable that is not conceptually distinct from them may lead us into the error of concluding that IQ explains the correlation of reading and arithmetic scores. Similarly, in political science, the methods discussed in this chapter might lead us into fallacies if we attempted to control the correlation of "alienation" and "vote" for "distrust of leaders," because "alienation" and "distrust of leaders" would conceptually overlap in most definitions of these terms.

EXERCISE

Table 13.11 provides data on U.S. Senators for 1973. COPE is the senator's rating by the AFL-CIO's Committee on Political Education, with 100 being the most favorable to the labor position. UNION is the percent of non-agricultural employees unionized in the senator's state. PARTY is the senator's party affiliation—R for Republican and D for Democrat.

As a first step, trichotomize the COPE and UNION data: (1) let $0-18$ = Low, $18.01-27.99$ = Medium, and 28.0 or more = High for UNION; (2) let $0-38$ = Low, $39-81$ = Medium, and $82-100$ = High for COPE.

Second, construct a table to investigate the hypothesis that the percent of unionized nonagricultural workers in the constituency of the senator determines his or her labor-related voting record, as measured by the COPE

TABLE 13.11   U.S. Senators, 1973

		Cope	Union	Party
Alabama	Allen	36	20.3	D
	Sparkman	70	20.3	D
Alaska	Gravel	86	27.1	D
	Stevens	60	27.1	R
Arizona	Fannin	20	17.6	R
	Goldwater	29	17.6	R
Arkansas	Fulbright	67	17.9	D
	McClellan	27	17.9	D
California	Cranston	90	30.5	D
	Tunney	82	30.5	D
Colorado	Haskell	90	20.5	D
	Dominick	9	20.5	R
Connecticut	Ribicoff	91	24.2	D
	Weicker	50	24.2	R
Delaware	Biden	80	22.6	D
	Roth	9	22.6	R
Florida	Chiles	73	13.9	D
	Gurney	30	13.9	R
Georgia	Nunn	40	16.2	D
	Talmadge	45	16.2	D
Hawaii	Inouye	91	28.1	D
	Fong	36	28.1	R
Idaho	Church	78	19.2	D
	McClure	20	19.2	R
Illinois	Stevenson	82	35.7	D
	Percy	75	35.7	R
Indiana	Bayh	91	35.6	D
	Hartke	91	35.6	D
Iowa	Clark	82	21.1	D
	Hughes	75	21.1	D
Kansas	Dole	27	16.6	R
	Pearson	67	16.6	R
Kentucky	Huddleston	82	27.3	D
	Cook	55	27.3	R
Louisiana	Johnston	50	18.4	D
	Long	82	18.4	D
Maine	Hathaway	73	18.4	D
	Muskie	82	18.4	D
Maryland	Beall	45	23.3	R
	Mathias	60	23.3	R
Massachusetts	Kennedy	91	25.6	D
	Brooke	89	25.6	R
Michigan	Hart	89	40.2	D
	Griffin	18	40.2	R

TABLE 13.11 (cont.)

Minnesota	Humphrey	90	28.9	D
	Mondale	90	28.9	D
Mississippi	Eastland	38	13.2	D
	Stennis	25	13.2	D
Missouri	Eagleton	80	35.9	D
	Symington	67	35.9	D
Montana	Mansfield	80	29.9	D
	Metcalf	82	29.9	D
Nebraska	Curtis	10	17.9	R
	Hruska	18	17.9	R
Nevada	Bible	82	32.8	D
	Cannon	82	32.8	D
New Hampshire	McIntyre	91	17.3	D
	Cotton	13	17.3	R
New Jersey	Williams	91	29.5	D
	Case	82	29.5	R
New Mexico	Montoya	91	14.8	D
	Domenici	18	14.8	R
New York	Buckley	11	35.6	R
	Javits	78	35.6	R
North Carolina	Ervin	27	7.8	D
	Helms	18	7.8	R
North Dakota	Burdick	82	17.2	D
	Young	45	17.2	R
Ohio	Saxbe	25	36.3	R
	Taft	38	36.3	R
Oklahoma	Bartlett	9	16.1	R
	Bellmon	27	16.1	R
Oregon	Hatfield	33	30.7	R
	Packwood	20	30.7	R
Pennsylvania	Schweicker	100	37.2	R
	Scott	55	37.2	R
Rhode Island	Pastore	100	26.1	D
	Pell	100	26.1	D
South Carolina	Hollings	60	9.6	D
	Thurmond	18	9.6	R
South Dakota	Abourezk	89	11.9	D
	McGovern	80	11.9	D
Tennessee	Baker	22	20.6	R
	Brock	30	20.6	R
Texas	Bentsen	64	14.4	D
	Tower	18	14.4	R
Utah	Moss	91	20.9	D
	Bennett	22	20.9	R

TABLE 13.11 (cont.)

Vermont	Aiken	73	16.2	R
	Stafford	73	16.2	R
Virginia	Byrd, Jr.	0	16.7	D
	Scott	22	16.7	R
Washington	Jackson	100	40.0	D
	Magnuson	100	40.0	D
West Virginia	Byrd	91	43.0	D
	Randolph	90	43.0	D
Wisconsin	Nelson	82	31.4	D
	Proxmire	82	31.4	D
Wyoming	McGee	89	17.7	D
	Hansen	18	17.7	R

ratings. Compute a measure of association (e.g., lambda) for this table. (Why shouldn't we compute a measure of significance?)

Third, construct subtables to test for the alternative hypothesis that party is an intervening variable between percent unionized and COPE votes. Compute measures of association for these subtables. What inferences do you make?

Fourth, use Goodman's method to analyze interactions among the three tables you have constructed. Which sets of interactions in the subtables contribute most to an explanation of the relationship in the original table? Which, if any, contribute to suppression of the relationship? (Why should we not compute Z_G?)

Fifth, assume that the COPE ratings are interval data. Test the same alternative hypothesis by partial correlation. Substitute r_{pb} for r in the formula for partial correlation, for the correlations of PARTY with COPE, and PARTY with UNION. Do you make the same inferences? What are the relative advantages and disadvantages of the two techniques?

14	Analysis of Variance and Covariance

Analysis of variance (ANOVA) is a common and powerful technique traditionally used in connection with experimental research designs, where errors can be randomized through the assignment of units to experimental groups on a random basis. In political science, most groups in which we may be interested (e.g., legislatures, communities) cannot be constructed at random from among individuals assigned by the researcher for this purpose. Nonetheless, because experimental research on small groups is done in political science, because political scientists must be able to understand psychological and sociological literature using ANOVA techniques, and because ANOVA is finding other, increasingly diverse applications in political science, it merits a chapter in this volume.

ONE-WAY ANALYSIS OF VARIANCE
(ONE INDEPENDENT VARIABLE)

Before we can consider the use of ANOVA in multivariate analysis, it is first necessary to understand simple analysis of variance, involving the use of just one independent and one dependent variable.

Simple analysis of variance is used for three main purposes:

1. To test whether an independent variable has any effect on a dependent variable. Specifically, ANOVA tests the null hypothesis that independent, random samples of n units each, from k classes of an independent variable, are drawn from the same population. For example, we may sample ten districts ($n=10$) in four regions of the country (independent variable = region; $k=4=$ East, South, Midwest, West) gathering data on the percentage of their vote for Nixon in 1972 (dependent variable = percentage of vote for Nixon in 1972). If, by ANOVA, we

reject the idea (null hypothesis) that the four samples came from the same underlying population, by the same token we reject the idea that the four regions are basically the same with regard to their vote for Nixon.

2. ANOVA is also a test of the difference of more than two sample means. Thus, it may be used when a z test among each of all possible pairs of sample means would be tedious (k samples involve $k(k-1)/2$ possible pairs).

3. ANOVA can be adapted to function as a measure of strength of association even when the dependent variable is only nominal in level. (This data-level advantage applies to the previous two purposes as well).

Rationale

If the variance of the dependent variable is the same *between* classes of the independent variable as it is *within* each class of the independent variable, then we have no reason not to think that the samples (each class is a sample) come from the same underlying population.

Statistic

The test statistic used in relation to ANOVA is the *F-ratio*:

$$F_0 = \frac{\text{between-groups variance estimate}}{\text{within-groups variance estimate}}$$

The observed *F*-ratio (F_0) must be as large or larger than the required *F*-ratio (F_r) found in Table VI in the Appendix, if we are to reject the null hypothesis that the samples do not come from different populations.

To read F_r in Table VI, one must know two degrees of freedom: $d.f._{BG}$, the degrees of freedom for the between-groups estimate, and $d.f._{WG}$ for the within-groups estimate:

$$d.f._{BG} = k - 1$$
$$d.f._{WG} = nk - k$$

where k = the number of independent variable classes (groups)

where n = the number of units per class

For *computational ease*, F_0 is computed according to a different but mathematically equivalent ratio, involving mean squares (MS_{BG} and MS_{WG}). In fact, the mean squares *are* the variance estimates. Their computation is discussed below. The mean squares equal the sum of squares (SS_{BG} and SS_{WG}) divided by their respective degrees of freedom.

Assumptions

As indicated at the outset, ANOVA requires stringent assumptions best approximated in experimental settings:

1. Samples must be independent. That is, observations in one sample (note that "samples" are the same as "classes," "groups," or "columns") must not affect the corresponding observations in the next sample. Samples are *not* independent when the data in one sample (class) are based on the same or matched units as in another sample (class).
2. The samples must be taken at random. For a test of randomness see the runs test.
3. The dependent variable must be normally distributed in each class of the independent variable (i.e., within each sample or group). For tests of normal distribution, see the chi-square goodness-of-fit test and the Kolmogorov-Smirnov goodness-of-fit test. Dependent data are interval.
4. The samples must have the same variances. ANOVA is very sensitive to this assumption. Note, therefore, that ANOVA is almost always employed after employing a test of homogeneity of variance, such as *Bartlett's test*, discussed later.
5. Error terms are assumed to be uncorrelated (this assumption is best met through experimental randomization of units to groups). In addition, error terms are assumed to be normally distributed and have a common variance.
6. Sources of variation in the dependent variable are assumed to be additive. [1]
7. ANOVA implies a causal model characterized by unidirectional flow of causation from independent to dependent variables, without feedback from the dependent to the independent variables. [2]

Note that one-way ANOVA tests whether sample groups share a common pattern of dispersion (i.e., seem to come from the same population by comparing variance estimates). Two-way ANOVA, to be discussed later, tests whether sample groups have similar centroids. Thus, two-way ANOVA is a slightly different test. Specifically, it is less sensitive to moderate violations of the homogeneity of variances assumption.

Finally, note that while variances must be equal in the assumption (No. 4) listed above, group means need not be.

Computation

Table 14.2 illustrates the manner in which the F-ratio is computed:

1. The data are in a table at the top of Table 14.2; there is one set of columns for each category of the independent (sample) variable: in the example, one for each region. The measurements of the dependent variable (votes for Nixon in %) are listed along with the squares of these measurements.

---

[1] For a discussion of additivity, see E. A. Haggard, *Intraclass Correlation and the Analysis of Variance* (New York: Dryden, 1958), pp. 46, 52–55. For *tests of additivity* and transforms used when the assumption of additivity is not met, see George Snedecor, *Statistical Methods* (Ames, Iowa: Iowa State Univ. Press, 1956), pp. 314–328.

[2] See H. P. Alker, "Statistics and Politics," in S. Lipset, ed., *Politics and the Social Sciences* (New York: Oxford, 1969), pp. 251–252.

2. The sum of measurements (Σx) is taken for each column, and then the grand sum of column sums is listed below ($\Sigma\Sigma x$). The same is done for the sum of squared measurements (Σx^2) and the corresponding grand sum ($\Sigma\Sigma x^2$).

3. The sum of measurements (Σx) is squared ($\Sigma x)^2$ and these squares for each column sums of measurements ($\Sigma\Sigma x$) is squared ($\Sigma\Sigma x)^2$.

5. The number of units (in the example, congressional districts) is $n = 10$; the number of classes, k, of the independent variable is $k = 4$ (i.e., the four regions).

6. Using n, k, and the sums in steps 1 through 4, the between-groups sum of squares (SS_{BG}) and the within-groups sum of squares (SS_{WG}), can be computed by using the formulas at the bottom of Table 14.2.

7. Degrees of freedom are computed as discussed on p. 369.

8. Then, thinking ahead to Bartlett's test of homogeneity of variance (which will be discussed later), we compute the following:
   a. The column averages (x), the sum of column averages $\Sigma(x)$,
   b. The square of column averages $(x)^2$, and the sum of these squares $\Sigma(x)^2$.
   c. The grand average of column averages $(\Sigma x/k) = x$.
   d. The column variances, $s^2 = \left(\frac{x^2}{n}\right) - x^2$

9. The results of the analysis of variance are presented in conventional format in Table 14.1. The observed F-ratio, F_o, is the ratio of mean squares, MS_{BG}/MS_{WG}. The mean squares, in turn, are the estimates of variance discussed earlier; they are the sum of squares divided by the corresponding degrees of freedom: $MS_{BG} = SS_{BG}/(k-1)$ and $MS_{WG} = SS_{WG}/(nk-k)$.

10. The F-ratio required for a given significance level, say the conventional .05 level, is read from Table VI in the Appendix. In this table, n_1 is the number of degrees of freedom associated with the larger mean square; n_2 is the number of degrees of freedom associated with the smaller mean square.

The required F-ratio at the .05 level is labelled $F_{r(.05)}$.

TABLE 14.1   Analysis of Variance of % of Vote for Nixon by Region

Source of Variation	d.f.	SS	MS
Between Groups (BG)	3	347.4	115.8
Within Groups (WG)	36	2,454.8	68.2
Total	39	2,802.2	
$F_o = 115.8/68.2 = 1.70$		$F_{r(.05)} = 2.87$	

Since Table 14.1 reveals that our computed F-ratio, F_0, is not as large as the required F-ratio at the .05 significance level, F_r, we fail to reject the null hypothesis that the regions differ. That is, the variance between groups is *not* so large compared to the variance within groups as to lead us to think the regions' data are drawn from different populations. (Note that as the variance within groups increases, since MS_{WG} is the denominator of the F-ratio, a given level of variation between groups, the numerator, will be found to be less significant).

Use of Total Sum of Squares as a Check in Computation   Since ANOVA involves tedious, error-prone computations when done by hand, it

TABLE 14.2   Computing Table for One-Way Analysis of Variance

Sample (Independent) Variable: Region

Dependent Variable: % for Nixon, 1972 — Units (Districts)	Northeast (NE) x	x^2	South (S) x	x^2	Midwest (MW) x	x^2	West (W) x	x^2
1	59.3	3516.5	73.8	5446.4	62.7	3931.3	65.2	4251.0
2	61.9	3831.6	73.5	5402.3	71.2	5069.4	54.0	2916.0
3	61.6	3794.6	68.1	4637.6	69.5	4830.3	51.2	2621.4
4	48.0	2304.0	69.0	4761.0	63.6	4045.0	52.5	2756.3
5	45.5	2070.3	75.2	5655.0	66.7	4448.9	65.2	4251.0
6	66.4	4409.0	55.6	3091.4	64.6	4173.2	72.4	5241.8
7	72.9	5314.4	57.6	3317.8	54.5	2970.3	56.4	3181.0
8	61.7	3806.9	56.1	3147.2	69.9	4886.0	46.2	2134.4
9	72.3	5227.3	77.8	6052.8	61.0	3721.0	64.3	4134.5
10	51.8	2683.2	50.9	2590.8	62.9	3956.4	60.2	3624.0

$n = 10$

$\Sigma x =$ 601.4 | 657.6 | 646.6 | 587.6

$(\Sigma x)^2 =$ 361,682.0 | 432,437.8 | 418,091.6 | 345,273.8

$\Sigma x^2 =$ 36,957.8 | 44,102.3 | 42,031.8 | 35,111.4

$\Sigma x/n = \bar{x} = $ 60.1 | 65.8 | 64.7 | 58.8; $\bar{x}^2 = $ 3,612.0 | 4,329.6 | 4,186.1 | 3,457.4

$\dfrac{x^2}{n} - \bar{x}^2 = s^2 = $ 83.8 | 80.6 | 17.1 | 53.7

$\Sigma\Sigma x = 2,493.2$ $(\Sigma\Sigma x)^2 = 6,216,046.2$ $\Sigma(\Sigma x)^2 = 1,557,485.2$

$\Sigma\Sigma x^2 = 158,203.3$ $\Sigma\bar{x}/k = \bar{x}_T = 62.4$

TABLE 14.2 (cont.)

$$\text{d.f.}_{BG} = k - 1 = 3 \qquad \text{d.f.}_{WG} = nk - k = 36$$

$$SS_{BG} = \left(\frac{\Sigma(\Sigma x)^2}{n}\right) - \left(\frac{(\Sigma\Sigma x)^2}{nk}\right) = \left(\frac{1{,}557{,}485.2}{10}\right) - \left(\frac{6{,}216{,}046.2}{40}\right) = 347.4$$

$$SS_{WG} = (\Sigma\Sigma x^2) - \left(\frac{\Sigma(\Sigma x)^2}{n}\right) = (158{,}203.3) - \left(\frac{1{,}557{,}485.2}{10}\right) = 2{,}434.8$$

is strongly advised that the researcher check his or her computations. One way to do this is to compute the total sum of squares, SS_T. If one has not made computational errors, SS_T should equal the sum of SS_{BG} and SS_{WG}. SS_T is computed as indicated below:

$$SS_T = (\Sigma\Sigma x^2) - \left[\frac{(\Sigma\Sigma x)^2}{nk}\right]$$

$$= 158,203.3 - \left[\frac{6,216,046.2}{4(10)}\right] = 2802.2$$

This number should be identical to that read in Table 14.1 for SS_T.

What if the Samples are not Equal in Size? When sample size, n, differs by class (column) of the independent variable, slightly different formulas are used. In these formulas, given below, n_i stands for the sample size in the ith column; when n_i appears in connection with a summation sign, Σ, one must sum for each column.

ANOVA Formulas When Sample Sizes Differ

$$SS_{BG} = \Sigma\left[\frac{(\Sigma x)^2}{n_i}\right] - \left[\frac{(\Sigma\Sigma x)^2}{\Sigma n_i}\right]$$

$$SS_{WG} = (\Sigma\Sigma x^2) - \Sigma\left[\frac{(\Sigma x)^2}{n_i}\right]$$

$$SS_T = (\Sigma\Sigma x^2) - \left[\frac{(\Sigma\Sigma x)^2}{\Sigma n_i}\right]$$

Bartlett's Test of Homogeneity of Variance

As mentioned earlier, ANOVA is quite sensitive to the assumption of each class (column) of the independent variable having the same variance. This is not to say that small deviations from this assumption are not routinely accepted by social scientists, but it is customary to test for homogeneity of variance.

The most frequent test is Barlett's test, illustrated in Table 14.3. Bartlett's test involves the following steps:

1. A six-column table is constructed, in which each row is a group (class) of the independent variable (region in our example). Column (1) lists the sample size of each group minus one (in our example, sample sizes are the same, but they needn't have been).
2. Column (2) lists the group variances, computed in Table 14.2.
3. Column (3) is the product of column (1) times column (2).

TABLE 14.3 Computing Table for Bartlett's Test of Homogeneity of Variance

Groups (Regions)	(1) $(n_i - 1)$	(2) (s_i^2)	(3) $[(n_i - 1)s_i^2]$	(4) $\log s_i^2$	(5) $[(n_i - 1)\log s_i^2]$	(6) $[1/(n_i - 1)]$
NE	9	83.8	754.2	1.9232	17.3088	.1111
S	9	80.6	725.4	1.9063	17.1567	.1111
MW	9	17.1	153.9	1.2330	11.0970	.1111
W	9	53.7	483.3	1.7300	15.5700	.1111

$\Sigma(n_i - 1) = 36$

$\log \Sigma(n_i - 1) = 1.5563$

$1/\Sigma(n_i - 1) = .0278$

d.f. $= k - 1 = 3$

$\Sigma(n_i - 1)s_i^2 = 2{,}116.8$

$\log \Sigma(n_i - 1)s_i^2 = 3.3237$

$\Sigma(n_i - 1)\log s_i^2 = 61.1325$

$\Sigma[1/(n_i - 1)] = .4444$

$$\chi^2_{BT} = \cfrac{2.302585 \left\{ \Sigma(n_i - 1)[\log \Sigma(n_i - 1)s_i^2 - \log \Sigma(n_i - 1)] - \Sigma(n_i - 1)\log s_i^2 \right\}}{1 + [\,\cfrac{1}{3(k-1)}\,]\{\Sigma[1/(n - 1)] - [1/\Sigma(n - 1)]\}}$$

$$= \frac{2.302585\,[34(3.3237 - 1.5563) - 61.1325]}{1 + [\frac{1}{3}(4 - 1)](.1111 - .0278)} = 5.7579$$

$$\chi^2_{r(.90)} = .58 \qquad\qquad \chi^2_{.10} = 6.3$$

4. Column (4) is the logarithm (to the base 10; i.e., the common logarithm) of column (2).

5. Column (5) is the product of column (1) times column (4).

6. Column (6) is the reciprocal of column (1).

7. Degrees of freedom in this test equal $(k = 1)$, where k is the number of classes of the independent variable.

8. The sum of column (1), logarithm of this sum, and reciprocal of this sum are computed.

9. The sum and logarithm of the sum of column (3) are computed.

10. The sums of columns (5) and (6) are also computed.

11. Bartlett's test uses the chi-square distribution, which Bartlett demonstrated to be the sampling distribution when ANOVA assumptions are met. Bartlett's test chi-square has a very complicated formula, shown in Table 14.3, but it can be easily computed using the sums from steps 8 through 10.

12. This value, X_{BT}^2, should be lower than the chi-square value in Table V of the Appendix for the .90 level, using $(k = 1)$ degrees of freedom.

Since the computed chi-square in Table 14.3 (5.76) is much higher than the required chi-square (.58), we cannot accept the hypothesis that there is no difference in column variances. (Note that the chi-square value in Table V of the Appendix for the .10 level is 6.3. If the computed chi-square is this large or larger, we could definitely reject the null hypothesis of no difference. Our computed value is too small for this. It lies between the .20 and .10 significance levels; thus it is our best guess that the variances are not the same, but we cannot conclude this. However, Bartlett's test is primarily concerned with proving the null hypothesis, so the main question is whether or not the computed chi-square is smaller than the required chi-square at the .90 level. Note also that some authors prefer a more stringent test, using the .95 level.)

Measures of Association Based on Analysis of Variance

The Coefficient of Nonlinear Correlation, Eta   The coefficient of non-linear correlation, eta, was discussed earlier in Chapter 12. Eta is the ratio of sum of squares between groups to sum of squares within groups. That is, it is the proportion of total variance accounted for by the variance between classes (groups) of the independent variable.

The Coefficient of Determination, Omega-Square   Omega-square, the coefficient of determination, is the proportion of variance in the dependent variable reduced by knowing the independent variable:

$$\omega^2 = \frac{SS_{BG} - (k-1)MS_{WG}}{SS_T + MS_{WG}}$$

Omega-square is interpreted similarly to the coefficient of linear determination, r^2. (Note that omega-square may be computed to be less than zero; in such cases it is set equal to zero).[3]

The Coefficient of Intraclass Correlation, r_I   The coefficient of intraclass correlation, r_I is "a measure of the relative homogeneity of scores within groups in relation to the total variation among all the scores in the table."[4]

$$r_I = \frac{\text{MS}_{\text{BG}} - \text{MS}_{\text{WG}}}{\text{MS}_{\text{BG}} + (n-1)\,\text{MS}_{\text{WG}}}$$

This coefficient will be *large* and *positive* when there is no variation within classes, but class means differ. It will be at its *largest negative* value when class means are the same, but there is great variation within classes. Its maximum value is positive 1.0, but its maximum negative value is dependent on sample size. The maximum negative value equals $[-1/(n-1)]$. A negative r_I, which means that between-group variation is less than what one would expect from the within-group variation, indicates that some third (control) variable has made the sampling nonrandom.[5] When sample sizes differ, n^* should be substituted for n:

$$n^* = [1/(k-1)]\left(\Sigma n_i - \frac{\Sigma n_i^2}{\Sigma n_i}\right)$$

The r_I coefficient is significant at the same level as F, and is a function of it:[6]

$$r_I = \frac{F-1}{F+(n-1)} \qquad\qquad F = \frac{1+(n-1)r_I}{1-r_I}$$

The Mean Intercolumn Correlation Coefficient, $\bar{r}$ The intraclass correlation coefficient, r_I, approximates the arithmetic mean of Pearson product-moment correlations ($\bar{r}$). Since k classes of the independent variable involve $k(k-1)/2$ pairs, there will be that many rs to average. Recall that Fisher's z transformation is used in averaging correlation coefficients.

The intraclass correlation coefficient, r_I, equals $\bar{r}$ (or r, if $k = 2$) if column means and variances are equalized. The product-moment correlation, r, and its average, $\bar{r}$, equalize means and variances by standardizing the data (subtracting the mean and dividing by the standard deviation).

[3]See Dennis Palumbo, *Statistics in Political and Behavioral Science* (New York: Appleton-Century-Crofts, 1969), pp. 239–240.
[4]Haggard, *Intraclass Correlation*, p. 6.
[5]Snedecor, *Statistical Methods*, p. 284.
[6]For computation of rank-order intraclass correlation, see Haggard, *Intraclass Correlation*, p. 6.

Consequently these statistics are not sensitive to differences in means and variances. Intraclass correlation, r_I, in contrast, is sensitive to such differences: specifically, r_I will decrease as such differences increase.

Haggard recommends computing r_I when scores in each column are of the same kind (e.g., each column is data on percentage of vote) and $\bar{r}$ when scores in each column differ in kind (e.g., one column is percentage of vote, another is income level, etc.). That is, product-moment correlation is a bivariate statistic, appropriate to two-variable situations, whereas intraclass correlation is univariate, appropriate to one-variable comparisons.

Relation of F-Ratio to t Test

When the number of sample groups (independent variable classes) is two, $F = t^2$, where t is the value in a test of two sample means.

Making Comparisons Between Subsets of the *k* Sample Groups

If we compute one-way ANOVA on a set of data and find that our F_o is significant, we are still left with the question, "Which of the k classes of the independent (sample) variable are different from which others, or is each equallly different from every other?"

As with other tests of significance, it is *not* appropriate to pick two classes (groups) out of the k groups and conduct a t test of difference of sample means, *if* the reason we have picked them is because we see their means differ greatly *after* we have computed the means. This is because k groups will allow $k(k - 1)/2$ pairs for comparison; thus, 7 groups allow 21 comparisons. If we set our significance level at the appropriate .05, then we would expect 1 out of these 21 comparisons to *seem* to be significant (less than the .05 level on a t test) even though it is not. (This is what the .05 level means: 1 chance in 20 of getting a result as strong or stronger just by chance of sampling).

Picking an Orthogonal Set of Comparisons in Advance   Picking a set of comparisons in advance of doing anything with our data helps avoid the fallacy just mentioned. If, in addition, that set is orthogonal, then the comparisons will partition the between-groups sum of squares. That is, the sum of squares between groups (SS_{BG}) for each comparison will sum to the overall sum of squares computed in analysis of variance for all k groups. *A set of comparisons is orthogonal* if:

1. no sum is used twice, *and if*
2. each sum is compared with another sum only if both are part of a previously mentioned sum (not counting the original sum of all k groups).

For our data, the following is an orthogonal set of comparisons:

1. $(E+MW+W)$ versus S
2. E versus $(MW+W)$
3. MW versus W

No sum is used twice, and each comparison partitions only one previously mentioned sum.

Note that the set of comparisons above is *not* the only one that would be orthogonal. Which set is chosen depends upon which comparisons are most relevant to the purposes of the researcher. For k groups, any orthogonal set of comparisons will have $(k-1)$ comparisons; this is the same as the number of degrees of freedom, d.f.$_{BG}$. The number of degrees of freedom associated with each comparison is always one ($1 =$ the number of sums, 2, in a given comparison, minus 1).

Since for each comparison degrees of freedom equal 1, then the SS_{BG} for each comparison will equal MS_{BG} (this is because MS_{BG} equals $SS_{BG}/d.f._{BG}$). The F-ratio for each comparison equals its MS_{BG} divided by the within-groups variance estimate, MS_{WG}, which was computed in the original analysis of variance for all k groups. For the example of four regional groups, E, S, MW, and W, the formulas in Table 14.4 illustrate the computations involved. The F-ratios for the various comparisons can then be used in the conventional manner to determine which are significant and which are not, regardless of whether or not the original F-ratio for all k groups showed the effect of the independent variable to be significant.

TABLE 14.4

Comparison	$SS'_{BG} = MS'_{BG}$ $F = \dfrac{MS'_{BG}}{MS_{WG}}$	
(E + MW + W) versus S	$\dfrac{(\Sigma x_E + \Sigma x_{MW} + \Sigma x_W)^2}{n_E + n_{MW} + n_W} + \dfrac{(\Sigma x_S)^2}{n_S} - \dfrac{(\Sigma\Sigma x)^2}{\Sigma n_i}$	F_1
E versus (MW + W)	$\dfrac{(\Sigma x_{MW} + \Sigma x_W)^2}{n_{MW} + n_W} + \dfrac{(\Sigma x_E)^2}{n_E} - \dfrac{(\Sigma x_{MW} + \Sigma x_W + \Sigma x_E)^2}{n_{MW} + n_W + n_E}$	F_2
MW versus W	$\dfrac{(\Sigma x_{MW})^2}{n_{MW}} + \dfrac{(\Sigma x_W)^2}{n_W} - \dfrac{(\Sigma x_{MW} + \Sigma x_W)^2}{n_M + n_W}$	F_3
MS_{WG} * computed in Table 14.2 * $MS_{WG} = \Sigma MS'_{WG}$		

Fixed versus Random Effects Models

The foregoing discussion of one-way analysis of variance assumes a "fixed effects" model: we assume that the k groups we analyze are the ones relevant to our research. In a "random effects" model, we assume the k groups are a random sample of all possible groups in which we might be interested. ANOVA for a random effects model is quite similar to the methods described above, but for purposes of brevity these procedures will not be discussed here. The reader is referred to other texts.[7]

Ordinal Data: Kruskal-Wallis One-Way Analysis of Variance by Ranks

The foregoing discussion also assumed that data on the dependent variable (percentage of vote for Nixon in the example) were interval in level. When this assumption is not met because the data are ordinal, or when the data are interval but are not normally distributed or not homogenous in variance, the Kruskal-Wallis test is commonly employed instead. In the Kruskal-Wallis test, the test statistic is H rather than F; a table of H is consulted in an analogous manner, with degrees of freedom equal to $(k - 1)$. Again, for purposes of brevity the reader is referred to other texts.[8] The elements of this test were outlined in Chapter 10.

TWO-WAY ANALYSIS OF VARIANCE (MORE THAN ONE INDEPENDENT VARIABLE)

Two-way analysis of variance (ANOVA) enables the researcher to examine the effect of more than one independent variable on a dependent variable. For the model in Figure 14.1, ANOVA enables us to determine (a) the effect

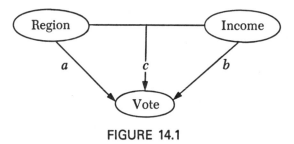

FIGURE 14.1

of region on vote, (b) the effect of income on vote, and (c) the effect on vote of the interaction between region and income. It will also enable us to assess

[7]Snedecor, *Statistical Methods*, pp. 259–282, for example.
[8]Sidney Siegel, *Nonparametric Statistics* (New York: McGraw-Hill, 1956), pp. 184–193.

the effect on vote of the "error term" (error involves measurement error plus the effect of variables not in the model, plus random error).

Rationale

If the variance associated with a given independent variable is not significantly greater than the variance associated with the error term, then we have no reason not to think that the samples (groups of the independent variable) come from the same underlying population. The same reasoning applies to the variance associated with the joint interaction of the independent variables. That is, the more the given variance exceeds the error variance, the higher the F-ratio, and the more significant the effect. NOTE: as in one-way ANOVA, MS_{WG} is taken as the estimate of error variance; "error sum of squares" is SS_{WG}.

Statistic

Thus two-way ANOVA uses the same statistic as one-way ANOVA —namely, the F-ratio. Table 14.6 presents the formulas for the relevant sums of squares (SS), degrees of freedom (d.f.), and F-ratios. As before, the F-ratios are ratios of estimates of variance (i.e., of mean squares, MS, where MS = SS/d.f.).

The relevant sums of squares include SS_{WG} (the within groups = the within subclass = the within cells = the error sum of squares) and SS_T (the total sum of squares), as in one-way ANOVA. Instead of just the sum of squares between groups (columns), SS_{BG}, we now have two statistics—SS_{BC} (the sum of squares between classes of the column independent variable) and SS_{BR} (the sum of squares between classes of the row independent variable). There is also the sum of squares associated with the joint or interaction effect of both independent variables on the dependent variable, SS_I. Finally, the sum of squares between subclasses, SS_{BS}, is necessary since it is a component in computing SS_I and SS_T.

Thus, the data in two-way ANOVA take the form of Table 14.5.

TABLE 14.5

		Regions			
		E	S	MW	W
Income Levels	High	x_i			
	Low				

In Table 14.5, x_i are the scores of the units (e.g., the percent of vote of the congressional districts).

Note: The number of scores, x_i, within each cell must be the same or proportional for the procedures described in Table 14.6. By proportional, we mean that the ratio of numbers of cases in a row of cells must equal the ratio of row marginals (or the ratio of numbers of cases in any column of cells must equal the ratio of column marginals). This requirement is easily arranged in experimental situations where the researcher is in a position to randomly assign given numbers of individuals to groups, but it is rarely met in nonexperimental research. The problem of disproportionate cell frequencies will be discussed later.

Note: Table 14.5 uses a forced dichotomy, income. In proper use of ANOVA in experimental research, this would not be done. Rather, a random sample of relatively narrow ranges would be selected and ANOVA computed as a mixed model, discussed below (e.g., in agricultural experiments using the variable "amount of irrigation," the research would not dichotomize into "above average" and "below average"; instead a random sample of specific rates of irrigation would be selected for experimental testing). Again, the application of ANOVA to nonexperimental research provides many problems.

Note: Table 14.6 contains a distinction between MS_{WG}, the "error" variance, and MS_{WG}', the corrected error variance. When the F-ratio reveals MS_I as *not* significant, corrected error variance must be substituted for error variance according to the following formula:

$$MS_{WG}' = (SS_{WG} + SS_I)/(n_t - k - r + 1)$$

When this substitution is made, the F test for the between-columns estimate of variance (MS_{BC}) and for the between-rows estimate of variance (MS_{BR}) is made as before.

Because computation is essentially identical to one-way ANOVA, and for reasons of space, a computational example will not be given here. In the computational formulas in Table 14.6, the sums Σx_k, Σx_r, Σx_t, and Σx_c stand, respectively, for the sum of observations in a given column, in a given row, in the whole table, and in a given cell. The numbers of observations corresponding to these sums are n_k, n_r, n_t, and n_c respectively. Finally, as before, k is the number of columns and r is the number of rows.

Interpretation

In multivariate analysis using two-way analysis of variance, the second independent variable is often the control variable. In Table 14.5, "income levels" might be considered the control variable. If "region," our initial independent variable, had a significant association with the dependent variable, percent of vote, then we might want to test whether some third variable such as income might not be an antecedent variable explaining both.

If two-way ANOVA shows a high interaction of the two independent variables, we cannot assume an additive causal model. That is, we cannot accept the model in Figure 14.2. This is not quite the same as accepting the

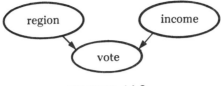

FIGURE 14.2

model in Figure 14.1. It is true that we could compute coefficients of intra-class correlation, r_I, for each of the arrows in Figure 14.1 (arrows a, b, and c), but we cannot equate between-columns, interaction, and between-rows effects with the causal assertions represented by these arrows. Since the effects of the two independent and one dependent variables cannot be separated in reality, we must conclude simply that when interaction is large, the main effects (the between-columns effect and the between-rows effect) cannot be interpreted in a simple (e.g., additive) way.

Thus ANOVA does not establish that income is an antecedent variable for region and vote; it merely rules out one possibility. However, in computing the interaction effect (see Table 14.6), our attention may be drawn to the cells with the largest sum of observation scores (Σx_c). By noting these cells, we may gain clues useful in reformulating an explanatory model to take account of which ranges of the independent variables contribute most to deviation from an additive model. For example, we may find that the cells that contribute the most to the interaction effect are those for the "South" region; when this column is deleted, interaction is low and an additive model sustained. We infer that a different explanatory model is necessary for the region "South."

However, these advantages may be obtained more directly by applying Goodman's method (recall Chapter 13), which, in addition, does not involve many of the stringent assumptions of analysis of variance. As Goodman's method is not yet common in political science, the alternatives to ANOVA most commonly chosen by political scientists are either multiple table and partial correlation analysis (see Chapter 13) or multiple correlation and multiple regression analysis (discussed in Chapter 15). The latter assume an interval level of measurement, unlike Goodman's method, but less-than-interval data are routinely dichotomized (made into what are called "dummy variables") for purposes of multivariate analysis.

In sum, analysis of variance enables us to estimate the effects of the column independent variable, the row independent variable, and the mutual interactive effect. Specifically, the total sum of squares (SS_T) will equal the sum of between-column, between-row, interaction, and error (within-groups) effects ($SS_{BC} + SS_{BR} + SS_I + SS_{WG}$). However, because of the difficulty of causal interpretation of these statistical effects and because

TABLE 14.6 Formulas for Two-Way Analysis of Variance When the Number of Observations per Cell is the Same or is Proportional to the Marginals

Sum of Squares	Corresponding Formula	Associated d.f.	F tests*
SS_{WG}	$SS_T - SS_{BS}$	$SS_{WG} = (n_t - kr)$ $SS_{WG'} = (n_t - kr) + (k-1)(r-1)$	
SS_{BC}	$\Sigma \left[\dfrac{(\Sigma x_k)^2}{n_k} \right] - \left[\dfrac{(\Sigma x_t)^2}{n_t} \right]$	$k - 1$	$\dfrac{MS_{BC}}{MS_{WG}}$ or $\dfrac{MS_{BC}}{MS_{WG'}}$
SS_{BR}	$\Sigma \left[\dfrac{(\Sigma x_r)^2}{n_r} \right] - \left[\dfrac{(\Sigma x_t)^2}{n_t} \right]$	$r - 1$	$\dfrac{MS_{BR}}{MS_{WG}}$ or $\dfrac{MS_{BR}}{MS_{WG'}}$
SS_I	$SS_{BS} - (SS_{BC} + SS_{BR})$	$(k-1)(r-1)$	$\dfrac{MS_I}{MS_{WG}}$
SS_T	$\Sigma (x_t^2) - \left[\dfrac{(\Sigma x_t)^2}{n_t} \right]$	$(n_t - 1)$	
SS_{BS}	$\left[\dfrac{(\Sigma x_c)^2}{n_c} \right] - \left[\dfrac{(\Sigma x_t)^2}{n_t} \right]$	$(kr - 1)$	

* Note that $MS_i = SS_i / \text{d.f.}_i$

of the many assumptions required in ANOVA, political scientists normally use other techniques. When these assumptions are met, however, as in experimental research, ANOVA is a powerful, common, and useful tool.

Other Considerations

What if the Number of Observations Per Cell Is Neither Equal nor Proportional? The foregoing procedures assume equal or proportional number of cases per cell. When this assumption is not met, various alternatives are employed.

First, one-way ANOVA may be computed for each category of the second independent variable (usually the control variable). This procedure requires a relatively large number of cases, much larger for a given level of significance than normal two-way ANOVA . Second, the researcher may: (a) substitute cell means for observations (i.e., have one observation per cell: the mean); (b) compute SS_{BC}, SS_{BR}, and SS_I with n_i equaling the number of means; (c) compute SS_{WC}, SS_T, and SS_{BS} with n equaling the number of observations; and (d) use a corrected MS_{WC} equal to MS_{WC} divided by the harmonic mean number of cases per cell (a harmonic mean is the reciprocal of the arithmetic mean of a set of reciprocals). Third, a more complex and sophisticated approach involves the methods of fitting constants and using weighted squares of means.[9] These methods are beyond the scope of this text.

Intraclass Correlation in Two-Way Analysis of Variance   Intraclass correlation, r_I, assumes many more forms in two-way ANOVA than the one form it took in one-way ANOVA. There is an r_I for the between-columns effect on the dependent variable, the between-rows effect, and the interaction effect. Moreover, like the F test, r_I is computed on a different basis dependent on whether the researcher assumes a fixed effects model (the classes of both independent variables are the ones in which we are interested), a random effects model (the classes of both are randomly selected classes from population of possible class), or a mixed model. Table 14.7 illustrates these differences (notation is as before).[10] The intraclass correlation coefficients computed for two-way analysis of variance may be used in studies of the reliability of test items in questionnaires and examinations.[11]

Ordinal Data   For ordinal data or data that are not normally distributed or samples that are dependent, Friedman two-way analysis of variance

---

[9]The second method is discussed in H. Walker and J. Lev, *Statistical Inference* (New York: Holt, 1953), ch. 3. The third method is discussed in T. Bancroft, *Topics in Intermediate Statistical Methods* (Ames, Iowa: Iowa State Univ. Press, 1968), pp. 16–65; and in K. Schuessler, *Analyzing Social Data* (Boston: Houghton-Mifflin, 1971), pp. 152–197.

[10]See Haggard, *Intraclass Correlation*, p. 60.

[11]See Haggard, ch. 6.

TABLE 14.7   *F* and r_I for Alternative Models of
Two-Way Analysis of Variance

Fixed Effects Model	F	r_I
Between columns	MS_{BC}/MS_{WG}	$\dfrac{MS_{BC} - MS_{WG}}{MS_{BC} + (k-1)MS_{WG}}$
Between rows	MS_{BR}/MS_{WG}	$\dfrac{MS_{BR} - MS_{WG}}{MS_{BR} + (k-1)MS_{WG}}$
Interaction (same in all models)	MS_I/MS_{WG}	$\dfrac{MS_I - MS_{WG}}{MS_I + (k-1)MS_{WG}}$
Random Effects Model	F	r_I
Between columns	MS_{BG}/MS_I	$\dfrac{MS_{BC} - MS_I}{MS_{BC} + (k-1)MS_I}$
Between Rows	MS_{BR}/MS_I	$\dfrac{MS_{BR} - MS_I}{MS_{BR} + (k-1)MS_I}$

Mixed Model A: Only column classes are random

Between Columns	same as fixed model
Between Rows	same as random model

Mixed Model B: Only row classes are random

Between Columns	same as random model
Between Rows	same as fixed model

is used. This is so rarely used in political science that it is not treated here.[12]

Three-Way Analysis of Variance   ANOVA techniques may be applied to more than two independent variables, as illustrated in Figure 14.3. Three independent variables involve main effects (the effects of each independent variable on the dependent variable), first-order interaction effects (the effects of each pair of independent variables), and a second-order interaction effect (the effect of all three independent variables). Similar reasoning (and difficulties of interpretation) arise in three-way ANOVA. Since each variable must be measured and sampled in conformity with the assumptions set forth earlier, three-way ANOVA is extremely rare in political science, although it is common in experimental research.[13]

[12]See Sidney Siegel, *Nonparametric Statistics for the Behavioral Sciences* (New York: McGraw-Hill, 1956), pp. 166–172; James Bradley, *Distribution-Free Statistical Tests* (Englewood Cliffs, N. J.: Prentice-Hall, 1968), pp. 123–129, 134–141; Virginia Senders, *Measurement and Statistics* (New York: Oxford, 1958), pp. 450–452.
[13]For discussion and illustration of 3-way ANOVA, see Quinn McNemar, *Psychological Statistics* (New York: John Wiley & Sons, 1962), pp. 318–345.

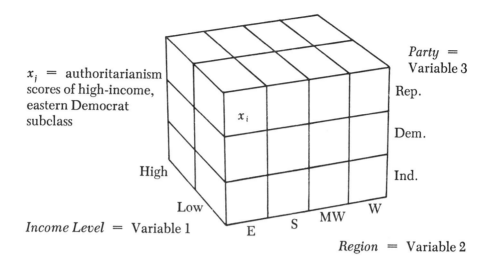

x_i = authoritarianism scores of high-income, eastern Democrat subclass

Party = Variable 3

Rep.

Dem.

Ind.

High

Low

Income Level = Variable 1

E   S   MW   W

Region = Variable 2

Relevant Mean Squares:

MS_{B1} —between income levels
MS_{B2} —between regions   } "main effects"
MS_{B3} —between parties

MS_{I12} —interaction of income and region
MS_{I13} —interaction of income and party   } 1st-order interactions
MS_{I23} —interaction of region and party

MS_{I123} --interaction of all three variables
MS_{WG} —within groups (error) sum of squares   } 2nd-order interaction

FIGURE 14.3   ANOVA With Three Independent Variables

ANALYSIS OF COVARIANCE

As discussed earlier, even two-way analysis of variance does not directly test the effect of a control variable. Analysis of covariance is a little-used procedure that is applicable in this instance. For a dependent variable (y), an independent variable (x), and a control variable (c), analysis of covariance uses regression analysis (discussed in Chapter 15) to "correct" the y values within each sample (group or class) of the independent variable, x. The result is that the researcher is able to assess the effect of a control variable on an independent variable, much as was discussed in the previous chapter. Moreover, unlike partial product-moment correlation, analysis of covariance may be adapted to avoid an assumption that the data are linearly related.

However, analysis of covariance does involve analysis of variance assumptions discussed previously (e.g., common variances) and more besides. Two additional assumptions are (1) that the sample populations (the classes of the control variable) have identical regression slopes and (2) that, for each class of the control variable, the sample populations have identical and normal distributions. Thus, analysis of covariance assumes that the independent and dependent variables are measured at the interval level, while the control variable is nominal or ordinal. As with analysis of variance, the error factor (including the effect of unmeasured variables) is assumed to vary independently of the measured explanatory variables. Subclasses need not have equal or proportional numbers of observations, however.

The results of the computation of analysis of covariance are interpreted in a manner similar to analysis of variance, except that the effect of one or more control variables is now included. That is, analysis of covariance may be thought of as analysis of variance on scores adjusted for the covariation of the independent and control variables.

Because of the rarity of analysis of covariance in political science and because of its use of regression techniques not yet introduced, the reader is referred to other texts for computation.[14] Except for the regression adjustment of initial scores, however, analysis of covariance is a relatively simple extension of analysis of variance in terms of computation.

EXERCISE

A researcher is interested in the effect of region and political party identification on support for the Vietnamese war. The researcher constructs and tests a Guttman scale of war support, scores of which are treated as interval in level. A stratified random sample of students at a large university is then taken, such that five students for each combination of region and party identification are sampled, with their war support scores listed in Table 14.8.

The researcher hypothesizes in advance that region and party identification influence war support in an independent, additive manner. Using analysis of variance techniques, is this hypothesis supported? Is the effect of region significant? Is the effect of party identification significant? How do you interpret the interaction effect? (Does this data set justify the assumption of homogeneity of variance?)

[14]See, for example, Snedecor, *Statistical Methods*, ch. 13; McNemar, *Psychological Statistics*, ch. 18; Bancroft, *Intermediate Statistical Methods*, ch. 6; and Schuessler, *Analyzing Social Data*, ch. 5.

TABLE 14.8

Party Identification	Region			
	East	South	Midwest	West
Republican	60	82	76	69
	79	69	55	42
	52	68	70	59
	40	81	82	77
	88	74	71	80
Independent	78	77	65	67
	42	68	81	52
	50	81	72	73
	61	55	64	49
	58	58	61	52
Democratic	58	59	61	38
	38	62	68	55
	46	67	71	49
	55	55	53	68
	39	73	66	70

15	# Multiple Correlation and Regression Analysis

Regression analysis is among the most common of the more advanced statistical techniques used by political scientists. Where the correlation coefficient, r, was a measure of the extent to which data for two variables fell in a straight line when plotted in a scatter diagram (recall Chapter 12), regression has to do with obtaining the formula that describes that line. For example, in Figure 15.1, the line for $y = 2x + 1$ is shown. More generally, a straight line is described by the formula: $y = bx + c$, where y is the dependent

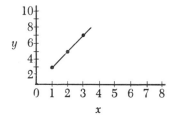

FIGURE 15.1

variable, x is the independent (predictor) variable, c is the constant (equal to the y-intercept—where the line crosses the y axis), and b is the regression coefficient.

Thus a regression coefficient is the slope of the straight line that best describes a set of points in a scatter diagram. (Later we will discuss *curvilinear* regression.) In the remainder of this chapter we will discuss the simple form of linear regression of the sort just described, multiple regression (more than one independent variable) and its cousin, multiple correlation, and briefly touch on some related topics in regression analysis.

Regression analysis helps us to better understand what correlation means, how multiple correlation (the correlation of a dependent variable with the combined effect of two or more independent variables) is computed, and how prediction equations are derived. Correlation is enough when we only want to know the level of association between variables, but when (as in model building) we want to predict one variable from another, we must have the actual equation of the line that describes the relationship: the regression equation.

SIMPLE LINEAR REGRESSION

What criterion should be used to draw the "best" summary line through points on a scatter diagram? In simple cases, one might well approximate the best solution by simply inspecting the diagram visually and drawing a line through it by intuition—the freehand or "black thread" method—although the subjectivity of this procedure makes it impossible to test "goodness." The best line is considered to be the one where squared vertical deviations of the points from the line are minimized.[1]

In least-squares regression, the first two statistics to be computed are the regression coefficient, b, and the constant, c. This is relatively simple, since the constant is a function of x and b, while b itself, the regression coefficient, is intimately related to the correlation coefficient. The correlation coefficient is a standardized regression coefficient, adjusted for the ratio of the standard deviations. The formulas given below are for the hypothesis that x causes or predicts y; if the reverse were hypothesized, the x and y in the formulas could be reversed and a different regression coefficient computed. Thus, every set of data has two usually different regression coefficients, b_{yx} and b_{xy}:

$$b_{yx} = \frac{\Sigma yx - n\bar{x}\bar{y}}{\Sigma(x-\bar{x})^2} = r\frac{s_x}{s_y}$$

$$= \frac{\Sigma xy - n\bar{x}\bar{y}}{\Sigma x^2 - [(\Sigma x)^2/n]} = \text{computational formula for } b$$

$$c_{yx} = \bar{y} - b_{yx}\bar{x}$$

To take an example with actual data shown in Table 15.1, we might hypothesize that unemployment (x) causes labor rioting (y), at least for the 1930s. Computation of the regression equation involves simply listing x and y, their products, and x^2, and finding the sum of these lists. From there it is a short step to substituting the observed values into the regression coefficient

---

[1]Deviations must be squared because there is always a horizontal line such that the sum of the raw deviations is zero.

TABLE 15.1

Year	Unemploy-ment (x)	Riots (y)	xy	x²	y²
1930	8.7%	3	26.1	75.69	9
1931	15.9	28	445.2	252.81	784
1932	23.6	21	495.6	556.96	441
1933	24.9	17	423.3	620.01	289
1934	21.7	37	802.9	470.89	1369
1935	20.1	30	603.0	404.01	900
1936	16.9	31	523.9	285.61	961
1937	14.3	22	314.6	204.49	484
1938	19.0	2	38.0	361.00	4
1939	17.2	9	154.8	295.84	81
$n=10$	$\Sigma x = 182.3$ $\bar{x} = 18.23$	$\Sigma y = 200$ $\bar{y} = 20$	$\Sigma xy = 3827.4$	$\Sigma x^2 = 3527.31$	$y^2 = 5322$

$$b_{yx} = \frac{\Sigma xy - n\bar{x}\bar{y}}{\Sigma x^2 - [(\Sigma x)^2/n]}$$

$$= \frac{3{,}827.40 - 3{,}646.00}{3{,}527.31 - (33{,}233.29/10)} = \frac{181.4}{203.98} = .889$$

$$c = \bar{y} - b_{yx}\bar{x} = 20.0 - .889(18.23) = 3.79$$

$$y = .889x + 3.79$$

equation; when the coefficient is computed it may be used in the second equation to derive the constant. The result is an equation that may be used to predict number of labor riots (y) from unemployment rate (x). For example, in a year in which unemployment was 10 percent we would expect 0.889(10) + 3.79, or approximately thirteen labor riots.

Standard Error of Estimate, s_{yx}

Computing the regression equation is not enough. We still must decide how *confident* we should be about our predictions using the equation. The standard error of estimate, s_{yx}, may be used on normally distributed interval data to answer this question. This statistic equals the root of the sum of the squared differences between observed minus expected y values, divided by $n - 2$:

$$s_{yx} = \sqrt{\frac{\Sigma (y_o - y_e)^2}{n - 2}} \quad \text{(definitional formula)}$$

The observed and expected y values are listed, their differences squared, summed, divided by $n - 2$, and the square root taken, in the definitional formula.

However, this is equivalent to another procedure that seems more complex but is actually easier, based on data already computed in arriving at the linear regression coefficient:

$$s_{yx} = \sqrt{\frac{\Sigma y^2 - [(\Sigma xy)^2 / \Sigma x^2]}{n - 2}} \quad \text{(computational formula)}$$

$$= \sqrt{\frac{5322 - (14{,}648{,}991/3{,}527.31)}{10 - 2}}$$

$$= \sqrt{\frac{5322 - 4153}{8}} = \sqrt{\frac{1169}{8}}$$

$$= 12.1$$

All that is necessary is to determine the sum of y^2, substitute the other values, and work the equation through. In this case the standard error of estimate is 12.1. This means that any y value (predicted number of riots) estimated by the regression equation will be within ± 12.1 of the real value 68 percent of the time, within ± 24.2 about 95 percent of the time.* Because n is small in this case, standard error of estimate is large, and we cannot be very confident about our predictions. At the 95-percent level, our estimate of 13 riots on the basis of 10 percent unemployment would have to be rephrased to 13 riots, ± 24! Clearly these wide confidence limits undermine the validity of our predictions. Because this is always a possibility, standard error of estimate must be given along with regression predictions, a procedure that is also applicable to multiple regression.

THE COEFFICIENTS COMPARED

What is the relationship between correlation, regression, and standard error of estimate?

Comparing purpose, correlation measures the amount (strength) of association; regression provides a prediction equation to estimate the dependent variable from data on the independent variable(s); and standard error of estimate gives us confidence limits on such estimates.

Comparing magnitude, a high absolute correlation coefficient means that a high *proportion* of the dependent variable is explained by the inde-

*Recall the section on the normal distribution and its applications in Chapter 8.

pendent variable; a high absolute regression coefficient means that a *large amount* of change in the dependent variable occurs when the independent variable changes; and a high standard error of estimate means that there is *much error* incurred in predicting the dependent variable from the independent variable.

For simple correlation of two variables, the correlation coefficient is the standardized regression coefficient, *beta* (β). Beta equals the regression coefficient, *b*, adjusted for the ratio of the standard deviations; it also equals the geometric mean of the two regression coefficients:

$$\beta_{yx} = r_{yx} = r_{xy} = b_{yx}(\frac{s_x}{s_y}) = b_{xy}(\frac{s_y}{s_x}) = \sqrt{b_{yx}b_{xy}}$$

Similarly:

$$r^2_{ij.k} = \beta_{ij.k}\,\beta_{ji.k}$$

Note that the regression coefficient, *b*, is the slope of the regression line. Remembering back to high school, the slope is the amount *y* changes for each unit change in *x*. Note also that there is no assurance that the slope would be the same for values of *x* higher or lower than the observed values of *x*; that is, our regression analysis pertains to predictions for the observed range of *x*–*x* and *y* *may* have a different sort of relationship outside this range. The range of *x*, of course, is the values *x* may assume between the lowest and highest observed *x* values inclusive. The regression coefficient, *b*, is the rate of change in *y* over the observed range of *x*.

Finally, note that simple regression makes the same *assumptions* as does product-moment correlation, *r*: interval data, linear relationship, homoscedasticity, common (normal) underlying distribution and variance. We also assume that the error term is uncorrelated with the independent variable and is normally distributed with a mean of zero. (The *error term* is the observed value of *y* minus the value of *y* predicted by the regression equation.)

What happens when assumptions are violated? Moderate violations of the assumptions of homoscedasticity and of normality of error term distribution appear to have little effect in most situations, assuming a reasonably large sample size. Substitution of ordinal for interval data, and other forms of measurement error, do lead to serious consequences for regression analysis estimates, however.[2] Nonlinearity also seriously undermines linear regression analysis, but, as will be discussed later, curvilinear regression procedures exist to handle such data. Since regression estimates may be seriously dis-

[2]George Bohrnstedt and Michael Carter, "Robustness in Regression Analysis," in H. Costner, ed., *Sociological Methodology 1971* (San Francisco: Jossey-Bass, 1971), pp. 118–146.

torted because of measurement error, wherever possible, reliability coefficients pertaining to one's measurement instruments should be presented when regression analysis is undertaken.[3]

MULTIPLE LINEAR REGRESSION AND MULTIPLE CORRELATION

Multiple regression is a way of predicting the dependent variable from two or more independent variables. Multiple correlation is a closely related statistic used in determining the proportion of variance of the dependent variable explained by two or more independent variables. Since computation of these statistics is so laborious that it is always done by computer, only the three-variable (one dependent, two independent) case will be discussed.

If x_1 is the dependent variable (e.g., number of labor riots) and x_2 and x_3 are the independent variables (e.g., unemployment and real wages), then the formula for the multiple regression line looks like this:

$$x_1 = b_{12.3}(x_2) + b_{13.2}(x_3) + c_{1.23}$$

The dependent variable equals the partial regression coefficient of the dependent with the first independent variable, controlling for the second, times the first independent variable, plus a similar quantity for the second independent variable, plus a constant. Computation of the partial regression coefficients involves computation of the simple regression coefficients first, after which the formulas below may be used to arrive at a prediction equation for the dependent variable:

$$b_{12.3} = b_{12} - (b_{13})(b_{32})/[1 - (b_{23})(b_{32})]$$
$$b_{13.2} = b_{13} - (b_{12})(b_{23})/[1 - (b_{32})(b_{23})]$$
$$c_{1.23} = \bar{x}_1 - b_{12.3}(\bar{x}_2) - b_{13.2}(\bar{x}_3)$$

Note that the beta weights can also be computed directly from the correlation matrix by solving a set of simultaneous equations. For the case of two predictor variables, and a dependent variable, y, these equations are:

$$\beta_1 + \beta_2 r_{12} = r_{y1}$$
$$\beta_1 r_{12} + \beta_2 = r_{y2}$$

---

[3]See the section on reliability coefficients in Chapter 12. Other forms of reliability coefficients and suggested method of correcting regression parameters are presented in Bohrnstedt and Carter, *supra*. See also "correction for attenuation," as listed in index.

For the case of three predictor variables, the equations are:

$$\beta_1 + \beta_2 r_{12} + \beta_3 r_{13} = r_{y1}$$

$$\beta_1 r_{12} + \beta_2 + \beta_3 r_{23} = r_{y2}$$

$$\beta_1 r_{13} + \beta_2 r_{23} + \beta_3 = r_{y3}$$

and so on for the case of regressions with more predictor variables.[4] In either method computation is ordinarily done by computer.

The partial b coefficients in such a prediction equation are called *unstandardized regression coefficients*. Because these are not affected by the range of the data, as are correlation coefficients, some have argued for their use as measures of association in explaining change. Their disadvantage, however, is that they cannot be compared to tell the relative importance of each independent variable in predicting the dependent variable. Therefore, *standardized regression coefficients*, also called *beta weights*, are obtained by multiplying the partial b coefficients by the ratio of the standard deviation of the independent variable to the standard deviation of the dependent variable. The formula for the standardized multiple regression line, where the data (x_1, x_2, x_3) are standardized, looks like this:

$$x_1 = b_{12.3} (s_2/s_1)(x_2) + b_{13.2} (s_3/s_1)(x_3) + c_{1.23}$$

The standardized formula will result in the following sort of equation:

$$\text{number of riots } (x_1) = .50 \times \text{unemployment rate } (x_2)$$
$$+ .10 \times \text{real wages } (x_3) + 3.9$$

Beta weights and b coefficients are, of course, partial regression coefficients whenever there are two or more independent variables. Such partial coefficients "hold constant" the effect of other independent variables in computing the regression weight to be assigned to the given independent variable. That is, such coefficients represent the regression of the given variable on the *residual* values of the dependent variable (residuals equal the original values minus the values estimated by the regression equation involving the other independent variables).

The relative importance of the independent (predictor) variables in a regression equation is the ratio of their beta weights. We use the b coefficients to make the actual predictions, but we use the β coefficients to compare the relative power of the independent variables. (See Chapter 18 for an important discussion of b compared to β coefficients.)

[4]See F. Kerlinger and E. Pedhazur, *Multiple Regression in Behavioral Research* (New York: Holt, Rinehart & Winston, 1973), pp. 60–63; and Norman Nie *et al.*, *SPSS: Statistical Package for the Social Sciences*, 2nd ed. (New York: McGraw-Hill, 1975), pp. 328–329.

Note that a relatively high β coefficient does not necessarily mean that the associated variable is the most important. This is because regression analysis assumes a causal model in which all relevant variables have been considered explicitly. That is, the regression coefficient will be relatively large if the associated variable has great apparent effect on the dependent variable, *or if unmeasured independent variables correlated with such a variable have an effect* on the dependent variable.

Multicollinearity

When two or more independent variables in regression analysis are highly correlated (e.g., above .80), the associated regression coefficients will have a large standard error. Since we cannot rely on the regression coefficients in such a situation, it becomes difficult or impossible to make causal inferences. That is, when multicollinearity exists we cannot use the ratio of the β weights to assess the relative importance of the independent variables. When the correlation of two independent variables is perfect (1.0), it is impossible to separate their effects on the dependent variable by regression analysis.

Time series data are particularly susceptible to multicollinearity since many variables increase over time, yielding high intercorrelations. It is also a common problem in research on economic variables. When multicollinearity is present, the researcher may choose to drop one of the highly correlated variables from the analysis (but remember the assumption noted above), or to conduct two or more analyses, dropping different variables to note the effect.[5] Neither approach constitutes a real "solution" to the problem, however; high multicollinearity indicates use of methods other than regression when the researcher's purpose is causal inference (as opposed to simple prediction). When regression analysis is pursued in spite of high multicollinearity, the researcher may be tempted into attaching undue theoretical significance to large variations in regression coefficients that are based on small differences in correlation.[6] In sum, regression analysis assumes that the independent variables are uncorrelated with unmeasured independent variables, not (or at least not highly) correlated with each other, and not themselves influenced by two-way causation with the dependent variable; moreover, these causal relations are assumed to be linear and additive.

[5]For further discussion, see David Huang, *Regression and Econometric Models* (New York: John Wiley & Sons, 1970), pp. 148–158. See also R. Althauser, "Multicollinearity and Non-Additive Regression Models," in H. Blalock, ed., *Causal Models in the Social Sciences* (New York: Aldine, 1971), ch. 26. Althauser advises against the use of regression models in which one independent variable is a multiplicative function of two or more others (e.g., where $x_3 = x_1 x_2$).

[6]See R. Gordon, "Issues in Multiple Regression," *American Journal of Sociology* 73, no. 5 (March 1968): 592–616.

Multiple Correlation

Multiple correlation, R, is the square root of the proportion of the variance in the dependent variable "explained" by the independent variables. Thus it is very closely related to standardized multiple regression. In the three-variable case, R may be computed directly from the formula:

$$R_{1.23} = \sqrt{r_{12}^2 + r_{13.2}^2(1 - r_{12}^2)}$$
$$= \sqrt{r_{12}^2 + r_{13}^2 - 2r_{12}r_{13}r_{23}/1 - r_{23}^2}$$

By using this formula with the data in Table 15.2, it may be shown that unemployment and real wages "explain" about 63.5 percent of the variance in labor rioting between 1927 and 1963. The *significance of multiple correlation*, R, is tested by the F test, where F is the ratio of proportion

TABLE 15.2

	x_1	x_2	x_3
Riots (x_1)	—	.768	−.662
Unemployment (x_2)	.768	—	−.651
Wages (x_3)	−.662	−.651	—

$$R_{1.23}^2 = \frac{r_{12}^2 + r_{13}^2 - 2r_{12}r_{13}r_{23}}{1 - r_{23}^2}$$

$$= \frac{(.768)^2 + (-.662)^2 - 2(.768)(-.662)(-.651)}{1 - (-.651)^2}$$

$$= .635$$

explained (R^2) to proportion not explained ($1 - R^2$). For Table 15.2, for degrees of freedom equal to k (the number of independent variables; 2 in this case) and $n - k - 1$ (where n is the number of units; 36 in this case, one for each year), computation of F is as follows:

$$F = R^2(n - k - 1) / (1 - R^2)k$$
$$= (.635)(36 - 2 - 1) / (.365)(2)$$
$$= 28.71$$

Looking in an F table for k (2) and $n - k - 1$ (33) degrees of freedom, a value of 3.29 is required for significance at the .05 level, and 5.31 for the .01 level. Since our computed F (28.71) is much larger, we may conclude that R is significant at the .01 level.

R-square is often called the coefficient of multiple determination, just as r^2 is termed the coefficient of determination: the percent of variance in the dependent variable "explained" by the independent variable(s).

Significance of b Coefficients

Earlier we discussed the significance of *b* coefficients in simple linear regression, and above we discussed the significance test for multiple correlation. But what is the test of significance for the regression coefficient in multiple regression (i.e., the test for partial regression coefficients and their corresponding β weights)?

The significance of partial *b* can be tested by the *t* test, where *t* equals the *b* coefficient divided by its standard error (normal tables may be consulted instead of *t* tables when *n* is 30 or more):

$$t_{b_i} = b_i / SE_{b_i}$$

where b_i = the *b* coefficient of the *i*th independent variable

SE_{b_i} = the standard error of the *i*th coefficient

$$SE_{b_i} = \sqrt{\frac{\Sigma d^2/(n-k-1)}{\Sigma(x_i - \bar{x})^2 (1 - R_i)^2}}$$

where *d* = the difference between the observed and predicted values of the dependent variable in the regression

d.f. $= n - k - 1$

= degrees of freedom in the *t* test

n = the number of units

k = the number of independent variables

x_i = the scores of the *i*th independent variable

$\bar{x}$ = the mean of the *i*th independent variable

R_i = the multiple correlation using the *i*th variable as a dependent variable and the remaining independent variables as the independent variables.

Note: This procedure is inappropriate when there is pretesting bias (e.g., when the *b* coefficients are from a regression equation from which some variables have been dropped because of their insignificant *t* levels on previous occasions).

Stepwise Regression

Stepwise regression is a method usually used with computers, whereby a regression equation is computed with one independent variable, a second equation is computed with two variables, then a third variable may be added, etc. First a correlation matrix is computed. The computer selects as the first independent variable that variable with the strongest correlation with the dependent variable and computes the first step regression equation. It then computes a partial correlation matrix, using the first independent variable as a control. The second independent variable chosen is that with the strongest partial correlation with the dependent variable, and the second step regression equation is computed. Then another partial correlation matrix is computed using the first two independent variables as controls; the third independent variable chosen is the one with the highest second-order partial correlation with the dependent variable. The fourth and later independent variables are chosen in an analogous manner.

Testing the Significance of Additional Variables in Stepwise Regression
Each step in stepwise regression yields a corresponding coefficient of multiple determination. The step for two independent variables yields the coefficient $R^2_{1.23}$; the step for $(m-1)$ independent variables yields the coefficient $R^2_{1.23...m}$. We may wish to know if adding one or more independent variables significantly increases R^2. For this we use the F test, as in the F test for multiple correlation; note that that is the test for the regression line as a whole):

$$F_{m-k} = \begin{array}{l}\text{the } F \text{ value for the significance of the difference in } R^2 \text{ levels} \\ \text{for the same dependent variable, using } m \text{ and } k \text{ independent} \\ \text{variables respectively, where } m > k.\end{array}$$

$$F_{m-k} = \frac{(R^2_{y.12...m} - R^2_{y.12...k})\,/\,(m-k)}{(1 - R^2_{y.12...m})\,/\,(n-m-1)}$$

where y = the dependent variable and
other notation as before.

d.f. $= (m - k)$ and $(n - m - 1)$

Note that this test is affected by the order in which variables are entered. The F test may show that adding a given independent variable may raise the R^2 level insignificantly, yet were it to be entered in an earlier step an opposite finding might be made. This would happen if the given independent variable were entered after an independent variable with which it was highly correlated.

Relation of Stepwise Regression to Part Correlation   The coefficient of multiple determination, R^2, may be interpreted as the sum of a series of correlation and part correlation coefficients (recall Chapter 12):

$$R^2_{y.12\ldots k} = r^2_{y1} + r^2_y(2.1) + \ldots + r^2_{y(k.12\ldots k-1)}$$

That is, the coefficient of multiple determination equals the coefficient of determination between the first independent variable and the dependent variable, plus the sum of part correlations squared for each successive independent variable, controlling for previously entered independent variables.[7]

Correction for Small Sample Size

As discussed earlier (in Chapter 12), correlation is sensitive to small sample size. Correlation statistics computed on the basis of small samples tend to overstate the degree of association. For small samples (e.g., under 100), the researcher should correct the coefficient of multiple determination by the following formula:[8]

$$\text{corrected } R^2 = R^{*2} = 1 - (1 - R^2)\left(\frac{n-1}{n-m}\right)$$

where R^2 = the uncorrected coefficient
of multiple determination

n = sample size

m = number of variables

Regression Analysis Using Dummy Variables

If a variable is a dichotomy (assumes the values of zero or 1), it may be used in regression analysis even though it is not interval in level (e.g., male = 0, female = 1). A nominal-level variable that assumes more than two values may be treated as a set of dichotomies (e.g., region, where "East" = 0 if the unit is not in the East, 1 if it is; "South" = 0 if the unit is not in the South, 1 if it is; and so on for as many regions as are included in the study). Through use of such *dummy variables*, regression analysis can be extended to nominal-level data. Similarly, ordinal data (scale ranks in a Guttman scale

[7]For further discussion, see F. Kerlinger and E. Pedhazur, *Multiple Regression in Behavioral Research* (New York: Holt, Rinehart, & Winston, 1973), pp. 65–72, 93–97.

[8]See J. P. Guilford, *Fundamental Statistics in Psychology and Education*, 4th ed. (New York: McGraw-Hill, 1965), pp. 400–401. See also the slightly more generalized version in Moredecai Ezekiel and Karl Fox, *Methods of Correlation and Regression Analysis*, 3rd ed. (New York: John Wiley & Sons, 1967), pp. 300–304.

of conservatism, for example) or interval data (age ranges, such as 10–19, 20–29, etc., for example) may be converted to sets of dummy variables as well.

Dummy variable analysis assumes that the dummy variables (e.g., regions, conservatism scale types, age ranges) are mutually exclusive. The dependent variable is assumed to be continuous and interval in level.[9] The dummy variables used are not exhaustive however (i.e., one region, scale rank, or age range must be omitted from the analysis).

The set of dummy variables is not exhaustive because of reasons pertaining to the previous discussion of multicollinearity. If a set of three dummy variables is exhaustive (all units must receive a *1* score on one variable and *0* scores on the others), then when we knoe a unit's score on the first two variables, we have predetermined its score on the third variable. In other words, the third variable would be a linear function of the first two, and this multicollinearity would lead to a high standard error undermining the interpretability of the regression coefficients.

Therefore, if there is one set of dummy variables, we must either drop one to make the set nonexhaustive or set the constant equal to zero. If there are two sets of dummy variables, we must drop one variable from each set or drop one from one set and set the constant equal to zero. For three sets we must drop one from each, or drop two and set the constant at zero; etc. In general, the preferred procedure is to drop one variable from each set. Alternatively, two or more nominal sets can be combined into one (e.g., sex and party identification can be combined into one set: male Republican, male Democrat, male Independent, female Republican, female Democrat, female Independent, from which set we must drop one).[10]

The omitted value in a dummy variable analysis is called the *reference category*. For example, if we are analyzing the nominal variable "party" in terms of dummy variables, such as Republican (0 = unit is not Republican, 1 = unit is Republican), Democrat (0 = is not; 1 = is), and Other, we may choose not to include the "Other" value. In this case "Other" is the reference category. If the party dummy variables are the only ones in the

---

[9]Discriminant analysis may be used for the case of a dichotomous dependent variable. See F. Kort, "Regression Analysis and Discriminant Analysis," *American Political Science Review* 67, no. 2 (June 1973): 555–559. See also William Klecka, "Discriminant Analysis," ch. 23 in Nie *et al.*, *SPSS*. An alternative method is presented in L. Goodman, "A Modified Multiple Regression Approach to the Analysis of Dichotomous Variables," *American Sociological Review* 37, no. 1 (February 1972): 28–46. See also Huang, *Regression and Econometric Models*, pp. 169–171. Dichotomous and larger dependent variable analysis is also treated in H. Theil, "On the Estimation of Relationships Involving Qualitative Variables," *American Journal of Sociology* 76, no. 1 (July 1970): 103–154, and in J. Coleman, "Multivariate Analysis for Attribute Data," in Edgar Borgatta, ed., *Sociological Methodology 1970* (San Francisco: Jossey-Bass, 1970), ch. 13.

[10]See H. Blalock, *Social Statistics*, 2nd ed. (New York: McGraw-Hill, 1972): 498–500; Huang, *Regression and Econometric Models*, pp. 163–169; and D. Suits, "Use of Dummy Variables in Regression Equations," *Journal of the American Statistical Association* 52, no. 280 (December 1957): 548–551.

regression, then the constant (the y intercept) is the estimated mean value of the dependent variable for the reference category, "Other." The regression coefficients for the values Republican and Democrat in the dummy variable analysis thus represent the differences from the mean value associated with the reference category. (That is, where the constant, c, is the estimate for "other," the estimate for Republican is this constant plus the regression coefficient for Republican). Dummy variable analysis therefore includes information on the nature of the "omitted" value.

Multiple Correlation for Ordinal Variables

In addition to the procedure for breaking an ordinal variable into a set of dummy variables for regression analysis,[11] other measures of multiple association exist when we are simply interested in obtaining a measure for ordinal data akin to R^2 (i.e., without also coming up with prediction equations).

***Kendall's Coefficient of Concordance,* W** W is a kind of multiple correlation for *ordinal* data, extending the function of rho and tau (Chapter 11) to more than two variables. The first step in computing W is to present a table of the ranked data, such as shown in Table 15.3, listing a number of

TABLE 15.3

	n	1	2	3	4	5	6
Riot rank		1	2	3	4	5	6
k Unemployment rank		1	4	3	5	2	6
Wage rank		3	2	1	4	5	6
	R_i	5	8	7	13	12	18

$$\Sigma R_i = 63 \qquad \bar{R} = 10.5$$

$$|R_i - \bar{R}| = 5.5 \quad 3.5 \quad 1.5$$
$$2.5 \quad 2.5 \quad 7.5$$

$$(R_i - \bar{R})^2 = 30.25 \quad 12.25 \quad 2.25$$
$$6.25 \quad 6.25 \quad 56.25$$

$$\Sigma (R_i - \bar{R})^2 = 113.5$$

$$W = \frac{\Sigma (R_i - \bar{R})^2}{k^2(n^3 - n)/12}$$

$$= \frac{113.5}{(3)^2(6^3 - 6)/12}$$

$$= 113.5/157.5$$

$$= .721$$

[11]On the debate over "ordinal regression," see K. MacDonald, "Ordinal Regression?" and attached bibliography, in *American Sociological Review* 38, no. 4 (August 1973): 494–495.

variables (k; 3 in the example) down the side and a number of units (n, 6 in the example) across the top.

If there were perfect association among the variables, then the column sums (R) should be $1k$, $2k$, $3k$, . . . , nk, when the dependent variable (riot rank, listed first) is ranked in order. Note that negatively correlated variables, like wages and rioting (rioting goes up as wages go down) must be reverse ranked in this procedure. That is, if perfect association held, the first column would have all 1s, the second all 2s, etc., adding in this case to 3, 6, 9 etc. Kendall's W is a measure of the extent to which this happens.

In computing W, the second step is to add up the columns, find the mean column total (equal to $\Sigma R_i/n$), subtract from each column total the mean column total, square these differences and add them up. This gives the numerator.

Third, the denominator is computed by placing the numbers for k (number of variables; note change in meaning) and n (number of units) in the formula and working it through. W is the second step divided by the third step, equal to .721 in this case.

Note that in the case of *ties*, average ranks may be used; since ties tend to lower W when they are numerous, an adjustment should be made. The adjustment for a large number of tied ranks is to subtract from the denominator in the formula for W an amount equal to

$$\Sigma (t^3 - t)/12$$

In this adjustment, t equals the number of ties at any given value for each row. In the first row, there may be three ties for first place, two ties for fourth place; in the second row, there may be two ties for second place and four ties for fourth place, etc. $-(t^3-t)/12$ is calculated for 3, 2, 2, 4, . . . ties and summed.

The *significance of* W may be tested by chi-square when n is 8 or higher. In this test, chi-square equals:

$$\chi_w^2 = \frac{\Sigma (R_i - \overline{R})^2}{kn(n+1)/12} \quad \text{where d.f.} = n - 1$$

The notation is the same as for the formula for W. If the chi-square value computed by this formula is as large as that in the chi-square table, W is considered significant. When n is 7 or less, a table of critical values of s (113.5 in Table 15.3) is as large as the critical value in the reference table (as it is in the example), then W is considered significant. Also available when n is small is a table of values of the coefficient of concordance significant at various levels, listing how high W must be to be significant at the .05 or .01 levels, for various n and k.

In *computing* the significance for W, the following formula is used:

$$\chi^2 = k\,(n - 1)\,W$$

This is mathematically equivalent to the earlier formula above, though easier to compute when W has already been computed.

CURVILINEAR REGRESSION

Curvilinear regression can easily involve complexities too advanced for treatment in this text, particularly when the researcher wishes to determine the *best*-fitting curve (regression line) for a set of data.[12] However, the procedures for checking to see whether or not certain common curvilinear relationships might not have *more* explanatory power than those uncovered by linear regression are relatively straightforward.

Testing for Curvilinearity

In discussing the correlation ratio (η), eta, we observed that curvilinearity existed to the extent that η^2 exceeded the coefficient of determination, r^2. But how *much* must this difference be for us to conclude that curvilinear regression would yield significantly better results than linear regression? The answer is given by the F test of significance:

$$F_{\eta - r} = \frac{(\eta^2 - r^2) / (k - 2)}{(1 - \eta^2) / (n - k)}$$

with d.f.$_1 = (k - 2)$ where n = the number of units

d.f.$_2 = (n - k)$ k = the number of classes (ranges) of the independent variable used in computing η.

Note that the conventional procedure is to test for curvilinearity of the relationship of the regression of the dependent variable (y) predicted on the basis of the independent variable (x), or "y on x" (b_{yx}). This procedure uses η_{yx}. It would also be possible, however, to test for the curvilinearity of "x on y" (using η_{xy}) if this suited our research purposes.

---

[12]More detailed treatment of curvilinear regression is presented in Kerlinger and Pedhazur, *Multiple Regression in Behavioral Research*, pp. 208–218; Ezekiel and Fox, *Correlation and Regression Analysis*, chs. 14–16; George Snedecor, *Statistical Methods* (Ames, Iowa: Iowa Univ. Press, 1956), ch. 15. These texts list additional, more advanced bibliography.

Fitting a Curve

If one or more independent variables shows a significant curvilinear relationship to the dependent variable in regression analysis, a curved rather than a straight regression will usually be preferable. One method for handling curvilinear relations has already been discussed: the data may be transformed in a curvilinear fashion, as by the use of logarithms (recall Chapter 7).

An alternative method is to treat exponential and other transformations of the independent variable(s) as additional variables in regression analysis. Before discussing this method it is necessary to describe briefly the nature of common curvilinear regression equations.

A *linear* regression equation of the type discussed at the beginning of the chapter takes the form:

$$y = bx + c$$

Here y is the dependent variable, x the independent, b the regression coefficient, and c the constant.

A *quadratic* regression equation describes a curve with one bend and takes the form:

$$y = b_1 x + b_2 x^2 + c$$

Political scientists would rarely use a higher-order regression equation, but for illustrative purposes, the third-degree regression equation, called a *cubic* equation and describing a curve with two bends, takes the following form:

$$y = b_1 x + b_2 x^2 + b_3 x^3 + c$$

The highest possible order of equation is $(k-1)$, where k is the number of values assumed by the independent variable, x (in such an equation, the last term before the constant would be $b_{k-1} x^{k-1}$). Eta-square may be thought of as the coefficient of multiple determination, R^2, for the highest-possible-order curvilinear regression.

How do we know which order polynomial to use? The rule is to use the lowest one that explains all but an insignificant amount of the explainable variance in the dependent variable. Ordinarily this will be the quadratic order polynomial.

Procedure   To compute curvilinear regression, use the observed values of x to generate x^2, x^3, and x^4 (one could keep going on up to x_i , but in practice it is almost always wasted effort to worry about relationships beyond the fourth level and, indeed, it is rare to use anything beyond the second level in political science). We may then treat the data for x^2 as the data for a second variable, the data for x^3 as data for a third variable, and the data for x^4 as those for a fourth variable. Then stepwise multiple regression can be performed on these four "variables," three of which are functions of the first.

For each step in stepwise regression we will get a value for R^2. When R^2 increases only an insignificant amount, we know it is not worth considering the variable added in that step. The significance test for difference of R^2 values was given earlier in this chapter.

For multiple curvilinear regression, we also compute the values for the powers of the additional variables. Since quadratic (second-order) relations are generally the highest considered in political science, we are usually using stepwise regression to find the coefficients in the following equation, in which y is the dependent variable and the x_is are the independent variables:

$$y = b_1 x_1 + b_2 x_1^2 + b_3 x_2 + b_4 x_2^2 + \cdots + b_{2n} x_n^2 + c$$

As before, the values for the second power of the independent variables are treated as additional variables.

Note that in addition to powers of the independent variables, other transforms such as reciprocals or logarithms might have been used.

Note also that the curve, whether linear or curvilinear, will describe a line going through a set of dots representing units of data in a way that maximizes R^2. But such a line will be more reliable for those portions of the curve that go through many dots (are based on many units or observations) than for those portions (usually the extremes) based on few units. The curve has no necessary reliability for portions based on no units (i.e., extrapolations outside the range of the observed data).

As mentioned above a major method for curvilinear regression is to "straighten" the data first by use of a logarithmic transformation. This procedure was discussed in Chapter 7. Edward Tufte has suggested that regressions on logarithmic-adjusted data approximate the following in interpretation: *

$y = \beta x + c$	A unit change in x corresponds to b units change in y
$\log y = \beta (\log x) + c$	A percentage change in x corresponds to b percentage change in y

*Edward R. Tufte, *Data Analysis for Politics and Policy* (Englewood Cliffs, N. J.: Prentice-Hall, 1974), pp. 108–134.

$$\log y = x + c$$

A unit change in x corresponds to b percentage change in y

$$y = (\log x) + c$$

A percentage change in x corresponds to b units change in y

Multicollinearity in Curvilinear Regression   While by definition a given variable, x, and its powers, x^2, x^3, . . . x^n, will not be linearly related, the regression technique outlined above may nonetheless involve some degree of multicollinearity. An alternative procedure is to undertake separate regressions using x, x^2, . . . , x^n each in turn in order to assess the relative effect of each power function on the prediction of the dependent variable. Similarly, separate multiplicative relations, xa, xb, . . . , xz, may be assessed in separate regressions.

This separate assessment gives us an idea of the relative predictive importance of the various power functions of a variable in polynomial regression analysis. To assess whether the addition of a power of a variable to a regression involving other powers of that variable is useful, the F test of difference of coefficients of multiple determination may be used, as discussed earlier. To the extent that there is multicollinearity, however, the relative sizes of the β weights are unreliable guides to the predictive importance of the various power functions of a given variable. That must be assessed through separate regressions as indicated above.[13]

CANONICAL CORRELATION

Multiple regression and multiple correlation involve the relation of several independent variables to one dependent variable. *Canonical correlation* is an extension of multiple correlation to cover the case of the relation of a set of several independent variables to another set of several dependent variables. While its computation is too complex to detail here, its rationale and interpretation can be set forth.

Using least-squares regression techniques, one can construct a composite, that is, a linear function of a given set of variables. Canonical correlation, R_c^2, can be thought of as the coefficient of multiple determination (R^2) between two composites. Paul Horst has extended this to *multiple canonical correlation*, for the relationship among more than two composites.[14]

[13]For further discussion of this method, technique of curvilinear regression, see Kerlinger and Pedhazur, *Multiple Regression in Behavioral Research*, pp. 208 ff.; Snedecor, *Statistical Methods*, pp. 452 ff.

[14]Paul Horst, "Relations Among m Sets of Measures," *Psychometrika* 26 no. 1 (June 1961): 129–149.

When canonical correlation is computed for a set of independent and a set of dependent variables, several R_c^2 coefficients are generated. The first one is the largest, representing the percent of variance shared by the two composites. This coefficient would be the same regardless of which of the two sets of variables is considered the dependent variable set. A second canonical correlation may then be computed for the variance remaining after this first step, yielding a second R_c^2. Similarly, a third coefficient may be computed for the variance remaining after the second step, and so on.

Chi-square procedures exist for testing the significance of each of these successively smaller R_c^2 coefficients. Often only the first coefficient is found to be significant, and in political science it would be very rare to find more than the third such coefficient to be significant.

The first R_c^2 coefficient is interpreted as a coefficient of shared variance of the independent and dependent composites on the basis of the first source of variance in the two sets. The second coefficient has the same interpretation for the second source of variance, and so on. That is, the several canonical correlation coefficients can be interpreted as a series of successively less important dimensions of the relationship of the two sets of variables.

For example, we might seek to compute canonical correlation for a set of measures of political participation (the dependent set: voter turnout by district, number of candidates for given offices, proportion of citizens contributing to campaign costs, etc.) and a set of measures of social characteristics (the independent set: income, education, ethnic composition, etc., for the districts in the study). We might find two significant canonical correlation coefficients, the first equal to .60 and the second equal to .30. These would be interpreted as two dimensions (two sources) of the variation between the two sets of variables. To name these two dimensions we would have to look at the canonical vector loadings (these correspond roughly to the regression coefficients, though they must be interpreted with greater caution). These loadings consist of a list of coefficients for each of the variables for a given R_c^2 coefficient. Just as the β weights can be compared in multiple regression analysis to assess the relative importance of predictor variables, so the vector loadings for standardized data can be compared to assess the relative importance of the different variables for a given R_c^2. By noting which variables are loaded most heavily on the first R_c^2 we are given a basis for labelling this dimension (source) of variance.

Using this reasoning we might find, for instance, that for the first R_c^2, the most heavily loaded independent variables were income and occupational status, and the most heavily loaded dependent variables were campaign contributions and extent of political advertising in local media. On a non-mathematical basis we might infer that this represented the economic dimension of variance. Similarly, we might use the loadings on the second R_c^2 to interpret the second course of variance for the two sets of variables.

Thus canonical correlation enables the researcher to obtain a measure of the degree of association between two sets of variables (usually conceived as an independent and dependent set) and to do so for each of the significant sources of variance for the two sets. Uncovering a small number of sources of variation or dimensions that characterize a large number of variables is a feature that canonical correlation has in common with factor analysis, discussed in the next chapter. Both procedures may be used in many cases. In canonical correlation the researcher specifies in advance which variables belong in which sets, and then seeks to measure the correlation of these sets on one or more dimensions. In factor analysis, in contrast, the researcher does not specify in advance which variables belong in which sets. Factor analysis is a procedure for uncovering the smallest number of underlying dimensions (factors) that explain all but an insignificant amount of the explainable variance of all the variables. In this procedure the factor loadings (which correspond in a loose way to vector loadings in canonical correlation and β weights in multiple regression) may be used as criteria for grouping the variables into sets, with sets corresponding to the factors.[15]

EXERCISE

For the data in the exercise in Chapter 13, compute the multiple correlation of UNION and PARTY as independent variables with COPE as a dependent variable. How does this compare with the correlations computed in the earlier exercise? Use the regression equation to compute the predicted COPE values or the first ten Senators. How close are these predicted values to the observed values? Is R^2 significant? Are both b coefficients significant? If you are doing this exercise on a computer, check to see if a second-order (curvilinear) equation would yield a better fit.

[15]For further reading on canonical correlation, see William Cooley and Paul Lohnes, *Multivariate Procedures for the Behavioral Sciences* (New York: John Wiley & Sons, 1962), ch. 3. Note that this volume contains examples of computer programs for correlation, multiple correlation and regression, and canonical correlation. See also John Van de Geer, *Introduction to Multivariate Analysis for the Social Sciences* (San Francisco: Freeman, 1971), ch. 14.

16 | Factor Analysis

Given a table showing the correlation of each variable with every other, what is the minimum number of underlying factors needed to account for all the relationships? Or, more simply, what variables share a common dimension with what other variables? These questions are treated through factor analysis.[1] The solution to a factor analysis problem yields a table of the sort shown in Table 16.1.

TABLE 16.1

Variable	Factor 1	Factor 2	Factor 3	Communality (h^2)
1	.1346	.4256	.6879*	.6726
2	.0327	−.7807*	.0717	.6158
3	−.4888	−.2762	.6780*	.7750
4	−.3770	−.2403	.7433*	.7526
5	.0968	.8170*	.0036	.6770
6	−.9416*	−.1128	.2431	.9586
7	−.8993*	−.1514	.2833	.9120
8	−.8202*	.0905	.0447	.6831
9	−.6050*	.5256	−.0486	.6448

* Indicates those variables most heavily loaded on a given factor.

For each variable, Table 16.1 shows the degree to which it is loaded* on each factor. For example, variable 2 is loaded −.7807 on factor 2. Table

[1] Compare multidimensional scaling (Chapter 9) and canonical correlation (Chapter 15), either of which may be an alternative to factor analysis.

*"Loaded" is a technical term roughly equivalent to "weighted"—it is discussed later in this chapter.

16.1 also shows the proportion of variance in the variable explained by all the factors together (the communalities; e.g., all three factors explain 61.58 percent of the variance in variable 2). Thus nine variables can be simplified into three underlying factors, a process of simplification that necessarily loses information. Factor 1 is associated with variables 6 to 9, factor 2 is most associated with variables 2 and 5, and factor 3 with variables 1, 3, and 4.

Especially in exploratory studies, the researcher may find it useful to form his or her hypotheses in terms of three underlying factors rather than using a more complicated model based on all of the variables. Factor analysis is sometimes used in causal modelling (discussed in Chapters 5, 13, 18) on the argument that variables grouped together in a model should tend to be loaded on the same underlying factors. Factor analysis is also used in validation of measurement instruments on the assumption that measures of the same concept should be loaded on the same factor.

In any use of factor analysis the crucial question is, of course, what do the factors represent? Factor analysis generates loadings of variables on underlying dimensions (factors), but it does not instruct the researcher as to what label to attach to these dimensions. The researcher must infer what the factors represent from observing which variables are loaded on them. For example, if variables 6 to 9 are education, income, occupational status, and level of political information, he might guess that factor 1 may represent an underlying socioeconomic factor. If variables 2 and 5 are support of larger federal role and Americans for Democratic Action ratings, factor 2 might be called a "liberalness" factor. Clearly, this is all very arbitrary, especially since variables may be loaded (like variable 9) on more than one factor. For this reason many social scientists believe factor analysis is best used in an exploratory way.

Interpreting the Communality, h^2, and the Factor Loadings, a_{ij}

The communality, h^2, is interpreted in a manner analogous to the coefficient of determination, r^2: it is the percent of variance in a given variable explained by all the factors underlying all the variables in the analysis. The communality of the dependent variable is sometimes called the "factor validity coefficient," discussed briefly in Chapter 11. When the communalities are low, the underlying factors do not account for much of the relationships among the variables in the analysis—we fail to conclude that the variables reflect a smaller number of underlying dimensions. Communalities will always be low when the intercorrelations among the variables are low.

Since factor analysis is based on correlation, it shares the same mathematical assumptions. Most forms of factor analysis generate uncorrelated factors.[2] When factors are uncorrelated we may assume that each represents

[2]Uncorrelated factors are generated by orthogonal rotation, correlated factors by oblique rotation. Rotation is discussed later in this chapter.

a distinctly different dimension. For uncorrelated factors, the communality equals the sum of squared factor loadings for a given variable:

$$h_i^2 = a_{i1}^2 + a_{i2}^2 + \bullet \bullet \bullet + a_{in}^2$$

where h_i^2 = the communality of the
ith variable

a_{ij} = the factor loadings of the
ith variable for factors
$j = 1$ through n

The factor loadings can be thought of as regression weights in the following regression equation:

$$z_i = a_{i1}F_1 + a_{i2}F_2 + \bullet \bullet \bullet \bullet + a_{in}F_n$$

where F_j = the factors, 1 through n

z_i = the standardized score on the ith variable

a_{ij} = as before

That is, when units are individuals in a given study, an individual's standardized score on a given variable is predicted by the sum of factor loadings times the individual's score on the several factors. The latter is predicted by the following regression equation: *

$$F_{jk} = a_{1j}z_{1k} + a_{2j}z_{2k} + \bullet \bullet \bullet \bullet + a_{nj}z_{mk}$$

where F_{jk} = the score of the kth individual
on the jth factor

a_{ij} = the factor coefficients of variables
$i = 1$ through m for the jth factor

z_{ik} = the standardized scores of the kth
individual on variables $i = 1$
through m

The researcher is unlikely to use such regression equations, but they illustrate the point that a factor may be thought of as a linear (regression) combination of a set of variables; and a variable may be thought of as a linear combination of a set of factors. More generally, we must remember

---

*Factor coefficients used in computing factor scores are a function of the factor loadings and the intercorrelations.

that factor analysis assumes *linear, additive effects,* as these regression equations indicate. If such assumptions are inappropriate to one's research, factor scores of individuals should not be computed.

Stinchombe's Heuristic Procedure for Interpreting h   When two variables measure the same thing, their correlation will equal the product of the roots of the communalities:

$$r_{ij} = h_i h_j \quad \text{where } r_{ij} = \text{the product-moment correlation of variables } i \text{ and } j$$

$$h_i, h_j \quad = \text{the square roots of the communalities for variables } i \text{ and } j \text{ respectively.}$$

This equality will hold when no other variable in the factor analysis is correlated significantly differently with variable i than with variable j.

We may test to see whether or not two variables seem to measure the same thing with respect to all other variables in the analysis by dividing the matrix of correlations of each variable with every other by the corresponding products of roots of communalities. That is, r_{12} may be divided by $h_1 h_2$; r_{13} may be divided by $h_1 h_3$; and so on for every correlation, r_{ij} divided by $h_i h_j$. Once this is done, we will have a new matrix of corrected correlations.

A pair of variables with a corrected correlation approaching 1 may be said to "measure the same thing" with respect to all the other variables in the analysis. A pair of variables with a corrected correlation approaching zero may be said to measure distinctly different things. A pair of variables with a corrected correlation approaching .707 ($r^2 = .50$) may be said to be maximally muddled; it is likely that such variables, which are neither redundant (measure the same thing) nor independent (measure distinctly unrelated things), will be the ones most interesting in causal modelling.

Stinchombe also points out that $h_i h_i = h_i^2 = $ the communality of variable i may be interpreted as an estimate of the item's reliability (i.e., an estimate of its correlation with another measure just like it, as with a similar item in a retest).[3]

Programming Options in Factor Analysis

Factor analysis is so complex in computation that it is virtually always done by computer, and for this reason the introductory mathematics of factor analysis are not given. Only a further discussion of the terms used in factor

---

[3]Arthur Stinchombe, "A Heuristic Procedure for Interpreting Factor Analysis," *American Sociological Review* 36, no. 6 (December 1971): 1080–1084.

analysis will be presented here, with special reference to decisions the researcher must make in selecting which factor analysis computer program to use for his or her data.

Nature of Analysis

The first decision involves the nature of the analysis undertaken. Typically the researcher is interested in uncovering a few (2 to 10) factors that underlie several (10 to 50) variables, with data based on many (100 to 1000) people. For example, what are the factors that underlie a set of 50 votes by 100 senators? This is known as the *R-technique*. Alternatively, the researcher might be interested in uncovering a few (2 to 10) factors that unite several persons (usually 10 to 50), with data based on many variables. For example, what are the factors uniting factions of Senate Democrats, based on data for at least 100 votes? This is called the *Q-technique*, and will enable identification of subgroups of like senators as measured by the 100 votes.

Thus the R-technique is based on the correlation of measures or variables for a population of persons on one occasion. The Q-technique is based on the correlation of persons, for a population of measures on one occasion. Two less used techniques remain: the P-technique and the O-technique. The P-technique is based on the correlation of measures for a population (a number) of occasions for one person. The P-technique might be used, for example, to study the changing composition of political indicators as measures over time. The *O-technique* is less common, involving the correlation of occasions for a population of measures for one person. The O-technique could be used to group occasions according to the ways they affect performance on a series of political measures or indicators as applied to one senator, for example.

Finally, the S-technique and the T-technique round out the logical possibilities. The *S-technique* is based on the correlation of persons for a number (population) of occasions on one measure. It addresses itself to a question of the sort, "Which groups of senators are homogeneous over time with regard to a particular measure, as a measure of support for larger federal role?" The *T-technique* involves the correlation of occasions for a population of persons for one measure. It is relevant to a question of the sort, "How may occasions be grouped according to how they, for a particular measure such as support for larger federal role, are associated with different cluster patterns of senators?"

The R-technique is by far the most common; O-, P-, S-, and T-techniques are rarely used in political science, although not because of methodological shortcomings. Which technique is used is solely a matter of what the researcher's question is. Whichever is chosen, the first step in factor analysis is to generate a correlation matrix of each variable with every other variable

(*R*-technique), each person with every other person (*Q*-technique), or whatever correlation is appropriate. Table 16.2 summarizes the various factor analysis techniques and their uses.

TABLE 16.2

Technique	Correlation of	For a Population of	Holding Constant
O	occasions	measures	one person
P	measures	occasions	one person
Q	persons	measures	one occasion
*R**	measures	persons	one occasion
S	persons	occasions	one measure
T	occasions	persons	one measure

*The *R*-technique is the one most commonly used in political science. It is particularly helpful in validating scale items. See Kent Smith, "Forming Composite Scales and Estimating Their Validity Through Factor Analysis," *Social Forces* 53, no. 2 (December 1974): 168=180.

Method of Extracting the Factors

Once the correlation matrix has been constructed, there remains the central question, "By what criteria are the factors to be extracted?" The *cluster method* is the simplest approach, akin to the "freehand method" in regression analysis, in that it does not result in a unique factor solution.

Assuming the *R*-technique[4] with a correlation of variables, the researcher begins with the two variables most correlated with each other and computes their *B* coefficient. *B* equals the ratio of the average of the correlations of each variable within the cluster with every other variable in the cluster $(\bar{G})$, to the average correlation of variables not in the cluster $(\bar{T})$, or $\bar{B} = \bar{G}/\bar{T}$. The first two variables are assumed to belong to the same factor. A third variable is selected, the one for which the sum of its correlations with each of the two variables already in the cluster is highest. The *B* coefficient is again computed, and if the addition of the third variable does not significantly lower the *B* coefficient, it too is considered to belong to the factor. This process is continued until addition of a variable significantly lowers the *B* coefficient. Then the process is repeated to extract a second factor, using the remaining variables not clustered in the first factor. The process is repeated for a third, fourth, or however many factors may be extracted.

The *centroid method* is more advanced, although it too fails to yield a unique solution for the minimum number of factors that can explain the correlation matrix. It is considered a fair approximation to the more accurate principal-components method discussed below, and is computationally far easier. One starts with the correlation matrix (*step 1*), using whatever kind

[4]The *R*-technique is assumed throughout the remainder of the discussion.

of correlation is appropriate to the nature of the analysis. Here, the R-technique is assumed. *Step 2* is simply to add up the correlations in each column. *Step 3* notes the highest correlation in each column, and in *step 4* this is added to the column sum of correlations. In *step 5*, m is computed, where m

TABLE 16.3 Centroid Method

Correlation Matrix

Step	Variable	1	2	3	4	5	
	1	—	.00	.20	.00	.40	
	2	.00	—	.30	.40	.60	
1	3	.20	.30	—	.00	.80	
	4	.00	.40	.00	—	.00	
	5	.40	.60	.80	.00	—	
2	$\Sigma r=$	.60	1.3	1.3	.40	1.8	
3	$r_{max}=$	.40	.6	.8	.40	.8	
4	$\Sigma r_t =$	1.0	1.9	2.1	.80	1.6	$\Sigma(\Sigma r_t)=7.4$
5	$m=1/\sqrt{\Sigma(\Sigma r_t)}=1/\sqrt{7.4}=.368$						
6	$m\Sigma r_t=$	.37	.70	.77	.29	.59	

		1	2	3	4	5	
	1 (.37)	—	−.26	−.08	−.11	.18	
	2 (.70)	−.26	—	−.24	−.20	−.19	First
7	3 (.77)	−.08	−.24	—	−.22	.35	Unreflected
	4 (.29)	−.11	.20	−.22	—	−.17	Residual
	5 (.59)	.18	.19	.35	−.17	—	Matrix

First Unreflected Residual Matrix

	Variable	1	2*	3	4*	5	
	1	—	−.26	−.08	−.11	.18	
	2*	−.26	—	−.24	.20	.19	
8	3	−.08	−.24	—	−.22	.35	
	4*	−.11	.20	−.22	—	−.17	
	5	.18	.19	.35	−.17	—	
9	$\Sigma r=$	−.27	−.11	−.19	−.30	.55	$\Sigma(\Sigma r)=-.32$
10	col. 4 reflected=	−.05	−.51	.25	.30*	.89	
11	col. 2 reflected=	.47	.51*	.73	.70	.51	

First Reflected Residual Matrix

	Variable	1	2	3	4	5	
	1	—	.26	−.08	.11	.18	
12	2	.26	—	.24	.20	−.19	
	3	−.08	.24	—	.22	.35	
	4	.11	.20	.22	—	.17	
	5	.18	−.19	.35	.17	—	
13	$\Sigma r=$	.47	.51	.73	.70	.51	
14	$r_{max}=$	.26	.26	.35	.22	.35	
15	$r_t=$	.73	.77	1.08	.99	.86	$\Sigma(\Sigma r_t)=4.43$
16	$m=1/\sqrt{\Sigma(\Sigma r_t)}=1/\sqrt{4.43}=.475$						
17	$m\Sigma r_t=$	.35	−.37	.51	−.47	.41	

is the reciprocal of the square root of the total of the sums computed in step 4. The value m is multiplied by each of the step 4 sums to give the values in *step 6*. These are the loadings of each variable on the first factor. Variable 1, for instance, has an unrotated loading of 0.37 on the first factor (rotation is discussed below).

In *step 7* the first residual correlation matrix is computed. Computing residuals is based on the fact that a correlation between variable A and variable B equals the factor loading of A on factor 1 times the loading of B on factor 1, plus the loading of A on factor 2 times B's loading on factor 2, . . . plus the factor loading of A on factor n, times the loading of B on factor n. In step 7, the entries in the first unreflected residual correlation matrix are obtained by multiplying the respective row and column factor loadings and subtracting that result from the original cell entry. For example, the entry in column 1, row 2 is obtained by multiplying the column loading (.37) times the row variable loading (.70), and subtracting the result (.26) from the original entry (.00), giving a residual loading of $-.26$.

Step 8 is simply to recopy these unreflected residual entries onto a new table. *Step 9* (as in step 2) is to add up the column residual correlations. If any of the sums in step 9 are negative, which is usually the case, it is necessary to *reflect* the residual matrix. If all are positive, the researcher can skip to step 14. *Reflection* is begun in *step 10* by taking the largest negative sum in step 9 ($-.30$, in column 4) and entering it as a positive value under the line for step 10. An asterisk is placed beside that column and row number to indicate its reflection. The other entries in step 10 are derived by doubling that row's entry for each column, changing its sign and adding it to the column sum computed in step 9. For example, the reflected value for the first column equals the unreflected residual entry ($-.11$), doubled ($-.22$), with its sign changed (.22), and added to the sum computed in step 9 $[.22 + (-.27) = -.05]$.

If any of the final entries in step 10 are negative, the process is repeated. *Step 11* is such a repetition, done for the highest negative value in step 10, namely the $-.51$ entry in column 2. Performed exactly as in step 10, this step results in sums that are all positive. Sometimes many repetitions are necessary, even requiring reflection of a column more than one time. Note that the one exception in repetitions of step 10 is that signs are *not* reversed before adding the doubled value for entries in columns that have previously been reflected once (or three or any odd number of times). In step 11, for example, the .20 entry in the second row, fourth column is left positive after it is doubled; it is then added to the .30 sum in step 10, to give a step 11 entry of .70.

Step 12 is to copy the first reflected residual correlation matrix. In absolute terms, the reflected matrix has exactly the same entries as the unreflected matrix. The difference is that it has different signs. The signs in the unreflected matrix (step 8) are reversed *if* they

1. Are in rows that have been reflected (and have an asterisk) but in columns that have *not* been reflected (and therefore do not have an asterisk),
2. Or, vice versa, are in reflected columns but not in reflected rows.

Steps 13 through *16* repeat steps 2 through 5, this time using the reflected residual matrix instead of the original correlation matrix. *Step 17* repeats step 6, giving the absolute values of the factor loadings of each variable on the *second* factor. The sign given each of these loadings depends on the number of times the variable column has been reflected:

1. If it was reflected once or an odd number of times, its sign is the reverse of its sign in the previous factor.
2. If it was not reflected or was reflected an even number of times, its sign remains the same as in the previous factor.

Further steps may be undertaken in a similar fashion to compute the second unreflected residual matrix, reflect it, and get the factor loadings for the third factor, and so on. The *communality*, h^2, for each variable equals the sum of the squared loadings of that variable on all the factors.

Thus, steps 6 and 17 in Table 16.3 give factor loadings which are interpreted as discussed at the beginning of the chapter, *after* these scores are rotated. Rotation is discussed below.

The *principal-components* or *principal-factor method* is more complicated than the centroid method, but is used in most computer programs for factor analysis because it gives a unique least-squares solution. That is, the principal-components (also called *principal-axis*) method first extracts the factor that accounts for the greatest variance, then extracts the factor accounting for the second greatest variance, and so on. The centroid method may well give more factors than are necessary to account for a given percentage of the variance. Several other methods of extracting factors are available, but these are rarely used in political science.[5]

Other Options Principal-component factor solutions start with a correlation matrix having unities (1s) on the main diagonal. The principal-factor solution starts with a correlation matrix having estimates of the

---

[5]A concise explanation of the principal-components method is found in Karl Schuessler, *Analyzing Social Data* (Boston: Houghton Mifflin, 1971), pp. 107–118. For a more detailed treatment see Benjamin Fruchter, *Introduction to Factor Analysis* (Princeton, N. J.: Van Nostrand, 1954), ch. 6.

communalities of each variable on the main diagonal. The former is appropriate if we can assume no measurement error; when, as is almost always the case, the researcher assumes measurement error, the latter is appropriate.

There are three common methods of estimating the communalities in a principal-factor solution: (1) use the highest column correlation (r) in place of the main diagonal unity (1) for that column; (2) use the coefficient of multiple determination (R^2) of the column variable as the dependent variable correlated with all the other variables as independent variables; or (3) use the principal-component method to generate communalities (h^2), then substitute these for the unities on the main diagonal and compute the factors (and communalities) again, substitute *these* communalities for the first communalities, and keep repeating the process till the communalities no longer change (this is called *principal factoring by iteration*). In general, method 3 is preferable to method 2, and method 2 is preferable to method 1.

Rao's Canonical Factoring   Some computer programs, such as the Statistical Package for the Social Sciences (SPSS), also provide other factoring options.[6] Though not yet much used in political science, one can be briefly mentioned here. *Canonical factoring* assumes the data used to compute the original correlations matrix are based on a random sample. This assumption leads to the expectation of sampling error, and to significance tests of difference between the observed data and the data as predicted by a factor solution. That is, canonical factoring computes the least number of factors that yield predictions not significantly different from the observed data. In this method the significance level (e.g., .05) is set arbitrarily by the researcher.

Number of Factors to Extract

Most factor analysis computer programs give the researcher some discretion over the number of factors to be computed. If a principal-components or principal-factors method is used, the later factors computed will account for less and less of the variance. Consequently, they will become more and more difficult to interpret. One procedure is to program the computer to compute a preselected number of factors (e.g., 5) on the assumption that factors beyond this number will be uninteresting.

A second common option programs the computer to stop computing factors when the next factor to be computed would add less than x^2 to the communalities (h^2). In this procedure, the researcher specifies x according to his or her particular research needs.

[6]N. Nie *et al. SPSS: Statistical Package for the Social Sciences 2nd Ed.* (New York: McGraw- Hill, 1975), ch. 24.

A third common method programs the computer to stop computing factors when the next factor to be computed would result in an *eigenvalue* less than an amount specified by the researcher (e.g., less than 1.0). An eigenvalue is the amount of variance explained by the given factor. The *trace* is the sum of eigenvalues (including eigenvalues for factors that fell below the criterion cutoff of 1.0, or whatever level was used) and represents the sum of variances explained by all factors. The *cumulative percent of trace* is the percent of the variance explained by the given factor plus any previously computed factor. A specified change in the cumulative percent of trace would also appear to be an appropriate cutoff criterion for specifying the number of factors to be computed.

Other less common criteria are the following. The *Tucker's phi* criterion is based on the significance of the decrease in the cell entries of reflected residual matrices. Using the notation given in the centroid method example, phi is $\Sigma \, (\Sigma r_i)$ for the $(n + 1)$th reflected residual matrix divided by the corresponding statistic for the nth residual matrix; if this phi coefficient is larger than $(N - 1)/(N + 1)$, where N is the number of variables, then there are at least n significant factors.

Coomb's Criterion is applicable only where the original correlation matrix contains no negative entries significantly different from zero. When the number of negative entries remaining in a residual table after reflection is not significantly different from the corresponding value in a table of critical values of Coomb's criterion, then enough factors have been extracted.

Humphrey's Rule is based on the significance of correlation. The factor is considered not significant unless the product of the two highest factor loadings exceeds two standard errors of a zero correlation coefficient.

While difficult to generalize, it would appear that the eigenvalue criterion is the one most commonly used in political science.

Regardless of the criterion chosen, the number of factors computed should be less than the least number of factors necessary to explain the inter-correlations among n variables, where these correlations have been set arbitrarily. This number, which we shall label f_{max}, can be computed by the following formula:

$$f_{max} = \frac{(2n + 1) - \sqrt{8n + 1}}{2}$$

where n = the number of variables

(In applying this formula, one should always round upward.) Thus, 3 variables can be explained by 1 factor even when the correlations are arbitrary (don't constrain each other); 4 variables by 2 factors; 5 or 6 variables by 3 factors; 7 variables by 4 factors; 8 variables by 5 factors; 9 or

10 variables by 6 factors; 25 variables by 19 factors; 50 variables by 41 factors; and 100 variables by 87 factors. From this it can be seen that factor analysis, which ordinarily generates no more than a dozen factors at most, is most different from what is possible even on the basis of arbitrary correlations when the number of variables is large.[7]

Method of Rotation

If the research involves n factors describing a number of variables, then one may conceive of the factors as vectors in n-dimensional space. Factor loadings describe the location of the variables with respect to these vectors, all of which meet at the origin of the n-dimensional coordinate system formed by the factors. Thus the factor vectors can be thought of as coordinate axes, and as such may be rotated about the origin. Such rotation will change the factor loadings, but the new loadings will be equivalent: both will generate the same correlation matrix. The new, rotated factor loadings, though mathematically equivalent, may be more interpretable. For example, rotation may maximize the loadings of some variables and minimize others, helping us to more clearly identify variables with factors.

The mathematics of factor rotation is beyond the scope of an introductory work, but a few terms may be set forth. First, the researcher may decide whether he or she wants orthogonal or oblique rotation. *Orthogonal rotation* has the advantage that it leaves each of the reference axes perpendicular (orthogonal) to one another, making each of the factors independent of one another. Thus the researcher can be sure that each factor underlying a set of variables is a completely different factor. *Oblique rotation* does not necessarily leave the axes perpendicular, and hence the factors are unlikely to be mutually independent. It has an advantage, however, in that the factors can account for more of the variance.

The choice between orthogonal and oblique rotation depends upon the researcher's purpose. If the researcher hypothesizes that his or her measures reflect two or more *unrelated* dimensions, then orthogonal rotation is appropriate—and the researcher will have the advantage that because the factors are assumed to be unrelated, hence distinct from each other, they will be easier to interpret.

If, however, the researcher assumes that his or her data reflect two or more *related* (correlated) dimensions, then oblique rotation is appropriate. But because the factors can no longer be assumed to be distinct from one another, the factor loadings will be difficult to interpret. Therefore, when oblique rotation is used it is common to undertake *second-order factor analysis*. Second-order factor analysis is simply the factor analysis of the

[7]Harry Harman, *Modern Factor Analysis*, 2nd ed. (Chicago: Univ. of Chicago Press, 1967), pp. 70–71.

matrix of intercorrelations among a set of oblique factors. It results in information on the degree to which oblique factors seem to reflect similar or different underlying dimensions. Such second-order factors are sometimes called "general factors," while first-order factors are called "primary factors." Ordinarily, second-order factoring is orthogonal. In sum, while oblique rotation prevents us from assuming that the factors we find are distinct from one another, second-order factor analysis helps us understand how the factors are similar and how they are different.

If orthogonal rotation is selected, the *varimax method* is usually used. This method rotates the reference axes to maximize the variance of the squared factor loadings for each factor. The result is that each factor tends to be identified clearly with some variables and clearly not with others; any given variable will be easier to be judged as loaded or not loaded on a given factor. Thus factors are more easily labelled since it will be clearer what variables are associated with them. The *quartimax* method maximizes the sum of factor loadings to the fourth power, with the effect that, except for a first factor on which many variables may be highly loaded (called a "general factor"), each variable will tend to be loaded on just one factor. *Biquartimax* or *equimax* solutions may be thought of as giving equal weight to the two criteria. Some programs also allow the researcher to specify an unequal weight, as in *orthomax-c*, where "c" is the percent of weight specified to be attached to the quartimax criterion, the remainder going to the varimax criterion.

If the rotation chosen is oblique, analogous methods exist. One set of methods is those using an *oblimin* criterion, which takes three forms: covarimin, quartimin, and biquartimin. *Covarimin* solutions tend to be the least oblique, *quartimin* the most. Therefore political scientists usually use *biquartimin* solutions, a standard option on most computer programs. Biquartimin solutions combine covarimin and quartimin considerations and are thought to avoid bias toward overorthogonality or overobliqueness when oblique rotation is desired. A second common method maximizes the kurtosis (peakedness) of a function of the frequency distribution of rotated factor loadings. This method, called the *oblimax* method, results in each variable tending to be heavily loaded on one factor only.

Graphic Output

Because the factors may be thought of as coordinate axes and because the factor loadings describe the position of variables in relation to these axes, factor analysis results can be presented in the form of a graph, rather than a table such as Table 16.1. There will be one such graph for each pair of dimensions (factors) in the analysis. For Factors 1 and 2 in Table 16.1, graphical output would look like Figure 16.1. While such a format provides no additional information in comparison with the conventional table output,

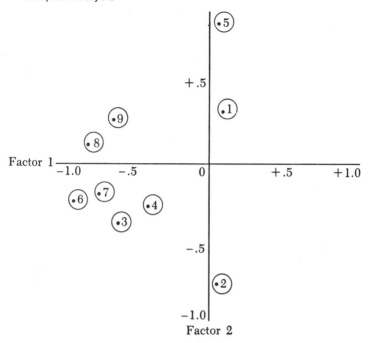

FIGURE 16.1   Graphical Presentation of Factor Loadings for
Variables 1 Through 9 (Circled) in Table 16.1

inspection of such graphs can give the researcher a quick insight into the relation between the factors and the variables loaded on them, the clustering of related variables, and the correlation of factors.

Nominal and Ordinal Data

Factor analysis is normally said to require interval-level data. The assumptions behind the correlation matrix on which factor analysis is built should be met, notably linearity and homoscedasticity of relationship. Pearsonian product-moment correlation is typically used on normally distributed metric data gathered by enumeration or random sample, although other product-moment correlation statistics may be used instead. Biserial or rank-difference correlations may be used as estimates of product-moment coefficients, if necessary. The phi coefficient should not be used, nor should different types of coefficients be mixed in a single correlation matrix. Because of this last restriction, dichotomous variables should not be mixed with continuous variables, and there is thus a limitation on the types of variables that can be placed together in factor analysis. On the other hand, it is unclear just how much conclusions are likely to be in error if these and other restrictions mentioned earlier are not met.[8] A linear, additive model requiring interval data is assumed throughout; where coefficients for nonmetric data are used, these are assumed to approximate the Pearsonian correlation were one able to measure the metric scale assumed to underlie one's nominal or ordinal data. Such an assumption must be justified on a nontechnical basis. Where such an assumption is made, the findings must be regarded as exploratory rather than conclusive.

RELATED TECHNIQUES

Multiple Regression of Factor Scores

In ordinary multiple regression analysis the researcher seeks to predict a dependent variable (or set of dependent variables in canonical correlation) on the basis of several independent variables which have been measured. By applying factor analysis to a large set of such measures, the researcher can compute a smaller number of underlying factors. These factors can be regarded as the "true" underlying variables for which the measures are only indicators. By computing the factor scores of the individuals in the study, the researcher can generate "new" data: the scores of each individual on each underlying variable (i.e., on each factor).[9] These scores can then be used as the data in regression analysis (or canonical correlation) and a dependent variable (or factor) can be predicted on the basis of several underlying (factor) variables. The coefficient of multiple determination, R^2, can be used to assess the explanatory power of the independent variables, and the beta weights to assess the relative importance one to the other.

This procedure introduces causal (asymmetric) considerations into factor analysis, which is otherwise essentially correlative in function. It is particularly appropriate when the assumptions of regression and factor analysis have been met, and when there is reason to think that the variables constructed by factor analysis will be more meaningful than the initial measures obtained by the researcher. Where a higher R^2 is obtained by multiple regression of factor scores than by multiple regression of initial scores, the variables that the latter are presumed to represent may stand in need of reconceptualization. That is, since variables constructed a posteriori by

---

[8]These technical requirements are frequently not determinants in social science decisions to use factor analysis. For a study treating rank data as interval and combining continuous with dichotomous variables in factor analysis, see R. Artz, R. Curtis, D. Fairbank, and E. Jackson, "Community Rank Stratification: A Factor Analysis," *American Sociological Review* 36, no. 6 (December 1971): 985–1002.

[9]On computing factor scores, see Nie *et al. SSPS*, p. 487; Harman, *Modern Factor Analysis*, pp. 70–71.

factor analysis explain the dependent variable(s) better than measures conceptualized and operationalized *a priori*, there is some indication that new conceptualizations more consistent with factor analysis results may be more powerful.

Smallest Space Analysis

Smallest space analysis is an alternative to factor analysis that can be used with ordinal data. SSA is a procedure for reducing n-space to m-space, where n is the number of initial variables and m is the smaller number of dimensions in a smallest-space solution. SSA solutions are ordinarily presented graphically, as in Figure 16.2.[10] Smallest space analysis starts with a

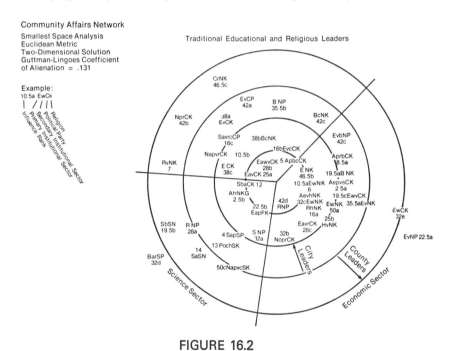

FIGURE 16.2

matrix of "distance coefficients" measuring the distance between objects. For example, the distance coefficients for a set of variables might be the set of correlation coefficients with their signs reversed (path coefficients may be used, as may sociometric or subjective estimates; signs are reversed to measure difference rather than similarity).

[10]James Lingoes, "A General Survey of the Guttman-Lingoes Nonmetric Program," in R. Shepard, K. Romney, and S. Nerlove, eds., *Multidimensional Scaling*, (New York: Seminar Press, 1972): 1: 54. Lingoes describes several variants of SSA programs (pp. 52–60).

SSA procedures then seek monotonic transformations of the data which preserve the rank order relations of distance among the variables while at the same time reducing the number of dimensions necessary to reproduce this information. Thus, SSA analysis can be used on metric data, but only information on the ordinal relations among metric measures is retained in the analysis.

SSA procedures involve two variants: the distance model and the vector model. The distance model maps distance ranks into the ranks of distance coefficients; the vector model maps ranks of scalar products into ranks of similarity indices, indirectly solving for communalities. The vector model most closely approximates ordinary factor analysis.

Smallest space analysis is a version of multidimensional scaling, discussed earlier. It determines the smallest space (number of dimensions) that can account for the ordinal variation in a set of data. The SSA solution is achieved through least-squares techniques, using the original measure of distance as one coordinate and the corresponding Euclidian distance in smallest space as the other dimension.[11] Scatter about this regression line can be measured by the correlation coefficient or the coefficient of alienation, K. K equals the square root of $(1 - r^2)$. To the extent K approaches zero, the original rank information can be predicted from distances in smallest space.[12] Therefore, the *coefficient of alienation* is a measure of the value of SSA. No convention has yet been set for how low K must be for SSA to be considered "good enough," but most published SSA-based articles have reported a K of .2 or less.

Smallest space analysis can be used to identify clusters of objects (e.g., individuals) in an n-space of variables, *or* to represent clusters of variables in an n-space of individuals. (This is analogous to the Q- and R-techniques, respectively, in factor analysis.) In Figure 16.2, data on community decision-making elites was presented by Edward Laumann and Franz Pappi.[13] In this diagram, data on five variables (influence rank, primary and secondary institutional sector, political party, and religion) are presented in two dimensions, with a coefficient of alienation of 0.131. Without needing to understand the authors' notation for these five variables, we may note that: (1) each set of letters and a number represents an individual—the diagram illustrates the clustering of individuals; (2) one can draw in concentric rings indicating degrees of centrality on the dimensions underlying the five variables (in this study, the authors assumed that centrality accompanied inte-

[11]See K. Bailey, "Polythetic Reduction of Monothetic Property Space," in H. Costner, ed., *Sociological Methodology 1972* (San Francisco: Jossey-Bass, 1972), p. 102.

[12]In most programs, a coefficient of monotonicity, analogous but not identical to r, is substituted for r in computing K. See L. Guttman, "A General Nonmetric Technique for Finding the Smallest Coordinate Space for a Configuration of Points," *Psychometrika* 33 (December 1968): 478–479.

[13]E. Laumann and F. Pappi, "New Directions in the Study of Community Elites," *American Sociological Review* 38, no. 2 (April 1973): 221.

grative importance in the network studied); and (3) one can draw radiating lines from the origin delimiting sectors—sectors will encompass individuals of varying degrees of centrality on the dimensions underlying the five variables, but who share a common direction with relation to the origin because they share some common trait, in this case occupational traits (science, economy, education and religion sectors). Thus smallest-space analysis offers a graphic method of analyzing and presenting information on the relationship of objects along certain underlying dimensions, analogous to Q-technique factor analysis graphically displayed, but without requiring many of the assumptions of that technique, notably interval-level data.

Other Techniques

Finally, it should be noted that Kruskal and Shepard have put forward a method on *nonmetric linear factor analysis*[14] and Carroll has described *polynomial factor analysis*, which is a nonlinear method of factor analysis.[15] While both are beyond the scope of the present text and are not yet much used in political science, the relaxed data requirements each involve suggest they will be increasingly popular in the future.

EXERCISE

Read and evaluate the usefulness of factor analysis in Jack E. Vincent, "Predicting Voting Patterns in the General Assembly," in *American Political Science Review* 65, no. 2 (June 1971): 471–498.

[14]See R. Shepard, "Metric Structures in Ordinal Data," in *Journal of Mathematical Psychology* 3 (1966): 287–315.
[15]See J. Carroll, "Polynomial Factor Analysis," *Proceedings of the American Psychological Association* 4 (1969): 103–104.

17	# Analysis of Time Series

Explanatory models in political science commonly involve theories of change over time.[1] Some of the techniques appropriate to analysis of time series have already been mentioned, such as panel studies and cohort analysis (Chapter 7) and regression (Chapter 15). This chapter discusses these techniques in greater detail and brings attention to other, related methods which are also helpful in analyzing political and social trends.

PANEL STUDIES

Panel studies involve measurements (e.g., attitude surveys of individuals) of the same subjects (i.e., the same individuals) at two or more points in time. The high cost of repeated measurements of a sample of individuals who may be difficult to reinterview tends to make this technique relatively rare in political science. Rather, it is popular in small-group experimental studies in which the researcher has some confidence in the availability of the subjects over time. Where panel studies are feasible, they yield more information than the alternative of using different subjects in the different points in time.

Table 17.1 illustrates some of the advantages of panel analysis. In this table, fictional data are presented for a sample of 1,000 individuals, taken at two points in time (before and after the 1972 election campaign and vote). For simplicity, only two variables are analyzed, both of which are dichotomies: party and candidate preference. Panel analysis can be extended to more than two points in time, variables, and values per variable, however.

[1] Cf. Eric Nordlinger, "Political Development: Time Sequences and Rates of Change," in *World Politics* 20 (April 1968): 494–520.

TABLE 17.1

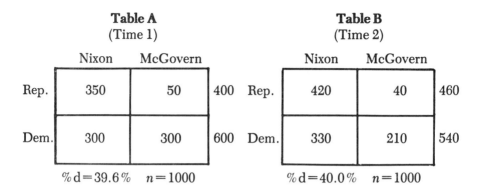

Table A
(Time 1)

	Nixon	McGovern	
Rep.	350	50	400
Dem.	300	300	600

%d=39.6%   n=1000

Table B
(Time 2)

	Nixon	McGovern	
Rep.	420	40	460
Dem.	330	210	540

%d=40.0%   n=1000

Table C
Time 2

		RN	RM	DN	DM	
	RN	350	0	0	0	350
	RM	10*	40	0	0*	50
Time 1	DN	40*	0	250	10*	300
	DM	20	0	80	200	300
		420	40	330	210	n=1000

Tables A and B represent the kind of information about the relation of party and candidate preference that we would obtain if we did *not* use panel data, but instead simply had two different samples of 1,000 persons each. On the basis of these tables we would note that there is a moderately strong relationship between the two variables, that the strength of this relationship as measured by percent difference did not change over time, and there was a net switch of 60 persons from the Democratic to the Republican Party and a net switch of 100 supporters from McGovern to Nixon. We might be tempted to infer that the 1972 election affected the attitudes of 10 percent of our population (100 persons), and of this 10 percent, some 60 percent (60 persons) changed party identification to conform to their new preferences.

Table C, which presents hypothetical panel data on the same subject, illustrates the danger of such inferences. In this table, all off-diagonal entries represent *turnover*—subjects who shifted values on one or both variables over time. Here we find that the election corresponds to an effect on 180 persons, 18 percent of the population, even though the *net effects* are the same as in Tables A and B. Thus, one important use of panel analysis is to understand turnover as well as net effect over time. For example, we can understand that the 60 persons who changed party identification were composed of two-thirds Nixon supporters who changed party and one-third former McGovern supporters who changed both preference and party.

This suggests a second important use of panel studies: they enable the identification of subjects who change over time. This gives the researcher the opportunity to conduct a more detailed analysis of a particularly interesting segment of the sample, perhaps through additional follow-up interviews.

Third, panel data enables the researcher to assess the relative effect of the two variables, using the ideas of role theory and cognitive dissonance discussed in Chapter 2. Table C of Table 17.1 shows that in Time 1 there were 350 individuals who held value-inconsistent beliefs: 50 Republicans for McGovern, and 300 Democrats for Nixon. Role theory predicts a strain toward consistency of belief over time. The researcher may be interested in determining whether party or candidate preference seems to exert the more potent pull toward consistency. For this data, the relevant comparisons involve the cells marked by an asterisk in Table C. The entries in these cells indicate that 20 persons resolved the inconsistency by changing candidate preference and 40 persons by changing party; 290 persons did not change toward consistent beliefs. Thus, while the data do not strongly support role theory predictions, they do suggest that in this instance candidate preference involved the more powerful effect.

Markov Chains Applied to Panel Data

A fourth line of inquiry appropriate to (but not limited to) panel data involves the use of Markov chains. A Markov chain is a series of states related by a series of sets of transition probabilities. Each state is a function of the transition probabilities from the immediately preceding state. For example, in Subtable C of Table 17.1, we see that the chance of a Democrat for Nixon in Time 1 becoming a Republican for Nixon in Time 2 is $40/300 = .13$; the chance of becoming a Republican for McGovern is zero; the chance of remaining a Democrat for Nixon is $250/300 = .83$; and the chance of becoming a Democrat for McGovern is $10/300 = .03$. By taking the cell entries as percentages of the row marginals we can derive all the transition probabilities in the same way. The set of such probabilities is called the *transition matrix.* The data for Time 1 and Time 2 provide the transition matrix from Time 2 to Time 3. This transition matrix is illustrated in Table 17.2. By multiplying the corresponding cells in subtable C of Table 17.1

TABLE 17.2

	RN	RM	DN	DM
RN	1.0	0	0	0
RM	.20	.80	0	0
DN	.13	0	.83	.03
DM	.07	0	.27	.67

with those of Table 17.2, we can obtain the following predicted distribution in some future Time 3 shown in Table 17.3. This procedure would be useful

TABLE 17.3

Time 3

		RN	RM	DN	DM
	RN	350	0	0	0
Time 2	RM	2	32	0	0
	DN	5	0	208	0
	DM	1	0	22	134

to political campaign advisers who might have monthly data on reactions, and who wished to extrapolate to the following month what would happen if trends of the previous month continued.

If actual data for Time 3 become available, a chi-square test might be applied to assess the extent to which the change process being studied is actually a Markov process. If it appears to be one, the researcher may wish to use Table 17.3 to compute the transition matrix needed to predict the distribution of responses in Time 4; this in turn can be used to get the matrix used in predicting Time 5; and so on, until a predicted table is not significantly different from the predicted table for the preceding time period. This final table, called the *equilibrium table*, represents the eventual outcome of a Markov process.

If the data do *not* seem to conform to a simple Markov process, the researcher may wish to compute the transition matrix on some other basis. For example, the transition probabilities might be computed on a longer basis. That is, instead of using the given time period and the immediately preceding one, the researcher can use the given time period and the initial one as the basis for computing the transition matrix used to predict the distribution for the time period following the given one. It is easy to think of many variants of modified Markov processes of this sort. More likely, however, is that a gap between actual and predicted distributions is due to the effect of unmeasured variables on the observed variables, to the effect between the observed variables not being Markovian in nature, and or to measurement errors.

Problems of Panel Analysis

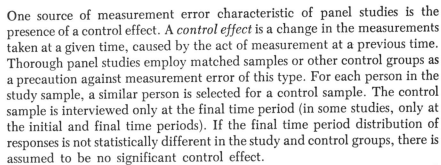

One source of measurement error characteristic of panel studies is the presence of a control effect. A *control effect* is a change in the measurements taken at a given time, caused by the act of measurement at a previous time. Thorough panel studies employ matched samples or other control groups as a precaution against measurement error of this type. For each person in the study sample, a similar person is selected for a control sample. The control sample is interviewed only at the final time period (in some studies, only at the initial and final time periods). If the final time period distribution of responses is not statistically different in the study and control groups, there is assumed to be no significant control effect.

A second major problem in panel analysis is called "sample mortality." *Sample mortality* refers to the percentage of respondents in the initial sample who are unavailable for testing at later time periods. Substitution of new subjects would undermine the very purpose of panel analysis and would not be appropriate. The only alternative for the researcher is a great deal of persistence and expense in obtaining interviews in later time periods.

To avoid the problem of time and expense incurred by panel studies, researchers may wish to turn to other methods. One "solution" would be to construct the distribution of measurements for previous time periods from the subjects' recollections at a given time period. While such recollections (e.g., the recollection of the subject's party identification in an earlier month) do provide some insight into change processes, memory is a notoriously error-prone factor. This is particularly true because subjects tend to reconstruct past attitudes and behaviors in a way that makes them consistent with present attitudes and behaviors and with a positive self-image.

Therefore, *cohort analysis* rather than reliance on recollections is the most common alternative to panel studies. Cohort analysis involves measurements over time, but the subjects in the later time periods are not the same as those in the earlier ones. Instead, more subjects are selected who would be the same age as the initial subjects. For example, persons aged 20–29 years in 1945 would be compared to persons aged 50–59 years in 1975, using comparable survey data for interviews conducted in 1945 and 1975.

Not only does cohort analysis return us to dependence on net effects rather than on turnover information, but in addition it is very difficult to separate the effects of position in the life cycle, membership in an age cohort (e.g., membership in the cohort associated with the 1940s baby boom), and historical time period (e.g., wartime periods compared to peacetime periods), although this need not constitute an insurmountable problem.[2]

In Table 17.4 we present a table for data on any variable, x, for various age cohorts using surveys taken at various historical periods. If x varies mainly with life cycle, then the cells within any given row will tend to have

TABLE 17.4

Age	Time of Survey			
	1940	1950	1960	1970
21–30	$x=40$			
31–40				
41–50				
51–60				
61–70				

[2]See K. Mason, W. Mason, H. Winsborough, and W. Poole, "Some Methodological Issues in Cohort Analysis of Archival Data," *American Sociological Review* 38, no. 2 (April 1973): 242–257.

For examples of cohort analysis, see Ronald Inglehart, "The Silent Revolution in Europe: Intergenerational Change in Post-Industrial Societies," *American Political Science Review* 65, no. 4 (December 1971): 991–1017; and G. Carlsson and K. Karlsson, "Age, Cohorts, and the Generation of Generations," *American Sociological Review* 35, no. 4 (August 1970): 710–718.

the same value (e.g., all four cells in the top row will be 40). If historical time period has the predominant effect, then the cells within any given column will tend to have the same value (e.g., all five cells in the first column will equal 40). If age cohort has the predominant effect, then the cells within any given diagonal will tend to have the same value, assuming the time between periods (columns) is the same as the time between age groups (rows; it is the same—10 years—in this example). That is, for the illustration in Table 17.4, the 31–40 age group in the 1950 survey would equal 40 on variable x; the 41–50 age groups in the 1960 survey would also equal 40; and the 51–60 age group in 1970 would equal 40. Techniques for assessing whether life cycle, age cohort, or historical period have the greatest effects on the variable have been developed by Mason, Mason, Winsborough, and Poole (see note 2). These techniques require interval data and other assumptions of regression analysis, which is the method used.

STOCHASTIC PROCESSES

Markov chains are an example of the more general subject of stochastic processes. A stochastic process is a series of states related to each other by the laws of probability. Markovian processes in particular assume (1) stationarity (the transition probabilities remain constant over time), (2) Markovian transitions (the probability of transition to a given state depends only on its current state and the transition matrix—it is not dependent on the history of its previous states), and (3) homogeneity (all subjects are governed by the same transition probabilities).[3] Although this process is beyond the scope of this chapter, it should be noted that various authors have developed techniques for stochastic models of change over time which do not require all the assumptions of Markov models.[4] Even where the researcher does not expect the assumptions of a Markov chain model to be met, however, the predictions derived from such a model can be used as a "base line," deviations from which become the object of analysis.[5]

[3]D. McFarland, "Intrageneration Social Mobility as a Markov Process," *American Sociological Review* 35, no. 3 (June 1970): 463–464.

[4]McFarland, *supra*, discusses heterogenous and nonstationary models; heterogenous models are also discussed in S. Spilerman, "The Analysis of Mobility Processes by the Introduction of Independent Variables into a Markov Chain," *American Journal of Sociology* 37, no. 3 (June 1972): 277–294. Models involving continuous time processes and changing population sizes are also treated in David Bartholomew, *Stochastic Models for Social Processes* (New York: John Wiley & Sons, 1967).

[5]See Spilerman, *supra*, p. 277. See also Thomas Fararo, "Stochastic Processes," in E. Borgatta, ed., *Sociological Methodology 1969* (San Francisco: Jossey-Bass, 1969), ch. 8.

TIME-LAG CORRELATION
ANALYSIS OF TIME SERIES

If the researcher has measurements at more than one point in time, certain causal inferences can be made on the basis of correlation and partial correlation coefficients. Figure 17.1 presents the possible correlations of two

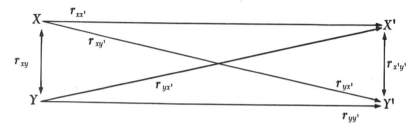

FIGURE 17.1

variables measured at two time intervals. When the two variables are measured at only one point in time, there is only one relevant correlation coefficient, r_{xy}. Even if we find that r_{xy} is high, we can make no statistical inference about whether X causes Y, Y causes X, or if there is reciprocal correlation. (If r_{xy} approaches zero, there may still be a causal effect if some unmeasured third variable exerts a suppressing force.)

As Figure 17.1 indicates, there are five additional correlation coefficients possible when two variables are measured at two points in time rather than just one. In comparing these coefficients, the following inferences may be made:

1. If X is hypothesized to be the predominant cause of Y, then $r_{xy'}$, should be greater than $r_{yx'}$, assuming a delayed effect.
2. If the X effect on Y is hypothesized to be a delayed effect, then $r_{xy'}$ should be greater than r_{xy} for $r_{x'y'}$.
3. If the X effect on Y is hypothesized to be immediate, then r_{xy} should equal $r_{x'y'}$ and both should be greater than $r_{xy'}$. (But this finding also supports the hypothesis that Y causes X.)
4. To the extent that X causes Y by a short-term effect, r_{xy} and $r_{x'y'}$ should approach $r_{xy'}$ where $r_{xy'}$ should be the largest in magnitude.
5. To the extent that X causes Y by a long-term effect, and r_{xy} and $r_{x'y'}$ should approach $r_{yx'}$, where $r_{yx'}$ should be the smallest in magnitude.

Because X will ordinarily be the best, or at least an important, predictor of X', and Y will be the best or an important predictor of Y', most authors prefer the use of partial rather than zero-order coefficients in time-lag analysis. The cross-lag correlation discussed above, therefore, should be considered a less rigorous rule-of-thumb method. The analogous expectations using partial correlation coefficients are:[6]

1. $r_{xy \cdot y}$ should be greater than $r_{yx' \cdot x}$;
2. $r_{xy \cdot y}$ should be greater than either r_{xy} or $r_{x'y'}$;
3. r_{xy} should equal $r_{x'y'}$ and both should be greater than $r_{xy \cdot y}$;
4. r_{xy} and $r_{x'y'}$ should approach $r_{xy'}$, which should be the largest in magnitude; and
5. r_{xy} and $r_{x'y'}$ should approach $r_{yx' \cdot x}$ which should be the smallest in magnitude.

Standardized versus Unstandardized Coefficients

As Bohrnstedt has noted, the researcher may wish to use unstandardized partial regression coefficients (b coefficients) instead of partial correlation coefficients under certain circumstances.[7] Standardized coefficients, such as correlation, partial correlation, and β coefficients, are affected not only by the causal relationship between two variables, X and Y, but also by their variance in the samples studied. Therefore, r_{xy} may differ from $r_{x'y'}$, for example, not because the causal relationship of X and Y has changed, but because X and Y have different variances in the second time period compared to the first. Unstandardized partial regression coefficients should be used in place of partial correlation coefficients when the researcher wishes to control for the effect of differing variances; the unstandardized coefficients will be relatively stable over samples of differing variation. On the other hand, if the researcher wishes to examine the percent of variance explained in a given sample (where that percent will depend in part on the variances of the variables), then use of partial correlation coefficients is recommended. Since both types of coefficient convey related, complementary information, the researcher may prefer to use both in conjunction.

Correction for Attenuation

As Bohrnstedt, among others, has also noted, correlation, partial correlation, and unstandardized partial regression coefficients used in time-lag comparisons should be corrected for measurement error.[8] This is called "correction for attenuation" since zero-order correlation coefficients based on data with measurement error will be attenuated or lower than the true correlation coefficients based on perfectly measured data. However, partial

---

[6]For further discussion, see D. Pelz and F. Andrews, "Detecting Causal Priorities in Panel Data," *American Sociological Review* 29, no. 6 (December 1964): 836–848. See also G. Bohrnstedt, "Observations on the Measurement of Change," in Borgatta, ed., *Sociological Methodology 1969*, ch. 4. Bohrnstedt advises against use of simple correlation coefficients in time-lag analysis.

[7]Bohrnstedt, *supra*, pp. 121–122. Recall the discussion of standardized versus unstandardized coefficients on p. 570 and Ch. 18, pp. 6–7. 22–4.

[8]*Ibid.*, pp. 126–128. See also the discussion in Ch. 18.

coefficients may be either higher *or* lower than their corrected counterparts (usually higher).

The corrected coefficients are:

$$r^*_{XY \cdot Y} = \frac{r_{YY} r_{XY'} - r_{XY} r_{YY'}}{\sqrt{r_{YY} - r^2_{XY}} \; \sqrt{r_{YY} - r^2_{YY'}}}$$

$$r^*_{XY} = r_{XY} / \sqrt{r_{XX} r_{YY}}$$

$$b^*_{XY' \cdot Y} = (\sigma_{X'} / \sigma_Y) \left(\frac{r_{YY} r_{XY'} - r_{XY} r_{YY'}}{r_{YY} - r^2_{XY}} \right)$$

$$\beta^*_{XY' \cdot Y} = (\sigma_X / \sigma_{Y'}) b^*_{XY' \cdot Y}$$

where   the coefficients with the asterisks are the corrected coefficients

r_{ii} are the reliability coefficients for the given variable

The researcher should use these corrections for attenuation with caution. In particular, it should be stressed that there are several methods for computing reliability coefficients, and all are usually differing estimates of the unknown "true" reliability. While the corrected coefficients are more appropriate for the causal inference assumption of perfect measurement, they must be treated as estimates in need of cross-validation rather than as unchallengeably "true" coefficients.

REGRESSION ANALYSIS OF TIME SERIES

Regression techniques are the obvious candidates for the most-favored approach to the analysis of time series. The "prediction equation" aspect of regression analysis meshes nicely with the popular use of time series for forecasting purposes. Moreover, the regression coefficient can be used as a simple measure of trend over time. That is, "time" may be used as a variable with values from zero (the first observation) to n (the observation in the last time period) and be regressed as a predictor variable using any other interval variable as the dependent variable. To the extent that the regression coefficient of "time" approaches zero, there is no linear trend in the dependent variable over time.

Regression is so popular that "time series analysis" is often equated with the use of regression techniques to decompose time series data into trend, cyclical, seasonal, and irregular components. This is, of course, a simplification since, as we have seen, many other techniques are appropriate to time series analysis and, indeed, the decomposition approach just mentioned involves other techniques in addition to regression. In this section we will outline the decomposition approach, discuss various uses of the results of decomposition, and conclude with some treatment of complications arising in this method.

Establishing a Secular Trend

Decomposition of a time series commonly results in five sets of data for a given variable: the original, observed data (X_o); the long-term, trend data (X_t); the shorter-term, cyclical data (X_c); the short-term, seasonal data (X_s); and the irregular, fluctuation data (X_f). More complex breakdowns are rare, especially in political science; many time series do not display all of these components (e.g., presidential election data has no seasonal component). In political science it is often impossible to do more than decompose a time series into trend data and data on irregular fluctuations about this trend.

The most common method for establishing trend data is as follows:

1. Time is used as a predictor variable for the dependent variable, x_o in a simple regression analysis (see Chapter 15). Ordinarily this is a linear regression, although logarithmic and other transforms of x_o (recall pp. 171 – 73) or other techniques of curvilinear regression may be used.
2. The resulting regression equation is used to predict the values of x_o for each time period observed. These predicted values are the trend data, x_t.
3. The residuals $(x_o - x_t)$ reflect the combined effect of cyclical, seasonal, and irregular fluctuation variance. This method of computing residuals is appropriate when x_o is assumed to be an *additive* function of x_t, x_c, x_s, and x_f.

   Sometimes, however, the researcher may wish to view x_o as a *multiplicative* function of its components. Such would be the case, for example, in a study of rioting if the effect of summer-month weather on frequency of rioting was much greater when it coincided with times of high unemployment than when it did not. (By contrast, an additive model would predict that seasonal *variation* in rioting would be the same regardless of unemployment level even though higher unemployment would increase *average* levels of rioting.) If a multiplicative model is assumed, residuals are computed by dividing x_o by x_t; computation of residuals in this manner is called *ratio detrending*. Ratio detrending seems to be more common in political science, presumably because researchers have thought multiplicative effects (the combined effect of two variables jointly is greater than the sum of their independent effects) to be more realistic in a variety of research contexts.

Before turning to further aspects of trend decomposition, it should be noted that regression is not the only technique used to determine the secular trend.

Other methods, especially popular before computers simplified the work of regression analysis, are the following:

1. *Freehand Curve-Fitting* X_o is plotted on graph paper and the researcher draws a "regression" line through the points on a visual/intuitive basis. As a simple rule-of-thumb method in exploratory stages of research, this approach yields satisfactory results in most cases.

2. *Semi-Average Method*   The average of X_o for the first half of the time periods is taken as one point and the average for the second half is taken as a second point. If done graphically, the "regression" line is the line connecting these two points, and values on the line are the values of X_t.

3. *Moving Averages*   Average values for certain ranges of X_o are substituted for the values of X_o, resulting in a "smoothed curve." The researcher first decides on the number of time intervals to constitute a range. This depends upon the research purpose. If the research purpose is to cancel out irregular, seasonal, and cyclical variations, then the selected range should be as long or longer in time duration as the longest hypothesized cyclical effect. In studies of American national politics, for example, a four-year moving average might be selected on the theory that cycles are geared to presidential campaigns (but this would not eliminate the possibility of longer-term cycles).

    Once a range of n time periods is selected, the average of the first n observations is computed and is assigned to the time period in the middle of the range of n periods. The following time period is assigned the average value of the 2nd to $(n + 1)$th observations. The next time period receives the average of the 3rd to $(n + 2)$th observations, and so on. (Note that this process involves the inability to compute average values for some of the first and last time periods.) After these average values are computed, they are plotted and connected by a line; interpolation and extrapolation of this line must be freehand. Values on this line are interpreted as the values of X_t.

4. *Weighted Moving Averages*   Although this is rare, it should be noted that weighted moving averages may also be used. In this method, the value of X_o at the given time period is given the most weight, the value at the previous time period is given a fraction of this weight, the value at the time two periods previous is given even less weight (usually the square of the fraction just mentioned), and so on for the range of n observations in time. The average of these weighted values is then assigned to the given time period. This method has the advantage of not necessitating the dropping of observations at the end of the series. As before, average values are plotted and connected by a line, values on which are interpreted as values of X_t.

Establishing Cyclical Effects

Further decomposition of a time series, after establishing the trend values, involves analysis of the residuals. In an additive model, X_t and X_s are subtracted from X_o and a moving average is applied to the remainder to eliminate irregular fluctuations. The resulting values are interpreted as the values of X_c, the cyclical values. In a multiplicative model, X_o is divided by X_t and X_s and moving averages are applied to obtain the estimates of X_c.

Since the computation of X_t and the use of moving averages has been set forth, calculation of the $\bar{x}_c$ values depends only on knowing how to compute the values of X_s. This is discussed below. Before turning to this subject, however, it is important to note that the mere fact one can obtain values for X_c emphatically *cannot* be taken to mean that there is a cyclical effect. The X_c values may simply represent random error disturbances not controlled by shorter-term factors reflected in X_s and the use of moving averages. To establish a cycle, the researcher must show that the values of X_c seem to reflect the effect of other variables in his or her explanatory model, or display a periodicity significantly different from chance variation.

Establishing Seasonal Effects

Seasonal effects are more important in economics than in political science. Where economists routinely deal with monthly data on employment, wage rates, and other economic variables, political scientists commonly deal with election and other data compiled annually or on a longer-term basis. Such data suppresses possible seasonal effects. Moreover, where employment is clearly related to season, for example, seasonal effects are rarely important in political science models.

If we wish to compute the seasonal effect values, X_s, from monthly time series data, the following is a conventional procedure:

1. Twelve-month moving average values of X_o are substituted for the original values of X_o. These averages are interpreted as the combined effects of trends and cycles. They also cancel out the effect of short-term, irregular fluctuations.

2. In a multiplicative model these moving averages are divided into the original X_o values. In an additive model, they are subtracted from X_o. The resulting values are interpreted as the combined effects of seasonal and longer-term irregular fluctuations.

3. The median moving average is computed for each month separately (i.e., the median of the averages of all the January observations is computed, then the median for February values, etc.). The median is preferred to the mean because it is less sensitive to extreme values, which are interpreted to represent random shocks in the time series. Thus all Januaries in the series will be assigned the same value (the median moving average of step 2 above), all Februaries, etc. These values are considered to be the values of X_s. (Thus seasonally adjusted data is X_o minus X_s in additive models and X_o divided by X_s in multiplicative models.)

Establishing Irregular Fluctuation Effects

Irregular fluctuation effects, X_f, are a residual. In an additive model, X_f is obtained by subtracting X_t, X_c, and X_s from X_o. In a multiplicative model,

X_f is obtained by dividing X_o by X_t, X_c, and X_s. The values of X_f are interpreted as reflections of random shocks, variables having a temporary or sporadic effect on X, and error factors.[9]

Interpretation of Decomposed Time Series

The values of the trend (X_t), cyclical (X_c), seasonal (X_s), and irregular fluctuation (X_f) components of a given variable (X_o) convey different information. It is self-evident that the graph of each of these values on the y-axis with "time" on the x-axis portrays in a simple manner the trend, cyclical, seasonal, and irregular fluctuation effects. From such a set of graphs one may readily see if there is an effect (no effect is indicated by a regression line with a slope of zero—a horizontal line); if the effect is linear or curvilinear (linearity is indicated when curvilinear regression fails to result in a significantly higher coefficient of multiple determination, R^2, than linear regression); if the effect is deterministic or involves high standard error (low error is indicated by the points being on or clustered close to the regression line or curve); and if the effect is homoscedastic (homoscedasticity is indicated by a similar degree of clustering or lack of clustering of points for one part of the regression line as compared to another; lack of homoscedasticity indicates the effect changes over time; see Bartlett's test).

The components of X_o may also give insight into its relation to other variables. For example the correlation of X_o with Y_o may approach zero, yet the correlation of X_t and Y_t may be very high. Yeomans gives the example of coal and oil consumption.[10] For this data, the observed correlation of coal and oil consumption by month was quite low (.20). The correlation of seasonal effects was very high (.98), however, reflecting common heavy use of both fuels in the winter. At the same time, the correlation of trends was strongly negative (-1.00), reflecting the tendency of oil to be substituted for coal as a fuel over the years. The opposing seasonal and trend effects were suppressed in the observed correlation of .2, which might have been used to conclude fallaciously that there was little relationship between coal and oil consumption. Similarly, such correlations of components of two variables can be used to gain greater insight into time-lag correlation and partial correlation analysis.

(Note that when linear regression is used to obtain the values of X_t, Y_t, and trend values for other variables, the correlation of two variables will be either plus or minus 1.0, unless there is no trend in one or both variables, in which case the correlation will be zero. This is because trend data obtained

[9]See K. Yeomans, *Statistics for the Social Scientist* (Baltimore: Penguin, 1968), vol. I, ch. 6 and vol. II, ch. 5; S. Kirkpatrick, *Quantitative Analysis of Political Data* (Columbus, Ohio: Merrill, 1974), ch. 5.

[10]Yeomans, *supra*, vol. I, p. 240.

by this technique are a perfect linear function of time; since each variable is perfectly linearly related to time, they will also be so related to each other).

Rather than seeking to reduce the relation between two time series or between two corresponding components of time series to a correlation coefficient, a simpler and in some ways more revealing procedure is to juxtapose the two time series (whether original data, trend data, cyclical data, or other data) on the same graph. In such a graph the x-axis is time, common to both variables, but the y-axis has two scales: one for each variable (e.g., unemployment percentages and riot frequencies). These scales may be placed at the right-hand and left-hand ends of the x-axis to facilitate reading the graph. Intuitive, visual observation of the two series plotted on the same graph enables the researcher to observe the correspondence of overall (observed value or raw score) effects, trend effects, cyclical effects, seasonal effects, and irregular fluctuation effects, depending on which set of time series is plotted.

Correction for Autocorrelation

Whenever regression techniques are used it is important to make some estimate of the reliability of the "prediction equations" calculated to derive, for example, the trend values of a variable. The standard error is the statistic used to make such an estimate. The sampling assumptions used in computing the standard error posit that regression residuals must be randomly distributed. For the regression line used to compute trend values, X_t, for example, the residuals are the differences between the originally observed values, X_o, and the trend values (thus the residuals equal $X_o - X_t$); these must be randomly distributed about each portion of the regression line (or about the regression surface in multiple regression). When this assumption cannot be met, the standard error of the regression (or correlation) coefficient will be larger in reality than it is computed to be by earlier formulas given which assume randomness of residuals.

TABLE 17.5

Year	Residual: Time 1 (z_t)	Residual: Time 2 (z_{t+1})	z_t^2	$z_t z_{t+1}$
1971	1.1	.4	1.21	.44
1972	.4	−.9	.16	−.36
1973	−.9	−3.1	.81	2.79
1974	−3.1	2.5	9.61	−7.75
1975	2.5	1.1	6.25	2.75
			$\Sigma = 18.04$	$\Sigma = -2.13$

$$r_a = (\Sigma z_t z_{t+1}) / \Sigma z_t^2 = -2.13/18.04 = -.12$$

The randomness of residuals assumption is violated when a significant degree of autocorrelation exists. *Autocorrelation* is the Pearsonian correlation of a time series with a time-lagged version of itself. Table 17.5 (see page 443) gives data for five years on the regression residuals of a given variable (z_t). The residuals lagged one year are given in the next column (z_{t+1}); the square of the initial residuals forms the third column, and the cross-product of the residual with its time lag the last column. Note that in forming the lagged series, the first entry of x_t becomes the last entry of z_{t+1}.

The autocorrelation of the series in Table 17.5 is computed immediately below the table to be $-.12$. The formula for autocorrelation is as follows:

$$r_a = \frac{(\Sigma z_t z_{t+1}) - (\Sigma z_t)^2 / n}{\Sigma z_t^2 - (\Sigma z_t)^2 / n}$$

Note that since regression residuals sum to zero, for this type data the above formula simplifies to that used under Table 17.5. Note also that some authors use this formula to define *serial correlation*. Following Ezekiel and Fox, however, we will use autocorrelation to refer to the correlation of a time series with a lagged version of itself, and reserve the term *serial correlation* for the correlation of the current values of one time series with the lagged values of another series.[11] Finally, note that the z_t values should not be confused with normalized z values discussed in earlier chapters.

Autocorrelation is assumed to exist in a time series if the autocorrelation coefficient is significant. Its significance level is determined by consulting a table of significance for the coefficient of autocorrelation, developed by R. L. Anderson.[12] Significant autocorrelation (.05 significance level) is said to exist if r_a exceeds .253 for sample size 5, .360 for size 10, .299 for 20, .208 for 50, and .154 for 100, for example. If r_a is negative, significant autocorrelation exists when r_a exceeds $-.753$ for sample size 5, $-.564$ for size 10, $-.399$ for 20, $-.248$ for 50, and $-.174$ for 100. For the five cases in Table 17.5, where an autocorrelation of $-.12$ was observed, we fail to conclude that significant autocorrelation exists since $-.12$ is not less than $-.753$. Therefore

---

[11]M. Ezekiel and K. Fox, *Methods of Correlation and Regression Analysis* (New York: John Wiley & Sons, 1959), p. 337n. Chapter 20 of this volume provides more detailed treatment of the topics presented above. Ezekiel and Fox also discuss von Neumann's Ratio, an alternate test of autocorrelation (pp. 337–340).

[12]Such a table is presented in Ezekiel and Fox, *supra*, p. 338. Original tables are found in R. L. Anderson, "Distribution of the Serial Correlation Coefficient," *Annals of Mathematical Statistics* 13, no. 1 (1942): 1–13. Anderson has also discussed a "non-circular formula for r_a (i.e., one "correcting" for the placement of the first value of z_t as the last value of z_{t+1}):

$$\text{corrected } r_a = \frac{\Sigma z_t z_{t+1} - [\,1/(n-1)(\Sigma z_t)(\Sigma z_{t+1})\,]}{\sqrt{\Sigma z_t^2 - [1/(n-1)(\Sigma z_t)^2]}\,\sqrt{\Sigma z_{t+1} - [1/(n-1)(\Sigma z_{t+1}^2)]}}$$

However, if autocorrelation is absent, then all residuals should be random and placement of the first z_t as the last z_{t+1} is justified.

we may use the conventional standard error formulas in our time series analysis.

The Durbin-Watson Test. Anderson's tables for testing the significance of the autocorrelation coefficient are similar in function to the Durbin-Watson d test:

$$d = \frac{\sum\limits_{t=2}^{n} (z_t - z_{t-1})^2}{\sum\limits_{t=1}^{n} (z_t^2)}$$

where the z values are regression estimate residuals, as in computing r_a

Thus, d is a ratio of the sum of squared differences in successive residuals. (If the time periods studied are not successive, differences for the gaps in the time sequences are omitted from the computation of d.) Low values of d indicate a similar successive regression estimate residuals, implying positive autocorrelation. More specifically:

$$d \cong 2(1 - r_a)$$

where r_a is the autocorrelation coefficient of the residuals as in Table 17.5

Given this approximate equality, d will equal 2 when autocorrelation is zero. To establish positive autocorrelation, d must be significantly less than 2; for negative autocorrelation, d must be significantly more than 2. Durbin and Watson have presented a table setting forth these limits, with values for d_l (the lower bound of d, less than which d must be to establish positive autocorrelation) and d_n (the upper bound). These bounds are interpreted as follows:

Value of d	Interpretation
$d < d_1$	positive autocorrelation at significant level
$d_1 < d < d_u$	positive autocorrelation at non-significant level
$d_u < d < (4 - d_u)$	accept null hypothesis (no autocorrelation)
$(4 - d_u) < d < (4 - d_1)$	negative autocorrelation at non-significant level
$d > (4 - d_1)$	negative autocorrelation at significant level

The Durbin-Watson test is designed for use with exogenous explanatory variables; when used with a lagged dependent variable, the test is biased toward Type II errors (accepting a false null hypothesis). Since the variable is assumed to be exogenous, the table of "Significance Points of the Durbin-Watson d' shows different values of d_l and d_n depending on k, the number of exogenous explanatory variables in the regression equating being analyzed. Such a table is given, for example, in E. J. Kane, *Economic Statistics and Econometrics* (New York: Harper and Row, 1968): p. 424, as well as numerous other econometrics texts. The original table appeared in *Biometrika*, Vol. 38 (1951): 159–177.

Note that the Durbin-Watson test also assumes normally distributed, homoscedastic, not autocorrelated error terms. For further reading, see M. M. Nerlove and K. F. Wallis, "Use of the Durbin-Watson Statistic in Inappropriate Situations," *Econometrica*, Vol. 34 (January 1966): 235–238.

Corrected Standard Error   If time series data are autocorrelated, then the regression estimates (i.e., the estimates of the trend data, X_t) will be less reliable and so, consequently, will be all estimates based upon manipulation of the observed data and the regression estimates (i.e., the estimates of X_o, X_s, and X_f). For example, the difference between our high and low estimates will be greater than if the data were not autocorrelated. (Recall that at the 95 percent confidence level, the high estimate is obtained by adding 1.96 standard errors of the partial b coefficient to the computed partial b coefficient, then using this upward-adjusted "prediction equation" to obtain the high estimate; when autocorrelation exists, the true standard errors will have a larger magnitude but estimated standard errors will understate true standard errors.)

Ezekiel and Fox note two neglected corrections of the standard error for autocorrelation.[13] Herman Wold gives the following formula for correction of the standard error of the partial regression coefficient:

$$S_{b*} = S_b \sqrt{1 + 2r_{a1} + 2r_{a2} + \cdots + 2r_{an}}$$

where S_b and S_{b*} are the uncorrected and corrected standard errors of the partial regression coefficient, b, respectively

r_{a1} is the autocorrelation coefficient lagged one time unit; r_{a2} is the autocorrelation coefficient lagged two units; etc.

[13]Ezekiel and Fox, *Methods of Correlation and Regression Analysis*, p. 335. The authors also note that for regressions based on first differences (the difference between the values at time n and at time $n - 1$) rather than original values, autocorrelation will typically be lower or not significant, *if* the variables being regressed are related by sharing common trends rather than by direct causal or logical interrelations (pp. 341–342).

In this formula it is rarely necessary to go beyond r_{a2} since correlation of residuals lagged more than two time units are ordinarily trivial.

Bartlett's correction of the standard error of the correlation coefficient between two time series is as follows: [14]

$$S_{c*} = S_c \sqrt{\frac{1 + (r_{a(x)})\,(r_{a(y)})}{1 - (r_{a(x)})\,(r_{a(y)})}}$$

> where S_{c*} and S_c are the corrected and uncorrected standard errors of correlation, respectively.
>
> $r_{a(x)}$ and $r_{a(y)}$ are the autocorrelations for two time series, x and y, respectively.

Both corrections increase the size of the computed standard error to reflect the lower reliability of results computed on autocorrelated data.

Correction by Generalized Least Squares

The corrections for autocorrelation cited above, although standard, tend to be quite conservative (minimizing the chance of Type I errors, but allowing considerable leeway for Type II errors). Douglas Hibbs has suggested generalized least squares (GLS) as a more accurate method of treating autocorrelation. GLS is a two-step process in which ordinary least-squares regression is used to obtain initial estimates of autocorrelative disturbances after which these values are used to transform variable scores preliminary to conventional regression analysis of time series. [15]

Relation of Autocorrelation to Markov Chain Models

Earlier in this chapter, Markov models of change were discussed as one approach to analysis of time series data. It was noted that a Markov model assumes that the distribution of values in a given point in time is a function of the distribution in the immediately preceding state and of the associated transition matrix. That is, in a Markov process a state at time n is influenced by the state at time $(n - 1)$ but *not* by earlier states such as $(n - 2)$ or greater time lags. If a time series reflects a Markov process, then the partial

---

[14]On standard error of correlation, see Ezekiel and Fox, *supra*, pp. 293–299; and on standard error of regression coefficients, pp. 281 ff. See also F. Kerlinger and E. Pedhazur, *Multiple Regression in Behavioral Research* (New York: Holt, Rinehart & Winston, 1973), pp. 66–70.

[15]See Douglas Hibbs, "Problems of Statistical Estimation and Causal Inference in Time-Series Regression Models," in H. L. Costner, ed., *Sociological Methodology 1973–1974* (San Francisco: Jossey-Bass, 1974), pp. 252–308.

autocorrelation of the observed series (z_t) with the same series lagged two time units (z_{t+2}), controlling for the same series lagged one time unit (z_{t+1}) should approach zero. That is, if only the immediately preceding state is determining, then there should be a zero partial correlation between a given state and an earlier state, controlling for the state immediately prior to the given one. Thus partial autocorrelation provides an easy though not conclusive test of whether a Markov process underlies given time series data.

COVARIANCE ANALYSIS OF TIME SERIES

Though outside the scope of this chapter, it should be noted that covariance analysis, noted earlier, is another appropriate if neglected tool in analysis of time series. Covariance analysis is useful in assessing the relative importance of effects between two variables over time ("between years") from effects at any given point in time ("within years"). Schuessler, for example, cites the case of crime and income: (1) within any year there is a negative relationship—the lower the income of an area, the higher the crime—but (2) over time (between years), there is a positive relationship—both income and crime are rising together over the years. As Schuessler notes, covariance analysis is thus useful in relating analyses by area to analyses by time.[16]

Without discussing the mathematics of covariance analysis, its essence can be understood and, indeed, much of usefulness can be obtained by considering how regression analysis can be displayed graphically. Suppose one has data by metropolitan district for income and crime, for fifteen districts at three points in time (e.g., 1965, 1970, 1975). Although for simplicity of illustration we have used few cases, more than fifteen observations would be used in practice. Figure 17.2 illustrates this hypothetical data, with the 1s corresponding to districts in 1965, 2s to districts in 1970, and 3s to 1975. Through each of these three sets of data one can draw a linear regression line (lines A, B, and C). A fourth line (line D) can be drawn connecting the mean values in each of the three sets.

From such a graph we can observe a number of things. First, we can see that the relation of crime and income over time is quite different from the relation at any one point in time. Obviously, this is not a contradiction but rather two aspects of the same relationship, both yielding useful information. Second, we can observe that the relationship between crime and income is changing over time, as indicated by the changing slopes of regression lines A, B, and C. And third, from observing the greater dispersion of observations (3s around A, 2s around B, 1s around C) for more

---

[16]Karl Schuessler, *Analysing Social Data* (Boston: Houghton Mifflin, 1971), pp. 238–246.

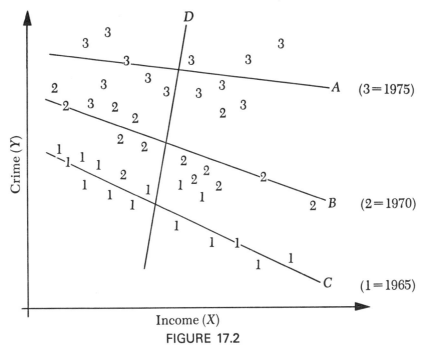

FIGURE 17.2

recent regressions, we may note that the relationship between the two variables is becoming weaker over time.

Analysis of variance (ANOVA) may be applied to appropriate time series data by simply treating time as the grouping variable. (Recall Chapter 14; time period rather than, say, region—the illustration in Chapter 14—would be the grouping variable.) Use of the F test would enable us to come to a decision about whether or not the data for any given year seem to be drawn from the same populations. If, for example, we find that the data are not significant by the F test, we fail to conclude that the time periods are different. Covariance analysis, however, has the advantage of more directly testing the effect of "time" as a control variable, whereas the causal interpretation of analysis of variance is more ambiguous.

EXERCISE

Read and evaluate the usefulness of time series analysis in Gerald Kramer, "Short-Term Fluctuations in U.S. Voting Behavior, 1896–1964," in the *American Political Science Review* 65, no. 1 (March 1971): 131–143. Since this represents a different use of regression analysis, compare it to the methods outlined in this chapter.

18 | Causal Modelling

In one sense, all forms of multivariate analysis are methods of causal modelling. That is, all may be used to gain information about the appropriateness of hypotheses about the direction and strength of causation in an explanatory model. Both multivariate analysis of tables (Chapter 13) and the use of partial correlation in testing causal hypotheses (also Chapter 13) are common forms of causal modelling. By causal modelling is meant a process that starts with the development of explanatory models (Chapter 6) and proceeds to their testing by various techniques, leading to possible revisions and new tests.

The sorts of partial correlation tests discussed in Chapter 13 can be extended to models with large numbers of variables. Arthur Goldberg has used such tests in examining a six-variable model of voting, illustrated in Table 18.1. The partial correlation technique consists of testing to see whether significant nonzero correlations (e.g., r_{41}) drop toward zero when relevant control variables are partialed (e.g., in comparing r_{41} with $r_{41.23}$). Relevant variables to use as controls in such partial correlations are those that appear in the model as anteceding or intervening variables. (Recall that anteceding variables are ones that cause two or more otherwise uncorrelated variables; intervening variables mediate the causal impact of one variable on another.)

Table 18.1 shows the predictions applicable to this six-variable model and presents the actual results. How close to zero must such results be before we conclude the data has an acceptable fit with the model? Unfortunately, there is no mathematical way of setting such a level, nor is there any standard, if arbitrary, convention. In most political science usage, however, a residual (actual result in Table 18.1) below .1 is often considered acceptable. Alternatively, one might accept any partial that dropped below a

TABLE 18.1

Variables

1—*FSC*—Father's Sociological Traits
2—*FPI*—Father's Party Identification
3—*RSC*—Respondent's Sociological Traits
4—*RPI*—Respondent's Party Identification
5—*RPA*—Respondent's Partisan Attitudes
6—*RV*—Respondent's Presidential Vote

Predicted Results	Actual Results
$r_{41.23} = 0$	.017
$r_{32.1} = 0$	.101
$r_{43.12} = 0$	.130
$r_{64.1235} = 0$	.365
$r_{62.1345} = 0$	−.022

Model

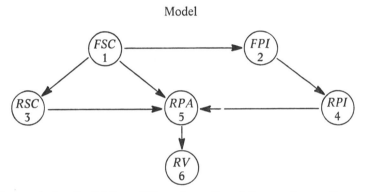

Source: Arthur S. Goldberg, "Discerning a Causal Pattern Among Data on Voting Behavior," *American Political Science Review* 60, no. 4 (December 1966): Fig. 1, p. 915. Reprinted by permission.

selected (e.g., .05) significance level. (For significance of partial correlation, see Chapter 12.) When actual results drop only part way toward zero, one has partial explanation, with the implications discussed earlier.

The limits associated with this technique are largely those associated with correlation: the assumption of interval-level data, linear relationships (unless transformations are specifically undertaken to reflect interactions and curvilinear relations), and the assumption of a multivariate normal distribution in significance testing. Moreover, in using a significance test criterion for accepting low residuals, it would be technically proper to accept such null hypotheses (the hypothesis that the residual is not different from zero) only for a high significance level (e.g., the .95 level). Many users find this criterion too stringent and therefore use the logically inappropriate lower level (e.g., .05; thus researchers are tempted to accept the hypothesis of no difference when difference is not demonstrably shown to be significant). Such significance tests also suffer from lack of comparability among samples, since the significance level for partial correlation depends upon sample size.

Other problems involve the necessity of assuming no two-way flows of causation, and of assuming recursivity. (A model is recursive if no variable is both a cause and an effect of another variable, either directly or indirectly.) Thus models involving reciprocal causation are not testable by this method. Also, it must be emphasized that this method need not yield a unique solution. That is, more than one explanatory model may be upheld by partial correlation analysis. Therefore the researcher should attempt to compute residuals for several different causal arrangements of his or her variables in order to assess which seems to be best supported by the data. Finally, the partial correlation technique assumes that error terms associated with each variable in the model are uncorrelated. These limitations have led to considerable criticism of the method,[1] but it remains a common technique in political science.[2]

In Chapter 13 we outlined common three-variable models in partial correlation analysis. Blalock has outlined the corresponding predictions for four-variable models, and these are presented in Figure 18.1.

FIGURE 18.1   Prediction Equations for Four-Variable Causal Models

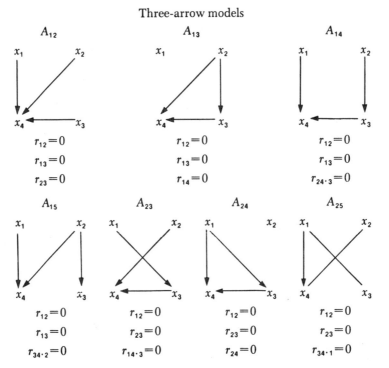

Three-arrow models

FIGURE 18.1 (cont.)

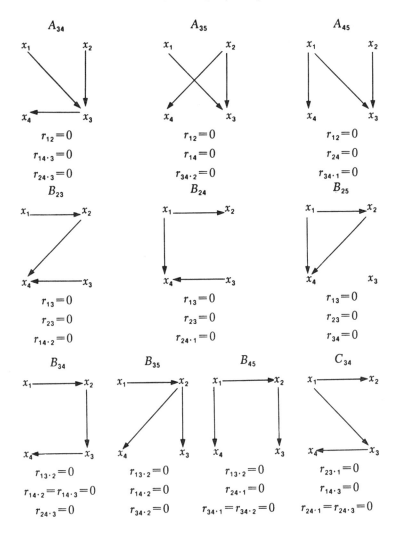

(*Source:* Adapted from H. M. Blalock, "Four-Variable Causal Models and Partial Correlations," *American Journal of Sociology* 68, no. 2 (September 1962): 186—188. Reprinted by permission.)

[1]For example, see R. Strauch, "The Fallacy of Causal Analysis," RAND Corporation Paper P-4618 (Santa Monica, Ca.: RAND Corp. April 1971). When relevant independent variables are omitted from the path model, ones which affect two or more of the endogenous variables, this assumption is always violated.

[2]For further reading, see H. Blalock, *Causal Inferences in Nonexperimental Research* (Chapel Hill, N. C.: Univ. of North Carolina, 1967); H. Blalock, "Theory-Building and Causal Inferences," in H. Blalock and A. Blalock, eds., *Methodology in Social Research* (New York: McGraw-Hill, 1968), ch. 5.

FIGURE 18.1 (cont.)

C_{35}

$r_{23 \cdot 1} = 0$
$r_{14 \cdot 2} = 0$
$r_{34 \cdot 1} = r_{34 \cdot 2} = 0$

C_{45}

$r_{23 \cdot 1} = 0$
$r_{24 \cdot 1} = 0$
$r_{34 \cdot 1} = 0$

D_{45}

$r_{14} = 0$
$r_{24} = 0$
$r_{34} = 0$

Four-arrow models

A_1

$r_{12} = 0$
$r_{13} = 0$

A_2

$r_{12} = 0$
$r_{23} = 0$

A_3

$r_{12} = 0$
$r_{14 \cdot 23} = 0$

A_4

$r_{12} = 0$
$r_{24 \cdot 13} = 0$

A_5

$r_{12} = 0$
$r_{34 \cdot 12} = 0$

B_2

$r_{13} = 0$
$r_{23} = 0$

B_3

$r_{13 \cdot 2} = 0$
$r_{14 \cdot 2} = 0$

B_4

$r_{13 \cdot 2} = 0$
$r_{24 \cdot 13} = 0$

B_5

$r_{13 \cdot 2} = 0$
$r_{34 \cdot 2} = 0$

C_3

$r_{23 \cdot 1} = 0$
$r_{14 \cdot 23} = 0$

C_4

$r_{23 \cdot 1} = 0$
$r_{24 \cdot 1} = 0$

C_5

$r_{23 \cdot 1} = 0$
$r_{34 \cdot 1} = 0$

FIGURE 18.1 (cont.)

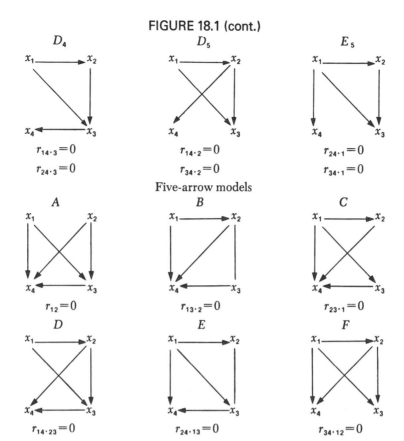

D_4 D_5 E_5

$r_{14 \cdot 3} = 0$ $r_{14 \cdot 2} = 0$ $r_{24 \cdot 1} = 0$

$r_{24 \cdot 3} = 0$ $r_{34 \cdot 2} = 0$ $r_{34 \cdot 1} = 0$

Five-arrow models

A   B   C

$r_{12} = 0$ $r_{13 \cdot 2} = 0$ $r_{23 \cdot 1} = 0$

D   E   F

$r_{14 \cdot 23} = 0$ $r_{24 \cdot 13} = 0$ $r_{34 \cdot 12} = 0$

PATH ANALYSIS

Path analysis is an extension of the same sort of causal reasoning as in partial correlation analysis, although it uses a different coefficient—the path coefficient. Before turning to this increasingly popular approach, it is necessary to understand the relation of this coefficient to ones already treated.

Partial Correlation, Standardized and Unstandardized Regression, and Path Coefficients: Their Interrelation

A correlation coefficient is a standardized regression coefficient in the case of two variables, and the partial correlation coefficient is the geometric mean of the two standardized regression coefficients.

$$r_{yx} = r_{xy} = \beta_{yx} = \beta_{xy} = b_{yx}\,(s_x/s_y) = b_{xy}\,(s_y/s_x)$$
$$r_{yx.z} = \sqrt{\beta_{yx.z}\,\beta_{xy.z}}$$

where r = Pearson's product-moment correlation
   b = the unstandardized regression coefficient
   β = the standardized regression coefficient
   s = the sample standard deviation

Path coefficients are standardized regression coefficients for the case of regressions using as independent variables only those variables that have a prior position on a causal diagram.

This procedure can be explained with regard to Figure 18.2. In this causal diagram, Variable A (social class) causes Variable B (education), which in turn causes Variable C (job status) and Variable D (job satisfaction); Variable C also causes Variable D. The path coefficient, p, represents the direct effect of one variable on another. The coefficient p_{ba} equals

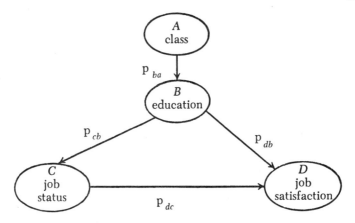

FIGURE 18.2

the standardized regression coefficient beta (β_{ba}), both of which equal the correlation coefficient, r, between Variables A and B. These equalities hold only for the direct causal relation in A and B (note that B has only one antecedent causal variable).

For later variables in the model in Figure 18.2, we must use a different approach. The path coefficient for the third variable in the model, p_{cb}, is the beta weight associated with Variable B in the regression of Variable C as the dependent variable and Variables A and B as the independent variables. (Note that A and B are the only antecedent causal variables with regard to C.) For the path coefficients associated with the fourth variable, p_{db} and p_{dc}, we take a similar approach: these are the beta weights associated with

Variables B and C respectively in the regression of Variable D as a dependent variable and Variables A, B, and C as the independent variables. (Note that A, B, and C are the antecedent causal variables with regard to D.)

To some extent, these coefficients serve similar functions. Consider the model in Figure 18.3 (analogous to Figure 18.2).

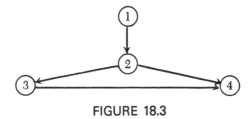

FIGURE 18.3

The partial correlation prediction equations for this model are:

$$r_{13.2} = 0$$
$$r_{14.23} = 0$$

We could describe this model as a set of regression equations, where Variable 1 is "given," associated only with an error term, e_1, which includes error ánd unmeasured variables' effects; Variable 2 would be predicted by Variable 1 plus the error term e_2; Variable 3 would be predicted by Variables 1 and 2 plus the error term, e_3; and so on, as follows:

$$z_1 = e_1$$
$$z_2 = b_{21}z_1 + e_2$$
$$z_3 = b_{31.2}z_1 + b_{32.1}z_2 + e_3$$
$$z_4 = b_{41.23}z_1 + b_{42.13}z_2 + b_{43.12}z_3 + e_4$$

where z_i = variables in standard scores, for
i = 1 through 4

e_i = error terms for variable
i = 1 through 4

Given the causal relationships indicated in Figure 18.3, we would predict that two of these unstandardized partial regression coefficients would be zero:

$$b_{31.2} = 0$$
$$b_{41.23} = 0$$

The corresponding standardized (β) coefficients would also be zero.

The nonzero standardized regression coefficients in this recursive model are the *path coefficients:*

$$p_{21} = \beta_{21}$$
$$p_{32} = \beta_{32.1}$$
$$p_{42} = \beta_{42.13}$$
$$p_{43} = \beta_{43.12}$$

These path coefficients can be considered the *direct effects* of one variable on another. In other words, the correlation, r, between two variables can be partitioned into two parts: a direct effect, indicated by the path coefficient; and an indirect effect or a combination of indirect effects, equal to the correlation minus the path coefficient $(r_{ij} - p_{ij})$: *

$$r_{21} = p_{21}$$
$$r_{32} = p_{32}$$
$$r_{42} = p_{42} + p_{43}r_{32}$$
$$r_{43} = p_{43} + p_{42}r_{32}$$

Thus, for example, the correlation of variables 2 and 4 is due to the direct effect of variable 2 on variable 4 (measured by the term p_{42}) plus the indirect effect of variable 2 on 4 by way of variable 3 (measured by the term $p_{42}p_{23}$). Since this is the only indirect path involving the endogenous variables (i.e., those variables caused by other variables in the model; variables 2, 3, and 4 in Figure 18.3), only r_{42} can be partitioned with this interpretation. The partition of r_{43} is computationally the same, but involves a different interpretation. Following the causal implications of the model in Figure 18.3, the correlation r_{43} can be decomposed into the direct effect of variable 3 on variable 4 (measured by p_{43}) and the spurious effect of variable 3 on variable 4 due to variables 3 and 4 having a common antecedent, variable 2 (this spurious effect is measured by the term $p_{42}p_{32}$).

Different causal arrows in Figure 18.3 would involve a different set of regressions and consequently different partitions of the correlation coefficients. For example, in Figure 18.4, the corresponding equations would be:

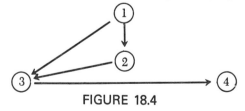

FIGURE 18.4

*Note that when there is no indirect effect $r_{ij} = p_{ij}$. Other wise, r_{ij} equals the direct effect plus the indirect effects (including the indirect effects of common anteceding variables).

$$p_{21} = \beta_{21} \qquad\qquad r_{21} = p_{21}$$

$$p_{31} = \beta_{31.2} \qquad\qquad r_{32} = p_{32} + p_{21}p_{31}$$

$$p_{32} = \beta_{32.1} \qquad\qquad r_{42} = p_{32}p_{43} + p_{21}p_{31}p_{43}$$

$$p_{43} = \beta_{43.21} \qquad\qquad r_{43} = p_{43}$$

Thus, depending upon how we model the variables, we will obtain different path estimates of the correlation coefficients. The models that provide the best path estimates are concluded to be the ones most consistent with the data. For example, if the observed r_{42} is closer to the expression $(p_{42} + p_{43}p_{32})$ in the path analysis for Figure 18.3 than it is to the expression $(p_{32}p_{43} - p_{21}p_{31}p_{43})$ for Figure 18.4, then the former model is considered to be better supported by the data, *provided* one accepts the same assumptions as for partial correlation analysis discussed earlier. If these assumptions, particularly the assumption of error terms uncorrelated with each other or with other endogenous variables, cannot be met, path analysis will lead to unreliable conclusions.

This technique of path analysis is akin to testing whether the predicted coefficients more nearly approach zero for one model compared to another in analysis using partial correlations or partial regression coefficients. In this sense the three types of coefficients can be used in a similar manner in testing models. Ordinarily the student will be interested in the use of a standardized measure, such as the correlation coefficients or path coefficients. Hubert Blalock has emphasized a major advantage of analysis using unstandardized regression coefficients, however: since they are not standardized, they reflect information on (1) the mean magnitude of the variable under study as well as (2) on the magnitude of change in one variable associated with a unit change in another variable. This information is comparable among populations regardless of whether or not the variables under study display the same variation in the different populations. To explain why a variable assumes a given average level in value, or to understand whether or not a relationship is constant in magnitude across populations of differing variances in the variables studied, an unstandardized measure would seem to be more useful. Of course the selection of such a measure means the researcher must forego other advantages associated with standardization: in correlation, for example, a measure that varies between zero and 1, has a meaning in terms of the proportion of variance explained, and is not affected by the magnitude of units of measurement (e.g., correlation will be the same whether income is measured in dollars or pounds, though the unstandardized regression coefficient will differ).[4] Assuming that a standardized procedure, involving path coefficients, is chosen, the sections below discuss this method more fully.

---

[4] H. Blalock, "Theory Building and Causal Inferences," in H. Blalock and A. Blalock, eds., *Methodology in Social Research*, pp. 186–192.

The general procedure in path analysis is to

1. Draw a recursive model of the phenomenon using variables for which appropriate data are available.
2. Specify the equations that describe the causal system in the model.
3. Derive values for the path coefficients by solution of these multiple equations.

Finally, of course, the path coefficients are used to aid the testing of models and the construction of theories.

Drawing a Recursive Model

Let us start with a simple three-variable model, the hypothesis that two independent variables, economic reversal (X_1) and intensity of social movement activity (X_2), cause the variation in the dependent variable, frequency of rioting (X_3). Assume that we have already gotten beyond the formidable problems of defining these terms and gathering valid measurements. Then our model would look like Figure 18.5, where X_a is a residual factor that includes the error factor.

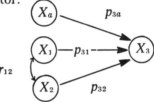

FIGURE 18.5

Note that we assume that the residual factor is uncorrelated with the independent variables. Given this sort of model, we can now express each of the relationships in equation form.

Note that this model, unlike those previously discussed (Figures 18.3 and 18.4), has *two* exogenous variables (i.e., variables that are not caused by other variables in the model; in Figure 18.5, variables 1 and 2 are exogenous). In such cases we show their correlation by a double-headed arrow as in Figure 18.5, indicating that we are not attempting to attribute causality between such variables.

Specifying Path Estimation Equations

First we can write the equation that says that the dependent variable is a function of the paths from the independent variables and the residual variable:

$$z_3 = p_{31}z_1 + p_{32}z_2 + p_{3a}z_a$$

where z_i = scores in normal form

Then we can write the equations that show that the correlations of the independent variables with the dependent variable are a function of the paths between a given independent variable and the dependent variable, plus the path between one independent variable and another:

$$r_{31} = p_{31} + p_{32}r_{12}$$

$$r_{32} = p_{32} + p_{31}r_{12}$$

Of course, all correlations can be computed quantitatively from the observed data, so we know these values from the start. The last equations to be written involve the dependent variable and the residual variable:

$$r_{33} = 1 = p_{31}r_{31} + p_{32}r_{32} + p_{3a}^2$$

$$p_{3a} = 1 - (p_{31}r_{31} + p_{32}r_{32}) = 1 - R^2$$

$$p_{3a} = 1 - R^2$$

R^2, of course, is the coefficient of multiple correlation, discussed in an earlier chapter. That is, it is the coefficient of the combined correlation of the independent variables (X_1 and X_2) with the dependent variable (X_3).

Before continuing to the third step, it should be pointed out that a parallel set of equations involving regression coefficients and path regression coefficients could also be written for the same model:

$$b_{31} = c_{31} + c_{32}b_{21}$$

$$b_{32} = c_{32} + c_{31}b_{12}$$

Deriving Values of the Path Coefficients

We are now in a position to solve the path estimation equations for p_{ij} by any of the standard algebraic means. This solution, clearly outlined by Kenneth Land, is as follows for the case of p_{31}.[5]
Start with the equation:

$$r_{31} = p_{31} + p_{32}r_{12}$$

Transform to place p_{31} to the left of the equal sign:

$$p_{31} = r_{31} - p_{32}r_{12}$$

[5]Kenneth Land, "Principles of Path Analysis," in E. Borgatta, ed., *Sociological Methodology 1969* (San Francisco: Jossey-Bass, 1969), ch. 1.

and by the same process,

$$p_{32} = r_{32} - p_{31}r_{12}$$

By substituting for p_{32} in the equation for p_{31} we get:

$$p_{31} = r_{31} - (r_{32} - p_{31}r_{12})r_{12}$$

$$= r_{31} - r_{32}r_{12} + p_{31}r_{12}r_{12}$$

Subtract $p_{31}\, r_{12}^2$ from both sides of the equation:

$$p_{31}(1 - r_{12}^2) = r_{31} - r_{32}r_{12}$$

Then solve for p_{31} by dividing each side by $(1 - r_{12}^2)$:

$$p_{31} = \frac{r_{31} - r_{32}r_{12}}{1 - r_{12}^2}$$

Determining Direct and Indirect Effects

Path coefficients are extremely useful in interpreting the meaning of correlation coefficients. In our hypothetical example, recall that X_1 was economic reversal (ER), X_2 was intensity of social movement action (SM), and the dependent variable X_3 was frequency of rioting (FR).

Also recall from the path estimation equations that

$$r_{31} = p_{31} + r_{12}p_{32}$$

That is, the correlation between rioting (FR) and economic reversal (ER) can be quantitatively divided into two parts, the first (p_{31}) representing *direct* effect of ER on FR, and the second $(r_{12}p_{32})$ representing the *indirect* effects of ER on FR due to ER's relation to other independent variables—in this case, to SM.*

Or to put it another way, the total indirect effect (TIE) of ER on FR is equal to

$$r_{12}p_{32} = TIE \text{ of 1 on 3} = r_{31} - p_{31}$$

---

*Note that "indirect effects" have two meanings, depending on whether the other independent variable(s) involved are intervening or antecedent. For a more detailed treatment of computation of direct and indirect effects see D. Alwin and R. Hauser, "The Decomposition of Effects in Path Analysis," *American Sociological Review* 40, no. 1 (February 1975): 37–47.

Note also that p_{3a} represents the proportion of the standard deviation in the dependent variable and p^2_{3a} represents the proportion of the variance in the dependent variable attributable to all causes including error other than the independent variables:

$$p^2_{3a} = \text{unexplained variance} = 1 - R^2$$

In fact, since there is unexplained variance (including error variance) in the independent variables as well as the dependent variables, our model should have looked like Figure 18.6.

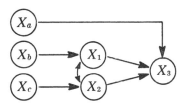

FIGURE 18.6

The paths from X_b to X_1 and from X_c to X_2 are computed the same as for that from X_a to X_3:

$$p_{3a} = \sqrt{1 - R^2} \qquad \text{where } R \text{ is } X_1 + X_2 \text{ on } X_3$$
$$p_{1b} = \sqrt{1 - R^2} \qquad \text{where } R \text{ is } X_2 + X_3 \text{ on } X_1$$
$$p_{2c} = \sqrt{1 - R^2} \qquad \text{where } R \text{ is } X_1 + X_3 \text{ on } X_2$$

In a complete path analysis diagram, every endogenous factor will have a residual term (e with a letter subscript). The path to this error term is estimated by $1 - R^2$, where R^2 is computed in the regression steps discussed earlier.

Assumptions Involved in Path Analysis

The researcher, of course, starts with the data in standardized score (Z) form. One must assume that the data are interval data. For example, if the analysis deals with a score representing negative attitudes created by riots, where one person scored 80 and another 40, that is assumed to mean that the first person is twice as negative as the second—in just the same way that eighty riots is twice as many as forty riots. Dichotomies can be used (male-female, white-nonwhite), but they are assumed to be real dichotomies, not arbitrary divisions of underlying continua. Land, Labovitz, and other social scientists have argued, however, that the treating of near-interval social science data as if they were interval does not ordinarily lead to significant errors.

The second assumption is that relationships among variables are homo-scedastic, linear, and additive. The researcher should draw scatter diagrams of the variables to visually assess the linearity of the data. Sometimes non-linear data can be transformed to linear form, as by applying logarithms to both sides of the equation.

Third, results will vary according to the causal assumptions. The model assumes that causation flows in the direction implied by the arrows. It also assumes that the causation occurs at one point in time, or at several points if a multistage model, as discussed by Land, is specified. That is, the path co-efficients cannot be used to prove whether the causal priorities hypothesized are "true" or not; they can only be used to aid further research, as by determining the path implications of two alternative causal arrangements of the variables.

Fourth, and implied in the third, is that all system inputs must be clearly presented and differentiated from the dependent variable. In addition, the causal priorities of the independent variables must be specified. No recipro-cal relations or feedback loops between variables are allowed.

Fifth, perhaps most important, the residual terms (in the example, those with letter subscripts) are assumed in each case to be uncorrelated with any of the other determining variables in the equation. Moreover, the residuals must be uncorrelated with one another, have mean values of zero, and be normally distributed.

Sixth, path analysis (and regression analysis) assumes that measurement error is taken into account. Specifically, correlation coefficients must be corrected for *attenuation*. (Attenuation is the "artificial" reduction in the magnitude of a correlation coefficient due to measurement error.) Correct-ing for attenuation bias can make a substantial difference in path analytic conclusions and should always be undertaken unless it is known that mea-surement error is negligible. In particular, it is incorrect to use the path

FIGURE 18.7

analytic prediction (i.e., the prediction that $r_{13} - p_{21} p_{32} = 0$) in testing a causal chain such as that in Figure 18.7 when correlations are uncorrected.

Correction for Attenuation

The standard correction for attenuation (the effect of measurement error) requires the use of reliability coefficients (recall Chapter 12) as measures of the degree of measurement error. A corrected correlation coefficient equals the corresponding uncorrected coefficient divided by the geometric mean of the reliability coefficients of the two variables involved:

$$r_{12}^* = r_{12}/\sqrt{r_{11}r_{22}}$$ where r_{12}^* = the corrected Pearson's r
r_{22} = the uncorrected Pearson's r

r_{11} and r_{22} = the reliability coefficients for variables 1 and 2

There are a number of methods of estimating the reliability coefficients, including test-retest methods and factor analytic methods discussed earlier.[6]

Testing the Significance of Path Coefficients

As in testing the significance of correlation coefficients, the F and t tests are used to test the significance of path coefficients. Recall also that if a large sample is involved, a statistic may be significant but nevertheless be so low that it is not strong or particularly important. The fact that the F and t tests are "parametric" (i.e., involve assumptions about the distribution of the variables) is the reason why the residuals must be assumed to be normally distributed.

The formula for testing the path coefficient p_{ij} would be:

$$F = \frac{p_{ij}^2(n-2)}{1 - p_{ij}^2}$$

In this formula p_{ij} represents the standard correlation coefficient between j and i, while n represents the number of observations made on i and j. One then takes this value of F, computes the two associated degrees of freedom

$$\text{d.f.}_1 = 1 \qquad\qquad \text{d.f.}_2 = n - 2,$$

---

[6]For an example of path analysis involving a discussion of correction for attenuation, see J. Kelley, "Causal Chain Models for the Socioeconomic Career," *American Sociological Review* 38, no. 4 (August 1973): 481–493.

A different approach to measurement error in path analysis is the use of multiple indicators for each construct. See H. Costner, "Theory, Deduction, and Rules of Correspondence," *American Journal of Sociology* 75, no. 2 (September 1969): 245–263. On the multiple indicator approach in partial correlation analysis, see J. Sullivan, "Multiple Indicators and Complex Causal Models," in H. Blalock, ed., *Causal Models*, ch. 18.

and consults a table of critical deviations of F for the .05 level and .01 level, or whatever level the researcher deems adequate. In consulting such a table he or she will see, for example, that at the .05 level for $n = 62$, F must be 4.00 or higher to consider the path coefficient significant ($p_{ij} = .25$ or higher would be significant in this case). For small samples, a t test would be used instead of an F test.

Using Tests of Significance in Model Building

Paths that are not statistically significant may, after an examination of the implications, be dropped from the model. That is, the F test can serve as a criterion for improving causal models if used in conjunction with path analysis. Since path coefficients measure only the *direct* contribution of one variable to another, this is preferable to the earlier method of deleting causal arrows in a model when the correlation between the variables was statistically insignificant.

Example: Unemployment, Real Wages, and Rioting

The data in this example are taken from a study of American labor disturbances between 1927 and 1963. For simplicity, only three variables will be considered: annual frequency of rioting ($RIOT$), the unemployment rate ($UEMP$), and adjusted weekly wages in 1947–49 dollars ($AWWG$). By methods discussed in the previous section on correlation, the product-moment correlation matrix shown in Table 18.2 was generated. These

TABLE 18.2

| | 1 | 2 | 3 |
Variable	UEMP	AWWG	RIOT
UEMP	1.000	−.651	.768
AWWG		1.000	−.662
RIOT			1.000

The multiple correlation R of $UEMP$ and $AWWG$ with $RIOT$ was .797

correlation coefficients are all significant above the .01 level.

As a first step, a hypothetical causal diagram is drawn with the correlation coefficients written in. (Figure 18.8*) If any of the correlation coeffi-

FIGURE 18.8

* @ is an error factor.

cients between variables linked in this causal diagram were not statistically significant, of course, the researcher would ordinarily rethink his model to adjust for this.

Step 2 is to specify the path estimation equations. These equations are the same as those worked earlier in this chapter, where it was shown that

$$p_{31} = \frac{r_{31} - r_{32} r_{12}}{1 - r_{12}^2}$$

By substituting the values of r derived from the data, we get:

$$p_{31} = \frac{.768 - (-.662)(-.651)}{1 - (-.651)^2} = \frac{.337}{.576} = .585$$

One of the path estimation equations derived previously was:

$$r_{32} = p_{32} + p_{31} r_{12}$$

By subtracting $p_{31} r_{12}$ from each side we obtain the formula for p_{32}:

$$p_{32} = r_{32} - p_{31} r_{12}$$

Since we already know the value of p_{31}, we can substitute the values:

$$p_{32} = -.662 - (.585)(-.651) = -.281$$

The last path, p_{3a}, is the root of 1 minus the multiple correlation, discussed earlier.

$$p_{3a} = \sqrt{1 - R^2} = \sqrt{1 - (.796)^2} = .604$$

At this point the casual model may be redrawn, writing in the path coefficients, after checking their significance on an F table. (Figure 18.9)

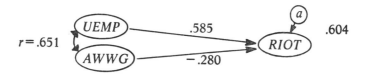

FIGURE 18.9

The last step involves *using path coefficients to partition the variance of the dependent variable:* this is possible because the correlation of the dependent variable with itself can be expressed as a function of path coefficients:

$$r_{33} = 1 = p_{31}r_{31} + p_{32}r_{32} + p_{3a}^2$$

By substituting the values derived above,   e get:

$$r_{33} = (.585)(.768) + (-.280)(-.662) + (.604)^2$$

$$= .449 + .185 + .365$$

$$\cong 1.00$$

Thus we can conclude that the path from unemployment to riot frequency accounted for .449 of the variance in rioting, changes in real wages accounted for another .185, and other factors not specified in the causal model, including error, accounted for the remaining .365 of the variation, assuming causality actually flowed in the direction indicated by the arrows. (Note that for purposes of simplicity of presentation, a correction for attenuation was not undertaken; a complete analysis would include such corrections prior to computing the path coefficients.)

Standard versus Concrete Path Coefficients

The foregoing discussion of path analysis assumed the use of standardized (beta) regression coefficients as the basis for computing the path coefficients, and these were used in conjunction with normalized (z-score) data. It is possible, however, to undertake a similar form of analysis using unstandardized (b) coefficients to compute the *concrete* path coefficients, using these in conjunction with raw (x-score) data.

The rationale for using concrete path coefficients in preference to standard path coefficients is the same as mentioned earlier in comparing analysis by unstandardized regression coefficients with analysis by correlation coefficients (which involve standardization). In summary, equal standardized coefficients for two independent variables mean that the variables have the same predictive power in the model, *but* the word "same" *assumes* that the variables have been made comparable by standardization.

As Schoenberg states:

> The following rule of thumb should be burned into the minds of all who would use path analysis methods: Paths may be compared only with those other paths that impinge on the same dependent variable (within the same set of data) to which it contributes variation. It is possible to multiply paths together and compare the result with a single path or with another path product as long as both paths end at the same dependent variable.... A path coefficient can also be directly interpreted as the increase in standard units in the dependent

variable if the independent variable increases by one standard unit and the other variables are held constant. This result again cannot be generalized beyond the sample or subsample from which it was computed since it is a function of the sample variances. [7]

That is, if we divide our data into two groups (e.g., whites and blacks) and then undertake a path analysis of a given model for each group, we might find the path coefficients for two corresponding paths to be equal. Can we conclude that the effect is equal in both groups? No—because standardized coefficients reflect not only the effect, but also the size of the variances of the variables. Unless the variances are the same in each group, the standardized path coefficients are not comparable.

Correspondingly, if differences in variances are taken into account through the use of unstandardized path coefficients (called concrete path coefficients or path regression coefficients), we will then find that paths reflecting "the same predictive power" by the criterion of equal standardized coefficients involve different actual effects (i.e., different raw-score effects). Specifically, paths involving variables with larger means or smaller standard deviation will be associated with greater raw-score effects. Thus, a concrete path coefficient can be interpreted as the increase in actual (raw-score) units in the dependent variable if the independent variable increases by one actual (raw-score) unit and other variables are held constant.

In conclusion, if we wish to compare effects to determine if they are the "same," we must decide what we mean by "the same." If we mean that a given percentage increase in raw scores *does* have the same magnitude effect on the raw scores of the dependent variable, then we should opt for un-standardized measures such as concrete path coefficients. If by "the same" we mean that a given percentage increase in raw scores *would* have the same effect on the dependent variable *if* the means and variances were equalized, then we should choose a standardized measure such as standard path coefficients. [8]

Problems of Causal Inference

Beyond previously mentioned problems associated with the assumptions of path analysis (e.g., interval data of high reliability, uncorrelated error terms, no feedback effects, and all the assumptions associated with regression

[7]Ronald Schoenberg, "Strategies for Meaningful Comparison," in H. Costner, ed., *Sociological Methodology 1972* (San Francisco: Jossey-Bass, 1972), p. 4.

[8]For further discussion of this point, see S. Wright, "Path Coefficients and Path Regressions: Alternative or Complementary Concepts?" in H. Blalock, ed., *Causal Models*, ch. 6. Wright argues that the two types of coefficient "correspond to different modes of interpretation which taken together give a deeper understanding of a situation than either can give itself" (p. 114).

analysis), David Heise has drawn attention to a problem of inference in path analysis which has not received sufficient consideration.[9]

Path analysis, as previously stated, assumes a recursive model. That is, the causal sequence of the variables is taken as a given (i.e., it is known which variable is variable 1, which variable 2, and so on) and each endogenous variable is linearly caused only by variables earlier in the sequence. Assuming a different sequence may result in different path coefficients and different conclusions. Thus path analysis assumes the causal sequence is correctly stated and tests to see if the data are consistent.

In a fully recursive system this test is not meaningful. A fully recursive system is one in which there are direct causal links (paths, or arrows in a causal diagram) from the first variable to each of the remaining variables, from the second variable to each of the later variables, from the third variable to each of the remaining ones, and so on until the dependent variable, which is last. Therefore, for k variables, a fully recursive system will involve $k(k - 1)/2$ paths, not counting paths from error terms. Figure 18.10 illustrates a fully recursive four-variable model:

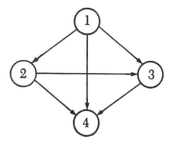

FIGURE 18.10

As discussed earlier, a model may be tested in path analysis by evaluating the degree to which the path coefficients can be used to predict the correlation coefficients. To the extent that there is a discrepancy between the observed correlations and the predicted correlations, one may conclude that the data do not support the path model. *But*, as Heise notes, "such a discrepancy can arise only when one has hypothesized a model more parsimonious than a full-scale recursive model, that is, when one has assumed some possible paths that might exist in the recursive model do not, in fact, exist."[10] That is, a fully recursive model will always lead to path coefficients which reproduce the correlations, even when the model is erroneous. Path analysis assumes that the causal sequence is correct in the model.

[9]David Heise, "Problems in Path Analysis and Causal Inference," in E. Borgatta, ed., *Sociological Methodology 1969*, ch. 2.
[10]*Ibid.*, p. 62.

Assuming a known causal sequence, path analysis can test whether or not a simpler model than the fully recursive model is supported by the data. The models in Figure 18.11 are such models, simpler than the full model of

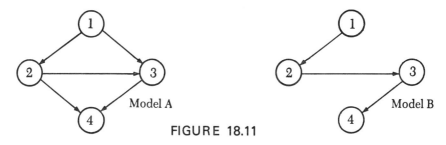

Model A

Model B

FIGURE 18.11

18.10. These simpler models, in effect, hypothesize that some of the path coefficients are zero; the test of these hypotheses is evaluation of the extent to which one can predict the correlations.

There is no mathematical criterion for determining when the discrepancies are small enough to accept the simplified model as consistent with the data. Significance tests are not appropriate since the need for high reliability calls for the use of large samples in path analysis, but large samples mean that a very small absolute discrepancy may well be found significant. *If* the researcher accepts the posited causal sequence and *if* he or she is satisfied that the discrepancies are "too large," then path analysis provides a criterion for rejecting an hypothesized model.

Often, however, the researcher will want to use path analysis to compare two simplified models of the same fully recursive system—for example, to compare Model A and Model B in Figure 18.11. As Heise notes, we cannot conclude that the model with the smaller discrepancies is better supported by the data. That is because the model that more nearly approximates the fully recursive model (Model A) will by this very characteristic tend to reproduce the correlation matrix better. If we find that the less recursive simple model (Model B) reproduces the correlations better than the more recursive simple model (Model A), we have no problem in accepting the former as more supported by the data by path analytic assumptions. But if the more recursive model better reproduces the correlations, we are left uncertain whether this is due to it being a better model or to it being a more nearly fully recursive model, or both.

Reciprocal Interactions

All the models discussed to this point have involved one-way causal arrows. Although too complex a topic to treat here, it should be noted that Wright and others have developed path analytic methods that allow reciprocal (two-way) causal hypotheses.[11] As Heise notes also, when the feedback effect involves a time lage, a recursive model may still be used (1) if one treats the given variable in time one as if it were a different variable from the same variable in time two, and (2) if one can assume that the error term of the given variable in time one is uncorrelated with the error term of the variable in time two.

Nominal and Ordinal Data

The previous discussion has also assumed that the data are measured at the interval level. It should be noted that methods analogous to path analysis have been developed for nominal and ordinal data. Smith has developed a procedure for path analysis using ordinal statistics (tau) which is quite similar to the interval-level techniques outlined above. In an empirical test of this method, Smith found that treatment of ordinal-level data as if it were interval for purposes of interval-level path analysis led to conclusions not supported by ordinal-level path analysis of the data he studied. Somers' work also supports this ordinal method.[12] Thomas Wilson has persuasively argued, however, that these procedures require an assumption of additivity not warranted by the data.[13] On the other hand, as Raoul Naroll has commented on this ongoing debate, violation of this assumption has not been shown to be an important source of error in practical applications and therefore use of partial tau in path analysis still seems a fruitful tool.[14] An alternative approach is found in the work of Leo Goodman.

Goodman has extended the methods of interaction analysis discussed in Chapter 13 to include techniques that are analogous to path analysis, except they are appropriate for dichotomous and polytomous data.[15] Interval-level path analysis of such data requires relaxing the assumptions of homoscedasticity and of a range not restricted to specific limits. As Goodman notes, his method does not require these assumptions.

[11]S. Wright, "The Treatment of Reciprocal Interaction, with or without Lag, in Path Analysis," in *Biometrics* (September 1960): 423–445. On reciprocal methods in regression analysis ("structural equations"), see M. Ezekiel and K. Fox, *Methods of Correlation and Regression Analysis* (New York: John Wiley & Sons, 1967), ch. 24.

[12]R. Smith, "Neighborhood Context and College Plans: An Ordinal Path Analysis," *Social Forces* 51, no. 2 (December 1972): 199–217; "Continuities in Ordinal Path Analysis," *Social Forces* 53, no. 2 (December 1974): 200–229. R. Somers, "Analysis of Partial Rank Correlation Measures Based on the Product-Moment Model," *Social Forces* 53, no. 2 (December 1974): 229–246.

[13]T. Wilson, "On 'Ordinal Path Analysis'," *Social Forces* 53, no. 1 (September 1974): 120–123; "On Interpreting Ordinal Analogies," *Social Forces* 53, no. 2 (December 1974): 196–199; "Reply to Smith and Somers," *Social Forces* 53, no. 2 (December 1974): 247–251.

[14]Raoul Naroll, "The Use of Ordinal Statistics in Causal Analysis of Correlations," *Social Forces* 53, no. 2 (December 1974): 251–253.

[15]L. Goodman, "Causal Analysis of Data from Panel Studies and Other Kinds of Surveys," *American Journal of Sociology* 78, no. 5 (March 1973): 1135–1191.

COMMONALITY ANALYSIS

One of the uses of path analysis is to partition the variance in a dependent variable into portions attributable to the various causal paths to it, including the path from the error term. Other techniques that serve the general function of partitioning the variance in a dependent variable are analysis of variance (Chapter 14) and commonality analysis.

Commonality analysis enables us to partition the variance in a dependent variable, y, into elements associated uniquely with each independent variable and each combination of independent variables and with the error term. For a four-variable model the result is as follows:

$$r_{yy} = 1 = U_1 + U_2 + U_3 + C_{12} + C_{13} + C_{23} + C_{123} + E$$

That is, the variance in the dependent variable, y, can be viewed as composed of elements associated with the unique contribution of each variable (U_i, where $i = 1, 2, 3$), the common contribution of each pair of independent variables (C_{ij}), the common contribution of all three variables (C_{ijk}), and the contribution of the error term (E). The common effects are called "interaction effects."

Commonality analysis is an extension of regression analysis, as is path analysis. Consequently, it involves the same assumptions. In particular it should be noted that the unique and common coefficients computed in commonality analysis (like regression and path coefficients) will often change dramatically if variables are added to or subtracted from the analysis. That is, the unique variance associated with a given independent variable will be a misleading estimate to the extent that relevant variables have been omitted from the analysis. An additional problem of commonality analysis is the large number of coefficients computed. By the probability rules discussed earlier (recall Chapter 8) we know that the number of coefficients in commonality analysis will be 2 , where n is the number of independent variables. Thus for a model with six independent variables, the variance in the dependent variable will be partitioned into sixty-four elements!

How are these elements computed?

1. The Error Component

The error component, E, is simply one minus the coefficient of multiple determination, R^2:

$$E = 1 - R^2_{y.123}$$

2. The Unique Components

The unique contributions of each variable considered separately, U_i, are equal to the amount each raises R^2 when it is entered last into a regression equation:

$$U_1 = R^2_{y.123} - R^2_{y.23}$$

$$U_2 = R^2_{y.123} - R^2_{y.13}$$

$$U_3 = R^2_{y.123} - R^2_{y.12}$$

3. The Common Components

Computation of the common elements is more complicated. The first step is to construct a mathematical expression in which each variable in the combination for which the common coefficient is sought is expressed as $(1 - X_i)$ and each variable not in the combination is listed after these terms. For the common coefficient C_{12} (involving the joint interaction of X_1 and X_2) in a model with three independent variables (X_1, X_2, X_3), the expression is as follows: [16]

$$-1 (1 - X_1)(1 - X_2) X_3 = -X_3 + X_1 X_3 + X_2 X_3 - X_1 X_2 X_3$$

The second step is to expand this expression by multiplying through, as illustrated above (note that -1 always precedes the first term in the expression to the left of the equal sign).

The third step is to replace the Xs in the expanded expression with the corresponding coefficients of multiple determination. This gives the expression for computing the common coefficient:

$$C_{12} = -R^2_{y.3} + R^2_{y.13} + R^2_{y.23} - R^2_{y.123}$$

We can find the other common terms in the same manner:

$$C_{13} = -R^2_{y.2} + R^2_{y.12} + R^2_{y.23} - R^2_{y.123}$$

$$C_{23} = -R^2_{y.1} + R^2_{y.12} + R^2_{y.13} - R^2_{y.123}$$

---

[16]For a more complete presentation of commonality analysis, including an example, see F. Kerlinger and E. Pedhazur, *Multiple Regression in Behavioral Research* (New York: Holt, Rinehart, & Winston, 1973): 297–305, on which the above discussion draws.

The common term for all three independent variables will involve a -1 which is ignored, but otherwise the computation is the same:

$$-1(1-X_1)(1-X_2)(1-X_3) \; = \; -1+X_1+X_2-X_1X_2+X_3-X_1X_3-X_2X_3+X_1X_2X_3$$

$$C_{123} \; = \; R^2_{y.1}+R^2_{y.2}-R^2_{y.12}+R^2_{y.3}-R^2_{y.13}-R^2_{y.23}+R^2_{y.123}$$

All the coefficients of multiple determination (R^2) can be computed by procedures outlined in Chapter 15.

Partitioning the variance by commonality analysis rather than path analysis is preferred when: (1) one cannot confidently posit the causal sequence assumed in path analysis or meet other assumptions of this method; (2) one can meet the assumptions of regression analysis (including absence of multicollinearity); and (3) the number of independent variables is not so great as to make the number (2^n) of commonality coefficients excessive. Such partitions of the variance in the dependent variable are more useful in assessing the relative predictive power of determinants than in making causal inferences, however.

SUMMARY

It is tempting to suppose that the most complicated techniques for analyzing data are somehow the best. But, of course, a moment's reflection should convince us that what is "best" depends upon our research purposes. Most political science writing will be more concerned with conceptual and substantive matters than with data manipulation. In these matters the topics discussed in the first several chapters of this volume are the more relevant. Even where quantitative analysis is possible, the quality of our data may dictate simple techniques, such as the analysis of tables and subtables. Such approaches should not be slighted as "unsophisticated" since, in many if not most political science research contexts, they will be the most appropriate. Only with data of the best quality and under quite stringent assumptions explicitly accepted may we fruitfully move on to more complex methods such as those discussed in this chapter.

EXERCISE

Read and evaluate the effectiveness of path analysis in John Child, "Strategies of Control and Organizational Behavior," in *Administrative Science Quarterly* 18, no. 1 (March 1973): 1–17.

If computer facilities are available, compute the path coefficients for Child's Figure 3 (p. 15) when you assume a different causal ordering of the variables, and compare your results with Child's. Then partition the variance in the dependent variable ("conflict") using commonality analysis, and compare the results by this method with those using path analysis.

Appendixes

Examples of Computer Programs

Every computer is different, and most university computer centers will have their own "prepackaged" programs for social science data. In using these programs, the researcher needs to understand only a minimum of programming. In fact, these are sometimes called "cookbook" programs, since it is only necessary to follow the directions! To give an idea of how these easy-to-use prepackaged programs work, three are presented here:

(1) a Fortran program that can be used on almost any computer system; (2) a prepackaged program supplied by I.B.M. for use on their smallest computer, the 1130; and (3) a prepackaged program used on large computers, using the Statistical Package in the Social Sciences (SPSS; the most common of the prepackaged programs used by political scientists).

A PROGRAM FOR CROSS-TABULATION AND CHI-SQUARE

The program for cross-tabulation and chi-square[1] is designed to construct up to 200 r-by-c tables, using up to 400 variables and an unlimited number of respondents, where the variables range from 0 to 9 in integers. Thus, if there are three levels of income and 5 levels of political attitude, the program would print a 3-by-5 table, giving also the chi-square significance for the table.

Step 1

Starting in column 1 of an IBM card, type up a "job card":

// JOB T

[1]The program for crosstabulation was written by Karl Deirup.

This card tells the computer your job is starting; if desired, or if your computer center requires it, you can also place your identification number (usually starting in column 51) and name (usually starting in column 63) on this card. The computer will then print these at the top of each page of the printout.

Step 2

After the job card comes a stack of program cards. This is the "prepackaged" part. As an illustration, these program cards are listed here, with a brief description of how the program works.

```
/ / FOR
*IOCS(CARD,1132PRINTER,DISK)
*ONE WORD INTEGERS
     DEFINE FILE 1 (20000, 1, U, NEXT)
     DIMENSION ISCOR(400,ANAME(400,2)KRT1(200),KRT2(200),
     1NROW(200),NCOL(200),INTRY(10,10),MARGR(10),MARGC(10),
     2CLMPC(10),RWMPC(10),PERCN(10,10)
```

(This part of the program sets aside space for 200 10-by-10 tables, 400 variables, and other space needed.)

```
 1 DO 10 I = 1, 400
10 ISCOR (I) = 0
   DO 11 I = 1, 20000, 400
11 WRITE (1'I) (ISCOR(J), J = 1, 400)
```

These cards set the spaces set aside for tables and variables equal to zero to begin with.

```
    READ (2, 101) NV, NCT, NDATA, ((ANAME(I,J), J = 1,2),
    I = 1, NV)
101 FORMAT (13,11X,13,11X,15/ (26A3,2X))
```

These direct the computer to read the first control card, discussed in step 3, plus name cards discussed in step 4.

```
    WRITE (3, 102) ((ANAME(I,J),J = 1,2),I = 1,NV)
102 FORMAT (1H1,2A3,14(1X,2A3)/15X,15(1X,2A3)
```

Computer is instructed to write variable names, for automatic listing of the first ten data cards.

```
    READ (2, 103) (KRT1(I), KRT2(I) NROW(I), NCOL(I), I = 1, NCT)
103 FORMAT (5(13, 2X, 13, 1X, 12, 2X, 12, 1X))
```

Computer reads the crosstab control cards discussed in step 5.

```
      DO 12 J = 1, NDATA
      READ (2, 104) (ISCOR(I), I = 1, NV)
104   FORMAT (7011,10X)
      WRITE (3,105) (ISCOR(I), I = 1, NV)
105   FORMAT (/(1517),15X)
      DO 12 I = 1, NCT
      IJK1 = KRT1(I)
      IJK2 = KRT2(I)
      M1 = 100*(I - 1) & 10*(ISCOR(IJK1)) & ISCOR(IJK2) &1
      READ (1'M1) M2
      M2 = M2 & 1
12    WRITE (1'M1) M2
```

These cards are a "DO loop" repeated once for each respondent and resulting in calculation of the entries in each cell. The first two cards after the initial DO 12 card enable the computer to read the data cards discussed in step 6. The next two cards provide for printing out data cards, and the remaining cards are a secondary DO loop within the main DO loop and are repeated once per table.

```
      JPGCH = 0
      DO 24 I = 1, NCT
      IJK1 = KRT1(I)
      IJK2 = KRT2(I)
      JPGCH = JPGCH - (17&3*NROW(I))
      IF (JPGCH) 14, 13, 13
13    WRITE (3, 106) (ANAME(IJK1,K), K = 1,2),IJK1,(ANAME(IJK2,K),K =
      1,2), 1IJK2
106   FORMAT (///////1X,2A3,' IS ROWS (', 13, 1H),3X,2A3, ' IS COLUMNS
      1(', 13,',')')
      GO TO 15
14    JPGCH = 57 = (11&3*NROW(I))
      WRITE(3,107)(ANAME(IJK1,K),K = 1,2),IJK1,(ANAME(IJK2,K),K = 1,2),
      1IJK2
107   FORMAT(1H1,2A3,' IS ROWS (',13,')'',3X,2A3,' IS COLUMNS
      1(',13,')')
```

This part of the program provides for centering tables on printout pages and for writing the heading of each table.

```
15    IR = NROW(I)
      IC = NCOL(I)
      DO 16 KR = 1,IR
```

```
      DO 16 KC = 1,IC
      M3 = 100*(I - 1) & 10*(KR - 1) &KC
 16   READ (1'M3) INTRY(KR,KC)
      ISUMC = 0
      DO 20 KC =  1,IC
      MARGC(KC) = 0
      DO 19 KR = 1,IR
 19   MARGC(KC) = MARGC(KC) & INTRY(KR,KC)
 20   ISUMC = ISUMC & MARGC(KC)
      DO 27 KC = 1, IC
 27   CLMPC(KC) = MARGC(KC)*100.0/ISUMC
      ISUMR = 0
      DO 18 KR =  1,IR
      MARGR(KR) = 0
      DO 17 KC = 1,IC
      PERCN(KR,KC) =  INTRY(KR,KC)*100.0/MARGC(KC)
 17   MARGR(KR) = MARGR(KR) & INTRY(KR,KC)
      RWMPC(KR) = MARGR(KR)*100.0/ISUMC
 18   ISUMR = ISUMR & MARGR(KR)
```

These DO loops read out all the cell entries for a table, calculate the column and row marginals, cell entries as a percent of column totals, and marginal totals as a percent of *N*.

```
      SUMR = ISUMR
      CHISQ = 0
      DO 21 KR  = 1,IR
      DO 21 KC = 1,IC
      EXPF = MARGR(KR)*MARGC(KC) / SUMR
 21   CHISQ = CHISQ & (INTRY(KR,KC) - EXPF)**2/EXPF
```

This section of the program calculates the chi-square value for each table.

```
      ICL = IC - 1
      WRITE (3,108)(KC, KC = 1, ICL)
108   FORMAT(/12X,'0',9I10)
      DO 22 KR = 1,IR
      KRL = KR - 1
      WRITE (3,109) KRL, (INTRY(KR,KC,)KC = 1,IC),MARGR(KR)
109   FORMAT (/1X, 13, 11I10)
 22   WRITE (3, 112) (PERCN(KR,KC),KC = 1,IC), RWMPC(KR)
112   FORMAT 9X,11(F6.1'PCT'))
      WRITE (3,110) (MARGC(KC),KC = 1,IC),ISUMR
110   FORMAT (//4X,11I10)
      WRITE (3,113) (CLMPC(KC),KC = 1,IC)
113   FORMAT (9X,10(F6.1'PCT'))
      IDF = (NROW(I) - 1)*(NCOL(I) - 1)
      WRITE (3,114) IDF
```

```
114  FORMAT ('0',13' DEGREES OF FREEDOM')
     IF (ISMR - ISUMC)23,24,23
 23  WRITE (3,111) ISUMR, ISUMC
111  FORMAT ('ERROR**SUM OF ROW MARGINALS = ',15,', SUM OF
   1 COLUMN MARGINALS = ',15)
 24  WRITE (3,115) CHISQ
115  FORMAT ('OCHI SQUARE = ',F9.3)
     CALL EXIT
     END
//XEQ
```

These cards provide for all the information to be printed out in table form, along with variable names, percentages, marginals, chi-square value and number of degrees of freedom.

Step 3

Now comes the "cookbook" part, telling the computer just what is wanted through "control cards." The first control card, immediately after the //XEQ card, tells the computer how many variables are on the data cards (cols. 1–3), how many tables are to be computed (cols. 15–17), and the number of respondents or units of data (cols. 29–33). For example:

015   VARIABLES 007 CROSSTABS 00125 UNITS OF DATA

Step 4

Next the variable names are listed, using six letters per variable name and a maximum of thirteen names per card, and using as many cards as are needed up to a maximum of 400 variable names. If no names are needed, just put in the appropriate number of blank IBM cards, the same number as if names were used. For example:

VAR001VAR002VAR003VAR004VAR005VAR006VAR007VAR008VAR009
VAR010

Step 5

The next control cards tell the computer which two variables are to be tabled in each table. The computer is told the number of the variable that is to be the row variable in the table (cols. 1–3), the number of the column variable (cols. 6–8), the number of rows to be in the table (cols. 10–11) and the number of columns (cols. 14–15). This sequence may be repeated to give instructions for 5 tables per card, using as many cards as are necessary for up to 200 tables. For example, to crosstabulate variable 1 by variable 2 in a 3-by-6 table, and to tabulate variable 6 by variable 5 in a 10-by-2 table:

001BY002(03BY06)006BY005(10BY02)

Step 6

After these control cards, the researcher then enters the data cards, where the variables range from 0 to 9 and are listed from column 1 to column 70, using as many data cards per respondent as are necessary. Columns 71–80 are reserved for a card identification number, if desired. (If the data are differently arranged, FORMAT 104 in the program may be changed.) Finally, some machines require a blank card at the end of the data. Providing the data cards, filling out a few control cards and a job card, and adding on the prepackaged program is all there is to it.[2]

A PROGRAM FOR STEPWISE LINEAR REGRESSION

IBM supplies "prepackaged" statistical programs, relatively easy to use even by those unfamiliar with programming. One of these is a program for stepwise linear regression. The IBM regression program for the 1130 can handle up to 30 variables, far more than used in most political science applications.

Step 1

The job card, the same as in crosstabulation.

Step 2

The prepackaged program, stored on a computer disk. This program is "called out" by copying the next two cards:

```
// XEQ REGR         01
*LOCALREGR,FMTRD,PRNTB,DATRD,MXRAD,TRAN
```

(This call-out routine comes in different versions, so the user must check with his computer center for the prepackaged programs in use there.)

---

[2]For other Fortran programs, see William Cooley and Paul Lohnes, *Multivariate Procedures for the Behavioral Sciences* (New York: John Wiley & Sons, 1962).

Step 3

An input-output units card, telling the computer what machines to use for reading-in data (cols. 1–2, usually '02' for the card reader as an input device); for output of computed matrices if desired (cols. 3–4, usually also '02') and the main output switch (cols. 5–6, usually '00' for printer output):

020200

Step 4

A job title card; whatever the researcher puts here will be printed at the top of each page of the output. A job number, which is arbitrary, goes in columns 1–4, and any title desired in columns 9–80:

0001   LABOR RIOTING REGRESSION

Step 5

An option card, where entries in columns 1–44 indicate choices the researcher may make about computation and output of the regression analysis. Columns 1–2 list the number of variables, columns 3–4 list the input type, etc. The user will find all this information in an "1130 Statistical System User's Manual." Among the options available is one to print out the correlation matrix of each variable with every other variable (cols. 21–22). Also columns 25–26 can be marked to instruct the computer to stop after computing the correlation matrix, not doing regression analysis at all. Thus, this is also a program for Pearsonian correlation. There is also an option for printing out the regression results after each step (cols. 25–26). In the first step the computer will compute a regression equation with the strongest correlated variable as an independent variable, in the second step two independent variables will be used, in the third step three, etc., until criteria are reached specified in the last three options. An option card would look like this:

0701000000000000000001020100010.010.010.0001

Step 6

Next come one or more variable name cards, the same as in step 4 of the crosstabulation program, except that only four letters are allowed per name:

RIOTWAGEUEMPSTRKVOTEPRTYHOME

Step 7

The next card is a variable format card, describing how the data are positioned on data cards. For example:

$$(14,I1,F2.0,1X,4F4.2,F4.0,1X,F2.1)$$

The format card above reads as follows: the data are arranged with a 4-digit identification number, a 1-digit identification number, a unit of data 2 digits long with zero digits to the right of the decimal, one space (1X), 4 units of data each 4 digits long and each with 2 of these digits to the right of the decimal, a unit 4 digits long with no digits to the right of the decimal, a space, and a last unit of data 2 digits long with one of these digits to the right of the decimal.

Step 8

Then the deck of cards is inserted. For the format in the above example, they would look like this:

```
00010128   1234234534564567111   22
00020249   0293847567483929222   33
etc.
```

Step 9

A card with a −1 entry in the first two columns is placed after the last data card, followed by a blank card, and the program is ready to run.

A PROGRAM FOR FACTOR ANALYSIS

Medium and larger-sized computer facilities usually carry a variety of prepackaged programs, of which one of the most common is the Statistical Package in the Social Sciences (SPSS).[3]

Step 1

As previously, the JOB card comes first. Its exact format will depend upon the practices at your local computer center.

[3]Norman Nie, Dale Bent, and Hadlai Hull, *SPSS: Statistical Package in the Social Sciences* (New York: McGraw-Hill, 1970).

Step 2

SPSS allows the user the option of giving his or her job or run a particular name, which is printed on each page of the output:

RUN NAME   DIMENSIONS OF 60 MUNICIPAL VARIABLES

All SPSS commands involve (1) a control word, starting in column 1 (RUN NAME), and (2) a specification field, starting in column 16 (DIMENSIONS OF . . .).

Step 3

Assuming one has already stored one's data under some file name (e.g., under the name URBAN) in one's area in the computer, all that is necessary next is to call that data out:

GET FILE   URBAN

Step 4

The next SPSS command instructs the computer to perform factor analysis on the URBAN data set:

FACTOR   VARIABLES = SES TO POLICE/TYPE = PA2

If socioeconomic status (SES) is the first variable and size of the police force (POLICE) is the last, then all variables will be entered into the factor analysis. SPSS provides other options whereby the user may list any combination of variables in his or her data set. After the variable list comes a slash, and then a specification of the type of factor analysis to be performed. In the example above, PA2 is the SPSS specification for principal factors using an iterative process to estimate the diagonal entries (recall Chapter 16).

Step 5

SPSS then provides options for the output of various statistics related to factor analysis:

STATISTICS   1, 2, 4

This instructs the SPSS system to compute statistics 1, 2, and 4 from a list of six possible statistics:

1. the correlation matrix,
2. communalities, eigenvalues, and proportion of variance,
3. unrotated principal factor matrix,
4. varimax rotated factor matrix,
5. factor-score coefficient matrix,
6. rotated factors in plot (graph) format.

Step 6

Finally, the user must signal the system that no more control commands are to be entered. This is done simply through the use of the FINISH card:

FINISH

In addition, the user's local computer center may require one or two cards signalling the end of the job.

Appendix B

TABLE I. Squares and Square Roots

Number	Square	Square root	Number	Square	Square root
1	1	1.0000	31	9 61	5.5678
2	4	1.4142	32	10 24	5.6569
3	9	1.7321	33	10 89	5.7446
4	16	2.0000	34	11 56	5.8310
5	25	2.2361	35	12 25	5.9161
6	36	2.4495	36	12 96	6.0000
7	49	2.6458	37	13 69	6.0828
8	64	2.8284	38	14 44	6.1644
9	81	3.0000	39	15 21	6.2450
10	1 00	3.1623	40	16 00	6.3246
11	1 21	3.3166	41	16 81	6.4031
12	1 44	3.4641	42	17 64	6.4807
13	1 69	3.6056	43	18 49	6.5574
14	1 96	3.7417	44	19 36	6.6332
15	2 25	3.8730	45	20 25	6.7082
16	2 56	4.0000	46	21 16	6.7823
17	2 89	4.1231	47	22 09	6.8557
18	3 24	4.2426	48	23 04	6.9282
19	3 61	4.3589	49	24 01	7.0000
20	4 00	4.4721	50	25 00	7.0711
21	4 41	4.5826	51	26 01	7.1414
22	4 84	4.6904	52	27 04	7.2111
23	5 29	4.7958	53	28 09	7.2801
24	5 76	4.8990	54	29 16	7.3485
25	6 25	5.0000	55	30 25	7.4162
26	6 76	5.0990	56	31 36	7.4833
27	7 29	5.1962	57	32 49	7.5498
28	7 84	5.2915	58	33 64	7.6158
29	8 41	5.3852	59	34 81	7.6811
30	9 00	5.4772	60	36 00	7.7460

Source: H. Sorenson, *Statistics for Students of Psychology and Education* (New York: McGraw-Hill Book Company, Inc., 1936), pp. 347–359, Table 72. Copyright © McGraw-Hill Book Company, Inc., with the kind permission of the author and publisher.

TABLE I.   Squares and Square Roots *(Continued)*

Number	Square	Square root	Number	Square	Square root
61	37 21	7.8102	101	1 02 01	10.0499
62	38 44	7.8740	102	1 04 04	10.0995
63	39 69	7.9373	103	1 06 09	10.1489
64	40 96	8.0000	104	1 08 16	10.1980
65	42 25	8.0623	105	1 10 25	10.2470
66	43 56	8.1240	106	1 12 36	10.2956
67	44 89	8.1854	107	1 14 49	10.3441
68	46 24	8.2462	108	1 16 64	10.3923
69	47 61	8.3066	109	1 18 81	10.4403
70	49 00	8.3666	110	1 21 00	10.4881
71	50 41	8.4261	111	1 23 21	10.5357
72	51 84	8.4853	112	1 25 44	10.5830
73	53 29	8.5440	113	1 27 69	10.6301
74	54 76	8.6023	114	1 29 96	10.6771
75	56 25	8.6603	115	1 32 25	10.7238
76	57 76	8.7178	116	1 34 56	10.7703
77	59 29	8.7750	117	1 36 89	10.8167
78	60 84	8.8318	118	1 39 24	10.8628
79	62 41	8.8882	119	1 41 61	10.9087
80	64 00	8.9443	120	1 44 00	10.9545
81	65 61	9.0000	121	1 46 41	11.0000
82	67 24	9.0554	122	1 48 84	11.0454
83	68 89	9.1104	123	1 51 29	11.0905
84	70 56	9.1652	124	1 53 76	11.1355
85	72 25	9.2195	125	1 56 25	11.1803
86	73 96	9.2736	126	1 58 76	11.2250
87	75 69	9.3274	127	1 61 29	11.2694
88	77 44	9.3808	128	1 63 84	11.3137
89	79 21	9.4340	129	1 66 41	11.3578
90	81 00	9.4868	130	1 69 00	11.4018
91	82 81	9.5394	131	1 71 61	11.4455
92	84 64	9.5917	132	1 74 24	11.4891
93	86 49	9.6437	133	1 76 89	11.5326
94	88 36	9.6954	134	1 79 56	11.5758
95	90 25	9.7468	135	1 82 25	11.6190
96	92 16	9.7980	136	1 84 96	11.6619
97	94 09	9.8489	137	1 87 69	11.7047
98	96 04	9.8995	138	1 90 44	11.7473
99	98 01	9.9499	139	1 93 21	11.7898
100	1 00 00	10.0000	140	1 96 00	11.8322

TABLE I. Squares and Square Roots (Continued)

Number	Square	Square root	Number	Square	Square root
141	1 98 81	11.8743	181	3 27 61	13.4536
142	2 01 64	11.9164	182	3 31 24	13.4907
143	2 04 49	11.9583	183	3 34 89	13.5277
144	2 07 36	12.0000	184	3 38 56	13.5647
145	2 10 25	12.0416	185	3 42 25	13.6015
146	2 13 16	12.0830	186	3 45 96	13.6382
147	2 16 09	12.1244	187	3 49 69	13.6748
148	2 19 04	12.1655	188	3 53 44	13.7113
149	2 22 01	12.2066	189	3 57 21	13.7477
150	2 25 00	12.2474	190	3 61 00	13.7840
151	2 28 01	12.2882	191	3 64 81	13.8203
152	2 31 04	12.3288	192	3 68 64	13.8564
153	2 34 09	12.3693	193	3 72 49	13.8924
154	2 37 16	12.4097	194	3 76 36	13.9284
155	2 40 25	12.4499	195	3 80 25	13.9642
156	2 43 36	12.4900	196	3 84 16	14.0000
157	2 46 49	12.5300	197	3 88 09	14.0357
158	2 49 64	12.5698	198	3 92 04	14.0712
159	2 52 81	12.6095	199	3 96 01	14.1067
160	2 56 00	12.6491	200	4 00 00	14.1421
161	2 59 21	12.6886	201	4 04 01	14.1774
162	2 62 44	12.7279	202	4 08 04	14.2127
163	2 65 69	12.7671	203	4 12 09	14.2478
164	2 68 96	12.8062	204	4 16 16	14.2829
165	2 72 25	12.8452	205	4 20 25	14.3178
166	2 75 56	12.8841	206	4 24 36	14.3527
167	2 78 89	12.9228	207	4 28 49	14.3875
168	2 82 24	12.9615	208	4 32 64	14.4222
169	2 85 61	13.0000	209	4 36 81	14.4568
170	2 89 00	13.0384	210	4 41 00	14.4914
171	2 92 41	13.0767	211	4 45 21	14.5258
172	2 95 84	13.1149	212	4 49 44	14.5602
173	2 99 29	13.1529	213	4 53 69	14.5945
174	3 02 76	13.1909	214	4 57 96	14.6287
175	3 06 25	13.2288	215	4 62 25	14.6629
176	3 09 76	13.2665	216	4 66 56	14.6969
177	3 13 29	13.3041	217	4 70 89	14.7309
178	3 16 84	13.3417	218	4 75 24	14.7648
179	3 20 41	13.3791	219	4 79 61	14.7986
180	3 24 00	13.4164	220	4 84 00	14.8324

TABLE I.   Squares and Square Roots *(Continued)*

Number	Square	Square root	Number	Square	Square root
221	4 88 41	14.8661	261	6 81 21	16.1555
222	4 92 84	14.8997	262	6 86 44	16.1864
223	4 97 29	14.9332	263	6 91 69	16.2173
224	5 01 76	14.9666	264	6 96 96	16.2481
225	5 06 25	15.0000	265	7 02 25	16.2788
226	5 10 76	15.0333	266	7 07 56	16.3095
227	5 15 29	15.0665	267	7 12 89	16.3401
228	5 19 84	15.0997	268	7 18 24	16.3707
229	5 24 41	15.1327	269	7 23 61	16.4012
230	5 29 00	15.1658	270	7 29 00	16.4317
231	5 33 61	15.1987	271	7 34 41	16.4621
232	5 38 24	15.2315	272	7 39 84	16.4924
233	5 42 89	15.2643	273	7 45 29	16.5227
234	5 47 56	15.2971	274	7 50 76	16.5529
235	5 52 25	15.3297	275	7 56 25	16.5831
236	5 56 96	15.3623	276	7 61 76	16.6132
237	5 61 69	15.3948	277	7 67 29	16.6433
238	5 66 44	15.4272	278	7 72 84	16.6733
239	5 71 21	15.4596	279	7 78 41	16.7033
240	5 76 00	15.4919	280	7 84 00	16.7332
241	5 80 81	15.5242	281	7 89 61	16.7631
242	5 85 64	15.5563	282	7 95 24	16.7929
243	5 90 49	15.5885	283	8 00 89	16.8226
244	5 95 36	15.6205	284	8 06 56	16.8523
245	6 00 25	15.6525	285	8 12 25	16.8819
246	6 05 16	15.6844	286	8 17 96	16.9115
247	6 10 09	15.7162	287	8 23 69	16.9411
248	6 15 04	15.7480	288	8 29 44	16.9706
259	6 20 01	15.7797	289	8 35 21	17.0000
250	6 25 00	15.8114	290	8 41 00	17.0294
251	6 30 01	15.8430	291	8 46 81	17.0587
252	6 35 04	15.8745	292	8 52 64	17.0880
253	6 40 09	15.9060	293	8 58 49	17.1172
254	6 45 16	15.9374	294	8 64 36	17.1464
255	6 50 25	15.9687	295	8 70 25	17.1756
256	6 55 36	16.0000	296	8 76 16	17.2047
257	6 60 49	16.0312	297	8 82 09	17.2337
258	6 65 64	16.0624	298	8 88 04	17.2627
259	6 70 81	16.0935	299	8 94 01	17.2916
260	6 76 00	16.1245	300	9 00 00	17.3205

TABLE I.   Squares and Square Roots *(Continued)*

Number	Square	Square root	Number	Square	Square root
301	9 06 01	17.3494	341	11 62 81	18.4662
302	9 12 04	17.3781	342	11 69 64	18.4932
303	9 18 09	17.4069	343	11 76 49	18.5203
304	9 24 16	17.4356	344	11 83 36	18.5472
305	9 30 25	17.4642	345	11 90 25	18.5742
306	9 36 36	17.4929	346	11 97 16	18.6011
307	9 42 49	17.5214	347	12 04 09	18.6279
308	9 48 64	17.5499	348	12 11 04	18.6548
309	9 54 81	17.5784	349	12 18 01	18.6815
310	9 61 00	17.6068	350	12 25 00	18.7083
311	9 67 21	17.6352	351	12 32 01	18.7350
312	9 73 44	17.6635	352	12 39 04	18.7617
313	9 79 69	17.6918	353	12 46 09	18.7883
314	9 85 96	17.7200	354	12 53 16	18.8149
315	9 92 25	17.7482	355	12 60 25	18.8414
316	9 98 56	17.7764	356	12 67 36	18.8680
317	10 04 89	17.8045	357	12 74 49	18.8944
318	10 11 24	17.8326	358	12 81 64	18.9209
319	10 17 61	17.8606	359	12 88 81	18.9473
320	10 24 00	17.8885	360	12 96 00	18.9737
321	10 30 41	17.9165	361	13 03 21	19.0000
322	10 36 84	17.9444	362	13 10 44	19.0263
323	10 43 29	17.9722	363	13 17 69	19.0526
324	10 49 76	18.0000	364	13 24 96	19.0788
325	10 56 25	18.0278	365	13 32 25	19.1050
326	10 62 76	18.0555	366	13 39 56	19.1311
327	10 69 29	18.0831	367	13 46 89	19.1572
328	10 75 84	18.1108	368	13 54 24	19.1833
329	10 82 41	18.1384	369	13 61 61	19.2094
330	10 89 00	18.1659	370	13 69 00	19.2354
331	10 95 61	18.1934	371	13 76 41	19.2614
332	11 02 24	18.2209	372	13 83 84	19.2873
333	11 08 89	18.2483	373	13 91 29	19.3132
334	11 15 56	18.2757	374	13 98 76	19.3391
335	11 22 25	18.3030	375	14 06 25	19.3649
336	11 28 96	18.3303	376	14 13 76	19.3907
337	11 35 69	18.3576	377	14 21 29	19.4165
338	11 42 44	18.3848	378	14 28 84	19.4422
339	11 49 21	18.4120	379	14 36 41	19.4679
340	11 56 00	18.4391	380	14 44 00	19.4936

TABLE I. Squares and Square Roots *(Continued)*

Number	Square	Square root	Number	Square	Square root
381	14 51 61	19.5192	421	17 72 41	20.5183
382	14 59 24	19.5448	422	17 80 84	20.5426
383	14 66 89	19.5704	423	17 89 29	20.5670
384	14 74 56	19.5959	424	17 97 76	20.5913
385	14 82 25	19.6214	425	18 06 25	20.6155
386	14 89 96	19.6469	426	18 14 76	20.6398
387	14 97 69	19.6723	427	18 23 29	20.6640
388	15 05 44	19.6977	428	18 31 84	20.6882
389	15 13 21	19.7231	429	18 40 41	20.7123
390	15 21 00	19.7484	430	18 49 00	20.7364
391	15 28 81	19.7737	431	18 57 61	20.7605
392	15 36 64	19.7990	432	18 66 24	20.7846
393	15 44 49	19.8242	433	18 74 89	20.8087
394	15 52 36	19.8494	434	18 83 56	20.8327
395	15 60 25	19.8746	435	18 92 25	20.8567
396	15 68 16	19.8997	436	19 00 96	20.8806
397	15 76 09	19.9249	437	19 09 69	20.9045
398	15 84 04	19.9499	438	19 18 44	20.9284
399	15 92 01	19.9750	439	19 27 21	20.9523
400	16 00 00	20.0000	440	19 36 00	20.9762
401	16 08 01	20.0250	441	19 44 81	21.0000
402	16 16 04	20.0499	442	19 53 64	21.0238
403	16 24 09	20.0749	443	19 62 49	21.0476
404	16 32 16	20.0998	444	19 71 36	21.0713
405	16 40 25	20.1246	445	19 80 25	21.0950
406	16 48 36	20.1494	446	19 89 16	21.1187
407	16 56 49	20.1742	447	19 98 09	21.1424
408	16 64 64	20.1990	448	20 07 04	21.1660
409	16 72 81	20.2237	449	20 16 01	21.1896
410	16 81 00	20.2485	450	20 25 00	21.2132
411	16 89 21	20.2731	451	20 34 01	21.2368
412	16 97 44	20.2978	452	20 43 04	21.2603
413	17 05 69	20.3224	453	20 52 09	21.2838
414	17 13 96	20.3470	454	20 61 16	21.3073
415	17 22 25	20.3715	455	20 70 25	21.3307
416	17 30 56	20.3961	456	20 79 36	21.3542
417	17 38 89	20.4206	457	20 88 49	21.3776
418	17 47 24	20.4450	458	20 97 64	21.4009
419	17 55 61	20.4695	459	21 06 81	21.4243
420	17 64 00	20.4939	460	21 16 00	21.4476

TABLE I. Squares and Square Roots *(Continued)*

Number	Square	Square root	Number	Square	Square root
461	21 25 21	21.4709	501	25 10 01	22.3830
462	21 34 44	21.4942	502	25 20 04	22.4054
463	21 43 69	21.5174	503	25 30 09	22.4277
464	21 52 96	21.5407	504	25 40 16	22.4499
465	21 62 25	21.5639	505	25 50 25	22.4722
466	21 71 56	21.5870	506	25 60 36	22.4944
467	21 80 89	21.6102	507	25 70 49	22.5167
468	21 90 24	21.6333	508	25 80 64	22.5389
469	21 99 61	21.6564	509	25 90 81	22.5610
470	22 09 00	21.6795	510	26 01 00	22.5832
471	22 18 41	21.7025	511	26 11 21	22.6053
472	22 27 84	21.7256	512	25 21 44	22.6274
473	22 37 29	21.7486	513	26 31 69	22.6495
474	22 46 76	21.7715	514	26 41 96	22.6716
475	22 56 25	21.7945	515	26 52 25	22.6936
476	22 65 76	21.8174	516	22 62 56	22.7156
477	22 75 29	21.8403	517	26 72 89	22.7376
478	22 84 84	21.8632	518	26 83 24	22.7596
479	22 94 41	21.8861	519	26 93 61	22.7816
480	23 04 00	21.9089	520	27 04 00	22.8035
481	23 13 61	21.9317	521	27 14 41	22.8254
482	23 23 24	21.9545	522	27 24 84	22.8473
483	23 32 89	21.9773	523	27 35 29	22.8692
484	23 42 56	22.0000	524	27 45 76	22.8910
485	23 52 25	22.0227	525	27 56 25	22.9129
486	23 61 96	22.0454	526	27 66 76	22.9347
487	23 71 69	22.0681	527	27 77 29	22.9565
488	23 81 44	22.0907	528	27 87 84	22.9783
489	23 91 21	22.1133	529	27 98 41	23.0000
490	24 01 00	22.1359	530	28 09 00	23.0217
491	24 10 81	22.1585	531	28 19 61	23.0434
492	24 20 64	22.1811	532	28 30 24	23.0651
493	24 30 49	22.2036	533	28 40 89	23.0868
494	24 40 36	22.2261	534	28 51 56	23.1084
495	24 50 25	22.2486	535	28 62 25	23.1301
496	24 60 16	22.2711	536	28 72 96	23.1517
497	24 70 09	22.2935	537	28 83 69	23.1733
498	24 80 04	22.3159	538	28 94 44	23.1948
499	24 90 01	22.3383	539	29 05 21	23.2164
500	25 00 00	22.3607	540	29 16 00	23.2379

TABLE I. Squares and Square Roots *(Continued)*

Number	Square	Square root	Number	Square	Square root
541	29 26 81	23.2594	581	33 75 61	24.1039
542	29 37 64	23.2809	582	33 87 24	24.1247
543	29 48 49	23.3024	583	33 98 89	24.1454
544	29 59 36	23.3238	584	34 10 56	24.1661
545	29 70 25	23.3452	585	34 22 25	24.1868
546	29 81 16	23.3666	586	34 33 96	24.2074
547	29 92 09	23.3880	587	34 45 69	24.2281
548	30 03 04	23.4094	588	34 57 44	24.2487
549	30 14 01	23.4307	589	34 69 21	24.2693
550	30 25 00	23.4521	590	34 81 00	24.2899
551	30 36 01	23.4734	591	34 92 81	24.3105
552	30 47 04	23.4947	592	35 04 64	24.3311
553	30 58 09	23.5160	593	35 16 49	24.3516
554	30 69 16	23.5372	594	35 28 36	24.3721
555	30 80 25	23.5584	595	35 40 25	24.3926
556	30 91 36	23.5797	596	35 52 16	24.4131
557	31 02 49	23.6008	597	35 64 09	24.4336
558	31 13 64	23.6220	598	35 76 04	24.4540
559	31 24 81	23.6432	599	35 88 01	24.4745
560	31 36 00	23.6643	600	36 00 00	24.4949
561	31 47 21	23.6854	601	36 12 01	24.5153
562	31 58 44	23.7065	602	36 24 04	24.5357
563	31 69 69	23.7276	603	36 36 09	24.5561
564	31 80 96	23.7487	604	36 48 16	24.5764
565	31 92 25	23.7697	605	36 60 25	24.5967
566	32 03 56	23.7908	606	36 72 36	24.6171
567	32 14 89	23.8118	607	36 84 49	24.6374
568	32 26 24	23.8328	608	36 96 64	24.6577
569	32 37 61	23.8537	609	37 08 81	24.6779
570	32 49 00	23.8747	610	37 21 00	24.6982
571	32 60 41	23.8956	611	37 33 21	24.7184
572	32 71 84	23.9165	612	37 45 44	24.7385
573	32 83 29	23.9374	613	37 57 69	24.7588
574	32 94 76	23.9583	614	37 69 96	24.7790
575	33 06 25	23.9792	615	37 82 25	24.7992
576	33 17 76	24.0000	616	37 94 56	24.8193
577	33 29 29	24.0208	617	38 06 89	24.8395
578	33 40 84	24.0416	618	38 19 24	24.8596
579	33 52 41	24.0624	619	38 31 61	24.8797
580	33 64 00	24.0832	620	38 44 00	24.8998

498   *Appendix B*

TABLE I.   Squares and Square Roots *(Continued)*

Number	Square	Square root	Number	Square	Square root
621	38 56 41	24.9199	661	43 69 21	25.7099
622	38 68 84	24.9399	662	43 82 44	25.7294
623	38 81 29	24.9600	663	43 95 69	25.7488
624	38 93 76	24.9800	664	44 08 96	25.7682
625	39 06 25	25.0000	665	44 22 25	25.7876
626	39 18 76	25.0200	666	44 35 56	25.8070
627	39 31 29	25.0400	667	44 48 89	25.8263
628	39 43 84	25.0599	668	44 62 24	25.8457
629	39 56 41	25.0799	669	44 75 61	25.8650
630	39 69 00	25.0998	670	44 89 00	25.8844
631	39 81 61	25.1197	671	45 02 41	25.9037
632	39 94 24	25.1396	672	45 15 84	25.9230
633	40 06 89	25.1595	673	45 29 29	25.9422
634	40 19 56	25.1794	674	45 42 76	25.9615
635	40 32 25	25.1992	675	45 56 25	25.9808
636	40 44 96	25.2190	676	45 69 76	26.0000
637	40 57 69	25.2389	677	45 83 29	26.0192
638	40 70 44	25.2587	678	45 96 84	26.0384
639	40 83 21	25.2784	679	46 10 41	26.0576
640	40 96 00	25.2982	680	46 24 00	26.0768
641	41 08 81	25.3180	681	46 37 61	26.0960
642	41 21 64	25.3377	682	46 51 24	26.1151
643	41 34 49	25.3574	683	46 64 89	26.1343
644	41 47 36	25.3772	684	46 78 56	26.1534
645	41 60 25	25.3969	685	46 92 25	26.1725
646	41 73 16	25.4165	686	47 05 96	26.1916
647	41 86 09	25.4362	687	47 19 69	26.2107
648	41 99 04	25.4558	688	47 33 44	26.2298
649	42 12 01	25.4755	689	47 47 21	26.2488
650	42 25 00	25.4951	690	47 61 00	26.2679
651	42 38 01	25.5147	691	47 74 81	26.2869
652	42 51 04	25.5343	692	47 88 64	26.3059
653	42 64 09	25.5539	693	48 02 49	26.3249
654	42 77 16	25.5734	694	48 16 36	26.3439
655	42 90 25	25.5930	695	48 30 25	26.3629
656	43 03 36	25.6125	696	48 44 16	26.3818
657	43 16 49	25.6320	697	48 58 09	26.4008
658	43 29 64	25.6515	698	48 72 04	26.4197
659	43 42 81	25.6710	699	48 86 01	26.4386
660	43 56 00	25.6905	700	49 00 00	26.4575

TABLE I. Squares and Square Roots *(Continued)*

Number	Square	Square root	Number	Square	Square root
701	49 14 01	26.4764	741	54 90 81	27.2213
702	49 28 04	26.4953	742	55 05 64	27.2397
703	49 42 09	26.5141	743	55 20 49	27.2580
704	49 56 16	26.5330	744	55 35 36	27.2764
705	49 70 25	26.5518	745	55 50 25	27.2947
706	49 84 36	26.5707	746	55 65 16	27.3130
707	49 98 49	26.5895	747	55 80 09	27.3313
708	50 12 64	26.6083	748	55 95 04	27.3496
709	50 26 81	26.6271	749	56 10 01	27.3679
710	50 41 00	26.6458	750	56 25 00	27.3861
711	50 55 21	26.6646	751	56 40 01	27.4044
712	50 69 44	26.6833	752	56 55 04	27.4226
713	50 83 69	26.7021	753	56 70 09	27.4408
714	50 97 96	26.7208	754	56 85 16	27.4591
715	51 12 25	26.7395	755	57 00 25	27.4773
716	51 26 56	26.7582	756	57 15 36	27.4955
717	51 40 89	26.7769	757	57 30 49	27.5136
718	51 55 24	26.7955	758	57 45 64	27.5318
719	51 69 61	26.8142	759	57 60 81	27.5500
720	51 84 00	26.8328	760	57 76 00	27.5681
721	51 98 41	26.8514	761	57 91 21	27.5862
722	52 12 84	26.8701	762	58 06 44	27.6043
723	52 27 29	26.8887	763	58 21 69	27.6225
724	52 41 76	26.9072	764	58 36 96	27.6405
725	52 56 25	26.9258	765	58 52 25	27.6586
726	52 70 76	26.9444	766	58 67 56	27.6767
727	52 85 29	26.9629	767	58 82 89	27.6948
728	52 99 84	26.9815	768	58 98 24	27.7128
729	53 14 41	27.0000	769	59 13 61	27.7308
730	53 29 00	27.0185	770	59 29 00	27.7489
731	53 43 61	27.0370	771	59 44 41	27.7669
732	53 58 24	27.0555	772	59 59 84	27.7849
733	53 72 89	27.0740	773	59 75 29	27.8029
734	53 87 56	27.0924	774	59 90 76	27.8209
735	54 02 25	27.1109	775	60 06 25	27.8388
736	54 16 96	27.1293	776	60 21 76	27.8568
737	54 31 69	27.1477	777	60 37 29	27.8747
738	54 46 44	27.1662	778	60 52 84	27.8927
739	54 61 27	27.1846	779	60 68 41	27.9106
740	54 76 00	27.2029	780	60 84 00	27.9285

TABLE I.   Squares and Square Roots *(Continued)*

Number	Square	Square root	Number	Square	Square root
781	60 99 61	27.9464	821	67 40 41	28.6531
782	61 15 24	27.9643	822	67 56 84	28.6705
783	61 30 89	27.9821	823	67 73 29	28.6880
784	61 46 56	28.0000	824	67 89 76	28.7054
785	61 62 25	28.0179	825	68 06 25	28.7228
786	61 77 96	28.0357	826	68 22 76	28.7402
787	61 93 69	28.0535	827	68 39 29	28.7576
788	62 09 44	28.0713	828	68 55 84	28.7750
789	62 25 21	28.0891	829	68 72 41	28.7924
790	62 41 00	28.1069	830	68 89 00	28.8097
791	62 56 81	28.1247	831	69 05 61	28.8271
792	62 72 64	28.1425	832	69 22 24	28.8444
793	62 88 49	28.1603	833	69 38 89	28.8617
794	63 04 36	28.1780	834	69 55 56	28.8791
795	63 20 25	28.1957	835	69 72 25	28.8964
796	63 36 16	28.2135	836	69 88 96	28.9137
797	63 52 09	28.2312	837	70 05 69	28.9310
798	63 68 04	28.2489	838	70 22 44	28.9482
799	63 84 01	28.2666	839	70 39 21	28.9655
800	64 00 00	28.2843	840	70 56 00	28.9828
801	64 16 01	28.3019	841	70 72 81	29.0000
802	64 32 04	28.3196	842	70 89 64	29.0172
803	64 48 09	28.3373	843	71 06 49	29.0345
804	64 64 16	28.3549	844	71 23 36	29.0517
805	64 80 25	28.3725	845	71 40 25	29.0689
806	64 96 36	28.3901	846	71 57 16	29.0861
807	65 12 49	28.4077	847	71 74 09	29.1033
808	65 28 64	28.4253	848	71 91 04	29.1204
809	65 44 81	28.4429	849	72 08 01	29.1376
810	65 61 00	28.4605	850	72 25 00	29.1548
811	65 77 21	28.4781	851	72 42 01	29.1719
812	65 93 44	28.4956	852	72 59 04	29.1890
813	66 09 69	28.5132	853	72 76 09	29.2062
814	66 25 96	28.5307	854	72 93 16	29.2233
815	66 42 25	28.5482	855	73 10 25	29.2404
816	66 58 56	28.5657	856	73 27 36	29.2575
817	66 74 89	28.5832	857	73 44 49	29.2746
818	66 91 24	28.6007	858	73 61 64	29.2916
819	67 07 61	28.6082	859	73 78 81	29.3087
820	67 24 00	28.6356	860	73 96 00	29.3258

TABLE I.   Squares and Square Roots *(Continued)*

Number	Square	Square root	Number	Square	Square root
861	74 13 21	29.3428	901	81 18 01	30.0167
862	74 30 44	29.3598	902	81 36 04	30.0333
863	74 47 69	29.3769	903	81 54 09	30.0500
864	74 64 96	29.3939	904	81 72 16	30.0666
865	74 82 25	29.4109	905	81 90 25	30.0832
866	74 99 56	29.4279	906	82 08 36	30.0998
867	75 16 89	29.4449	907	82 26 49	30.1164
868	75 34 24	29.4618	908	82 44 64	30.1330
869	75 51 61	29.4788	909	82 62 81	30.1496
870	75 69 00	29.4958	910	82 81 00	30.1662
871	75 86 41	29.5127	911	82 99 21	30.1828
872	76 03 84	29.5296	912	83 17 44	30.1993
873	76 21 29	29.5466	913	83 35 69	30.2159
874	76 38 76	29.5635	914	83 53 96	30.2324
875	76 56 25	29.5804	915	83 72 25	30.2490
876	76 73 76	29.5973	916	83 90 56	30.2655
877	76 91 29	29.6142	917	84 08 89	30.2820
878	77 08 84	29.6311	918	84 27 24	30.2985
879	77 26 41	29.6479	919	84 45 61	30.3150
880	77 44 00	29.6648	920	84 64 00	30.3315
881	77 61 61	29.6816	921	84 82 41	30.3480
882	77 79 24	29.6985	922	85 00 84	30.3645
883	77 96 89	29.7153	923	85 19 29	30.3809
884	78 14 56	29.7321	924	85 37 76	30.3974
885	78 32 25	29.7489	925	85 56 25	30.4138
886	78 49 96	29.7658	926	85 74 76	30.4302
887	78 67 69	29.7825	927	85 93 29	30.4467
888	78 85 44	29.7993	928	86 11 84	30.4631
889	79 03 21	29.8161	929	86 30 41	30.4795
890	79 21 00	29.8329	930	86 49 00	30.4959
891	79 38 81	29.8496	931	86 67 61	30.5123
892	79 56 64	29.8664	932	86 86 24	30.5287
893	79 74 49	29.8831	933	87 04 89	30.5450
894	79 92 36	29.8998	934	87 23 56	30.5614
895	80 10 25	29.9166	935	87 42 25	30.5778
896	80 28 16	29.9333	936	87 60 96	30.5941
897	80 46 09	29.9500	937	87 79 69	30.6105
898	80 64 04	29.9666	938	87 98 44	30.6268
899	80 82 01	29.9833	939	88 17 21	30.6431
900	81 00 00	30.0000	940	88 36 00	30.6594

TABLE I.   Squares and Square Roots *(Continued)*

Number	Square	Square root	Number	Square	Square root
941	88 54 81	30.6757	971	94 28 41	31.1609
942	88 73 64	30.6920	972	94 47 84	31.1769
943	88 92 49	30.7083	973	94 67 29	31.1929
944	89 11 36	30.7246	974	94 86 76	31.2090
945	89 30 25	30.7409	975	95 06 25	31.2250
946	89 49 16	30.7571	976	95 25 76	31.2410
947	89 68 09	30.7734	977	95 45 29	31.2570
948	89 87 04	30.7896	978	95 64 84	31.2730
949	90 06 01	30.8058	979	95 84 41	31.2890
950	90 25 00	30.8221	980	96 04 00	31.3050
951	90 44 01	30.8383	981	96 23 61	31.3209
952	90 63 04	30.8545	982	96 43 24	31.3369
953	90 82 09	30.8707	983	96 62 89	31.3528
954	91 01 16	30.8869	984	96 82 56	31.3688
955	91 20 25	30.9031	985	97 02 25	31.3847
956	91 39 36	30.9192	986	97 21 96	31.4006
957	91 58 49	30.9354	987	97 41 69	31.4166
958	91 77 64	30.9516	988	97 61 44	31.4325
959	91 96 81	30.9677	989	97 81 21	31.4484
960	92 16 00	30.9839	990	98 01 00	31.4643
961	92 35 21	31.0000	991	98 20 81	31.4802
962	92 54 44	31.0161	992	98 40 64	31.4960
963	92 73 69	31.0322	993	98 60 49	31.5119
964	92 92 96	31.0483	994	98 80 36	31.5278
965	93 12 25	31.0644	995	99 00 25	31.5436
966	93 31 56	31.0805	996	99 20 16	31.5595
967	93 50 89	31.0966	997	99 40 09	31.5753
968	93 70 24	31.1127	998	99 60 04	31.5911
969	93 89 61	31.1288	999	99 80 01	31.6070
970	94 09 00	31.1448	1000	100 00 00	31.6228

TABLE II.   Table of Probabilities Associated with Values as Small as Observed Values of *x* in the Binomial Test

N \ x	0	1	2	3	4	5	6	7	8	9	10	11	12	13	14	15
5	031	188	500	812	969	†										
6	016	109	344	656	891	984	†									
7	008	062	227	500	773	938	992	†								
8	004	035	145	363	637	855	965	996	†							
9	002	020	090	254	500	746	910	980	998	†						
10	001	011	055	172	377	623	828	945	989	999	†					
11		006	033	113	274	500	726	887	967	994	†	†				
12		003	019	073	194	387	613	806	927	981	997	†	†			
13		002	011	046	133	291	500	709	867	954	989	998	†	†		
14		001	006	029	090	212	395	605	788	910	971	994	999	†	†	
15			004	018	059	151	304	500	696	849	941	982	996	†	†	†
16			002	011	038	105	227	402	598	773	895	962	989	998	†	†
17			001	006	025	072	166	315	500	685	834	928	975	994	999	†
18			001	004	015	048	119	240	407	593	760	881	952	985	996	999
19				002	010	032	084	180	324	500	676	820	916	968	990	998
20				001	006	021	058	132	252	412	588	748	868	942	979	994
21				001	004	013	039	095	192	332	500	668	808	905	961	987
22					002	008	026	067	143	262	416	584	738	857	933	974
23					001	005	017	047	105	202	339	500	661	798	895	953
24					001	003	011	032	076	154	271	419	581	729	846	924
25						002	007	022	054	115	212	345	500	655	788	885

†1.0 or approximately 1.0.

Source: Adapted from *Statistical Inference* by Helen M. Walker and Joseph Lev. Copyright, 1953, by Holt, Rinehart and Winston, Inc. Reprinted by permission of Holt, Rinehart and Winston, Inc.

TABLE III.   Areas of the Normal Curve

$\frac{x}{\sigma}$	.00	.01	.02	.03	.04	.05	.06	.07	.08	.09
0.0	.0000	.0040	.0080	.0120	.0159	.0199	.0239	.0279	.0319	.0359
0.1	.0398	.0438	.0478	.0517	.0557	.0596	.0636	.0675	.0714	.0753
0.2	.0793	.0832	.0871	.0910	.0948	.0987	.1026	.1064	.1103	.1141
0.3	.1179	.1217	.1255	.1293	.1331	.1368	.1406	.1443	.1480	.1517
0.4	.1554	.1591	.1628	.1664	.1700	.1736	.1772	.1808	.1844	.1879
0.5	.1915	.1950	.1985	.2019	.2054	.2088	.2123	.2157	.2190	.2224
0.6	.2257	.2291	.2324	.2357	.2389	.2422	.2454	.2486	.2518	.2549
0.7	.2580	.2612	.2642	.2673	.2704	.2734	.2764	.2794	.2823	.2852
0.8	.2881	.2910	.2939	.2967	.2995	.3023	.3051	.3078	.3106	.3133
0.9	.3159	.3186	.3212	.3238	.3264	.3289	.3315	.3340	.3365	.3389
1.0	.3413	.3438	.3461	.3485	.3508	.3531	.3554	.3577	.3599	.3621
1.1	.3643	.3665	.3686	.3718	.3729	.3749	.3770	.3790	.3810	.3830
1.2	.3849	.3869	.3888	.3907	.3925	.3944	.3962	.3980	.3997	.4015
1.3	.4032	.4049	.4066	.4083	.4099	.4115	.4131	.4147	.4162	.4177
1.4	.4192	.4207	.4222	.4236	.4251	.4265	.4279	.4292	.4306	.4319
1.5	.4332	.4345	.4357	.4370	.4382	.4394	.4406	.4418	.4430	.4441
1.6	.4452	.4463	.4474	.4485	.4495	.4505	.4515	.4525	.4535	.4545
1.7	.4554	.4564	.4573	.4582	.4591	.4599	.4608	.4616	.4625	.4633
1.8	.4641	.4649	.4656	.4664	.4671	.4678	.4686	.4693	.4699	.4706
1.9	.4713	.4719	.4726	.4732	.4738	.4744	.4750	.4758	.4762	.4767
2.0	.4772	.4778	.4783	.4788	.4793	.4798	.4803	.4808	.4812	.4817
2.1	.4821	.4826	.4830	.4834	.4838	.4842	.4846	.4850	.4854	.4857
2.2	.4861	.4865	.4868	.4871	.4875	.4878	.4881	.4884	.4887	.4890
2.3	.4893	.4896	.4898	.4901	.4904	.4906	.4909	.4911	.4913	.4916
2.4	.4918	.4920	.4922	.4925	.4927	.4929	.4931	.4932	.4934	.4936
2.5	.4938	.4940	.4941	.4943	.4945	.4946	.4948	.4949	.4951	.4952
2.6	.4953	.4955	.4956	.4957	.4959	.4960	.4961	.4962	.4963	.4964
2.7	.4965	.4966	.4967	.4968	.4969	.4970	.4971	.4972	.4973	.4974
2.8	.4974	.4975	.4976	.4977	.4977	.4978	.4979	.4980	.4980	.4981
2.9	.4981	.4982	.4983	.4984	.4984	.4984	.4985	.4985	.4986	.4986
3.0	.49865	.4987	.4987	.4988	.4988	.4988	.4989	.4989	.4989	.4990
3.1	.49903	.4991	.4991	.4991	.4992	.4992	.4992	.4992	.4993	.4993
4.0	.49997									

Source: "Table of Areas of the Normal Curve," in H. Arkin and R. Colton, An Outline of Statistical Methods, 4th ed. (New York: Barnes and Noble, 1939). By permission of Harper & Row.

TABLE IV.   Distribution of t

df	Level of significance for one-tailed test					
	.10	.05	.025	.01	.005	.0005
	Level of significance for two-tailed test					
	.20	.10	.05	.02	.01	.001
1	3.078	6.314	12.706	31.821	63.657	636.619
2	1.886	2.920	4.303	6.965	9.925	31.598
3	1.638	2.353	3.182	4.541	5.841	12.941
4	1.533	2.132	2.776	3.747	4.604	8.610
5	1.476	2.015	2.571	3.365	4.032	6.859
6	1.440	1.943	2.447	3.143	3.707	5.959
7	1.415	1.895	2.365	2.998	3.499	5.405
8	1.397	1.860	2.306	2.896	3.355	5.041
9	1.383	1.833	2.262	2.821	3.250	4.781
10	1.372	1.812	2.228	2.764	3.169	4.587
11	1.363	1.796	2.201	2.718	3.106	4.437
12	1.356	1.782	2.179	2.681	3.055	4.318
13	1.350	1.771	2.160	2.650	3.012	4.221
14	1.345	1.761	2.145	2.624	2.977	4.140
15	1.341	1.753	2.131	2.602	2.947	4.073
16	1.337	1.746	2.120	2.583	2.921	4.015
17	1.333	1.740	2.110	2.567	2.898	3.965
18	1.330	1.734	2.101	2.552	2.878	3.922
19	1.328	1.729	2.093	2.539	2.861	3.883
20	1.325	1.725	2.086	2.528	2.845	3.850
21	1.323	1.721	2.080	2.518	2.831	3.819
22	1.321	1.717	2.074	2.508	2.819	3.792
23	1.319	1.714	2.069	2.500	2.807	3.767
24	1.318	1.711	2.064	2.492	2.797	3.745
25	1.316	1.708	2.060	2.485	2.787	3.725
26	1.315	1.706	2.056	2.479	2.779	3.707
27	1.314	1.703	2.052	2.473	2.771	3.690
28	1.313	1.701	2.048	2.467	2.763	3.674
29	1.311	1.699	2.045	2.462	2.756	3.659
30	1.310	1.697	2.042	2.457	2.750	3.646
40	1.303	1.684	2.021	2.423	2.704	3.551
60	1.296	1.671	2.000	2.390	2.660	3.460
120	1.289	1.658	1.980	2.358	2.617	3.373
∞	1.282	1.645	1.960	2.326	2.576	3.291

Source: Abridged from Table III of R. A. Fisher and F. Yates, *Statistical Tables for Biological, Agricultural and Medical Research*, 6th ed., published by Longman Group Ltd., London (previously published by Oliver & Boyd, Edinburgh), by permission of the authors and publishers.

TABLE V.   Distribution of χ^2

Probability

df	.99	.98	.95	.90	.80	.70	.50	.30	.20	.10	.05	.02	.01	.001
1	.0³157	.0⁴628	.00393	.0158	.0642	.148	.455	1.074	1.642	2.706	3.841	5.412	6.635	10.827
2	.0201	.0404	.103	.211	.446	.713	1.386	2.408	3.219	4.605	5.991	7.824	9.210	13.815
3	.115	.185	.352	.584	1.005	1.424	2.366	3.665	4.642	6.251	7.815	9.837	11.341	16.268
4	.297	.429	.711	1.064	1.649	2.195	3.357	4.878	5.989	7.779	9.488	11.668	13.277	18.465
5	.554	.752	1.145	1.610	2.343	3.000	4.351	6.064	7.289	9.236	11.070	13.388	15.086	20.517
6	.872	1.134	1.635	2.204	3.070	3.828	5.348	7.231	8.558	10.645	12.592	15.033	16.812	22.457
7	1.239	1.564	2.167	2.833	3.822	4.671	6.346	8.383	9.803	12.017	14.067	16.622	18.475	24.322
8	1.646	2.032	2.733	3.490	4.594	5.527	7.344	9.524	11.030	13.362	15.507	18.168	20.090	26.125
9	2.088	2.532	3.325	4.168	5.380	6.393	8.343	10.656	12.242	14.684	16.919	19.679	21.666	27.877
10	2.558	3.059	3.940	4.865	6.179	7.267	9.342	11.781	13.442	15.987	18.307	21.161	23.209	29.588
11	3.053	3.609	4.575	5.578	6.989	8.148	10.341	12.899	14.631	17.275	19.675	22.618	24.725	31.264
12	3.571	4.178	5.226	6.304	7.807	9.034	11.340	14.011	15.812	18.549	21.026	24.054	26.217	32.909
13	4.107	4.765	5.892	7.042	8.634	9.926	12.340	15.119	16.985	19.812	22.362	25.472	27.688	34.528
14	4.660	5.368	6.571	7.790	9.467	10.821	13.339	16.222	18.151	21.064	23.685	26.873	29.141	36.123
15	5.229	5.985	7.261	8.547	10.307	11.721	14.339	17.322	19.311	22.307	24.996	28.259	30.578	37.697
16	5.812	6.614	7.962	9.312	11.152	12.624	15.338	18.418	20.465	23.542	26.296	29.633	32.000	39.252
17	6.408	7.255	8.672	10.085	12.002	13.531	16.338	19.511	21.615	24.769	27.587	30.995	33.409	40.790
18	7.015	7.906	9.390	10.865	12.857	14.440	17.338	20.601	22.760	25.989	28.869	32.346	34.805	42.312
19	7.633	8.567	10.117	11.651	13.716	15.352	18.338	21.689	23.900	27.204	30.144	33.687	36.191	43.820
20	8.260	9.237	10.851	12.443	14.578	16.266	19.337	22.775	25.038	28.412	31.410	35.020	37.566	45.315
21	8.897	9.915	11.591	13.240	15.445	17.182	20.337	23.858	26.171	29.615	32.671	36.343	38.932	46.797
22	9.542	10.600	12.338	14.041	16.314	18.101	21.337	24.939	27.301	30.813	33.924	37.659	40.289	48.268
23	10.196	11.293	13.091	14.848	17.187	19.021	22.337	26.018	28.429	32.007	35.172	38.968	41.638	49.728
24	10.856	11.992	13.848	15.659	18.062	19.943	23.337	27.096	29.553	33.196	36.415	40.270	42.980	51.179
25	11.524	12.697	14.611	16.473	18.940	20.867	24.337	28.172	30.675	34.382	37.652	41.566	44.314	52.620
26	12.198	13.409	15.379	17.292	19.820	21.792	25.336	29.246	31.795	35.563	38.885	42.856	45.642	54.052
27	12.879	14.125	16.151	18.114	20.703	22.719	26.336	30.319	32.912	36.741	40.113	44.140	46.963	55.476
28	13.565	14.847	16.928	18.939	21.588	23.647	27.336	31.391	34.027	37.916	41.337	45.419	48.278	56.893
29	14.256	15.574	17.708	19.768	22.475	24.577	28.336	32.461	35.139	39.087	42.557	46.693	49.588	58.302
30	14.953	16.306	18.493	20.599	23.364	25.508	29.336	33.530	36.250	40.256	43.773	47.962	50.892	59.703

For larger values of df, the expression $\sqrt{2\chi^2} - \sqrt{2df - 1}$ may be used as a normal deviate with unit variance, remembering that the probability for χ^2 corresponds with that of a single tail of the normal curve.

Source: Taken from Table IV of R. A. Fisher and F. Yates, *Statistical Tables for Biological, Agricultural and Medical Research*, 6th ed., published by Longman Group Ltd., London (previously published by Oliver & Boyd, Edinburgh), by permission of the authors and publishers.

TABLE VI.   Distribution of F

$p = .05$

n_1 \ n_2	1	2	3	4	5	6	8	12	24	∞
1	161.4	199.5	215.7	224.6	230.2	234.0	238.9	243.9	249.0	254.3
2	18.51	19.00	19.16	19.25	19.30	19.33	19.37	19.41	19.45	19.50
3	10.13	9.55	9.28	9.12	9.01	8.94	8.84	8.74	8.64	8.53
4	7.71	6.94	6.59	6.39	6.26	6.16	6.04	5.91	5.77	5.63
5	6.61	5.79	5.41	5.19	5.05	4.95	4.82	4.68	4.53	4.36
6	5.99	5.14	4.76	4.53	4.39	4.28	4.15	4.00	3.84	3.67
7	5.59	4.74	4.35	4.12	3.97	3.87	3.73	3.57	3.41	3.23
8	5.32	4.46	4.07	3.84	3.69	3.58	3.44	3.28	3.12	2.93
9	5.12	4.26	3.86	3.63	3.48	3.37	3.23	3.07	2.90	2.71
10	4.96	4.10	3.71	3.48	3.33	3.22	3.07	2.91	2.74	2.54
11	4.84	3.98	3.59	3.36	3.20	3.09	2.95	2.79	2.61	2.40
12	4.75	3.88	3.49	3.26	3.11	3.00	2.85	2.69	2.50	2.30
13	4.67	3.80	3.41	3.18	3.02	2.92	2.77	2.60	2.42	2.21
14	4.60	3.74	3.34	3.11	2.96	2.85	2.70	2.53	2.35	2.13
15	4.54	3.68	3.29	3.06	2.90	2.79	2.64	2.48	2.29	2.07
16	4.49	3.63	3.24	3.01	2.85	2.74	2.59	2.42	2.24	2.01
17	4.45	3.59	3.20	2.96	2.81	2.70	2.55	2.38	2.19	1.96
18	4.41	3.55	3.16	2.93	2.77	2.66	2.51	2.34	2.15	1.92
19	4.38	3.52	3.13	2.90	2.74	2.63	2.48	2.31	2.11	1.88
20	4.35	3.49	3.10	2.87	2.71	2.60	2.45	2.28	2.08	1.84
21	4.32	3.47	3.07	2.84	2.68	2.57	2.42	2.25	2.05	1.81
22	4.30	3.44	3.05	2.82	2.66	2.55	2.40	2.23	2.03	1.78
23	4.28	3.42	3.03	2.80	2.64	2.53	2.38	2.20	2.00	1.76
24	4.26	3.40	3.01	2.78	2.62	2.51	2.36	2.18	1.98	1.73
25	4.24	3.38	2.99	2.76	2.60	2.49	2.34	2.16	1.96	1.71
26	4.22	3.37	2.98	2.74	2.59	2.47	2.32	2.15	1.95	1.69
27	4.21	3.35	2.96	2.73	2.57	2.46	2.30	2.13	1.93	1.67
28	4.20	3.34	2.95	2.71	2.56	2.44	2.29	2.12	1.91	1.65
29	4.18	3.33	2.93	2.70	2.54	2.43	2.28	2.10	1.90	1.64
30	4.17	3.32	2.92	2.69	2.53	2.42	2.27	2.09	1.89	1.62
40	4.08	3.23	2.84	2.61	2.45	2.34	2.18	2.00	1.79	1.51
60	4.00	3.15	2.76	2.52	2.37	2.25	2.10	1.92	1.70	1.39
120	3.92	3.07	2.68	2.45	2.29	2.17	2.02	1.83	1.61	1.25
∞	3.84	2.99	2.60	2.37	2.21	2.09	1.94	1.75	1.52	1.00

Values of n_1 and n_2 represent the degrees of freedom associated with the larger and smaller estimates of variance respectively.

Source: Taken from Table V of R. A. Fisher and F. Yates, *Statistical Tables for Biological, Agricultural and Medical Research*, 6th ed., published by Longman Group Ltd., London (previously published by Oliver & Boyd, Edinburgh), by permission of the authors and publishers.

TABLE VI.   Distribution of F *(Continued)*

$$p = .01$$

n_1 \ n_2	1	2	3	4	5	6	8	12	24	∞
1	4052	4999	5403	5625	5764	5859	5981	6106	6234	6366
2	98.49	99.01	99.17	99.25	99.30	99.33	99.36	99.42	99.46	99.50
3	34.12	30.81	29.46	28.71	28.24	27.91	27.49	27.05	26.60	26.12
4	21.20	18.00	16.69	15.98	15.52	15.21	14.80	14.37	13.93	13.46
5	16.26	13.27	12.06	11.39	10.97	10.67	10.27	9.89	9.47	9.02
6	13.74	10.92	9.78	9.15	8.75	8.47	8.10	7.72	7.31	6.88
7	12.25	9.55	8.45	7.85	7.46	7.19	6.84	6.47	6.07	5.65
8	11.26	8.65	7.59	7.01	6.63	6.37	6.03	5.67	5.28	4.86
9	10.56	8.02	6.99	6.42	6.06	5.80	5.47	5.11	4.73	4.31
10	10.04	7.56	6.55	5.99	5.64	5.39	5.06	4.71	4.33	3.91
11	9.65	7.20	6.22	5.67	5.32	5.07	4.74	4.40	4.02	3.60
12	9.33	6.93	5.95	5.41	5.06	4.82	4.50	4.16	3.78	3.36
13	9.07	6.70	5.74	5.20	4.86	4.62	4.30	3.96	3.59	3.16
14	8.86	6.51	5.56	5.03	4.69	4.46	4.14	3.80	3.43	3.00
15	8.68	6.36	5.42	4.89	4.56	4.32	4.00	3.67	3.29	2.87
16	8.53	6.23	5.29	4.77	4.44	4.20	3.89	3.55	3.18	2.75
17	8.40	6.11	5.18	4.67	4.34	4.10	3.79	3.45	3.08	2.65
18	8.28	6.01	5.09	4.58	4.25	4.01	3.71	3.37	3.00	2.57
19	8.18	5.93	5.01	4.50	4.17	3.94	3.63	3.30	2.92	2.49
20	8.10	5.85	4.94	4.43	4.10	3.87	3.56	3.23	2.86	2.42
21	8.02	5.78	4.87	4.37	4.04	3.81	3.51	3.17	2.80	2.36
22	7.94	5.72	4.82	4.31	3.99	3.76	3.45	3.12	2.75	2.31
23	7.88	5.66	4.76	4.26	3.94	3.71	3.41	3.07	2.70	2.26
24	7.82	5.61	4.72	4.22	3.90	3.67	3.36	3.03	2.66	2.21
25	7.77	5.57	4.68	4.18	3.86	3.63	3.32	2.99	2.62	2.17
26	7.72	5.53	4.64	4.14	3.82	3.59	3.29	2.96	2.58	2.13
27	7.68	5.49	4.60	4.11	3.78	3.56	3.26	2.93	2.55	2.10
28	7.64	5.45	4.57	4.07	3.75	3.53	3.23	2.90	2.52	2.06
29	7.60	5.42	4.54	4.04	3.73	3.50	3.20	2.87	2.49	2.03
30	7.56	5.39	4.51	4.02	3.70	3.47	3.17	2.84	2.47	2.01
40	7.31	5.18	4.31	3.83	3.51	3.29	2.99	2.66	2.29	1.80
60	7.08	4.98	4.13	3.65	3.34	3.12	2.82	2.50	2.12	1.60
120	6.85	4.79	3.95	3.48	3.17	2.96	2.66	2.34	1.95	1.38
∞	6.64	4.60	3.78	3.32	3.02	2.80	2.51	2.18	1.79	1.00

Values of n_1 and n_2 represent the degrees of freedom associated with the larger and smaller estimates of variance respectively.

TABLE VI.   Distribution of F *(Continued)*

$p = .001$

n_2 \ n_1	1	2	3	4	5	6	8	12	24	∞
1	405284	500000	540379	562500	576405	585937	598144	610667	623497	636619
2	998.5	999.0	999.2	999.2	999 3	999.3	999.4	999.4	999.5	999.5
3	167.5	148.5	141.1	137.1	134.6	132.8	130.6	128.3	125.9	123.5
4	74.14	61.25	56.18	53.44	51.71	50.53	49.00	47.41	45.77	44.05
5	47.04	36.61	33.20	31.09	29.75	28.84	27.64	26.42	25.14	23.78
6	35.51	27.00	23.70	21.90	20.81	20.03	19.03	17.99	16.89	15.75
7	29.22	21.69	18.77	17.19	16.21	15.52	14.63	13.71	12.73	11.69
8	25.42	18.49	15.83	14.39	13.49	12.86	12.04	11.19	10.30	9.34
9	22.86	16.39	13.90	12.56	11.71	11.13	10.37	9.57	8.72	7.81
10	21.04	14.91	12.55	11.28	10.48	9.92	9.20	8.45	7.64	6.76
11	19.69	13.81	11.56	10.35	9.58	9.05	8.35	7.63	6.85	6.00
12	18.64	12.97	10.80	9.63	8.89	8.38	7 71	7.00	6.25	5.42
13	17.81	12.31	10.21	9.07	8.35	7.86	7.21	6.52	5.78	4.97
14	17.14	11.78	9 73	8.62	7.92	7.43	6.80	6.13	5.41	4.60
15	16.59	11.34	9.34	8.25	7.57	7.09	6.47	5.81	5.10	4.31
16	16.12	10.97	9.00	7.94	7.27	6.81	6.19	5.55	4.85	4.06
17	15.72	10.66	8.73	7.68	7.02	6.56	5.96	5.32	4.63	3.85
18	15.38	10.39	8.49	7.46	6.81	6.35	5.76	5.13	4.45	3.67
19	15.08	10.16	8.28	7.26	6.61	6.18	5.59	4.97	4.29	3.52
20	14.82	9.95	8.10	7.10	6.46	6.02	5.44	4.82	4.15	3.38
21	14.59	9.77	7.94	6.95	6.32	5.88	5.31	4.70	4.03	3.26
22	14.38	9.61	7.80	6.81	6.19	5.76	5.19	4.58	3.92	3.15
23	14.19	9.47	7.67	6.69	6.08	5.65	5.09	4.48	3.82	3.05
24	14.03	9.34	7.55	6.59	5 98	5.55	4.99	4.39	3.74	2.97
25	13.88	9.22	7.45	6.49	5.88	5.46	4.91	4.31	3.66	2.89
26	13.74	9.12	7.36	6.41	5.80	5.38	4.83	4.24	3.59	2.82
27	13.61	9.02	7.27	6.33	5.73	5.31	4.76	4.17	3.52	2.75
28	13.50	8.93	7.19	6.25	5 66	5.24	4.69	4.11	3.46	2.70
29	13.39	8.85	7.12	6.19	5.59	5.18	4.64	4.05	3.41	2.64
30	13.29	8.77	7.05	6.12	5.53	5.12	4.58	4.00	3.36	2.59
40	12.61	8.25	6.60	5.70	5.13	4.73	4.21	3.64	3.01	2.23
60	11.97	7.76	6.17	5.31	4.76	4.37	3.87	3.31	2.69	1.90
120	11.38	7.31	5.79	4.95	4.42	4.04	3.55	3.02	2.40	1.56
∞	10.83	6.91	5.42	4.62	4.10	3.74	3.27	2.74	2.13	1.00

Values of n_1 and n_2 represent the degrees of freedom associated with the larger and smaller estimates of variance respectively.

TABLE VII.   Random Numbers

Line/Col.	(1)	(2)	(3)	(4)	(5)	(6)	(7)	(8)	(9)	(10)	(11)	(12)	(13)	(14)
1	10480	15011	01536	02011	81647	91646	69179	14194	62590	36207	20969	99570	91291	90700
2	22368	46573	25595	85393	30995	89198	27982	53402	93965	34095	52666	19174	39615	99505
3	24130	48360	22527	97265	76393	64809	15179	24830	49340	32081	30680	19655	63348	58629
4	42167	93093	06243	61680	07856	16376	39440	53537	71341	57004	00849	74917	97758	16379
5	37570	39975	81837	16656	06121	91782	60468	81305	49684	60672	14110	06927	01263	54613
6	77921	06907	11008	42751	27756	53498	18602	70659	90655	15053	21916	81825	44394	42880
7	99562	72905	56420	69994	98872	31016	71194	18738	44013	48840	63213	21069	10634	12952
8	96301	91977	05463	07972	18876	20922	94595	56869	69014	60045	18425	84903	42508	32307
9	89579	14342	63661	10281	17453	18103	57740	84378	25331	12566	58678	44947	05585	56941
10	85475	36857	43342	53988	53060	59533	38867	62300	08158	17983	16439	11458	18593	64952
11	28918	69578	88231	33276	70997	79936	56865	05859	90106	31595	01547	85590	91610	78188
12	63553	40961	48235	03427	49626	69445	18663	72695	52180	20847	12234	90511	33703	90322
13	09429	93969	52636	92737	88974	33488	36320	17617	30015	08272	84115	27156	30613	74952
14	10365	61129	87529	85689	48237	52267	67689	93394	01511	26358	85104	20285	29975	89868
15	07119	97336	71048	08178	77233	13916	47564	81056	97735	85977	29372	74461	28551	90707
16	51085	12765	51821	51259	77452	16308	60756	92144	49442	53900	70960	63990	75601	40719
17	02368	21382	52404	60268	89368	19885	55322	44819	01188	65255	64835	44919	05944	55157
18	01011	54092	33362	94904	31273	04146	18594	29852	71585	85030	51132	01915	92747	64951
19	52162	53916	46369	58586	23216	14513	83149	98736	23495	64350	94738	17752	35156	35749
20	07056	97628	33787	09998	42698	06691	76988	13602	51851	46104	88916	19509	25625	58104
21	48663	91245	85828	14346	09172	30168	90229	04734	59193	22178	30421	61666	99904	32812
22	54164	58492	22421	74103	47070	25306	76468	26384	58151	06646	21524	15227	96909	44592
23	32639	32363	05597	24200	13363	38005	94342	28728	35806	06912	17012	64161	18296	22851
24	29334	27001	87637	87308	58731	00256	45834	15398	46557	41135	10367	07684	36188	18510
25	02488	33062	28834	07351	19731	92420	60952	61280	50001	67658	32586	86679	50720	94953
26	81525	72295	04839	96423	24878	82651	66566	14778	76797	14780	13300	87074	79666	95725
27	29676	20591	68086	26432	46901	20849	89768	81536	86645	12659	92259	57102	80428	25280
28	00742	57392	39064	66432	84673	40027	32832	61362	98947	96067	64760	64584	96096	98253
29	05366	04213	25669	26422	44407	44048	37937	63904	45766	66134	75470	66520	34693	90449
30	91921	26418	64117	94305	26766	25940	39972	22209	71500	64568	91402	42416	07844	69618
31	00582	04711	87917	77341	42206	35126	74087	99547	81817	42607	43808	76655	62028	76630
32	00725	69884	62797	56170	86324	88072	76222	36086	84637	93161	76038	65855	77919	88006
33	69011	65797	95876	55293	18988	27354	26575	08625	40801	59920	29841	80150	12777	48501
34	25976	57948	29888	88604	67917	48708	18912	82271	65424	69774	33611	54262	85963	03547
35	09763	83473	73577	12908	30883	18317	28290	35797	05998	41688	34952	37888	38917	88050
36	91567	42595	27958	30134	04024	86385	29880	99730	55536	84855	29080	09250	79656	73211
37	17955	56349	90999	49127	20044	59931	06115	20542	18059	02008	73708	83517	36103	42791
38	46503	18584	18845	49618	02304	51038	20655	58727	28168	15475	56942	53389	20562	87338
39	92157	89634	94824	78171	84610	82834	09922	25417	44137	48413	25555	21246	35509	20468
40	14577	62765	35605	81263	39667	47358	56873	56307	61607	49518	89656	20103	77490	18062
41	98427	07523	33362	64270	01638	92477	66969	98420	04880	45585	46565	04102	46880	45709
42	34914	63976	88720	82765	34476	17032	87589	40836	32427	70002	70663	88863	77775	69348
43	70060	28277	39475	46473	23219	53416	94970	25832	69975	94884	19661	72828	00102	66794
44	53976	54914	06990	67245	68350	82948	11398	42878	80287	88267	47363	46634	06541	97809
45	76072	29515	40980	07391	58745	25774	22987	80059	39911	96189	41151	14222	60697	59583
46	90725	52210	83974	29992	65831	38857	50490	83765	55657	14361	31720	57375	56228	41546
47	64364	67412	33339	31926	14883	24413	59744	92351	97473	89286	35931	04110	23726	51900
48	08962	00358	31662	25388	61642	34072	81249	35648	56891	69352	48373	45578	78547	81788
49	95012	68379	93526	70765	10593	04542	76463	54328	02349	17247	28865	14777	62730	92277
50	15664	10493	20492	38391	91132	21999	59516	81652	27195	48223	46751	22923	32261	85653

Source: Reprinted from Samuel M. Selby, *Standard Mathematical Tables* 21st ed. (Cleveland: The Chemical Rubber Co., 1973), pp. 626–627, "A Table of 14,000 Random Units." Copyright © by The Chemical Rubber Co. Used by permission of the Chemical Rubber Co.

TABLE VII. Random Numbers (*continued*)

Line/Col.	(1)	(2)	(3)	(4)	(5)	(6)	(7)	(8)	(9)	(10)	(11)	(12)	(13)	(14)
51	16408	81899	04153	53381	79401	21438	83035	92350	36693	31238	59649	91754	72772	02338
52	18629	81953	05520	91962	04739	13092	97662	24822	94730	06496	35090	04822	86772	98289
53	73115	35101	47498	87637	99016	71060	88824	71013	18735	20286	23153	72924	35165	43040
54	57491	16703	23167	49323	45021	33132	12544	41035	80780	45393	44812	12515	98931	91202
55	30405	83946	23792	14422	15059	45799	22716	19792	09983	74353	68668	30429	70735	25499
56	16631	35006	85900	98275	32388	52390	16815	69298	82732	38480	73817	32523	41961	44437
57	96773	20206	42559	78985	05300	22164	24369	54224	35083	19687	11052	91491	60383	19746
58	38935	64202	14349	82674	66523	44133	00697	35552	35970	19124	63318	29686	03387	59846
59	31624	76384	17403	53363	44167	64486	64758	75366	76554	31601	12614	33072	60332	92325
60	78919	19474	23632	27889	47914	02584	37680	20801	72152	39339	34806	08930	85001	87820
61	03931	33309	57047	74211	63445	17361	62825	39908	05607	91284	68833	25570	38818	46920
62	74426	33278	43972	10119	89917	15665	52872	73823	73144	88662	88970	74492	51805	99378
63	09066	00903	20795	95452	92648	45454	09552	88815	16553	51125	79375	97596	16296	66092
64	42238	12426	87025	14267	20979	04508	64535	31355	86064	29472	47689	05974	52468	16834
65	16153	08002	26504	41744	81959	65642	74240	56302	00033	67107	77510	70625	28725	34191
66	21457	40742	29820	96783	29400	21840	15035	34537	33310	06116	95240	15957	16572	06004
67	21581	57802	02050	89728	17937	37621	47075	42080	97403	48626	68995	43805	33386	21597
68	55612	78095	83197	33732	05810	24813	86902	60397	16489	03264	88525	42786	05269	92532
69	44657	66999	99324	51281	84463	60563	79312	93454	68876	25471	93911	25650	12682	73572
70	91340	84979	46949	81973	37949	61023	43997	15263	80644	43942	89203	71795	99533	50501
71	91227	21199	31935	27022	84067	05462	35216	14486	29891	68607	41867	14951	91696	85065
72	50001	38140	66321	19924	72163	09538	12151	06878	91903	18749	34405	56087	82790	70925
73	65390	05224	72958	28609	81406	39147	25549	48542	42627	45233	57202	94617	23772	07896
74	27504	96131	83944	41575	10573	08619	64482	73923	36152	05184	94142	25299	84387	34925
75	37169	94851	39117	89632	00959	16487	65536	49071	39782	17095	02330	74301	00275	48280
76	11508	70225	51111	38351	19444	66499	71945	05422	13442	78675	84081	66938	93654	59894
77	37449	30362	06694	54690	04052	53115	62757	95348	78662	11163	81651	50245	34971	52924
78	46515	70331	85922	38329	57015	15765	97161	17869	45349	61796	66345	81073	49106	79860
79	30986	81223	42416	58353	21532	30502	32305	86482	05174	07901	54339	58861	74818	46942
80	63798	64995	46583	09765	44160	78128	83991	42865	92520	83531	80377	35909	81250	54238
81	82486	84846	99254	67632	43218	50076	21361	64816	51202	88124	41870	52689	51275	83556
82	21885	32906	92431	09060	64297	51674	64126	62570	26123	05155	59194	52799	28225	85762
83	60336	98782	07408	53458	13564	59089	26445	29789	85205	41001	12535	12133	14645	23541
84	43937	46891	24010	25560	86355	33941	25786	54990	71899	15475	95434	98227	21824	19585
85	97656	63175	89303	16275	07100	92063	21942	18611	47348	20203	18534	03862	78095	50136
86	03299	01221	05418	38982	55758	92237	26759	86367	21216	98442	08303	56613	91511	75928
87	79626	06486	03574	17668	07785	76020	79924	25651	83325	88428	85076	72811	22717	50585
88	85636	68335	47539	03129	65651	11977	02510	26113	99447	68645	34327	15152	55230	93448
89	18039	14367	61337	06177	12143	46609	32989	74014	64708	00533	35398	58408	13261	47908
90	08362	15656	60627	36478	65648	16764	53412	09013	07832	41574	17639	82163	60859	75567
91	79556	29068	04142	16268	15387	12856	66227	38358	22478	73373	88732	09443	82558	05250
92	92608	82674	27072	32534	17075	27698	98204	63863	11951	34648	88022	56148	34925	57031
93	23982	25835	40055	67006	12293	02753	14827	22235	35071	99704	37543	11601	35503	85171
94	09915	96306	05908	97901	28395	14186	00821	80703	70426	75647	76310	88717	37890	40129
95	50937	33300	26695	62247	69927	76123	50842	43834	86654	70959	79725	93872	28117	19233
96	42488	78077	69882	61657	34136	79180	97526	43092	04098	73571	80799	76536	71255	64239
97	46764	86273	63003	93017	31204	36692	40202	35275	57306	55543	53203	18098	47625	88684
98	03237	45430	55417	63282	90816	17349	88298	90183	36600	78406	06216	95787	42579	90730
99	86591	81482	52667	61583	14972	90053	89534	76036	49199	43716	97548	04379	46370	28672
100	38534	01715	94964	87288	65680	43772	39560	12918	86537	62738	19636	51132	25739	56947

TABLE VIII.   Critical Values of D in the Kolmogorov-
Smirnov One-Sample Test

Sample size (N)	Level of significance for D = maximum $|F_0(X) - S_N(X)|$				
	.20	.15	.10	.05	.01
1	.900	.925	.950	.975	.995
2	.684	.726	.776	.842	.929
3	.565	.597	.642	.708	.828
4	.494	.525	.564	.624	.733
5	.446	.474	.510	.565	.669
6	.410	.436	.470	.521	.618
7	.381	.405	.438	.486	.577
8	.358	.381	.411	.457	.543
9	.339	.360	.388	.432	.514
10	.322	.342	.368	.410	.490
11	.307	.326	.352	.391	.468
12	.295	.313	.338	.375	.450
13	.284	.302	.325	.361	.433
14	.274	.292	.314	.349	.418
15	.266	.283	.304	.338	.404
16	.258	.274	.295	.328	.392
17	.250	.266	.286	.318	.381
18	.244	.259	.278	.309	.371
19	.237	.252	.272	.301	.363
20	.231	.246	.264	.294	.356
25	.21	.22	.24	.27	.32
30	.19	.20	.22	.24	.29
35	.18	.19	.21	.23	.27
Over 35	$\dfrac{1.07}{\sqrt{N}}$	$\dfrac{1.14}{\sqrt{N}}$	$\dfrac{1.22}{\sqrt{N}}$	$\dfrac{1.36}{\sqrt{N}}$	$\dfrac{1.63}{\sqrt{N}}$

Source: F. J. Massey, Jr., "The Kolmogorov-Smirnov Test of Goodness of Fit," *Journal of the American Statistical Association,* vol. 46, p. 70, 1951, with the kind permission of the author and publisher.

TABLE IX.   Critical Values of *r* in the Runs Test

Given in the bodies of Table A and Table B are various critical values of *r* for various values of n_1 and n_2. For the one-sample runs test, any value of *r* which is equal to or smaller than that shown in Table A or equal to or larger than that shown in Table B is significant at the .05 level. For the Wald-Wolfowitz two-sample runs test, any value of *r* which is equal to or smaller than that shown in Table A is significant at the .05 level.

Table A

n_1 \ n_2	2	3	4	5	6	7	8	9	10	11	12	13	14	15	16	17	18	19	20
2											2	2	2	2	2	2	2	2	2
3			2	2	2	2	2	2	2	2	2	2	3	3	3	3	3	3
4			2	2	2	3	3	3	3	3	3	3	3	4	4	4	4	4
5		2	2	3	3	3	3	3	4	4	4	4	4	4	4	5	5	5
6	2	2	3	3	3	3	4	4	4	4	5	5	5	5	5	5	6	6
7	2	2	3	3	3	4	4	5	5	5	5	5	6	6	6	6	6	6
8	2	3	3	3	4	4	5	5	5	6	6	6	6	6	7	7	7	7
9	2	3	3	4	4	5	5	5	6	6	6	7	7	7	7	8	8	8
10	2	3	3	4	5	5	5	6	6	7	7	7	7	8	8	8	8	9
11	2	3	4	4	5	5	6	6	7	7	7	8	8	8	9	9	9	9
12	2	2	3	4	4	5	6	6	7	7	7	8	8	8	9	9	9	10	10
13	2	2	3	4	5	5	6	6	7	7	8	8	9	9	9	10	10	10	10
14	2	2	3	4	5	5	6	7	7	8	8	9	9	9	10	10	10	11	11
15	2	3	3	4	5	6	6	7	7	8	8	9	9	10	10	11	11	11	12
16	2	3	4	4	5	6	6	7	8	8	9	9	10	10	11	11	11	12	12
17	2	3	4	4	5	6	7	7	8	9	9	10	10	11	11	11	12	12	13
18	2	3	4	5	5	6	7	8	8	9	9	10	10	11	11	12	12	13	13
19	2	3	4	5	6	6	7	8	8	9	10	10	11	11	12	12	13	13	13
20	2	3	4	5	6	6	7	8	9	9	10	10	11	12	12	13	13	13	14

Source: Taken from Frieda A. Swed and Churchill Eisenhart, "Tables for Testing Randomness of Grouping in a Sequence of Alternatives," *Annals of Mathematical Statistics,* vol. 14, pp. 83–86, 1943, with the kind permission of the authors and publisher.

TABLE IX.   Critical Values of *r* in the Runs Test (*continued*)

Table B

n_1 \ n_2	2	3	4	5	6	7	8	9	10	11	12	13	14	15	16	17	18	19	20
2																			
3																			
4				9	9														
5			9	10	10	11	11												
6			9	10	11	12	12	13	13	13	13								
7				11	12	13	13	14	14	14	14	15	15	15					
8				11	12	13	14	14	15	15	16	16	16	16	17	17	17	17	17
9					13	14	14	15	16	16	16	17	17	18	18	18	18	18	18
10					13	14	15	16	16	17	17	18	18	18	19	19	19	20	20
11					13	14	15	16	17	17	18	19	19	19	20	20	20	21	21
12					13	14	16	16	17	18	19	19	20	20	21	21	21	22	22
13						15	16	17	18	19	19	20	20	21	21	22	22	23	23
14						15	16	17	18	19	20	20	21	22	22	23	23	23	24
15						15	16	18	18	19	20	21	22	22	23	23	24	24	25
16							17	18	19	20	21	21	22	23	23	24	25	25	25
17							17	18	19	20	21	22	23	23	24	25	25	25	26
18							17	18	19	20	21	22	23	24	25	25	26	26	27
19							17	18	20	21	22	23	23	24	25	26	26	27	27
20							17	18	20	21	22	23	24	25	25	26	27	27	28

TABLE X. Probabilities Associated With Values As Small As Observed Values of U in the Mann-Whitney Test

$N_2 = 3$				$N_2 = 4$				
U \ N_1	1	2	3	U \ N_1	1	2	3	4
0	.250	.100	.050	0	.200	.067	.028	.014
1	.500	.200	.100	1	.400	.133	.057	.029
2	.750	.400	.200	2	.600	.267	.114	.057
3		.600	.350	3		.400	.200	.100
4			.500	4		.600	.314	.171
5			.650	5			.429	.243
6				6			.571	.343
7				7				.443
8				8				.557

$N_2 = 5$						$N_2 = 6$						
U \ N_1	1	2	3	4	5	U \ N_1	1	2	3	4	5	6
0	.167	.047	.018	.008	.004	0	.143	.036	.012	.005	.002	.001
1	.333	.095	.036	.016	.008	1	.286	.071	.024	.010	.004	.002
2	.500	.190	.071	.032	.016	2	.428	.143	.048	.019	.009	.004
3	.667	.286	.125	.056	.028	3	.571	.214	.083	.033	.015	.008
4		.429	.196	.095	.048	4		.321	.131	.057	.026	.013
5		.571	.286	.143	.075	5		.429	.190	.086	.041	.021
6			.393	.206	.111	6		.571	.274	.129	.063	.032
7			.500	.278	.155	7			.357	.176	.089	.047
8			.607	.365	.210	8			.452	.238	.123	.066
9				.452	.274	9			.548	.305	.165	.090
10				.548	.345	10				.381	.214	.120
11					.421	11				.457	.268	.155
12					.500	12				.545	.331	.197
13					.579	13					.396	.242
14						14					.465	.294
15						15					.535	.350
16						16						.409
17						17						.469
18						18						.531

Source: H. B. Mann and D. R. Whitney, "On a Test of Whether One of Two Random Variables is Stochastically Larger than the Other," *Annals of Mathematical Statistics,* vol. 18, pp. 52–54, 1947, with the kind permission of the authors and publisher.

TABLE X.   Probabilities Associated With Values As Small
As Observed Values of U in the Mann-Whitney
Test (*continued*)

$N_2 = 7$

N_1 U	1	2	3	4	5	6	7
0	.125	.028	.008	.003	.001	.001	.000
1	.250	.056	.017	.006	.003	.001	.001
2	.375	.111	.033	.012	.005	.002	.001
3	.500	.167	.058	.021	.009	.004	.002
4	.625	.250	.092	.036	.015	.007	.003
5		.333	.133	.055	.024	.011	.006
6		.444	.192	.082	.037	.017	.009
7		.556	.258	.115	.053	.026	.013
8			.333	.158	.074	.037	.019
9			.417	.206	.101	.051	.027
10			.500	.264	.134	.069	.036
11			.583	.324	.172	.090	.049
12				.394	.216	.117	.064
13				.464	.265	.147	.082
14				.538	.319	.183	.104
15					.378	.223	.130
16					.438	.267	.159
17					.500	.314	.191
18					.562	.365	.228
19						.418	.267
20						.473	.310
21						.527	.355
22							.402
23							.451
24							.500
25							.549

TABLE X. Probabilities Associated With Values As Small As Observed Values of *U* in the Mann-Whitney Test (*continued*)

$$N_2 = 8$$

U \ N₁	1	2	3	4	5	6	7	8
0	.111	.022	.006	.002	.001	.000	.000	.000
1	.222	.044	.012	.004	.002	.001	.000	.000
2	.333	.089	.024	.008	.003	.001	.001	.000
3	.444	.133	.042	.014	.005	.002	.001	.001
4	.556	.200	.067	.024	.009	.004	.002	.001
5		.267	.097	.036	.015	.006	.003	.001
6		.356	.139	.055	.023	.010	.005	.002
7		.444	.188	.077	.033	.015	.007	.003
8		.556	.248	.107	.047	.021	.010	.005
9			.315	.141	.064	.030	.014	.007
10			.387	.184	.085	.041	.020	010
11			.461	.230	.111	.054	.027	.014
12			.539	.285	.142	.071	.036	.019
13				.341	.177	.091	.047	.025
14				.404	.217	.114	.060	.032
15				.467	.262	.141	.076	.041
16				.533	.311	.172	.095	.052
17					.362	.207	.116	.065
18					.416	.245	.140	.080
19					.472	.286	.168	.097
20					.528	.331	.198	.117
21						.377	.232	.139
22						.426	.268	.164
23						.475	.306	.191
24						.525	.347	.221
25							.389	.253
26							.433	.287
27							.478	.323
28							.522	.360
29								.399
30								.439
31								.480
32								.520

TABLE XI.   Table of Critical Values of *U* in the Mann-Whitney Test

Critical Values of *U* for a One-tailed Test at $\alpha = .05$ or for a
Two-tailed Test at $\alpha = .10$

n_2 \ n_1	9	10	11	12	13	14	15	16	17	18	19	20
1											0	0
2	1	1	1	2	2	2	3	3	3	4	4	4
3	3	4	5	5	6	7	7	8	9	9	10	11
4	6	7	8	9	10	11	12	14	15	16	17	18
5	9	11	12	13	15	16	18	19	20	22	23	25
6	12	14	16	17	19	21	23	25	26	28	30	32
7	15	17	19	21	24	26	28	30	33	35	37	39
8	18	20	23	26	28	31	33	36	39	41	44	47
9	21	24	27	30	33	36	39	42	45	48	51	54
10	24	27	31	34	37	41	44	48	51	55	58	62
11	27	31	34	38	42	46	50	54	57	61	65	69
12	30	34	38	42	47	51	55	60	64	68	72	77
13	33	37	42	47	51	56	61	65	70	75	80	84
14	36	41	46	51	56	61	66	71	77	82	87	92
15	39	44	50	55	61	66	72	77	83	88	94	100
16	42	48	54	60	65	71	77	83	89	95	101	107
17	45	51	57	64	70	77	83	89	96	102	109	115
18	48	55	61	68	75	82	88	95	102	109	116	123
19	51	58	65	72	80	87	94	101	109	116	123	130
20	54	62	69	77	84	92	100	107	115	123	130	138

*Adapted and abridged from Tables 1, 3, 5, and 7 of Auble, D., "Etended tables for the Mann-Whitney statistic," *Bulletin of the Institute of Educational Research at Indiana University* 1, no. 2, (1953), with the kind permission of the publisher.

TABLE XI. Table of Critical Values of *U* in the Mann-Whitney Test (cont.)

Critical Values of U for a One-tailed Test at $\alpha = .025$ of for a
Two-tailed Test at $\alpha = .05$

n_1 \ n_2	9	10	11	12	13	14	15	16	17	18	19	20
1												
2	0	0	0	1	1	1	1	1	2	2	2	2
3	2	3	3	4	4	5	5	6	6	7	7	8
4	4	5	6	7	8	9	10	11	11	12	13	13
5	7	8	9	11	12	13	14	15	17	18	19	20
6	10	11	13	14	16	17	19	21	22	24	25	27
7	12	14	16	18	20	22	24	26	28	30	32	34
8	15	17	19	22	24	26	29	31	34	36	38	41
9	17	20	23	26	28	31	34	37	39	42	45	48
10	20	23	26	29	33	36	39	42	45	48	52	55
11	23	26	30	33	37	40	44	47	51	55	58	62
12	26	29	33	37	41	45	49	53	57	61	65	69
13	28	33	37	41	45	50	54	59	63	67	72	76
14	31	36	40	45	50	55	59	64	67	74	78	83
15	34	39	44	49	54	59	64	70	75	80	85	90
16	37	42	47	53	59	64	70	75	81	86	92	98
17	39	45	51	57	63	67	75	81	87	93	99	105
18	42	48	55	61	67	74	80	86	93	99	106	112
19	45	52	58	65	72	78	85	92	99	106	113	119
20	48	55	62	69	76	83	90	98	105	112	119	127

TABLE XI.   Table of Critical Values of U in the Mann-Whitney Test (cont.)

Critical Values of U for a One-tailed Test at $\alpha = .01$ or for a
Two-tailed Test at $\alpha = .02$

n_2 / n_1	9	10	11	12	13	14	15	16	17	18	19	20
1												
2					0	0	0	0	0	0	1	1
3	1	1	1	2	2	2	3	3	4	4	4	5
4	3	3	4	5	5	6	7	7	8	9	9	10
5	5	6	7	8	9	10	11	12	13	14	15	16
6	7	8	9	11	12	13	15	16	18	19	20	22
7	9	11	12	14	16	17	19	21	23	24	26	28
8	11	13	15	17	20	22	24	26	28	30	32	34
9	14	16	18	21	23	26	28	31	33	36	38	40
10	16	19	22	24	27	30	33	36	38	41	44	47
11	18	22	25	28	31	34	37	41	44	47	50	53
12	21	24	28	31	35	38	42	46	49	53	56	60
13	23	27	31	35	39	43	47	51	55	59	63	67
14	26	30	34	38	43	47	51	56	60	65	69	73
15	28	33	37	42	47	51	56	61	66	70	75	80
16	31	36	41	46	51	56	61	66	71	76	82	87
17	33	38	44	49	55	60	66	71	77	82	88	93
18	36	41	47	53	59	65	70	76	82	88	94	100
19	38	44	50	56	63	69	75	82	88	94	101	107
20	40	47	53	60	67	73	80	87	93	100	107	114

TABLE XI. Table of Critical Values of *U* in the Mann-Whitney Test (cont.)

Critical Values of *U* for a One-tailed Test at $\alpha = .001$ or for a
Two-tailed Test at $\alpha = .002$

n_1 \ n_2	9	10	11	12	13	14	15	16	17	18	19	20
1												
2												
3									0	0	0	0
4		0	0	0	1	1	1	2	2	3	3	3
5	1	1	2	2	3	3	4	5	5	6	7	7
6	2	3	4	4	5	6	7	8	9	10	11	12
7	3	5	6	7	8	9	10	11	13	14	15	16
8	5	6	8	9	11	12	14	15	17	18	20	21
9	7	8	10	12	14	15	17	19	21	23	25	26
10	8	10	12	14	17	19	21	23	25	27	29	32
11	10	12	15	17	20	22	24	27	29	32	34	37
12	12	14	17	20	23	25	28	31	34	37	40	42
13	14	17	20	23	26	29	32	35	38	42	45	48
14	15	19	22	25	29	32	36	39	43	46	50	54
15	17	21	24	28	32	36	40	43	47	51	55	59
16	19	23	27	31	35	39	43	48	52	56	60	65
17	21	25	29	34	38	43	47	52	57	61	66	70
18	23	27	32	37	42	46	51	56	61	66	71	76
19	25	29	34	40	45	50	55	60	66	71	77	82
20	26	32	37	42	48	54	59	65	70	76	82	88

TABLE XII.   Percentage Cutoff Points for Cluster-Bloc Analysis: Simple Indices of Identical Voting*

No. of	Significance Levels for Single-Tailed Tests							
	Disagreement				Agreement			
Votes	.001	.01	.025	.05	.05	.025	.01	.001
2	—	—	—	—	—	—	—	—
3	—	—	—	—	—	—	—	—
4	—	—	—	—	—	—	—	—
5	—	—	—	0.0	100.00	—	—	—
6	—	—	0.0	0.0	100.00	100.00	—	—
7	—	0.0	0.0	0.0	100.00	100.00	100.00	—
8	—	0.0	0.0	12.50	87.50	100.00	100.00	—
9	—	0.0	11.11	11.11	88.88	88.88	100.00	—
10	0.0	0.0	10.00	10.00	90.00	90.00	100.00	100.00
11	0.0	9.09	9.09	18.18	81.82	90.91	90.91	100.00
12	0.0	8.33	16.67	16.67	83.33	83.33	91.67	100.00
13	0.0	7.69	15.38	23.08	76.92	84.62	92.31	100.00
14	7.14	14.29	14.29	21.43	78.57	85.71	85.71	92.86
15	6.67	13.33	20.00	20.00	80.00	80.00	86.67	93.33
16	6.25	12.50	18.75	25.00	75.00	81.25	87.50	93.75
17	5.88	17.65	23.53	23.53	76.47	76.47	82.35	94.12
18	11.11	16.67	22.22	27.78	72.22	77.78	83.33	88.89
19	10.53	21.05	21.05	26.32	73.68	78.95	78.95	89.47
20	10.00	20.00	25.00	25.00	75.00	75.00	80.00	90.00
21	14.29	19.05	23.81	28.57	71.43	76.19	80.95	85.71
22	13.64	22.73	22.73	27.27	72.73	77.27	77.27	86.36
23	13.04	21.74	26.09	30.43	69.57	73.91	78.26	86.96
24	16.67	20.83	25.00	29.17	70.83	75.00	79.17	83.33
25	16.00	24.00	28.00	28.00	72.00	72.00	76.00	84.00
26	15.38	23.08	26.92	30.77	69.23	73.08	76.92	84.62
27	18.52	25.93	29.93	29.63	70.37	74.07	74.07	81.48
28	17.86	25.00	28.57	32.14	67.86	71.43	75.00	82.14
29	17.24	24.14	27.59	31.03	68.97	72.41	75.86	82.76
30	20.00	26.67	30.00	33.33	66.67	70.00	73.33	80.00
35	22.86	28.57	31.43	34.29	65.71	68.57	71.43	77.14
40	22.50	30.00	32.50	35.00	65.00	67.50	70.00	77.50
45	24.44	31.11	33.33	35.56	64.44	66.67	68.89	75.56
50	26.00	32.00	34.00	36.00	64.00	64.00	68.00	74.00
55	27.27	32.73	34.55	36.36	63.64	65.45	67.27	72.73
60	28.33	33.33	35.00	38.33	61.67	65.00	66.67	71.67
65	29.23	33.85	36.92	38.46	61.54	63.08	66.15	70.77
70	30.00	34.29	37.14	38.57	61.43	62.86	65.71	70.00
75	30.67	34.67	37.33	38.67	61.33	62.67	65.33	69.33
80	31.25	36.25	37.50	40.00	60.00	62.50	63.75	68.75

*Probability of Agreement = 0.500; Probability of Disagreement = 0.500.
Source: Expanded version of Peter Willetts, "Cluster-Bloc Analysis and Statistical Inference," *American Political Science Review* 66, no. 2 (June 1972): 574. Expansion supplied by the author, and reprinted with the kind permission of the author and publisher.

TABLE XII.A.   Cutoff Points for Cluster-Bloc Analysis or Issue-Set Analysis with Simple Indices on the Assumption of Random Voting

No. of Votes	Significance Levels for Single-Tailed Tests							
	Disagreement				Agreement			
	.001	.01	.025	.05	.05	.025	.01	.001
85	31.76	36.47	37.65	40.00	60.00	62.35	63.53	68.24
90	32.22	36.67	38.89	40.00	60.00	61.11	63.33	67.78
95	33.68	36.84	38.95	40.00	60.00	61.05	63.16	66.32
100	34.00	37.00	39.00	41.00	59.00	61.00	63.00	66.00
105	34.29	38.10	39.05	40.95	59.05	60.95	61.90	65.71
110	34.55	38.18	40.00	40.91	59.09	60.00	61.82	65.45
115	34.78	38.26	40.00	41.74	58.26	60.00	61.74	65.22
120	35.00	38.33	40.00	41.67	58.33	60.00	61.67	65.00
125	35.20	39.20	40.80	41.60	58.40	59.20	60.80	64.80
130	35.38	39.23	40.77	42.31	57.69	59.23	60.77	64.62
135	36.30	39.26	40.74	42.22	57.78	59.26	60.74	63.70
140	36.43	39.29	40.71	42.14	57.86	59.29	60.71	63.57
145	36.55	40.00	41.38	42.76	57.24	58.62	60.00	63.45
150	36.67	40.00	41.33	42.67	57.33	58.67	60.00	63.33
155	36.77	40.00	41.29	42.58	57.42	58.71	60.66	63.23
160	37.50	40.00	41.88	43.13	56.87	58.12	60.00	62.50
165	37.58	40.61	41.82	43.03	56.97	58.18	59.39	62.42
170	37.65	40.59	41.76	42.94	57.06	58.24	59.41	62.35
175	37.71	40.57	42.29	43.43	56.57	57.71	59.43	62.29
180	37.78	40.56	42.22	43.33	56.67	57.78	59.44	62.22
185	38.38	41.08	42.16	43.24	56.76	57.84	58.92	61.62
190	38.42	41.05	42.63	43.68	56.32	57.37	58.95	61.58
195	38.46	41.03	42.56	43.59	56.41	57.44	58.97	61.54
200	38.50	41.50	42.50	43.50	56.60	57.50	58.50	61.50
205	38.54	41.46	42.44	43.90	56.10	57.56	58.54	61.46
210	39.05	41.43	42.86	43.81	56.19	57.14	58.57	60.95
215	39.07	41.40	42.79	43.72	56.28	57.21	58.60	60.93
220	39.09	41.82	42.73	44.09	55.91	57.27	58.18	60.91
225	39.11	41.78	43.11	44.00	56.00	56.89	58.22	60.89
230	39.57	41.74	43.04	44.35	55.65	56.96	58.26	60.43
235	39.57	42.13	42.98	44.26	55.74	57.02	57.87	60.43
240	39.58	42.08	43.33	44.17	55.83	56.67	57.92	60.42
245	39.59	42.04	43.27	44.49	55.51	56.73	57.96	60.41
250	40.00	42.40	43.60	44.40	55.60	56.40	57.60	60.00

TABLE XIII.   Probabilities Associated with Values As Large As
Observed Values of S in the Kendall Rank Correlation Coefficient

S	Values of N				S	Values of N		
	4	5	8	9		6	7	10
0	.625	.592	.548	.540	1	.500	.500	.500
2	.375	.408	.452	.460	3	.360	.386	.431
4	.167	.242	.360	.381	5	.235	.281	.364
6	.042	.117	.274	.306	7	.136	191	.300
8		.042	.199	.238	9	.068	.119	.242
10		.0083	.138	.179	11	.028	.068	.190
12			.089	.130	13	.0083	.035	.146
14			.054	.090	15	.0014	.015	.108
16			.031	.060	17		.0054	.078
18			.016	.038	19		.0014	.054
20			.0071	.022	21		.00020	.036
22			.0028	.012	23			.023
24			.00087	.0063	25			.014
26			.00019	.0029	27			.0083
28			.000025	.0012	29			.0046
30				.00043	31			.0023
32				.00012	33			.0011
34				.000025	35			.00047
36				.0000028	37			.00018
					39			.000058
					41			.000015
					43			.0000028
					45			.00000028

Source: Taken from M. G. Kendall, *Rank Correlation Methods* (London: Charles Griffin & Co., Ltd., 1962), Appendix Table 1, p. 173, with the kind permission of the publisher.

TABLE XIV. Table of Critical Values of T in the Wilcoxon Matched-Pairs Signed-ranks Test

One-sided	Two-sided	N=5	N=6	N=7	N=8	N=9	N=10	N=11	N=12	N=13	N=14	N=15	N=16
P=.05	P=.10	1	2	4	6	8	11	14	17	21	26	30	36
P=.025	P=.05		1	2	4	6	8	11	14	17	21	25	30
P=.01	P=.02			0	2	3	5	7	10	13	16	20	24
P=.005	P=.01				0	2	3	5	7	10	13	16	19

One-sided	Two-sided	N=17	N=18	N=19	N=20	N=21	N=22	N=23	N=24	N=25	N=26	N=27	N=28
P=.05	P=.10	41	47	54	60	68	75	83	92	101	110	120	130
P=.025	P=.05	35	40	46	52	59	66	73	81	90	98	107	117
P=.01	P=.02	28	33	38	43	49	56	62	69	77	85	93	102
P=.005	P=.01	23	28	32	37	43	49	55	61	68	76	84	92

One-sided	Two-sided	N=29	N=30	N=31	N=32	N=33	N=34	N=35	N=36	N=37	N=38	N=39
P=.05	P=.10	141	152	163	175	188	201	214	228	242	256	271
P=.025	P=.05	127	137	148	159	171	183	195	208	222	235	250
P=.01	P=.02	111	120	130	141	151	162	174	186	198	211	224
P=.005	P=.01	100	109	118	128	138	149	160	171	183	195	208

One-sided	Two-sided	N=40	N=41	N=42	N=43	N=44	N=45	N=46	N=47	N=48	N=49	N=50
P=.05	P=.10	287	303	319	336	353	371	389	408	427	446	466
P=.025	P=.05	264	279	295	311	327	344	361	379	397	415	434
P=.01	P=.02	238	252	267	281	297	313	329	345	362	380	398
P=.005	P=.01	221	234	248	262	277	292	307	323	339	356	373

TABLE XV.   Critical Values of Pearson's r

Levels of Significance

	.1	.05	.02	.01	.001
1	.98769	.99692	.999507	.999877	.9999989
2	.90000	.95000	.98000	.990000	.99900
3	.8054	.8783	.93433	.95873	.99116
4	.7293	.8114	.8822	.91720	.97406
5	.6694	.7545	.8329	.8745	.95074
6	.6215	.7067	.7887	.8343	.92493
7	.5822	.6664	.7498	.7977	.8982
8	.5494	.6319	.7155	.7646	.8721
9	.5214	.6021	.6851	.7348	.8471
10	.4973	.5760	.6581	.7079	.8233
11	.4762	.5529	.6339	.6835	.8010
12	.4575	.5324	.6120	.6614	.7800
13	.4409	.5139	.5923	.6411	.7603
14	.4259	.4973	.5742	.6226	.7420
15	.4124	.4821	.5577	.6055	.7246
16	.4000	.4683	.5425	.5897	.7084
17	.3887	.4555	.5285	.5741	.6932
18	.3783	.4438	.5155	.5614	.6787
19	.3687	.4329	.5034	.5487	.6652
20	.3598	.4227	.4921	.5368	.6524
25	.3233	.3809	.4451	.4869	.5974
30	.2960	.3494	.4093	.4487	.5541
35	.2746	.3246	.3810	.4182	.5189
40	.2573	.3044	.3578	.3932	.4896
45	.2428	.2875	.3384	.3721	.4648
50	.2306	.2732	.3218	.3541	.4433
60	.2108	.2500	.2948	.3248	.4078
70	.1954	.2319	.2737	.3017	.3799
80	.1829	.2172	.2565	.2830	.3568
90	.1726	.2050	.2422	.2673	.3375
100	.1638	.1946	.2301	.2540	.3211

Source: Abridged from Table VII of R. A. Fisher and F. Yates, *Statistical Tables for Biological, Agricultural and Medical Research*, 6th ed., published by Longman Group Ltd., London (previously published by Oliver & Boyd, Edinburgh), by permission of the authors and publishers.

On Writing Political Science Papers

Politics may not be a science, but its study involves quite a bit more than journalism. There are no laws that *guarantee* good results, but the following are some guidelines for writing successful political science papers.

CHOOSING A TOPIC

Choosing a topic sounds obvious, yet many people do a bad job. A good paper will choose a clear *analytic topic*. That is, you should do more than select an area and write about it. You should even try to do more than select a question to be pondered. Sometimes descriptive or speculative papers are desired, to be sure, but most often you should pose a *hypothesis*, gather evidence, and come to conclusions about the validity of your hypothesis.

For example, a paper describing in a historical manner how Nixon was elected is usually a bad topic. A paper asking "Why was Nixon elected?" is a bit better, but is still not sharp enough. An analytic paper might pose the hypothesis that "Nixon was elected because of popular reaction against the Vietnam war under Johnson," and seek to prove or disprove this hypothesis. A good paper tries to prove something in a logical way—not just describe or speculate about something. This means you must pose a clear hypothesis at the outset.

FORMING AN OUTLINE

Outlining is not something "just for high school." If you can do it in your head, fine, but you really need to think out your paper in advance. For most of us, this means writing an outline. Obviously this will depend on the topic, but a typical paper will have the following general form:

A. INTRODUCTION
   1. Statement of the hypothesis
   2. Brief (historical)background, showing importance
   3. Proposed method of analysis, integrated with proposed outline of remainder of paper
B. BODY
   1. The hypothesis in operationalized form
   2. Alternative hypotheses
   3. Evidence on relationships, assessing significance, strength, and validity of data
   4. Use of control variables as check
   5. Accepting or rejecting the hypothesis
C. CONCLUSION
   1. Brief summary of findings
   2. Implications for political theory or larger framework

SETTING UP THE HYPOTHESIS

It is not enough to pick an analytic topic and have a clear outline—you need to proceed logically as well. The first step, thinking clearly about your hypothesis, is the crucial one. First, make clear what, specifically, it is that you are trying to explain (what is your *dependent variable*). In a short paper it is a good idea to have just one dependent variable—for instance, Nixon's being elected—not McCarthy's failure to get the nomination as well. If you need to explain more than one thing, then you should have more than one proof, clearly distinguishing them.

After making your dependent variable clear, you should then clearly identify the *other variables* you are going to use in explaining the dependent variable. For instance, in explaining why Nixon was elected, are you going to examine variables like traditional partisan identifications, economic indicators, campaign spending, riots, foreign policy activity, personality factors, running mates, political organization, student movements, interest groups, other variables? State clearly which variables you are going to examine and explain why they are the more important. You should also explain why you are going to exclude other variables from your analysis.

Third, *operationalize your variables*. This is a very common problem with student (and professional!) papers. It is clear enough what the dependent variable in this example is: Nixon's being elected—although even here, you should decide if you are trying to explain his being elected at all, or the margin by which he was elected. But what are "economic factors," for example? Such umbrella terms must be broken into more specific variables like unemployment, cost of living, income levels. Even then, such variables must be given specific, empirical meaning. Which of the different indicators of cost of living are you going to use? You may want to use a variable like "alienation," but how, exactly, do you know it when you see it?

Fourth, *identify the causal relationships* among your variables. It is not enough to say that A and B cause X, because this could mean one of several

$A \rightarrow B \rightarrow X$	$A \rightarrow X \leftarrow B$	$\begin{matrix} A \\ B \end{matrix} \!\! > \rightarrow X$
Hypothesis 1	Hypothesis 2	Hypothesis 3

things. In hypothesis 1, it is asserted that A causes B, which in turn causes X. Hypothesis 2 asserts that A causes X, and B independently causes X. Hypothesis 3 asserts that the joint relation of A and B causes X. If you allow for more than three variables and if you allow for two-way (mutual) causation, identifying causal relationships becomes quite complex. Often a pictorial diagram is a real convenience. But going through this procedure becomes important when you go to gather evidence. The kind of evidence you need will depend on what exactly your hypothetical model is.

Fifth, specify the *alternative hypotheses.* You can usually assume that more than one hypothesis will fit any given set of data. Just because you show that the data fit your hypothesis, your task is not complete. Other theories may well fit the data too. Ultimately, you can never prove that your hypothesis is true; you can only show that alternative hypotheses are unsupported by the data and are therefore untrue. A good political science paper will therefore raise alternative hypotheses to the central one. Such alternatives may be drawn from examining the work of other writers, or from one's imagination. Creatively forming the central hypothesis *and* reasonable alternative hypotheses is half the job of writing a political science paper. The other half is gathering evidence to show that your hypothesis is supported and the alternatives are not.

GATHERING EVIDENCE

Before you can select the types of evidence you need, you must have gone through the preceding steps. In doing so, you will have had to consider two things. First, the *level of your analysis:* are you going to explain the dependent variable on the level of biological factors (aggressive instincts, physical needs directly acted upon), ecological (demographic trends, herding), psychological (frustrations, needs), economic (relations to production, income), political (power, authority), social (group pressure), cultural (values, norms), or some combination? Second, the *method of analysis;* comparisons over time, comparisons across space; inductive, deductive; qualitative, quantitative.

Choosing the method of analysis always depends on the specific problem. As an example, in studying power distribution, one can study particular decisions and trace relationships exhibited therein. One can ask people who they think holds power. Or one can assume that benefits indicate how power is distributed and therefore examine how benefits are distributed. And if you want to generalize, you will have to have evidence for different time periods and/or different cultures.

There is an almost infinite variety of *kinds of evidence;* archives, printed matter, surveys, interviews, participant observation, physical traces. In gathering evidence, a few rules of thumb are important:

1. The most common source of evidence in student papers is books. In using this source, focus on the author's actual evidence, not his conclusions or opinions. This sounds simple, but few observe this rule of thumb.

2. Periodicals are the next most common source, and definitely should be used in a thorough paper. But remember two points:
    a. Focus first on articles in scholarly journals, not tidbits from *Time* and *Life.*
    b. Try to consult sources representing different sides of the debate. If you're writing about another country, try to include authors from that country. If you're writing about the labor movement, include union sources, just as you would include business sources on business or communist sources on Communism (don't go to the other extreme, obviously).

3. Bring statistical evidence to bear where appropriate. Many neglect sources such as the *City and County Data Book, America Votes, Handbook of World Indicators,* city, state, and country handbooks issued annually, labor and other federal department data, *Historical Statistics of the U.S. from Colonial Times to the Present,* annual presidential reports, or even the *Census.*

4. If you plan at the outset, interviewing, mail questionnaires, or even some sample surveying is possible in student papers. Remember, you don't have to rely on data collected by others—often you can collect your own.

PRESENTING EVIDENCE ON THE HYPOTHESIS

There will probably be several relationships in question in your analysis, specified when you identified the causal relationships. In presenting your evidence, deal with the different relationships in question in some kind of logical order. One such order would be to start by presenting the evidence on relationships furthest from the dependent variable in your causal model, and· work toward relationships directly involving the dependent variable.

Whatever logical order you choose, in presenting your evidence you should address three questions:

1. *Significance*—Are you sure that the evidence you have collected isn't just the result of chance?

2. *Association*—Is the evidence in support of the relationship you have posited strong enough to be consistent with your model?

3. *Validity*—Would the evidence be the same at another time or place? Are you really measuring what you think you are? Is the surface relationship spurious because of variables omitted from the model? If your data are quantitative, there are statistical tests of significance and measures of association that may be used.

Of course, one should avoid *fallacies*. What is true for one group may not be true for another. What is true for one group may not be true overall, or vice versa. What is true between groups may not be true within groups; for example, states that are Catholic might tend to be Democratic, yet within any state there might be no relation between religion and vote—if Protestants voted Democratic in predominantly Catholic states and Catholics voted Republican in predominantly Protestant states. One may legitimately compare ideal with ideal or reality with reality, but not ideal with reality—not socialist ideal with capitalist practice, or vice versa.

USING CONTROL VARIABLES

A crucial part of determining the validity of any relationships you assert is showing they hold even when other variables are held constant (controlled). Unemployment may be associated with rioting, but does this relation hold when income is controlled for? Catholicism may correlate with voting Democratic, but does this hold when social class is taken as a control?

	Catholic	Protestant
Democratic	1a	1b
Republican	1c	1d

Low Socioeconomic Status

	Catholic	Protestant
Democratic	2a	2b
Republican	2c	2d

High Socioeconomic Status

	Catholic	Protestant
Democratic	3a	3b
Republican	3c	3d

FIGURE C.1

In Figure C.1, we may find Catholicism is associated with voting Democratic and Protestantism with voting Republican (most examples in boxes 1a or 1d, few or none in 1b or 1c). If you want to control for another variable, say socioeconomic status, divide your examples or evidence into those dealing with low socioeconomic cases and those dealing with high cases. If the examples are still concentrated in the a and d boxes (in tables 2 and 3), then the relationship holds even when socioeconomic status is controlled for. This may be done in a qualitative way with descriptive examples, or in a quantitative way with aggregate data. In statistics, control variables may be handled by multivariate analysis or partial correlation, among others.

ACCEPTING OR REJECTING YOUR HYPOTHESIS

The preceding steps should lead logically to your conclusion—acceptance or rejection of your hypothesis. The soundness of the evidence gathered will, of course, determine the assurance with which you come to a conclusion. You will want to show that the evidence leads to rejection of the alternative hypotheses formed earlier but is consistent with your own views. This whole process is not, of course, as mechanical as these notes might suggest, nor need it be quantitatively oriented or even follow the suggested outline. But the elements of logical proof must be present in a sound social science paper.

DRAWING IMPLICATIONS

Aside from avoiding various fallacies and keeping one's generalizations within those warranted by the kind of evidence one has gathered, a good political science paper should attempt to relate its findings to existing political science literature, to contemporary issues, or to some larger framework. Relations to disciplines other than political science should not be neglected. At the same time, the limits of the study should be made explicit; don't overstate a good case.

Index

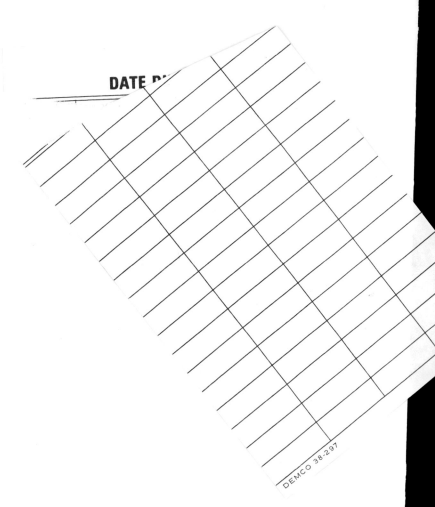

DATE D

DEMCO 38-297